SURVEY
OF ACCOUNTING

FOURTH EDITION

CARL S. WARREN
Professor Emeritus of Accounting
University of Georgia, Athens

SOUTH-WESTERN
CENGAGE Learning

Australia • Brazil • Japan • Korea • Mexico • Singapore • Spain • United Kingdom • United States

SOUTH-WESTERN
CENGAGE Learning

Survey of Accounting, Fourth Edition
Carl S. Warren

VP/Editorial Director: Jack W. Calhoun

Editor-in-Chief: Rob Dewey

Executive Editor: Sharon Oblinger

Developmental Editor: Aaron Arnsparger

Marketing Manager: Steven E. Joos

Content Project Manager: Joanna Grote

Manager, Editorial Media: John Barans

Technology Project Manager: Scott Hamilton

Senior Frontlist Buyer: Doug Wilke

Production Service: LEAP Publishing Services, Inc.

Composition Service: Macmillan Publishing Solutions

Art Director: Stacy Jenkins Shirley

Internal Designer: cmiller design

Cover Designer: cmiller design

Cover Image: Getty Images

For product information and technology assistance, contact us at
Cengage Learning Academic Resource Center, 1-800-423-0563

For permission to use material from this text or product,
submit all requests online at **www.cengage.com/permissions**
Further permissions questions can be emailed to
permissionrequest@cengage.com

Library of Congress Control Number: 2007942234
Student Edition ISBN-13: 978-0-324-65826-2
Student Edition ISBN-10: 0-324-65826-5
Instructor's Edition ISBN-13: 978-0-324-65827-9
Instructor's Edition ISBN-10: 0-324-65827-3

South-Western Cengage Learning
5191 Natorp Boulevard
Mason, OH 45040
USA

Cengage Learning products are represented in Canada by Nelson Education, Ltd.

For your course and learning solutions, visit **academic.cengage.com**
Purchase any of our products at your local college store or at our preferred online store **www.ichapters.com**

Printed in Canada
1 2 3 4 5 6 7 12 11 10 09 08

Preface

Survey of Accounting, Fourth Edition, is designed for a one-term introductory accounting course. It provides an overview of the basic topics in financial and managerial accounting, without the extraneous accounting principles topics that must be skipped or otherwise modified to fit into a one-term course. Written for students who have no prior knowledge of accounting, this text emphasizes how accounting reports are used by managers, investors, and other business stakeholders.

Hallmark Features

The fourth edition of this text continues to emphasize elements designed to help instructors and to enhance the learning experience of students. These features include the following:

- **Integrated Financial Statement Framework** shows how transactions impact each of the three primary financial statements and stresses the integrated nature of accounting

- **Infographic art** examples help students visualize important accounting concepts within the chapter

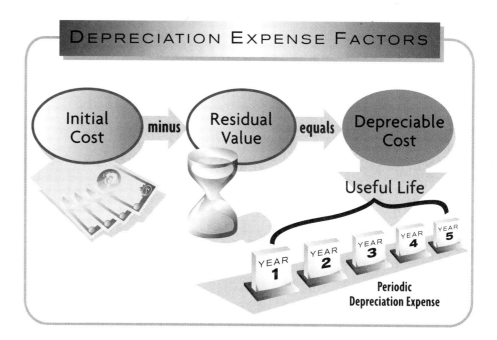

- **Illustrative Problems** help students apply what they learn by walking them through problems that cover the most important concepts addressed within the chapter.

Illustrative Problem

Hawley Inc. manufactures Product S for national distribution. The standard costs for the manufacture of Product S were as follows:

	Standard Costs	Actual Costs
Direct materials	1,500 pounds at $35	1,600 pounds at $32
Direct labor	4,800 hours at $11	4,500 hours at $11.80
Factory overhead	Rates per labor hour, based on 100% of normal capacity of 5,500 labor hours:	
	Variable cost, $2.40	$12,300 variable cost
	Fixed cost, $3.50	$19,250 fixed cost

Instructions

1. Determine the quantity variance, price variance, and total direct materials cost variance for Product S.
2. Determine the time variance, rate variance, and total direct labor cost variance for Product S.
3. Appendix: Determine the controllable variance, volume variance, and total factory overhead cost variance for Product S.

Solution

1.   *Direct Materials Cost Variance*

Quantity variance:		
Actual quantity	1,600 pounds	
Standard quantity	1,500	
Variance—unfavorable	100 pounds × standard price, $35	$ 3,500
Price variance:		
Actual price	$32.00 per pound	
Standard price	35.00	
Variance—favorable	$ (3.00) per pound × actual quantity, 1,600	(4,800)
Total direct materials cost variance—favorable		$(1,300)

- **"Integrity, Objectivity, and Ethics in Business"** features describe real-world ethics situations, emphasizing the importance of not only knowing how to apply accounting concepts learned in the course but also how to apply those concepts ethically as well as with integrity and objectivity.

INTEGRITY, OBJECTIVITY, AND ETHICS IN BUSINESS

A Good Corporate Citizen

Many argue that it is good business for a company to be a good corporate citizen and contribute to the welfare of the society and the local community in which it operates. The Hershey Company has a long history of such involvement that includes the establishment and operation of the Milton Hershey School for disadvantaged children. The school is funded by an endowment of over $5 billion of The Hershey Company's stock. In addition, Hershey gives nonprofit, charitable organizations cash awards of $200 for each employee who can document 100 hours of

volunteer work for the organization. Hershey also recently donated $500,000 over 5 years to scholarships for minority students in south-central Pennsylvania. The money will be used to fund scholarships of $5,000 a year for 20 students living within the region.

Sources: Bill Sutton, "Donations to Aid Minority Students," *The Patriot-News*, November 12, 2004, and "Hershey Throws Greenline a Kiss," *The Commercial Appeal*, September 26, 2004.

■ **"How Businesses Make Money"** vignettes emphasize practical ways in which businesses apply accounting concepts when generating profit strategies.

HOW BUSINESSES MAKE MONEY

Where's Rudolph?

In future years, holiday shoppers won't find as many seasonal products as they have in the past. For example, The Hershey Company has decided not to rely as heavily on seasonal products such as Christmas-colored candies. Hershey and other retailers don't want to be stuck with excess seasonal, time-limited products that they might have to discount heavily in after-holiday sales. Instead, retailers are using "limited edition" items during the year that don't have natural time boundaries.

Customers are often willing to pay premium prices for such limited editions, which also increases demand for the original brands and showcases innovative products. For example, Hershey's sales rose last year with the aid of limited edition white chocolate Reese's and inside-out Reese's.

Source: Pallavi Gogoi, "Avoiding Retail's Post-Holiday Blues," *BusinessWeek Online*, November 23, 2004.

■ **An attractive design** engages students and clearly presents the material. The Integrated Financial Statement Framework benefits from this pedagogically sound use of color, as each statement within the framework is shaded to reinforce the integrated nature of accounting.

Integrated Financial Statement (IFS) Approach

This framework clearly demonstrates the impact of transactions on the balance sheet, income statement, and the statement of cash flows and the corresponding relationship among these financial statements. The IFS framework moves the student from the simple to the complex and explains the how and why of financial statements.

Chapter 1 introduces students to this integration in the form of actual company financials from The Hershey Company, a well-known business.

EXHIBIT 8   *Integrated Financial Statements*

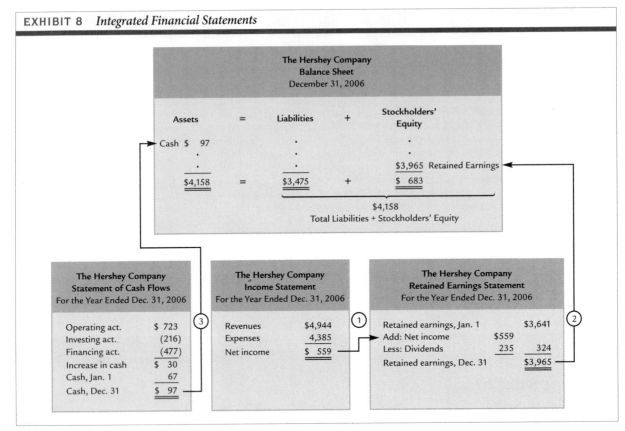

Chapter 2 then begins with an example format of the integrated framework used throughout the financial chapters. Students early on in the course will gain a greater understanding of how important trends or events can impact a company's financial statements, which adds valuable insight into the financial condition of a business.

EXHIBIT 1   *Integrated Financial Statement Framework*

Statement of Cash Flows	Balance Sheet							Income Statement
	Assets	=	Liabilities	+	Stockholders' Equity			
	Assets	=	Liabilities	+	Capital Stock	+	Retained Earnings	
Transactions	XXX		XXX		XXX		XXX	
	XXX		XXX		XXX		XXX	

Statement of Cash Flows		Income Statement	
+/− Operating activities	XXX	Revenues	XXX
+/− Investing activities	XXX	Expenses	XXX
+/− Financing activities	XXX	Net income or loss	XXX
Increase or decrease in cash	XXX		
Beginning cash	XXX		
Ending cash	XXX		

INTEGRATED FINANCIAL STATEMENT FRAMEWORK

The primary focus up front is on cash transactions, which helps eliminate confusion for students who oftentimes have difficulty determining whether an event or transaction should be recorded.

Transaction (d) During the first month of operations, Family Health Care earns patient fees of $5,500, receiving the amount in cash. The effect of this transaction is an inflow of cash flows from operating activities of $5,500. Thus, a positive $5,500 is entered in the statement of cash flows column as an operating activity. Since cash has been received, cash is increased by $5,500 under the balance sheet column for assets. Fees earned of $5,500 is a revenue item that is entered in the income statement column as a positive amount. Since net income retained in the business increases stockholders' equity (retained earnings) and since revenues contribute to net income, $5,500 is also entered as an increase in retained earnings in the stockholders' equity column of the balance sheet. Entering the increases of $5,500 for cash and retained earnings in the balance sheet columns retains the equality of the accounting equation. The effect of this transaction on Family Health Care's financial statements is summarized below.

Statement of Cash Flows	Balance Sheet									Income Statement
	Assets			=	Liabilities	+	Stockholders' Equity			
	Cash	+	Land	=	Notes Payable	+	Capital Stock	+	Retained Earnings	
Balances	4,000		12,000		10,000		6,000			
d. Fees earned	5,500								5,500	d.
Balances	9,500		12,000		10,000		6,000		5,500	

Statement of Cash Flows		Income Statement	
d. Operating	5,500	d. Fees earned	5,500

Fourth Edition Changes and Enhancements

- All real-world company financial data in the relevant text chapters has been updated to recent year (2006) financials. This includes The Hershey Company, Home Depot, Starbucks, and Microsoft, among other real-world examples that are included in the text.

- Data and solutions to all end-of-chapter exercises and problems have been updated. In some cases, new special activities have been added to stimulate group discussion or to delve into ethical situations.

- Chapter 4 now clarifies terminology regarding transportation out and delivery expenses. In addition, a new exhibit has been added to this chapter that depicts changes in current operating assets and liabilities.

- Chapter 6 includes a newly reworked discussion of the LIFO vs. FIFO example for Deere and Company.

- Chapter 10, "Accounting Systems for Manufacturing Businesses," now includes a new continuing example that highlights Legend Guitars. The discussion starts with a brief introduction of materials, factory labor, and factory overhead costs, with a new exhibit that shows the guitar-making operations of the company. The chapter then moves into a discussion of job order cost systems in which the cost flows associated with the production process of guitars (from materials to work in process to finished goods inventory) are shown and thoroughly explained.

- *Survey of Accounting, 4e,* now offers a new online homework solution for students, CengageNOW *Express*, which includes all end-of-chapter exercises and problems.

- Webtutor on Blackboard (or WebCT) now includes access to several new videos developed specifically for managerial accounting topics. Select videos from the Experience Accounting Video library, which include current, cutting-edge companies such as Hard Rock Café and Cold Stone Creamery, are available via Webtutor.

Elements Retained

The fourth edition of *Survey of Accounting* preserves the past edition features that were well received by the marketplace. These features include the following:

- The basics of accounting are presented in an easy-to-understand manner, without stressing the use of debits and credits.

- Double-entry accounting systems (debits and credits) are covered in Appendix A at the back of the text.

- "The Role of Accounting in Business" begins the text. This chapter includes an introduction to business that discusses types of businesses, forms of business, business strategies, the value chain of a business, and business stakeholders. The business activities of financing, investing, and operating are discussed, followed by an introduction to the role of accounting in business and financial statements.

- The cash and accrual bases of accounting are discussed and illustrated, using a continuing illustration, Family Health Care.

- The usefulness of the accrual basis of accounting over the cash basis in evaluating and predicting future business performance is discussed and illustrated.

- Contemporary accounting systems for service, merchandising, and manufacturing businesses are described and illustrated.

- Real-world companies are illustrated throughout the text and are included in many end-of-chapter exercises, problems, and activities.

- Managerial control and reporting topics provide a basic framework for understanding how accounting systems help satisfy managerial decision-making needs and how accounting systems can be used to control business operations.

- The end-of-chapter materials contain a wide variety of assignments for students, including short exercises covering key concepts in each chapter. On average, each chapter contains 15–20 discussion questions, over 20 exercises, 5–6 problems, and 5–8 activities.

- Icons in the end-of-chapter materials indicate which activities have an accompanying enhanced spreadsheet template. In addition, some activities are tagged to show a focus on ethical situations or whether the activity is appropriate for group work.

SPREADSHEET　　**ETHICS**　　**GROUP**

Technology

Just What You Need to Know and Do NOW! CengageNOW *Express*™ for Warren *Survey of Accounting* is an online homework solution that delivers better student outcomes—NOW! CengageNOW *Express* focuses on the textbook homework that is central to success in accounting with streamlined course start-up, straightforward assignment creation, automatic grading and tracking student progress, and instant feedback for students.

- **Streamlined Course Start-Up**—All brief exercises, exercises, problems, and comprehensive problems are available immediately for students to practice.

- **Straightforward Assignment Creation**—Users can select required exercises and problems, and CengageNOW *Express* automatically applies faculty-approved Accounting Homework Options.

- **Automatic grading and tracking student progress**—CengageNOW *Express* grades and captures students' scores to easily monitor their progress. Export the grade book to Excel for easy data management.

- **Instant feedback for students**—Students stay on track with instructor-written hints and immediate feedback with every assignment. Links to the e-book, animated exercise demonstrations, and Excel spreadsheets from specific assignments are ideal for student review.

WebTutor on Blackboard and WebCT

WebTUTOR™

Jumpstart your course with customizable, rich-text-specific content within your Course Management System!

- **Jumpstart**—a WebTutor cartridge into their Course Management System.

- **Customizable**—Easily blend, add, edit, reorganize, or delete content.

- **Content**—Text-specific quizzing, weblinks, discussion topics, videos, and more.

Whether you want to Web-enable your class or put an entire course online, WebTutor delivers!

Supplements for the Instructor

The supplements described below are available on a single CD-ROM as well as in print form. In addition, except for the Test Bank, these supplements can be downloaded from the text's Web site. Visit the Warren home page (academic.cengage.com/accounting/warren) to harness the power of the Internet in accounting education for both you and your students.

Solutions Manual—The Solutions Manual contains answers to all questions, exercises, problems, and activities in the text.

PowerPoint™ Lecture Presentations—These presentations enhance lecture quality and shorten preparation time. Each chapter's slides outline the chapter content and feature key exhibits from the text.

Test Bank—The Test Bank contains a wealth of short-answer questions, problems, and discussion questions, with complete solutions. Each question is tagged to a chapter objective and assigned a level of difficulty for quick reference. The test bank questions have also been tagged to both AACSB and AICPA core competencies as an additional tool to aid in assessing student progress relative to these standards.

ExamView®—A computerized version of the Test Bank allows instructors to quickly and easily customize tests for their students. Instructors can add or edit questions, instructions, and answers and select questions (randomly, numerically, by objective, or by difficulty) by previewing them on screen. Instructors can also create and administer quizzes and tests online, whether over the Internet, a local area network (LAN), or a wide area network (WAN). This program is located on the Instructor's Resource CD-ROM and is compatible with Microsoft® Windows.

Instructor's Manual—Each chapter contains a list of key terms, a lecture outline, transparency masters, class participation ideas, supplemental examples and illustrations, and selected group learning activities. **For added flexibility, the Instructor's Manual also contains a supplement to Appendix A in the text that converts selected exercises and problems to journal entry (d/cr) format for instructors who wish to stress this approach in the course.** Solutions to these converted activities are also provided.

Instructor's Resource CD-ROM with ExamView® (ISBN: 0-324-65829-X)—Key instructor ancillaries (Solutions Manual, Instructor's Manual, Test Bank, ExamView, and PowerPoint™ presentation slides) are provided on a CD-ROM—giving instructors the ultimate tool for customizing lectures and presentations. The Test Bank files on the CD-ROM are provided in ExamView® format.

Supplements for Students

Survey of Accounting Companion Web Site (academic.cengage.com/accounting/warren)—The Web site for the fourth edition continues to offer you and your students even more resources for teaching and learning. Among the many elements available to students are:

- Quizzes that offer feedback
- Crossword puzzles that provide fun testing of vocabulary knowledge
- Repeated objectives from the chapter, to serve as a study aid to keep clear focus on the core goals

Enhanced Excel® Templates—These templates are provided for selected long or complicated end-of-chapter exercises and problems and provide assistance to the student as they set up and work the problem. Certain cells are coded to display a red asterisk when an incorrect answer is entered, which helps students stay on track. Selected problems that can be solved using these templates are designated by an icon. These helpful templates appear on both the student Web site at academic.cengage.com/accounting/warren. (Solutions for the Excel® Templates are available only from your instructor.)

SPREADSHEET

Additional Resources

InfoTrac® College Edition—With this resource, students can receive anytime, anywhere online access to a database of full-text articles from hundreds of popular and scholarly periodicals, such as *Newsweek, Fortune, Entrepreneur, Journal of Accountancy,* and *Nation's Business,* among others. Students can use its fast and easy search tools to find relevant news and analytical information among the tens of thousands of articles in the database—updated daily and going back as far as four years—all at a single Web site. InfoTrac is a great way to expose students to online research techniques, with the security that the content is academically based and reliable. An InfoTrac College Edition subscription card can be packaged free with new copies of this text. For more information, visit academic.cengage.com/infotrac.

An Introduction to Accounting, Business Processes, and ERP (by Phil Reckers, Julie Smith David, and Harriet MacCracken, all of Arizona State University)—Utilizing JD Edwards software demos, an industry-leading ERP company, students will experience an overview of the use of ERP software for accounting and business processes. They will not only learn the advantages of technology in accessing business information but will also learn to apply it in three different business models. After each module, student learning is reinforced by quizzing. Equip your students with this class-tested and easy-to-use experience to help them meet the ever-changing challenges of business and technology!

Ethics in the Post-Enron Age (by Iris and Bruce Stuart of California State University—Fullerton)—With the Enron/Andersen debacle, ethics is becoming an increasingly important (and interesting) part of accounting education. This timely supplement contains ethics cases based on real situations in the business world. Examples include cases tied to Enron, Global Crossing, and Boston Chicken. Identifying ethical dilemmas and projecting their resolution will allow students to develop essential skills for success in their future careers.

Business & Professional Ethics for Accountants, 4e (by Leonard J. Brooks of the University of Toronto)—This textbook provides real-world examples of ethical issues in the workplace, examining why ethical issues occur while discussing the strategies utilized to make the most ethical decisions possible. BUSINESS & PROFESSIONAL ETHICS examines the background and nature of the new stakeholder-support era of corporate and professional accountability and governance and provides insights into the development of sound patterns of behavior on the part of directors, executives, and accountants.

Contemporary Auditing: Real Issues and Cases, 6te (by Michael C. Knapp of the University of Oklahoma)— This candid and even-handed approach to obstacles in the auditing profession will teach students how to "think like an auditor." Students will learn how to recognize and understand the critical factors and circumstances that determine the outcome of audits. Knapp's *Contemporary Auditing: Real Issues and Cases* is the only auditing textbook that relies exclusively on "real world" auditing cases to demonstrate vividly and with clarity the true nature of the work environment and work roles of independent auditors.

Acknowledgments

Many people deserve thanks for their contributions to this text over the last several editions. James Emig, of Villanova University, was an outstanding resource for his careful verification of the end-of-chapter materials. Leslie Kauffman, at LEAP Publishing Services, carefully took on the development of many of the text supplements. The comments from the following reviewers also influenced recent editions of the text:

Ajay Adhikari
American University—Kogod School of Business

Kenneth Callow
Bay Path College

Carol Coman
California Lutheran University

Anita Feller
University of Illinois at Urbana—Champaign

Rhonda Gilreath
Tiffin University

Connie Hylton
George Mason University

D. Donald Kent, Jr.
SUNY Brockport

Ronald Kilgore
University of Tennessee—Martin

Janet Mabon
University of Oregon

Janice Marsteller
University of Toledo

Les Price
Pierce College
University of Puget Sound
Seattle University

Mike Slaughbaugh
Indiana University—Purdue University Fort Wayne

Kortney White
Arkansas State University

Your comments and suggestions as you use this text are sincerely appreciated.

Carl S. Warren

About the Author

Carl S. Warren

Dr. Carl S. Warren is Professor Emeritus of Accounting at the University of Georgia, Athens. For over twenty-five years, Professor Warren has taught all levels of accounting classes. In recent years, Professor Warren has focused his teaching efforts on principles of accounting and auditing courses. Professor Warren has taught classes at the University of Iowa, Michigan State University, and University of Chicago. Professor Warren received his doctorate degree (PhD) from Michigan State University and his undergraduate (BBA) and masters (MA) degrees from the University of Iowa. During his career, Professor Warren published numerous articles in professional journals, including *The Accounting Review, Journal of Accounting Research, Journal of Accountancy, The CPA Journal,* and *Auditing: A Journal of Practice & Theory*. Professor Warren's outside interests include writing short stories and novels, oil painting, handball, golf, skiing, backpacking, and fly-fishing.

Brief Contents

Contents

Appendix A

Double_Entry Accounting System 607

The Role of Accounting in Business

Learning Objectives

After studying this chapter, you should be able to:

Obj 1
Describe the types and forms of businesses, how businesses make money, and business stakeholders.

Obj 2
Describe the three business activities of financing, investing, and operating.

Obj 3
Define accounting and describe its role in business.

Obj 4
Describe and illustrate the basic financial statements and how they interrelate.

Obj 5
Describe eight accounting concepts underlying financial reporting.

When two teams pair up for a game of football, there is often a lot of noise. The band plays, the fans cheer, and fireworks light up the scoreboard. Obviously, the fans are committed and care about the outcome of the game. Just like fans at a football game, the owners of a business want their business to "win" against their competitors in the marketplace. Although having our football team win can be a source of pride, winning in the marketplace goes beyond pride and has many tangible benefits. Companies that are winners are better able to serve customers, provide good jobs for employees, and make more money for the owners.

An example of such a successful company is the *The Hershey Company*, founded by Milton Hershey in the early 1900s. The Hershey Company is America's leading chocolate manufacturer, producing more than a billion pounds of chocolate products each year. In addition to Hershey chocolate bars, the company sells candy under such brands as Reese's, Twizzlers®, York®, Almond Joy®, and Kit Kat®.

As we begin our study of accounting in this chapter, we will first discuss the nature, types, and activities of businesses, such as Hershey's. In doing so, we describe business stakeholders, such as the owners, customers, and employees. We conclude the chapter by discussing the role of accounting in business, including financial statements, basic accounting concepts, and how to use financial statements to evaluate a business's performance.

Obj 1

Describe the types and forms of businesses, how businesses make money, and business stakeholders.

The Nature of Business

You are familiar with many large companies, such as ***General Motors***, ***Barnes & Noble***, and ***AT&T***. You are also familiar with many local businesses, such as gas stations, grocery stores, and restaurants. You may work for one of these businesses. But what do they have in common that identifies them as businesses?

In general, a **business** is an organization in which basic resources (inputs), such as materials and labor, are assembled and processed to provide goods or services (outputs) to customers.[1] Businesses come in all sizes, from a local coffeehouse to General Motors, which sells several billion dollars worth of cars and trucks each year. The customers of a business are individuals or other businesses who purchase goods or services in exchange for money or other items of value. In contrast, a church is not a business because those who receive its services are not obligated to pay for them.

The objective of most businesses is to maximize profits by providing goods or services that meet customer needs. Profit is the difference between the amount received from customers for goods or services provided and the amount paid for the inputs used to provide the goods or services. Some businesses operate with an objective other than to maximize profits. The objective of such not-for-profit businesses is to provide some benefit to society, such as medical research or conservation of natural resources. In other cases, governmental units such as cities operate water works or sewage treatment plants on a not-for-profit basis. Our focus in this text will be on businesses operated to earn a profit. However, many of the concepts and principles also apply to not-for-profit businesses.

Types of Businesses

There are three different types of businesses that are operated for profit: manufacturing, merchandising, and service businesses. Each type of business has unique characteristics.

Manufacturing businesses change basic inputs into products that are sold to individual customers. Examples of manufacturing businesses and some of their products are shown below.

Manufacturing Business	*Product*
General Motors	Automobiles, trucks, vans
General Mills	Breakfast cereals
Boeing	Jet aircraft
Nike	Athletic shoes
Coca-Cola	Beverages
Sony	Stereos, televisions, radios

Merchandising businesses also sell products to customers. However, they do not make the products but purchase them from other businesses (such as manufacturers). In this sense, merchandisers bring products and customers together. Examples of merchandising businesses and some of the products they sell are shown below.

Merchandising Business	*Product*
Wal-Mart	General merchandise
Toys"R"Us	Toys
Barnes & Noble	Books
Best Buy	Consumer electronics
Amazon.com	Books

---

[1] A list of key terms appears at the end of each chapter in the text.

Service businesses provide services rather than products to customers. Examples of service businesses and the types of services they offer are shown below.

Service Business	Service
Disney	Entertainment
Delta Air Lines	Transportation
Marriott	Hospitality and lodging
Merrill Lynch	Financial
Google	Internet search

Forms of Business

A business is normally organized as one of four different forms: proprietorship, partnership, corporation, or limited liability company. A **proprietorship** is owned by one individual. More than 70% of the businesses in the United States are organized as proprietorships. The popularity of this form is due to the ease and low cost of organizing. The primary disadvantage of proprietorships is that the financial resources available to the business are limited to the individual owner's resources. Small local businesses such as hardware stores, repair shops, laundries, restaurants, and maid services are often organized as proprietorships.

As a business grows and requires more financial and managerial resources, it may become a partnership. A **partnership** is owned by two or more individuals. Like proprietorships, small local businesses such as automotive repair shops, music stores, beauty shops, and men's and women's clothing stores may be organized as partnerships. Currently, about 10% of the businesses in the United States are organized as partnerships.

Like proprietorships, a partnership may outgrow its ability to finance its operations. As a result, it may become a corporation. A **corporation** is organized under state or federal statutes as a separate legal entity. The ownership of a corporation is divided into shares of stock. A corporation issues the stock to individuals or other businesses, who then become owners or stockholders of the corporation.

A primary advantage of the corporate form is the ability to obtain large amounts of resources by issuing shares of stock, which are ownership rights in the corporation. For this reason, most companies that require large investments in equipment and facilities are organized as corporations. For example, Toys"R"Us has raised over $800 million by issuing shares of common stock to finance its operations. Other examples of corporations include *Yahoo!*, *Ford*, *Apple Computer*, *Coca-Cola*, and *Starbucks*.

About 20% of the businesses in the United States are organized as corporations. However, since most large companies are organized as corporations, over 90% of the total dollars of business receipts are received by corporations. Thus, corporations have a major influence on the economy.

A **limited liability company** (LLC) combines attributes of a partnership and a corporation in that it is organized as a corporation, but it can elect to be taxed as a partnership. In addition, its owners' (or members') liability is limited to their investment in the business.

In addition to the ease of formation and ability to raise large amounts of capital, the legal liability, taxes, and limitation on life are important considerations in choosing a form of business organization. For sole proprietorships and partnerships, the owners have unlimited liability to creditors and for other debts of the company. For corporations and limited liability companies, the owners' liability is limited to the amount invested in the company. Corporations are taxed as separate legal entities, while the income of sole proprietorships, partnerships, and limited liability companies is passed through to the owners and taxed on the owners' tax returns. As separate legal entities, corporations also continue on, regardless of the lives of the individual owners. In contrast, sole proprietorships, partnerships, and limited liability companies may terminate their existence with the death of an individual owner.

The characteristics of sole proprietorships, partnerships, corporations, and limited liability companies discussed in this section are summarized here.

Organizational Form	Ease of Formation	Legal Liability	Taxation	Limitation on Life of Entity	Access to Capital
Proprietorship	Simple	No limitation	Nontaxable (pass-through) entity	Yes	Limited
Partnership	Simple	No limitation	Nontaxable (pass-through) entity	Yes	Average
Corporation	Complex	Limited liability	Taxable entity	No	Extensive
Limited Liability Company	Moderate	Limited liability	Nontaxable (pass-through) entity by election	Yes	Average

The three types of businesses we discussed earlier—manufacturing, merchandising, and service—may be either proprietorships, partnerships, corporations, or limited liability companies. However, businesses that require a large amount of resources, such as many manufacturing businesses, are corporations. Likewise, most large retailers such as **Wal-Mart, Sears,** and **JC Penney** are corporations. Because most large businesses are corporations, they tend to dominate the economic activity in the United States. For this reason, we focus our attention in this text on the corporate form of organization. However, many of the concepts and principles that we discuss also apply to proprietorships and partnerships.

How Do Businesses Make Money?

The goal of a business is to make money by providing goods or services to customers. How does it decide which products or services to offer its customers? For example, should Best Buy offer warranty and repair services to its customers? Many factors influence this decision. Ultimately, however, the decision is based on how the business plans to gain an advantage over its competitors, and in doing so, make money and maximize its profits. *Profits* are the excess of revenues from selling services or products over the cost of providing those services or products as illustrated below.

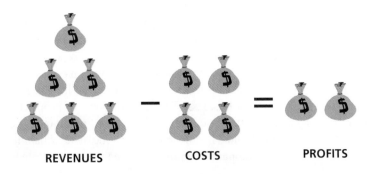

REVENUES   COSTS   PROFITS

Businesses try to maximize their profits by generating high revenues, low costs, and thus, high profits. However, a business's competitors are also trying to do the same and, thus, a business can only maximize its profits by gaining an advantage over its competitors. So, how can a business accomplish this?

Generally, businesses gain an advantage over their competitors by using either a low-cost or a premium-price emphasis. Under a *low-cost emphasis,* a business designs and produces products or services at a lower cost than its competitors. Wal-Mart and **Southwest Airlines** are examples of businesses with a low-cost emphasis. Such businesses sell no-frills, standardized products and services.

Under a *premium-price emphasis,* a business tries to design and produce products or services that serve unique market needs, allowing it to charge premium prices. For example, customers may perceive a product or service as unique based upon quality, reliability, image, or design. **John Deere**, **Tommy Hilfiger**, and **BMW** are examples of businesses that charge premium prices for their products. To illustrate, John Deere emphasizes the reliability of its lawn equipment, Tommy Hilfiger emphasizes the unique image of its clothing, and BMW emphasizes the unique driving style and prestige of its automobiles.

Since businesses are highly competitive, it is difficult for them to sustain a competitive advantage over time. For example, a primary concern of a business using a low-cost emphasis is that a competitor may copy its low-cost methods or develop technological advances that enable it to achieve even lower costs. A primary concern of a business using a premium-price emphasis is that a competitor may develop products with characteristics perceived as more desirable by customers.

Examples of how businesses use the low-cost and premium-price emphases to try to gain advantages over one another include the following:

- Local pharmacies try to develop personalized relationships with their customers. By doing so, they are able to charge premium (higher) prices. In contrast, Wal-Mart's pharmacies use the low-cost emphasis and compete on cost.
- Grocery stores such as **Kroger** and **Safeway** also try to develop personalized relationships with their customers. One way they do this is by issuing magnetic cards to preferred customers to establish brand loyalty. The cards also allow the stores to track consumer preferences and buying habits for use in purchasing and advertising campaigns. In doing so, Kroger and Safeway hope to compete on a premium-price basis against Wal-Mart Supercenters, which use a low-cost emphasis.

INTEGRITY, OBJECTIVITY, AND ETHICS IN BUSINESS

A Good Corporate Citizen

Many argue that it is good business for a company to be a good corporate citizen and contribute to the welfare of the society and the local community in which it operates. The Hershey Company has a long history of such involvement that includes the establishment and operation of the Milton Hershey School for disadvantaged children. The school is funded by an endowment of over $5 billion of The Hershey Company's stock. In addition, Hershey gives nonprofit, charitable organizations cash awards of $200 for each employee who can document 100 hours of volunteer work for the organization. Hershey also recently donated $500,000 over 5 years to scholarships for minority students in south-central Pennsylvania. The money will be used to fund scholarships of $5,000 a year for 20 students living within the region.

Sources: Bill Sutton, "Donations to Aid Minority Students," *The Patriot-News*, November 12, 2004, and "Hershey Throws Greenline a Kiss," *The Commercial Appeal*, September 26, 2004.

- *Honda* advertises the reliability and quality ratings of its automobiles and is thus able to charge premium prices. Similarly, *Volvo's* premium-price emphasis uses safety as the unique characteristic of its automobiles. In contrast, *Hyundai* and *Kia* use a low-cost emphasis.
- *Harley-Davidson* emphasizes that its motorcycles are "Made in America" and promotes its "rebel" image in implementing a premium-price emphasis. This allows Harley-Davidson to charge higher prices for its motorcycles than does Honda, *Yamaha*, or *Suzuki*.

Some well-known businesses struggle to find their competitive advantages. For example, JC Penney and Sears have difficulty competing on low costs against Wal-Mart, *Goody's Family Clothing*, *Kohl's*, *T.J. Maxx*, and *Target*. At the same time, JC Penney and Sears have difficulty charging premium prices for their merchandise against competitors such as *The Gap*, *Old Navy*, *Eddie Bauer*, and *Talbot's*. Likewise, Delta Air Lines and *United Airlines* have difficulty competing against low-cost airlines such as Southwest and *JetBlue*. At the same time, Delta and United don't offer any unique services for which their passengers are willing to pay a premium price.

Exhibit 1 summarizes the characteristics of the low-cost and premium-price emphases. Common examples of businesses that employ each emphasis are also listed.

EXHIBIT 1   *Business Emphasis and Industries*

Business Emphasis	Industry					
	Airline	Freight	Automotive	Retail	Financial Services	Hotel
Low cost	Southwest	Union Pacific	Saturn	Sam's Clubs	Ameritrade	Super 8
Premium price	Virgin Atlantic	FedEx	BMW	Talbot's	Morgan Stanley	Ritz-Carlton

Business Stakeholders

A company's business emphasis, often termed a strategy, directly affects its economic performance. For example, *Kmart* was unsuccessful in implementing a business emphasis that would allow it to compete effectively against Wal-Mart. The result was that Kmart filed for bankruptcy protection in early 2002, and Kmart stakeholders, including employees, creditors, and stockholders, suffered.

HOW BUSINESSES MAKE MONEY

Where's Rudolph?

In future years, holiday shoppers won't find as many seasonal products as they have in the past. For example, The Hershey Company has decided not to rely as heavily on seasonal products such as Christmas-colored candies. Hershey and other retailers don't want to be stuck with excess seasonal, time-limited products that they might have to discount heavily in after-holiday sales. Instead, retailers are using "limited edition" items during the year that don't have natural time boundaries.

Customers are often willing to pay premium prices for such limited editions, which also increases demand for the original brands and showcases innovative products. For example, Hershey's sales rose last year with the aid of limited edition white chocolate Reese's and inside-out Reese's.

Source: Pallavi Gogoi, "Avoiding Retail's Post-Holiday Blues," *BusinessWeek Online*, November 23, 2004.

A **business stakeholder** is a person or entity that has an interest in the economic performance and well-being of a business. For example, stockholders, suppliers, customers, and employees are all stakeholders in a corporation. Business stakeholders can be classified into one of the four categories illustrated in Exhibit 2 below.

EXHIBIT 2	*Business Stakeholders*	
Business Stakeholder	**Interest in the Business**	**Examples**
Capital market stakeholders	Providers of major financing for the business	Banks, owners, stockholders
Product or service market stakeholders	Buyers of products or services and vendors to the business	Customers and suppliers
Government stakeholders	Collect taxes and fees from the business and its employees	Federal, state, and city governments
Internal stakeholders	Individuals employed by the business	Employees and managers

Capital market stakeholders provide the major financing for a business in order for it to begin and continue its operations. Banks and other long-term creditors have an economic interest in recovering the amount they loaned the business plus interest. Owners and stockholders want to maximize the economic value of their investments. Capital market stakeholders expect to receive a return on their investments proportionate to the degree of risk they are taking. Since banks and long-term creditors have first preference to the assets in case the business fails, their risk is less than that of the owners; thus, their overall return is lower.

Product or service market stakeholders include customers who purchase the business's products or services as well as the vendors who supply inputs to the business. Customers have an economic interest in the continued success of the business. For example, in the early 2000s, customers of the Internet provider **@*home.com*** were initially unable to retrieve their e-mail or connect with the Internet when @home.com declared bankruptcy. Customers who purchase advance tickets on Delta Air Lines have an economic interest in whether Delta will continue in business. Similarly, suppliers are stakeholders in the continued success of their customers. Suppliers may invest in technology or other capital equipment to meet a customer's buying and manufacturing specifications. If a customer fails or cuts back on purchases during downturns, suppliers may see their business decline also. This was the case for **Delphi**, a major supplier to General Motors, during GM's downturn in 2005.

Various governments have an interest in the economic performance of businesses. As a result, city and state governments often provide incentives for businesses to locate within their jurisdictions. City, county, state, and federal governments collect taxes from businesses within their jurisdictions. The better a business does, the more taxes the government can collect. In addition, workers are taxed on their wages. In contrast, workers who are laid off and unemployed can file claims for unemployment compensation, which results in a financial burden for the government.

Internal stakeholders include individuals employed by the business. The managers are those individuals who the owners have authorized to operate the business. Managers are primarily evaluated on the economic performance of the business. The managers of businesses that perform poorly are often fired by the owners. Thus, managers have an incentive to maximize the economic value of the business. Owners may offer managers salary contracts that are tied directly to how well the business performs. For example, a manager might receive a percentage of the profits or a percentage of the increase in profits.

Employees provide services to the company they work for in exchange for pay. Thus, employees have an interest in the economic performance of the business because their jobs depend upon it. During business downturns, it is not unusual for a business to lay off workers for extended periods of time. In the extreme, a business may fail and the employees may lose their jobs permanently. Employee labor unions often use the good economic performance of a business to argue for wage increases. In contrast, businesses often use poor economic performance to argue for employee concessions such as wage decreases.

Some examples of business stakeholders mentioned in the prior paragraphs are illustrated below.

Stakeholders

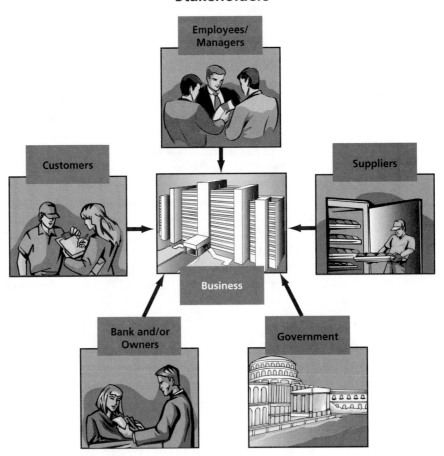

Business Activities

Obj **2**

Describe the three business activities of financing, investing, and operating.

Regardless of whether the company is *Microsoft* or *General Electric*, all businesses are engaged in the activities of financing, investing, and operating, as shown at the top of the next page. First, a business must obtain the necessary funds to finance the costs to organize, pay legal fees, and pay other startup costs. Next, a business must invest funds in the necessary assets such as buildings and equipment to begin operations. For example, Milton Hershey invested in the German chocolate-making machinery he saw at the Chicago International Exposition. Finally, a business must utilize its assets and

Business Activities

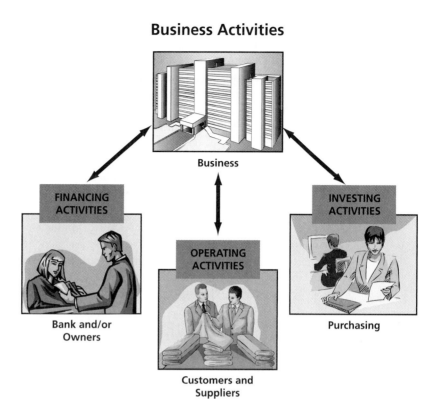

resources to implement its business emphasis. Milton Hershey's business emphasis was to mass-produce chocolate candies at an affordable cost.

As we will discuss later in this chapter, a major role of accounting is to provide stakeholders with information on the financing, investing, and operating activities of businesses. Financial statements are one source of such information.

Financing Activities

Financing activities involve obtaining funds to begin and operate a business. Businesses seek financing through the use of capital markets. This financing may take the form of borrowing or issuing shares of ownership. Most major businesses use both means of financing.

When a business borrows money, it incurs a liability. A **liability** is a legal obligation to repay the amount borrowed according to the terms of the borrowing agreement. For example, when you use your credit card, you incur an obligation to pay the issuer (bank). When a business borrows from a vendor or supplier, the liability is called an **account payable**. In such cases, the business is buying on credit and promising to pay according to the terms set forth by the vendor or supplier. Most vendors and suppliers require payment within a relatively short time, such as 30 days. As of December 31, 2006, The Hershey Company reported approximately $156 million of accounts payable.

A business may borrow money by issuing bonds. *Bonds* are sold to investors and normally require repayment with interest at a specific time in the future. Bonds are a type of long-term financing, with a face amount that is normally due after several years have passed. In contrast, the interest on bonds is normally paid semiannually. Bond obligations are reported as **bonds payable**, and any interest that is due is reported as **interest payable**. Examples of well-known companies that have bonds outstanding include American Telephone and Telegraph (AT&T), John Deere, and *Xerox*.

Most large corporations also borrow money by issuing a note payable. A **note payable** requires payment of the amount borrowed plus interest. Notes payable may be issued either on a short-term or a long-term basis.

A business may finance its operations by issuing shares of ownership. For a corporation, shares of ownership are issued in the form of shares of stock. Although corporations may issue a variety of different types of stock, the basic type of stock issued to owners is called **common stock**. For our purposes, we will use the term **capital stock** to include all the types of stock a corporation may issue.[2] Investors who purchase the stock are referred to as **stockholders**.

The claims of creditors and stockholders on the corporation's resources are different. The resources owned by a business (corporation) are called its **assets**. In case of a corporation's liquidation or bankruptcy, creditors have first claim on its assets. Only after the creditors' claims are satisfied can the stockholders obtain corporate assets. In addition, while creditors expect to receive timely payments of their claims, which may include interest, stockholders are not entitled to regular payments. However, many corporations distribute earnings to stockholders on a regular basis as long as the claims of creditors are being satisfied. These distributions of earnings to stockholders are called **dividends**.

Investing Activities

Once financing has been obtained, a business uses **investing activities** to obtain the necessary assets to start and operate the business. Depending upon the nature of the business, a variety of different assets must be purchased. For example, Milton Hershey purchased the German chocolate-making machinery and later constructed a building to house the Hershey operations. In addition to machinery and buildings, other assets could include computers, office furnishings, trucks, and automobiles. Although most assets have physical characteristics, such as equipment, some assets are intangible in nature. For example, a business may purchase patent rights for use in a manufacturing process or product.

A business may acquire assets through financing activities when the business acquires cash through borrowing or issuing shares of stock. Cash is used to purchase assets through investing activities, such as in the preceding paragraph. Finally, assets may be acquired through operating activities, as we will describe in the next section.

Assets may take a variety of different forms. For example, tangible assets include cash, land, property, plant, and equipment. Assets may also include intangible items, such as rights to patents and rights to payments from customers. Rights to payments from customers are called **accounts receivable**. Other intangible assets, such as goodwill, copyrights, or patents, are often grouped together and reported as **intangible assets**. A business may also prepay for items such as insurance or rent. Such items, which are assets until they are consumed, are normally reported as **prepaid expenses**.

Operating Activities

Once resources have been acquired, a business uses **operating activities** to implement its business emphasis. Hershey's emphasis was to mass-produce and distribute chocolate candies at affordable prices. When Hershey sold its chocolates, it received revenue from its customers. **Revenue** is the increase in assets from selling products or services. Revenues are often identified according to their source. For example, revenues received from selling products are called *sales*. Revenues received from providing services are called *fees*.

[2]Types of stock are discussed in Chapter 8, "Liabilities and Stockholders' Equity."

To earn revenue, a business incurs costs, such as wages of employees, salaries of managers, rent, insurance, advertising, freight, and utilities. Costs used to earn revenue are called **expenses**. Depending upon the nature of the cost, expenses may be identified in a variety of ways. For example, the cost of products sold is often referred to as the *cost of merchandise sold, cost of sales,* or *cost of goods sold.* Other expenses are often classified as either *selling expenses* or *administrative expenses.* Selling expenses include those costs directly related to the selling of a product or service. For example, selling expenses include such costs as sales salaries, sales commissions, freight, and advertising costs. Administrative expenses include other costs not directly related to the selling, such as officer salaries and other costs of the corporate office.

As we will discuss later in this chapter, by comparing the revenues for a period with the related expenses, you can determine whether the business earned net income or incurred a net loss. A **net income** results when revenues exceed expenses. A **net loss** results when expenses exceed revenues.

What Is Accounting and Its Role in Business?

Obj **3**

Define accounting and describe its role in business.

How do stakeholders get information about the financing, investing, and operating activities of a business? This is the role of accounting. Accounting provides information for managers to use in operating the business. In addition, accounting provides information to other stakeholders to use in assessing the economic performance and condition of the business.

In a general sense, **accounting** can be defined as an information system that provides reports to stakeholders about the economic activities and condition of a business. We will focus our discussions in this text on accounting and its role in business. However, many of the concepts in this text also apply to individuals, governments, and other types of organizations. For example, individuals must account for activities such as hours worked, checks written, and bills due. Stakeholders for individuals include creditors, dependents, and the government. A main interest of the government is making sure that individuals pay the proper taxes.

Accounting is sometimes called the "language of business." This is because accounting is the means by which business information is communicated to the stakeholders. For example, accounting reports summarizing the profitability of a new product help Coca-Cola's management decide whether to continue offering the new product for sale. Likewise, financial analysts use accounting reports in deciding whether to recommend the purchase of Coca-Cola's stock. Banks use accounting reports in deciding the amount of credit to extend to Coca-Cola. Suppliers use accounting reports in deciding whether to offer credit for Coca-Cola's purchases of supplies and raw materials. State and federal governments use accounting reports as a basis for assessing taxes on Coca-Cola.

As we described above, accounting serves many purposes for business. A primary purpose is to summarize the financial performance of the firm for external users, such as banks and governmental agencies. The branch of accounting that is associated with preparing reports for users external to the business is termed *financial accounting.* Accounting also can be used to guide management in making decisions about the business. This branch of accounting is called *managerial accounting.* Financial and managerial accounting overlap in many areas. For example, financial reports for external users are often used by managers in considering the impact of their decisions.

In this text, we focus on financial accounting. The two major objectives of financial accounting are:

1. To report the financial condition of a business at a point in time.
2. To report changes in the financial condition of a business over a period of time.

The relationship between the two financial accounting objectives is shown in Exhibit 3. You may think of the first objective as a still photograph (snapshot) of the business and the second objective as a moving picture (video) of the business. The first objective measures the financial status of a business. This measure is used by stakeholders to evaluate the business's financial health at a point in time. The second objective measures the change in the financial condition of a business for a period of time. This measure is used by stakeholders to predict how a business may perform in the future.

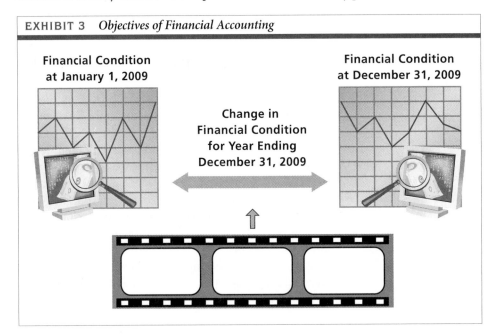

EXHIBIT 3   *Objectives of Financial Accounting*

Financial Condition at January 1, 2009

Change in Financial Condition for Year Ending December 31, 2009

Financial Condition at December 31, 2009

The objectives of accounting are satisfied by (1) recording the economic events affecting a business and then (2) summarizing the impact of these events on the business in financial reports, called **financial statements**. We will describe and illustrate the basic financial statements next.

Financial Statements

Obj 4

Describe and illustrate the basic financial statements and how they interrelate.

Financial statements report the financial condition of a business at a point in time and changes in the financial condition over a period of time. The four basic financial statements and their relationship to the two objectives of financial accounting are listed below.[3]

Financial Statement	Financial Accounting Objective
Income statement	Reports change in financial condition
Retained earnings statement	Reports change in financial condition
Balance sheet	Reports financial condition
Statement of cash flows	Reports change in financial condition

[3]Instead of the retained earnings statement, companies often prepare a statement of stockholders' equity. This statement reports changes in retained earnings as well as changes in other stockholders' equity items. We describe and illustrate the statement of stockholders' equity in a later chapter, after we have discussed stockholders' equity in more detail.

The income statement is normally prepared first, followed by the retained earnings statement, the balance sheet, and the statement of cash flows. The nature of each statement is described below.

- **Income statement**—A summary of the revenue and the expenses for a specific period of time, such as a month or a year.
- **Retained earnings statements**—A summary of the changes in the earnings retained in the corporation for a specific period of time, such as a month or a year.
- **Balance sheet**—A list of the assets, liabilities, and stockholders' equity as of a specific date, usually at the close of the last day of a month or a year.
- **Statement of cash flows**—A summary of the cash receipts and cash payments for a specific period of time, such as a month or a year.

In the next section, we describe and illustrate the preceding four financial statements for The Hershey Company. Our objective in this section is to introduce you to the financial statements that we will be studying throughout this text. In later chapters, we will expand upon these concepts and terminology. The four financial statements are illustrated in Exhibits 4–7. The data for the statements were adapted from the annual report of The Hershey Company.[4]

Income Statement

The income statement reports the change in financial condition due to the operations of a business. The time period covered by the income statement may vary depending upon the needs of the stakeholders. Public corporations are required to file quarterly and annual income statements with the Securities and Exchange Commission. The income statement shown in Exhibit 4 for The Hershey Company is for the year ended December 31, 2006.

EXHIBIT 4 *Income Statement: The Hershey Company*

THE HERSHEY COMPANY
Income Statement
For the Year Ended December 31, 2006 (in millions)

Revenues:		
Sales		$4,944
Expenses:		
Cost of sales	$3,077	
Selling and administrative	860	
Interest	116	
Income taxes	317	
Business realignment and asset impairment expenses	15	4,385
Net income		$ 559

Since the focus of business operations is to generate revenues, the income statement begins by listing the revenues for the period. During 2006, Hershey generated sales of over $4.9 billion. These sales are listed under the revenue caption. You should note that the numbers shown in Exhibit 4 are expressed in millions of dollars. It is common for large corporations to express their financial statements in thousands or millions of dollars.

---

[4]The financial statements for The Hershey Company can be found at **http://www.hersheys.com** by clicking on "Investor Relations."

Following the revenues, the expenses that were used in generating the revenues are listed. For Hershey, these expenses include cost of sales, selling and administrative, interest, income taxes, and business realignment and asset impairment expenses. By reporting the expenses and the related revenues for a period, the expenses are said to be matched against the revenues. This is known in accounting as the *matching concept*. We will further discuss this concept later in this chapter.

When revenues exceed expenses for a period, the business has *net income*. If expenses exceed revenues, the business has a *net loss*. Reporting net income means that the business increased its net assets through its operations. That is, the assets created by the revenues coming into the business exceeded the assets used in generating the revenues. The objective of most businesses is to maximize net income or profit. A net loss means that the business decreased its net assets through its operations. While a business might survive in the short run by reporting net losses, in the long run a business must report net income to survive.

During 2006, Hershey earned net income of almost $560 million. Is this good or bad? Certainly, net income is better than a net loss. However, the stakeholders must assess the economic performance of the corporation according to their own standards. For example, a creditor might be satisfied that the net income is sufficient to assure that it will be repaid. On the other hand, a stockholder might not be satisfied if the corporation's profitability is less than its competitors' profitability. Throughout this text, we describe various methods of assessing corporate performance.

Retained Earnings Statement

The retained earnings statement reports changes in financial condition due to changes in retained earnings during a period. **Retained earnings** is the portion of a corporation's net income that is retained in the business. A corporation may retain all of its net income for use in expanding operations, or it may pay a portion or all of its net income to stockholders as dividends. For example, high-growth companies like Google Inc. and *Sirius Satellite Radio* do not distribute dividends to stockholders; instead, they retain profits for future expansion. In contrast, more mature corporations like Coca-Cola or General Electric routinely pay their stockholders a regular dividend. Thus, investors such as retirees who desire the comfort of a routine dividend payment might invest in Coca-Cola or General Electric. In contrast, younger and more aggressive growth-oriented investors might invest in Google or Sirius.

Since retained earnings depend upon net income, the time period covered by the retained earnings statement is the same period as the income statement. Thus, the retained earnings statement for Hershey shown in Exhibit 5 is for the year ended December 31, 2006.

EXHIBIT 5   *Retained Earnings Statement: The Hershey Company*

THE HERSHEY COMPANY
Retained Earnings Statement
For the Year Ended December 31, 2006 (in millions)

Retained earnings, January 1, 2006		$3,641
Add net income	$559	
Less dividends	235	
Increase in retained earnings		324
Retained earnings, December 31, 2006		$3,965

You should note that dividends are reported in Hershey's retained earnings statement rather than in the income statement. This is because dividends are not an expense, but are a distribution of net income to stockholders. During 2006, Hershey distributed (declared) dividends of $235 million and retained $324 million of its net income in the business. Thus, Hershey's retained earnings increased from $3,641 million to $3,965 million during 2006.

Balance Sheet

The balance sheet reports the financial condition as of a point in time. This is in contrast to the income statement, the retained earnings statement, and the statement of cash flows that report changes in financial condition. The financial condition of a business as of a point in time is measured by its total assets and claims or rights to those assets. Thus, the financial condition of a business can be represented as follows:

$$\text{Assets} = \text{Claims (Rights to the Assets)}$$

The claims on a business's assets consist of rights of creditors who have loaned money or extended credit to the business and the rights of stockholders who have invested in the business. As we discussed earlier, the rights of creditors are liabilities. The rights of stockholders are referred to as **stockholders' equity**, which is sometimes referred to as **owners' equity**. Thus, the assets and the claims on those assets can be presented in equation form as follows:

$$\text{Assets} = \text{Liabilities} + \text{Stockholders' Equity}$$

This equation is called the **accounting equation**. As we shall discover in later chapters, accounting information systems are developed using this equation as their foundation.

The balance sheet, sometimes called the statement of financial condition, is prepared using the framework of the accounting equation. That is, assets are listed first and added to arrive at total assets. Liabilities are then listed and added to arrive at total liabilities. Stockholders' equity items are listed next and added to arrive at total stockholders' equity. Finally, the total assets must equal the combined total liabilities and stockholders' equity. In other words, the accounting equation must balance; hence, the name *balance sheet*. The balance sheet for The Hershey Company as of December 31, 2006, is shown in Exhibit 6.

As of December 31, 2006, Hershey had total assets of $4.2 billion, of which creditors had claims of $3.5 billion and stockholders had claims of $0.7 billion. One use of the balance sheet by creditors is to determine whether the corporation's assets are sufficient to ensure that they will be paid their claims. In Hershey's case, as of December 31, 2006, the assets of the corporation exceed the creditors' claims by $0.7 billion. Therefore, the creditors are reasonably assured that their claims will be repaid.

Statement of Cash Flows

The statement of cash flows reports the change in financial condition due to the changes in cash during a period. During 2006, Hershey's net cash increased by $30 million, as shown in Exhibit 7.

Earlier in this chapter, we discussed the three business activities of financing, investing, and operating. Any changes in cash must be related to one of these three activities. Thus, the statement of cash flows is organized by reporting the changes in each of these three activities, as shown in Exhibit 7.

EXHIBIT 6   Balance Sheet: The Hershey Company

THE HERSHEY COMPANY
Balance Sheet
December 31, 2006 (in millions)

Assets

Cash	$ 97
Accounts receivable	523
Inventories	649
Prepaid expenses	149
Property, plant, and equipment	1,651
Intangibles	642
Other assets	447
Total assets	$ 4,158

Liabilities

Accounts payable	$ 156
Accrued liabilities	454
Notes and other debt	2,579
Income taxes payable	286
Total liabilities	$ 3,475

Stockholders' Equity

Capital stock	$ 360
Retained earnings	3,965
Repurchased stock and other equity items	(3,642)
Total stockholders' equity	$ 683
Total liabilities and stockholders' equity	$ 4,158

EXHIBIT 7   Statement of Cash Flows: The Hershey Company

THE HERSHEY COMPANY
Statement of Cash Flows
For the Year Ended December 31, 2006 (in millions)

Net cash flows from operating activities	$ 723
Cash flows from investing activities:	
Investments in property, plant, and equipment	$(216)
Net cash flows used in investing activities	$(216)
Cash flows from financing activities:	
Cash receipts from financing activities, including debt	$ 544
Dividends paid to stockholders	(235)
Repurchase of stock	(622)
Other, including repayment of debt	(164)
Net cash flows used in financing activities	$(477)
Net increase in cash during 2006	$ 30
Cash as of January 1, 2006	67
Cash as of December 31, 2006	$ 97

In the statement of cash flows, the net cash flows from operating activities is reported first, because cash flows from operating activities are a primary analysis focus for most business stakeholders. For example, creditors are interested in determining whether the company's operating activities are generating enough positive cash flow to repay their debts. Likewise, stockholders are interested in the company's ability to pay dividends. A business cannot survive in the long term unless it generates positive cash flows from operating activities. Thus, employees, managers, and other stakeholders interested in the long-term viability of the business also focus upon the cash flows from operating activities. During 2006, Hershey's operations generated a positive net cash flow of $723 million.

Because of the impact investing activities have on the operations of a business, the cash flows from investing activities are presented following the cash flows from operating activities section. Any cash receipts from selling property, plant, and equipment would be reported in this section. Likewise, any purchases of property, plant, and equipment would be reported as cash payments. Companies that are expanding rapidly, such as startup companies, will normally report negative net cash flows from investing activities. In contrast, companies that are downsizing or selling segments of the business may report positive net cash flows from investing activities.

As shown in Exhibit 7, Hershey reported negative net cash flows from investing activities of $216 million. This negative net cash flow was from the purchase of property, plant, and equipment. Thus, it appears that Hershey is expanding operations.

Cash flows from financing activities are reported next. Any cash receipts from issuing debt or stock would be reported in this section as cash receipts. Likewise, paying debt or dividends would be reported as cash payments. Business stakeholders can analyze cash flows from financing activities to determine whether a business is changing its financing policies.

Hershey paid dividends of $235 million and repaid debt of $164 million. Cash of $544 million was received from financing activities that included additional borrowing from creditors. Finally, Hershey purchased its own stock at a cost of $622 million. A company may purchase its own stock if the corporate management believes its stock is undervalued or for providing stock to employees or managers as part of an incentive (stock option) plan.[5]

The statement of cash flows is completed by determining the increase or decrease in cash flows for the period by adding the net cash flows from operating, investing, and financing activities. Hershey reported a net increase in cash of $30 million. This increase or decrease is added to or subtracted from the cash at the beginning of the period to determine the cash as of the end of the period. Thus, Hershey began the year with $67 million in cash and ended the year with $97 million in cash.

So what does the statement of cash flows reveal about The Hershey Company during 2006? The statement reveals that Hershey generated over $723 million in cash flows from its operations while using cash to expand its operations and pay dividends to stockholders. Overall, Hershey appears to be in a strong operating position to generate cash and pay its creditors.

Integrated Financial Statements

As we mentioned earlier, financial statements are prepared in the order of the income statement, retained earnings statement, balance sheet, and statement of cash flows. Preparing them in this order is important because the financial statements are integrated.

[5]We will discuss the accounting for a company's purchase of its own stock in a later chapter.

EXHIBIT 8 *Integrated Financial Statements*

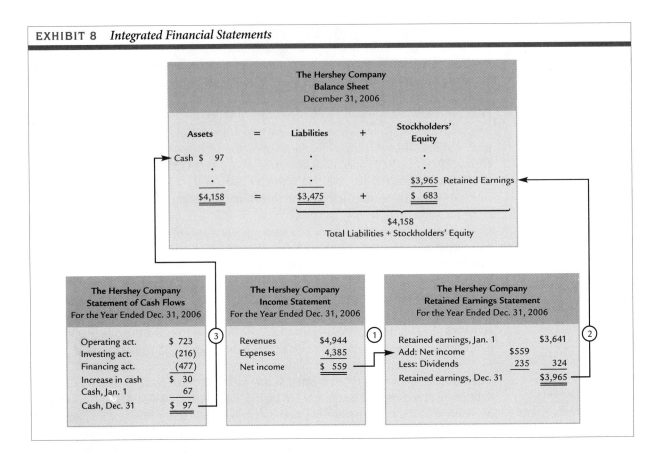

Based upon The Hershey Company's financial statements in Exhibits 4–7, this integration is shown in Exhibit 8 as follows:[6]

1. The income and retained earnings statements are integrated. The net income or net loss appearing on the income statement also appears on the retained earnings statement as either an addition (net income) to or deduction (net loss) from the beginning retained earnings. To illustrate, Hershey's net income of $559 million is also reported on the retained earnings statement as an addition to the beginning retained earnings.

2. The retained earnings statement and the balance sheet are integrated. The retained earnings at the end of the period on the retained earnings statement also appears on the balance sheet as a part of stockholders' equity. To illustrate, Hershey's retained earnings of $3,965 million as of December 31, 2006, is also reported on the balance sheet.

3. The balance sheet and statement of cash flows are integrated. The cash on the balance sheet also appears as the end-of-period cash on the statement of cash flows. To illustrate, the cash of $97 million reported on Hershey's balance sheet is also reported as the end-of-period cash on the statement of cash flows.

The preceding integration is important in analyzing financial statements and the possible impact of economic events or transactions on a business. In addition, this integration serves as a check on whether the financial statements have been prepared correctly. For example, if the ending cash on the statement of cash flows doesn't agree with the balance sheet cash, then an error exists.

[6]Depending upon the method of preparing cash flows from operating activities, net income may also appear on the statement of cash flows. This link and the method of preparing the statement of cash flows, called "the indirect method," is illustrated in a later chapter. In addition, as we will illustrate in Chapter 2, cash flows from operating activities may equal net income.

Obj 5

Describe eight accounting concepts underlying financial reporting.

Accounting Concepts

In the preceding section, we described and illustrated the four basic corporate financial statements. Just as the rules of football determine the proper manner of scoring touchdowns, accounting "rules," called **generally accepted accounting principles (GAAP)**, determine the proper content of financial statements. GAAP are necessary so that stakeholders can compare the financial condition and operating results across companies and across time. If the management of a company could prepare financial statements as they saw fit, the comparability between companies and across time periods would be difficult, if not impossible. In other words, this would be like allowing a football team to determine the point-count for a touchdown every time it scored.

As shown on the following page, GAAP support and determine the content of the financial statements. GAAP are established in the United States by the **Financial Accounting Standards Board (FASB)**.[7] In establishing GAAP, the FASB publishes *Statements of Financial Accounting Standards*. The FASB establishes GAAP by relying on eight supporting accounting concepts.

Understanding these concepts that support the FASB pronouncements is essential for analyzing and interpreting financial statements. We discuss these concepts next. We conclude this section by describing recent financial reporting frauds, the accounting concepts that were violated, and underlying contributing factors.

Business Entity Concept

A business entity could be an individual, a not-for-profit organization such as a church, or a for-profit company such as a real estate agency. The **business entity concept** applies accounting to a specific entity for which stakeholders need economic data. Once the entity is identified, the accountant can determine which economic data and activities should be analyzed, recorded, and summarized in the financial statements for stakeholders.

The accounting for The Hershey Company, a for-profit corporation, is separated from the accounting for other entities. For example, the accounting for transactions and events of individual stockholders, creditors, or other Hershey stakeholders are not included in The Hershey Company's financial statements. Only the transactions and events of the corporation as a separate entity are included in Hershey's financial statements.

Cost Concept

The **cost concept** determines the amount initially entered into the accounting records for purchases. For example, assume that Hershey purchased land for $2 million as a site for a future plant. The cost of the land to Hershey is the amount that would be entered into the accounting records. The seller may have been asking $2.3 million for the land up to the time of the sale. The land may have been assessed for property tax purposes at $1.5 million. A month after purchasing the land, Hershey may have received an offer of $2.4 million for the land. The only amount that affects the accounting records and the financial statements is the $2 million purchase price.

Going Concern Concept

In most cases, the amount of time that a business will be able to continue in operation is not known, so an assumption must be made. A business normally expects to continue operating for an indefinite period of time. This is called the **going concern concept**.

---

[7]The Securities and Exchange Commission (SEC) also has authority to set accounting principles for publicly held corporations. In almost all cases, the SEC adopts the principles established by the FASB.

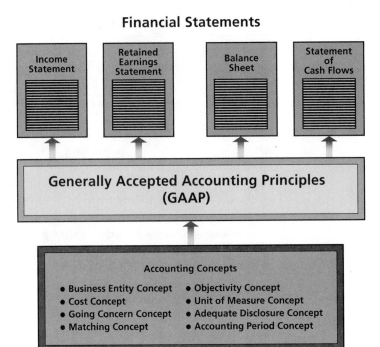

Financial Statements

The going concern concept affects the recording of transactions and thus affects the financial statements. For example, the going concern concept justifies the use of the cost concept for recording purchases, such as the land purchased by Hershey in the preceding example. In this example, Hershey plans to build a plant on the land. Since Hershey does not plan to sell the land, reporting changes in the market value of the land is irrelevant. That is, the amount Hershey could sell the land for if it discontinued operations or went out of business is not important because Hershey plans to continue its operations.

If, however, there is strong evidence that a business is planning to discontinue its operations, then the accounting records should show the values expected to be received. For example, the assets and liabilities of businesses in receivership or bankruptcy are valued from a quitting concern or liquidation point of view, rather than from the going concern point of view.

Matching Concept

In accounting, revenues for a period are matched with the expenses incurred in generating the revenues. Under this **matching concept**, revenues are normally recorded at the time of the sale of the product or service. This recording of revenues is often referred to as *revenue recognition*. At the point of sale, the sale price has been agreed upon, the buyer acquires ownership of the product or acquires the service, and the seller has a legal claim against the buyer for payment.

The following excerpt from the notes to Hershey's annual report describes when Hershey records sales:

> The Corporation records sales when . . . a . . . customer order with a fixed price has been received, . . . the product has been shipped, . . . there is no further obligation to assist in the resale of the product, and collectibility (of the account receivable) is reasonably assured.

Objectivity Concept

The **objectivity concept** requires that entries in the accounting records and the data reported on financial statements be based on objective evidence. If this concept is ignored, the confidence of users of the financial statements cannot be maintained. For example, evidence such as invoices and vouchers for purchases, bank statements for the amount of cash in the bank, and physical counts of supplies on hand support the accounting records. Such evidence is objective and verifiable. In some cases, judgments, estimates, and other subjective factors may have to be used in preparing financial statements. In such situations, the most objective evidence available should be used.

Unit of Measure Concept

In the United States, the **unit of measure concept** requires that all economic data be recorded in dollars. Other relevant, nonfinancial information may also be recorded, such as terms of contracts. However, it is only through using dollar amounts that the various transactions and activities of a business can be measured, summarized, reported, and compared. Money is common to all business transactions and thus is the unit of measurement for reporting.

Adequate Disclosure Concept

Financial statements, including related footnotes and other disclosures, should contain all relevant data a reader needs to understand the financial condition and performance of a business. This is called the **adequate disclosure concept**. Nonessential data should be excluded in order to avoid clutter. For example, the balance of each cash account is usually not reported separately. Instead, the balances are grouped together and reported as one total.

Accounting Period Concept

The process in which accounting data are recorded and summarized in financial statements is a period process. Data are recorded, and the income statement, retained earnings statement, and statement of cash flows are prepared for a period of time such as a month or a year. The balance sheet is then prepared as of the end of the period. After the accounting process is completed for one period, a new period begins and the accounting process is repeated for the new period. This process is based on the **accounting period concept**. Hershey's financial statements shown in Exhibits 4–7 illustrate the accounting period concept for the year ending December 31, 2006.

The financial history of a business may be shown by a series of balance sheets and income statements. If the life of a business is expressed by a line moving from left to right, this series of financial statements may be graphed as follows:

FINANCIAL HISTORY OF A BUSINESS

Income statement for the year ended Dec. 31, 2007 — DEC. 31 **2007**

Balance sheet Dec. 31, 2007

Income statement for the year ended Dec. 31, 2008 — DEC. 31 **2008**

Balance sheet Dec. 31, 2008

Income statement for the year ended Dec. 31, 2009 — DEC. 31 **2009**

Balance sheet Dec. 31, 2009

Responsible Reporting

The reliability of the financial reporting system is important to the economy and for the ability of businesses to raise money from investors. That is, stockholders and creditors require accurate financial reporting before they will invest their money. Scandals and financial reporting frauds in the early 2000s threatened the confidence of U.S. investors. Exhibit 9 is a partial list of some of the financial reporting frauds and abuses.

The companies listed in Exhibit 9 were caught in the midst of ethical lapses that led to fines, firings, and criminal or civil prosecution. The second column of Exhibit 9 identifies the accounting concept that was violated in committing these unethical business practices. For example, the **WorldCom** fraud involved reporting various expense items as though they were assets. This is a violation of the matching concept and resulted in overstating income and assets. The third column of the table identifies some of the results of these events. In most cases, senior and midlevel executives lost their jobs and

EXHIBIT 9	*Accounting Fraud in the 2000s*	
Company	*Concept Violated*	*Result*
Adelphia	*Business Entity Concept:* Rigas family treated the company assets as their own.	Bankruptcy. Rigas family members convicted of fraud and lost their investment in the company.
AIG	*Business Entity Concept:* Compensation transactions with an off-shore company that should have been disclosed on AIG's books.	CEO (Chief Executive Officer) resigned. AIG paid $126 million in fines.
AOL and **PurchasePro**	*Matching Concept:* Back-dated contracts to inflate revenues.	Civil charges filed against senior executives of both companies. $500 million fine.
Computer Associates	*Matching Concept:* Fraudulently inflating revenues.	CEO and senior executives indicted. Five executives pled guilty. $225 million fine.
Enron	*Business Entity Concept:* Treated transactions as revenue, when they should have been treated as debt.	Bankruptcy. Criminal charges against senior executives. Over $60 billion in stock market losses.
Fannie Mae	*Accounting Period Concept:* Managing earnings by shifting expenses between periods.	CEO and CFO fired. $9 billion in restated earnings.
HealthSouth	*Matching Concept:* $4 billion in false entries to overstate revenues.	Senior executives face regulatory *and* civil charges.
Quest	*Matching Concept:* Improper recognition of $3 billion in revenue.	CEO and six other executives charged with "massive financial fraud." $250 million SEC fine.
Tyco	*Adequate Disclosure Concept:* Failure to disclose secret loans to executives that were subsequently forgiven.	CEO forced to resign and was convicted in criminal proceedings.
WorldCom	*Matching Concept:* Improperly treated expenses as assets.	Bankruptcy. Criminal conviction of CEO and CFO. Over $100 billion in stock market losses. Directors fined $18 million.
Xerox	*Matching Concept:* Recognized $3 billion in revenue in periods earlier than should have been recognized.	$10 million fine to SEC. Six executives fined $22 million.

were sued by upset investors. In some cases, the executives also were criminally prosecuted and are serving prison terms.

What went wrong for these companies and executives? The answer to this question involves the following three factors:

1. Individual character
2. Firm culture
3. Laws and enforcement

Individual Character   Executives often face pressures from senior managers to meet company and analysts' expectations. In many of the cases in Exhibit 9, executives initially justified small violations to avoid such pressures. However, these small lies became big lies as the hole was dug deeper and deeper. By the time the abuses were discovered, the misstatements became sufficient to wreck lives and ruin businesses. For example, David Myers, the former controller of WorldCom, in testifying about his recording of improper transactions, stated the following:

> "I didn't think that it was the right thing to do, but I had been asked by Scott (Sullivan, the VP of Finance) to do it."[8]

Individual character is important. It embraces honesty, integrity, and fairness in the face of pressure to hide the truth.

Firm Culture   By their behavior and attitude, senior managers of a company set the firm culture. As explained by one author, when leaders of companies are put on a pedestal, "they begin to believe they and their organizations are one-of-a-kind, that they're changing the face of the industry. They desire entitlements beyond any other C.E.O.'s (chief executive officers)."[9] In most of the firms shown in Exhibit 9, the senior managers created a culture of greed and indifference to the truth. This culture flowed down to lower-level managers, creating an environment of shortcuts, greed, and lies that ultimately resulted in financial fraud.

Laws and Enforcement   Many blamed the lack of laws and enforcement for contributing to the financial reporting abuses described in Exhibit 9. For example, Eliot Spitzer, attorney general of New York, stated the following:

> "A key lesson from the recent scandals is that the checks on the system simply have not worked. The honor code among CEOs didn't work. Board oversight didn't work. Self-regulation was a complete failure."[10]

As a result, Congress enacted new laws, and enforcement efforts have increased since the early 2000s. For example, the Sarbanes-Oxley Act of 2002 (SOX) was enacted. SOX established a new oversight body for the accounting profession, called the Public Company Accounting Oversight Board (PCAOB). In addition, SOX established standards for independence, corporate responsibility, enhanced financial disclosures, and corporate accountability.

---

[8]Susan Pulliam, "Crossing the Line: At Center of Fraud, WorldCom Official Sees Life Unravel," *The Wall Street Journal,* March 24, 2005, p. A1.

[9]Tim Race, "New Economy Executives Are Smitten, and Undone by Their Own Images," *New York Times,* July 7, 2002. Quote attributed to Professor Jay A. Conger.

[10]Eliot Spitzer, "Strong Law Enforcement Is Good for the Economy," *The Wall Street Journal,* April 5, 2005, p. A18.

Key Points

1. **Describe the types and forms of businesses, how businesses make money, and business stakeholders.**

   The three types of businesses operated for profit include manufacturing, merchandising, and service businesses. Such businesses may be organized as proprietorships, partnerships, corporations, and limited liability companies. A business may make money (profits) by gaining an advantage over its competitors using a low-cost or a premium-price emphasis. Under a *low-cost emphasis*, a business designs and produces products or services at a lower cost than its competitors. Under a *premium-price emphasis*, a business tries to design products or services that possess unique attributes or characteristics for which customers are willing to pay more. A business's economic performance is of interest to its stakeholders. Business stakeholders include four categories: capital market stakeholders, product or service market stakeholders, government stakeholders, and internal stakeholders.

2. **Describe the three business activities of financing, investing, and operating.**

   All businesses engage in financing, investing, and operating activities. Financing activities involve obtaining funds to begin and operate a business. Investing activities involve obtaining the necessary resources to start and operate the business. Operating activities involve using the business's resources according to its business emphasis.

3. **Define accounting and describe its role in business.**

   Accounting is an information system that provides reports to stakeholders about the economic activities and condition of a business. Accounting is the "language of business."

4. **Describe and illustrate the basic financial statements and how they interrelate.**

   The principal financial statements of a corporation are the income statement, the retained earnings statement, the balance sheet, and the statement of cash flows. The income statement reports a period's net income or net loss, which also appears on the retained earnings statement. The ending retained earnings reported on the retained earnings statement is also reported on the balance sheet. The ending cash balance is reported on the balance sheet and the statement of cash flows.

5. **Describe eight accounting concepts underlying financial reporting.**

   The eight accounting concepts discussed in this chapter include the business entity, cost, going concern, matching, objectivity, unit of measure, adequate disclosure, and accounting period concepts.

Key Terms

Account payable

Accounting

Accounting equation

Accounting period concept

Accounts receivable

Adequate disclosure concept

Assets

Balance sheet

Bonds payable

Business

Business entity concept

Business stakeholder

Capital stock

Common stock

Corporation

Cost concept

Dividends

Expenses

Financial Accounting Standards Board (FASB)

Financial statements

Financing activities

Generally accepted accounting principles (GAAP)

Going concern concept

Income statement

Intangible assets

Interest payable

Investing activities

Liabilities

Limited liability company (LLC)

Manufacturing

Matching concept

Merchandising

Net income

Net loss

Note payable	Prepaid expenses	Service
Objectivity concept	Proprietorship	Statement of cash flows
Operating activities	Retained earnings	Stockholders
Owners' equity	Retained earnings statement	Stockholders' equity
Partnership	Revenue	Unit of measure concept

Illustrative Problem

The financial statements at the end of Spratlin Consulting's first month of operations follow.

SPRATLIN CONSULTING
Income Statement
For the Month Ended June 30, 2008

Fees earned		$36,000
Operating expenses:		
Wages expense	$12,000	
Rent expense	7,640	
Utilities expense	(a)	
Miscellaneous expense	1,320	
Total operating expenses		23,120
Net income		$ (b)

SPRATLIN CONSULTING
Retained Earnings Statement
For the Month Ended June 30, 2008

Net income for June	$ (c)
Less dividends	(d)
Retained earnings, June 30, 2008	$ (e)

SPRATLIN CONSULTING
Balance Sheet
June 30, 2008

Assets	
Cash	$ 5,600
Land	50,000
Total assets	$ (f)
Liabilities	
Accounts payable	$ 1,920
Stockholders' Equity	
Capital stock	(g)
Retained earnings	(h)
Total stockholders' equity	$ (i)
Total liabilities and stockholders' equity	$ (j)

(continued)

SPRATLIN CONSULTING
Statement of Cash Flows
For the Month Ended June 30, 2008

Cash flows from operating activities:		
Cash received from customers	$36,000	
Deduct cash payments for operating expenses	(k)	
Net cash flows from operating activities		$14,800
Cash flows from investing activities:		
Cash payments for acquisition of land		(l)
Cash flows from financing activities:		
Cash received from issuing capital stock	$48,000	
Deduct dividends	7,200	
Net cash flows from financing activities		(m)
Net cash flow and June 30, 2008 cash balance		$ (n)

Instructions

By analyzing how the four financial statements are integrated, determine the proper amounts for (a) through (n).

Solution

a. Utilities expense, $2,160 ($23,120 − $12,000 − $7,640 − $1,320)
b. Net income, $12,880 ($36,000 − $23,120)
c. Net income, $12,880 (same as b)
d. Dividends, $7,200 (from statement of cash flows)
e. Retained earnings, $5,680 ($12,880 − $7,200)
f. Total assets, $55,600 ($5,600 + $50,000)
g. Capital stock, $48,000 (from the statement of cash flows)
h. Retained earnings, $5,680 (same as e)
i. Total stockholders' equity, $53,680 ($48,000 + $5,680)
j. Total liabilities and stockholders' equity, $55,600 ($1,920 + $53,680) (same as f)
k. Cash payments for operating expenses, $21,200 ($36,000 − $14,800)
l. Cash payments for acquisition of land, $50,000 (from balance sheet)
m. Net cash flows from financing activities, $40,800 ($48,000 − $7,200)
n. Net cash flow and June 30, 2008 cash balance, $5,600 ($14,800 − $50,000 + $40,800)

Self-Examination Questions   *(Answers appear at the end of chapter.)*

1. A profit-making business operating as a separate legal entity and in which ownership is divided into shares of stock is known as a:
    A. proprietorship.
    B. service business.
    C. partnership.
    D. corporation.

2. The resources owned by a business are called:
    A. assets.
    B. liabilities.
    C. the accounting equation.
    D. stockholders' equity.

3. A listing of a business entity's assets, liabilities, and stockholders' equity as of a specific date is:
   A. a balance sheet.
   B. an income statement.
   C. the retained earnings statement.
   D. a statement of cash flows.

4. If total assets are $20,000 and total liabilities are $12,000, the amount of stockholders' equity is:
   A. $32,000.
   B. ($32,000).
   C. ($8,000).
   D. $8,000.

5. If revenue was $45,000, expenses were $37,500, and dividends were $10,000, the amount of net income or net loss would be:
   A. $45,000 net income.
   B. $7,500 net income.
   C. $37,500 net loss.
   D. $2,500 net loss.

Class Discussion Questions

1. What is the objective of most businesses?

2. What is the difference between a manufacturing business and a merchandising business? Give an example of each type of business.

3. What is the difference between a manufacturing business and a service business? Is a restaurant a manufacturing business, a service business, or both?

4. Why are most large companies like **Microsoft**, **Pepsi**, **Caterpillar,** and **AutoZone** organized as corporations?

5. Both **KIA** and **Porsche** produce and sell automobiles. Describe and contrast the business emphasis of KIA and Porsche.

6. Assume that a friend of yours operates a family-owned pharmacy. A **Super Wal-Mart** is scheduled to open in the next several months that will also offer pharmacy services. What business emphasis would your friend use to compete with the Super Wal-Mart pharmacy?

7. What services does **eBay** offer to its customers?

8. A business's stakeholders can be classified into capital market, product or service market, government, and internal stakeholders. Will the interests of all the stakeholders within a classification be the same? Use bankers and stockholders of the capital market as an example in answering this question.

9. The three business activities are financing, investing, and operating. Using **United Airlines**, give an example of a financing, investing, and operating activity.

10. What is the role of accounting in business?

11. Briefly describe the nature of the information provided by each of the following financial statements: the income statement, the retained earnings statement, the balance sheet, and the statement of cash flows. In your descriptions, indicate whether each of the financial statements covers a period of time or is for a specific date.

12. For the year ending February 3, 2007, **The Limited Inc.** had revenues of $10,671 million and total expenses of $9,995 million. Did The Limited (a) incur a net loss or (b) realize net income?

13. What particular item of financial or operating data appears on both the income statement and the retained earnings statement? What item appears on both the balance sheet and the retained earnings statement? What item appears on both the balance sheet and statement of cash flows?

14. Becky Woods is the owner of City Delivery Service. Recently, Becky paid interest of $4,000 on a personal loan of $50,000 that she used to begin the business. Should City Delivery Service record the interest payment? Explain.

15. On March 10, Reliable Repair Service extended an offer of $75,000 for land that had been priced for sale at $90,000. On March 25, Reliable Repair Service accepted the seller's counteroffer of $80,000. Describe how Reliable Repair Service should record the land.

16. Land with an assessed value of $475,000 for property tax purposes is acquired by a business for $600,000. Seven years later, the plot of land has an assessed value of $550,000 and the business receives an offer of $900,000 for it. Should the monetary amount assigned to the land in the business records now be increased?

Exercises

E1-1

Types of businesses

Obj 1

Indicate whether each of the following companies is primarily a service, merchandise, or manufacturing business. If you are unfamiliar with the company, you may use the Internet to locate the company's home page or use the finance Web site of Yahoo.com.

1. *Alcoa*
2. *AT&T*
3. *Boeing*
4. *Caterpillar*
5. *Citigroup*
6. *CVS*
7. *Dow Chemical*
8. *FedEx*
9. *First Republic Bank*
10. *Ford Motor*
11. *The Gap*
12. *Hilton Hotels*
13. *H&R Block Inc.*
14. *Procter & Gamble*
15. *Sears Roebuck*

E1-2

Business emphasis

Obj 1

Identify the primary business emphasis of each of the following companies as (a) a low-cost emphasis or (b) a premium-price emphasis. If you are unfamiliar with the company, you may use the Internet to locate the company's home page or use the finance Web site of Yahoo.com.

1. *BMW*
2. *Charles Schwab*
3. *Circuit City Stores*
4. *Coca-Cola*
5. *Dollar General*
6. *Goldman Sachs Group*
7. *Home Depot*
8. *Maytag*
9. *Nike*
10. *Office Depot*
11. *Sara Lee*
12. *Southwest Airlines*

E1-3

Accounting equation

Obj 4

✓ Coca-Cola, $16,920

The total assets and total liabilities of *Coca-Cola* and *PepsiCo* are shown here.

	Coca-Cola (in millions)	PepsiCo (in millions)
Assets	$29,963	$29,930
Liabilities	13,043	14,483

Determine the stockholders' equity of each company.

E1-4

Accounting equation

Obj 4

✓ eBay, $10,905

The total assets and total liabilities of *eBay Inc.* and *Estée Lauder Inc.* are shown here.

	eBay Inc. (in millions)	Estée Lauder Inc. (in millions)
Assets	$13,494	$3,784
Liabilities	2,589	2,162

Determine the stockholders' equity of each company.

E1-5

Accounting equation

Obj 4

✓ a. $190,000

Determine the missing amount for each of the following:

	Assets	=	*Liabilities*	+	*Stockholders' Equity*
a.	X	=	$ 70,000	+	$120,000
b.	$ 45,000	=	X	+	$ 10,000
c.	$320,000	=	$115,000	+	X

E1-6

Accounting equation

Obj 4

✓ a. $4,138

Determine the missing amounts (in thousands) for the condensed balance sheets shown below.

	The Limited	FedEx Corporation	Ford Motor Co.
Assets	$7,093	$ (b)	$278,554
Liabilities	(a)	11,179	282,019
Stockholders' equity	2,955	11,511	(c)

E1-7

Net income and dividends

Obj 4

The income statement of a corporation for the month of November indicates a net income of $200,000. During the same period, $225,000 in cash dividends were paid.

Would it be correct to say that the business incurred a net loss of $25,000 during the month? Discuss.

E1-8

Net income and stockholders' equity for four businesses

Obj 4

✓ Company E: Net income, $80,000

Four different companies, E, F, G, and H, show the same balance sheet data at the beginning and end of a year. These data, exclusive of the amount of owners' equity, are summarized as follows:

	Total Assets	Total Liabilities
Beginning of the year	$600,000	$240,000
End of the year	960,000	520,000

On the basis of the above data and the following additional information for the year, determine the net income (or loss) of each company for the year. (*Hint:* First determine the amount of increase or decrease in stockholders' equity during the year.)

Company E: No additional capital stock was issued, and no dividends were paid.
Company F: No additional capital stock was issued, but dividends of $48,000 were paid.
Company G: Capital stock of $120,000 was issued, but no dividends were paid.
Company H: Capital stock of $120,000 was issued, and dividends of $48,000 were paid.

E1-9

Accounting equation and income statement

Obj 4

✓ 1. $3,375,600

Staples, Inc., is a leading office products distributor, with retail stores in the United States, Canada, Asia, Europe, and South America. The following financial statement data were adopted from Staples' financial statements as of February 3, 2007 and January 28, 2006:

	2007 (in thousands)	2006 (in thousands)
Total assets	$ 8,397,265	$7,676,589
Total liabilities	(1)	3,251,118
Total stockholders' equity	5,021,665	(2)
Sales	18,160,789	
Cost of goods sold	12,966,788	
Selling and administrative expenses	3,716,517	
Other income and (expense)	(5,835)	
Income tax expense	497,972	

a. Determine the missing data indicated for (1) and (2).
b. Using the income statement data for 2007, determine the amount of net income or loss.

E1-10
Balance sheet items

Obj 4

From the following list of selected items taken from the records of Metro Appliance Service as of a specific date, identify those that would appear on the balance sheet.

1. Accounts Payable	6. Supplies
2. Capital Stock	7. Supplies Expense
3. Cash	8. Utilities Expense
4. Fees Earned	9. Wages Expense
5. Land	10. Wages Payable

E1-11
Income statement items

Obj 4

Based on the data presented in Exercise 1-10, identify those items that would appear on the income statement.

E1-12
Financial statement items

Obj 4

Identify each of the following items as (a) an asset, (b) a liability, (c) revenue, (d) an expense, or (e) a dividend:

1. Amounts due from customers	6. Equipment
2. Amounts owed vendors	7. Note payable owed to the bank
3. Cash on hand	8. Rent paid for the month
4. Cash paid to stockholders	9. Sales commissions paid to salespersons
5. Cash sales	10. Wages paid to employees

E1-13
Retained earnings statement

Obj 4

SPREADSHEET

✓ Retained earnings,
June 30, 2008: $478,800

Financial information related to Fresca Company for the month ended June 30, 2008, is as follows:

Net income for June	$ 93,800
Dividends during June	25,000
Retained earnings, June 1, 2008	410,000

Prepare a retained earnings statement for the month ended June 30, 2008.

E1-14
Income statement

Obj 4

SPREADSHEET

✓ Net income: $156,000

Boutique Services was organized on May 1, 2008. A summary of the revenue and expense transactions for May follows:

Fees earned	$375,000
Wages expense	140,000
Miscellaneous expense	4,000
Rent expense	60,000
Supplies expense	15,000

Prepare an income statement for the month ended May 31.

E1-15
Missing amounts from balance sheet and income statement data

Obj 4

✓ (a) $78,150

One item is omitted in each of the following summaries of balance sheet and income statement data for four different corporations, W, X, Y, and Z.

	W	X	Y	Z
Beginning of the year:				
Assets	$360,000	$250,000	$160,000	$ (d)
Liabilities	216,000	130,000	121,600	450,000
End of the year:				
Assets	447,000	350,000	144,000	930,000
Liabilities	195,000	110,000	128,000	510,000
During the year:				
Additional issue of capital stock	(a)	50,000	16,000	150,000
Dividends	24,000	16,000	(c)	225,000
Revenue	118,650	(b)	184,000	420,000
Expenses	64,800	64,000	196,000	480,000

Determine the missing amounts, identifying them by letter. [*Hint:* First determine the amount of increase or decrease in owners' (stockholders') equity during the year.]

E1-16

Balance sheets, net income

Obj 4

SPREADSHEET

✓ b. $90,850

Financial information related to Midas Interiors for March and April 2008 is as follows:

	March 31, 2008	April 30, 2008
Accounts payable	$ 30,800	$ 33,200
Accounts receivable	68,000	78,250
Capital stock	37,500	37,500
Retained earnings	?	?
Cash	120,000	204,000
Supplies	6,000	5,000

a. Prepare balance sheets for Midas Interiors as of March 31 and as of April 30, 2008.
b. Determine the amount of net income for April, assuming that no additional capital stock was issued and no dividends were paid during the month.
c. Determine the amount of net income for April, assuming that no additional capital stock was issued but dividends of $25,000 were paid during the month.

E1-17

Financial statements

Obj 4

Each of the following items is shown in the financial statements of *ExxonMobil Corporation.* Identify the financial statement (balance sheet or income statement) in which each item would appear.

a. Accounts payable
b. Cash equivalents
c. Crude oil inventory
d. Equipment
e. Exploration expenses
f. Income taxes payable
g. Investments
h. Long-term debt
i. Marketable securities
j. Notes and loans payable
k. Operating expenses
l. Prepaid taxes
m. Retained earnings
n. Sales
o. Selling expenses

E1-18

Statement of cash flows

Obj 4

Indicate whether each of the following cash activities would be reported on the statement of cash flows as (a) an operating activity, (b) an investing activity, or (c) a financing activity.

1. Sold excess office equipment
2. Paid rent
3. Paid for office equipment
4. Issued capital stock
5. Sold services
6. Paid for advertising
7. Paid officers' salaries
8. Issued a note payable
9. Paid rent
10. Paid dividends

E1-19

Statement of cash flows

Obj 4

Indicate whether each of the following activities would be reported on the statement of cash flows as (a) an operating activity, (b) an investing activity, or (c) a financing activity.

1. Cash received from investment by stockholders
2. Cash received from fees earned
3. Cash paid for land
4. Cash paid for expenses

E1-20

Statement of cash flows

Obj 4

SPREADSHEET

✓ Net cash flows from operating activities, $109,080

Eduardo Inc. was organized on July 1, 2009. A summary of cash flows for July follows.

Cash receipts:	
Cash received from customers	$169,200
Cash received for capital stock	648,000
Cash received from note payable	72,000
Cash payments:	
Cash paid out for expenses	$ 60,120
Cash paid out for purchase of equipment	540,000
Cash paid as dividends	36,000

Prepare a statement of cash flows for the month ended July 31, 2009.

E1-21

Using financial statements

Obj 4

A company's stakeholders often differ in their financial statement focus. For example, some stakeholders focus primarily on the income statement, while others may focus primarily on the statement of cash flows or the balance sheet. For each of the following situations, indicate which financial statement would be the likely focus for the stakeholder. Choose either the income statement, balance sheet, or the statement of cash flows and justify your choice.

> **Situation One:** Assume that you are considering investing in eBay (capital market stakeholder).
>
> **Situation Two:** Assume that you are considering purchasing a personal computer from **Dell.**
>
> **Situation Three:** Assume that you are a banker for Citigroup (capital market stakeholder), considering whether to grant a major credit line (loan) to Wal-Mart. The credit line will allow Wal-Mart to borrow up to $400 million for a 5-year period at the market rate of interest.
>
> **Situation Four:** Assume that you are employed by Sara Lee Corporation (product market stakeholder) and are considering whether to extend credit for a 60-day period to a new grocery store chain that has recently opened throughout the Midwest.
>
> **Situation Five:** Assume that you are considering taking a job (internal stakeholder) with either Sears or JC Penney.

E1-22

Financial statement items

Obj 4

Starbucks Corporation purchases and roasts high-quality whole bean coffees and sells them, along with fresh, rich-brewed coffees and a variety of other complementary items, primarily through company-operated retail stores.

The following items were adapted from the annual report of Starbucks Corporation for the period ending October 1, 2006:

	In thousands
1. Accounts payable	$ 340,937
2. Accounts receivable	224,271
3. Accrued taxes payable	94,010
4. Additions to property, plant, and equipment	771,230
5. Inventories	636,222

	In thousands
6. Cost of sales	$3,178,791
7. Depreciation and amortization expenses	387,211
8. General and administrative expenses	473,023
9. Income tax expense	324,770
10. Net cash provided by operating activities	1,131,633
11. Net sales	7,786,942
12. Other income (loss)	106,228
13. Other expenses	277,301
14. Property, plant, and equipment	2,287,899
15. Retained earnings (October 1, 2006)	2,151,084
16. Store operating expenses	2,687,815

Using the following notations, indicate on which financial statement you would find each of the preceding items. (*Note:* An item may appear on more than one statement.)

IS	Income statement
RE	Retained earnings statement
BS	Balance sheet
SCF	Statement of cash flows

E1-23

Income statement

Obj 4

✓ Net income, $564,259

Based on the ***Starbucks Corporation*** financial statement data shown in Exercise 1-22, prepare an income statement for the year ending October 1, 2006.

E1-24

Financial statement items

Obj 4

Though the ***McDonald's*** menu of hamburgers, cheeseburgers, the Big Mac®, Quarter Pounder®, the Filet-O-Fish®, and Chicken McNuggets® is easily recognized, McDonald's financial statements may not be as familiar. The following items were adapted from a recent annual report of McDonald's Corporation:

1. Accounts payable
2. Accrued interest payable
3. Capital stock outstanding
4. Cash
5. Cash provided by operations
6. Food and packaging costs used in operations
7. Income tax expense
8. Interest expense
9. Inventories
10. Long-term debt payable

11. Net income
12. Net increase in cash
13. Notes payable
14. Notes receivable
15. Occupancy and rent expense
16. Payroll expense
17. Prepaid expenses not yet used in operations
18. Property and equipment
19. Retained earnings
20. Sales

Identify the financial statement on which each of the preceding items would appear. An item may appear on more than one statement. Use the following notations:

IS	Income statement
RE	Retained earnings statement
BS	Balance sheet
SCF	Statement of cash flows

E1-25

Financial statements

Obj 4

✓ Correct amount of total
assets is $195,000

Pacific Realty, organized August 1, 2009, is owned and operated by Dawn Cordell. How many
errors can you find in the following financial statements for Pacific Realty, prepared after its first
month of operations? Assume that the cash balance on August 31, 2009, is $46,600 and that cash
flows from operating activities is reported correctly.

PACIFIC REALTY
Income Statement
August 31, 2009

Sales commissions		$308,400
Operating expenses:		
Office salaries expense	$172,600	
Rent expense	31,200	
Miscellaneous expense	2,200	
Automobile expense	7,900	
Total operating expenses		213,900
Net income		$134,500

DAWN CORDELL
Retained Earnings Statement
August 31, 2008

Retained earnings, August 1, 2009	$ 17,800
Less dividends during August	12,000
	$ 5,800
Net income for the month	134,500
Retained earnings, August 31, 2009	$140,300

Balance Sheet
For the Month Ended August 31, 2009

Assets		
Cash		$ 46,600
Accounts payable		12,500
Land		60,000
Total assets		$119,100
Liabilities		
Accounts receivable		$ 81,200
Prepaid expenses		7,200
Stockholders' Equity		
Capital stock	$100,000	
Retained earnings	140,300	240,300
Total liabilities and stockholders' equity		$328,700

Statement of Cash Flows
August 31, 2009

Cash flows from operating activities:		
Cash received from customers	$227,200	
Cash paid for operating expenses	208,600	
Net cash flow from operating activities		$ 18,600
Cash flows from financing activities:		
Cash received from issuance of capital stock	$100,000	
Dividends paid to stockholders	(12,000)	
Net cash flow from financing activities		88,000
Net cash flow and cash balance as of		
August 31, 2009		$106,600

E1-26

Accounting concepts

Obj 5

Match each of the following statements with the appropriate accounting concept. Some concepts may be used more than once, while others may not be used at all. Use the notations shown to indicate the appropriate accounting concept.

Accounting Concept	Notation
Accounting period concept	P
Adequate disclosure concept	D
Business entity concept	B
Cost concept	C
Going concern concept	G
Matching concept	M
Objectivity concept	O
Unit of measure concept	U

Statements

1. Personal transactions of owners are kept separate from the business.
2. Changes in the use of accounting methods from one period to the next are described in the notes to the financial statements.
3. This concept supports relying on an independent actuary (statistician), rather than the chief operating officer of the corporation, to estimate a pension liability.
4. Assume that a business will continue forever.
5. This concept justifies recording only transactions that are expressed in dollars.
6. Material litigation involving the corporation is described in a footnote.
7. If this concept was ignored, the confidence of users in the financial statements could not be maintained.
8. Monthly utilities costs are reported as expenses along with the monthly revenues.
9. The changes in financial condition are reported at the end of the month.
10. Land worth $800,000 is reported at its original purchase price of $220,000.

E1-27

Business entity concept

Obj 5

Glacier Sports sells hunting and fishing equipment and provides guided hunting and fishing trips. Glacier Sports is owned and operated by Ben Chambless, a well-known sports enthusiast and hunter. Ben's wife, Julie, owns and operates Fashion Boutique, a women's clothing store. Ben and Julie have established a trust fund to finance their children's college education. The trust fund is maintained by San Marcos City Bank in the name of the children, Renee and Keith.

For each of the following transactions, identify which of the entities listed should record the transaction in its records.

Entities	
G	Glacier Sports
S	San Marcos City Bank
F	Fashion Boutique
X	None of the above

1. Julie purchased two dozen spring dresses from a San Marcos designer for a special spring sale.
2. Ben paid for dinner and a movie to celebrate their fifteenth wedding anniversary.
3. Ben paid a local doctor for his annual physical, which was required by the workmens' compensation insurance policy carried by Glacier Sports.
4. Ben received a cash advance from customers for a guided hunting trip.
5. Julie deposited a $4,000 personal check in the trust fund at San Marcos City Bank.
6. Julie purchased mutual fund shares as an investment for the children's trust.
7. Ben paid for an advertisement in a hunters' magazine.

(continued)

8. Julie donated several dresses from inventory for a local charity auction for the benefit of a women's abuse shelter.
9. Julie paid her dues to the YWCA.
10. Ben paid a breeder's fee for a Brittany spaniel to be used as a hunting guide dog.

Problems

P1-1

Income statement, retained earnings statement, and balance sheet

Obj 4

SPREADSHEET

✓ 1. Net income: $222,200

The amounts of the assets and liabilities of Aloha Travel Service at November 30, 2008, the end of the current year, and its revenue and expenses for the year are listed below. The retained earnings were $140,000, and the capital stock was $60,000 at December 1, 2007, the beginning of the current year. Dividends of $120,000 were paid during the current year.

Accounts payable	$ 48,800
Accounts receivable	125,400
Cash	212,200
Fees earned	1,052,800
Miscellaneous expense	11,800
Rent expense	151,200
Supplies	13,400
Supplies expense	28,400
Taxes expense	22,400
Utilities expense	90,000
Wages expense	526,800

Instructions

1. Prepare an income statement for the current year ended November 30, 2008.
2. Prepare a retained earnings statement for the current year ended November 30, 2008.
3. Prepare a balance sheet as of November 30, 2008.

P1-2

Missing amounts from financial statements

Obj 4

SPREADSHEET

✓ j. $121,320

The financial statements at the end of La Jolla Realty's first month of operations are shown below.

LA JOLLA REALTY
Income Statement
For the Month Ended April 30, 2008

Fees earned		$56,400
Operating expenses:		
Wages expense	$ (a)	
Rent expense	5,760	
Supplies expense	4,800	
Utilities expense	3,240	
Miscellaneous expense	1,980	
Total operating expenses		28,680
Net income		$ (b)

LA JOLLA REALTY
Retained Earnings Statement
For the Month Ended April 30, 2008

Net income for April		$ (c)
Less dividends		(d)
Retained earnings, April 30, 2008		$ (e)

LA JOLLA REALTY
Balance Sheet
April 30, 2008

Assets

Cash	$35,400
Supplies	2,400
Land	(f)
Total assets	$ (g)

Liabilities

Accounts payable	$ 2,880

Stockholders' Equity

Capital stock	$ (h)	*12,3∠0*
Retained earnings	(i)	(j)
Total liabilities and stockholders' equity		$ (k)

LA JOLLA REALTY
Statement of Cash Flows
For the Month Ended April 30, 2008

Cash flows from operating activities:		
Cash received from customers	$ (l)	
Deduct cash payments for expenses and payments to creditors	28,200	
Net cash flows from operating activities		$ (m)
Cash flows from investing activities:		
Cash payments for acquisition of land		86,400
Cash flows from financing activities:		
Cash received from issuing capital stock	$108,000	
Deduct dividends	14,400	
Net cash flows from financing activities		(n)
Net cash flow and April 30, 2008 cash balance		$ (o)

Instructions

O = m⁻

1. Would you classify a realty business like La Jolla Realty as a manufacturing, merchandising, or service business?
2. By analyzing the interrelationships between the financial statements, determine the proper amounts for (a) through (o).

P1-3

Income statement, retained earnings statement, and balance sheet

Obj 4

SPREADSHEET

✓ 1. Net income, $1,377

The following financial data were adapted from the annual report of **Best Buy Inc.** for the period ending March 3, 2007:

	In millions
Accounts payable	$ 5,745
Capital stock	694
Cash	3,793
Cost of goods sold	27,165
Income tax expense	752
Inventories	4,028
Investments	318
Goodwill and other intangible assets	1,000
Other assets	945
Other liabilities	1,624
Other revenue (net)	130
Property, plant, and equipment	2,938
Receivables	548

(continued)

	In millions
Sales	35,934
Selling, general, and administrative expenses	6,770 ✳

Instructions

1. Prepare Best Buy's income statement for the year ending March 3, 2007.
2. Prepare Best Buy's retained earnings statement for the year ending March 3, 2007. (*Note:* The retained earnings at March 3, 2006, was $4,304. During the year, Best Buy paid dividends of $174.)
3. Prepare a balance sheet as of March 3, 2007, for Best Buy.

P1-4

Statement of cash flows

Obj 4

SPREADSHEET

✓ Net increase in cash, $2,901

The following cash data were adapted from the annual report of **Apple Computer Inc.** for the period ended September 30, 2006. The cash balance as of September 30, 2005, was $3,491 (in millions).

	In millions
Receipts from capital stock	$ 324
Payments for property, plant, and equipment	657
Receipts from sale of other investments (net)	1,014
Net cash flows from operating activities	2,220

Instructions

Prepare Apple's statement of cash flows for the year ended September 30, 2006.

P1-5

Financial statements, including statement of cash flows

Obj 4

SPREADSHEET

✓ 1. Net income, $236,250

eWare Corporation began operations on January 1, 2009, as an online retailer of computer software and hardware. The following financial statement data were taken from eWare's records at the end of its first year of operations, December 31, 2009.

Accounts payable	$ 31,500
Accounts receivable	50,400 okay
Capital stock	262,500
Cash	?
Cash payments for operating activities	735,000
Cash receipts from operating activities	878,850
Cost of sales	420,000
Dividends	26,250
Income tax expense	147,000
Income taxes payable	21,000
Interest expense	15,750
Inventories	94,500
Note payable (due in 2015)	105,000 okay
Property, plant, and equipment	396,900
Retained earnings	?
Sales	929,250
Selling and administrative expense	110,250

Instructions

1. Prepare an income statement for the year ended December 31, 2009.
2. Prepare a retained earnings statement for the year ended December 31, 2009.
3. Prepare a balance sheet as of December 31, 2009.
4. Prepare a statement of cash flows for the year ended December 31, 2009.

Activities

A1-1

Integrity, objectivity, and ethics at The Hershey Company

ETHICS

The management of ***The Hershey Company*** has asked union workers in two of their highest cost Pennsylvania plants to accept higher health insurance premiums and take a wage cut. The worker's portion of the insurance cost would double from 6% of the premium to 12%. In addition, workers hired after January 2000 would have their hourly wages cut by $4, which would be partially offset by a 2% annual raise. Management says that the plants need to be more cost competitive. The management has indicated that if the workers accept the proposal that the company would invest $30 million to modernize the plants and move future projects to the plants. Management, however, has refused to guarantee more work at the plants if the workers approve the proposal. If the workers reject the proposal, management implies that they would move future projects to other plants and that layoffs might be forthcoming. Do you consider management's actions ethical?

Source: Susan Govzdas, "Hershey to Cut Jobs or Wages," *Central Penn Business Journal,* September 24, 2004.

A1-2

Ethics and professional conduct in business

GROUP

ETHICS

Monica Orgeta, president and owner of Star Enterprises, applied for a $250,000 loan from Carmel National Bank. The bank requested financial statements from Star Enterprises as a basis for granting the loan. Monica has told her accountant to provide the bank with a balance sheet. Monica has decided to omit the other financial statements because there was a net loss during the past year.

In groups of three or four, discuss the following questions:

1. Is Monica behaving in a professional manner by omitting some of the financial statements?
2. a. What types of information about their businesses would owners be willing to provide bankers? What types of information would owners not be willing to provide?
   b. What types of information about a business would bankers want before extending a loan?
   c. What common interests are shared by bankers and business owners?

A1-3

How businesses make money

GROUP

Assume that you are the chief executive officer for ***Pilgrim's Pride Corporation***, a national poultry producer. The company's operations include hatching chickens through the use of breeder stock and feeding, raising, and processing the mature chicks into finished products. The finished products include breaded chicken nuggets and patties and deboned, skinless, and marinated chicken. Pilgrim's Pride Corporation sells its products to schools, military services, fast-food chains, and grocery stores.

In groups of four or five, discuss the following business emphasis and risk issues:

1. In a commodity business like poultry production, what do you think is the dominant business emphasis? What are the implications in this dominant emphasis for how you would run Pilgrim's Pride Corporation?
2. Identify at least two major business risks for operating Pilgrim's Pride Corporation.
3. How could Pilgrim's Pride Corporation try to differentiate its products?

A1-4

Net income versus cash flow

On January 3, 2009, Dr. Abraham Brody established Second Opinion, a medical practice organized as a professional corporation. The following conversation occurred the following September between Dr. Brody and a former medical school classmate, Dr. Janice Martin, at an American Medical Association convention in Paris, France.

Dr. Martin: Abraham, good to see you again. Why didn't you call when you were in Las Vegas? We could have had dinner together.

(continued)

Dr. Brody: Actually, I never made it to Las Vegas this year. My wife and kids went up to our Lake Tahoe condo twice, but I got stuck in New York. I opened a new consulting practice this January and haven't had any time for myself since.

Dr. Martin: I heard about it . . . Second . . . something . . . right?

Dr. Brody: Yes, Second Opinion. My wife chose the name.

Dr. Martin: I've thought about doing something like that. Are you making any money? I mean, is it worth your time?

Dr. Brody: You wouldn't believe it. I started by opening a bank account with $40,000, and my August bank statement has a balance of $120,000. Not bad for eight months—all pure profit.

Dr. Martin: Maybe I'll try it in Las Vegas. Let's have breakfast together tomorrow and you can fill me in on the details.

Comment on Dr. Brody's statement that the difference between the opening bank balance ($40,000) and the August statement balance ($120,000) is pure profit.

A1-5
The accounting equation

Obtain the annual reports for three well-known companies, such as **Ford Motor Co., General Motors, IBM, Microsoft,** or **Amazon.com.** These annual reports can be obtained from the library, the company's Web site under "Investor Relations," **http://finance.yahoo.com** (type in the company name for Get Quotes), or the company's 10-K filing with the Securities and Exchange Commission at **http://www.sec.gov/**.

To obtain annual report information, click on "Search for Company Filings." Next, click on "Historical EDGAR Archives." Key in the company name. EDGAR will list the reports available for the company. Click on the 10-K (or 10-K405) report for the year you want to download. If you wish, you can save the whole 10-K report to a file and then open it with your word processor.

Examine the balance sheet for each company and determine the total assets, liabilities, and stockholders' equity. Verify that total assets equal the total of the liabilities plus stockholders' equity.

A1-6
Hershey's annual report

The financial statements of **The Hershey Company** are shown in Exhibits 4 through 7 of this chapter. Based upon these statements, answer the following questions.

1. What are Hershey's sales (in millions)?
2. What is Hershey's cost of sales (in millions)?
3. What is Hershey's net income (in millions)?
4. What is Hershey's percent of the cost of sales to sales? Round to one decimal place.
5. The percent that a company adds to its cost of sales to determine the selling price is called a markup. What is Hershey's markup percent? Round to one decimal place.
6. What is the percentage of net income to sales for Hershey? Round to one decimal place.

A1-7
Income statement analysis

The following data (in thousands of dollars) were adapted from the December 31, 2006, financial statements of **Tootsie Roll Industries Inc.:**

Sales	$495,990
Cost of goods sold	310,507
Net income	65,919

1. What is Tootsie Roll's percent of the cost of sales to sales? Round to one decimal place.
2. The percent a company adds to its cost of sales to determine selling price is called a markup. What is Tootsie Roll's markup percent? Round to one decimal place.
3. What is the percentage of net income to sales for Tootsie Roll? Round to one decimal place.
4. Compare your answer to (3) with that of The Hershey Company in Activity 1-6. What are your conclusions?

A1-8

Financial analysis of Enron Corporation

Enron Corporation, headquartered in Houston, Texas, provides products and services for natural gas, electricity, and communications to wholesale and retail customers. Enron's operations are conducted through a variety of subsidiaries and affiliates that involve transporting gas through pipelines, transmitting electricity, and managing energy commodities. The following data were taken from Enron's December 31, 2000, financial statements:

	In millions
Total revenues	$100,789
Total costs and expenses	98,836
Operating income	1,953
Net income	979
Total assets	65,503
Total liabilities	54,033
Total stockholders' equity	11,470
Net cash flows from operating activities	4,779
Net cash flows from investing activities	(4,264)
Net cash flows from financing activities	571
Net increase in cash	1,086

At the end of 2000, the market price of Enron's stock was approximately $83 per share. As of April 17, 2005, Enron's stock was selling for $0.03 per share.

Review the preceding financial statement data and search the Internet for articles on Enron Corporation. Briefly explain why Enron's stock dropped so dramatically in such a short time.

Answers to Self-Examination Questions

1. **D** A corporation, organized in accordance with state or federal statutes, is a separate legal entity in which ownership is divided into shares of stock (answer D). A proprietorship (answer A) is an unincorporated business owned by one individual. A service business (answer B) provides services to its customers. It can be organized as a proprietorship, partnership, or corporation. A partnership (answer C) is an unincorporated business owned by two or more individuals.

2. **A** The resources owned by a business are called assets (answer A). The debts of the business are called liabilities (answer B), and the equity of the owners is called stockholders' equity (answer D). The relationship between assets, liabilities, and stockholders' equity is expressed as the accounting equation (answer C).

3. **A** The balance sheet is a listing of the assets, liabilities, and stockholders' equity of a business at a specific date (answer A). The income statement (answer B) is a summary of the revenue and expenses of a business for a specific period of time. The retained earnings statement (answer C) summarizes the changes in retained earnings

during a specific period of time. The statement of cash flows (answer D) summarizes the cash receipts and cash payments for a specific period of time.

4. **D** The accounting equation is:

   Assets = Liabilities + Stockholders' Equity

   Therefore, if assets are $20,000 and liabilities are $12,000, stockholders' equity is $8,000 (answer D), as indicated in the following computation:

Assets	= Liabilities + Stockholders' Equity
+$20,000	= +$12,000 + Stockholders' Equity
+$20,000 − $12,000	= Stockholders' Equity
+$8,000	= Stockholders' Equity

5. **B** Net income is the excess of revenue over expenses, or $7,500 (answer B). If expenses exceed revenue, the difference is a net loss. Dividends are the opposite of the stockholders investing in the business and do not affect the amount of net income or net loss.

CHAPTER 2

Basic Accounting Concepts

Learning Objectives

After studying this chapter, you should be able to:

Obj 1

Describe the basic elements of a financial accounting system.

Obj 2

Analyze, record, and summarize transactions for a corporation's first period of operations.

Obj 3

Prepare financial statements for a corporation's first period of operations.

Obj 4

Analyze, record, and summarize transactions for a corporation's second period of operations.

Obj 5

Prepare financial statements for a corporation's second period of operations.

Suppose you receive $100 as a result of some event. Does it make a difference what the event is? Yes, it does! If you receive $100 for your birthday, it's a gift. If you receive $100 as a result of working part time for a week, then it's the result of your effort. If you receive $100 as a loan, then it's money that you have to pay back in the future. If you received $100 as a result of selling your stereo, then it's the result of giving up something tangible. Thus, we see that the $100 received can be associated with different types of events, and that these events have different meanings to you. You'd much rather receive a $100 gift than a $100 loan, given the choice. Likewise, a company and its stakeholders would view events such as these differently.

Wm. Wrigley Jr. Company receives cash in return for providing a very simple but widely used product: chewing gum. Wm. Wrigley Jr. Company's stakeholders are interested in its future financial condition and success. As we discussed in Chapter 1, the financial condition and changes in financial condition of a business are assessed through analyzing financial statements. In this chapter, we continue our discussion of financial statements. We begin by describing the basic elements of a financial accounting system that will enable the preparation of financial statements. We then distinguish types of accounting systems and illustrate the simplest form of an accounting system using receipts and payments of cash. In doing so, this chapter will serve as the foundation for our later discussions of modern accounting systems and financial reporting.

Elements of an Accounting System

A financial accounting system is designed to produce financial statements. You should recall from Chapter 1 that the basic financial statements are the income statement, retained earnings statement, balance sheet, and statement of cash flows. So what are the basic elements of an accounting system that will enable the preparation of these statements?

The basic elements of a **financial accounting system** include (1) a set of rules for determining what, when, and the amount that should be recorded for economic events, (2) a framework for preparing financial statements, and (3) one or more controls to determine whether errors may have arisen in the recording process. These basic elements are found in all financial accounting systems—from a local retailer or hardware store to *Microsoft*, *Sony*, *Boeing*, and Wrigley.

Rules

A set of rules for determining what, when, and the amount that should be recorded for an entity's economic events are derived from the eight concepts we discussed in Chapter 1. These concepts form the foundation for generally accepted accounting principles. Throughout this text, we describe and illustrate generally accepted accounting principles based upon these eight concepts.

A **transaction** is an economic event that under generally accepted accounting principles affects an element of the financial statements and, therefore, must be recorded. A transaction may affect one, two, or more elements of the financial statements. For example, equipment purchased for cash affects only assets. That is, one asset (equipment) increases while another asset (cash) decreases. If, on the other hand, the equipment is purchased on credit, both assets (equipment) and liabilities (accounts or notes payable) increase.

Framework

In order to prepare financial statements, transactions must be analyzed, recorded, and summarized using a framework. The accounting equation provides a starting point for designing such a framework. You should recall from Chapter 1 that the accounting equation is expressed as follows:

$$\text{Assets} = \text{Liabilities} + \text{Stockholders' Equity}$$

An *integrated financial statement approach* is used for analyzing, recording, and summarizing transactions by expanding the accounting equation as shown in Exhibit 1. This is done by including columns for the statement of cash flows, balance sheet, and income statement.

The left-hand column in Exhibit 1 shows the effects of transactions on the statement of cash flows. Each cash transaction is recorded and classified into operating, investing, and financing activities as a basis for preparing the statement of cash flows. The cash amount at the beginning of the period plus or minus the cash flows from operating, investing, and financing activities equals the end-of-period cash. This end-of-period cash amount is reported as an asset on the balance sheet. Thus, the statement of cash flows is integrated with the balance sheet.

The far right-hand column in Exhibit 1 records and summarizes revenue and expense transactions as a basis for preparing the income statement. Recall, net income, which is revenue less expenses, affects retained earnings. Thus, revenue and expense transactions are also recorded under the retained earnings column of the balance sheet. By doing so, the balance sheet is integrated with the income statement.

EXHIBIT 1   *Integrated Financial Statement Framework*

Statement of Cash Flows	Balance Sheet				Income Statement
	Assets = Liabilities +		Stockholders' Equity		
	Assets = Liabilities +		Capital Stock +	Retained Earnings	
Transactions	XXX	XXX	XXX	XXX	
	XXX	XXX	XXX	XXX	

Statement of Cash Flows		Income Statement	
+/− Operating activities	XXX	Revenues	XXX
+/− Investing activities	XXX	Expenses	XXX
+/− Financing activities	XXX	Net income or loss	XXX
Increase or decrease in cash	XXX		
Beginning cash	XXX		
Ending cash	XXX		

> **INTEGRATED FINANCIAL STATEMENT FRAMEWORK**

Exhibit 1 also illustrates the importance of the balance sheet as the connecting link between the statement of cash flows and the income statement.[1] Later in this chapter, we illustrate the use of this integrated financial statement approach for analyzing, recording, and summarizing transactions.

You will find the integrated financial statement approach, shown in Exhibit 1, an invaluable aid in analyzing the financial condition and changes in financial condition of a company. This is because, without understanding how a company's financial statements are prepared and integrated, you may miss important trends or events. To illustrate, assume a company reports net income (profits) on its income statement. This might lead you to mistakenly conclude that the company's operations are doing well and no major changes are necessary. In fact, if the company has negative net cash flows from operations, it may be headed toward bankruptcy. This is why it is essential to analyze all the financial statements and why we emphasize the integrated financial statement approach throughout this text.

Controls

The integrated financial statement approach shown in Exhibit 1 has built-in controls that transactions are analyzed, recorded, and summarized correctly. Specifically, the accounting equation ensures that total assets must equal total liabilities plus total stockholders' equity on the balance sheet. If at the end of the period this equality does not hold, then an error has occurred in either recording or summarizing transactions. For example, if a $10,000 purchase of equipment for cash is incorrectly recorded as an increase in both equipment and cash, the total assets will exceed the total liabilities and stockholders' equity by $20,000 at the end of the period. Likewise, if equipment was increased by $10,000, but cash was not decreased by $10,000, the total assets will exceed total liabilities and stockholders' equity by $10,000 at the end of the period. In both cases, the inequality of the equation will indicate that an error has occurred in the recording process.

[1]In Chapter 3, we describe and illustrate how balance sheet elements can be used to reconcile net cash flows from operating activities with net income.

HOW BUSINESSES MAKE MONEY

Got the Flu? Why Not Chew Some Gum?

Facing a slumping market for sugared chewing gum, such as Juicy Fruit and Doublemint, Wm. Wrigley Jr. Company is reinventing itself by expanding its product lines and introducing new chewing gum applications. Wrigley's new products include sugarless breath mints and more powerful flavored mint chewing gum, like Extra Polar Ice. In addition, Wrigley is experimenting with health-care applications of chewing gum. Wrigley's Health Care Division has already developed Surpass, an antacid chewing gum to compete with Rolaids and Mylanta. Wrigley is also developing a cold-relief chewing gum and a gum that would provide dental benefits, such as whitening teeth and reducing plaque. Given that the U.S. population is aging, the company figures that people might prefer chewing gum to taking pills for sore throats, colds, or the flu. The effects of these new initiatives will ultimately be reflected in Wrigley's financial statements.

Source: Adapted from "A Young Heir Has New Plans at Old Company," by David Barboza, *New York Times,* August 28, 2001.

The equality of the equation at the end of the period doesn't necessarily mean that no errors have occurred. For example, assume that a business purchased $10,000 of equipment on credit and recorded the transaction as an increase in equipment of $10,000. However, instead of increasing the liabilities by $10,000, the transaction was recorded as a $10,000 decrease in cash. In this case, the accounting equation still balances, even though cash and liabilities are understated by $10,000.

The integrated financial statement approach provides two additional controls. First, the ending cash amount shown in the statement of cash flows column must agree with the end-of-period cash amount shown under assets in the balance sheet column. Second, the net income or loss from the income statement column must agree with the net effects of revenues and expenses on retained earnings.[2]

Recording a Corporation's First Period of Operations

Obj 2

Analyze, record, and summarize transactions for a corporation's first period of operations.

Using the integrated financial statement framework shown in Exhibit 1, we will illustrate the recording of transactions for a corporation's first period of operations. We will assume that on September 1, 2009, Lee Landry, M.D., organizes a professional corporation to practice general medicine. The business is to be known as Family Health Care, P.C., where P.C. refers to professional corporation. We describe each transaction or group of similar transactions during September, the first month of operations. We then illustrate how Exhibit 1 can be used to analyze, record, and summarize the effects of these transactions on the financial statements. We begin with Dr. Landry's investment to establish the business.

Transaction (a)   Dr. Landry deposits $6,000 in a bank account in the name of Family Health Care, P.C., in return for shares of stock in the corporation. We refer to stock issued to owners (stockholders) such as Lee Landry as capital stock. The effect of this transaction is to increase cash from financing activities by $6,000 under the statement of cash flows column. Increases are recorded as positive numbers, while decreases are recorded as negative numbers. In addition, the transaction increases assets (cash) in the left side of the accounting equation under the balance sheet column by $6,000. To balance the equation, the stockholders' equity (capital stock) on the right side of the equation is increased by the same amount. Since no revenues or expenses are affected,

[2]We discuss additional accounting controls in Chapter 4.

there are no entries under the income statement column. The effect of this transaction on Family Health Care's financial statements is shown below.

Statement of Cash Flows	Balance Sheet					Income Statement
	Assets	=	Liabilities	+	Stockholders' Equity	
	Cash	=		+	Capital Stock	
a. Investment by Dr. Landry	6,000				6,000	

Statement of Cash Flows

a. Financing	6,000

Note that the equation relates only to the business, Family Health Care, P.C. Lee Landry's personal assets (such as a home or a personal bank account) and personal liabilities are excluded from the equation. The business is treated as a separate entity, with cash of $6,000 and stockholders' equity of $6,000.

Transaction (b)   Family Health Care's next transaction is to borrow $10,000 from First National Bank to finance its operations. To borrow the $10,000, Lee Landry signed a note payable in the name of Family Health Care. The note payable is a liability or a claim on assets that Family Health Care must satisfy (pay) in the future. In addition, the note payable requires the payment of interest of $100 per month until the note is due in full on September 30, 2014. At the end of September, we will record the payment of $100 of interest.

The effect of this transaction is to increase cash from financing activities by $10,000 under the statement of cash flows column. In addition, cash is increased and liabilities (notes payable) are increased under the balance sheet columns. Observe how this transaction changed the mix of assets and liabilities on the balance sheet but did not change Family Health Care's stockholders' equity. That is, assets minus liabilities still equals stockholders' equity of $6,000 on the balance sheet. Since no revenues or expenses are affected, no entries are made under the income statement column. The effect of this transaction on Family Health Care's financial statements is shown below.

Statement of Cash Flows	Balance Sheet					Income Statement
	Assets	=	Liabilities	+	Stockholders' Equity	
	Cash	=	Notes Payable	+	Capital Stock	
Balances	6,000				6,000	
b. Loan from bank	10,000		10,000			
Balances	16,000		10,000		6,000	

Statement of Cash Flows

b. Financing	10,000

Transaction (c)   Next, Family Health Care buys land for $12,000 cash. The land is located near a new suburban hospital that is under construction. Lee Landry plans to rent office space and equipment for several months. When the hospital is completed, Family Health Care will build on the land.

The effect of this transaction is an outflow of cash as an investing activity. Thus, a negative $12,000 is entered in the statement of cash flows column as an investing activity. On the balance sheet, the purchase of the land changes the makeup of the assets, but it does not change the total assets. That is, cash is decreased and land is increased by $12,000. The effect of this transaction on Family Health Care's financial statements is shown below.

Statement of Cash Flows	Assets			=	Liabilities	+	Stockholders' Equity	Income Statement
	Cash	+	Land	=	Notes Payable	+	Capital Stock	
Balances	16,000				10,000		6,000	
c. Purchase of land	−12,000		12,000					
Balances	4,000		12,000		10,000		6,000	

Statement of Cash Flows		
c. Investing	−12,000	

Transactions (b) and (c) have not improved the stockholders' equity of Family Health Care. They have simply changed the mix of assets and increased the liability, notes payable. However, the objective of businesses is to improve stockholders' equity through operations.

Transaction (d)   During the first month of operations, Family Health Care earns patient fees of $5,500, receiving the amount in cash. The effect of this transaction is an inflow of cash flows from operating activities of $5,500. Thus, a positive $5,500 is entered in the statement of cash flows column as an operating activity. Since cash has been received, cash is increased by $5,500 under the balance sheet column for assets. Fees earned of $5,500 is a revenue item that is entered in the income statement column as a positive amount. Since net income retained in the business increases stockholders' equity (retained earnings) and since revenues contribute to net income, $5,500 is also entered as an increase in retained earnings in the stockholders' equity column of the balance sheet. Entering the increases of $5,500 for cash and retained earnings in the balance sheet columns retains the equality of the accounting equation. The effect of this transaction on Family Health Care's financial statements is summarized below.

Statement of Cash Flows	Assets			=	Liabilities	+	Stockholders' Equity				Income Statement
	Cash	+	Land	=	Notes Payable	+	Capital Stock	+	Retained Earnings		
Balances	4,000		12,000		10,000		6,000				
d. Fees earned	5,500								5,500	d.	
Balances	9,500		12,000		10,000		6,000		5,500		

Statement of Cash Flows			Income Statement	
d. Operating	5,500		d. Fees earned	5,500

Transaction (e)   For Family Health Care, the expenses paid during the month were as follows: wages, $1,125; rent, $950; utilities, $450; interest, $100; and miscellaneous, $275. Miscellaneous expenses include small amounts paid for such items as postage due and newspaper and magazine purchases.

The effect of this transaction is an outflow of cash of $2,900 for operating activities. Thus, a negative $2,900 is entered in the statement of cash flows column as an operating activity. Expenses have the opposite effect as revenues on net income and retained earnings. As a result, each of the expenses is listed as a negative amount in the income statement column. Finally, a negative $2,900 is also entered in the cash and retained earnings columns of the balance sheet. The effect of this transaction on Family Health Care's financial statements is summarized below.

Statement of Cash Flows	Assets			=	Liabilities	+	Stockholders' Equity			Income Statement
	Cash	+	Land	=	Notes Payable	+	Capital Stock	+	Retained Earnings	
Balances	9,500		12,000		10,000		6,000		5,500	
e. Paid expenses	−2,900								−2,900	e.
Balances	6,600		12,000		10,000		6,000		2,600	

Statement of Cash Flows

e. Operating	−2,900

Income Statement

e. Wages expense	−1,125
Rent expense	−950
Utilities expense	−450
Interest expense	−100
Misc. expense	−275

Transaction (f)   At the end of the month, Family Health Care pays $1,500 to stockholders (Dr. Lee Landry) as dividends. Dividends are distributions of business earnings to stockholders.

The effect of this transaction is an outflow of cash of $1,500 for financing activities. Thus, a negative $1,500 is entered in the statement of cash flows column as a financing activity. In addition, the cash and retained earnings are decreased under the balance sheet column, by $1,500. The effect of this transaction on Family Health Care's financial statements is summarized below.

Statement of Cash Flows	Assets			=	Liabilities	+	Stockholders' Equity			Income Statement
	Cash	+	Land	=	Notes Payable	+	Capital Stock	+	Retained Earnings	
Balances	6,600		12,000		10,000		6,000		2,600	
f. Paid dividends	−1,500								−1,500	
Balances	5,100		12,000		10,000		6,000		1,100	

Statement of Cash Flows

f. Financing	−1,500

You should be careful not to confuse dividends with expenses. Dividends do not represent assets consumed or services used in the process of earning revenues. The decrease in stockholders' equity from dividends is listed in the equation under "Retained Earnings." This is because dividends are considered a distribution of earnings to the owners.

INTEGRITY, OBJECTIVITY, AND ETHICS IN BUSINESS

A History of Ethical Conduct

The Wrigley Company has a long history of integrity, objectivity, and ethical conduct. When pressured to become part of a cartel, known as the Chewing Gum Trust, the company founder, William Wrigley Jr., said, "We prefer to do business by fair and square methods or we prefer not to do business at all." In 1932, Phillip K. Wrigley, called "PK" by his friends, became president of the Wrigley Company after his father, William Wrigley Jr., died. PK also was president of the Chicago Cubs, which played in Wrigley Field. He was financially generous to his players and frequently gave them advice on and off the field. However, as a man of integrity and high ethical standards, PK docked (reduced) his salary as president of the Wrigley Company for the time he spent working on Cubs related activities and business.

Source: St. Louis Post-Dispatch, "Sports—Backpages," January 26, 2003.

The transactions of Family Health Care are summarized in Exhibit 2. The transactions are identified by letter, and the balances are shown as of the end of September. You should note that under the balance sheet columns the accounting equation balances. That is, total assets of $17,100 ($5,100 + $12,000) equals total liabilities plus stockholders' equity of $17,100 ($10,000 + $6,000 + $1,100).

In reviewing the preceding illustration and Exhibit 2, you should note the following, which apply to all types of businesses:

1. The balance sheet reflects the accounting equation (assets = liabilities + stockholders' equity).
2. The two sides of the balance sheet (accounting equation) are always equal.

EXHIBIT 2 *Family Health Care Summary of Transactions for September*

Statement of Cash Flows	Assets			=	Liabilities	+	Stockholders' Equity			Income Statement
	Cash	+	Land	=	Notes Payable	+	Capital Stock	+	Retained Earnings	
a. Investment by Dr. Landry	6,000						6,000			
b. Loan from bank	10,000				10,000					
c. Purchase of land	−12,000		12,000							
d. Fees earned	5,500								5,500	d.
e. Paid expenses	−2,900								−2,900	e.
f. Paid dividends	−1,500								−1,500	
Balances, Sept. 30	5,100		12,000		10,000		6,000		1,100	

Statement of Cash Flows		Income Statement	
a. Financing	6,000	d. Fees earned	5,500
b. Financing	10,000	e. Wages expense	−1,125
c. Investing	−12,000	Rent expense	−950
d. Operating	5,500	Utilities expense	−450
e. Operating	−2,900	Interest expense	−100
f. Financing	−1,500	Misc. expense	−275
Increase in cash and Sept. 30 cash	5,100	Net income	2,600

3. Every transaction affects (increases or decreases) one or more of the balance sheet elements—assets, liabilities, or stockholders' equity.
4. A transaction may or may not affect (increase or decrease) an element of the statement of cash flows or the income statement. Some transactions affect elements of both statements, some transactions affect only one statement and not the other, and some transactions affect neither statement.
5. The effect of every *cash* transaction increases or decreases the asset cash on the balance sheet. Every cash transaction also increases or decreases an operating, investing, or financing activity on the statement of cash flows.
6. The net increase or decrease in cash for the period shown in the statement of cash flows ($5,100 in Exhibit 2) agrees with the ending cash balance shown on the balance sheet. In this illustration, this resulted because it was the entity's first period of operations. In future periods, the net increase (decrease) in cash will be added to (subtracted from) the beginning cash balance to equal the ending cash balance. This ending cash balance will appear in both the statement of cash flows and balance sheet.
7. The stockholders' equity is increased by amounts invested by stockholders (capital stock).
8. Revenues increase stockholders' equity (retained earnings) and expenses decrease stockholders' equity (retained earnings). The effects of revenue and expense transactions are also shown in the income statement column.
9. Stockholders' equity (retained earnings) is decreased by dividends distributed to stockholders.
10. The change in retained earnings for the period is the net income minus dividends. For a net loss, the change in retained earnings is the net loss plus dividends.
11. The statement of cash flows is linked to the balance sheet through cash (an asset).
12. The income statement is linked to the balance sheet through revenues and expenses (net income or loss), which affects retained earnings.

Exhibit 3 summarizes the effects of the various transactions affecting stockholders' equity.

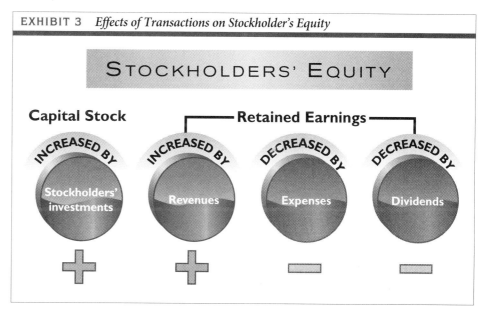

EXHIBIT 3   *Effects of Transactions on Stockholder's Equity*

Financial Statements for a Corporation's First Period of Operations

Obj 3

Prepare financial statements for a corporation's first period of operations.

In Exhibit 2, the September transactions for Family Health Care are listed in the order that they occurred. This exhibit, however, is not very user-friendly in that it does not group and summarize like transactions together. As we described and illustrated in Chapter 1, the accounting reports that provide this summarized information are financial statements. Such financial statements can easily be prepared from the integrated financial statement framework shown in Exhibit 2.

The September financial statements for Family Health Care are illustrated in Exhibit 4. The data for the statements were taken from Exhibit 2.

The income statement is normally prepared first using the income statement column of Exhibit 2. The income statement is prepared first because the net income or loss is needed to prepare the retained earnings statement. The retained earnings statement is prepared next because the ending balance of retained earnings is needed for preparing the balance sheet. The retained earnings statement is prepared using the income statement and the amount recorded for dividends for the period. The balance sheet is prepared next using the balances as of September 30 shown in Exhibit 2. The statement of cash flows is normally prepared last using the statement of cash flows column of Exhibit 2. You should note that each financial statement is identified by the name of the business, the title of the statement, and the date or period of time.

EXHIBIT 4   *Family Health Care Financial Statements for September*

FAMILY HEALTH CARE, P.C.
Income Statement
For the Month Ended September 30, 2009

Fees earned		$5,500
Operating expenses:		
Wages expense	$1,125	
Rent expense	950	
Utilities expense	450	
Interest expense	100	
Miscellaneous expense	275	
Total operating expenses		2,900
Net income		$2,600

FAMILY HEALTH CARE, P.C.
Retained Earnings Statement
For the Month Ended September 30, 2009

Net income for September	$2,600
Less dividends	1,500
Retained earnings, September 30, 2009	$1,100

FAMILY HEALTH CARE, P.C.
Balance Sheet
September 30, 2009

Assets

Cash		$ 5,100
Land		12,000
Total assets		$17,100

Liabilities

Notes payable		$10,000

Stockholders' Equity

Capital stock	$6,000	
Retained earnings	1,100	7,100
Total liabilities and stockholders' equity		$17,100

FAMILY HEALTH CARE, P.C.
Statement of Cash Flows
For the Month Ended September 30, 2009

Cash flows from operating activities:			
Cash received from customers		$ 5,500	
Deduct cash payments for expenses		2,900	
Net cash flow from operating activities			$ 2,600
Cash flows from investing activities:			
Cash payments for acquisition of land			(12,000)
Cash flows from financing activities:			
Cash received from sale of capital stock	$ 6,000		
Cash received from notes payable	10,000	$16,000	
Deduct cash dividends		1,500	
Net cash flow from financing activities			14,500
Net increase in cash			$ 5,100
September 1, 2009, cash balance			0
September 30, 2009, cash balance			$ 5,100

Income Statement

As shown in Exhibit 4, the income statement for Family Health Care reports fees earned of $5,500, total operating expenses of $2,900, and net income of $2,600. The $5,500 of fees earned was taken from the income statement column of Exhibit 2. Likewise, the expenses were summarized from the income statement column of Exhibit 2 and reported under the heading "Operating expenses." The expenses were listed in order of size, beginning with the largest expense. Miscellaneous expense is usually shown as the last item, regardless of the amount. The total operating expenses were then subtracted from the fees earned to arrive at the net income of $2,600. The effect of this net income will be to increase retained earnings and stockholders' equity.

Retained Earnings Statement

Since Family Health Care has been in operation for only one month, it has no retained earnings at the beginning of September. The ending September balance is the change in retained earnings that results from net income and dividends. This change, $1,100, will be the beginning retained earnings balance for October.

Balance Sheet

The amounts of Family Health Care's assets, liabilities, and stockholders' equity as of September 30 appear on the last line of the balance sheet columns of Exhibit 2. The balance sheet is prepared as shown in Exhibit 4.

In the liabilities section of Family Health Care's balance sheet, notes payable is the only liability. When there are two or more categories of liabilities, each should be listed and the total amount of liabilities reported. Liabilities should be presented in the order that they will be paid in cash. Thus, the notes payable due in 2014 will be listed after the obligations that are due in shorter time periods.

For Family Health Care, the September 30, 2009, stockholders' equity consists of $6,000 of capital stock and retained earnings of $1,100. The retained earnings amount is also reported on the retained earnings statement.

Statement of Cash Flows

Family Health Care's statement of cash flows for September is prepared from the statement of cash flows column of Exhibit 2. Cash increased from a zero balance at the beginning of the month to $5,100 at the end of the month. Part of this $5,100 increase in cash was a result of cash flows from operating activities of $2,600.

In addition to cash inflows of $2,600 from operating activities, Family Health Care spent $12,000 of cash for investing activities involving the purchase of land. This cash outflow related to investing activities was financed by an increased investment of $6,000 by Dr. Landry and $10,000 borrowed through a note payable at First National Bank. Family Health Care also distributed $1,500 in cash dividends during September.

Integration of Financial Statements

Exhibit 5 shows the integration of Family Health Care's financial statements for September. The ending cash balance of $5,100 on the balance sheet equals the ending cash balance reported on the statement of cash flows. The net income of $2,600 is reported on the income statement and the retained earnings statement. The ending retained earnings of $1,100 is reported in the retained earnings statement and the balance sheet. The cash flows from operating activities of $2,600 reported on the statement of cash flows equals the net income on the income statement. However, as we illustrate and explain in the next chapter, while cash flows from operating activities and net income are related they are normally not equal.

EXHIBIT 5   *Family Health Care Integrated Financial Statements for September*

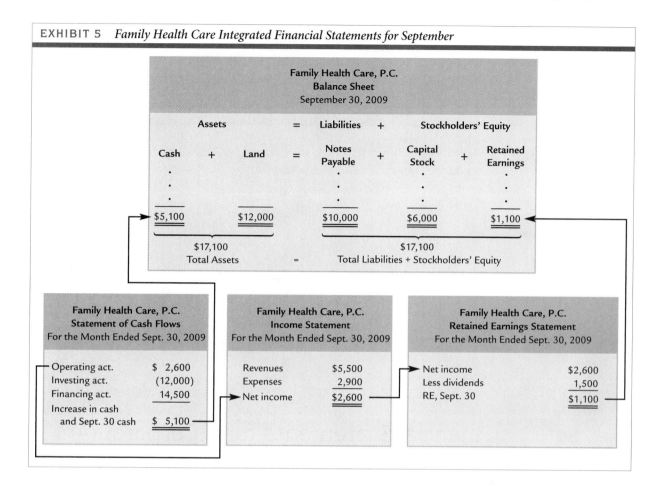

Recording a Corporation's Second Period of Operations

Obj 4

Analyze, record, and summarize transactions for a corporation's second period of operations.

To reinforce your understanding of recording transactions and preparing financial statements, we continue with Family Health Care's October transactions. During October, Family Health Care entered into the following transactions:

a. Received fees of $6,400 in cash.
b. Paid expenses in cash, as follows: wages, $1,370; rent, $950; utilities, $540; interest, $100; and miscellaneous, $220.
c. Paid dividends of $1,000 in cash.

The preceding October transactions have been analyzed and entered into a summary of transactions for October, as shown in Exhibit 6. You should note that the balance sheet columns of Exhibit 6 begin with the ending balances as of September 30, 2009. This is because the balance sheet reports the cumulative total of the entity's assets, liabilities, and stockholders' equity since its inception. In other words, as of October 1, Family Health Care has cash of $5,100, land of $12,000, notes payable of $10,000, capital stock of $6,000, and retained earnings of $1,100. In contrast, the statement of cash flows and the income statement report only transactions for the period.

EXHIBIT 6   *Family Health Care Summary of Transactions for October*

Statement of Cash Flows	Balance Sheet							Income Statement
	Assets		=	Liabilities	+	Stockholders' Equity		
	Cash	+ Land	=	Notes Payable	+	Capital Stock	+ Retained Earnings	
Balances, Oct. 1	5,100	12,000		10,000		6,000	1,100	
a. Fees earned	6,400						6,400	a.
b. Paid expenses	−3,180						−3,180	b.
c. Paid dividends	−1,000						−1,000	
Balances, Oct. 31	7,320	12,000		10,000		6,000	3,320	

Statement of Cash Flows			Income Statement	
a. Operating	6,400		a. Fees earned	6,400
b. Operating	−3,180		b. Wages expense	−1,370
c. Financing	−1,000		Rent expense	−950
Increase in cash	2,220		Utilities expense	−540
			Interest expense	−100
			Misc. expense	−220
			Net income	3,220

Financial Statements for a Corporation's Second Period of Operations

Obj 5

Prepare financial statements for a corporation's second period of operations.

Family Health Care's financial statements for October are shown in Exhibit 7. These statements were prepared from the integrated financial statement framework shown in Exhibit 6.

The income statement for October reports net income of $3,220. This is an increase of $620, or 23.8% ($620/$2,600), from September's net income of $2,600. This increase in net income was due to fees increasing from $5,500 to $6,400, a $900, or 16.4%

EXHIBIT 7   *Family Health Care Financial Statements for October*

FAMILY HEALTH CARE, P.C.
Income Statement
For the Month Ended October 31, 2009

Fees earned		$6,400
Operating expenses:		
Wages expense	$1,370	
Rent expense	950	
Utilities expense	540	
Interest expense	100	
Miscellaneous expense	220	
Total operating expenses		3,180
Net income		$3,220

FAMILY HEALTH CARE, P.C.
Retained Earnings Statement
For the Month Ended October 31, 2009

Retained earnings, October 1, 2009		$1,100
Net income for October	$3,220	
Less dividends	1,000	2,220
Retained earnings, October 31, 2009		$3,320

FAMILY HEALTH CARE, P.C.
Balance Sheet
October 31, 2009

Assets		
Cash		$ 7,320
Land		12,000
Total assets		$19,320
Liabilities		
Notes payable		$10,000
Stockholders' Equity		
Capital stock	$6,000	
Retained earnings	3,320	9,320
Total liabilities and stockholders' equity		$19,320

FAMILY HEALTH CARE, P.C.
Statement of Cash Flows
For the Month Ended October 31, 2009

Cash flows from operating activities:	
Cash received from customers	$ 6,400
Deduct cash payments for expenses	3,180
Net cash flow from operating activities	$ 3,220
Cash flows from investing activities	0
Cash flows from financing activities:	
Deduct cash dividends	(1,000)
Net increase in cash	$ 2,220
October 1, 2009, cash balance	5,100
Ocober 31, 2009, cash balance	$ 7,320

($900/$5,500), increase from September. At the same time, total operating expenses increased only $280, or 9.7% ($280/$2,900). This suggests that Family Health Care's operations are profitable and expanding.

The retained earnings statement reports an increase in retained earnings of $2,220. This increase is the result of net income ($3,220) less the dividends ($1,000) paid to Dr. Landry.

The balance sheet shows that total assets increased from $17,100 on September 30, 2009, to $19,320 on October 31. This increase of $2,220 was due to an increase in cash from operations of $3,220 less the dividends of $1,000 that were paid to Dr. Landry. Total liabilities remained the same, but retained earnings and stockholders' equity increased by $2,220.

The statement of cash flows shows net cash receipts from operations of $3,220 and a cash payment for dividends of $1,000. The ending cash balance of $7,320 also appears on the October 31 balance sheet. The integration of these statements is shown in Exhibit 8.

EXHIBIT 8 *Family Health Care Integrated Financial Statements for October*

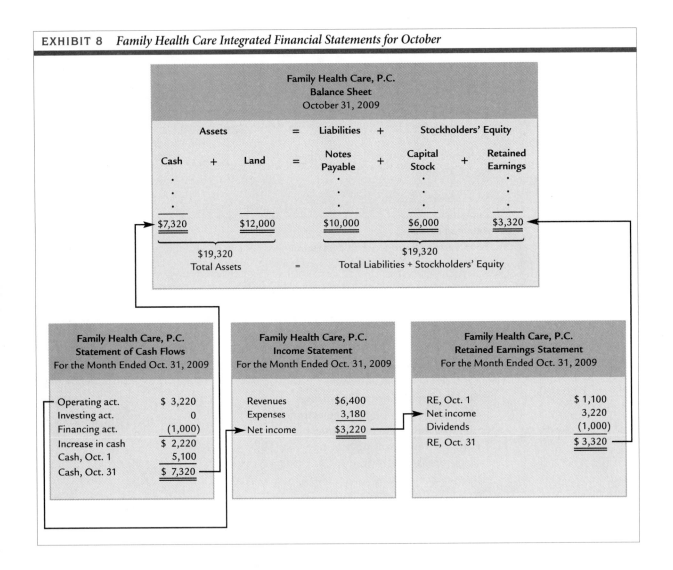

Key Points

1. **Describe the basic elements of a financial accounting system.**

   The basic elements of a financial accounting system include (1) a set of rules for determining what should be recorded, when it should be recorded, and the amount that should be recorded for economic events, (2) a framework for facilitating preparation of financial statements, and (3) one or more controls to determine whether errors may have arisen in the recording process.

2. **Analyze, record, and summarize transactions for a corporation's first period of operations.**

   Using the integrated financial statement framework, September transactions for Family Health Care are recorded and summarized in Exhibit 2.

3. **Prepare financial statements for a corporation's first period of operations.**

   The financial statements for Family Health Care for September, its first period of operations, are shown in Exhibit 4.

4. **Analyze, record, and summarize transactions for a corporation's second period of operations.**

   Using the accounting equation as a basic framework, October transactions for Family Health Care are recorded and summarized in Exhibit 6.

5. **Prepare financial statements for a corporation's second period of operations.**

   The financial statements for Family Health Care for October, its second period of operations, are shown in Exhibit 7.

Key Terms

Financial accounting system

Transaction

Illustrative Problem

Beth Sumner established an insurance agency on April 1, 2009, and completed the following transactions during April:

a. Opened a business bank account in the name of Sumner Insurance Inc., with a deposit of $15,000 in exchange for capital stock.
b. Borrowed $8,000 by issuing a note payable.
c. Received cash from fees earned, $11,500.
d. Paid rent on office and equipment for the month, $3,500.
e. Paid automobile expenses for the month, $650, and miscellaneous expenses, $300.
f. Paid office salaries, $1,400.
g. Paid interest on the note payable, $60.
h. Purchased land as a future building site, $20,000.
i. Paid dividends, $1,000.

Instructions

1. Indicate the effect of each transaction and the balances after each transaction, using the integrated financial statement framework.
2. Prepare an income statement and retained earnings statement for April.
3. Prepare a balance sheet as of April 30, 2009.
4. Prepare a statement of cash flows for April.

Solution

(1)

Statement of Cash Flows	Assets			=	Liabilities	+	Stockholders' Equity			Income Statement
				Balance Sheet						
	Cash	+	Land	=	Notes Payable	+	Capital Stock	+	Retained Earnings	
a. Investment	15,000						15,000			
b. Issued note payable	8,000				8,000					
Balances	23,000				8,000		15,000			
c. Fees earned	11,500								11,500	*c.*
Balances	34,500				8,000		15,000		11,500	
d. Rent expense	−3,500								−3,500	*d.*
Balances	31,000				8,000		15,000		8,000	
e. Paid expenses	−950								−950	*e.*
Balances	30,050				8,000		15,000		7,050	
f. Paid salary expense	−1,400								−1,400	*f.*
Balances	28,650				8,000		15,000		5,650	
g. Paid interest expense	−60								−60	*g.*
Balances	28,590				8,000		15,000		5,590	
h. Purchased land	−20,000		20,000							
Balances	8,590		20,000		8,000		15,000		5,590	
i. Paid dividends	−1,000								−1,000	
Balances, April 30	7,590		20,000		8,000		15,000		4,590	

Statement of Cash Flows			**Income Statement**	
a. Financing	15,000		*c.* Fees earned	11,500
b. Financing	8,000		*d.* Rent expense	−3,500
c. Operating	11,500		*e.* Auto expense	−650
d. Operating	−3,500		*e.* Misc. expense	−300
e. Operating	−950		*f.* Salary expense	−1,400
f. Operating	−1,400		*g.* Interest expense	−60
g. Operating	−60		Net income	5,590
h. Investing	−20,000			
i. Financing	−1,000			
Increase in cash and April 30 cash	7,590			

(2)

SUMNER INSURANCE, INC.
Income Statement
For the Month Ended April 30, 2009

Revenues:		
Fees earned		$11,500
Expenses:		
Rent expense	$3,500	
Salaries expense	1,400	
Automotive expense	650	
Interest expense	60	
Miscellaneous expense	300	
Total expenses		5,910
Net income		$ 5,590

SUMNER INSURANCE, INC.
Retained Earnings Statement
For the Month Ended April 30, 2009

Net income	$5,590
Less dividends	1,000
Retained earnings, April 30, 2009	$4,590

(3)

SUMNER INSURANCE, INC.
Balance Sheet
April 30, 2009

Assets		
Cash		$ 7,590
Land		20,000
Total assets		$27,590
Liabilities		
Note payable		$ 8,000
Stockholders' Equity		
Capital stock	$15,000	
Retained earnings	4,590	
Total stockholders' equity		19,590
Total liabilities and stockholders' equity		$27,590

(4)

SUMNER INSURANCE, INC.
Statement of Cash Flows
For the Month Ended April 30, 2009

Cash flows from operating activities:		
Cash receipts from operating activities		$11,500
Cash payments for operating activities		5,910
Net cash flows from operating activities		$ 5,590
Cash flows from investing activities:		
Cash payments for land		(20,000)
Cash flows from financing activities:		
Cash receipts from issuing capital stock	$15,000	
Cash receipts from note payable	8,000	
Cash payments for dividends	(1,000)	
Net cash flows used in financing activities		22,000
Net increase in cash during April		$ 7,590
Cash as of April 1, 2009		0
Cash as of April 30, 2009		$ 7,590

Self-Examination Questions   *(Answers appear at end of chapter.)*

1. The purchase of land for $50,000 cash was incorrectly recorded as an increase in land and an increase in notes payable. Which of the following statements is correct?
   A. The accounting equation will not balance because cash is overstated by $50,000.
   B. The accounting equation will not balance because notes payable are overstated by $50,000.
   C. The accounting equation will not balance because assets will exceed liabilities by $50,000.
   D. Even though a recording error has been made, the accounting equation will balance.

2. The receipt of $8,000 cash for fees earned was recorded by Langley Consulting as an increase in cash of $8,000 and a decrease in retained earnings (revenues) of $8,000. What is the effect of this error on the accounting equation?
   A. Total assets will exceed total liabilities and stockholders' equity by $8,000.
   B. Total assets will be less than total liabilities and stockholders' equity by $8,000.
   C. Total assets will exceed total liabilities and stockholders' equity by $16,000.
   D. The error will not affect the accounting equation.

3. If total assets increased $20,000 during a period and total liabilities increased $12,000 during the same period, the amount and direction (increase or decrease) of the change in stockholders' equity for that period is:
   A. a $32,000 increase.
   B. a $32,000 decrease.
   C. an $8,000 increase.
   D. an $8,000 decrease.

4. If revenue was $90,000, expenses were $75,000, and dividends were $20,000, the amount of net income or net loss would be:
   A. $90,000 net income.
   B. $15,000 net income.
   C. $75,000 net loss.
   D. $5,000 net loss.

5. Which of the following transactions changes only the mix of assets and does not affect liabilities or stockholders' equity?
   A. Borrowed $40,000 from First National Bank.
   B. Purchased land for cash.
   C. Received $3,800 for fees earned.
   D. Paid $4,000 for office salaries.

Class Discussion Questions

1. What are the basic elements of a financial accounting system? Do these elements apply to all businesses from a local restaurant to Apple Computer? Explain.

2. Provide an example of a transaction that affects
   (a) only one element of the accounting equation,
   (b) two elements of the accounting equation, (c) three elements of the accounting equation.

3. Indicate whether the following error would cause the accounting equation to be out of balance and, if so, indicate how it would be out of balance. The payment of utilities of $1,800 was recorded as a decrease in cash of $1,800 and a decrease in retained earnings (utilities expense) of $8,100.

4. For each of the following errors, indicate whether the error would cause the accounting equation to be out of balance, and if so, indicate how it would be out of balance. (a) The purchase of land for $100,000 cash was recorded as an increase in land of $100,000 and a decrease in cash of $10,000. (b) The receipt of $9,000 for fees earned was recorded as an increase in cash of $9,000 and an increase in liabilities of $9,000.

5. What is a primary control for determining the accuracy of a business's record keeping?

6. Global Consulting Services acquired land 4 years ago for $50,000. Global recently signed an agreement to sell the land for $125,000. In accordance with the sales agreement, the buyer transferred $125,000 to Global's bank account on July 9. How would elements of the accounting equation be affected by the sale?

7. (a) How does the payment of dividends of $39,000 affect the three elements of the accounting equation? (b) Is net income affected by the payment of dividends? Explain.

8. Assume that Miramar Consulting erroneously recorded the payment of $18,000 of dividends as salary expense. (a) How would this error affect the equality of the accounting equation? (b) How would this error affect the income statement, retained earnings statement, balance sheet, and statement of cash flows?

9. Assume that Elite Realty Inc. borrowed $100,000 from City Bank and Trust. In recording the transaction, Elite erroneously recorded the receipt as an increase in cash, $100,000, and an increase in fees earned, $100,000. (a) How would this error affect the equality of the accounting equation? (b) How would this error affect the income statement, retained earnings statement, balance sheet, and statement of cash flows?

10. Assume that as of January 1, 2009, Sorrento Consulting has total assets of $600,000 and total liabilities of $180,000. As of December 31, 2009, Sorrento has total liabilities of $220,000 and total stockholders' equity of $500,000. (a) What was Sorrento's stockholders' equity as of December 31, 2008? (b) Assume that Sorrento did not pay any dividends during 2009. What was the amount of net income for 2009?

11. Using the January 1 and December 31, 2009, data given in Question 10, answer the following question. If Sorrento paid $17,500 of dividends during 2009, what was the amount of net income for 2009?

Exercises

E2-1

Accounting equation

Obj 1

✓ a. $2,850,000

Determine the missing amount for each of the following:

	Assets	=	Liabilities	+	Stockholders' Equity
a.	X	=	$750,000	+	$2,100,000
b.	$450,000	=	X	+	$375,000
c.	$190,000	=	$58,000	+	X

E2-2

Accounting equation

Obj 1

✓ a. $26,210

The Walt Disney Company had the following assets and liabilities (in millions) as of September 30, 2005.

Assets	$53,158
Liabilities	26,948

a. Determine the stockholders' equity of Walt Disney as of September 30, 2005.
b. If assets increased by $6,840 and stockholders' equity increased by $5,610, what was the increase or decrease in liabilities for the year ending September 30, 2006?

(continued)

c.   What were the total assets, liabilities, and stockholders' equity as of September 30, 2006?

d.   Based upon your answer to (c), does the accounting equation balance?

E2-3

Accounting equation

Obj 1

✓ a. $1,270

Campbell Soup Co. had the following assets and liabilities (in millions) as of July 31, 2005.

Assets	$6,776
Liabilities	5,506

a.   Determine the stockholders' equity of Campbell Soup as of July 31, 2005.

b.   If assets increased by $1,094 and liabilities increased by $596, what was the increase or decrease in stockholders' equity for the year ending July 30, 2006?

c.   What were the total assets, liabilities, and stockholders' equity as of July 30, 2006?

d.   Based upon your answer to (c), does the accounting equation balance?

E2-4

Accounting equation

Obj 1

✓ a. $853

One item is omitted in each of the following summaries of balance sheet and income statement data (in millions) for *Google* and *Verizon Communications* as of December 31, 2006 and 2005.

	Google	*Verizon*
December 31, 2005:		
Assets	$10,272	(e)
Liabilities	(a)	(f)
Stockholders' equity	(b)	$ 39,680
Increase (Decrease) in assets, liabilities, and stockholders' equity during 2006:		
Assets	$ 8,202	(g)
Liabilities	581	$ 11,819
Stockholders' equity	7,621	(h)
December 31, 2006:		
Assets	(c)	$188,804
Liabilities	$ 1,434	(i)
Stockholders' equity	(d)	48,535

Determine the amounts of the missing items (a) through (i).

E2-5

Accounting equation

Obj 1

✓ b. $490,000

Selby Hinkle is the sole stockholder and operator of Osaka, a motivational consulting business. At the end of its accounting period, December 31, 2007, Osaka has assets of $800,000 and liabilities of $375,000. Using the accounting equation and considering each case independently, determine the following amounts:

a.   Stockholders' equity, as of December 31, 2007.

b.   Stockholders' equity, as of December 31, 2008, assuming that assets increased by $125,000 and liabilities increased by $60,000 during 2008.

c.   Stockholders' equity, as of December 31, 2008, assuming that assets decreased by $100,000 and liabilities increased by $40,000 during 2008.

d.   Stockholders' equity, as of December 31, 2008, assuming that assets increased by $80,000 and liabilities decreased by $200,000 during 2008.

e.   Net income (or net loss) during 2008, assuming that as of December 31, 2008, assets were $910,000, liabilities were $400,000, and there were no dividends and no additional capital stock was issued.

E2-6
Effects of transactions on stockholders' equity

Objs 2, 4

For **Kroger Co.**, indicate whether the following transactions would (1) increase, (2) decrease, or (3) have no effect on stockholders' equity.

a. Borrowed money from the bank.
b. Paid creditors.
c. Made cash sales to customers.
d. Purchased store equipment.
e. Paid dividends.

f. Paid store rent.
g. Paid interest expense.
h. Sold store equipment at a loss.
i. Received interest income.
j. Paid taxes.

E2-7
Effects of transactions on accounting equation

Objs 1, 2, 4

Describe how the following business transactions affect the three elements of the accounting equation.

a. Issued capital stock for cash.
b. Purchased land for cash.
c. Received cash for services performed.

d. Borrowed cash at local bank.
e. Paid for utilities used in the business.

E2-8
Effects of transactions on accounting equation

Objs 1, 2, 4

✓ (1) Assets decreased $20,000

A vacant lot acquired for $200,000, on which there is a balance owed of $120,000, is sold for $300,000 in cash. The seller pays the $120,000 owed. What is the effect of these transactions on the total amount of the seller's (1) assets, (2) liabilities, and (3) stockholders' equity?

E2-9
Effects of transactions on stockholders' equity

Objs 2, 4

Indicate whether each of the following types of transactions will (a) increase stockholders' equity or (b) decrease stockholders' equity.

1. Received cash for fees earned.
2. Issued capital stock for cash.
3. Paid cash for utilities expense.

4. Paid cash for rent expense.
5. Paid cash dividends.

E2-10
Transactions

Objs 1, 2, 4

Juniper Delivery Service had the following selected transactions during May:

1. Received cash from issuance of capital stock, $50,000.
2. Received cash for providing delivery services, $18,000.
3. Paid advertising expense, $1,000.
4. Billed customers for delivery services, $35,000.
5. Purchased supplies for cash, $2,100.
6. Paid creditors, $2,000.
7. Paid rent for May, $2,000.
8. Received cash from customers on account, $16,700.
9. Determined that the cost of supplies on hand was $1,200; therefore, $900 of supplies had been used during the month.
10. Paid dividends, $1,500.

Indicate the effect of each transaction on the accounting equation by listing the numbers identifying the transactions, (1) through (10), in a vertical column, and inserting at the right of each number the appropriate letter from the following list:

a. Increase in an asset, decrease in another asset.
b. Increase in an asset, increase in a liability.

(continued)

c.   Increase in an asset, increase in stockholders' equity.
d.   Decrease in an asset, decrease in a liability.
e.   Decrease in an asset, decrease in stockholders' equity.

E2-11

Nature of transactions

Objs 1, 2, 4

✓ b. $6,000

Dude Peng operates his own catering service. Summary financial data for August are presented in equation form as follows. Each line designated by a number indicates the effect of a transaction on the balance sheet. Each increase and decrease in owners' equity, except transaction (4), affects net income.

	Cash	+	Land	=	Liabilities	+	Capital Stock	+	Retained Earnings
Bal.	15,000		50,000		10,000		10,000		45,000
1.	+20,000								+20,000
2.	−18,000		+18,000						
3.	−6,000								−6,000
4.	−2,000								−2,000
Bal.	9,000		68,000		10,000		10,000		57,000

a.   Describe each transaction.
b.   What is the amount of net decrease in cash during the month?
c.   What is the amount of net increase in retained earnings during the month?
d.   What is the amount of the net income for the month?
e.   How much of the net income for the month was retained in the business?
f.   What is the amount of net cash flows from operating activities?
g.   What is the amount of net cash flows from investing activities?
h.   What is the amount of net cash flows from financing activities?

E2-12

Net income and dividends

Objs 3, 5

The income statement of a corporation for the month of February indicates a net income of $263,000. During the same period, $300,000 in cash dividends were paid.

Would it be correct to say that the business incurred a net loss of $37,000 during the month? Discuss.

E2-13

Net income and stockholders' equity for four businesses

Objs 1, 3, 5

✓ Company U: Net income, $99,000

Four different companies, S, T, U, and V, show the same balance sheet data at the beginning and end of a year. These data, exclusive of the amount of stockholders' equity, are summarized as follows:

	Total Assets	Total Liabilities
Beginning of the year	$315,000	$132,000
End of the year	582,000	255,000

On the basis of the preceding data and the following additional information for the year, determine the net income (or loss) of each company for the year. (*Suggestion:* First determine the amount of increase or decrease in stockholders' equity during the year.)

Company S: No additional capital stock was issued, and no dividends were paid.
Company T: No additional capital stock was issued, but dividends of $30,000 were paid.
Company U: Capital stock of $45,000 was issued, but no dividends were paid.
Company V: Capital stock of $45,000 was issued, and dividends of $30,000 were paid.

E2-14

Missing amounts from balance sheet and income statement data

Objs 1, 3, 5

✓ a. $207,000

One item is omitted from each of the following summaries of balance sheet and income statement data for four different corporations, I, J, K, and L.

	I	*J*	*K*	*L*
Beginning of the year:				
Assets	$360,000	$ 95,000	$100,000	(d)
Liabilities	234,000	45,000	80,000	$150,000
End of the year:				
Assets	$810,000	$125,000	$120,000	$310,000
Liabilities	450,000	35,000	105,000	170,000
During the year:				
Additional issue of				
capital stock	(a)	$ 22,000	$ 10,000	$ 50,000
Dividends	$ 36,000	8,000	(c)	75,000
Revenue	225,000	(b)	175,000	140,000
Expenses	162,000	52,000	177,000	160,000

Determine the amounts of the missing items, identifying them by letter. (*Suggestion:* First determine the amount of increase or decrease in stockholders' equity during the year.)

E2-15

Net income, retained earnings, and dividends

Objs 3, 5

✓ a. $513 increase

Use the following data (in millions); for **Gap Inc.** for the year ending February 3, 2007, to answer the following questions:

Retained earnings, January 28, 2006	$8,133
Retained earnings, February 3, 2007	8,646
Net cash from operating activities	1,250
Net decrease in cash	(5)

a. Determine the net increase or decrease in retained earnings during the year ending February 3, 2007.
b. If dividends are $265 during the year, what was the net income or loss for Gap for the year ending February 3, 2007?

E2-16

Balance sheet, net income, and cash flows

Objs 3, 5

SPREADSHEET

✓ b. $115,500

Financial information related to Atrium Interiors for October and November of 2009 is as follows:

	October 31, 2009	*November 30, 2009*
Notes payable	$105,000	$157,500
Land	278,500	462,500
Capital stock	63,000	94,500
Retained earnings	?	?
Cash	89,000	83,500

a. Prepare balance sheets for Atrium Interiors as of October 31 and November 30, 2009.
b. Determine the amount of net income for November, assuming that dividends of $21,000 were paid.
c. Determine the net cash flows from operating activities.
d. Determine the net cash flows from investing activities.
e. Determine the net cash flows from financing activities.
f. Determine the net increase or decrease in cash.

E2-17

Income statement

Objs 3, 5

SPREADSHEET

✓ Net income, $40,500

After its first month of operation, the following amounts were taken from the accounting records of Sandcastle Realty Inc. as of June 30, 2009.

Capital stock	$18,000	Notes payable	$54,000
Cash	38,700	Rent expense	10,800
Dividends	7,200	Retained earnings	0
Interest expense	3,600	Salaries expense	16,200
Land	66,600	Sales commissions	89,100
Miscellaneous expense	4,500	Utilities expense	13,500

Prepare an income statement for the month ending June 30, 2009.

E2-18

Retained earnings statement

Objs 3, 5

SPREADSHEET

✓ Retained earnings, June 30, 2009, $33,300

Using the financial data shown in Exercise 2-17 for Sandcastle Realty Inc., prepare a retained earnings statement for the month ending June 30, 2009.

E2-19

Balance sheet

Objs 3, 5

SPREADSHEET

✓ Total assets, $105,300

Using the financial data shown in Exercise 2-17 for Sandcastle Realty Inc., prepare a balance sheet as of June 30, 2009.

E2-20

Statement of cash flows

Objs 3, 5

SPREADSHEET

✓ Net cash flows from operating activities, $40,500

Using the financial data shown in Exercise 2-17 for Sandcastle Realty Inc., prepare a statement of cash flows for the month ending June 30, 2009.

E2-21

Effects of transactions on accounting equation

Objs 1, 2, 4

Describe how transactions of **Lucent Technologies Inc.** would affect the three elements of the accounting equation.

a. Received cash from issuing stock.
b. Made cash sales.
c. Received cash from the issuance of long-term debt.
d. Paid research and development expenses for the current year.
e. Purchased machinery and equipment for cash.

f. Received proceeds from selling a portion of manufacturing operations for a gain on the sale.
g. Paid off long-term debt.
h. Paid employee pension expenses for the current year.
i. Paid taxes.
j. Paid officer salaries.
k. Paid selling expenses.
l. Paid dividends.

E2-22

Statement of cash flows

Objs 3, 5

Based upon the financial transactions for Lucent Technologies Inc. shown in Exercise 2-21, indicate whether the transaction would be reported in the cash flows from operating, investing, or financing sections of the statement of cash flows.

Problems

P2-1

Transactions and financial statements

Objs 1, 2, 3

SPREADSHEET

✓ 3. Net income, $5,400

Renee Berg established an insurance agency on January 1, 2009, and completed the following transactions during January:

a. Opened a business bank account in the name of Berg Insurance Inc., with a deposit of $20,000 in exchange for capital stock.
b. Borrowed $15,000 by issuing a note payable.
c. Received cash from fees earned, $11,500.
d. Paid rent on office and equipment for the month, $2,000.
e. Paid automobile expense for the month, $1,200, and miscellaneous expense, $600.
f. Paid office salaries, $2,200.
g. Paid interest on the note payable, $100.
h. Purchased land as a future building site, $30,000.
i. Paid dividends, $1,500.

Instructions

1. Indicate the effect of each transaction and the balances after each transaction, using the integrated financial statement framework.
2. Briefly explain why the stockholders' investments and revenues increased stockholders' equity, while dividends and expenses decreased stockholders' equity.
3. Prepare an income statement and retained earnings statement for January.
4. Prepare a balance sheet as of January 31, 2009.
5. Prepare a statement of cash flows for January.

P2-2

Transactions and financial statements

Objs 1, 2, 3

SPREADSHEET

✓ 1. Net income, $10,250

Gary McReynolds established CPU Computer Services on August 1, 2009. The effect of each transaction and the balances after each transaction for August are shown in the integrated financial statement framework at the top of the next page.

Instructions

1. Prepare an income statement for the month ended August 31, 2009.
2. Prepare a retained earnings statement for the month ended August 31, 2009.
3. Prepare a balance sheet as of August 31, 2009.
4. Prepare a statement of cash flows for the month ended August 31, 2009.

(continued)

Statement of Cash Flows	Balance Sheet									Income Statement
	Asset		=	Liabilities	+	Stockholders' Equity				
	Cash	+	Land	=	Notes Payable	+	Capital Stock	+	Retained Earnings	
a. Investment	30,000						30,000			
b. Fees earned	18,000								18,000	b.
Balances	48,000						30,000		18,000	
c. Rent expense	−2,500								−2,500	c.
Balances	45,500						30,000		15,500	
d. Issued notes payable	10,000				10,000					
Balances	55,500				10,000		30,000		15,500	
e. Purchased land	−40,000		40,000							
Balances	15,500		40,000		10,000		30,000		15,500	
f. Paid expenses	−1,650								−1,650	f.
Balances	13,850		40,000		10,000		30,000		13,850	
g. Paid salary expense	−3,600								−3,600	g.
Balances	10,250		40,000		10,000		30,000		10,250	
h. Paid dividends	−2,000								−2,000	
Balances, Aug. 31	8,250		40,000		10,000		30,000		8,250	

Statement of Cash Flows

a. Financing	30,000
b. Operating	18,000
c. Operating	−2,500
d. Financing	10,000
e. Investing	−40,000
f. Operating	−1,650
g. Operating	−3,600
h. Financing	−2,000
Increase in cash	8,250

Income Statement

b. Fees earned	18,000
c. Rent expense	−2,500
f. Auto expense	−950
f. Misc. expense	−700
g. Salary expense	−3,600
Net income	10,250

P2-3

Financial statements

Objs 2, 3

SPREADSHEET

✓ 1. Net income, $86,625

The following amounts were taken from the accounting records of Caravan Services, Inc., as of March 31, 2009. Caravan Services began its operations on April 1, 2008.

Capital stock	$ 10,500
Cash	28,875
Dividends	5,250
Fees earned	240,975
Interest expense	1,260
Land	78,750
Miscellaneous expense	7,140
Notes payable	15,750
Rent expense	25,200
Salaries expense	68,250
Taxes expense	18,900
Utilities expense	33,600

Instructions

1. Prepare an income statement for the year ending March 31, 2009.
2. Prepare a retained earnings statement for the year ending March 31, 2009.
3. Prepare a balance sheet as of March 31, 2009.
4. Prepare a statement of cash flows for the year ending March 31, 2009.

P2-4

Financial statements

Obj 5

SPREADSHEET

✓ 1. Net income, $96,070

After its second year of operations, the following amounts were taken from the accounting records of Caravan Services, Inc., as of March 31, 2010. Caravan Services began its operations on April 1, 2008 (see Problem 2-3).

Capital stock	$ 26,250
Cash	?
Dividends	15,750
Fees earned	266,800
Interest expense	1,680
Land	147,000
Miscellaneous expense	7,350
Notes payable	21,000
Rent expense	29,400
Salaries expense	73,500
Taxes expense	21,000
Utilities expense	37,800

Instructions

1. Prepare an income statement for the year ending March 31, 2010.
2. Prepare a retained earnings statement for the year ending March 31, 2010.
   (*Note:* The retained earnings at April 1, 2009, was $81,375.)
3. Prepare a balance sheet as of March 31, 2010.
4. Prepare a statement of cash flows for the year ending March 31, 2010.
   (*Hint:* You should compare the asset and liability amounts of March 31, 2010, with those of March 31, 2009, to determine cash used in investing and financing activities. See Problem 2-3 for the March 31, 2009, balance sheet amounts.)

P2-5

Missing amounts from financial statements

Objs 3, 5

SPREADSHEET

✓ a. $78,000

The financial statements at the end of Panda Realty, Inc.'s first month of operation are shown here. By analyzing the interrelationships between the financial statements, fill in the proper amounts for (a) through (s).

PANDA REALTY, INC.
Income Statement
For the Month Ended October 31, 2009

Fees earned		$ (a)
Operating expenses:		
Wages expense	$22,080	
Rent expense	12,000	
Utilities expense	(b)	
Interest expense	1,200	
Miscellaneous expense	2,640	
Total operating expenses		45,000
Net income		$ (c)

(continued)

PANDA REALTY, INC.
Retained Earnings Statement
For the Month Ended October 31, 2009

Retained earnings, October 1, 2009		$ (d)
Net income for October	$33,000	
Less dividends	(e)	(f)
Retained earnings, October 31, 2009		$ (g)

PANDA REALTY, INC.
Balance Sheet
October 31, 2009

Assets

Cash		$ (h)
Land		120,000
Total assets		$159,000

Liabilities

Notes payable		$ 72,000

Stockholders' Equity

Capital stock	$ (i)	
Retained earnings	(j)	(k)
Total liabilities and stockholders' equity		$ (l)

PANDA REALTY, INC.
Statement of Cash Flows
For the Month Ended October 31, 2009

Cash flows from operating activities:			
Cash received from customers		$78,000	
Deduct cash payments for expenses		45,000	
Net cash flows from operating activities			$ (m)
Cash flows from investing activities:			
Cash payment for purchase of land			(120,000)
Cash flows from financing activities:			
Cash received from sale of capital stock	$60,000		
Cash received from notes payable	(n)	$ (o)	
Deduct cash dividends		6,000	
Net cash flows from financing activities			(p)
Net increase in cash			$ (q)
October 1, 2009, cash balance			(r)
October 31, 2009, cash balance			$ (s)

P2-6

Financial statements

Objs 3, 5

Granite Realty, Inc., organized May 1, 2009, is operated by Cecelia Hawkins. How many errors can you find in the following financial statements for Granite Realty, Inc., prepared after its first month of operation?

GRANITE REALTY, INC.
Income Statement
May 31, 2009

Sales commissions		$184,400
Operating expenses:		
Office salaries expense	$32,600	
Rent expense	15,200	
Automobile expense	7,000	
Dividends	4,000	
Miscellaneous expense	3,100	
Total operating expenses		61,900
Net income		$82,500

CECELIA HAWKINS
Retained Earnings Statement
May 31, 2008

Net income for the month	$82,500
Retained earnings, May 31, 2008	$82,500

Balance Sheet
For the Month Ended May 31, 2009

Assets		
Cash		$ 121,700
Notes payable		40,000
Total assets		$ 161,700
Liabilities		
Land		$ 80,800
Stockholders' Equity		
Capital stock	$40,000	
Retained earnings	82,500	122,500
Total liabilities and stockholders' equity		$203,300

GRANITE REALTY, INC.
Statement of Cash Flows
May 31, 2009

Cash flows from operating activities:	
Cash receipts from sales commissions	$ 184,400
Cash flows from investing activities:	
Cash payments for land	(80,800)
Cash flows from financing activities:	
Cash receipts from retained earnings	162,500
Net increase in cash during May	$266,100
Cash as of May 1, 2009	0
Cash as of May 31, 2009	$266,100

Activities

A2-1

Business emphasis

Assume that you are considering developing a nationwide chain of women's clothing stores. You have contacted a Seattle-based firm that specializes in financing new business ventures and enterprises. Such firms, called venture capital firms, finance new businesses in exchange for a percentage of the ownership.

1. In groups of four or five, discuss the different business emphases that you might use in your venture.
2. For each emphasis you listed in (1), provide an example of a real-world business using the same emphasis.
3. What percentage of the ownership would you be willing to give the venture capital firm in exchange for its financing?

A2-2

Cash accounting

Maria Avey and Tina Bishop both graduated from State University in June 2009. After graduation, Tina took a job as a staff accountant in the San Francisco office of ***Ernst & Young***, an international public accounting firm. Maria began working as a manager in Hays Electronics, a wholesale computer hardware and software company, but left after only nine months to start her own consulting business. The following conversation took place between Maria and Tina at an Ernst & Young alumni function.

Maria: Tina, good to see you again.

Tina: Yes. It doesn't seem like it's been almost two years since we graduated.

Maria: That's for sure. It seems like only yesterday we were listening to that boring commencement speaker. I don't even remember his name . . . Oscar somebody. Are you still working for Ernst & Young?

Tina: Yes, it's been great. I've worked on over 15 companies . . . it's been a fantastic learning experience. Each client has a different culture, management team, problems, and personality. I've learned something new every day. How about you? Are you still working for Hays Electronics?

Maria: No, I quit after nine months. My customers really didn't know what they needed for computer systems . . . so . . . I quit and started a consulting business. I feel like I'm helping my customers more now than I did before. Besides, I like being my own boss.

Tina: What's the name of your business?

Maria: Avey Consulting. It's been amazing. I started with my savings of $4,000 a year ago. My last bank statement showed I've got more than $80,000—"pure profit" of $76,000 in only a year.

Tina: That's unbelievable! If you ever need a CPA firm, keep us in mind.

Maria: Sure. What are friends for anyway?

Comment on Maria's statement that she's earned $76,000 "pure profit" in only a year.

A2-3

Cash flows

Amazon.com, an Internet retailer, was incorporated in the early 1990s and opened its virtual doors on the Web shortly thereafter. On the statement of cash flows, would you expect Amazon.com's net cash flows from operating, investing, and financing activities to be positive or negative for its first 3 years of operation? Use the following format for your answers, and briefly explain your logic.

	Year 1	Year 2	Year 3
Net cash flows from operating activities	negative		
Net cash flows from investing activities			
Net cash flows from financing activities			

A2-4

Financial information

Yahoo.com's finance Internet site provides summary financial information about public companies, such as stock quotes, recent financial filings with the Securities and Exchange Commission, and recent news stories. Go to Yahoo.com's financial Web site (**http://finance.yahoo.com/**) and enter Wm. Wrigley J. Company's stock symbol, WWY. Answer the following questions concerning Wm. Wrigley Jr. Company by clicking on the various items under the tab "More Reports for WWY."

1. At what price did Wrigley's stock last trade?
2. What is the 52-week range of Wrigley's stock?
3. When was the last time Wrigley's stock hit a 52-week high?
4. Over the last six months, has there been any insider selling or buying of Wrigley's stock?
5. Who is the chief executive officer of Wm. Wrigley Jr. Company, and how old is the president?
6. What was the salary of the president of Wm. Wrigley Jr. Company?
7. What is the annual dividend of Wrigley's stock?
8. How many current broker recommendations are strong buy, buy, hold, sell, or strong sell? What is the average of the broker recommendations?
9. What is the net cash flow from operations for this year?
10. What is the operating margin for this year?

A2-5

Analyzing financial information

In the March 30, 2005, issue of the *Chicago Sun-Times*, there is an article by Eric Herman, entitled "Wrigley Opening Facilities Here and Around the World." Read the article and answer the following questions:

1. Is the article favorable, neutral, or unfavorable regarding future prospects for Wm. Wrigley Jr. Company?
2. Would you invest in Wm. Wrigley Jr. Company's stock based only upon this article? If not, what additional information would you want?
3. Would it be a prudent investment strategy to only rely upon published financial statements in deciding to invest in a company's stock?
4. What sources do you think financial analysts use in making investment decisions and recommendations?

Answers to Self-Examination Questions

1. D Even though a recording error has been made, the accounting equation will balance (answer D). However, assets (cash) will be overstated by $50,000, and liabilities (notes payable) will be overstated by $50,000. Answer A is incorrect because although cash is overstated by $50,000, the accounting equation will balance. Answer B is incorrect because although notes payable are overstated by $50,000, the accounting equation will balance. Answer C is incorrect because the accounting equation will balance and assets will not exceed liabilities.

2. C Total assets will exceed total liabilities and stockholders' equity by $16,000. This is because stockholders' equity (retained earnings) was decreased instead of increased by $8,000. Thus, stockholders' equity will be understated by a total of $16,000.

3. C The accounting equation is:

Assets = Liabilities + Stockholders' Equity

Therefore, if assets increased by $20,000 and liabilities increased by $12,000, stockholders' equity must have increased by $8,000 (answer C), as indicated in the following computation:

Assets	=	Liabilities + Stockholders' Equity
+ $20,000	=	$12,000 + Stockholders' Equity
+ $20,000 − $12,000	=	Stockholders' Equity
+ $8,000	=	Stockholders' Equity

4. B Net income is the excess of revenue over expenses, or $15,000 (answer B). If expenses exceed revenue, the difference is a net loss. Dividends are the opposite of the stockholders' investing in the business and do not affect the amount of net income or net loss.

5. B The purchase of land for cash changes the mix of assets and does not affect liabilities or stockholders' equity (answer B). Borrowing cash from a bank (answer A) increases assets and liabilities. Receiving cash for fees earned (answer C) increases cash and stockholders' equity (retained earnings). Paying office salaries (answer D) decreases cash and stockholders' equity (retained earnings).

CHAPTER 3

Accrual Accounting Concepts

Learning Objectives

After studying this chapter, you should be able to:

Obj 1

Describe basic accrual accounting concepts, including the matching concept.

Obj 2

Use accrual concepts of accounting to analyze, record, and summarize transactions.

Obj 3

Describe and illustrate the end-of-period adjustment process.

Obj 4

Prepare financial statements using accrual concepts of accounting, including a classified balance sheet.

Obj 5

Describe how the accrual basis of accounting enhances the interpretation of financial statements.

Do you subscribe to any magazines? Most of us subscribe to one or more magazines such as *Cosmopolitan*, *Sports Illustrated*, *Golf Digest*, *Newsweek*, or *Rolling Stone*. Magazines usually require us to prepay the yearly subscription price before we receive any issues. When should the magazine company record revenue from the subscriptions? As we discussed in Chapter 2, sometimes revenues are earned and expenses are incurred at the point cash changes hands. However, for many transactions, such as magazine subscriptions, the revenue is earned when the magazine is delivered. Large corporations are required to account for revenues and expenses when the benefit is substantially provided or consumed, which may not necessarily occur when cash is either received or paid.

For example, **Wendy's International, Inc.,** records revenues when cash is received at the cash register from meal sales. However, the ingredient costs associated with each meal are recorded at the time the meal is sold, not when the various ingredients are purchased. With over 6,000 restaurants, Wendy's has become a successful company, climbing to the third largest fast-food chain in the United States.

In this chapter, we continue our discussion of financial statements and financial reporting systems. In doing so, we focus on accrual concepts of accounting that are used by all major businesses, such as Wendy's. Our discussions will include how to record transactions under accrual accounting concepts, update accounting records, and prepare accrual financial statements. Because all large companies, and many small ones, use accrual concepts of accounting, a thorough understanding of this topic is important for your business studies and future career.

Basic Accrual Accounting Concepts, Including the Matching Concept

Obj 1

Describe basic accrual accounting concepts, including the matching concept.

In Chapter 2, we illustrated the recording of transactions for Family Health Care for the months of September and October. In these illustrations, we used many of the accounting concepts described in Chapter 1. For example, under the business entity concept, we accounted for Family Health Care as a separate entity, independent of the owner-manager, Dr. Lee Landry. Under the cost concept, we recorded the purchase of land at the amount paid for it. Consistent with the going concern concept, we did not revalue the land for increases or decreases in its market value, but retained the land in the accounting records at its original cost. We also employed the accounting period, full disclosure, objectivity, and unit of measurement concepts in preparing financial statements for Family Health Care.

The one accounting concept that we did not emphasize in Chapter 2 was the matching concept. This is because all the transactions in Chapter 2 were structured so that cash was either received or paid. We did this to simplify the recording of transactions and the preparation of financial statements. For example, all revenues were received in cash at the time the services were rendered and all expenses were paid in cash at the time they were incurred.

In the real world, cash may be received or paid at a different time from when revenues are earned or expenses are incurred. In fact, companies often earn revenues before or after cash is received and incur expenses before or after cash is paid. For example, a company might spend months or years developing land for a business complex or subdivision. During the development of the land, the company has to pay for materials, wages, insurance, and other construction items. At the same time, cash might not be received until portions of the development are sold. Thus, if revenues were recorded only when cash is received and expenses recorded only when cash is paid, the company would report a series of losses on its income statement during the development of the land. In this case, the income statements would not provide a realistic picture of the company's operations. In fact, the development might be highly successful and the early losses misleading.

Accrual accounting concepts are designed to reflect a company's financial performance during a period and avoid misleading results that could arise from the timing of cash receipts and payments such as those described in the preceding paragraph. At the same time, accrual accounting recognizes the importance of reporting cash flows through its emphasis on preparing and reporting the statement of cash flows.

HOW BUSINESSES MAKE MONEY

Not Cutting Corners

Have you ever ordered a hamburger from Wendy's and noticed that the meat patty is square? The square meat patty reflects a business emphasis instilled in Wendy's by its founder, Dave Thomas. Mr. Thomas emphasized offering high-quality products at a fair price in a friendly atmosphere, without "cutting corners"; hence, the square meat patty. In the highly competitive fast-food industry, Dave Thomas's approach has enabled Wendy's to become the third largest fast-food restaurant chain in the world, with annual sales of over $7 billion.

Source: Douglas Martin, "Dave Thomas, 69, Wendy's Founder, Dies," *New York Times*, January 9, 2002.

Under the accrual concepts of accounting, transactions are recorded as they occur and thus affect the accounting equation (assets, liabilities, and stockholders' equity). Since the receipt or payment of cash affects assets (cash), all cash receipts and payments are recorded in the accounts under accrual concepts. However, under the accrual concepts, transactions are also recorded even though cash is not received or paid until a later point. For example, Family Health Care may provide services to patients who are covered by health insurance. It then files a claim with the insurance company for the payment. In this case, revenue is recognized when the services are provided, and the services are said to be provided "on account." Likewise, a business may purchase supplies from a vendor, with terms that allow the business to pay for the purchase within a time period, such as ten days. In this case, the supplies are said to be purchased "on account." Each of the preceding illustrations represents a business transaction that affects elements of the accounting equation and is therefore recorded under accrual concepts, *even though cash is not received or paid* at the time of the transaction.

In accounting, we often use the term "recognized" to refer to when a transaction is recorded. *Under accrual concepts of accounting, revenue is recognized when it is earned.* For Family Health Care, revenue is earned when services have been provided to the patient. At this point, the revenue earning process is complete, and the patient is legally obligated to pay for the services.

Under the accrual concepts, the matching concept plays an important role in determining when expenses are recorded. When revenues are earned and recorded, all expenses incurred in generating the revenues must also be recorded, regardless of whether cash has been paid. In this way, revenues and expenses are matched and the net income or net loss for the period can be determined. This is an application of the matching concept that we discussed in Chapter 1. That is, expenses are recognized and recorded in the same period as the related revenues that they generated and, thus, net income (loss) can be accurately determined.

Accrual concepts recognize liabilities at the time the business incurs the obligation to pay for the services or goods purchased. For example, the purchase of supplies on account would be recorded when the supplies are received and the business has incurred the obligation to pay for the supplies.

Using Accrual Concepts of Accounting for Family Health Care's November Transactions

Obj 2

Use accrual concepts of accounting to analyze, record, and summarize transactions.

To illustrate accrual concepts of accounting, we will use the following November 2009 Family Health Care transactions.

a. On November 1, received $1,800 from ILS Company as rent for the use of Family Health Care's land as a temporary parking lot from November 2009 through March 2010.
b. On November 1, paid $2,400 for an insurance premium on a 2-year, general business policy.
c. On November 1, paid $6,000 for an insurance premium on a six-month medical malpractice policy.
d. Dr. Landry invested an additional $5,000 in the business in exchange for capital stock.
e. Purchased supplies for $240 on account.

f. Purchased $8,500 of office equipment. Paid $1,700 cash as a down payment, with the remaining $6,800 ($8,500 − $1,700) due in five monthly installments of $1,360 ($6,800/5) beginning January 1.
g. Provided services of $6,100 to patients on account.
h. Received $5,500 for services provided to patients who paid cash.
i. Received $4,200 from insurance companies, which paid on patients' accounts for services that have been provided.
j. Paid $100 on account for supplies that had been purchased.
k. Expenses paid during November were as follows: wages, $2,790; rent, $800; utilities, $580; interest, $100; and miscellaneous, $420.
l. Paid dividends of $1,200 to stockholders (Dr. Landry).

In analyzing and recording the November transactions for Family Health Care, we use the integrated financial statement framework that we used in Chapter 2. In so doing, we record increases and decreases for each financial statement element. These separate elements are referred to as **accounts**.

Transaction (a)   *On November 1, received $1,800 from ILS Company as rent for the use of Family Health Care's land as a temporary parking lot from November 2009 through March 2010.* In this transaction, Family Health Care entered into a rental agreement for the use of its land. The agreement required the payment of the rental fee of $1,800 in advance. The rental agreement also gives ILS Company the option of renewing the agreement for another four months.

How does this transaction affect the accounts (elements) of the balance sheet, and how should it be recorded? Since cash has been received, cash is increased by $1,800, but what other account should be increased or decreased? Family Health Care has agreed to rent the land to ILS Company for five months and thus has incurred a liability to provide this service—rental of the land. If Family Health Care canceled the agreement on November 1, after accepting the $1,800, it would have to repay that amount to ILS Company. Thus, Family Health Care should record this transaction as an increase in cash and an increase in a liability for $1,800. Because the liability relates to rent that has been paid in cash, but not yet earned, it is recorded as **unearned revenue**, as shown below.

Statement of Cash Flows	Cash	+	Land	=	Notes Payable	+	Unearned Revenue	+	Capital Stock	+	Retained Earnings	Income Statement
Balances, Nov. 1	7,320		12,000		10,000				6,000		3,320	
a. Received rent in advance	1,800						1,800					
Balances	9,120		12,000		10,000		1,800		6,000		3,320	

Statement of Cash Flows
a. Operating   1,800

As time passes, the liability will decrease, and Family Health Care will earn rental revenue. For example, at the end of November, one-fifth of the $1,800 ($360) will have been earned. Later in this chapter, we will discuss how to record the $360 of earned rent revenue at the end of November.

You should note that the November 1 balances shown in the preceding integrated financial statement spreadsheet are the ending balances from October. That is, the cash balance of $7,320 is the ending cash balance as of October 31, 2009. Likewise, the other balances are carried forward from the preceding month. In this sense, the accounting equation represents a cumulative history of the financial results of the business. In addition, the receipt of cash has the effect of increasing cash flows from operating activities on the statement of cash flows.

Transaction (b) *On November 1, paid $2,400 for an insurance premium on a 2-year, general business policy.* This insurance policy covers a variety of possible risks to the business, such as fire and theft. By paying the premium, Family Health Care has purchased an asset, insurance coverage, in exchange for cash. Thus, the mix of assets has changed and cash flows from operating activities decreases by $2,400. However, the prepaid insurance coverage is unique in that it expires with the passage of time. At the end of the 2-year period, the asset will have been used up, and the insurance policy will be completely expired. Such assets are called **prepaid expenses** or **deferred expenses**. Thus, the purchase of the insurance coverage is recorded as prepaid insurance, as shown below.

		Balance Sheet								
Statement of Cash Flows		Assets		=	Liabilities		+	Stockholders' Equity		Income Statement
	Cash +	Prepaid Insurance +	Land =	Notes Payable +	Unearned Revenue +	Capital Stock +	Retained Earnings	
Balances	9,120		12,000	10,000	1,800	6,000	3,320	
b. Paid insurance for 2 yrs.	−2,400	2,400						
Balances	6,720	2,400	12,000	10,000	1,800	6,000	3,320	

Statement of Cash Flows
b. Operating   −2,400

Later in this illustration, we will discuss how such accounts are updated at the end of an accounting period to reflect the portion of the asset that has expired.

Transaction (c) *On November 1, paid $6,000 for an insurance premium on a six-month medical malpractice policy.* This transaction is similar to transaction (b), except that Family Health Care has purchased medical malpractice insurance that is renewable every six months. The transaction is recorded as follows:

		Balance Sheet								
Statement of Cash Flows		Assets		=	Liabilities		+	Stockholders' Equity		Income Statement
	Cash +	Prepaid Insurance +	Land =	Notes Payable +	Unearned Revenue +	Capital Stock +	Retained Earnings	
Balances	6,720	2,400	12,000	10,000	1,800	6,000	3,320	
c. Paid insurance for 6 mos.	−6,000	6,000						
Balances	720	8,400	12,000	10,000	1,800	6,000	3,320	

Statement of Cash Flows
c. Operating   −6,000

Transaction (d) *Dr. Landry invested an additional $5,000 in the business in exchange for capital stock.* This transaction is similar to the one in which Dr. Landry initially established Family Health Care. It is recorded as shown on the top of page 84.

Statement of Cash Flows	Balance Sheet						Income Statement
	Assets		= Liabilities	+ Stockholders' Equity			
	Cash +	Prepaid Insurance + Land	= Notes Payable +	Unearned Revenue +	Capital Stock +	Retained Earnings	
Balances	720	8,400 12,000	10,000	1,800	6,000	3,320	
d. Issued capital stock	5,000				5,000		
Balances	5,720	8,400 12,000	10,000	1,800	11,000	3,320	

Statement of Cash Flows	
d. Financing	5,000

Transaction (e)   *Purchased supplies for $240 on account.* This transaction is similar to transactions (b) and (c), in that purchased supplies are assets until they are used up in generating revenue. Family Health Care has purchased and received the supplies, with a promise to pay in the near future. Such liabilities that are incurred in the normal operations of the business are called **accounts payable**. The transaction is recorded by increasing the asset supplies and increasing the liability accounts payable, as shown here.

Statement of Cash Flows	Balance Sheet								Income Statement
	Assets			= Liabilities		+ Stockholders' Equity			
	Cash +	Prepaid Insurance +	Supplies + Land	= Notes Payable +	Accounts Payable +	Unearned Revenue +	Capital Stock +	Retained Earnings	
Balances	5,720	8,400	12,000	10,000		1,800	11,000	3,320	
e. Purchased supplies			240		240				
Balances	5,720	8,400	240 12,000	10,000	240	1,800	11,000	3,320	

Transaction (f)   *Purchased $8,500 of office equipment. Paid $1,700 cash as a down payment, with the remaining $6,800 (8,500 − $1,700) due in five monthly installments of $1,360 ($6,800/5) beginning January 1.* In this transaction, the asset office equipment is increased by $8,500, cash is decreased by $1,700, notes payable is increased by $6,800, and cash flows from investing activities is decreased by $1,700. The transaction is recorded as follows:

Statement of Cash Flows	Balance Sheet									Income Statement
	Assets				= Liabilities		+ Stockholders' Equity			
	Cash +	Prepaid Insur. +	Supp. +	Office Equip. + Land	= Notes Pay. +	Accts. Pay. +	Unearned Revenue +	Capital Stock +	Retained Earnings	
Balances	5,720	8,400	240		12,000	10,000	240	1,800	11,000	3,320	
f. Purchased office equip.	−1,700			8,500		6,800				
Balances	4,020	8,400	240	8,500 12,000	16,800	240	1,800	11,000	3,320	

Statement of Cash Flows	
f. Investing	−1,700

Transaction (g) *Provided services of $6,100 to patients on account.* This transaction is similar to the revenue transactions that we recorded in September and October, except that the services have been provided on account. Family Health Care will collect cash from the patients' insurance companies in the future. Such amounts that are to be collected in the future and that arise from the normal operations of a business are called **accounts receivable**. Since a valid claim exists for future collection, accounts receivable are assets, and the transaction would be recorded as shown below.

Statement of Cash Flows												Income Statement
	Balance Sheet											
	Assets						=	Liabilities			+ Stockholders' Equity	
	Cash +	Accts. Rec. +	Prepaid Insur. +	Supp. +	Office Equip. +	Land =	Notes Pay. +	Accts. Pay. +	Unearned Revenue +	Capital Stock +	Retained Earnings	
Balances	4,020		8,400	240	8,500	12,000	16,800	240	1,800	11,000	3,320	
g. Fees earned on acct.		6,100									6,100	g.
Balances	4,020	6,100	8,400	240	8,500	12,000	16,800	240	1,800	11,000	9,420	

Income Statement

g. Fees earned 6,100

Transaction (h) *Received $5,500 for services provided to patients who paid cash.* This transaction is similar to the revenue transactions that we recorded in September and October and is recorded as follows.

Statement of Cash Flows												Income Statement
	Balance Sheet											
	Assets						=	Liabilities			+ Stockholders' Equity	
	Cash +	Accts. Rec. +	Prepaid Insur. +	Supp. +	Office Equip. +	Land =	Notes Pay. +	Accts. Pay. +	Unearned Revenue +	Capital Stock +	Retained Earnings	
Balances	4,020	6,100	8,400	240	8,500	12,000	16,800	240	1,800	11,000	9,420	
h. Fees earned for cash	5,500										5,500	h.
Balances	9,520	6,100	8,400	240	8,500	12,000	16,800	240	1,800	11,000	14,920	

Statement of Cash Flows

h. Operating 5,500

Income Statement

h. Fees earned 5,500

Transaction (i) *Received $4,200 from insurance companies, which paid on patients' accounts for services that have been provided.* In this transaction, cash is increased and the accounts receivable is decreased by $4,200. Thus, only the mix of assets changes, and the transaction is recorded as follows.

Statement of Cash Flows												Income Statement
	Balance Sheet											
	Assets						=	Liabilities			+ Stockholders' Equity	
	Cash +	Accts. Rec. +	Prepaid Insur. +	Supp. +	Office Equip. +	Land =	Notes Pay. +	Accts. Pay. +	Unearned Revenue +	Capital Stock +	Retained Earnings	
Balances	9,520	6,100	8,400	240	8,500	12,000	16,800	240	1,800	11,000	14,920	
i. Collected cash on acct.	4,200	−4,200										
Balances	13,720	1,900	8,400	240	8,500	12,000	16,800	240	1,800	11,000	14,920	

Statement of Cash Flows

i. Operating 4,200

Transaction (j) *Paid $100 on account for supplies that had been purchased.* This transaction reduces the cash and the accounts payable by $100, as shown below.

Statement of Cash Flows	Balance Sheet									Stockholders' Equity		Income Statement
	Assets						=	Liabilities		+		
	Cash +	Accts. Rec. +	Prepaid Insur. +	Supp. +	Office Equip. +	Land =	Notes Pay. +	Accts. Pay. +	Unearned Revenue +	Capital Stock +	Retained Earnings	
Balances	13,720	1,900	8,400	240	8,500	12,000	16,800	240	1,800	11,000	14,920	
j. Paid on account	−100							−100				
Balances	13,620	1,900	8,400	240	8,500	12,000	16,800	140	1,800	11,000	14,920	

Statement of Cash Flows
j. Operating   −100

Transaction (k) *Expenses paid during November were as follows: wages, $2,790; rent, $800; utilities, $580; interest, $100; and miscellaneous, $420.* This transaction is similar to the expense transaction that we recorded for Family Health Care in September and October. It is recorded as follows.

Statement of Cash Flows	Balance Sheet									Stockholders' Equity		Income Statement
	Assets						=	Liabilities		+		
	Cash +	Accts. Rec. +	Prepaid Insur. +	Supp. +	Office Equip. +	Land =	Notes Pay. +	Accts. Pay. +	Unearned Revenue +	Capital Stock +	Retained Earnings	
Balances	13,620	1,900	8,400	240	8,500	12,000	16,800	140	1,800	11,000	14,920	
k. Paid expenses	−4,690										−4,690	k.
Balances	8,930	1,900	8,400	240	8,500	12,000	16,800	140	1,800	11,000	10,230	

Statement of Cash Flows
k. Operating   −4,690

Income Statement
k. Wages expense   −2,790
   Rent expense   −800
   Utilities expense   −580
   Interest expense   −100
   Misc. expense   −420

Transaction (l) *Paid dividends of $1,200 to stockholders (Dr. Landry).* This transaction is similar to the dividends transactions of September and October. It is recorded as follows.

Statement of Cash Flows	Balance Sheet									Stockholders' Equity		Income Statement
	Assets						=	Liabilities		+		
	Cash +	Accts. Rec. +	Prepaid Insur. +	Supp. +	Office Equip. +	Land =	Notes Pay. +	Accts. Pay. +	Unearned Revenue +	Capital Stock +	Retained Earnings	
Balances	8,930	1,900	8,400	240	8,500	12,000	16,800	140	1,800	11,000	10,230	
l. Paid dividends	−1,200										−1,200	
Balances	7,730	1,900	8,400	240	8,500	12,000	16,800	140	1,800	11,000	9,030	

Statement of Cash Flows
l. Financing   −1,200

Obj 3

Describe and illustrate the end-of-period adjustment process.

The Adjustment Process

Accrual concepts of accounting require the accounting records to be updated prior to preparing financial statements. This updating process, called the **adjustment process**, is necessary to properly match revenues and expenses. This is an application of the matching concept.

Adjustments are necessary because, at any point in time, some accounts (elements) of the accounting equation will not be up to date. For example, as time passes, prepaid insurance will expire and supplies will be used in operations. However, it is not efficient to record the daily expiration of prepaid insurance or the daily usage of supplies. Rather, the accounting records are normally updated just prior to preparing the financial statements.

You may wonder why we were able to prepare the September and October financial statements for Family Health Care in Chapter 2 without recording any adjustments. The answer is that in September and October, Family Health Care only entered into cash transactions. When all of a party's transactions are cash transactions, no adjustments are necessary. However, Family Health Care had accrual transactions in November. Thus, we must now address the adjustment process.

Deferrals and Accruals

The financial statements are affected by two types of adjustments—deferrals and accruals. Whether a deferral or an accrual, each adjustment will affect a balance sheet account and an income statement account.

Deferrals are created by recording a transaction in a way that delays or defers the recognition of an expense or a revenue. Common examples of deferrals are described below.

- **Prepaid expenses** or **deferred expenses** are items that initially have been recorded as assets but are expected to become expenses over time or through the normal operations of the business. For Family Health Care, prepaid insurance is an example of a deferral that will normally require adjustment. Other examples include supplies, prepaid advertising, and prepaid interest. *McDonald's Corporation* reported over $300 million of prepaid expenses and other current assets on a recent balance sheet.
- **Unearned revenues** or **deferred revenues** are items that initially have been recorded as liabilities but are expected to become revenues over time or through the normal

INTEGRITY, OBJECTIVITY, AND ETHICS IN BUSINESS

Dave's Legacy

When Dave Thomas, founder of Wendy's, died in 2002, he left behind a corporate culture of integrity and high ethical conduct. When asked to comment on Dave's death, Jack Schuessler, chairman and chief executive officer of Wendy's, stated:

"People (could) relate to Dave, that he was honest and has integrity and he really cares about people. . . . There is no replacing Dave Thomas. . . . So you are left with . . . the values that he gave us . . . and you take care of the customer every day like Dave would want us to and good things will happen."

"He's [Dave Thomas] taught us so much that when we get stuck, we can always look back and ask ourselves, how would Dave handle it?"

In a recent discussion of corporate earnings with analysts, Kerrii Anderson, chief financial officer of Wendy's, stated: "We're confident about the future because of our unwavering commitment to our core values, such as quality food, superior restaurant operations, continuous improvement, and *integrity to doing the right thing* (emphasis added)."

Sources: Neil Cavuto, "Wendy's CEO—Interview," *Fox News: Your World,* February 11, 2002; "Q1 2003 Wendy's International Earnings Conference Call—Final," *Financial Disclosure Wire,* April 24, 2003.

operations of the business. For Family Health Care, unearned rent is an example of a deferred revenue. Other examples include tuition received in advance by a school, an annual retainer fee received by an attorney, premiums received in advance by an insurance company, and magazine subscriptions received in advance by a publisher. On a recent balance sheet, ***Microsoft Corporation*** reported over $12 billion of deferred revenue related to its software.

Accruals are created when a revenue or expense has been earned or incurred, but has not been recorded at the end of the accounting period. Accruals are normally the result of revenue being earned or an expense being incurred before any cash is received or paid. One such situation occurs when employees earn wages before the end of the year, but are not paid until after year-end. For example, employee wages may be paid and recorded every Friday, but the accounting period may end on a Tuesday. Thus, at the end of the accounting period, the company owes the employees for their wages on Monday and Tuesday that will be paid on the following Friday. At the end of the accounting period, these wages have been incurred by the company, but have not yet been recorded or paid. Thus, the amount of the wages for Monday and Tuesday is an accrual. Other examples of accruals are described below.

- **Accrued expenses** or accrued liabilities are expenses that have been incurred but have not been recorded in the accounts. An example of an accrued expense is accrued interest on notes payable at the end of a period. Other examples include accrued utility expenses and taxes. On a recent balance sheet, ***Home Depot*** reported over $1.3 billion of accrued salaries and related expenses and over $1.9 billion of other accrued expenses.
- **Accrued revenues** or accrued assets are revenues that have been earned but have not been recorded in the accounts. An example of an accrued revenue is fees for services that an attorney has provided but has not billed to the client at the end of the period. Other examples include accrued interest on notes receivable and accrued rent on property rented to others.

Exhibit 1 summarizes the nature of deferrals and accruals and the need for adjustments in order to prepare financial statements.

Adjustments for Family Health Care

We now analyze the accounts for Family Health Care at the end of November to determine whether any adjustments are necessary. Specifically, we will focus on the following adjustment data, which are typical for most businesses.

Deferred expenses:
1. Prepaid insurance expired, $1,100.
2. Supplies used, $150.
3. Depreciation on office equipment, $160.

Deferred revenue:
4. Unearned revenue earned, $360.

Accrued expense:
5. Wages owed but not paid to employees, $220.

Accrued revenue:
6. Services provided but not billed to insurance companies, $750.

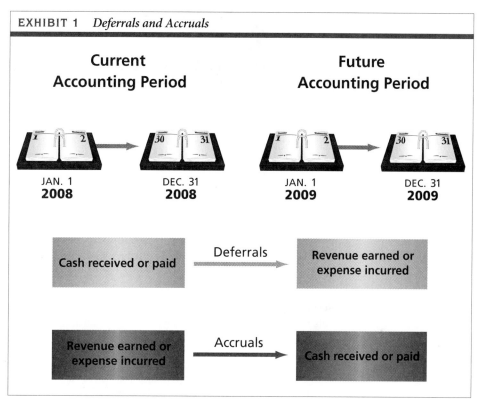

EXHIBIT 1 *Deferrals and Accruals*

Adjustment 1 (Prepaid Insurance)   This first adjustment recognizes that a portion of the prepaid insurance purchased November 1 expired during November. Family Health Care prepaid two policies—a general business policy for $2,400 (transaction b) and a malpractice policy for $6,000 (transaction c). The general business policy is a 2-year policy expiring at a rate of $100 ($2,400 ÷ 24) per month. The malpractice policy is a six-month policy that expires at a rate of $1,000 ($6,000 ÷ 6) per month. The total expired prepaid insurance is thus $1,100 ($100 + $1,000). This adjustment is recorded below.

Statement of Cash Flows	Balance Sheet											Income Statement
	Assets					=	Liabilities		+	Stockholders' Equity		
	Cash +	Accts. Rec. +	Prepaid Insur. +	Supp. +	Office Equip. +	Land =	Notes Pay. +	Accts. Pay. +	Unearned Revenue +	Capital Stock +	Retained Earnings	
Balances	7,730	1,900	8,400	240	8,500	12,000	16,800	140	1,800	11,000	9,030	
a1. Insurance expense			−1,100								−1,100	*a1.*
Balances	7,730	1,900	7,300	240	8,500	12,000	16,800	140	1,800	11,000	7,930	

Income Statement
a1. Insurance exp.   −1,100

Adjustment 2 (Supplies)   This adjustment recognizes the portion of the $240 of supplies purchased during November that have been used. For November, $150 of the supplies were used, leaving $90 of supplies remaining for use during the coming months. Thus, after recording the adjustment, the accounting records should show supplies expense of $150 for November and supplies on hand (an asset) of $90. The second adjustment is recorded as shown at the top of the next page.

Statement of Cash Flows		Balance Sheet											Income Statement
		Assets						=	Liabilities			+ Stockholders' Equity	
	Cash +	Accts. Rec. +	Prepaid Insur. +	Supp. +	Office Equip. +	Land =	Notes Pay. +	Accts. Pay. +	Unearned Revenue +	Capital Stock +	Retained Earnings	
Balances	7,730	1,900	7,300	240	8,500	12,000	16,800	140	1,800	11,000	7,930	
a2. Supplies expense				−150							−150	a2.
Balances	7,730	1,900	7,300	90	8,500	12,000	16,800	140	1,800	11,000	7,780	

Income Statement	
a2. Supplies exp.	−150

Adjustment 3 (Depreciation) This adjustment recognizes that fixed assets such as office equipment lose their ability to provide service over time. This reduction in the ability of a fixed asset to provide service is called **depreciation**. However, it is difficult to objectively determine the physical decline in the ability of fixed assets to provide service. For this reason, accountants estimate the amount of the cost of long-term assets that becomes expense over the asset's useful life. In a later chapter, we will discuss methods of estimating depreciation. In this chapter, we simply assume that the amount of November depreciation for the office equipment is $160.

To maintain a record of the initial cost of a fixed asset for tax and other purposes, the fixed asset (office equipment) is not reduced directly. Instead, an offsetting or contra asset account, called **accumulated depreciation**, is included in the accounting equation. On the balance sheet, the accumulated depreciation will be subtracted from the original cost of the fixed asset. Thus, the third adjustment is recorded as follows.

Statement of Cash Flows		Balance Sheet												Income Statement
		Assets							=	Liabilities			+ Stockholders' Equity	
	Cash +	Accts. Rec. +	Prepaid Insur. +	Supp. +	Office Equip. −	Acc. Dep. +	Land =	Notes Pay. +	Accts. Pay. +	Unearned Revenue +	Capital Stock +	Retained Earnings	
Balances	7,730	1,900	7,300	90	8,500		12,000	16,800	140	1,800	11,000	7,780	
a3. Depreciation exp.						−160						−160	a3.
Balances	7,730	1,900	7,300	90	8,500	−160	12,000	16,800	140	1,800	11,000	7,620	

Income Statement	
a3. Depreciation exp.	−160

Note that the accumulated depreciation account is subtracted in determining the total assets. We should also note three other points related to Adjustment 3. First, land is not depreciated, since it usually does not lose its ability to provide service. Second, the cost of the equipment can be thought of as a deferred expense, since it is recognized as an expense over the equipment's useful life. Third, the cost of the fixed asset less the balance of its accumulated depreciation is called the asset's *carrying value* or *book value*. For example, the carrying value of the office equipment, after the preceding adjustment, is $8,340 ($8,500 − $160).

Adjustment 4 (Unearned Rent) This adjustment recognizes that a portion of the unearned revenue is earned by the end of November. That is, of the $1,800 received for rental of the land for five months (November through March), one-fifth, or $360, would have been earned as of November 30. The fourth adjustment recognizes this decrease in the unearned revenue and the increase in the rental revenue, as shown below.

Statement of Cash Flows				Balance Sheet											Income Statement
				Assets				=		Liabilities		+	Stockholders' Equity		
	Cash +	Accts. Rec. +	Prepaid Insur. +	Supp. +	Office Equip. −	Acc. Dep. +	Land =	Notes Pay. +	Accts. Pay. +		Unearned Revenue +	Capital Stock +	Retained Earnings	
Balances	7,730	1,900	7,300	90	8,500	−160	12,000	16,800	140		1,800	11,000	7,620	
a4. Rent revenue											−360		360	a4.
Balances	7,730	1,900	7,300	90	8,500	−160	12,000	16,800	140		1,440	11,000	7,980	

Income Statement

a4. Rent revenue 360

Adjustment 5 (Accrued Wages Expense) This adjustment recognizes that as of November 30, employees of Family Health Care may have worked one or more days for which they have not been paid. It is rare that the employees are paid the same day that the accounting period ends. Thus, at the end of an accounting period, it is normal for businesses to owe wages to their employees. This is what we defined as an accrued expense earlier in our discussion. The fifth adjustment is recorded by increasing wages payable, a liability, and deducting wages expense from retained earnings, as shown here.

Statement of Cash Flows				Balance Sheet												Income Statement
				Assets				=		Liabilities			+	Stockholders' Equity		
	Cash +	Accts. Rec. +	Prepaid Insur. +	Supp. +	Office Equip. −	Acc. Dep. +	Land =	Notes Pay. +	Accts. Pay. +	Wages Pay. +	Unearned Revenue +	Capital Stock +	Retained Earnings	
Balances	7,730	1,900	7,300	90	8,500	−160	12,000	16,800	140		1,440	11,000	7,980	
a5. Wages exp.										220			−220	a5.
Balances	7,730	1,900	7,300	90	8,500	−160	12,000	16,800	140	220	1,440	11,000	7,760	

Income Statement

a5. Wages expense −220

Adjustment 6 (Accrued Fees Earned) This adjustment recognizes that Family Health Care has provided services to patients that have not yet been billed. Such services are usually provided near the end of the month. This adjustment is recorded by increasing accounts receivable and fees earned, as shown at the top of the next page.

Statement of Cash Flows	Balance Sheet													Income Statement
				Assets				=	Liabilities			+	Stockholders' Equity	
	Cash +	Accts. Rec. +	Prepaid Insur. +	Supp. +	Office Equip. −	Acc. Dep. +	Land =	Notes Pay. +	Accts. Pay. +	Wages Pay. +	Unearned Revenue +	Capital Stock +	Retained Earnings	
Balances	7,730	1,900	7,300	90	8,500	−160	12,000	16,800	140	220	1,440	11,000	7,760	
a6. Fees earned		750											750	a6.
Balances	7,730	2,650	7,300	90	8,500	−160	12,000	16,800	140	220	1,440	11,000	8,510	

Income Statement
a6. Fees earned   750

The November transactions and adjustments for Family Health Care are summarized in Exhibit 2.

Financial Statements

In Chapter 2, we prepared financial statements for Family Health Care for September and October. In this section, we describe and illustrate financial statements for November, using accrual concepts of accounting. These financial statements are shown in Exhibits 3, 4, 5, and 6. They are based on the summary of transactions and adjustments shown in Exhibit 2.

Income Statement

The income statement shown in Exhibit 3 is prepared by summarizing the revenue and expense transactions listed under the income statement column of Exhibit 2. The operating income is determined by deducting the operating expenses from the fees earned from normal operations. The other income—rental revenue—is then added to determine the net income for November.

As reported on the income statement, *revenues* are a result of providing services or selling products to customers. Examples of revenues include fees earned, fares earned, commissions revenue, interest revenue, and rent revenue.

Revenues from the primary operations of the business are normally reported separately from other revenue. For example, Family Health Care has two types of revenues for November, fees earned and rental revenue. Since the primary operation of the business is providing services to patients, rental revenue is reported under the heading of "Other income."

Expenses on the income statement are assets used up or services consumed in the process of generating revenues. Expenses are matched against their related revenues to determine the net income or net loss for a period. Examples of typical expenses include wages expense, rent expense, utilities expense, supplies expense, and miscellaneous expense. Expenses not related to the primary operations of the business are sometimes reported as "Other expense." Interest expense is an example of an expense that may be reported separately as an Other expense.

EXHIBIT 2   *Family Health Care Summary of Transactions and Adjustments for November*

Statement of Cash Flows	Balance Sheet											Stockholders' Equity		Income Statement
	Assets						=	Liabilities				+		
	Cash +	Accts. Rec. +	Prepaid Insur. +	Supp. +	Office Equip. −	Acc. Dep. +	Land =	Notes Pay. +	Accts. Pay. +	Wages Pay. +	Unearned Revenue +	Capital Stock +	Retained Earnings	
Balances, Nov. 1	7,320						12,000	10,000				6,000	3,320	
a. Rental rev.	1,800										1,800			
b. Paid insurance	−2,400		2,400											
c. Paid insurance	−6,000		6,000											
d. Investment	5,000											5,000		
e. Pur. supplies				240					240					
f. Pur. off. equip.	−1,700				8,500				6,800					
g. Fees earned		6,100											6,100	g.
h. Fees earned	5,500												5,500	h.
i. Collected cash	4,200	−4,200												
j. Paid on acct.	−100								−100					
k. Paid expenses	−4,690												−4,690	k.
l. Dividends	−1,200												−1,200	
a1. Insurance exp.			−1,100										−1,100	a1.
a2. Supplies exp.				−150									−150	a2.
a3. Deprec. exp						−160							−160	a3.
a4. Rental revenue											−360		360	a4.
a5. Wages exp.										220			−220	a5.
a6. Fees earned		750											750	a6.
Balances, Nov. 30	7,730	2,650	7,300	90	8,500	−160	12,000	16,800	140	220	1,440	11,000	8,510	

Statement of Cash Flows			Income Statement		
a. Operating	1,800		g. Fees earned	6,100	
b. Operating	−2,400		h. Fees earned	5,500	
c. Operating	−6,000		k. Wages exp.	−2,790	
d. Financing	5,000		Rent exp.	−800	
f. Investing	−1,700		Utilities exp.	−580	
h. Operating	5,500		Interest exp.	−100	
i. Operating	4,200		Misc. exp.	−420	
j. Operating	−100		a1. Insur. exp.	−1,100	
k. Operating	−4,690		a2. Supplies exp.	−150	
l. Financing	−1,200		a3. Deprec. exp.	−160	
Increase in cash	410		a4. Rental rev.	360	
Nov. 1 cash bal.	7,320		a5. Wages exp.	−220	
Nov. 30 cash bal.	7,730		a6. Fees earned	750	
			Net income	6,390	

EXHIBIT 3   *Family Health Care Income Statement for November*

FAMILY HEALTH CARE, P.C.
Income Statement
For the Month Ended November 30, 2009

Fees earned		$12,350
Operating expenses:		
Wages expense	$3,010	
Insurance expense	1,100	
Rent expense	800	
Utilities expense	580	
Depreciation expense	160	
Supplies expense	150	
Interest expense	100	
Miscellaneous expense	420	
Total operating expenses		6,320
Operating income		$ 6,030
Other income:		
Rental revenue		360
Net income		$ 6,390

Retained Earnings Statement

The retained earnings statement shown in Exhibit 4 is prepared by adding the November net income (from the income statement), less the November dividends, to the beginning amount of retained earnings. This ending amount of retained earnings is included on the balance sheet.

EXHIBIT 4   *Family Health Care Retained Earnings Statement for November*

FAMILY HEALTH CARE, P.C.
Retained Earnings Statement
For the Month Ended November 30, 2009

Retained earnings, November 1, 2009		$3,320
Net income for November	$6,390	
Less dividends	1,200	5,190
Retained earnings, November 30, 2009		$8,510

Balance Sheet

The balance sheet shown in Exhibit 5 is prepared from the ending balances shown in the Balance Sheet columns of Exhibit 2. The balance sheet shown in Exhibit 5 is a **classified balance sheet**. As the term implies, a classified balance sheet is prepared with various sections, subsections, and captions that aid in its interpretation and analysis. In the following paragraphs, we describe some of these sections and subsections.

Assets are resources such as physical items or rights that are owned by the business. Examples of physical assets include cash, supplies, buildings, equipment, and land. Examples of rights are patent rights or rights to services (prepaid items). Physical assets of

EXHIBIT 5   *Family Health Care Balance Sheet for November*

FAMILY HEALTH CARE, P.C.
Balance Sheet
November 30, 2009

Assets			
Current assets:			
Cash		$ 7,730	
Accounts receivable		2,650	
Prepaid insurance		7,300	
Supplies		90	
Total current assets			$17,770
Fixed assets:			
Office equipment	$8,500		
Less accumulated depreciation	160	$ 8,340	
Land		12,000	
Total fixed assets			20,340
Total assets			$38,110
Liabilities			
Current liabilities:			
Accounts payable		$ 140	
Wages payable		220	
Notes payable		6,800	
Unearned revenue		1,440	
Total current liabilities			$ 8,600
Long-term liabilities:			
Notes payable			10,000
Total liabilities			$18,600
Stockholders' Equity			
Capital stock		$11,000	
Retained earnings		8,510	
Total stockholders' equity			19,510
Total liabilities and stockholders' equity			$38,110

a long-term nature are referred to as **fixed assets**. Rights that are long term in nature are called **intangible assets.**

Assets are normally divided into classes in preparing a classified balance sheet. Three of these classes are (1) current assets, (2) fixed assets, and (3) intangible assets.

Cash and other assets that are expected to be converted to cash or sold or used up within 1 year or less, through the normal operations of the business, are called **current assets**. In addition to cash, the current assets normally include accounts receivable, notes receivable, supplies, and other prepaid expenses. Accounts receivable and notes receivable are current assets because they will usually be converted to cash within 1 year or less. **Notes receivable** are written claims against debtors who promise to pay the amount of the note and interest at an agreed-upon rate. A note receivable is the creditor's view of a note payable transaction. As shown in Exhibit 5, Family Health Care has current assets of cash, accounts receivable, prepaid insurance, and supplies as of November 30, 2009.

The fixed assets section may also be labeled as property, plant, and equipment, or plant assets. Fixed assets include equipment, machinery, buildings, and land. Except for land, such fixed assets depreciate over a period of time, as we discussed earlier in this chapter. The cost less accumulated depreciation for each major type of fixed asset is normally reported on the classified balance sheet. As of November 30, 2009, Family Health Care's fixed assets consist of office equipment and land.

Intangible assets represent rights, such as patent rights, copyrights, and goodwill. Goodwill arises from such factors as name recognition, location, product quality, reputation, and managerial skill. Goodwill is recorded and reported on the balance sheet when a company purchases another company at a premium price above the normal cost of the purchased company's assets. For example, goodwill was recognized when *eBay Inc*. purchased *PayPal Inc*. Family Health Care has no intangible assets as of November 30.

Liabilities are amounts owed to outsiders (creditors). Liabilities are often identified on the balance sheet by titles that include the word *payable*. Examples of liabilities include notes payable and wages payable.

Liabilities are normally divided into two classes on a classified balance sheet. These classes are (1) current liabilities and (2) long-term liabilities.

Liabilities that will be due within a short time (usually 1 year or less) and that are to be paid out of current assets are called **current liabilities**. The most common current liabilities are notes payable and accounts payable. Other current liabilities reported on the classified balance sheet include wages payable, interest payable, taxes payable, and unearned revenue.

Liabilities that will not be due for a long time (usually more than 1 year) are called **long-term liabilities**. Long-term liabilities are reported below the current liabilities. As long-term liabilities come due and are to be paid within 1 year, they are reported as current liabilities. If they are to be renewed rather than paid, they would continue to be classified as long term. When an asset is pledged as security for a long-term liability, the obligation may be called a *mortgage note payable* or a *mortgage payable*.

Family Health Care's current and long-term liabilities as of November 30, 2009, are shown in Exhibit 5. You should note that $6,800 of the notes payable is due within the next year and therefore is reported as a current liability. The remainder of the notes payable, $10,000, is not due until 2014 and thus is reported as a long-term liability. Family Health Care's other current liabilities consist of accounts payable, wages payable, and unearned revenue.

Stockholders' equity is the stockholders' rights to the assets of the business. For a corporation, the stockholders' equity consists of capital stock and retained earnings. The stockholders' equity section of a classified balance sheet reports each of these two financial statement accounts separately. The capital stock amount on the balance sheet of $11,000 results from adding the additional investment during November of $5,000 to the beginning amount of capital stock of $6,000. The ending retained earnings of $8,510 comes from the retained earnings statement.

Statement of Cash Flows

The statement of cash flows shown in Exhibit 6 is prepared by summarizing the cash transactions shown in the statement of cash flows column of Exhibit 2. The net cash flow from operations is computed by adding the cash receipts from revenue transactions and subtracting the cash payments for operating transactions. These items are

EXHIBIT 6   *Family Health Care Statement of Cash Flows for November*

FAMILY HEALTH CARE P.C.
Statement of Cash Flows
For the Month Ended November 30, 2009

Cash flows from operating activities:		
Cash received from patients	$ 9,700	
Cash received from rental of land	1,800	$ 11,500
Deduct cash payments for expenses		(13,190)
Net cash flow used in operating activities		$ (1,690)
Cash flows from investing activities:		
Purchase of office equipment		(1,700)
Cash flows from financing activities:		
Additional issuance of capital stock	$ 5,000	
Deduct cash dividends	(1,200)	
Net cash flow from financing activities		3,800
Net increase in cash		$ 410
November 1, 2009 cash balance		7,320
November 30, 2009 cash balance		$ 7,730

identified in the statement of cash flows column of Exhibit 2 as operating activities. The cash received from revenue transactions consists of $9,700 ($5,500 + $4,200) received from patients and $1,800 received from rental of the land. The cash payments for operating transactions of $13,190 ($2,400 + $6,000 + $100 + $4,690) is determined by adding the negative cash payments related to operating activities shown in the statement of cash flows column of Exhibit 2. The purchase of the office equipment is treated as a separate cash outflow from investment activities. The receipt of the additional investment and the payment of dividends are reported as cash flows from financing activities.

Integration of Financial Statements

Exhibit 7 shows the integration of Family Health Care's financial statements for November. The reconciliation of net income and net cash flows from operations is shown in the appendix at the end of this chapter.

Obj 5

Accrual and Cash Bases of Accounting

Describe how the accrual basis of accounting enhances the interpretation of financial statements.

The financial statements of Family Health Care for November were prepared under accrual accounting concepts. Entities that use accrual accounting concepts for recording transactions and preparing financial statements are said to use the *accrual basis of accounting*. The accrual basis of accounting is used by large businesses and is required of publicly held corporations such as ***Amazon.com***, eBay, and ***Wm. Wrigley Jr. Company.***

Entities that record transactions only when cash is received or paid are said to use the cash basis of accounting. Individuals and small businesses often use the *cash basis of*

EXHIBIT 7   *Integrated Financial Statements—Family Health Care*

Family Health Care, P.C.
Balance Sheet
November 30, 2009

	Assets	=	Liabilities	+	Stockholders' Equity	
	Cash				**Capital Stock**	**Retained Earnings**
	.		.		.	.
	.		.		.	.
	.		.		.	.
	$7,730		$18,600		$11,000	$8,510

$38,110
Total Assets

$38,110
Total Liabilities + Stockholders' Equity

=

Family Health Care, P.C.
Statement of Cash Flows
For the Month Ended Nov. 30, 2009

Operating act.	$(1,690)
Investing act.	(1,700)
Financing act.	3,800
Increase in cash	$ 410
Cash, Nov. 1	7,320
Cash, Nov. 30	$ 7,730

Family Health Care, P.C.
Income Statement
For the Month Ended Nov. 30, 2009

Revenues	$12,350
Expenses	6,320
Operating income	$ 6,030
Other income	360
Net income	$ 6,390

Family Health Care, P.C.
Retained Earnings Statement
For the Month Ended Nov. 30, 2009

RE, Nov. 1	$ 3,320
Net income	6,390
Dividends	(1,200)
RE, Nov. 30	$ 8,510

Reconciliation of cash flows from operations and net income (see appendix to this chapter)

accounting.[1] For example, you probably use a cash basis because your checkbook is your primary accounting record. You keep track of your deposits (cash receipts) and checks (cash payments). Periodically, your bank sends you a statement that you use to verify the accuracy of your record keeping.

Using the Cash Basis of Accounting

Under the **cash basis of accounting**, a business records only transactions involving increases or decreases of its cash. To illustrate, assume that a real estate agency sells a $300,000 piece of property on December 28, 2008. In selling the property,

[1]Some businesses use modified-cash bases of accounting. These bases of accounting are covered in advanced accounting texts.

the agency earns a commission of 8% of the selling price. However, the agency does not receive the $24,000 commission check until January 3, 2009. Under the cash basis, the real estate agency will not record the commission (revenue) until January 3, 2009.

Under the cash basis, expenses are recorded only when cash is paid. For example, a December cellular phone bill that is paid in January would be recorded as a January expense, not a December expense. Thus, under the cash basis, the matching concept does not determine when expenses are recorded. That is, expenses are recorded when paid in cash, not necessarily in the period when the revenue is earned. As a result, adjusting entries are not required under the cash basis.

Using the Accrual Basis of Accounting

Under the **accrual basis of accounting**, revenue is recorded as it is earned, regardless of when cash is received. To illustrate, using the preceding example, the real estate agency would record the commission (revenue) of $24,000 as earned on December 28, 2008, even though the check (cash) is not received until January 3, 2009. Once revenue has been earned and recorded, any expenses that have been incurred in generating the revenue are recorded and thus matched against that revenue. For example, a December cellular phone bill would be recorded in December as an increase in expenses and liabilities, even though it is not paid until January. In this way, the December phone expense is matched against the revenue it helped generate in December. We used the accrual basis of accounting to record the November transactions of Family Health Care. In addition, as we illustrated earlier in this chapter, the accrual basis requires adjusting entries to update the accounting records at the end of the period. Exhibit 8 summarizes the basic differences of how revenue and expenses are recorded under the cash and accrual bases of accounting.

EXHIBIT 8	*Cash versus Accrual Accounting*	
	Cash Basis	**Accrual Basis**
Revenue is recorded	When cash is received	When revenue is earned
Expense is recorded	When cash is paid	When expense is incurred in generating revenue
Adjusting entries	Not required	Required in order to prepare financial statements

Family Health Care under the Cash and Accrual Bases of Accounting

All the transactions for Family Health Care in Chapter 2 involved the receipt or payment of cash. As a result, the financial statements shown in Chapter 2 for Family Health Care would be the same as those reported under the cash basis of accounting. In this chapter, however, Family Health Care entered into transactions that used accrual accounting concepts. As a result, the November financial statements shown in Exhibits 3 through 6 differ from those prepared using the cash basis of accounting.

One of the major differences in financial statements prepared under the accrual and cash bases of accounting involves the reporting of net income and net cash flows from operations. Under the cash basis of accounting, net income and net cash flows from operations are the same. For example, in Chapter 2, net income and net cash flows from operations for September and October for Family Health Care were $2,600 and $3,220. In contrast, under the accrual basis of accounting, net income and net cash flows from operations may be significantly different. This is shown in Exhibit 3 where Family Health Care reports net income of $6,390 for November while reporting net cash flows from operations of ($1,690). This difference is due to the effects of accrual and deferrals.[2]

Importance of Accrual Basis of Accounting

The use of the accrual basis of accounting is essential for assessing and interpreting the financial performance of an entity. To illustrate, we have summarized the net cash flows from operations and net income for Family Health Care below.

	Net Cash Flow from Operations	Net Income
September	$ 2,600	$2,600
October	3,220	3,220
November	(1,690)	6,390

Under the cash basis, the cash flows from operating activities and the net income for November would be reported as a negative amount (loss) of $1,690. While this might be interpreted as an unfavorable trend, the accrual basis better reflects what is really happening to Family Health Care. Since September, revenues have more than doubled, increasing from $5,500 to $12,350, and net income has more than doubled. Thus, the accrual basis reflects Family Health Care as a profitable, rapidly expanding business. This illustrates why net income is generally a better predictor of the long-term profitability of a business than is net cash flows from operations.

Such differences between the cash basis and the accrual basis illustrate why generally accepted accounting principles require the accrual basis for all but the very smallest businesses. You should recognize, however, that the net cash flow from operating activities is an important amount that is useful to readers of the financial statements. For this reason, generally accepted accounting principles require reporting cash flows. For example, in the long run, a business will go bankrupt if it continually experiences negative cash flows from operations, even though it may report net income. In other words, a business must generate positive cash flows from operations in order to survive. In the case of Family Health Care, the negative cash flows from operations for November was due in large measure to prepaying insurance premiums of $8,400. Thus, the negative cash flows from operations is temporary for Family Health Care and not a matter of major concern. This illustrates why the financial statements must be analyzed and interpreted together, rather than individually, and why we use the integrated financial statements approach throughout this text. For example, long-run profitability is best analyzed by focusing on the net income reported under the accrual basis, while the availability of cash to pay debts as they become due is best analyzed by focusing on the net cash flows from operating activities.

---

[2]A formal reconciliation of net cash flows from operations and the net income is shown in the appendix at the end of this chapter.

The Accounting Cycle for the Accrual Basis of Accounting

The process that begins with analyzing transactions and ends with preparing the accounting records for the next accounting period is called the **accounting cycle**. The most important output of the accounting cycle is the financial statements. The basic steps in the accounting cycle are shown below.

1. *Identifying, analyzing, and recording* the effects of transactions on the accounting equation (financial statement accounts).
2. *Identifying, analyzing, and recording* adjustment data.
3. *Preparing* financial statements.

We have described and illustrated steps 1–3 in this chapter. Using the integrated financial statement framework, the ending balances for the balance sheet elements (columns) become the beginning balances for the next accounting period.[3] Steps 1–3 are then repeated for the next accounting period.

Appendix — *Reconciliation: Net Cash Flows from Operations and Net Income*[4]

In Chapter 2, we illustrated financial statements for Family Health Care for September and October 2009. Because all the September and October transactions were cash transactions, the net cash flows from operating activities shown on the statement of cash flows equals the net income shown in the income statements. For example, Exhibits 4 and 7 in Chapter 2 report net cash flows from operating activities and net income of $2,600 and $3,220 for September and October. When all of an entity's transactions are cash transactions or when an entity uses the cash basis of accounting, net cash flows from operating activities will always equal net income. This is not true, however, under the accrual basis of accounting.

During November and December, Family Health Care used the accrual basis of accounting. The November financial statements are illustrated in Exhibits 3 through 6 of this chapter. The December financial statements for Family Health Care are illustrated in the Illustrative Problem at the end of this chapter. The net cash flows from operating activities and net income for November and December are shown here.

	Net Cash Flows from Operating Activities	Net Income
November	$(1,690)	$ 6,390
December	8,760	10,825

Under the accrual basis, net cash flows from operating activities will normally not be the same as net income. The difference can be reconciled by considering the effects of accruals and deferrals on the income statement. Exhibit 9 illustrates the November reconciliation of Family Health Care's net income with operating cash flows from operations.

---

[3]In double-entry accounting systems such as described in Appendix A, at the end of the text, another step is necessary to complete the accounting cycle. This fourth step, called the closing process, involves transferring balances of revenues, expenses, and dividends to retained earnings. This step is unnecessary when using the integrated financial statements framework.

[4]This reconciliation is referred to as the indirect method of reporting cash flows from operations.

In Exhibit 9, we begin with net income. We then add or deduct the effects of accruals or deferrals that influenced net income under the accrual basis but did not result in the receipt or payment of cash. We thus arrive at net cash flows from operating activities.

EXHIBIT 9   *November's Reconciliation of Net Income and Cash Flows from Operations*

Net income		$ 6,390
Add:		
Depreciation expense	$ 160	
Increase in accounts payable	140	
Increase in wages payable	220	
Increase in unearned revenue	1,440	1,960
Deduct:		
Increase in accounts receivable	$(2,650)	
Increase in prepaid insurance	(7,300)	
Increase in supplies	(90)	(10,040)
Net cash flows from operating activities		$ (1,690)

The effect of an accrual or deferral on the income statement and net income is reflected in its net increase or decrease during the period. For example, during November, depreciation expense of $160 was recorded (a deferred expense) and thus deducted in arriving at net income. Yet, no cash was paid. Thus, to arrive at cash flows from operations, depreciation expense is added back to net income. Likewise, accounts payable increased during November by $140, and a related expense was recorded. But again, no cash was paid. Similarly, wages payable increased during November by $220, and the related wages expense was deducted in arriving at net income. However, the $220 was not paid until the next month. Thus, for November, the increases of $140 in accounts payable and $220 in wages payable are added back to net income.

The increase in unearned revenue of $1,440 represents unearned revenue for four months for land rented to ILS Company. ILS Company initially paid Family Health Care $1,800 in advance. Of the $1,800, one-fifth ($360) was recorded as revenue for November. However, under the cash basis, the entire $1,800 would have been recorded as revenue. Therefore, $1,440 (the increase in the unearned revenue) is added back to net income to arrive at cash flows from operations.

During November, accounts receivable increased by $2,650 and thus was recorded as part of revenue in arriving at net income. However, no cash was received. Thus, this increase in accounts receivable is deducted in arriving at cash flows from operations.

The increase in prepaid insurance represents an $8,400 payment of cash for insurance premiums. During November, only $1,100 of the premiums is deducted in arriving at net income. Therefore, the remaining $7,300 (the increase in prepaid insurance) is deducted in arriving at cash flows from operations. Similarly, the increase in supplies of $90 is deducted.

You may have noticed a pattern in how we reconciled net income to net cash flows from operations. First, depreciation expense was added. Next, increases in current assets related to operations were deducted, while increases in current liabilities related to operations were added. The increase in the current liability for notes payable of $6,800 was not included in the reconciliation. This is because the notes payable is related to the purchase of office equipment, which, in the statement of cash flows, is an investing activity rather than an operating activity.

During November, all the current asset and liability accruals and deferrals related to operations were increases. This was because Family Health Care used the cash basis during October, so there were no deferrals or accruals at the beginning of November. In future periods, there would be both increases and decreases in these items. These increases and decreases would be added or subtracted to arrive at cash flows from operations, as shown in Exhibit 10.

EXHIBIT 10 *Reconciling Items*		
Net income		$XXX
Add:		
Depreciation expense	$XXX	
Increases in current liabilities from operations	XXX	
Decreases in current assets from operations	XXX	XXX
Deduct:		
Increases in current assets from operations	$XXX	
Decreases in current liabilities from operations	XXX	XXX
Net cash flows from operations		$XXX

For example, a decrease in accounts receivable implies that cash was collected and thus would be added. In contrast, a decrease in accounts payable implies that cash was paid and thus would be deducted.

Key Points

1. **Describe basic accrual accounting concepts, including the matching concept.**

   Under accrual concepts of accounting, revenue is recognized when it is earned. When revenues are earned and recorded, all expenses incurred in generating the revenues are recorded so that revenues and expenses are properly matched in determining the net income or loss for the period. Liabilities are recorded at the time a business incurs the obligation to pay for the services or goods purchased.

2. **Use accrual concepts of accounting to analyze, record, and summarize transactions.**

   Using the integrated financial statement framework, November transactions for Family Health Care are recorded. Family Health Care's November transactions involve accrual accounting transactions.

3. **Describe and illustrate the end-of-period adjustment process.**

   The accrual concepts of accounting require the accounting records to be updated prior to preparing financial statements. This updating process, called the adjustment process, is necessary to match revenues and expenses. The adjustment process involves two types of adjustments—deferrals and accruals. Adjustments for deferrals may involve deferred expenses or deferred revenues. Adjustments for accruals may involve accrued expenses or accrued revenues.

4. **Prepare financial statements using accrual concepts of accounting, including a classified balance sheet.**

A classified balance sheet includes sections for current assets; property, plant, and equipment (fixed assets); and intangible assets. Liabilities are classified as current liabilities or long-term liabilities. The income statement normally reports sections for revenues, operating expenses, other income and expense, and net income.

5. **Describe how the accrual basis of accounting enhances the interpretation of financial statements.**

The net cash flows from operating activities and net income will differ under the accrual basis of accounting.

Under the accrual basis, net income is a better indicator of the long-term profitability of a business. For this reason, the accrual basis of accounting is required by generally accepted accounting principles, except for very small businesses. The accrual basis reports the effects of operations on cash flows through the reporting of net cash flows from operating activities on the statement of cash flows.

The accounting cycle is the process that begins with the analysis of transactions and ends with preparing the accounting records for the next accounting period. The basic steps in the accounting cycle are (1) identifying, analyzing, and recording the effects of transactions on the accounting equation; (2) identifying, analyzing, and recording adjustment data; and (3) preparing financial statements.

Key Terms

Account	Adjustment process	Fixed assets
Accounting cycle	Cash basis of accounting	Intangible assets
Accounts payable	Classified balance sheet	Liabilities
Accounts receivable	Current assets	Long-term liabilities
Accrual basis of accounting	Current liabilities	Notes receivable
Accruals	Deferrals	Prepaid expenses
Accrued expense	Deferred expenses	Stockholders' equity
Accrued revenue	Deferred revenues	Unearned revenues
Accumulated depreciation	Depreciation	

Illustrative Problem

Assume that the December transactions for Family Health Care are as follows:

a. Received cash of $1,900 from patients for services provided on account during November.
b. Provided services of $10,800 on account.
c. Received $6,500 for services provided for patients who paid cash.
d. Purchased supplies on account, $400.
e. Received $6,900 from insurance companies that paid on patients' accounts for services that had been previously billed.
f. Paid $310 on account for supplies that had been purchased.
g. Expenses paid during December were as follows: wages, $4,200, including $220 accrued at the end of November; rent, $800; utilities, $610; interest, $100; and miscellaneous, $520.
h. Paid dividends of $1,200 to stockholders (Dr. Landry).

Instructions

1. Record the December transactions, using the integrated financial statement framework as shown below. The beginning balances of December 1 have already been entered. After each transaction, you should enter a balance for each item. The transactions are recorded similarly to those for November. You should note that in transaction (g), the $4,200 of wages paid includes wages of $220 that were accrued at the end of November. Thus, only $3,980 ($4,200 – $220) should be recorded as wages expense for December. The remaining $220 reduces the wages payable. You should also note that the balance of retained earnings on December 1, $8,510, is the balance on November 30.

Statement of Cash Flows	Balance Sheet													Income Statement
	Assets							=	Liabilities				+ Stockholders' Equity	
	Cash +	Accts. Rec. +	Prepaid Insur. +	Supp. +	Office Equip. −	Acc. Dep. +	Land =	Notes Pay. +	Accts. Pay. +	Wages Pay. +	Unearned Revenue +	Capital Stock +	Retained Earnings	
Balances, Dec. 1	7,730	2,650	7,300	90	8,500	−160	12,000	16,800	140	220	1,440	11,000	8,510	

2. The adjustment data for December are as follows:

Deferred expenses:
1. Prepaid insurance expired, $1,100.
2. Supplies used, $275.
3. Depreciation on office equipment, $160.

Deferred revenues:
4. Unearned revenue earned, $360.

Accrued expense:
5. Wages owed employees but not paid, $340.

Accrued revenue:
6. Services provided but not billed to insurance companies, $1,050.

Enter the adjustments in the integrated financial statement framework. Identify each adjustment by "a" and the number of the related adjustment item. For example, the adjustment for prepaid insurance should be identified as (a1).

3. Prepare the December financial statements, including the income statement, retained earnings statement, balance sheet, and statement of cash flows.
4. (Appendix) Reconcile the December net income with the net cash flows from operations. (*Note:* In computing increases and decreases in amounts, use adjusted balances.)

Solution

1 and 2. Family Health Care summary of transactions and adjustments for December:

(continued)

Statement of Cash Flows		Cash +	Accts. Rec. +	Prepaid Insur. +	Supp. +	Office Equip. −	Acc. Dep. +	Land =	Notes Pay. +	Accts. Pay. +	Wages Pay. +	Unearned Revenue +	Capital Stock +	Retained Earnings	Income Statement
	Balance Sheet														
				Assets				**=**		**Liabilities**	**+**		**Stockholders' Equity**		
	Balances, Dec. 1	7,730	2,650	7,300	90	8,500	−160	12,000	16,800	140	220	1,440	11,000	8,510	
a.	Collected cash	1,900	−1,900												
	Balances	9,630	750	7,300	90	8,500	−160	12,000	16,800	140	220	1,440	11,000	8,510	
b.	Fees earned		10,800											10,800	b.
	Balances	9,630	11,550	7,300	90	8,500	−160	12,000	16,800	140	220	1,440	11,000	19,310	
c.	Fees earned	6,500												6,500	c.
	Balances	16,130	11,550	7,300	90	8,500	−160	12,000	16,800	140	220	1,440	11,000	25,810	
d.	Pur. supplies				400					400					
	Balances	16,130	11,550	7,300	490	8,500	−160	12,000	16,800	540	220	1,440	11,000	25,810	
e.	Collected cash	6,900	−6,900												
	Balances	23,030	4,650	7,300	490	8,500	−160	12,000	16,800	540	220	1,440	11,000	25,810	
f.	Paid accts. pay.	−310								−310					
	Balances	22,720	4,650	7,300	490	8,500	−160	12,000	16,800	230	220	1,440	11,000	25,810	
g.	Paid expenses	−6,230									−220			−6,010	g.
	Balances	16,490	4,650	7,300	490	8,500	−160	12,000	16,800	230	0	1,440	11,000	19,800	
h.	Paid dividends	−1,200												−1,200	
	Balances	15,290	4,650	7,300	490	8,500	−160	12,000	16,800	230	0	1,440	11,000	18,600	
a1.	Insurance exp.			−1,100										−1,100	a1.
	Balances	15,290	4,650	6,200	490	8,500	−160	12,000	16,800	230	0	1,440	11,000	17,500	
a2.	Supplies exp.				−275									−275	a2.
	Balances	15,290	4,650	6,200	215	8,500	−160	12,000	16,800	230	0	1,440	11,000	17,225	
a3.	Deprec. exp.						−160							−160	a3.
	Balances	15,290	4,650	6,200	215	8,500	−320	12,000	16,800	230	0	1,440	11,000	17,065	
a4.	Rental revenue											−360		360	a4.
	Balances	15,290	4,650	6,200	215	8,500	−320	12,000	16,800	230	0	1,080	11,000	17,425	
a5.	Wages exp.										340			−340	a5.
	Balances	15,290	4,650	6,200	215	8,500	−320	12,000	16,800	230	340	1,080	11,000	17,085	
a6.	Fees earned		1,050											1,050	a6.
	Balances, Dec. 31	15,290	5,700	6,200	215	8,500	−320	12,000	16,800	230	340	1,080	11,000	18,135	

Statement of Cash Flows

a. Operating	1,900
c. Operating	6,500
e. Operating	6,900
f. Operating	−310
g. Operating	−6,230
h. Financing	−1,200
Net increase in cash	7,560
Beginning cash bal.	7,730
Ending cash bal.	15,290

Income Statement

b. Fees earned	10,800
c. Fees earned	6,500
g. Wages exp.	−3,980
Rent exp.	−800
Utilities exp.	−610
Interest exp.	−100
Misc. exp.	−520
a1. Insur. exp.	−1,100
a2. Supplies exp.	−275
a3. Deprec. exp.	−160
a4. Rental rev.	360
a5. Wages exp.	−340
a6. Fees earned	1,050
Net income	10,825

3.

FAMILY HEALTH CARE, P.C.
Income Statement
For the Month Ended December 31, 2009

Fees earned		$18,350
Operating expenses:		
Wages expense	$4,320	
Insurance expense	1,100	
Rent expense	800	
Utilities expense	610	
Supplies expense	275	
Depreciation expense	160	
Interest expense	100	
Miscellaneous expense	520	
Total operating expenses		7,885
Operating income		$10,465
Other income:		
Rental revenue		360
Net income		$10,825

FAMILY HEALTH CARE, P.C.
Retained Earnings Statement
For the Month Ended December 31, 2009

Retained earnings, December 1, 2009		$ 8,510
Net income for December	$10,825	
Less dividends	1,200	9,625
Retained earnings, December 31, 2009		$18,135

FAMILY HEALTH CARE, P.C.
Statement of Cash Flows
For the Month Ended December 31, 2009

Cash flows from operating activities:	
Cash received from patients	$15,300
Deduct cash payments for expenses	(6,540)
Net cash flows from operating activities	$ 8,760
Cash flows from financing activities:	
Deduct cash dividends	(1,200)
Net increase in cash	$ 7,560
December 1, 2009 cash balance	7,730
December 31, 2009 cash balance	$15,290

(continued)

FAMILY HEALTH CARE, P.C.
Balance Sheet
December 31, 2009

Assets

Current assets:

Cash		$15,290	
Accounts receivable		5,700	
Prepaid insurance		6,200	
Supplies		215	
Total current assets			$27,405

Fixed assets:

Office equipment	$8,500		
Less accumulated depreciation	320	$ 8,180	
Land		12,000	
Total fixed assets			20,180
Total assets			$47,585

Liabilities

Current liabilities:

Accounts payable		$ 230	
Wages payable		340	
Notes payable		6,800	
Unearned revenue		1,080	
Total current liabilities			$ 8,450

Long-term liabilities:

Notes payable			10,000
Total liabilities			$18,450

Stockholders' Equity

Capital stock		$11,000	
Retained earnings		18,135	
Total stockholders' equity			29,135
Total liabilities and stockholders' equity			$47,585

4. December's reconciliation of net income with net cash flows from operations:

Net income		$10,825
Add:		
Depreciation expense	$ 160	
Increase in accounts payable	90	
Increase in wages payable	120	
Decrease in prepaid insurance	1,100	1,470
Deduct:		
Increase in accounts receivable	$(3,050)	
Increase in supplies	(125)	
Decrease in unearned revenue	(360)	(3,535)
Net cash flows from operating activities		$ 8,760

Self-Examination Questions   *(Answers appear at end of chapter.)*

1. Assume that a lawyer bills her clients $15,000 on June 30, 2009, for services rendered during June. The lawyer collects $8,500 of the billings during July and the remainder in August. Under the accrual basis of accounting, when would the lawyer record the revenue for the fees?
   A. June, $15,000; July, $0; and August, $0
   B. June, $0; July, $6,500; and August, $8,500
   C. June, $8,500; July, $6,500; and August, $0
   D. June, $0; July, $8,500; and August, $6,500

2. On January 24, 2009, Niche Consulting collected $5,700 it had billed its clients for services rendered on December 31, 2008. How would you record the January 24 transaction, using the accrual basis?
   A. Increase Cash, $5,700; decrease Fees Earned, $5,700
   B. Increase Accounts Receivable, $5,700; increase Fees Earned, $5,700
   C. Increase Cash, $5,700; decrease Accounts Receivable, $5,700
   D. Increase Cash, $5,700; increase Fees Earned, $5,700

3. Which of the following items represents a deferral?
   A. Prepaid insurance
   B. Wages payable
   C. Fees earned
   D. Accumulated depreciation

4. If the supplies account indicated a balance of $2,250 before adjustment on May 31 and supplies on hand at May 31 totaled $950, the adjustment would be:
   A. increase Supplies, $950; decrease Supplies Expense, $950.
   B. increase Supplies, $1,300; decrease Supplies Expense, $1,300.
   C. increase Supplies Expense, $950; decrease Supplies, $950.
   D. increase Supplies Expense, $1,300; decrease Supplies, $1,300.

5. The balance in the unearned rent account for Jones Co. as of December 31 is $1,200. If Jones Co. failed to record the adjusting entry for $600 of rent earned during December, the effect on the balance sheet and income statement for December would be:
   A. assets understated by $600; net income overstated by $600.
   B. liabilities understated by $600; net income understated by $600.
   C. liabilities overstated by $600; net income understated by $600.
   D. liabilities overstated by $600; net income overstated by $600.

Class Discussion Questions

1. Would **General Electric** and **Xerox** use the cash basis or the accrual basis of accounting? Explain.

2. How are revenues and expenses reported on the income statement under (a) the cash basis of accounting and (b) the accrual basis of accounting?

3. Fees for services provided are billed to a customer during 2008. The customer remits the amount owed in 2009. During which year would the revenues be reported on the income statement under (a) the cash basis? (b) the accrual basis?

4. Employees performed services in 2008, but the wages were not paid until 2009. During which year would the wages expense be reported on the income statement under (a) the cash basis? (b) the accrual basis?

5. Which of the following accounts would appear only in an accrual basis accounting system, and which could appear in either a cash basis or an accrual basis accounting system? (a) Capital Stock, (b) Fees Earned, (c) Accounts Payable, (d) Land, (e) Utilities Expense, and (f) Accounts Receivable.

6. Is the land balance before the accounts have been adjusted the amount that should normally be reported on the balance sheet? Explain.

7. Is the supplies balance before the accounts have been adjusted the amount that should normally be reported on the balance sheet? Explain.

8. Why are adjustments needed at the end of an accounting period?

9. Identify the four different categories of adjustments frequently required at the end of an accounting period.

10. If the effect of an adjustment is to increase the balance of a liability account, which of the following statements describes the effect of the adjustment on the other account?
   a. Increases the balance of a revenue account.
   b. Increases the balance of an expense account.
   c. Increases the balance of an asset account.

11. If the effect of an adjustment is to increase the balance of an asset account, which of the following statements describes the effect of the adjustment on the other account?

   a. Increases the balance of a revenue account.
   b. Increases the balance of a liability account.
   c. Increases the balance of an expense account.

12. Does every adjustment have an effect on determining the amount of net income for a period? Explain.

13. (a) Explain the purpose of the two accounts: Depreciation Expense and Accumulated Depreciation. (b) Is it customary for the balances of the two accounts to be equal? (c) In what financial statements, if any, will each account appear?

14. Describe the nature of the assets that compose the following sections of a balance sheet: (a) current assets, (b) property, plant, and equipment.

Exercises

E3-1

Transactions using accrual accounting

Obj 2

Holistic Care is owned and operated by Sara Lucas, the sole stockholder. During March 2009, Holistic Care entered into the following transactions:

   a. Sara Lucas invested $15,000 in Holistic Care in exchange for capital stock.
   b. Paid $4,800 for an insurance premium on a 1-year policy.
   c. Purchased supplies on account, $750.
   d. Received fees of $21,500 during March.
   e. Paid expenses as follows: wages, $6,000; rent, $2,500; utilities, $1,100; and miscellaneous, $600.
   f. Paid dividends of $2,000.

Record the preceding transactions using the integrated financial statement framework. After each transaction, you should enter a balance for each item.

E3-2

Adjustment process

Obj 3

SPREADSHEET

Using the data from Exercise 3-1, record the adjusting entries at the end of March to record the insurance expense and supplies expense. There were $400 of supplies on hand as of March 31. Identify the adjusting entry for insurance as (a1) and supplies as (a2).

E3-3

Financial statements

Obj 4

SPREADSHEET

Using the data from Exercises 3-1 and 3-2, prepare financial statements for March, including income statement, retained earnings statement, balance sheet, and statement of cash flows.

E3-4

Reconcile net income and net cash flows from operations.

App

Using the income statement and statement of cash flows you prepared in Exercise 3-3, reconcile net income with the net cash flows from operations.

E3-5

Accrual basis of accounting

Obj 2

Sherry Kerr established Espresso Services, P.C., a professional corporation, on January 1 of the current year. Espresso Services offers financial planning advice to its clients. The effect of each transaction on the balance sheet and the balances after each transaction for January are as follows. Each increase or decrease in stockholders' equity, except transaction (h), affects net income.

	Assets			=	Liabilities	+	Stockholders' Equity	
	Cash	+ Receivable +	Supplies	=	Accounts Payable	+	Capital Stock	+ Retained Earnings
a.	+30,000						+30,000	
b.			+1,200		+1,200			
Bal.	30,000		1,200		1,200		30,000	
c.	−900				−900			
Bal.	29,100		1,200		300		30,000	
d.	+18,500							+18,500
Bal.	47,600		1,200		300		30,000	18,500
e.	−10,000							−10,000
Bal.	37,600		1,200		300		30,000	8,500
f.			−800					−800
Bal.	37,600		400		300		30,000	7,700
g.		+2,000						+2,000
Bal.	37,600	2,000	400		300		30,000	9,700
h.	−1,800							−1,800
Bal.	35,800	2,000	400		300		30,000	7,900

a. Describe each transaction.
b. What is the amount of the net income for January?

E3-6

Classify accruals and deferrals

Obj 3

Classify the following items as (a) deferred expense (prepaid expense), (b) deferred revenue (unearned revenue), (c) accrued expense (accrued liability), or (d) accrued revenue (accrued asset).

1. Fees received but not yet earned.
2. Utilities owed but not yet paid.
3. Subscriptions received in advance by a magazine publisher.
4. Fees earned but not yet received.
5. Taxes owed but payable in the following period.
6. Salary owed but not yet paid.
7. Supplies on hand.
8. A 2-year premium paid on a fire insurance policy.

E3-7

Classify adjustments

Obj 3

The following accounts were taken from the unadjusted trial balance of Dobro Co., a congressional lobbying firm. Indicate whether or not each account would normally require an adjusting entry. If the account normally requires an adjusting entry, use the following notation to indicate the type of adjustment:

AE—Accrued Expense
AR—Accrued Revenue

(continued)

DR—Deferred Revenue
DE—Deferred Expense

To illustrate, the answer for the first account is as follows.

Account	*Answer*
Accounts Receivable	Normally requires adjustment (AR).
Accumulated Depreciation	
Cash	
Dividends	
Interest Payable	
Interest Receivable	
Land	
Office Equipment	
Prepaid Insurance	
Supplies Expense	
Unearned Fees	
Wages Expense	

E3-8

Adjustment for supplies

Obj 3

✓ a. $1,175

Answer each of the following independent questions concerning supplies and the adjustment for supplies. (a) The balance in the supplies account, before adjustment at the end of the year, is $1,850. What is the amount of the adjustment if the amount of supplies on hand at the end of the year is $675? (b) The supplies account has a balance of $380, and the supplies expense account has a balance of $1,560 at December 31, 2009. If 2009 was the first year of operations, what was the amount of supplies purchased during the year?

E3-9

Adjustment for prepaid insurance

Obj 3

The prepaid insurance account had a balance of $3,600 at the beginning of the year. The account was increased for $4,800 for premiums on policies purchased during the year. What is the adjustment required at the end of the year for each of the following independent situations: (a) the amount of unexpired insurance applicable to future periods is $2,700, (b) the amount of insurance expired during the year is $4,150? For (a) and (b), indicate each account affected, whether the account is increased or decreased, and the amount of the increase or decrease.

E3-10

Adjustment for unearned fees

Obj 3

The balance in the unearned fees account, before adjustment at the end of the year, is $10,800. What is the adjustment if the amount of unearned fees at the end of the year is $3,600? Indicate each account affected, whether the account is increased or decreased, and the amount of the increase or decrease.

E3-11

Adjustment for unearned revenue

Obj 3

For the year ending June 30, 2006, Microsoft Corporation reported short-term unearned revenue of $9,138 million. For the year ending June 30, 2006, Microsoft also reported total revenues of $44,282 million. (a) Assuming that Microsoft recognized $2,000 million of unearned revenue during the year, what entry for unearned revenue did Microsoft make during the year? Indicate each account affected, whether the account is increased or decreased, and the amount of the increase or decrease. (b) What percentage of total revenues is the short-term unearned revenue as of June 30, 2006? Round to one decimal place.

E3-12

Effect of omitting adjustment

Obj 3

At the end of June, the first month of the business year, the usual adjustment transferring rent earned to a revenue account from the unearned rent account was omitted. Indicate which items will be incorrectly stated, because of the error, on (a) the income statement for June and (b) the balance sheet as of June 30. Also indicate whether the items in error will be overstated or understated.

E3-13

Adjustment for accrued salaries

Obj 3

Canyon Realty Co. pays weekly salaries of $12,000 on Friday for a five-day week ending on that day. What is the adjustment at the end of the accounting period, assuming that the period ends (a) on Tuesday, (b) on Wednesday? Indicate each account affected, whether the account is increased or decreased, and the amount of the increase or decrease.

E3-14

Determine wages paid

Obj 3

The balances of the two wages accounts at December 31, after adjustments at the end of the first year of operations, are Wages Payable, $11,250, and Wages Expense, $575,200. Determine the amount of wages paid during the year.

E3-15

Effect of omitting adjustment

Obj 3

Accrued salaries of $3,900 owed to employees for December 30 and 31 are not considered in preparing the financial statements for the year ended December 31, 2008. Indicate which items will be erroneously stated, because of the error, on (a) the income statement for December 2008 and (b) the balance sheet as of December 31, 2008. Also indicate whether the items in error will be overstated or understated.

E3-16

Effect of omitting adjustment

Obj 3

Assume that the error in Exercise 3-15 was not corrected and that the $3,900 of accrued salaries was included in the first salary payment in January 2009. Indicate which items will be erroneously stated, because of failure to correct the initial error, on (a) the income statement for January 2009 and (b) the balance sheet as of January 31, 2009.

E3-17

Effects of errors on financial statements

Obj 3

For a recent period, **Circuit City Stores** reported accrued expenses of $464,511,000. For the same period, Circuit City reported income before income taxes of $151,112,000. If accrued expenses had not been recorded, what would have been the income (loss) before income taxes?

E3-18

Effects of errors on financial statements

Obj 3

The balance sheet for **Ford Motor Company** as of December 31, 2006, includes $82,518 million of accrued expenses as liabilities. Before taxes, Ford Motor Company reported a loss of $15,051 million. If the accruals had not been recorded at December 31, 2006, how much would income or loss before taxes have been for the year ended December 31, 2006?

E3-19

Effects of errors on financial statements

Obj 3

✓ b. $236,350

The accountant for Glacier Medical Co., a medical services consulting firm, mistakenly omitted adjusting entries for (a) unearned revenue earned during the year ($5,750) and (b) accrued wages ($2,800).

a. Indicate the effect of each error, considered individually, on the income statement for the current year ended December 31. Also indicate the effect of each error on the December 31 balance sheet. Set up a table similar to the following, and record your answers by inserting the dollar amount in the appropriate spaces. Insert a zero if the error does not affect the item.

	Error (a)		Error (b)	
	Over-stated	Under-stated	Over-stated	Under-stated
1. Revenue for the year would be	$	$	$	$
2. Expenses for the year would be	$	$	$	$
3. Net income for the year would be	$	$	$	$
4. Assets at December 31 would be	$	$	$	$
5. Liabilities at December 31 would be	$	$	$	$
6. Stockholders' equity at December 31 would be	$	$	$	$

b. If the net income for the current year had been $233,400, what would be the correct net income if the proper adjustments had been made?

E3-20

Adjustment for accrued fees

Obj 3

At the end of the current year, $27,100 of fees have been earned but have not been billed to clients.

a. What is the adjustment to record the accrued fees? Indicate each account affected, whether the account is increased or decreased, and the amount of the increase or decrease.
b. If the cash basis rather than the accrual basis had been used, would an adjustment have been necessary? Explain.

E3-21

Adjustments for unearned and accrued fees

Obj 3

The balance in the unearned fees account, before adjustment at the end of the year, is $175,000. Of these fees, $69,500 have been earned. In addition, $20,000 of fees have been earned but have not been billed. What are the adjustments (a) to adjust the unearned fees account and (b) to record the accrued fees? Indicate each account affected, whether the account is increased or decreased, and the amount of the increase or decrease.

E3-22

Effect of deferred revenue

Obj 3

✓ a. $126 million

Time Warner Inc. reported deferred revenue of $2,018 million and $2,144 million as of December 31, 2006 and 2005, respectively. For the year ending December 31, 2006, Time Warner reported total revenues of $44,224 million. (a) What was the amount of the adjustment for unearned revenue for 2006? (b) What would have been total revenues under the cash basis after considering the effect of (a)?

E3-23

Effect on financial statements of omitting adjustment

Obj 3

The adjustment for accrued fees was omitted at August 31, the end of the current year. Indicate which items will be in error, because of the omission, on (a) the income statement for the current year and (b) the balance sheet as of August 31. Also indicate whether the items in error will be overstated or understated.

E3-24

Adjustment for depreciation

Obj 3

The estimated amount of depreciation on equipment for the current year is $9,000. (a) How is the adjustment recorded? Indicate each account affected, whether the account is increased or decreased, and the amount of the increase or decrease. (b) If the adjustment in (a) was omitted, which items would be erroneously stated on (1) the income statement for the year and (2) the balance sheet as of December 31?

E3-25

Adjustments

Obj 3

Zimmatic Company is a consulting firm specializing in pollution control. The following adjustments were made for Zimmatic Company:

Account	Adjustments Increase (Decrease)
Accounts Receivable	$ 10,600
Supplies	(1,800)
Prepaid Insurance	(2,750)
Accumulated Depreciation—Equipment	3,200
Wages Payable	4,500
Unearned Rent	(1,700)
Fees Earned	10,600
Wages Expense	4,500
Supplies Expense	1,800
Rent Revenue	1,700
Insurance Expense	2,750
Depreciation Expense	3,200

Identify each of the six pairs of adjustments. For each adjustment, indicate the account, whether the account is increased or decreased, and the amount of the adjustment. No account is affected by more than one adjustment. Use the following format. The first adjustment is shown as an example.

Adjustment	Account	Increase or Decrease	Amount
1.	Accounts Receivable	Increase	$10,600
	Fees Earned	Increase	10,600

E3-26

Book value of fixed assets

Obj 4

Barnes & Noble Inc. reported *Property, Plant, and Equipment* of $2,303,331,000 and *Accumulated Depreciation* of $1,497,275,000 at February 3, 2007.

a. What was the book value of the fixed assets at February 3, 2007?
b. Would the book values of Barnes & Noble's fixed assets normally approximate their fair market values?

E3-27

Classify assets

Obj 4

Identify each of the following as (a) a current asset or (b) property, plant, and equipment:

1. Accounts Receivable
2. Building
3. Cash
4. Office Equipment
5. Prepaid Insurance
6. Supplies

E3-28

Balance sheet classification

Obj 4

At the balance sheet date, a business owes a mortgage note payable of $720,000, the terms of which provide for monthly payments of $6,000. Explain how the liability should be classified on the balance sheet.

E3-29

Classified balance sheet

Obj 4

✓ Total assets, $91,000

Redox Co. offers personal weight reduction consulting services to individuals. After all the accounts have been closed on November 30, 2008, the end of the current fiscal year, the balances of selected accounts from the ledger of Redox Co. are as follows:

Accounts Payable	$ 7,600	Prepaid Insurance	$ 5,800
Accounts Receivable	17,500	Prepaid Rent	3,600
Accum. Depreciation—Equipment	16,800	Retained Earnings	56,000
Capital Stock	25,000	Salaries Payable	1,400
Cash	?	Supplies	1,500
Equipment	65,000	Unearned Fees	1,000

Prepare a classified balance sheet that includes the correct balance for Cash.

E3-30

Classified balance sheet

Obj 4

✓ Total assets, $971,174

La-Z-Boy Inc. is one of the world's largest manufacturers of furniture that is best known for its reclining chairs. The following data (in thousands) were adapted from the 2006 annual report of La-Z-Boy Inc.:

Accounts payable	$ 85,561
Accounts receivable	270,578
Accrued expenses	132,005
Accumulated depreciation	288,308
Capital stock	263,958
Cash	24,089
Intangible assets	75,720
Inventories	238,826
Debt due within one year*	10,844
Long-term debt**	173,368
Other assets**	51,066
Other assets**	100,909
Other long-term liabilities**	59,051
Property, plant, and equipment	498,294
Retained earnings	246,387

(continued)

For the preceding items, (*) indicates that the item is current in nature, while (**) indicates that the item is long-term in nature.

Prepare a classified balance sheet as of April 29, 2006.

E3-31

Balance sheet

Obj 4

List the errors you find in the following balance sheet. Prepare a corrected balance sheet.

CASA SERVICES CO.
Balance Sheet
For the Year Ended July 31, 2008

Assets		
Current assets:		
Cash	$ 4,000	
Accounts payable	9,300	
Supplies	1,600	
Prepaid insurance	4,800	
Land	90,000	
Total current assets		$109,700
Property, plant, and equipment:		
Building	$ 75,000	
Equipment	30,000	
Total property, plant, and equipment		105,000
Total assets		$214,700
Liabilities		
Current liabilities:		
Accounts receivable	$ 13,600	
Accumulated depreciation—building	18,200	
Accumulated depreciation—equipment	10,800	
Net loss	7,500	
Total liabilities		$ 50,100
Stockholders' Equity		
Wages payable	$ 2,700	
Capital stock	30,000	
Retained earnings	148,000	
Total stockholders' equity		180,700
Total liabilities and stockholders' equity		$214,700

Problems

P3-1

Accrual basis accounting

Obj 2

`SPREADSHEET`

Emerald Health Care Inc. is owned and operated by Dr. Julie Weinstein, the sole stockholder. During March 2009, Emerald Health Care entered into the following transactions:

Mar. 1 Received $12,000 from Moloney Company as rent for the use of a vacant office in Emerald Health Care's building. Moloney paid the rent six months in advance.

  1 Paid $5,400 for an insurance premium on a general business policy.

  6 Purchased supplies of $1,425 on account.

  9 Collected $13,500 for services provided to customers on account.

  11 Paid creditors $2,400 on account.

  18 Invested an additional $40,000 in the business in exchange for capital stock.

  20 Billed patients $37,200 for services provided on account.

25 Received $10,000 for services provided to customers who paid cash.

30 Paid expenses as follows: wages, $18,000; utilities, $5,250; rent on medical equipment, $4,000; interest, $400; and miscellaneous, $1,000.

30 Paid dividends of $3,000 to stockholders (Dr. Weinstein).

Instructions

Analyze and record the March transactions for Emerald Health Care Inc. using the integrated financial statement framework. Record each transaction by date and show the balance for each item after each transaction. The March 1, 2009, balances for the balance sheet are shown below.

		Assets							=	Liabilities				+	Stockholders' Equity	
	Cash +	Accts. Rec. +	Pre. Ins. +	Supp. +	Building −	Acc. Dep. +	Land =			Accts. Pay. +	Un. Rev. +	Wages Pay. +	Notes Pay. +		Capital Stock +	Ret. Earn.
Bal.,Mar.1	15,600	20,250	540	840	135,000	−10,800	67,500	5,700		0	0	54,000			60,000	109,230

P3-2

Adjustment process

Obj 3

SPREADSHEET

Adjustment data for Emerald Health Care Inc. for March are as follows:

1. Insurance expired, $720.
2. Supplies on hand on March 31, $775.
3. Depreciation on building, $2,000.
4. Unearned rent revenue earned, $1,200.
5. Wages owed employees but not paid, $2,250.
6. Services provided but not billed to patients, $6,000.

Instructions

Based upon the transactions recorded in March for Problem 3-1, record the adjustments for March using the integrated financial statement framework.

P3-3

Financial statements

Obj 4

SPREADSHEET

✓ 1. Net income, $19,290

Data for Emerald Health Care for March are provided in Problems 3-1 and 3-2.

Instructions

Prepare an income statement, retained earnings statement, and a classified balance sheet for March. The notes payable is due in 2013.

P3-4

Statement of cash flows

Obj 4

SPREADSHEET

✓ Net cash flows from operating activities, ($950)

Data for Emerald Health Care for March are provided in Problems 3-1, 3-2, and 3-3.

Instructions

1. Prepare a statement of cash flows for March.
2. Reconcile the net cash flows from operating activities with the net income for March. (*Hint:* See the appendix to this chapter and use adjusted balances in computing increases and decreases in accounts.)

P3-5

Adjustments and errors

Obj 3

SPREADSHEET

✓ Corrected net income, $244,450

At the end of October, the first month of operations, the following selected data were taken from the financial statements of Michael Han, Attorney-at-Law, P.C.

Net income for October	$240,000
Total assets at October 31	750,000
Total liabilities at October 31	250,000
Total stockholders' equity at October 31	500,000

(continued)

In preparing the financial statements, adjustments for the following data were overlooked:

a. Unbilled fees earned at October 31, $12,800.
b. Depreciation of equipment for October, $4,000.
c. Accrued wages at October 31, $3,100.
d. Supplies used during October, $1,250.

Instructions

Determine the correct amount of net income for October and the total assets, liabilities, and stockholders' equity at October 31. In addition to indicating the corrected amounts, indicate the effect of each omitted adjustment by setting up and completing a columnar table similar to the following. Adjustment (a) is presented as an example.

	Net Income	Total Assets	Total Liabilities	Total Stockholders' Equity
Reported amounts	$240,000	$750,000	$250,000	$500,000
Corrections:				
Adjustment (a)	+12,800	+12,800	0	+12,800
Adjustment (b)	_____	_____	_____	_____
Adjustment (c)	_____	_____	_____	_____
Adjustment (d)	_____	_____	_____	_____
Corrected amounts	═══════	═══════	═══════	═══════

P3-6

Adjustment process and financial statements

Objs 3, 4

SPREADSHEET

✓ 2. Net income, $121,300

Adjustment data for Launderland Inc. for the year ended July 31, 2009, are as follows:

a. Wages accrued but not paid at July 31, $2,700.
b. Depreciation of equipment during the year, $14,000.
c. Laundry supplies on hand at July 31, $2,000.
d. Insurance premiums expired, $4,500.

Instructions

1. Using the following integrated financial statement framework, record each adjustment to the appropriate accounts identifying each adjustment by its letter. After all adjustments are recorded, determine the balances.

					Balance Sheet						
Statement of Cash Flows			Assets			=	Liabilities	+	Stockholders' Equity		Income Statement
	Cash +	Laundry Supplies +	Prepaid Insurance +	Laundry Equip. −	Acc. Deprec. =	Accts. Payable +	Wages Payable +	Capital Stock +	Retained Earnings	
Balances, July 31, 2009.	48,000	9,000	6,000	250,000	−60,000	7,000	0	50,000	196,000	

Statement of Cash Flows

Operating (Revenues)	315,000
Financing (Capital Stock)	25,000
Operating (Expenses)	−220,000
Investing (Equipment)	−80,000
Financing (Dividends)	−5,000
Net increase in cash	35,000
Beginning cash balance, Aug. 1, 2008	13,000
Ending cash balance, July 31, 2009	$48,000

Income Statement

July	Laundry revenue	315,000
	Wages expense	−110,000
	Rent expense	−30,000
	Utilities expense	−18,000
	Misc. expense	−7,500

2. Prepare an income statement and retained earnings statement for the year ended July 31, 2009. The retained earnings balance as of August 1, 2008, was $51,500.
3. Prepare a classified balance sheet as of July 31, 2009.
4. Prepare a statement of cash flows for the year ended July 31, 2009.

Activities

A3-1

Accrued revenue

The following is an excerpt from a conversation between Mario Cedric and Omar Farah just before they boarded a flight to London on **Northwest Airlines**. They are going to London to attend their company's annual sales conference.

Mario: Omar, aren't you taking an introductory accounting course at college?

Omar: Yes, I decided it's about time I learned something about accounting. You know, our annual bonuses are based upon the sales figures that come from the accounting department.

Mario: I guess I never really thought about it.

Omar: You should think about it! Last year, I placed a $500,000 order on December 27. But when I got my bonus, the $500,000 sale wasn't included. They said it hadn't been shipped until January 4, so it would have to count in next year's bonus.

Mario: A real bummer!

Omar: Right! I was counting on that bonus including the $500,000 sale.

Mario: Did you complain?

Omar: Yes, but it didn't do any good. Seth, the head accountant, said something about matching revenues and expenses. Also, something about not recording revenues until the sale is final. I figure I'd take the accounting course and find out whether he's just jerking me around.

Mario: I never really thought about it. When do you think Northwest Airlines will record its revenues from this flight?

Omar: Mmm . . . I guess it could record the revenue when it sells the ticket . . . or . . . when the boarding passes are taken at the door . . . or . . . when we get off the plane . . . or when our company pays for the tickets . . . or . . . I don't know. I'll ask my accounting instructor.

Discuss when Northwest Airlines should recognize the revenue from ticket sales to properly match revenues and expenses.

A3-2

Adjustments for financial statements

Several years ago, your brother opened Balboa Repair Services. He made a small initial investment and added money from his personal bank account as needed. He withdrew money for living expenses at irregular intervals. As the business grew, he hired an assistant. He is now considering adding more employees, purchasing additional service trucks, and purchasing the building he now rents. To secure funds for the expansion, your brother submitted a loan application to the bank and included the most recent financial statements, shown below, prepared from accounts maintained by a part-time bookkeeper.

BALBOA REPAIR SERVICES
Income Statement
For the Year Ended October 31, 2008

Service revenue		$124,920
Less: Rent paid	$30,000	
Wages paid	27,750	
Supplies paid	7,650	
Utilities paid	4,800	
Insurance paid	3,600	
Miscellaneous payments	3,200	77,000
Net income		$ 47,920

(continued)

BALBOA REPAIR SERVICES
Balance Sheet
October 31, 2008

Assets	
Cash	$16,725
Amounts due from customers	9,150
Truck	45,000
Total assets	$70,875
Equities	
Stockholders' equity	$70,875

After reviewing the financial statements, the loan officer at the bank asked your brother if he used the accrual basis of accounting for revenues and expenses. Your brother responded that he did and that is why he included an account for "Amounts Due from Customers." The loan officer then asked whether or not the accounts were adjusted prior to the preparation of the statements. Your brother answered that they had not been adjusted.

1. Why do you think the loan officer suspected that the accounts had not been adjusted prior to the preparation of the statements?
2. Indicate possible accounts that might need to be adjusted before an accurate set of financial statements could be prepared.

A3-3

Business emphasis

GROUP

Assume that you and two friends are debating whether to open an automotive and service retail chain that will be called Auto-Mart. Initially, Auto-Mart will open three stores locally, but the business plan anticipates going nationwide within 5 years.

Currently, you and your future business partners are debating whether to focus Auto-Mart on a "do-it-yourself" or "do-it-for-me" business. A do-it-yourself business emphasizes the sale of retail auto parts that customers will use themselves to repair and service their cars. A do-it-for-me business emphasizes the offering of maintenance and service for customers.

1. In groups of three or four, discuss whether to implement a do-it-yourself or do-it-for-me business emphasis. List the advantages of each emphasis and arrive at a conclusion as to which emphasis to implement.
2. Provide examples of real-world businesses that use do-it-yourself or do-it-for-me business emphases.

A3-4

Cash basis income statement

The following operating data (in thousands) were adapted from the 2006 SEC 10-K filings of *Walgreen* and *CVS*:

	CVS		Walgreen	
	2006	**2005**	**2006**	**2005**
Accounts receivable	$2,651,700	$2,080,700	$2,062,700	$1,396,300
Accounts payable	4,813,700	3,988,900	5,755,300	4,481,000

1. Using the preceding data, adjust the operating income for CVS and Walgreen to an adjusted cash basis. For 2006, the operating income for CVS was $1,368,900 and for Walgreen's it was $1,750,600 (in thousands). (*Hint:* To convert to a cash basis, you need to compute the change in each accrual accounting item shown and then either add or subtract the change to the operating income.)

2. Compute the net difference between the operating income under the accrual and cash bases.
3. Express the net difference in (2) as a percent of operating income under the accrual basis.
4. Which company's operating income, CVS's or Walgreen's, is closer to the cash basis?
5. Do you think most analysts focus on operating income or net income in assessing the long-term profitability of a company? Explain.

A3-5

Analysis of income and cash flows

The following data (in millions) for 2006, 2005, and 2004 were taken from 10-K filings with the Securities and Exchange Commission:

	2006	2005	2004
Company A			
Revenues	$24,088	$23,104	$21,962
Operating income	6,308	6,085	5,698
Net income	5,080	4,872	4,847
Net cash flows from operating activities	5,957	6,423	5,968
Net cash flows from investing activities	(1,700)	(1,496)	(503)
Net cash flows from financing activities	(6,583)	(6,785)	(2,261)
Total assets	29,963	29,427	31,327
Company B			
Revenues	$17,171	$16,191	$15,002
Operating income (loss)	58	(2,001)	(3,308)
Net income (loss)	(6,203)	(3,818)	(5,198)
Net cash flows from operating activities	993	175	(1,123)
Net cash flows from investing activities	(361)	(460)	(220)
Net cash flows from financing activities	(606)	830	636
Total assets	19,622	20,039	21,801
Company C			
Revenues	$10,711	$ 8,490	$ 6,921
Operating income	389	432	440
Net income	190	359	588
Net cash flows from operating activities	702	733	567
Net cash flows from investing activities	(333)	(778)	(318)
Net cash flows from financing activities	(400)	(193)	(97)
Total assets	4,363	3,696	3,249
Company D			
Revenues	$66,111	$60,553	$56,434
Operating income (loss)	2,236	2,035	847
Net income (loss)	1,115	958	(100)
Net cash flows from operating activities	2,351	2,192	2,230
Net cash flows from investing activities	(1,587)	(1,279)	(1,608)
Net cash flows from financing activities	(785)	(847)	(737)
Total assets	21,215	20,482	20,491

1. Match each of the following companies with the data for Company A, B, C, or D:

   Amazon.com
   Coca-Cola Inc.
   Delta Air Lines
   Kroger

2. Explain the logic underlying your matches.

Answers to Self-Examination Questions

1. **A**   Under the accrual basis of accounting, revenues are recorded when the services are rendered. Since the services were rendered during June, all the fees should be recorded on June 30 (answer A). This is an example of accrued revenue. Under the cash basis of accounting, revenues are recorded when the cash is collected, not necessarily when the fees are earned. Thus, no revenue would be recorded in June, $8,500 of revenue would be recorded in July, and $6,500 of revenue would be recorded in August (answer D). Answers B and C are incorrect and are not used under either the accrual or cash bases.

2. **C**   The collection of a $5,700 accounts receivable is recorded as an increase in Cash, $5,700, and a decrease in Accounts Receivable, $5,700 (answer C). The initial recording of the fees earned on account is recorded as an increase in Accounts Receivable and an increase in Fees Earned (answer B). Services rendered for cash are recorded as an increase in Cash and an increase in Fees Earned (answer D). Answer A is incorrect and would result in the accounting equation being out of balance because total assets would exceed total liabilities and stockholders' equity by $11,400.

3. **A**   A deferral is the delay in recording an expense already paid, such as prepaid insurance (answer A). Wages payable (answer B) is considered an accrued expense or accrued liability. Fees earned (answer C) is a revenue item. Accumulated depreciation (answer D) is a contra account to a fixed asset.

4. **D**   The balance in the supplies account, before adjustment, represents the amount of supplies available during the period. From this amount ($2,250) is subtracted the amount of supplies on hand ($950) to determine the supplies used ($1,300). The used supplies is recorded as an increase in Supplies Expense, $1,300, and a decrease in Supplies, $1,300 (answer D).

5. **C**   The failure to record the adjusting entry increasing Rent Revenue, $600, and decreasing Unearned Rent, $600, would have the effect of overstating liabilities by $600 and understating net income by $600 (answer C).

CHAPTER 4

Accounting for Merchandising Businesses

Learning Objectives

After studying this chapter, you should be able to:

Obj 1
Distinguish the activities and financial statements of a service business from those of a merchandising business.

Obj 2
Describe and illustrate the financial statements of a merchandising business.

Obj 3
Describe the accounting for the sale of merchandise.

Obj 4
Describe the accounting for the purchase of merchandise.

Obj 5
Describe the accounting for transportation costs and sales taxes.

Obj 6
Illustrate the dual nature of merchandising transactions.

Obj 7
Describe the accounting for merchandise shrinkage.

Twenty years ago music was purchased at the "record store." No longer. Today, CDs can be purchased at retail stores such as *Best Buy*, *Borders*, *Wal-Mart*, *Sam Goodys*, and *Disc Exchange;* through online retailers, such as *CD Universe* and *CDNow*, and as individual MP3 downloads from services such as *Apple's* iTunes© and *Real's* Rhapsody©. The way we buy goods (and services) has undergone significant changes and will continue to change with consumer tastes and technology. For example, an established retailer like *JC Penney* is faced with a rapidly changing competitive landscape with the emergence of (1) discount merchandising, (2) category killers, and (3) Internet retailing.

Wal-Mart, which led the development of discount merchandising, has become the world's largest retailer. Wal-Mart's growth is centered on providing the consumer with everyday discount pricing over a broad array of household products. Category killers include *Toys"R"Us* (toys), Best Buy (electronics), *Home Depot* (home improvement), and *Office Depot* (office supplies), which provide a wide selection of attractively priced goods within a particular product segment. Internet retailers, such as *Amazon.com* and *Lands' End* (now part of *Sears*), allow time-conscious consumers to shop quickly and effortlessly. JC Penney has had to adapt its retailing model in order to respond to all these changes.

Merchandising will undoubtedly continue to evolve as consumer lifestyles and technologies change in the future. In this chapter, we introduce you to the accounting issues unique to merchandisers. We emphasize merchandisers at this point in the text because merchandising is significant in its own right, and because even nonmerchandisers have accounting issues similar to those discussed in this chapter.

Obj 1

Distinguish the activities
and financial statements
of a service business from
those of a merchandising
business.

Merchandise Operations

In prior chapters, we described and illustrated how businesses report their financial condition and changes in financial condition using the cash and accrual bases of accounting. In those chapters, we focused on service businesses. In this chapter, we describe and illustrate the accounting for merchandise operations.[1]

How do the operating activities of a service business, such as a consulting firm, law practice, or architectural firm, differ from those of a merchandising business, such as Home Depot or Wal-Mart? The differences are best illustrated by focusing on the income statements of the two types of businesses.

The condensed income statement of ***Jackson Hewitt Tax Service Inc.*** is shown in Exhibit 1.[2] Jackson Hewitt is a service business that primarily offers tax planning and preparation to its customers.

EXHIBIT 1   *Jackson Hewitt Income Statement*

JACKSON HEWITT TAX SERVICE INC.
Condensed Income Statement
For the Year Ended April 30, 2007
(in thousands)

Revenue	$293,196
Operating expenses	177,446
Operating income	$115,750
Other income and (expense)	(8,224)
Income before taxes	$107,526
Income taxes	42,146
Net income	$ 65,380

The condensed income statement of ***Home Depot Inc.*** is shown in Exhibit 2.[3] Home Depot is the world's largest home improvement retailer and the second largest retailer in the United States based on net sales volume.

The revenue activities of a service business involve providing services to customers. On the income statement for a service business, the revenues from services are reported as revenues or fees earned. The operating expenses incurred in providing services are subtracted from the revenues to arrive at operating income. Any other income or expense is then added or subtracted to arrive at income before taxes. Net income is determined by subtracting income taxes. Exhibit 1 shows that Jackson Hewitt earned operating profits of $115,750 (thousand) based on revenues of $293,196 (thousand). Adding other income and subtracting income taxes results in net income of $65,380 (thousand).

In contrast, the revenue activities of a merchandising business involve the buying and selling of merchandise. A merchandise business must first purchase merchandise to sell to its customers. The revenue received for merchandise sold to customers less any merchandise returned or any discounts is reported as net sales. The related cost of

---

[1]The closing process, which is not illustrated, is similar to that for a service business, which is referenced in Chapter 3, footnote 3 on page 101.
[2]Adapted from Jackson Hewitt's 10-K filing with the Securities and Exchange Commission.
[3]Adapted from Home Depot's 10-K filing with the Securities and Exchange Commission.

EXHIBIT 2	*Home Depot Income Statement*

HOME DEPOT INC.
Condensed Income Statement
For the Year Ended January 28, 2007
(in millions)

Net sales	$90,837
Cost of merchandise sold	61,054
Gross profit	$29,783
Operating expenses	20,110
Operating income	$ 9,673
Other income and (expense)	(365)
Income before taxes	$ 9,308
Income taxes	3,547
Net income	$ 5,761

merchandise sold is then determined and matched against the net sales. Gross profit is determined by subtracting the cost of merchandise sold from net sales. Gross profit gets its name from the fact that it is the profit before deducting operating expenses. Operating expenses are then subtracted in arriving at operating income. Like a service business, other income or expense is then added or subtracted to arrive at income before taxes. Subtracting income taxes yields net income.

Exhibit 2 shows that Home Depot earned a gross profit of $29,783 (million) based on net sales of $90,837 (million). Operating expenses reduce gross profit to an operating income of $9,673 (million). Subtracting other expense and subtracting income taxes results in net income of $5,761 (million).

In addition to operating and income statement differences, merchandise inventory on hand (not sold) at the end of the accounting period is reported on the balance sheet as **merchandise inventory**. Since merchandise is normally sold within a year, it is reported as a current asset on the balance sheet.

HOW BUSINESSES MAKE MONEY

Under One Roof at JC Penney

Most businesses cannot be all things to all people. Businesses must seek a position in the marketplace to serve a unique customer need. Companies that are unable to do this can be squeezed out of the marketplace. The mall-based department store has been under pressure from both ends of the retail spectrum. At the discount store end of the market, Wal-Mart has been a formidable competitor. At the high end, specialty retailers have established strong presence in identifiable niches, such as electronics and apparel. Over a decade ago, JC Penney abandoned its "hard goods," such as electronics and sporting goods, in favor of providing "soft goods" because of the emerging strength of specialty retailers in the hard good segments. JC Penney is positioning itself against these forces by *"exceeding the fashion, quality, selection, and service components of the discounter, equaling the merchandise intensity of the specialty store, and providing the selection and 'under one roof' shopping convenience of the department store."* JC Penney's merchandise emphasis is focused toward customers it terms the "modern spender" and "starting outs." It views these segments as most likely to value its higher-end merchandise offered under the convenience of "one roof."

Financial Statements for a Merchandising Business

Obj 2

Describe and illustrate the financial statements of a merchandising business.

In this section, we illustrate the financial statements for NetSolutions, a retailer of computer hardware and software. During 2009, we assume that Chris Clark organized Net-Solutions with a business emphasis of offering personalized service to individuals and small businesses who are upgrading or purchasing new computer systems. NetSolutions' personal service before the sale will include a no-obligation, on-site assessment of the customer's computer needs. By providing tailor-made solutions, personalized service, and follow-up, Chris feels that NetSolutions can compete effectively against larger retailers, such as Best Buy or Office Depot.

Multiple-Step Income Statement

The 2010 income statement for NetSolutions is shown in Exhibit 3.[4] This form of income statement, called a **multiple-step income statement**, contains several sections, subsections, and subtotals.

Sales is the total amount charged customers for merchandise sold, including cash sales and sales on account. Both sales returns and allowances and sales discounts are subtracted in arriving at net sales.

Sales returns and allowances are granted by the seller to customers for damaged or defective merchandise. For example, rather than have a buyer return merchandise, a seller may offer a $500 allowance to the customer as compensation for damaged merchandise. Sales returns and allowances are recorded when the merchandise is returned or when the allowance is granted by the seller.

Sales discounts are granted by the seller to customers for early payment of amounts owed. For example, a seller may offer a customer a 2% discount on a sale of $10,000 if the customer pays within ten days. If the customer pays within the ten-day period, the seller receives cash of $9,800 and the buyer receives a discount of $200 ($10,000 × 2%). Sales discounts are recorded when the customer pays the bill.

Net sales is determined by subtracting sales returns and allowances and sales discounts from sales. Rather than reporting sales, sales returns and allowances, and sales discounts as shown in Exhibit 3, many companies report only net sales.

Cost of merchandise sold is the cost of the merchandise sold to customers. To illustrate the determination of the cost of merchandise sold, assume that NetSolutions purchased $340,000 of merchandise during the last half of 2009. If the inventory at December 31, 2009, the end of the year, is $59,700, the cost of the merchandise sold during 2009 is $280,300, as shown below.

Purchases	$340,000
Less merchandise inventory, December 31, 2009	59,700
Cost of merchandise sold	$280,300

As we discussed in the preceding paragraphs, sellers may offer customers sales discounts for early payment of their bills. Such discounts are referred to as **purchase discounts**

---

[4]We use the NetSolutions income statement for 2010 as a basis for illustration because, as will be shown, it allows us to better illustrate the computation of the cost of merchandise sold.

EXHIBIT 3 *Multiple-Step Income Statement*

NETSOLUTIONS
Income Statement
For the Year Ended December 31, 2010

Revenue from sales:			
Sales		$720,185	
Less: Sales returns and allowances	$ 6,140		
Sales discounts	5,790	11,930	
Net sales			$708,255
Cost of merchandise sold			525,305
Gross profit			$182,950
Operating expenses:			
Selling expenses:			
Sales salaries expense	$56,230		
Advertising expense	10,860		
Depr. expense—store equipment	3,100		
Miscellaneous selling expense	630		
Total selling expenses		$ 70,820	
Administrative expenses:			
Office salaries expense	$21,020		
Rent expense	8,100		
Depr. expense—office equipment	2,490		
Insurance expense	1,910		
Office supplies expense	610		
Misc. administrative expense	760		
Total administrative expenses		34,890	
Total operating expenses			105,710
Income from operations			$ 77,240
Other income and expense:			
Rent revenue		$ 600	
Interest expense		(2,440)	(1,840)
Income before taxes			$ 75,400
Income taxes			15,000
Net income			$ 60,400

by the buyer. Purchase discounts reduce the cost of merchandise. A buyer may return merchandise to the seller (a **purchase return**), or the buyer may receive a reduction in the initial price at which the merchandise was purchased (a **purchase allowance**). Like purchase discounts, purchase returns and allowances reduce the cost of merchandise purchased during a period. In addition, transportation costs paid by the buyer for merchandise also increase the cost of merchandise purchased.

To continue the illustration, assume that during 2010 NetSolutions purchased additional merchandise of $521,980. It received credit for purchase returns and allowances of $9,100, took purchase discounts of $2,525, and paid transportation costs of $17,400. The purchase returns and allowances and the purchase discounts are deducted from the total purchases to yield the *net purchases*. The transportation costs, termed **transportation in**, are added to the net purchases to yield the *cost of merchandise purchased* of $527,755, as shown at the top of the next page.

Purchases		$521,980
Less: Purchase returns and allowances	$9,100	
Purchase discounts	2,525	11,625
Net purchases		$510,355
Add transportation in		17,400
Cost of merchandise purchased		$527,755

The ending inventory of NetSolutions on December 31, 2009, $59,700, becomes the beginning inventory for 2010. This beginning inventory is added to the cost of merchandise purchased to yield **merchandise available for sale**. The ending inventory, which is assumed to be $62,150, is then subtracted from the merchandise available for sale to yield the cost of merchandise sold of $525,305, as shown in Exhibit 4.

The cost of merchandise sold was determined by deducting the merchandise on hand at the end of the period from the merchandise available for sale during the period. The merchandise on hand at the end of the period is determined by taking a physical count of inventory on hand. This method of determining the cost of merchandise sold and the amount of merchandise on hand is called the **periodic method** of accounting for merchandise inventory. Under the periodic method, the inventory records do not show the amount available for sale or the amount sold during the period. In contrast, under the **perpetual method** of accounting for merchandise inventory, each purchase and sale of merchandise is recorded in the inventory and the cost of merchandise sold accounts. As a result, the amount of merchandise available for sale and the amount sold are continuously (perpetually) disclosed in the inventory records.

Most large retailers and many small merchandising businesses use computerized perpetual inventory systems. Such systems normally use bar codes, such as the one on the back of this textbook. An optical scanner reads the bar code to record merchandise purchased and sold. Merchandise businesses using a perpetual inventory system report the cost of merchandise sold as a single line on the income statement, as shown in Exhibit 2 for Home Depot. Merchandise businesses using the periodic inventory method report the cost of merchandise sold by using the format shown in Exhibit 4. Because of its wide use, we will use the perpetual inventory method throughout the remainder of this chapter.

EXHIBIT 4   *Cost of Merchandise Sold*

Merchandise inventory, January 1, 2010			$ 59,700
Purchases		$521,980	
Less: Purchase returns and allowances	$9,100		
Purchase discounts	2,525	11,625	
Net purchases		$510,355	
Add transportation in		17,400	
Cost of merchandise purchased			527,755
Merchandise available for sale			$587,455
Less merchandise inventory, December 31, 2010			62,150
Cost of merchandise sold			$525,305

Gross profit is determined by subtracting the cost of merchandise sold from net sales. Exhibit 3 shows that NetSolutions reported gross profit of $182,950 in 2010. *Operating income*, sometimes called **income from operations**, is determined by subtracting operating expenses from gross profit. Most merchandising businesses classify operating expenses as either selling expenses or administrative expenses. Expenses that are incurred directly in the selling of merchandise are **selling expenses**. They include such expenses as salespersons' salaries, store supplies used, depreciation of store equipment, and advertising. Expenses incurred in the administration or general operations of the business are **administrative expenses** or *general expenses*. Examples of these expenses are office salaries, depreciation of office equipment, and office supplies used. Credit card expense is also normally classified as an administrative expense. Although selling and administrative expenses may be reported separately, many companies report operating expenses as a single item.

Other income and expense is reported on NetSolutions' income statement in Exhibit 3. Revenue from sources other than the primary operating activity of a business is classified as **other income**. In a merchandising business, these items include income from interest, rent, and gains resulting from the sale of fixed assets.

Expenses that cannot be traced directly to operations are identified as **other expense**. Interest expense that results from financing activities and losses incurred in the disposal of fixed assets are examples of these items.

Other income and other expense are offset against each other on the income statement, as shown in Exhibit 3. If the total of other income exceeds the total of other expense, the difference is added to income from operations to determine net income. If the reverse is true, the difference is subtracted from income from operations.

Single-Step Income Statement

An alternate form of income statement is the **single-step income statement**. As shown in Exhibit 5, the income statement for NetSolutions deducts the total of all expenses *in one step* from the total of all revenues.

EXHIBIT 5   *Single-Step Income Statement*

NETSOLUTIONS		
Income Statement		
For the Year Ended December 31, 2010		
Revenues:		
Net sales		$708,255
Rent revenue		600
Total revenues		$708,855
Expenses:		
Cost of merchandise sold	$525,305	
Selling expenses	70,820	
Administrative expenses	34,890	
Interest expense	2,440	
Income taxes	15,000	
Total expenses		648,455
Net income		$ 60,400

The single-step form emphasizes total revenues and total expenses as the factors that determine net income. A criticism of the single-step form is that such amounts as gross profit and income from operations are not readily available for analysis.

Retained Earnings Statement

The retained earnings statement for NetSolutions is shown in Exhibit 6. This statement is prepared in the same manner that we described previously for a service business.

EXHIBIT 6 *Retained Earnings Statement for Merchandising Business*		
NETSOLUTIONS		
Retained Earnings Statement		
For the Year Ended December 31, 2010		
Retained earnings, January 1, 2010		$128,800
Net income for year	$60,400	
Less dividends	18,000	
Increase in retained earnings		42,400
Retained earnings, December 31, 2010		$171,200

Balance Sheet

As we discussed and illustrated in previous chapters, the balance sheet may be presented in a downward sequence in three sections. This form of balance sheet is called the **report form**.[5] The report form of balance sheet for NetSolutions is shown in Exhibit 7. In this balance sheet, note that merchandise inventory at the end of the period is reported as a current asset and that the current portion of the note payable is $5,000.

Statement of Cash Flows

The statement of cash flows for NetSolutions is shown in Exhibit 8 on page 134. It indicates that cash increased during 2010 by $11,450. This increase is generated from a positive cash flow from operating activities of $47,120, which is partially offset by negative cash flows from investing and financing activities of $12,670 and $23,000, respectively.

The net cash flows from operating activities is shown in Exhibit 8 using a method known as the **indirect method**. This method, which reconciles net income with net cash flows from operating activities, is widely used among publicly held corporations.[6] Finally, you should note that the December 31, 2010, cash balance reported on the statement of cash flows agrees with the amount reported for cash on the December 31, 2010, balance sheet shown in Exhibit 7.

The integration of NetSolutions' financial statements is shown in Exhibit 9 on page 135.

[5]The balance sheet may also be presented in an account form, with assets on the left-hand side and the liabilities and stockholders' equity on the right-hand side.
[6]The preparation of the statement of cash flows using the indirect method is further discussed and illustrated in the appendix to this chapter.

EXHIBIT 7   *Report Form of Balance Sheet*

NETSOLUTIONS
Balance Sheet
December 31, 2010

Assets

Current assets:

Cash		$ 52,950	
Accounts receivable		76,080	
Merchandise inventory		62,150	
Office supplies		480	
Prepaid insurance		2,650	
Total current assets			$ 194,310

Property, plant, and equipment:

Land		$ 20,000	
Store equipment	$ 27,100		
Less accumulated depreciation	5,700	21,400	
Office equipment	$ 15,570		
Less accumulated depreciation	4,720	10,850	
Total property, plant, and equipment			52,250
Total assets			$ 246,560

Liabilities

Current liabilities:

Accounts payable		$ 22,420	
Note payable (current portion)		5,000	
Salaries payable		1,140	
Unearned rent		1,800	
Total current liabilities:			$ 30,360

Long-term liabilities:

Note payable (final payment due 2019)			20,000
Total liabilities			$ 50,360

Stockholders' Equity

Capital stock		$ 25,000	
Retained earnings		171,200	196,200
Total liabilities and stockholders' equity			$ 246,560

Obj **3**

Describe the accounting
for the sale of
merchandise.

Sales Transactions

In the remainder of this chapter, we illustrate transactions that affect the financial statements of a merchandising business. These transactions affect the reporting of net sales, cost of merchandise sold, gross profit, and merchandise inventory.

Sales

A business may sell merchandise for cash. Cash sales are normally rung up (entered) on a cash register and recorded in the accounts by increasing cash and sales. Under the perpetual inventory system, the cost of merchandise sold and the reduction in merchandise inventory should also be recorded at the time of sale. In this way, the

EXHIBIT 8 *Statement of Cash Flows for Merchandising Business*

NETSOLUTIONS
Statement of Cash Flows
For the Year Ended December 31, 2010

Cash flows from operating activities:		
Net income		$ 60,400
Add: Depreciation expense—store equipment	$ 3,100	
Depreciation expense—office equipment	2,490	
Decrease in office supplies	120	
Decrease in prepaid insurance	350	
Increase in accounts payable	8,150	14,210
Deduct:		
Increase in accounts receivable	$(24,080)	
Increase in merchandise inventory	(2,450)	
Decrease in salaries payable	(360)	
Decrease in unearned rent	(600)	(27,490)
Net cash flows from operating activities		$ 47,120
Cash flows from investing activities:		
Purchase of store equipment	$ (7,100)	
Purchase of office equipment	(5,570)	
Net cash flows from investing activities		(12,670)
Cash flows from financing activities:		
Payment of note payable	$ (5,000)	
Payment of dividends	(18,000)	
Net cash flows from financing activities		(23,000)
Net increase in cash		$ 11,450
January 1, 2010 cash balance		41,500
December 31, 2010 cash balance		$ 52,950

merchandise inventory account will indicate the amount of merchandise on hand (not sold). To illustrate, assume that on January 3, NetSolutions sells merchandise for $1,800 that cost $1,200. The effect on the accounts and financial statements of these cash sales is as follows:

		Balance Sheet						**Income Statement**
Statement of Cash Flows		**Assets**	**=**	**Liabilities**	**+**	**Stockholders' Equity**		
	Cash	**+ Merchandise Inventory =**			**+**	**Retained Earnings**		
Jan. 3.	1,800	−1,200				600		Jan. 3.

Statement of Cash Flows	
Jan. 3. Operating	1,800

Income Statement	
Jan. 3. Sales	1,800
Cost of merch. sold	−1,200
Net income	600

EXHIBIT 9   *Integrated Financial Statements*

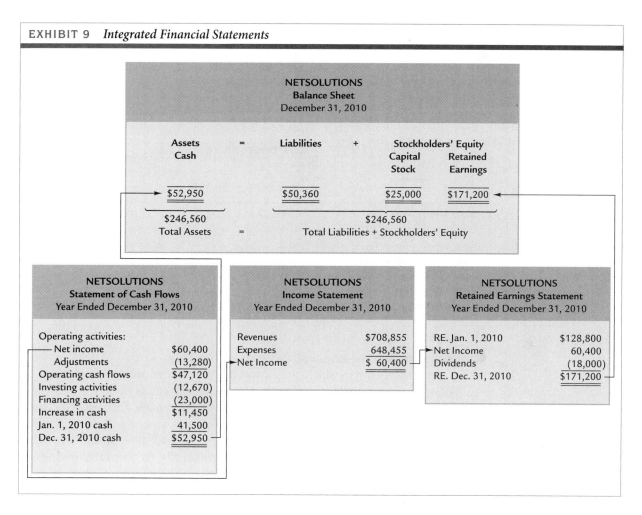

Sales made to customers using credit cards issued by banks, such as MasterCard or VISA, are treated as *cash sales*. The record of the sale is electronically sent to a clearing-house for credit card transactions. The clearinghouse processes the sale by contacting the bank that issued the credit card. Within one or two days, the seller's bank account is increased by the amount of the sale.

Retailers are charged service fees for credit card sales. The seller records these service fees as increases to an expense account and decrease to cash.

A business can sell merchandise on account. The effect of sales on account is similar to that for cash sales except that Accounts Receivable is increased instead of Cash. When the customer pays the amount, Accounts Receivable is decreased and Cash is increased.

Sales Discounts

The terms of a sale are normally indicated on the **invoice** or bill that the seller sends to the buyer. An example of a sales invoice for NetSolutions is shown in Exhibit 10.

The terms for when payments for merchandise are to be made, agreed on by the buyer and the seller, are called the **credit terms**. If payment is required on delivery, the terms are *cash or net cash*. Otherwise, the buyer is allowed an amount of time, known as the **credit period**, in which to pay.

The credit period usually begins with the date of the sale as shown on the invoice. If payment is due within a stated number of days after the date of the invoice, such as

EXHIBIT 10   *Invoice*

106-8

net **SOLUTIONS**   Invoice

5101 Washington Ave.
Cincinnati, OH 45227–5101

Made in U.S.A.

SOLD TO	CUSTOMER'S ORDER NO. & DATE
Omega Technologies 1000 Matrix Blvd. San Jose, CA 95116–1000	412 Jan. 10, 2010

DATE SHIPPED	HOW SHIPPED AND ROUTE	TERMS	INVOICE DATE
Jan. 12, 2010	US Express Trucking Co.	2/10, n/30	Jan. 12, 2010

FROM	F.O.B.		
Cincinnati	Cincinnati		

QUANTITY	DESCRIPTION	UNIT PRICE	AMOUNT
10	3COM Megahertz 10/100 Lan PC Card	150.00	1,500.00

30 days, the terms are *net 30 days.* These terms may be written as *n/30.*[7] If payment is due by the end of the month in which the sale was made, the terms are written as *n/eom.*

As a means of encouraging the buyer to pay before the end of the credit period, the seller may offer a discount. For example, a seller may offer a 2% discount if the buyer pays within 10 days of the invoice date. If the buyer does not take the discount, the total amount is due within 30 days. These terms are expressed as *2/10, n/30* and are read as *2% discount if paid within 10 days, net amount due within 30 days.* Using the information from the invoice in Exhibit 10, the credit terms of 2/10, n/30 are summarized below.

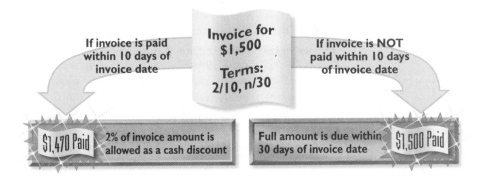

Discounts taken by the buyer for early payment are recorded as sales discounts by the seller. Since managers may want to know the amount of the sales discounts for a period, the seller normally records the sales discounts in a separate account. The sales discounts account is a *contra* (or *offsetting*) account to Sales. To illustrate, assume that cash is received within the discount period (10 days) from the credit sale of $1,500, shown on the invoice in Exhibit 10. The effect on the accounts and financial statements of the receipt of the cash is as follows:

---

[7]The word *net* as used here does not have the usual meaning of a number after deductions have been subtracted, as in *net income.*

Statement of Cash Flows	Balance Sheet						Income Statement
	Assets	=	Liabilities	+	Stockholders' Equity		
	Cash	+	Accounts Receivable	=		+	Retained Earnings	
Jan. 22.	1,470		−1,500				−30	Jan. 22.

Statement of Cash Flows		Income Statement	
Jan. 22. Operating	1,470	Jan. 22. Sales discounts	−30

Sales Returns and Allowances

Merchandise sold may be returned to the seller (sales return). In addition, because of defects or for other reasons, the seller may reduce the initial price at which the goods were sold (sales allowance). If the return or allowance is for a sale on account, the seller usually issues the buyer a **credit memorandum**. This memorandum shows the amount of and the reason for the seller's credit to an account receivable. A credit memorandum issued by NetSolutions is illustrated below.

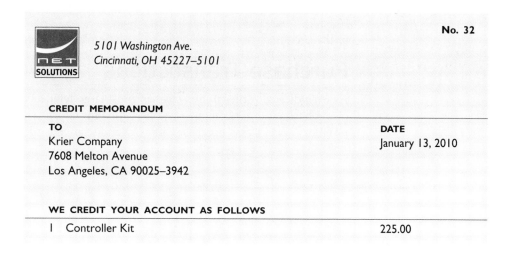

		No. 32
NET SOLUTIONS	5101 Washington Ave. Cincinnati, OH 45227–5101	

CREDIT MEMORANDUM

TO	DATE
Krier Company 7608 Melton Avenue Los Angeles, CA 90025–3942	January 13, 2010

WE CREDIT YOUR ACCOUNT AS FOLLOWS

1	Controller Kit	225.00

Like sales discounts, sales returns and allowances reduce sales revenue. They also result in additional shipping and other expenses. Since managers often want to know the amount of returns and allowances for a period, the seller records sales returns and allowances in a separate account. Sales Returns and Allowances is a *contra* (or *offsetting*) account to Sales.

The seller increases Sales Returns and Allowances for the amount of the return or allowance. If the original sale was on account, the seller decreases Accounts Receivable. Since the merchandise inventory is kept up to date in a perpetual system, the seller adds the cost of the returned merchandise to the merchandise inventory account. The seller must also decrease the cost of returned merchandise to the cost of merchandise sold account, since this account was increased when the original sale was recorded. To illustrate, assume that the cost of the merchandise returned in the preceding credit memorandum was $140. The effect on the accounts and financial statements of the issuance of the credit memorandum and the receipt of the returned merchandise is as follows:

Statement of Cash Flows	Balance Sheet						Income Statement
	Assets		=	Liabilities	+	Stockholders' Equity	
	Accounts Receivable	+	Merchandise Inventory	=		+	Retained Earnings	
Jan. 13.	−225		140				−85	Jan. 13.

Income Statement	
Jan. 13. Sales returns & allowances	−225
Cost of merch. sold	140
Net income	−85

What if the buyer pays for the merchandise and the merchandise is later returned? In this case, the seller may issue a credit and apply it against other accounts receivable owed by the buyer, or the cash may be refunded. If the credit is applied against the buyer's other receivables, the seller records entries similar to those preceding. If cash is refunded for merchandise returned or for an allowance, the seller increases Sales Returns and Allowances and decreases Cash.

Obj 4

Purchase Transactions

Describe the accounting for the purchase of merchandise.

As we indicated earlier in this chapter, most large retailers and many small merchandising businesses use computerized perpetual inventory systems. Under the perpetual inventory system, cash purchases of merchandise are recorded as follows:

Statement of Cash Flows	Balance Sheet						Income Statement
	Assets		=	Liabilities	+	Stockholders' Equity	
	Cash	+	Merchandise Inventory	=				
Jan. 3.	−2,510		2,510					

Statement of Cash Flows	
Jan. 3. Operating	−2,510

Purchases of merchandise on account are recorded as increases of merchandise inventory and accounts payable.

Purchase Discounts

Purchase discounts taken by the buyer for early payment of an invoice reduce the cost of the merchandise purchased. Under the perpetual inventory system, the buyer initially increases the merchandise inventory account for the amount of the invoice. When paying the invoice, the buyer decreases the merchandise inventory account for the amount of the discount. In this way, the merchandise inventory shows the *net* cost to the buyer. For example, the effects on the accounts and financial

INTEGRITY, OBJECTIVITY, AND ETHICS IN BUSINESS

The Case of the Fraudulent Price Tags

One of the challenges for a retailer is policing its sales return policy. There are many ways in which customers can unethically or illegally abuse such policies. In one case, a couple was accused of attaching **Marshall's** store price tags to cheaper merchandise bought or obtained elsewhere. The couple then returned the cheaper goods and received the substantially higher refund amount. Company security officials discovered the fraud and had the couple arrested after they had allegedly bilked the company for over $1 million.

statements of paying the invoice shown in Exhibit 10 at the end of the discount period is as follows:

Statement of Cash Flows	Balance Sheet					Income Statement
	Assets		=	Liabilities	+ Stockholders' Equity	
	Cash	+	Merchandise Inventory =	Accounts Payable		
Jan. 22.	−1,470		−30	−1,500		

Statement of Cash Flows	
Jan. 22. Operating	−1,470

If the invoice shown in Exhibit 10 is not paid during the discount period, the payment is recorded as a decrease in Cash and Accounts Payable for $1,500.

Purchase Returns and Allowances

When merchandise is returned (purchase return) or a price adjustment is requested (purchase allowance), the buyer (debtor) usually sends the seller a letter or a debit memorandum. A **debit memorandum**, shown below, informs the seller of the amount the

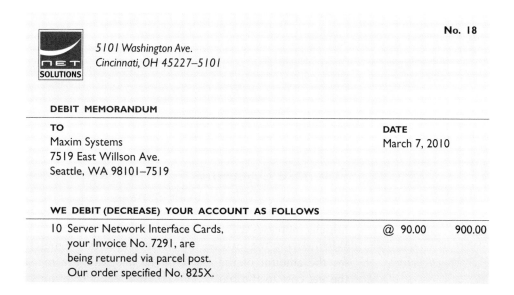

		No. 18
net SOLUTIONS	5101 Washington Ave. Cincinnati, OH 45227–5101	

DEBIT MEMORANDUM

TO Maxim Systems 7519 East Willson Ave. Seattle, WA 98101–7519	**DATE** March 7, 2010

WE DEBIT (DECREASE) YOUR ACCOUNT AS FOLLOWS

10 Server Network Interface Cards, your Invoice No. 7291, are being returned via parcel post. Our order specified No. 825X.	@ 90.00	900.00

buyer proposes to decrease to the account payable due the seller. It also states the reasons for the return or the request for a price reduction.

The buyer may use a copy of the debit memorandum as the basis for recording the return or allowance or wait for approval from the seller (creditor). In either case, the buyer must decrease Accounts Payable and increase Merchandise Inventory. To illustrate, the effect on the accounts and financial statements of the return of the merchandise indicated in the preceding debit memorandum is shown below.

Statement of Cash Flows	Balance Sheet				Income Statement
	Assets	=	Liabilities	+ Stockholders' Equity	
	Merchandise Inventory		Accounts Payable		
Mar. 7.	−900		−900		

When a buyer returns merchandise or has been granted an allowance prior to paying the invoice, the amount of the debit memorandum is deducted from the invoice amount. The amount is deducted before the purchase discount is computed. For example, assume that on May 2, NetSolutions purchases $5,000 of merchandise from Delta Data Link, subject to terms 2/10, n/30. On May 4, NetSolutions returns $3,000 of the merchandise, and on May 12, NetSolutions pays the original invoice less the return. NetSolutions would pay Delta Data Link $1,960 as shown below.

Invoice	$5,000
Less return	3,000
Amount due before discount	$2,000
Less discount ($2,000 × 2%)	40
Amount due within discount period	$1,960

The effect on the accounts and financial statements of paying the invoice on May 12 is as follows:

Statement of Cash Flows	Balance Sheet					Income Statement
	Assets	=	Liabilities	+ Stockholders' Equity		
	Cash +	Merchandise Inventory =	Accounts Payable			
May 12.	−1,960	−40	−2,000			

Statement of Cash Flows
May 12. Operating   −1,960

Obj 5

Transportation Costs and Sales Taxes

Describe the accounting for transportation costs and sales taxes.

Merchandise businesses incur transportation costs in selling and purchasing merchandise. In addition, a retailer must collect sales taxes in most states. In this section, we briefly discuss the unique aspects of accounting for transportation costs and sales taxes.

Transportation Costs

The terms of a sale should indicate when the ownership (title) of the merchandise passes to the buyer. This point determines which party, the buyer or the seller, must pay the transportation costs.[8]

The ownership of the merchandise may pass to the buyer when the seller delivers the merchandise to the transportation company or freight carrier. For example, **DaimlerChrysler** records the sale and the transfer of ownership of its vehicles to dealers when the vehicles are shipped from the factory. In this case, the terms are said to be **FOB (free on board) shipping point**. This term means that the dealer pays the transportation costs from the shipping point (factory) to the final destination. Such costs are part of the dealer's total cost of purchasing inventory and should be added to the cost of the inventory by increasing Merchandise Inventory.

To illustrate, assume that on June 10, NetSolutions buys merchandise from Magna Data on account, $900, terms FOB shipping point, and pays the transportation cost of $50. The effect on the accounts and financial statements of these transactions is as follows:

Statement of Cash Flows		Balance Sheet						Income Statement
		Assets		=	Liabilities	+	Stockholders' Equity	
	Cash	+	Merchandise Inventory	=	Accounts Payable			
June 10.	−50		950		900			

Statement of Cash Flows	
June 10. Operating	−50

The ownership of the merchandise may pass to the buyer when the buyer receives the merchandise. In this case, the terms are said to be **FOB (free on board) destination**. This term means that the seller delivers the merchandise to the buyer's final destination, free of transportation charges to the buyer. The seller thus pays the transportation costs to the final destination. The seller increases Delivery Expense, or Transportation Out, which is reported on the seller's income statement as an expense.

Shipping terms, the passage of title, and whether the buyer or seller is to pay the transportation costs are summarized in Exhibit 11.

---

[8]The passage of title also determines whether the buyer or seller must pay other costs, such as the cost of insurance, while the merchandise is in transit.

EXHIBIT 11   *Transportation Terms*

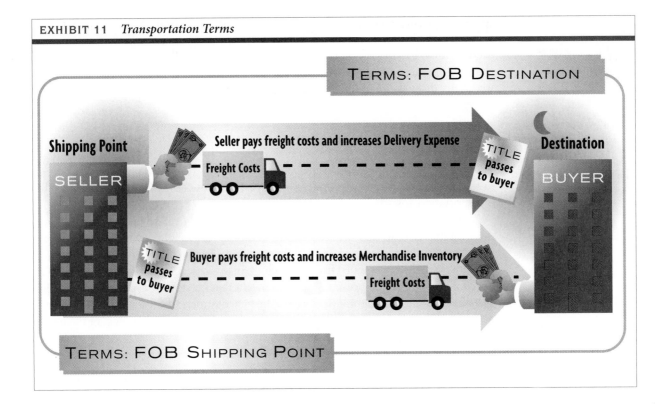

Sales Taxes

Almost all states and many other taxing units levy a tax on sales of merchandise.[9] The liability for the sales tax is incurred when the sale is made.

At the time of a cash sale, the seller collects the sales tax. When a sale is made on account, the seller charges the tax to the buyer by increasing Accounts Receivable. The seller increases the sales account for the amount of the sale and increases the tax to Sales Tax Payable. Normally on a regular basis, the seller pays to the taxing unit the amount of the sales tax collected. The seller records such a payment by decreasing Sales Tax Payable and Cash.

Obj **6**

Illustrate the dual nature of merchandising transactions.

Dual Nature of Merchandise Transactions

Each merchandising transaction affects a buyer and a seller. In the following illustration, we show how the same transactions would be recorded by both the seller and the buyer. In this example, the seller is Scully Company and the buyer is Burton Co.

---

[9]Businesses that purchase merchandise for resale to others are normally exempt from paying sales taxes on their purchases. Only final buyers of merchandise normally pay sales taxes.

On July 1, Scully Company sold merchandise on account to Burton Co., $7,500, terms FOB destination; 2/10, n/30. The cost of the merchandise sold was $4,500.

Scully Company (Seller)

Statement of Cash Flows	Balance Sheet					Income Statement
	Assets		= Liabilities	+	Stockholders' Equity	
	Accounts Receivable +	Merchandise Inventory =			+	Retained Earnings	
July 1.	7,500	−4,500				3,000	July 1.

	Income Statement	
July 1.	Sales	7,500
	Cost of merch. sold	−4,500
	Net income	3,000

Burton Co. (Buyer)

Statement of Cash Flows	Balance Sheet					Income Statement
	Assets	=	Liabilities	+	Stockholders' Equity	
	Merchandise Inventory	=	Accounts Payable			
July 1.	7,500		7,500			

On July 5, Scully Company pays transportation charges of $300 for delivery of the merchandise sold on July1 to Burton Co.

Scully Company (Seller)

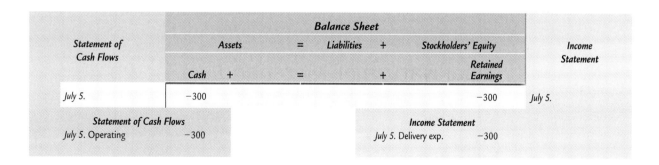

Statement of Cash Flows	Balance Sheet					Income Statement
	Assets	=	Liabilities	+	Stockholders' Equity	
	Cash +	=		+	Retained Earnings	
July 5.	−300				−300	July 5.

Statement of Cash Flows			Income Statement	
July 5. Operating	−300		July 5. Delivery exp.	−300

Burton Co. (Buyer)
No effect on the accounts and financial statements.

On July 6, Scully Company issues a credit memorandum for $1,000 for merchandise returned by Burton Co. The cost of the merchandise returned was $600.

Scully Company (Seller)

	Balance Sheet					
Statement of Cash Flows	Assets	=	Liabilities	+	Stockholders' Equity	Income Statement
	Accounts Receivable + Merchandise Inventory =			+	Retained Earnings	
July 6.	−1,000 600				−400	July 6.

	Income Statement	
July 6.	Sales retns. & allow.	−1,000
	Cost of merch. sold	−600
	Net income	−400

Burton Co. (Buyer)

	Balance Sheet					
Statement of Cash Flows	Assets	=	Liabilities	+	Stockholders' Equity	Income Statement
	Merchandise Inventory	=	Accounts Payable			
July 6.	−1,000		−1,000			

On July 11, Scully Company received payment from Burton Co. less discount.

Scully Company (Seller)

	Balance Sheet					
Statement of Cash Flows	Assets	=	Liabilities	+	Stockholders' Equity	Income Statement
	Cash + Accounts Receivable =			+	Retained Earnings	
July 11.	6,370 −6,500				−130	July 11.

Statement of Cash Flows			Income Statement	
July 11. Operating	6,370		July 11. Sales discounts	−130

Burton Co. (Buyer)

	Balance Sheet					
Statement of Cash Flows	Assets	=	Liabilities	+	Stockholders' Equity	Income Statement
	Cash + Merchandise Inventory =		Accounts Payable			
July 11.	−6,370 −130		−6,500			

Statement of Cash Flows	
July 11. Operating	−6,370

Merchandise Shrinkage

Obj 7

Describe the accounting for merchandise shrinkage.

Under the perpetual inventory system, a separate merchandise inventory account is maintained in the ledger. During the accounting period, this account shows the amount of merchandise for sale at any time. However, merchandising businesses could experience some loss of inventory due to shoplifting, employee theft, or errors in recording or counting inventory. As a result, the **physical inventory** taken at the end of the accounting period could differ from the amount of inventory shown in the inventory records. Normally, the amount of merchandise for sale, as indicated by the balance of the merchandise inventory account, is higher than the total amount of merchandise counted during the physical inventory. For this reason, the difference is often called **inventory shrinkage** or *inventory shortage*. One recent study estimated that inventory shrinkage exceeds $30 billion annually in the United States.

To illustrate, NetSolutions' inventory records, called the **book inventory**, indicate that $63,950 of merchandise should be available for sale on December 31, 2010. The physical inventory taken on December 31, 2010, however, indicates that only $62,150 of merchandise is actually available for sale. The inventory shrinkage for the year ending December 31, 2010, is $1,800 as shown:

December 31, 2010 unadjusted book inventory	$63,950
December 31, 2010 physical inventory	62,150
Inventory shrinkage	$ 1,800

The effect of the shrinkage on the accounts and financial statements follows.

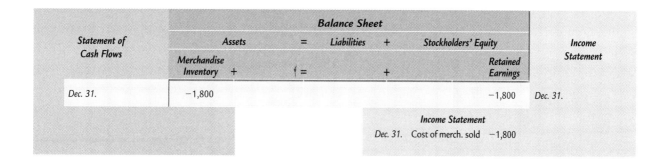

Appendix   *Statement of Cash Flows: The Indirect Method*

NetSolutions' statement of cash flows for the year ended December 31, 2010, is shown in Exhibit 8. The operating activities section of this statement was prepared using a method known as the *indirect method*. This method is used by over 90% of publicly held companies.

The use of the indirect method only affects net cash flows from operating activities. The other method of preparing the net cash flows from operating activities section is called the *direct method*. The direct method analyzes each transaction and its effect on cash flows. In contrast, the indirect method analyzes only the changes in accounts.

A major reason that the indirect method is so popular is that it is normally less costly to use. However, regardless of whether the indirect or direct method is used, the reporting of net cash flows from investing and financing activities is not affected. In this appendix, we illustrate the use of the indirect method of preparing the statement of cash flows.

The indirect method reconciles net income with net cash flows from operating activities. Net income is adjusted for the effects of accruals and deferrals that affected the net income but did not result in the receipt or payment of cash. The resulting amount is the net cash flows from operating activities.

The indirect method converts net income determined under the accrual basis of accounting to what it would have been under the cash basis of accounting. In other words, net cash flows from operating activities is equivalent to net income using the cash basis of accounting.

To illustrate, depreciation expense is deducted in arriving at net income but does not involve any cash payments. Thus, depreciation expense is added to net income under the indirect method. Likewise, assume that accounts receivable increases during the period by $10,000. This increase is included in the period's revenue and thus increases net income. However, cash was not collected. Thus, an increase in accounts receivable must be deducted from net income under the indirect method.

The typical adjustments to convert net income to net cash flows from operating activities, using the indirect method, are shown in Exhibit 12.

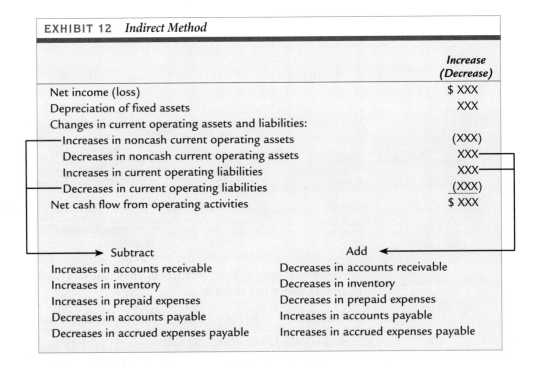

EXHIBIT 12   *Indirect Method*

	Increase (Decrease)
Net income (loss)	$ XXX
Depreciation of fixed assets	XXX
Changes in current operating assets and liabilities:	
⎯Increases in noncash current operating assets	(XXX)
Decreases in noncash current operating assets	XXX⎯
Increases in current operating liabilities	XXX⎯
⎯Decreases in current operating liabilities	(XXX)
Net cash flow from operating activities	$ XXX

⟶ Subtract	Add ⟵
Increases in accounts receivable	Decreases in accounts receivable
Increases in inventory	Decreases in inventory
Increases in prepaid expenses	Decreases in prepaid expenses
Decreases in accounts payable	Increases in accounts payable
Decreases in accrued expenses payable	Increases in accrued expenses payable

You should note that, except for depreciation, the adjustments in Exhibit 12 are for changes in the current assets and the current liabilities. This is because changes in the current assets and the current liabilities are related to operations and thus net income. For example, changes in inventories are related to sales, while changes in accounts payable are related to expenses.

Cash Flows from Operating Activities

To prepare the operating activities section for NetSolutions' statement of cash flows, we need to determine depreciation and the changes in the current assets and the liabilities during the year. This information is included in Exhibit 13, which shows the comparative balance sheets for NetSolutions as of December 31, 2010 and 2009, and related changes.

Based on Exhibit 13, the net cash flows from operating activities is shown below.

Net income		$ 60,400
Depreciation expense—store equipment	$ 3,100	
Depreciation expense—office equipment	2,490	
Changes in current operating assets and liabilities:		
Increase in accounts receivable	(24,080)	
Increase in merchandise inventory	(2,450)	
Decrease in office supplies	120	
Decrease in prepaid insurance	350	
Increase in accounts payable	8,150	
Decrease in salaries payable	(360)	
Decrease in unearned rent	(600)	(13,280)
Net cash flows from operating activities		$ 47,120

The depreciation expense of $3,100 for store equipment is determined from the increase in the accumulated depreciation for store equipment. Likewise, the depreciation expense of $2,490 for office equipment is determined from the increase in the accumulated depreciation for office equipment. The changes in the current assets and the current liabilities are also taken from Exhibit 13.

Cash Flows Used for Investing Activities

The cash flows for investing activities section can also be prepared by analyzing the changes in the accounts shown in Exhibit 13. For NetSolutions, the cash flows used for investing activities is composed of two items. First, additional store equipment of $7,100 was purchased, as shown by the increase in the store equipment. Likewise, additional office equipment of $5,570 was purchased. Thus, cash of $12,670 was used for investing activities, as shown in Exhibit 8.

Cash Flows Used for Financing Activities

The cash flows for financing activities can also be determined from Exhibit 13. For NetSolutions, the cash flows used for financing activities is composed of two items. First, dividends of $18,000 are reported on the retained earnings statement shown in Exhibit 6. Since no dividends payable appears on the balance sheets, cash dividends of $18,000 must have been paid during the year. In addition, notes payable decreased by $5,000 during the year, so cash must have been used in paying off $5,000 of the notes. Thus, cash of $23,000 was used for financing activities, as shown in Exhibit 8.

EXHIBIT 13   *NetSolutions' Comparative Balance Sheets*

NETSOLUTIONS
Balance Sheets

| | December 31, | | Changes |
	2010	2009	Increase (Decrease)
Assets			
Current assets:			
Cash	$ 52,950	$ 41,500	$11,450
Accounts receivable	76,080	52,000	24,080
Merchandise inventory	62,150	59,700	2,450
Office supplies	480	600	(120)
Prepaid insurance	2,650	3,000	(350)
Total current assets	$194,310	$156,800	$37,510
Property, plant, and equipment:			
Land	$ 20,000	$ 20,000	$ 0
Store equipment	27,100	20,000	7,100
Accumulated depreciation—store equipment	(5,700)	(2,600)	(3,100)
Office equipment	15,570	10,000	5,570
Accumulated depreciation—office equipment	(4,720)	(2,230)	(2,490)
Total property, plant, and equipment	$ 52,250	$ 45,170	$ 7,080
Total assets	$246,560	$201,970	$44,590
Liabilities			
Current liabilities:			
Accounts payable	$ 22,420	$ 14,270	$ 8,150
Notes payable (current portion)	5,000	5,000	0
Salaries payable	1,140	1,500	(360)
Unearned rent	1,800	2,400	(600)
Total current liabilities	$ 30,360	$ 23,170	$ 7,190
Long-term liabilities:			
Notes payable (final payment due 2019)	20,000	25,000	(5,000)
Total liabilities	$ 50,360	$ 48,170	$ 2,190
Stockholders' Equity			
Capital stock	$ 25,000	$ 25,000	$ 0
Retained earnings	171,200	128,800	42,400
Total stockholders' equity	$196,200	$153,800	$42,400
Total liabilities and stockholders' equity	$246,560	$201,970	$44,590

Key Points

1. **Distinguish the activities and financial statements of a service business from those of a merchandising business.**

   The revenue activities of a service enterprise involve providing services to customers. In contrast, the revenue activities of a merchandising business involve the buying and selling of merchandise.

2. **Describe and illustrate the financial statements of a merchandising business.**

   The multiple-step income statement of a merchandiser reports sales, sales returns and allowances, sales discounts, and net sales. The cost of the merchandise sold is subtracted from net sales to determine the gross profit. The cost of merchandise sold is determined by using either the periodic or perpetual inventory method. Operating income is determined by subtracting operating expenses from gross profit. Operating expenses are normally classified as selling or administrative expenses. Net income is determined by subtracting income taxes and other expense and adding other income. The income statement may also be reported in a single-step form. The retained earnings statement and the statement of cash flows are similar to those for a service business. The balance sheet reports merchandise inventory at the end of the period as a current asset.

3. **Describe the accounting for the sale of merchandise.**

   Sales of merchandise for cash or on account are recorded by increasing Sales. The cost of merchandise sold and the reduction in merchandise inventory are also recorded for the sale. For sales of merchandise on account, the credit terms can allow sales discounts for early payment. Such discounts are recorded by the seller as an increase in Sales Discounts. Sales discounts are reported as a deduction from the amount initially recorded in Sales. Likewise, when merchandise is returned or a price adjustment is granted, the seller increases Sales Returns and Allowances.

   Under the perpetual inventory system, the cost of merchandise sold and the reduction of merchandise inventory on hand are recorded at the time of sale. In this way, the merchandise inventory account indicates the amount of merchandise on hand at all times.

   Likewise, any returned merchandise is recorded in the merchandise inventory account with a related reduction in the cost of merchandise sold.

4. **Describe the accounting for the purchase of merchandise.**

   Purchases of merchandise for cash or on account are recorded by increasing Merchandise Inventory. For purchases of merchandise on account, the credit terms can allow cash discounts for early payment. Such purchase discounts are viewed as a reduction in the cost of the merchandise purchased. When merchandise is returned or a price adjustment is granted, the buyer decreases Merchandise Inventory.

5. **Describe the accounting for transportation costs and sales taxes.**

   When merchandise is shipped FOB shipping point, the buyer pays the transportation costs and increases Merchandise Inventory. When merchandise is shipped FOB destination, the seller pays the transportation costs and increases Delivery Expense or Transportation Out.

   The liability for sales tax is incurred when the sale is made and is recorded by the seller as an increase in the sales taxes payable account. When the amount of the sales tax is paid to the taxing unit, Sales Tax Payable and Cash are decreased.

6. **Illustrate the dual nature of merchandising transactions.**

   Each merchandising transaction affects a buyer and a seller. The illustration in this chapter shows how the same transactions would be recorded by both.

7. **Describe the accounting for merchandise shrinkage.**

   The physical inventory taken at the end of the accounting period could differ from the amount of inventory shown in the inventory records. The difference, called *inventory shrinkage,* requires an adjusting entry increasing Cost of Merchandise Sold and decreasing Merchandise Inventory. After this entry has been recorded, the adjusted Merchandise Inventory (book inventory) in the accounting records agrees with the actual physical inventory at the end of the period.

Key Terms

Administrative expenses

Book inventory

Cost of merchandise sold

Credit memorandum

Credit period

Credit terms

Debit memorandum

FOB (free on board) destination

FOB (free on board) shipping point

Gross profit

Income from operations (operating income)

Indirect method

Inventory shrinkage

Invoice

Merchandise available for sale

Merchandise inventory

Multiple-step income statement

Net sales

Other expense

Other income

Periodic inventory method

Perpetual inventory method

Physical inventory

Purchase discounts

Purchase return or allowance

Report form

Sales

Sales discounts

Sales returns and allowances

Selling expenses

Single-step income statement

Illustrative Problem

The following selected accounts and their current balances appear in the ledger of Sciatic Co. for the fiscal year ended July 31, 2010:

Cash	$123,000	Sales	$1,028,000
Accounts Receivable	96,800	Sales Returns and Allowances	18,480
Merchandise Inventory	140,000	Sales Discounts	17,520
Office Supplies	4,480	Cost of Merchandise Sold	620,000
Prepaid Insurance	2,720	Sales Salaries Expense	138,560
Office Equipment	68,000	Advertising Expense	35,040
Accumulated Depreciation—		Depreciation Expense—	
Office Equipment	10,240	Store Equipment	5,120
Store Equipment	122,400	Miscellaneous Selling Expense	1,280
Accumulated Depreciation—		Office Salaries Expense	67,320
Store Equipment	27,360	Rent Expense	25,080
Accounts Payable	44,480	Depreciation Expense—	
Salaries Payable	1,920	Office Equipment	10,160
Note Payable		Insurance Expense	3,120
(final payment due 2016)	44,800	Office Supplies Expense	1,040
Capital Stock	75,000	Miscellaneous Administrative	
Retained Earnings	301,600	Expense	1,280
Dividends	28,000	Interest Expense	4,000

Instructions

1. Prepare a multiple-step income statement.
2. Prepare a retained earnings statement.
3. Prepare a report form of balance sheet, assuming that the current portion of the note payable is $6,000.
4. Prepare a single-step income statement.

Solution

1.

SCIATIC CO.
Income Statement
For the Year Ended July 31, 2010

Revenue from sales:			
Sales		$1,028,000	
Less: Sales returns and allowances	$ 18,480		
Sales discounts	17,520	36,000	
Net sales			$992,000
Cost of merchandise sold			620,000
Gross profit			$372,000
Operating expenses:			
Selling expenses:			
Sales salaries expense	$138,560		
Advertising expense	35,040		
Depreciation expense—store equipment	5,120		
Miscellaneous selling expense	1,280		
Total selling expenses		$ 180,000	
Administrative expenses:			
Office salaries expense	$ 67,320		
Rent expense	25,080		
Depreciation expense—office equipment	10,160		
Insurance expense	3,120		
Office supplies expense	1,040		
Miscellaneous administrative expense	1,280		
Total administrative expenses		108,000	
Total operating expenses			288,000
Income from operations			$ 84,000
Other expense:			
Interest expense			4,000
Net income			$ 80,000

2.

SCIATIC CO.
Retained Earnings Statement
For the Year Ended July 31, 2010

Retained earnings, August 1, 2009		$301,600
Net income for the year	$80,000	
Less dividends	28,000	
Increase in retained earnings		52,000
Retained earnings, July 31, 2010		$353,600

(continued)

3.

SCIATIC CO.
Balance Sheet
July 31, 2010

Assets

Current assets:			
Cash		$123,000	
Accounts receivable		96,800	
Merchandise inventory		140,000	
Office supplies		4,480	
Prepaid insurance		2,720	
Total current assets			$367,000
Property, plant, and equipment:			
Office equipment	$ 68,000		
Less accumulated depreciation	10,240	$ 57,760	
Store equipment	$122,400		
Less accumulated depreciation	27,360	95,040	
Total property, plant, and equipment			152,800
Total assets			$519,800

Liabilities

Current liabilities:			
Accounts payable		$ 44,480	
Note payable (current portion)		6,000	
Salaries payable		1,920	
Total current liabilities			$ 52,400
Long-term liabilities:			
Note payable (final payment due 2016)			38,800
Total liabilities			$ 91,200

Stockholders' Equity

Capital stock		$ 75,000	
Retained earnings		353,600	428,600
Total liabilities and stockholders' equity			$519,800

4.

SCIATIC CO.
Income Statement
For the Year Ended July 31, 2010

Revenues:		
Net sales		$992,000
Expenses:		
Cost of merchandise sold	$620,000	
Selling expenses	180,000	
Administrative expenses	108,000	
Interest expense	4,000	
Total expenses		912,000
Net income		$ 80,000

Self-Examination Questions *(Answers appear at end of chapter.)*

1. If merchandise purchased on account is returned, the buyer can inform the seller of the details by issuing:
   A. a debit memorandum
   B. a credit memorandum
   C. an invoice
   D. a bill

2. If merchandise is sold on account to a customer for $1,000, terms FOB shipping point, 1/10, n/30, and the seller prepays $50 in transportation costs, the amount of the discount for early payment would be:
   A. $0   C. $10.00
   B. $5.00   D. $10.50

3. The income statement in which the total of all expenses is deducted from the total of all revenues is termed:
   A. multiple-step form   C. account form
   B. single-step form   D. report form

4. On a multiple-step income statement, the excess of net sales over the cost of merchandise sold is called:
   A. operating income
   B. income from operations
   C. gross profit
   D. net income

5. As of December 31, 2008, Ames Corporation's physical inventory was $275,000 and its book inventory was $290,000. The effect of the inventory shrinkage on the accounts is:
   A. to increase cost of merchandise sold and inventory by $15,000.
   B. to increase cost of merchandise sold and decrease inventory by $15,000.
   C. to decrease cost of merchandise sold and increase inventory by $15,000.
   D. to decrease cost of merchandise sold and inventory by $15,000.

Class Discussion Questions

1. What distinguishes a merchandising business from a service business?

2. Can a business earn a gross profit but incur a net loss? Explain.

3. In computing the cost of merchandise sold, does each of the following items increase or decrease that cost? (a) transportation costs, (b) beginning merchandise inventory, (c) purchase discounts, (d) ending merchandise inventory.

4. Describe how the periodic method differs from the perpetual method of accounting for merchandise inventory.

5. Differentiate between the multiple-step and the single-step forms of the income statement.

6. What are the major advantages and disadvantages of the single-step form of income statement compared to the multiple-step statement?

7. What type of revenue is reported in the Other income section of the multiple-step income statement?

8. How does the accounting for sales to customers using bank credit cards, such as MasterCard and VISA, differ from accounting for cash sales to customers?

9. What is the meaning of (a) 1/10, n/30; (b) n/90; (c) n/eom?

10. What is the nature of (a) a credit memorandum issued by the seller of merchandise, (b) a debit memorandum issued by the buyer of merchandise?

11. Who bears the transportation costs when the terms of sale are (a) FOB shipping point, (b) FOB destination?

12. When you purchase a new car, the "sticker price" includes a "destination" charge. Are you purchasing the car FOB shipping point or FOB destination? Explain.

13. Pembroke Office Equipment, which uses a perpetual inventory system, experienced a normal inventory shrinkage of $13,762. What accounts would be increased and decreased to record the adjustment for the inventory shrinkage at the end of the accounting period?

14. Assume that Pembroke Office Equipment in Question 13 experienced an abnormal inventory shrinkage of $215,650. Pembroke Office Equipment has decided to record the abnormal inventory shrinkage so that it would be separately disclosed on the income statement. What account would be increased for the abnormal inventory shrinkage?

Exercises

E4-1

Determining gross profit

Obj 1

During the current year, merchandise is sold for $2,850,750. The cost of the merchandise sold is $1,995,525.

a. What is the amount of the gross profit?
b. Compute the gross profit percentage (gross profit divided by sales).
c. Will the income statement necessarily report a net income? Explain.

E4-2

Determining cost of merchandise sold

Obj 1

For the year ending March 3, 2007, **Best Buy** reported revenue of $35,934 million. Its gross profit was $8,769 million. What was the amount of Best Buy's cost of merchandise sold?

E4-3

Identify items missing in determining cost of merchandise sold

Obj 2

For (a) through (d), identify the items designated by "X" and "Y."

a. Purchases − (X + Y) = Net purchases.
b. Net purchases + X = Cost of merchandise purchased.
c. Merchandise inventory (beginning) + Cost of merchandise purchased = X.
d. Merchandise available for sale − X = Cost of merchandise sold.

E4-4

Cost of merchandise sold and related items

Obj 2

✓ a. Cost of merchandise sold, $1,218,300

The following data were extracted from the accounting records of Meniscus Company for the year ended June 30, 2008:

Merchandise inventory, July 1, 2007	$ 183,250
Merchandise inventory, June 30, 2008	200,100
Purchases	1,279,600
Purchases returns and allowances	41,200
Purchases discounts	20,500
Sales	1,800,000
Transportation in	17,250

a. Prepare the cost of merchandise sold section of the income statement for the year ended June 30, 2008, using the periodic inventory system.
b. Determine the gross profit to be reported on the income statement for the year ended June 30, 2008.

E4-5

Cost of merchandise sold

Obj 2

✓ Correct cost of merchandise sold, $820,500

Identify the errors in the following schedule of cost of merchandise sold for the current year ended March 31, 2008:

Cost of merchandise sold:			
Merchandise inventory, March 31, 2008			$135,750
Purchases		$852,100	
Plus: Purchases returns and allowances	$10,500		
Purchases discounts	8,000	18,500	
Gross purchases		$870,600	
Less transportation in		7,500	
Cost of merchandise purchased			863,100
Merchandise available for sale			$998,850
Less merchandise inventory, April 1, 2007			115,150
Cost of merchandise sold			$883,700

E4-6

Income statement for merchandiser

Obj 2

For the fiscal year, sales were $4,125,800, sales discounts were $380,000, sales returns and allowances were $186,750, and the cost of merchandise sold was $2,475,500.

a. What was the amount of net sales?
b. What was the amount of gross profit?

E4-7

Income statement for merchandiser

Obj 2

The following expenses were incurred by a merchandising business during the year. In which expense section of the income statement should each be reported: (a) selling, (b) administrative, or (c) other?

1. Advertising expense.
2. Depreciation expense on store equipment.
3. Insurance expense on office equipment.
4. Interest expense on notes payable.
5. Rent expense on office building.
6. Salaries of office personnel.
7. Salary of sales manager.
8. Sales supplies used.

E4-8

Single-step income statement

Obj 2

✓ Net income: $451,450

Summary operating data for The Voodoo Company during the current year ended November 30, 2008, are as follows: cost of merchandise sold, $2,175,350; administrative expenses, $500,000; interest expense, $23,200; rent revenue, $30,000; net sales, $4,000,000; and selling expenses, $880,000. Prepare a single-step income statement.

E4-9

Multiple-step income statement

Obj 2

✓ a. Net income: $137,500

On August 31, 2008, the balances of the accounts appearing in the ledger of The Bent Needle Company, a furniture wholesaler, are as follows:

Administrative Expenses	$125,000	Notes Payable	$ 25,000
Building	512,500	Office Supplies	10,600
Cash	48,500	Salaries Payable	3,220
Cost of Merchandise Sold	700,000	Sales	1,275,000
Interest Expense	7,500	Sales Discounts	20,000
Capital Stock	568,580	Sales Returns and Allowances	80,000
Dividends	25,000	Selling Expenses	205,000
Merchandise Inventory	130,000	Store Supplies	7,700

a. Prepare a multiple-step income statement for the year ended August 31, 2008.
b. Compare the major advantages and disadvantages of the multiple-step and single-step forms of income statements.

E4-10

Determining amounts for items omitted from income statement

Obj 2

✓ a. $30,000

✓ h. $690,000

Two items are omitted in each of the following four lists of income statement data. Determine the amounts of the missing items, identifying them by letter.

Sales	$400,000	$500,000	$1,000,000	$ (g)
Sales returns and allowances	(a)	15,000	(e)	30,500
Sales discounts	20,000	8,000	40,000	37,000
Net sales	350,000	(c)	910,000	(h)
Cost of merchandise sold	(b)	285,000	(f)	540,000
Gross profit	200,000	(d)	286,500	150,000

E4-11

Multiple-step income statement

Obj 2

Identify the errors in the following income statement:

THE EUCLIDIAN COMPANY
Income Statement
For the Year Ended March 31, 2008

Revenue from sales:			
Sales		$7,127,500	
Add: Sales returns and allowances	$112,300		
Sales discounts	60,000	172,300	
Gross sales			$7,299,800
Cost of merchandise sold			4,175,100
Income from operations			$3,124,700
Expenses:			
Selling expenses		$ 710,000	
Administrative expenses		525,000	
Delivery expenses		18,100	
Total expenses			1,253,100
			$1,871,600
Other expense:			
Interest revenue			80,000
Gross profit			$1,791,600

E4-12

Sales returns and allowances

Obj 3

During the year, sales returns and allowances totaled $172,100. The cost of the merchandise returned was $100,300. The accountant recorded all the returns and allowances by decreasing the sales account and decreasing Cost of Merchandise Sold for $172,100.

Was the accountant's method of recording returns acceptable? Explain. In your explanation, include the advantages of using a sales returns and allowances account.

E4-13

Sales-related transactions

Obj 3

After the amount due on a sale of $18,500, terms 2/10, n/eom, is received from a customer within the discount period, the seller consents to the return of the entire shipment. The cost of the merchandise returned was $11,100. (a) What is the amount of the refund owed to the customer? (b) Illustrate the effects on the accounts and financial statements of the return and the refund.

E4-14

Sales-related transactions

Obj 3

✓ d. $9,654

Merchandise is sold on account to a customer for $9,200, terms FOB shipping point, 2/10, n/30. The seller paid the transportation costs of $638. Determine the following: (a) amount of the sale, (b) amount debited to Accounts Receivable, (c) amount of the discount for early payment, and (d) amount due within the discount period.

E4-15

Purchase-related transaction

Obj 4

Hushpuppy Company purchased merchandise on account from a supplier for $6,750, terms 2/10, n/30. Hushpuppy Company returned $1,500 of the merchandise and received full credit.

a. If Hushpuppy Company pays the invoice within the discount period, what is the amount of cash required for the payment?
b. Under a perpetual inventory system, what account is decreased by Hushpuppy Company to record the return?

E4-16

Purchase-related transactions

Obj 4

A retailer is considering the purchase of 100 units of a specific item from either of two suppliers. Their offers are as follows:

A: $375 a unit, total of $37,500, 2/10, n/30, plus transportation costs of $1,050.
B: $380 a unit, total of $38,000, 1/10, n/30, no charge for transportation.

Which of the two offers, A or B, yields the lower price?

E4-17

Purchase-related transactions

Obj 4

✓ (c) Cash, decreased $7,350

Madamé Co., a women's clothing store, purchased $10,000 of merchandise from a supplier on account, terms FOB destination, 2/10, n/30. Madamé Co. returned $2,500 of the merchandise, receiving a credit memorandum, and then paid the amount due within the discount period. Illustrate the effects on the accounts and financial statements of Madamé Co. to record (a) the purchase, (b) the merchandise return, and (c) the payment.

E4-18

Purchase-related transactions

Obj 4

✓ (e) Cash, increased $1,410

Illustrate the effects on the accounts and financial statements of the following related transactions of La Paz Company:

a. Purchased $18,400 of merchandise from Harbin Co. on account, terms 2/10, n/30.
b. Paid the amount owed on the invoice within the discount period.
c. Discovered that $4,500 of the merchandise was defective and returned items, receiving credit.
d. Purchased $3,000 of merchandise from Harbin Co. on account, terms n/30.
e. Received a check for the balance owed from the return in (c), after deducting for the purchase in (d).

E4-19

Determining amounts to be paid on invoices

Obj 5

✓ a. $6,435

Determine the amount to be paid in full settlement of each of the following invoices, assuming that credit for returns and allowances was received prior to payment and that all invoices were paid within the discount period.

	Merchandise	Transportation Paid by Seller		Returns and Allowances
a.	$ 8,000	—	FOB shipping point, 1/10, n/30	$1,500
b.	2,900	$125	FOB shipping point, 2/10, n/30	400
c.	3,850	—	FOB destination, 2/10, n/30	—
d.	15,000	—	FOB destination, n/30	2,500
e.	5,000	275	FOB shipping point, 2/10, n/30	1,000

E4-20

Sales tax

Obj 5

✓ c. $12,932

A sale of merchandise on account for $12,200 is subject to a 6% sales tax. (a) Should the sales tax be recorded at the time of sale or when payment is received? (b) What is the amount of the sale? (c) What is the amount of the increase to Accounts Receivable? (d) What is the title of the account to which the $732 ($12,200 × 6%) is recorded?

E4-21

Sales tax transactions

Obj 5

Illustrate the effects on the accounts and financial statements of recording the following selected transactions:

a. Sold $15,750 of merchandise on account, subject to a sales tax of 8%. The cost of the merchandise sold was $9,450.
b. Paid $29,183 to the state sales tax department for taxes collected.

E4-22

Sales-related transactions

Obj 3

Sellers Co., a furniture wholesaler, sells merchandise to Beyer Co. on account, $14,500, terms 2/10, n/30. The cost of the merchandise sold is $8,800. Sellers Co. issues a credit memorandum for $3,750 for merchandise returned and subsequently receives the amount due within the discount period. The cost of the merchandise returned is $2,100. Illustrate the effects on the accounts and financial statements of Sellers Co. for (a) the sale, including the cost of the merchandise sold, (b) the credit memorandum, including the cost of the returned merchandise, and (c) the receipt of the check for the amount due from Beyer Co.

E4-23

Purchase-related transactions

Obj 4

Based on the data presented in Exercise 4-22, illustrate the effects on the accounts and financial statements of Beyer Co. for (a) the purchase, (b) the return of the merchandise for credit, and (c) the payment of the invoice within the discount period.

E4-24

Adjusting entry for merchandise inventory shrinkage

Obj 7

Teramycin Inc.'s perpetual inventory records indicate that $715,275 of merchandise should be on hand on January 31, 2008. The physical inventory indicates that $698,150 of merchandise is actually on hand. Illustrate the effects on the accounts and financial statements of the inventory shrinkage for Teramycin Inc. for the year ended January 31, 2008.

Problems

P4-1

Multiple-step income statement and report form of balance sheet

SPREADSHEET

Obj 2

✓ 1. Net income: $120,000

GROUP

The following selected accounts and their current balances appear in the ledger of Magic Vinyl Co. for the fiscal year ended March 31, 2008:

Cash	$ 184,500	Sales	$1,542,000
Accounts Receivable	145,200	Sales Returns and Allowances	27,720
Merchandise Inventory	210,000	Sales Discounts	26,280
Office Supplies	6,720	Cost of Merchandise Sold	930,000
Prepaid Insurance	4,080	Sales Salaries Expense	207,840
Office Equipment	102,000	Advertising Expense	52,560
Accumulated Depreciation—		Depreciation Expense—	
Office Equipment	15,360	Store Equipment	7,680
Store Equipment	183,600	Miscellaneous Selling Expense	1,920
Accumulated Depreciation—		Office Salaries Expense	100,980
Store Equipment	41,040	Rent Expense	37,620
Accounts Payable	66,720	Depreciation Expense—	
Salaries Payable	2,880	Office Equipment	15,240
Note Payable		Insurance Expense	4,680
(final payment due 2018)	67,200	Office Supplies Expense	1,560
Capital Stock	75,000	Miscellaneous Administrative	
Retained Earnings	489,900	Expense	1,920
Dividends	42,000	Interest Expense	6,000

Instructions

1. Prepare a multiple-step income statement.
2. Prepare a retained earnings statement.
3. Prepare a report form of balance sheet, assuming that the current portion of the note payable is $9,000.
4. Briefly explain (a) how multiple-step and single-step income statements differ and (b) how report-form and account-form balance sheets differ.

P4-2

Single-step income statement

Obj 2

SPREADSHEET

Selected accounts and related amounts for Magic Vinyl Co. for the fiscal year ended March 31, 2008, are presented in Problem 4-1.

Instructions

1. Prepare a single-step income statement in the format shown in Exhibit 5.
2. Prepare a retained earnings statement.

P4-3

Sales-related transactions

Objs 3, 5

The following selected transactions were completed by Cardroom Supplies Co., which sells office supplies primarily to wholesalers and occasionally to retail customers.

Jan. 2. Sold merchandise on account to Glickman Co., $5,600, terms FOB shipping point, n/eom. The cost of merchandise sold was $3,100.

8. Sold merchandise on account to Kibler Company, $10,000, terms FOB destination, 1/10, n/30. The cost of merchandise sold was $6,500.
16. Sold merchandise on account to Bryan Co., $12,000, terms FOB shipping point, 1/10, n/30. The cost of merchandise sold was $7,200.
18. Received check for amount due from Kibler Star Company for sale on January 8.
19. Issued credit memorandum for $3,000 to Bryan Co. for merchandise returned from sale on January 16. The cost of the merchandise returned was $1,800.
26. Received check for amount due from Bryan Co. for sale on January 16 less credit memorandum of January 19 and discount.
31. Paid Speedy Delivery Service $1,875 for merchandise delivered during January to customers under shipping terms of FOB destination.
31. Received check for amount due from Glickman Co. for sale of January 2.

Instructions

Illustrate the effects of each of the preceding transactions on the accounts and financial statements of Cardroom Supplies Co. Identify each transaction by date.

P4-4

Purchase-related transactions

Objs 4, 5

The following selected transactions were completed by Scat Trak Co. during July of the current year:

July 3. Purchased merchandise from Phillips Co., $13,800, terms FOB destination, 2/10, n/30.
    6. Issued debit memorandum to Phillips Co. for $1,900 of merchandise returned from purchase on July 3.
   10. Purchased merchandise from Cleghorne Company, $18,000, terms FOB shipping point, n/eom.
   10. Paid transportation charges of $500 on July 10 purchase from Cleghorne Company.
   13. Paid Phillips Co. for invoice of July 3, less debit memorandum of July 6 and discount.
   31. Paid Cleghorne Company for invoice of July 10.

Instructions

Illustrate the effects of each of the preceding transactions on the accounts and financial statements of Scat Trak Co. Identify each transaction by date.

P4-5

Sales-related and purchase-related transactions for seller and buyer

Obj 6

The following selected transactions were completed during April between Sallis Company and Byce Company:

April 8. Sallis Company sold merchandise on account to Byce Company, $21,600, terms FOB destination, 1/15, n/eom. The cost of the merchandise sold was $13,000.
    8. Sallis Company paid transportation costs of $879 for delivery of merchandise sold to Byce Company on April 8.
   12. Byce Company returned $5,000 of merchandise purchased on account on April 8 from Sallis Company. The cost of the merchandise returned was $2,900.
   23. Byce Company paid Sallis Company for purchase of April 8, less discount and less return of April 12.
   24. Sallis Company sold merchandise on account to Byce Company, $15,000, terms FOB shipping point, n/eom. The cost of the merchandise sold was $9,000.
   26. Byce Company paid transportation charges of $400 on April 24 purchase from Sallis Company.
   30. Byce Company paid Sallis Company on account for purchase of April 24.

Instructions

Illustrate the effects of each of the preceding transactions on the accounts and financial statements of (1) Sallis Company and (2) Byce Company. Identify each transaction by date.

For the year ending December 31, 2009, Mildew Systems Inc. reported net income of $90,600 and paid dividends of $27,000. Comparative balance sheets as of December 31, 2009 and 2008, are as follows:

MILDEW SYSTEMS INC.
Balance Sheets

	December 31, 2009	December 31, 2008	Changes Increase (Decrease)
Assets			
Current assets:			
Cash	$ 79,425	$ 62,250	$17,175
Accounts receivable	114,120	78,000	36,120
Merchandise inventory	93,225	89,550	3,675
Office supplies	720	900	(180)
Prepaid insurance	3,975	4,500	(525)
Total current assets	$ 291,465	$235,200	$56,265
Property, plant, and equipment:			
Land	$ 30,000	$ 30,000	$ 0
Store equipment	40,650	30,000	10,650
Accumulated depreciation—			
store equipment	(8,550)	(3,900)	(4,650)
Office equipment	23,355	15,000	8,355
Accumulated depreciation—			
office equipment	(7,080)	(3,345)	(3,735)
Total property, plant,			
and equipment	$ 78,375	$ 67,755	$10,620
Total assets	$ 369,840	$302,955	$66,885
Liabilities			
Current liabilities:			
Accounts payable	$ 33,630	$ 21,405	$12,225
Notes payable (current portion)	7,500	7,500	0
Salaries payable	1,710	2,250	(540)
Unearned rent	2,700	3,600	(900)
Total current liabilities	$ 45,540	$ 34,755	$10,785
Long-term liabilities:			
Notes payable			
(final payment due 2015)	30,000	37,500	(7,500)
Total liabilities	$ 75,540	$ 72,255	$ 3,285
Stockholders' Equity			
Capital stock	$ 37,500	$ 37,500	$ 0
Retained earnings	256,800	193,200	63,600
Total stockholders' equity	$ 294,300	$230,700	$63,600
Total liabilities and stockholders' equity	$ 369,840	$302,955	$66,885

Instructions

1. Prepare a statement of cash flows, using the indirect method.
2. Why is depreciation added to net income in determining net cash flows from operating activities? Explain.

Activities

A4-1

Ethics and professional conduct in business

ETHICS

On February 24, 2008, Lawn Ranger Company, a garden retailer, purchased $40,000 of corn seed, terms 2/10, n/30, from Nebraska Farm Co. Even though the discount period had expired, Corey Gilbert subtracted the discount of $800 when he processed the documents for payment on March 25, 2008.

    Discuss whether Corey Gilbert behaved in a professional manner by subtracting the discount, even though the discount period had expired.

A4-2

Purchases discounts and accounts payable

The Eclipse Video Store Co. is owned and operated by Jared Helms. The following is an excerpt from a conversation between Jared Helms and Allison Fain, the chief accountant for The Eclipse Video Store:

Jared: Allison, I've got a question about this recent balance sheet.

Allison: Sure, what's your question?

Jared: Well, as you know, I'm applying for a bank loan to finance our new store in Winterville, and I noticed that the accounts payable are listed as $85,000.

Allison: That's right. Approximately $78,000 of that represents amounts due our suppliers, and the remainder is miscellaneous payables to creditors for utilities, office equipment, supplies, etc.

Jared: That's what I thought. But as you know, we normally receive a 2% discount from our suppliers for earlier payment, and we always try to take the discount.

Allison: That's right. I can't remember the last time we missed a discount.

Jared: Well, in that case, it seems to me the accounts payable should be listed minus the 2% discount. Let's list the accounts payable due suppliers as $76,440, rather than $78,000. Every little bit helps. You never know. It might make the difference between getting the loan and not.

How would you respond to Jared Helms' request?

A4-3

Determining cost of purchases

The following is an excerpt from a conversation between Kate Fleming and Bob Dent. Kate is debating whether to buy a stereo system from Design Sound, a locally owned electronics store, or Big Sound Electronics, an online electronics company.

Kate: Bob, I don't know what to do about buying my new stereo.

Bob: What's the problem?

Kate: Well, I can buy it locally at Design Sound for $580.00. However, Big Sound Electronics has the same system listed for $599.99.

Bob: So what's the big deal? Buy it from Design Sound.

Kate: It's not quite that simple. Big Sound said something about not having to pay sales tax, since I was out-of-state.

Bob: Yes, that's a good point. If you buy it at Design Sound, they'll charge you 8% sales tax.

Kate: But Big Sound Electronics charges $18.99 for shipping and handling. If I have them send it next-day air, it'll cost $24.99 for shipping and handling.

Bob: I guess it is a little confusing.

Kate: That's not all. Design Sound will give an additional 1% discount if I pay cash. Otherwise, they will let me use my VISA, or I can pay it off in three monthly installments.

Bob: Anything else???

Kate: Well . . . Big Sound says I have to charge it on my VISA. They don't accept checks.

Bob: I am not surprised. Many online stores don't accept checks.

Kate: I give up. What would you do?

1. Assuming that Big Sound Electronics doesn't charge sales tax on the sale to Kate, which company is offering the best buy?
2. What might be some considerations other than price that might influence Kate's decision on where to buy the stereo system?

A4-4
Sales discounts

Your sister operates Emigrant Parts Company, an online boat parts distributorship that is in its third year of operation. The income statement shown below was recently prepared for the year ended July 31, 2008:

EMIGRANT PARTS COMPANY
Income Statement
For the Year Ended July 31, 2008

Revenues:		
Net sales		$800,000
Interest revenue		10,000
Total revenues		$810,000
Expenses:		
Cost of merchandise sold	$520,000	
Selling expenses	90,000	
Administrative expenses	48,550	
Interest expense	15,000	
Total expenses		673,550
Net income		$136,450

Your sister is considering a proposal to increase net income by offering sales discounts of 2/15, n/30, and by shipping all merchandise FOB shipping point. Currently, no sales discounts are allowed and merchandise is shipped FOB destination. It is estimated that these credit terms will increase net sales by 15%. The ratio of the cost of merchandise sold to net sales is expected to be 65%. All selling and administrative expenses are expected to remain unchanged, except for store supplies, miscellaneous selling, office supplies, and miscellaneous administrative expenses, which are expected to increase proportionately with increased net sales. The amounts of these preceding items for the year ended July 31, 2008, were as follows:

Store supplies expense	$12,000
Miscellaneous selling expense	3,000
Office supplies expense	2,000
Miscellaneous administrative expense	1,000

The other income and other expense items will remain unchanged. The shipment of all merchandise FOB shipping point will eliminate all delivery expense, which for the year ended July 31, 2008, was $18,750.

1. Prepare a projected single-step income statement for the year ending July 31, 2009, based on the proposal. Assume all sales are collected within the discount period.
2. a. Based on the projected income statement in (1), would you recommend the implementation of the proposed changes?
   b. Describe any possible concerns you may have related to the proposed changes described in (1).

A4-5
Shopping for a television

GROUP

Assume that you are planning to purchase a 50-inch Plasma television. In groups of three or four, determine the lowest cost for the television, considering the available alternatives and the advantages and disadvantages of each alternative. For example, you could purchase locally, through mail order, or through an Internet shopping service. Consider such factors as delivery charges, interest-free financing, discounts, coupons, and availability of warranty services. Prepare a report for presentation to the class.

Answers to Self-Examination Questions

1. **A** A debit memorandum (answer A), issued by the buyer, indicates the amount the buyer proposes to decrease to the accounts payable account. A credit memorandum (answer B), issued by the seller, indicates the amount the seller proposes to decrease to the accounts receivable account. An invoice (answer C) or a bill (answer D), issued by the seller, indicates the amount and terms of the sale.

2. **C** The amount of discount for early payment is $10 (answer C), or 1% of $1,000. Although the $50 of transportation costs paid by the seller is increased to the customer's account, the customer is not entitled to a discount on that amount.

3. **B** The single-step form of income statement (answer B) is so named because the total of all expenses is deducted in one step from the total of all revenues. The multiple-step form (answer A) includes numerous sections and subsections with several subtotals. The account form (answer C) and the report form (answer D) are two common forms of the balance sheet.

4. **C** Gross profit (answer C) is the excess of net sales over the cost of merchandise sold. Operating income (answer A) or income from operations (answer B) is the excess of gross profit over operating expenses. Net income (answer D) is the final figure on the income statement after all revenues and expenses have been reported.

5. **B** The inventory shrinkage, $15,000, is the difference between the book inventory, $290,000, and the physical inventory, $275,000. The effect of the inventory shrinkage on the accounts is to increase cost of merchandise sold and decrease inventory by $15,000.

CHAPTER 5

Sarbanes-Oxley, Internal Control, and Cash

Learning Objectives

After studying this chapter, you should be able to:

Obj 1
Describe the Sarbanes-Oxley Act of 2002 and its impact on internal controls and financial reporting.

Obj 2
Describe and illustrate the objectives and elements of internal control.

Obj 3
Describe and illustrate the application of internal controls to cash.

Obj 4
Describe the nature of a bank account and its use in controlling cash.

Obj 5
Describe and illustrate the use of a bank reconciliation in controlling cash.

Obj 6
Describe the accounting for special-purpose cash funds.

Obj 7
Describe and illustrate the reporting of cash and cash equivalents in the financial statements.

Once a month, you may receive a bank statement that lists the deposits and withdrawals that have been added to and subtracted from your account balance. If you wrote any checks, the statement may also be accompanied by copies of your canceled checks.

New forms of payment are now arising that don't involve checks at all. Retailers, such as grocery stores, now allow customers to pay for merchandise by swiping their bank cards at checkout, causing an immediate transfer of funds out of a bank account. Banks are allowing regular monthly bills, such as utility bills, to be paid directly out of a checking account, using electronic fund transfers. Internet payments can be made by using services such as **PayPal**®, which will make payments to third parties directly out of a checking account. In all of these cases, you need to verify actual fund transfers with the correct amounts by comparing your bank statement with electronic invoices, receipts, and other evidence of payment.

Many banks are making real-time checking account information available on the Internet to account owners. Thus, account owners using this feature are now able to manage and control their accounts in a more timely way.

In this chapter, we will discuss how companies control their cash and other assets. We begin by discussing the importance of the Sarbanes-Oxley Act that was passed by Congress to improve the financial controls and reporting practices of companies.

Obj 1

Describe the Sarbanes-Oxley Act of 2002 and its impact on internal controls and financial reporting.

Sarbanes-Oxley Act of 2002

During the *Enron*, *WorldCom*, *Tyco*, *Adelphia*, and other financial scandals of the early 2000s, stockholders, creditors, and other investors lost millions and in some cases billions of dollars.[1] The resulting public outcry led Congress to pass the **Sarbanes-Oxley Act of 2002**. This act, referred to simply as *Sarbanes-Oxley,* is considered one of the most important and significant laws affecting publicly held companies in recent history. Although Sarbanes-Oxley applies only to companies whose stock is traded on public exchanges, referred to as *publicly held companies,* it has become the standard for assessing the financial controls and reporting of all companies.

Sarbanes-Oxley's purpose is to restore public confidence and trust in the financial statements of companies. In doing so, Sarbanes-Oxley emphasizes the importance of effective internal control.[2] **Internal control** is broadly defined as the procedures and processes used by a company to safeguard its assets, process information accurately, and ensure compliance with laws and regulations.

Sarbanes-Oxley requires companies to maintain strong and effective internal controls over the recording of transactions and the preparing of financial statements. Such controls are important because they deter fraud and prevent misleading financial statements, as shown in the following illustration:

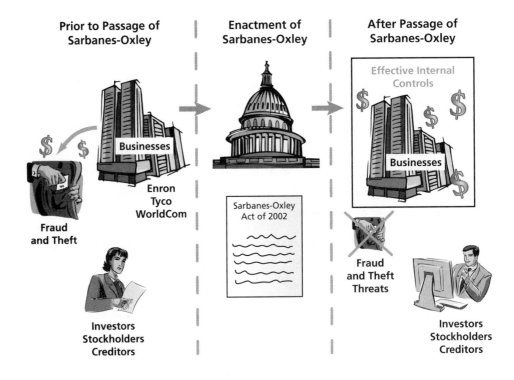

Sarbanes-Oxley not only requires companies to maintain strong and effective internal controls, but it also requires companies and their independent accountants to report

---

[1]Exhibit 9 in Chapter 1 briefly summarizes these scandals.
[2]Sarbanes-Oxley also has important implications for corporate governance and the regulation of the public accounting profession. In this chapter, we focus on the internal control implications of Sarbanes-Oxley.

on the effectiveness of the company's internal controls.[3] These reports are required to be filed with the company's annual 10-K report with the Securities and Exchange Commission. The act also encourages companies to include these reports in their annual reports to stockholders. An example of such a report by the management of ***General Electric Company (GE)*** is shown in Exhibit 1.

EXHIBIT 1   *Sarbanes-Oxley Report General Electric Company*

Management's Annual Report on Internal Control over Financial Reporting

The management of General Electric Company is responsible for establishing and maintaining adequate internal control over financial reporting for the company. With the participation of the Chief Executive Officer and the Chief Financial Officer, our management conducted an evaluation of the effectiveness of our internal control over financial reporting based on the framework and criteria established in Internal Control—Integrated Framework, issued by the Committee of Sponsoring Organizations. . . . Based on this evaluation, our management has concluded that our internal control over financial reporting was effective. . . .

General Electric Company's independent [accountant] auditor, KPMG LLP, a registered public accounting firm, has [also] issued an audit report on our management's assessment of our internal control over financial reporting.

JEFFREY R. IMMELT
Chairman of the Board
and Chief Executive Officer

KEITH S. SHERIN
Senior Vice President, Finance
and Chief Financial Officer

GE based its assessment and evaluation of internal controls upon *Internal Control—Integrated Framework,* which was issued by the Committee of Sponsoring Organizations. This framework is the widely accepted standard by which companies design, analyze, and evaluate internal controls. For this reason, we use this framework in the next section of this chapter as a basis for our discussion of internal controls.

Internal Control

Obj **2**

Describe and illustrate the objectives and elements of internal control.

As indicated in the prior section, effective internal controls are required by Sarbanes-Oxley. In addition, effective internal controls help businesses guide their operations and prevent theft and other abuses. For example, assume that you own and manage a lawn care service. Your business uses several employee teams, and you provide each team with a vehicle and lawn equipment. What issues might you face as a manager in controlling the operations of this business? Below are some examples.

- Lawn care must be provided on time.
- The quality of lawn care services must meet customer expectations.
- Employees must provide work for the hours they are paid.
- Lawn care equipment should be used for business purposes only.
- Vehicles should be used for business purposes only.
- Customers must be billed and payments collected for services rendered.

How would you address these issues? You could, for example, develop a schedule at the beginning of each day and then inspect the work at the end of the day to verify that

---

[3]These reporting requirements are required under Section 404 of the act. As a result, these requirements and reports are often referred to as 404 requirements and 404 reports.

it was completed according to quality standards. You could have "surprise" inspections by arriving on-site at random times to verify that the teams are working according to schedule. You could require employees to "clock in" at the beginning of the day and "clock out" at the end of the day to make sure that they are paid for hours worked. You could require the work teams to return the vehicles and equipment to a central location to prevent unauthorized use. You could keep a log of odometer readings at the end of each day to verify that the vehicles have not been used for "joy riding." You could bill customers after you have inspected the work and then monitor the collection of all receivables. All of these are examples of internal control.

In this section, we describe and illustrate internal control using the framework developed by the Committee of Sponsoring Organizations, which was formed by five major business associations. The committee's deliberations were published in *Internal Control—Integrated Framework.*[4] This framework, cited by GE in Exhibit 1, has become the standard by which companies design, analyze, and evaluate internal control. We describe and illustrate the framework by first describing the objectives of internal control and then showing how these objectives can be achieved through the five elements of internal control.

Objectives of Internal Control

The objectives of internal control are to provide reasonable assurance that: (1) assets are safeguarded and used for business purposes, (2) business information is accurate, and (3) employees comply with laws and regulations. These objectives are illustrated below.

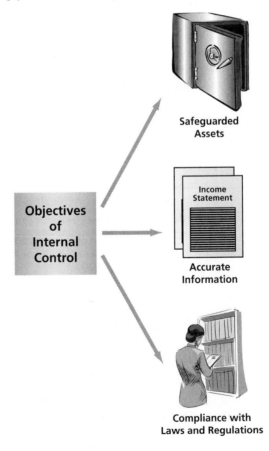

[4]*Internal Control—Integrated Framework* by the Committee of Sponsoring Organizations (COSO) of the Treadway Commission, 1992.

Internal control can safeguard assets by preventing theft, fraud, misuse, or misplacement. One of the most serious breaches of internal control is employee fraud. **Employee fraud** is the intentional act of deceiving an employer for personal gain. Such deception may range from purposely overstating expenses on a travel expense report to embezzling millions of dollars through complex schemes.

Accurate information is necessary for operating a business successfully. The safeguarding of assets and accurate information often go hand-in-hand. The reason is that employees attempting to defraud a business will also need to adjust the accounting records in order to hide the fraud.

Businesses must comply with applicable laws, regulations, and financial reporting standards. Examples of such standards and laws include environmental regulations, contract terms, safety regulations, and generally accepted accounting principles (GAAP).

Elements of Internal Control

How does management achieve its internal control objectives? Management is responsible for designing and applying five **elements of internal control** to meet the three internal control objectives. These elements are (1) the control environment, (2) risk assessment, (3) control procedures, (4) monitoring, and (5) information and communication.[5]

The elements of internal control are illustrated in Exhibit 2. In this exhibit, these elements form an umbrella over the business to protect it from control threats. The

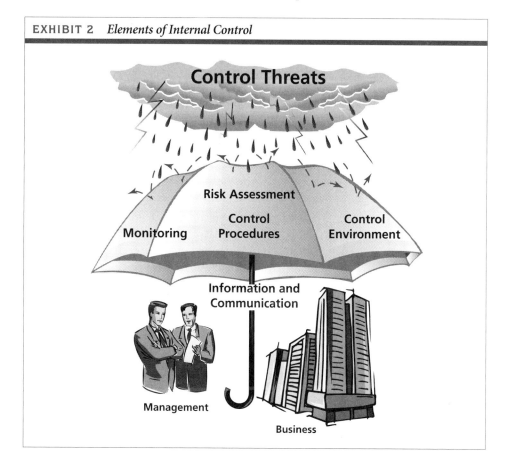

EXHIBIT 2   *Elements of Internal Control*

Control Threats

Risk Assessment

Monitoring   Control Procedures   Control Environment

Information and Communication

Management

Business

[5]Ibid., 12–14.

business's control environment is represented by the size of the umbrella. Risk assessment, control procedures, and monitoring are the fabric that keeps the umbrella from leaking. Information and communication link the umbrella to management. In the following paragraphs, we discuss each of these elements.

Control Environment

A business's control environment is the overall attitude of management and employees about the importance of controls. One of the factors that influences the control environment is *management's philosophy and operating style*. A management that overemphasizes operating goals and deviates from control policies may indirectly encourage employees to ignore controls. For example, the pressure to achieve revenue targets may encourage employees to fraudulently record sham sales. On the other hand, a management that emphasizes the importance of controls and encourages adherence to control policies will create an effective control environment.

Control Environment

CEO

employees

Management's Philosophy and Operating Style

Organizational Structure

Personnel Policies

The business's *organizational structure*, which is the framework for planning and controlling operations, also influences the control environment. For example, a department store chain might organize each of its stores as separate business units. Each store manager has full authority over pricing and other operating activities. In such a structure, each store manager has the responsibility for establishing an effective control environment.

Personnel policies also affect the control environment. Personnel policies involve the hiring, training, evaluation, compensation, and promotion of employees. In addition, job descriptions, employee codes of ethics, and conflict-of-interest policies are part of the personnel policies. Such policies can enhance the internal control environment if they provide reasonable assurance that only competent, honest employees are hired and retained.

To illustrate the importance of the control environment, consider the case where the head of a bank's loan department perpetrated a fraud by accepting kickbacks from customers with poor credit ratings. As a result, the bank lost thousands of dollars from bad loans. After discovering the fraud, the bank president improved the bank's control environment by implementing a program that allowed employees to report suspicious conduct anonymously. In addition to encouraging employees to report suspicious conduct, the employees were warned that employee fraud might occur anywhere and involve anyone.

Risk Assessment

All organizations face risks. Examples of risk include changes in customer requirements, competitive threats, regulatory changes, changes in economic factors such as interest rates, and employee violations of company policies and procedures. Management should assess these risks and take necessary actions to control them, so that the objectives of internal control can be achieved.

Once risks are identified, they can be analyzed to estimate their significance, to assess their likelihood of occurring, and to determine actions that will minimize them. For example, the manager of a warehouse operation may analyze the risk of employee back injuries, which might give rise to lawsuits. If the manager determines that the risk is significant, the company may purchase back support braces for its warehouse employees and require them to wear the braces.

Control Procedures

Control procedures are established to provide reasonable assurance that business goals will be achieved, including the prevention of fraud. In the following paragraphs, we will briefly discuss control procedures that can be integrated throughout the accounting system. These procedures are listed in Exhibit 3.

EXHIBIT 3 *Internal Control Procedures*

Control Threats

CONTROL PROCEDURES:
Competent personnel, rotating duties, and mandatory vacations
Separating responsibilities for related operations
Separating operations, custody of assets, and accounting
Proofs and security measures

Management

Business

INTEGRITY, OBJECTIVITY, AND ETHICS IN BUSINESS

Tips on Preventing Employee Fraud in Small Companies

- Do not have the same employee write company checks and keep the books. Look for payments to vendors you don't know or payments to vendors whose names appear to be misspelled.

- If your business has a computer system, restrict access to accounting files as much as possible. Also, keep a backup copy of your accounting files and store it at an off-site location.

- Be wary of anybody working in finance that declines to take vacations. They may be afraid that a replacement will uncover fraud.

- Require and monitor supporting documentation (such as vendor invoices) before signing checks.

- Track the number of credit card bills you sign monthly.

- Limit and monitor access to important documents and supplies, such as blank checks and signature stamps.

- Check W-2 forms against your payroll annually to make sure you're not carrying any fictitious employees.

- Rely on yourself, not on your accountant, to spot fraud.

Source: Steve Kaufman, "Embezzlement Common at Small Companies," Knight-Ridder Newspapers, reported in *Athens Daily News/Athens Banner-Herald*, March 10, 1996, p. 4D.

Competent Personnel, Rotating Duties, and Mandatory Vacations   The successful operation of an accounting system requires procedures to ensure that people are able to perform the duties to which they are assigned. Hence, it is necessary that all accounting employees be adequately trained and supervised in performing their jobs. It may also be advisable to rotate duties of clerical personnel and mandate vacations for nonclerical personnel. These policies encourage employees to adhere to prescribed procedures. In addition, existing errors or fraud may be detected. For example, numerous cases of employee fraud have been discovered after a long-term employee, who never took vacations, missed work because of an illness or other unavoidable reasons.

To illustrate, consider the case where a bank officer who was not required to take vacations stole approximately $5 million over 16 years by printing fake certificates of deposit. The officer would then issue the fake certificate to the customer and pocket the customer's money. After discovering the theft, the bank began requiring all employees to take vacations.

Separating Responsibilities for Related Operations   To decrease the possibility of inefficiency, errors, and fraud, the responsibility for related operations should be divided among two or more persons. For example, the responsibilities for purchasing, receiving, and paying for computer supplies should be divided among three persons or departments. If the same person orders supplies, verifies the receipt of the supplies, and pays the supplier, the following abuses are possible:

1. Orders may be placed on the basis of friendship with a supplier, rather than on price, quality, and other objective factors.
2. The quantity and quality of supplies received may not be verified, thus causing payment for supplies not received or poor-quality supplies.
3. Supplies may be stolen by the employee.
4. The validity and accuracy of invoices may be verified carelessly, thus causing the payment of false or inaccurate invoices.

The "checks and balances" provided by dividing responsibilities among various departments requires no duplication of effort. The business documents prepared by one department are designed to coordinate with and support those prepared by other departments.

To illustrate, consider the case where an accounts payable clerk created false invoices and submitted them for payment. The clerk obtained the resulting checks, opened a bank account, and cashed the checks under an assumed name. The clerk was able to steal thousands of dollars because no one was required to approve the payments other than the accounts payable clerk.

Separating Operations, Custody of Assets, and Accounting   Control policies should establish the responsibilities for various business activities. To reduce the possibility of errors and fraud, the responsibilities for operations, custody of assets, and accounting should be separated. The accounting records then serve as an independent check on the individuals who have custody of the assets and who engage in the business operations. For example, the employees entrusted with handling cash receipts from credit customers should not record cash receipts in the accounting records. To do so would allow employees to borrow or steal cash and hide the theft in the records. Likewise, if those engaged in operating activities also record the results of operations, they could distort the accounting reports to show favorable results. For example, a store manager whose year-end bonus is based upon operating profits might be tempted to record fictitious sales in order to receive a larger bonus.

To illustrate, consider the case where a payroll clerk was responsible for preparing the payroll and distributing the payroll checks. The clerk stole almost $40,000 over two months by preparing duplicate payroll checks and checks for fictitious part-time employees. After the theft was detected, the duties of preparing payroll checks and distributing payroll checks were assigned to separate employees.

Proofs and Security Measures   Proofs and security measures should be used to safeguard assets and ensure reliable accounting data. This control procedure applies to many different techniques, such as authorization, approval, and reconciliation procedures. For example, employees who travel on company business may be required to obtain a department manager's approval on a travel request form.

Other examples of control procedures include the use of bank accounts and other measures to ensure the safety of cash and valuable documents. A cash register that displays the amount recorded for each sale and provides the customer a printed receipt can be an effective part of the internal control structure. An all-night convenience store could use the following security measures to deter robberies:

1. Locate the cash register near the door, so that it is fully visible from outside the store; have two employees work late hours; employ a security guard.
2. Deposit cash in the bank daily, before 5 p.m.
3. Keep only small amounts of cash on hand after 5 p.m. by depositing excess cash in a store safe that can't be opened by employees on duty.
4. Install cameras and alarm systems.

To illustrate, consider the case where someone stole thousands of dollars in parking fines from a small town. Citizens would pay their parking fines by placing money in ticket envelopes and putting them in a locked box outside the town hall. The key to the locked box was not safeguarded and was readily available to a variety of people. As

INTEGRITY, OBJECTIVITY, AND ETHICS IN BUSINESS

The Theft at Perini Corporation

The financial vice president of **Perini Corporation** received a disturbing call from one of the company's banks. The bank reported that Perini's bank account was substantially overdrawn. Perini, a large construction company based near Boston, had never overdrawn any of its bank accounts in over twenty-five years. Shortly thereafter, another of Perini's banks called and reported that its Perini account was also overdrawn. A review of the recent bank statements, which had been lying around unreconciled for two weeks, revealed canceled checks of more than $1.1 million that had not been recorded.

Perini kept its unused checks in an unlocked room. Perini also kept its supply of coffee cups in the same room, where every clerk and secretary had access to them. A quick review revealed two missing boxes of checks.

Perini used a checkwriting machine that automatically signed the vice president's name. Unfortunately, Perini didn't implement the controls suggested by its accountant. Instead, the machine-processed checks were placed in an unlocked box, there was no reconciliation of the counter on the machine with the number of checks that should have been written, and the keys to lock the machine were not carefully safeguarded. The vice president said that such controls were "too much trouble," even though one purpose of controls is to help insure integrity in business. Whoever stole the money was never discovered.

a result, the person who stole the money was never discovered. The town later gave one person the responsibility of safeguarding the key and emptying the locked box.

Monitoring

Monitoring the internal control system locates weaknesses and improves control effectiveness. The internal control system can be monitored either through ongoing efforts by management or by separate evaluations. Ongoing monitoring efforts may include observing both employee behavior and warning signs from the accounting system. The indicators shown in Exhibit 4 may be clues to internal control problems.[6]

Separate monitoring evaluations are generally performed when there are major changes in strategy, senior management, business structure, or operations. In large businesses, internal auditors who are independent of operations normally are responsible for monitoring the internal control system. Internal auditors can report issues and concerns to an audit committee of the board of directors, who are independent of management. In addition, external auditors also evaluate internal control as a normal part of their annual financial statement audit.

Information and Communication

Information and communication are essential elements of internal control. Information about the control environment, risk assessment, control procedures, and monitoring is needed by management to guide operations and ensure compliance with reporting, legal, and regulatory requirements. Management can also use external information to assess events and conditions that impact decision making and external reporting. For example, management uses information from the Financial Accounting Standards Board (FASB) to assess the impact of possible changes in reporting standards.

[6]Edwin C. Bliss, "Employee Theft," *Boardroom Reports*, July 15, 1994, pp. 5–6.

EXHIBIT 4   *Indicators of Internal Control Problems*

CLUES TO POTENTIAL PROBLEMS

Warning signs with regard to people

1. Abrupt change in lifestyle (without winning the lottery).
2. Close social relationships with suppliers.
3. Refusing to take a vacation.
4. Frequent borrowing from other employees.
5. Excessive use of alcohol or drugs.

Warning signs from the accounting system

1. Missing documents or gaps in transaction numbers (could mean documents are being used for fraudulent transactions).
2. An unusual increase in customer refunds (refunds may be phony).
3. Differences between daily cash receipts and bank deposits (could mean receipts are being pocketed before being deposited).
4. Sudden increase in slow payments (employee may be pocketing the payment).
5. Backlog in recording transactions (possibly an attempt to delay detection of fraud).

Obj **3**

Describe and illustrate the application of internal controls to cash.

Cash Controls over Receipts and Payments

Cash includes coins, currency (paper money), checks, money orders, and money on deposit that is available for unrestricted withdrawal from banks and other financial institutions. Normally, you can think of cash as anything that a bank would accept for deposit in your account. For example, a check made payable to you could normally be deposited in a bank and thus is considered cash.

We will assume in this chapter that a business maintains only *one* bank account, represented in the ledger as *Cash*. In practice, however, a business may have several bank accounts, such as one for general cash payments and another for payroll. For each of its bank accounts, the business will maintain a ledger account, one of which may be called *Cash in Bank—First Bank*, for example. It will also maintain separate ledger accounts for special-purpose cash funds, such as travel reimbursements. We will introduce some of these other cash accounts later in this chapter.

Because of the ease with which money can be transferred, cash is the asset most likely to be diverted and used improperly by employees. In addition, many transactions either directly or indirectly affect the receipt or the payment of cash. Businesses must therefore design and use controls that safeguard cash and control the authorization of cash transactions. In the following paragraphs, we will discuss these controls.

Control of Cash Receipts

To protect cash from theft and misuse, a business must control cash from the time it is received until it is deposited in a bank. Businesses normally receive cash from two main sources: (1) customers purchasing products or services and (2) customers making payments on account. For example, fast-food restaurants, such as **McDonald's**, **Wendy's**, and **Burger King**, receive cash primarily from over-the-counter sales to customers. Mail-order and Internet retailers, such as **Lands' End**, **Orvis**, **L.L. Bean**, and **Amazon.com**, receive cash primarily through electronic funds transfers from credit card companies.

Cash Received from Cash Sales   Regardless of the source of cash receipts, every business must properly safeguard and record its cash receipts. One of the most important controls to protect cash received in over-the-counter sales is a cash register. When a clerk (cashier) enters the amount of a sale, the cash register normally displays the amount. This is a control to ensure that the clerk has charged you the correct amount. You also receive a receipt to verify the accuracy of the amount.

At the beginning of a work shift, each cash register clerk is given a cash drawer that contains a predetermined amount of cash for making change for customers. The amount in each drawer is sometimes called a *change fund*. At the end of the shift, the clerk and the supervisor count the cash in that clerk's cash drawer. The amount of cash in each drawer should equal the beginning amount of cash plus the cash sales for the day. However, errors in recording cash sales or errors in making change cause the amount of cash on hand to differ from this amount. Such differences are recorded in a **cash short and over account**.

At the end of the accounting period, a negative balance in the cash short and over account is included in Miscellaneous Expense in the income statement. A positive balance is included in the Other Income section. If a clerk consistently has significant cash short and over amounts, the supervisor may require the clerk to take additional training.

HOW BUSINESSES MAKE MONEY

The Lion King

How many ways does **The Walt Disney Company** earn revenues from *The Lion King*?

The answer includes ticket sales for the animated motion picture and any sequels, DVD sales, music soundtrack sales, ticket sales for the Broadway play, tickets and concession sales for Disney on Ice®, merchandise and apparel sales, theme park attractions, cable television programming, and video game sales—to name just a few. Disney's business approach is to develop a character, such as the Lion King, and then develop multiple ways to earn revenues from this key asset. Often, Disney will develop new channels of distribution in order to

support the breadth of product offshoots, such as a cable channel, merchandise store, Broadway theater, or theme park.

Overall, the preceding approach has been very successful in earning money for Disney. However, this approach is based on continual development of new characters from which to build a product universe. This is Disney's key challenge as it moves toward the world of computer animation.

Source: Adrian J. Slywotzky, David J. Morrison, and Bob Andelman, *The Profit Zone: How Strategic Business Design Will Lead You to Tomorrow's Profits* (New York: Random House, 1997).

After a cash register clerk's cash has been counted and recorded on a memorandum form, the cash is then placed in a store safe in the Cashier's Department until it can be deposited in the bank. The supervisor forwards the clerk's cash register receipts to the Accounting Department, where they serve as the basis for recording the transactions for the day as shown below.

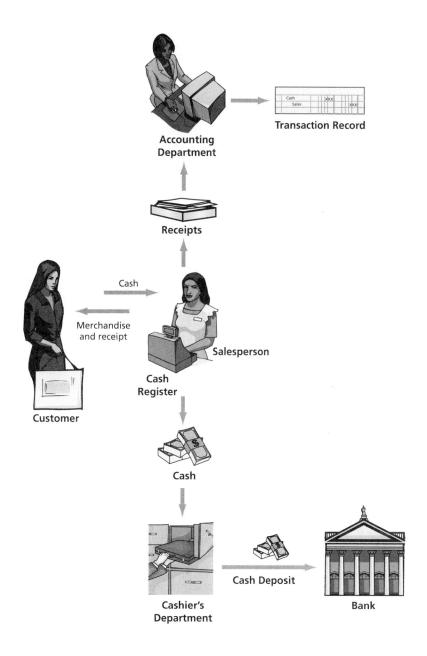

Some retail companies use debit card systems to transfer and record the receipt of cash. In a debit card system, a customer pays for goods at the time of purchase by presenting a plastic card. The card authorizes the electronic transfer of cash from the customer's checking account to the retailer's bank account.

Cash Received in the Mail　　Cash is received in the mail when customers pay their bills. This cash is usually in the form of checks and money orders. Most companies' invoices are designed so that customers return a portion of the invoice, called a *remittance advice,* with their payment. The employee who opens the incoming mail should initially compare the amount of cash received with the amount shown on the remittance advice. If a customer does not return a remittance advice, an employee prepares one. Like the cash register, the remittance advice serves as a record of cash initially received. It also helps ensure that the posting to the customer's account is accurate. Finally, as a control, the employee opening the mail normally also stamps checks and money orders "For Deposit Only" in the bank account of the business.

All cash received in the mail is sent to the Cashier's Department. An employee there combines it with the receipts from cash sales and prepares a bank deposit ticket. The remittance advices and their summary totals are delivered to the Accounting Department. An accounting clerk then prepares the records of the transactions and posts them to the customer accounts.

When cash is deposited in the bank, the bank normally stamps a duplicate copy of the deposit ticket with the amount received. This bank receipt is returned to the Accounting Department, where a clerk compares the receipt with the total amount that should have been deposited. This control helps ensure that all the cash is deposited and that no cash is lost or stolen on the way to the bank. Any shortages are thus promptly detected.

Separating the duties of the Cashier's Department, which handles cash, and the Accounting Department, which records cash, is a control. If Accounting Department employees both handle and record cash, an employee could steal cash and change the accounting records to hide the theft.

Cash Received by EFT　　Cash may also be received from customers through **electronic funds transfers (EFTs)**. For example, customers may authorize automatic electronic transfers from their checking accounts to pay monthly bills for such items as cell phone, cable, Internet, and electric services. In such cases, the company sends the customer's bank a signed form from the customer authorizing the monthly electronic transfers from the customer's checking account to the company's bank account. Each month, the company electronically notifies the customer's bank of the amount of the transfer and the date the transfer should take place. On the due date, the company records the electronic transfer as a receipt of cash to its bank account and posts the amount paid to the customer's account.

Most companies encourage automatic electronic transfers by customers for several reasons. First, electronic transfers are less costly than receiving cash payments through the mail since the employee handling of cash is eliminated. Second, electronic transfers enhance internal controls over cash since the cash is received directly by the bank without the handling of cash by employees. Thus, potential theft of cash is eliminated. Finally, electronic transfers reduce late payments from customers and speed up the processing of cash receipts.

Control of Cash Payments

The control of cash payments should provide reasonable assurance that payments are made for only authorized transactions. In addition, controls should ensure that cash is used efficiently. For example, controls should ensure that all available discounts, such as purchase discounts, are taken.

In a small business, an owner/manager may authorize payments based upon personal knowledge of goods and services purchased. In a large business, however, the duties of purchasing goods, inspecting the goods received, and verifying the invoices are usually performed by different employees. These duties must be coordinated to ensure that checks for proper payments are made to creditors. One system used for this purpose is the voucher system.

Voucher System   A **voucher system** is a set of procedures for authorizing and recording liabilities and cash payments. A **voucher** is any document that serves as proof of authority to pay cash or issue an electronic funds transfer. For example, an invoice properly approved for payment could be considered a voucher. In many businesses, however, a voucher is a special form for recording relevant data about a liability and the details of its payment.

A voucher is normally prepared after all necessary supporting documents have been received. For example, when a voucher is prepared for the purchase of goods, the voucher should be supported by the supplier's invoice, a purchase order, and a receiving report. After a voucher is prepared, it is submitted to the proper manager for approval. Once approved, the voucher is recorded in the accounts and filed by due date. Upon payment, the voucher is recorded in the same manner as the payment of an account payable.

A voucher system may be either manual or computerized. In a computerized system, properly approved supporting documents (such as purchase orders and receiving reports) would be entered directly into computer files. At the due date, the checks would be automatically generated and mailed to creditors. At that time, the voucher would be automatically transferred to a paid voucher file.

Cash Paid by EFT   Cash can also be paid by electronic funds transfer systems by using computers rather than paper money or checks. For example, a company may pay its employees by means of EFT. Under such a system, employees may authorize the deposit of their payroll checks directly into checking accounts. Each pay period, the business electronically transfers the employees' net pay to their checking accounts through the use of computer systems and networks. Likewise, many companies are using EFT systems to pay their suppliers and other vendors.

Electronic funds payments are also becoming more widely accepted by individuals. For example, **TeleCheck Services Inc.**, and PayPal offer online real-time check payment options for purchases made over the Internet. "It is apparent from the rapid growth of online sales that many consumers are as comfortable writing checks for Internet purchases as they are at their local brick-and-mortar store," explains the chief executive officer of TeleCheck.

Bank Accounts

Obj 4
Describe the nature of a bank account and its use in controlling cash.

Most of you are familiar with bank accounts. You probably have a checking account at a local bank, credit union, savings and loan association, or other financial institution. In this section, we discuss the use of bank accounts by businesses. We then discuss the use of bank accounts as an additional control over cash.

Use of Bank Accounts

A business often maintains several bank accounts. For example, a business with several branches or retail outlets such as *Sears* or *The Gap Inc.* will often maintain a bank account for each location. In addition, businesses usually maintain a separate bank account for payroll and other special purposes.

A major reason that businesses use bank accounts is for control purposes. Use of bank accounts reduces the amount of cash on hand at any one time. For example, many merchandise businesses deposit cash receipts twice daily to reduce the amount of cash on hand that is susceptible to theft. Likewise, using a payroll account allows for paying employees by check or electronic funds transfer rather than by distributing a large amount of cash each payroll period.

In addition to reducing the amount of cash on hand, bank accounts provide an independent recording of cash transactions that can be used as a verification of the business's recording of transactions. That is, the use of bank accounts provides a double recording of cash transactions. The company's cash account corresponds to the bank's liability (deposit) account for the company. As we will discuss and illustrate in the next section, this double recording of cash transactions allows for a reconciliation of the cash account on the company's records with the cash balance recorded by the bank.

Finally, the use of bank accounts facilitates the transfer of funds. For example, electronic funds transfer systems require bank accounts for the transfer of funds between companies. Within a company, cash can be transferred between bank accounts through the use of wire transfers. In addition, online banking allows companies to transfer funds and pay bills electronically as well as monitor their cash balances on a real-time basis.

Bank Statement

Banks usually maintain a record of all checking account transactions. A summary of all transactions, called a **bank statement**, is mailed to the depositor or made available online, usually each month. Like any account with a customer or a creditor, the bank statement shows the beginning balance, additions, deductions, and the balance at the end of the period. A typical bank statement is shown in Exhibit 5.

The depositor's checks or copies of the checks received by the bank during the period may accompany the bank statement, arranged in order of payment. If paid checks are returned, they are stamped "Paid," together with the date of payment. Many banks no longer return checks or check copies with bank statements. Instead, the check payment information is available online. Other entries that the bank has made in the depositor's account are described as debit or credit memorandums on the statement.

The depositor's checking account balance *in the bank records* is a liability. A credit memorandum entry on the bank statement indicates an increase in the depositor's account. Likewise, a debit memorandum entry on the bank statement indicates a decrease in the depositor's account. This relationship is shown in the illustration on page 182.

A bank increases the depositor's account (liability) by issuing credit memoranda for deposits made by electronic funds transfer, for collections of notes receivable for the depositor, for proceeds for a loan to the depositor, for interest earned on the depositor's

EXHIBIT 5   *Bank Statement*

MEMBER FDIC   PAGE   1

VALLEY NATIONAL BANK   ACCOUNT NUMBER   1627042
OF LOS ANGELES
                                      FROM 6/30/09   TO 7/31/09
LOS ANGELES, CA 90020-4253   **(310)555-5151**
                                      BALANCE   4,218.60

                                   22 DEPOSITS   13,749.75

        POWER NETWORKING   52 WITHDRAWALS   14,698.57
        1000 Belkin Street
        Los Angeles, CA 90014-1000 3 OTHER DEBITS
                                      AND CREDITS   90.00CR

                                      NEW BALANCE   3,359.78

* – – CHECKS AND OTHER DEBITS – – – * – – – DEPOSITS – – * – – DATE – – * – – BALANCE – – *					
819.40	122.54		585.75	07/01	3,862.41
369.50	732.26	20.15	421.53	07/02	3,162.03
600.00	190.70	52.50	781.30	07/03	3,100.13
25.93	160.00		662.50	07/05	3,576.70
921.20	NSF 300.00		503.18	07/07	2,858.68
32.26	535.09		ACH 932.00	07/29	3,404.40
21.10	126.20		705.21	07/30	3,962.31
	SC 18.00		MS 408.00	07/30	4,352.31
26.12	ACH 1,615.13		648.72	07/31	3,359.78

        EC — ERROR CORRECTION   ACH — AUTOMATED CLEARING HOUSE
        MS — MISCELLANEOUS
        NSF — NOT SUFFICIENT FUNDS   SC — SERVICE CHARGE

        * * *   * * *   * * *

        THE RECONCILEMENT OF THIS STATEMENT WITH YOUR RECORDS IS ESSENTIAL.
        ANY ERROR OR EXCEPTION SHOULD BE REPORTED IMMEDIATELY.

account, and to correct bank errors. A bank decreases the depositor's account (liability) by issuing debit memoranda for payments made by electronic funds transfer, for service charges, for customers' checks returned for not sufficient funds, and to correct bank errors.

Customers' checks returned for not sufficient funds, called *NSF checks*, are checks that were initially deposited but were not paid when they were presented to the customer's bank for payment. Since the bank initially increased the depositor's account when the check was deposited, the bank decreases the depositor's account by a debit memorandum when the check is returned without payment. We discuss the accounting for NSF checks later in this chapter.

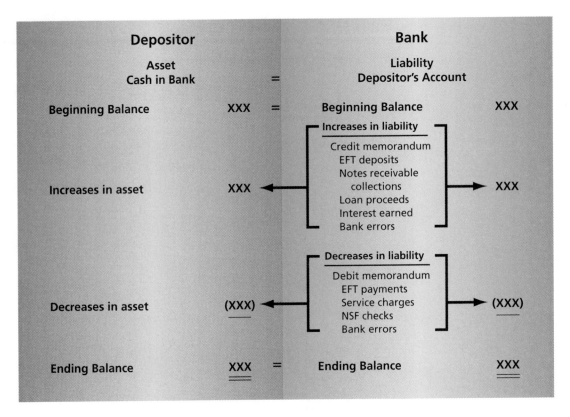

The reason for a credit or debit memorandum is indicated on the bank statement. For example, Exhibit 5 identifies the following types of credit and debit memorandum entries:

EC — Error correction to correct bank error.
NSF — Not sufficient funds check.
SC — Service charge.
ACH — Automated Clearing House entry for electronic funds transfer.
MS — Miscellaneous item such as collection of a note receivable on behalf of the depositor or receipt of loan proceeds by the depositor from the bank.

In the preceding list, we have included the notation "ACH" for electronic funds transfers. ACH is a network for clearing electronic funds transfers among individuals, companies, and banks.[7] Because electronic funds transfers may be either deposits or payments, ACH entries may indicate either an increase in or a decrease to the depositor's account. Likewise, entries to correct bank errors and miscellaneous items may indicate an increase in or a decrease to the depositor's account.

Bank Accounts as a Control over Cash

As we mentioned earlier, a bank account is one of the primary tools a company uses to control cash. For example, companies often require that all cash receipts be initially deposited in a bank account. Likewise, companies usually use checks or bank account transfers to make all cash payments, except for very small amounts. When such a system is used, there is a double record of cash transactions—one by the company and the other by the bank.

[7]For further information on ACH, see **http://www.nacha.org/About/** and click on "What is ACH?"

A company can use a bank statement to compare the cash transactions recorded in its accounting records to those recorded by the bank. The cash balance shown by a bank statement is usually different from the cash balance shown in the accounting records of the company, as shown in Exhibit 6.

EXHIBIT 6   *Power Networking's Records and Bank Statement*

Bank Statement		
Beginning Balance		$ 4,218.60
Additions:		
Deposits	$ 13,749.75	
Miscellaneous	408.00	14,157.75
Deductions:		
Checks	$14,698.57	
NSF Check	300	
Service Charge	18	15,016.57
Ending Balance		$ 3,359.78

Power Networking Records	
Beginning Balance	$ 4,227.60
Deposits	14,565.95
Checks	16,243.56
Ending Balance	$ 2,549.99

Power Networking should determine the reason for the difference in these two amounts.

This difference in the two cash balances may be the result of a delay by either party in recording transactions. For example, there is a time lag of one day or more between the date a check is written and the date that it is presented to the bank for payment. If the company mails deposits to the bank or uses the night depository, a time lag between the date of the deposit and the date that it is recorded by the bank is also probable. The bank may also increase or decrease the company's account for transactions about which the company will not be informed until later.

The difference may be the result of errors made by either the company or the bank in recording transactions. For example, the company may incorrectly post to Cash a check written for $4,500 as $450. Likewise, a bank may incorrectly record the amount of a check.

INTEGRITY, OBJECTIVITY, AND ETHICS IN BUSINESS

Check Fraud

Check fraud involves counterfeiting, altering, or otherwise manipulating the information on checks in order to fraudulently cash a check. According to the **National Check Fraud Center**, check fraud and counterfeiting are among the fastest growing problems affecting the financial system, generating over $10 billion in losses annually. Criminals perpetrate the fraud by taking blank checks from your checkbook, finding a canceled check in the garbage, or removing a check you have mailed to pay bills. Consumers can prevent check fraud by carefully storing blank checks, placing outgoing mail in postal mailboxes, and shredding canceled checks.

Obj 5

Describe and illustrate the
use of a bank reconciliation
in controlling cash.

Bank Reconciliation

For effective control, the reasons for the difference between the cash balance on the bank statement and the cash balance in the accounting records should be analyzed by preparing a bank reconciliation. A **bank reconciliation** is an analysis of the items and amounts that cause the cash balance reported in the bank statement to differ from the balance of the cash account in the ledger in order to determine the adjusted cash balance.

A bank reconciliation is usually divided into two sections. The first section, referred to as the bank section, begins with the cash balance according to the bank statement and ends with the adjusted balance. The second section, referred to as the company section, begins with the cash balance according to the company's records and ends with the adjusted balance. The two amounts designated as the adjusted balance must be equal. The content of the bank reconciliation is shown below.

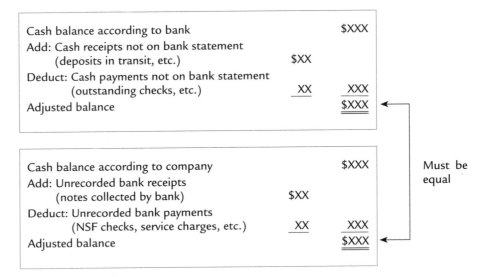

Cash balance according to bank		$XXX
Add: Cash receipts not on bank statement		
(deposits in transit, etc.)	$XX	
Deduct: Cash payments not on bank statement		
(outstanding checks, etc.)	XX	XXX
Adjusted balance		$XXX

Cash balance according to company		$XXX
Add: Unrecorded bank receipts		
(notes collected by bank)	$XX	
Deduct: Unrecorded bank payments		
(NSF checks, service charges, etc.)	XX	XXX
Adjusted balance		$XXX

Must be equal

The following steps are useful in finding the reconciling items and determining the adjusted balance of Cash:

1. Compare each deposit listed on the bank statement with unrecorded deposits appearing in the preceding period's reconciliation and with the current period's deposits. *Add deposits not recorded by the bank to the balance according to the bank statement.*
2. Compare paid checks with outstanding checks appearing on the preceding period's reconciliation and with recorded checks. *Deduct checks outstanding that have not been paid by the bank from the balance according to the bank statement.*
3. Compare bank credit memorandums to recorded cash receipts. For example, a bank would issue a credit memorandum for a note receivable and interest that it collected for a company. *Add credit memorandums that have not been recorded to the balance according to the company's records.*
4. Compare bank debit memorandums to recorded cash payments. For example, a bank normally issues debit memorandums for service charges and check printing charges. A bank also issues debit memorandums for not sufficient funds checks. NSF checks are normally charged back to the customer as an account receivable. *Deduct debit memorandums that have not been recorded from the balance according to the company's records.*

5. List any errors discovered during the preceding steps. For example, if an amount has been recorded incorrectly by the company, the amount of the error should be added to or deducted from the cash balance according to the company's records. Similarly, errors by the bank should be added to or deducted from the cash balance according to the bank statement.

To illustrate a bank reconciliation, we will use the bank statement for Power Networking in Exhibit 5. This bank statement shows a balance of $3,359.78 as of July 31. The cash balance in Power Networking's ledger as of the same date is $2,549.99. The following reconciling items are revealed by using the steps as outlined above:

Deposit of July 31, not recorded on bank statement	$ 816.20
Checks outstanding: No. 812, $1,061.00; No. 878, $435.39; No. 883, $48.60	1,544.99
Customer's note plus interest of $8 collected by bank (credit memorandum), not recorded	408.00
Check from customer (Thomas Ivey) returned by bank because of insufficient funds (NSF)	300.00
Bank service charges (debit memorandum), not recorded	18.00
Check No. 879 for $732.26 to Taylor Co. on account, recorded as $723.26	9.00

The bank reconciliation, based on the bank statement and the reconciling items, is shown in Exhibit 7.

EXHIBIT 7   *Bank Reconciliation for Power Networking*

POWER NETWORKING
Bank Reconciliation
July 31, 2009

Cash balance according to bank statement		$3,359.78
Add deposit of July 31, not recorded by bank		816.20
		$4,175.98
Deduct outstanding checks:		
No. 812	$1,061.00	
No. 878	435.39	
No. 883	48.60	1,544.99
Adjusted balance		$2,630.99 ←
Cash balance according to Power Networking records		$2,549.99
Add note and interest collected by bank		408.00
		$2,957.99
Deduct: Check returned because of insufficient funds	$ 300.00	
Bank service charge	18.00	
Error in recording Check No. 879	9.00	327.00
Adjusted balance		$2,630.99 ←

No adjustments are necessary on the company's records as a result of the information included in the bank section of the reconciliation. This section begins with the cash balance according to the bank statement. However, the bank should be notified of any errors that need to be corrected on its records.

Any items in the company's section of the bank reconciliation must be recorded in the company's accounts. For example, adjustments should be recorded for any unrecorded bank memorandums and any company errors. The effects of the adjustments on the accounts and financial statements of Power Networking, based on the preceding bank reconciliation, are as follows:

Statement of Cash Flows	Balance Sheet						Income Statement
	Assets		=	Liabilities	+	Stockholders' Equity	
	Cash	+	Notes Receivable =		+	Retained Earnings	
July 31.	408		−400			8	July 31.

Statement of Cash Flows			Income Statement	
July 31. Operating	408		July 31. Interest income	8

Statement of Cash Flows	Balance Sheet						Income Statement
	Assets		=	Liabilities	+	Stockholders' Equity	
	Cash	+	Accounts Receivable =	Accounts Payable	+	Retained Earnings	
July 31.	−327		300	−9		−18	July 31.

Statement of Cash Flows			Income Statement	
July 31. Operating	−327		July 31. Misc. expense	−18

After the preceding adjustments have been recorded, the cash account will have a balance of $2,630.99. This balance agrees with the adjusted cash balance shown on the bank reconciliation. This is the amount of cash available as of July 31 and the amount that would be reported on Power Networking's July 31 balance sheet.

Although businesses may reconcile their bank accounts in a slightly different format from what we described above, the objective is the same: to control cash by reconciling

INTEGRITY, OBJECTIVITY, AND ETHICS IN BUSINESS

Bank Error in Your Favor

You may sometime have a bank error in your favor, such as a misposted deposit. Such errors are not a case of "found money," as in the Monopoly® game. Bank control systems quickly discover most errors and make automatic adjustments. Even so, you have a legal responsibility to report the error and return the money to the bank.

the company's records to the records of an independent outside source, the bank. In doing so, any errors or misuse of cash may be detected.

For effective control, the bank reconciliation should be prepared by an employee who does not take part in or record cash transactions. When these duties are not properly separated, mistakes are likely to occur, and it is more likely that cash will be stolen or otherwise misapplied. For example, an employee who takes part in all of these duties could prepare and cash an unauthorized check, omit it from the accounts, and omit it from the reconciliation.

Obj **6**

Special-Purpose Cash Funds

Describe the accounting for special-purpose cash funds.

It is usually not practical for a business to write checks to pay small amounts, such as postage. Yet, these small payments may occur often enough to add up to a significant total amount. Thus, it is desirable to control such payments. For this purpose, a special cash fund, called a **petty cash fund**, is used.

A petty cash fund is established by first estimating the amount of cash needed for payments from the fund during a period, such as a week or a month. After necessary approvals, a check is written and cashed for this amount. The money obtained from cashing the check is then given to an employee, called the petty cash custodian, who is authorized to disburse monies from the fund. For control purposes, the company may place restrictions on the maximum amount and the types of payments that can be made from the fund. Each time monies are paid from petty cash, the custodian records the details of the payment on a petty cash receipt form.

The petty cash fund is normally replenished at periodic intervals or when it is depleted or reaches a minimum amount. When a petty cash fund is replenished, the accounts are adjusted by summarizing the petty cash receipts. A check is then written for this amount, payable to petty cash.

To illustrate normal petty cash fund entries, assume that a petty cash fund of $500 is established on August 1. The effect on the accounts and financial statements of recording this transaction is as follows:

Statement of Cash Flows	Balance Sheet						Income Statement
	Assets		=	Liabilities	+	Stockholders' Equity	
	Cash	+	Petty Cash	=			
Aug. 1.	−500		500				

At the end of August, the petty cash receipts indicate expenditures for the following items: office supplies, $380; postage (office supplies), $22; store supplies, $35; and miscellaneous administrative expense, $30. The effect on the accounts and financial statements of replenishing the petty cash fund on August 31 is as follows:

Statement of Cash Flows	Balance Sheet							Income Statement
	Assets				=	Liabilities +	Stockholders' Equity	
	Cash	+	Office Supplies	+	Store Supplies	=	+	Retained Earnings	
Aug. 31.	−467		402		35			−30	Aug. 31.

Statement of Cash Flows		Income Statement	
Aug. 31. Operating	−467	Aug. 31. Misc. admin. expense	−30

Replenishing the petty cash fund restores it to its original amount of $500. You should note that there is no adjustment to Petty Cash when the fund is replenished. Petty Cash is adjusted only if the amount of the fund is later increased or decreased.

In addition, businesses often use other cash funds to meet special needs, such as travel expenses for salespersons. For example, each salesperson might be given $200 for travel-related expenses. Periodically, the salesperson submits a detailed expense report and the travel funds are replenished. Also, as we discussed earlier in this chapter, retail businesses use change funds for making change for customers. Finally, most businesses use a payroll bank account to pay employees. Such cash funds are called **special-purpose funds**.

A special-purpose cash fund is initially established by first estimating the amount of cash needed for payments from the fund during a period, such as a week or a month. After necessary approvals, a check is written and cashed for this amount. The money obtained from cashing the check is then given to an employee, called the custodian, who is authorized to disburse monies from the fund. For control purposes, the company may place restrictions on the maximum amount and the types of payments that can be made from the fund.

Financial Statement Reporting of Cash

Obj 7

Describe and illustrate the reporting of cash and cash equivalents in the financial statements.

Cash is the most liquid asset, and therefore it is listed as the first asset in the Current Assets section of the balance sheet. Most companies present only a single cash amount on the balance sheet by combining all their bank and cash fund accounts.

A company may have cash in excess of its operating needs. In such cases, the company normally invests in highly liquid investments in order to earn interest. These investments are called **cash equivalents**.[8] Examples of cash equivalents include U.S. Treasury Bills, notes issued by major corporations (referred to as commercial paper), and money market funds. Companies that have invested excess cash in cash equivalents usually report *Cash and cash equivalents* as one amount on the balance sheet.

To illustrate, **Microsoft Corp**. disclosed the details of its cash and cash equivalents in the notes to its financial statements as follows:

---

[8]To be classified a cash equivalent, according to FASB Statement 95, the investment is expected to be converted to cash within 90 days.

(in millions)	June 30, 2007	June 30, 2006
Cash and cash equivalents:		
Cash	$3,040	$3,248
Money market mutual funds	132	288
Commercial paper	179	3,150
U.S. government and agency securities	1	14
Corporate notes and bonds	2,425	—
Municipal securities	334	14
	$6,111	$6,714

Banks may require companies to maintain minimum cash balances in their bank accounts. Such a balance is called a *compensating balance*. This requirement is often imposed by the bank as a part of a loan agreement or line of credit. A *line of credit* is a preapproved amount the bank is willing to lend to a customer upon request. If significant, compensating balance requirements should be disclosed in notes to the financial statements.

Key Points

1. **Describe the Sarbanes-Oxley Act of 2002 and its impact on internal controls and financial reporting.**

   The purpose of the Sarbanes-Oxley Act of 2002 is to restore public confidence and trust in the financial statements of companies. Sarbanes-Oxley requires companies to maintain strong and effective internal controls over the recording of transactions and the preparing of financial statements. Sarbanes-Oxley also requires companies and their independent accountants to report on the effectiveness of a company's internal controls.

2. **Describe and illustrate the objectives and elements of internal control.**

   The objectives of internal control are to provide reasonable assurance that (1) assets are safeguarded and used for business purposes, (2) business information is accurate, and (3) laws and regulations are complied with. The elements of internal control are the control environment, risk assessment, control procedures, monitoring, and information and communication.

3. **Describe and illustrate the application of internal controls to cash.**

   One of the most important controls to protect cash received in over-the-counter sales is a cash register. A remittance advice is a control for cash received through the mail. Separating the duties of handling cash and recording cash is also a control. A voucher system is a control system for cash payments that uses a set of procedures for authorizing and recording liabilities and cash payments. Many companies use electronic funds transfers to enhance their control over cash receipts and cash payments.

4. **Describe the nature of a bank account and its use in controlling cash.**

   Businesses use bank accounts as a means of controlling cash. Bank accounts reduce the amount of cash on hand and facilitate the transfer of cash between businesses and locations. In addition, banks send monthly statements to their customers, summarizing all of the transactions for the month. The bank statement allows a business to reconcile the cash transactions recorded in the accounting records to those recorded by the bank.

5. **Describe and illustrate the use of a bank reconciliation in controlling cash.**

The first section of the bank reconciliation begins with the cash balance according to the bank statement. This balance is adjusted for the company's changes in cash that do not appear on the bank statement and for any bank errors. The second section begins with the cash balance according to the company's records. This balance is adjusted for the bank's changes in cash that do not appear on the company's records and for any company errors. The adjusted balances for the two sections must be equal. No adjustments are necessary on the company's records as a result of the information included in the bank section of the bank reconciliation. However, the items in the company section require adjustments on the company's records.

6. **Describe the accounting for special-purpose cash funds.**

Businesses often use special-purpose cash funds, such as a petty cash fund or travel funds, to meet specific needs. Each fund is initially established by cashing a check for the amount of cash needed. The cash is then given to a custodian who is authorized to disburse monies from the fund. At periodic intervals or when it is depleted or reaches a minimum amount, the fund is replenished and the disbursements recorded.

7. **Describe and illustrate the reporting of cash and cash equivalents in the financial statements.**

Cash is listed as the first asset in the Current Assets section of the balance sheet. Companies that have invested excess cash in highly liquid investments usually report *Cash and cash equivalents* on the balance sheet.

Key Terms

Bank reconciliation	Electronic funds transfer (EFT)	Sarbanes-Oxley Act of 2002
Bank statement	Elements of internal control	Special-purpose fund
Cash	Employee fraud	Voucher
Cash equivalents	Internal control	Voucher system
Cash short and over account	Petty cash fund	

Illustrative Problem

The bank statement for Urethane Company for June 30, 2009, indicates a balance of $9,143.11. All cash receipts are deposited each evening in a night depository, after banking hours.

The accounting records indicate the following summary data for cash receipts and payments for June:

Cash balance as of June 1	$ 3,943.50
Total cash receipts for June	28,971.60
Total amount of checks issued in June	28,388.85

Comparing the bank statement and the accompanying canceled checks and memorandums with the records reveals the following reconciling items:

a. The bank had collected for Urethane Company $1,030 on a customer's note left for collection. The face of the note was $1,000.
b. A deposit of $1,852.21, representing receipts of June 30, had been made too late to appear on the bank statement.
c. Checks outstanding totaled $5,265.27.

d. A check drawn for $139 had been incorrectly charged by the bank as $157.
e. A check for $30 returned with the statement had been recorded in the company's records as $240. The check was for the payment of an obligation to Avery Equipment Company for the purchase of office supplies on account.
f. Bank service charges for June amounted to $18.20.

Instructions

1. Prepare a bank reconciliation for June.
2. Record the effects on the accounts and financial statements that should be made by Urethane Company based upon the bank reconciliation.

Solution

1.

URETHANE COMPANY
Bank Reconciliation
June 30, 2009

Cash balance according to bank statement		$ 9,143.11
Add: Deposit of June 30 not recorded by bank	$1,852.21	
Bank error in charging check as $157 instead of $139	18.00	1,870.21
		$11,013.32
Deduct: Outstanding checks		5,265.27
Adjusted balance		$ 5,748.05
Cash balance according to company's records		$ 4,526.25*
Add: Proceeds of note collected by bank, including $30 interest	$1,030.00	
Error in recording check	210.00	1,240.00
		$ 5,766.25
Deduct: Bank service charges		18.20
Adjusted balance		$ 5,748.05

*$3,943.50 + $28,971.60 − $28,388.85

2.

Statement of Cash Flows	Balance Sheet						Income Statement
	Assets		=	Liabilities	+	Stockholders' Equity	
	Cash	+ Notes Receivable	=	Accounts Payable	+	Retained Earnings	
June 30.	1,240.00	−1,000.00		210.00		30.00	June 30.

Statement of Cash Flows		Income Statement	
June 30. Operating	1,240.00	June 30. Interest revenue	30.00

(continued)

Statement of Cash Flows	Balance Sheet						Income Statement
	Assets	=	Liabilities	+	Stockholders' Equity		
	Cash	=		+		Retained Earnings	
June 30.	−18.20					−18.20	June 30.

Statement of Cash Flows			Income Statement	
June 30. Operating	−18.20		June 30. Misc. admin. exp.	−18.20

Self-Examination Questions *(Answers appear at end of chapter.)*

1. Which of the following is *not* an element of internal control?
   A. Control environment
   B. Monitoring
   C. Compliance with laws and regulations
   D. Control procedures

2. The bank erroneously charged Tropical Services' account for $450.50 for a check that was correctly written and recorded by Tropical Services as $540.50. To reconcile the bank account of Tropical Services at the end of the month, you would:
   A. add $90 to the cash balance according to the bank statement.
   B. add $90 to the cash balance according to Tropical Services' records.
   C. deduct $90 from the cash balance according to the bank statement.
   D. deduct $90 from the cash balance according to Tropical Services' records.

3. In preparing a bank reconciliation, the amount of checks outstanding would be:
   A. added to the cash balance according to the bank statement.
   B. deducted from the cash balance according to the bank statement.
   C. added to the cash balance according to the company's records.
   D. deducted from the cash balance according to the company's records.

4. Adjustments to the company's records based on the bank reconciliation are required for:
   A. additions to the cash balance according to the company's records.
   B. deductions from the cash balance according to the company's records.
   C. both A and B.
   D. neither A nor B.

5. A petty cash fund is:
   A. used to pay relatively small amounts.
   B. established by estimating the amount of cash needed for disbursements of relatively small amounts during a specified period.
   C. reimbursed when the amount of money in the fund is reduced to a predetermined minimum amount.
   D. all of the above.

Class Discussion Questions

1. (a) Why did Congress pass the Sarbanes-Oxley Act of 2002? (b) What was the purpose of the Sarbanes-Oxley Act of 2002?

2. Define *internal control*.

3. (a) Name and describe the five elements of internal control. (b) Is any one element of internal control more important than another?

4. How does a policy of rotating clerical employees from job to job aid in strengthening the control procedures within the control environment? Explain.

5. Why should the responsibility for a sequence of related operations be divided among different persons? Explain.

6. Why should the employee who handles cash receipts not have the responsibility for maintaining the accounts receivable records? Explain.

7. In an attempt to improve operating efficiency, one employee was made responsible for all purchasing, receiving, and storing of supplies. Is this organizational change wise from an internal control standpoint? Explain.

8. The ticket seller at a movie theater doubles as a ticket taker for a few minutes each day while the ticket taker is on a break. Which control procedure of a business's system of internal control is violated in this situation?

9. Why should the responsibility for maintaining the accounting records be separated from the responsibility for operations? Explain.

10. Assume that Susan Clayton, accounts payable clerk for Eagle Inc., stole $60,000 by paying fictitious invoices for goods that were never received. The clerk set up accounts in the names of the fictitious companies and cashed the checks at a local bank. Describe a control procedure that would have prevented or detected the fraud.

11. Before a voucher for the purchase of merchandise is approved for payment, supporting documents should be compared to verify the accuracy of the liability. Give an example of a supporting document for the purchase of merchandise.

12. The accounting clerk pays all obligations by prenumbered checks. What are the strengths and weaknesses in the internal control over cash payments in this situation?

13. The balance of Cash is likely to differ from the bank statement balance. What two factors are likely to be responsible for the difference?

14. What is the purpose of preparing a bank reconciliation?

15. Do items reported as a credit memorandum on the bank statement represent (a) additions made by the bank to the company's balance or (b) deductions made by the bank from the company's balance? Explain.

16. Gustafson Inc. has a petty cash fund of $1,500. (a) Since the petty cash fund is only $1,500, should Gustafson Inc. implement controls over petty cash? (b) What controls, if any, could be used for the petty cash fund?

17. (a) How are cash equivalents reported in the financial statements? (b) What are some examples of cash equivalents?

Exercises

E5-1

Sarbanes-Oxley internal control report

Obj 1

Locate a copy of the Sarbanes-Oxley Act of 2002 on the Web. Scan the Act and read Section 404. What does Section 404 require of management's internal control report?

E5-2

Internal controls

Objs 2, 3

Tyler Kirsch has recently been hired as the manager of Dark Canyon Coffee. Dark Canyon Coffee is a national chain of franchised coffee shops. During his first month as store manager, Tyler encountered the following internal control situations:

a. Dark Canyon Coffee has one cash register. Prior to Tyler's joining the coffee shop, each employee working on a shift would take a customer order, accept payment, and then prepare the order. Tyler made one employee on each shift responsible for taking orders and accepting the customer's payment. Other employees prepare the orders.

b. Since only one employee uses the cash register, that employee is responsible for counting the cash at the end of the shift and verifying that the cash in the drawer matches the amount of cash sales recorded by the cash register. Tyler expects each cashier to balance the drawer to the penny *every* time—no exceptions.

c. Tyler caught an employee putting a box of 100 single-serving tea bags in his car. Not wanting to create a scene, Tyler smiled and said, "I don't think you're putting those tea bags on the right shelf. Don't they belong inside the coffee shop?" The employee returned the tea bags to the stockroom.

State whether you agree or disagree with Tyler's method of handling each situation and explain your answer.

E5-3

Internal controls

Objs 2, 3

Rare Earth Clothing is a retail store specializing in women's clothing. The store has established a liberal return policy for the holiday season in order to encourage gift purchases. Any item purchased during November and December may be returned through January 31, with a receipt, for cash or exchange. If the customer does not have a receipt, cash will still be refunded for any item under $100. If the item is more than $100, a check is mailed to the customer.

Whenever an item is returned, a store clerk completes a return slip, which the customer signs. The return slip is placed in a special box. The store manager visits the return counter approximately once every two hours to authorize the return slips. Clerks are instructed to place the returned merchandise on the proper rack on the selling floor as soon as possible.

This year, returns at Rare Earth Clothing have reached an all-time high. There are a large number of returns under $100 without receipts.

a. How can sales clerks employed at Rare Earth Clothing use the store's return policy to steal money from the cash register?
b. What internal control weaknesses do you see in the return policy that make cash thefts easier?
c. Would issuing a store credit in place of a cash refund for all merchandise returned without a receipt reduce the possibility of theft? List some advantages and disadvantages of issuing a store credit in place of a cash refund.
d. Assume that Rare Earth Clothing is committed to the current policy of issuing cash refunds without a receipt. What changes could be made in the store's procedures regarding customer refunds in order to improve internal control?

E5-4

Internal controls for bank lending

Objs 2, 3

First Capone Bank provides loans to businesses in the community through its Commercial Lending Department. Small loans (less than $125,000) may be approved by an individual loan officer, while larger loans (greater than $125,000) must be approved by a board of loan officers. Once a loan is approved, the funds are made available to the loan applicant under agreed-upon terms. The president of First Capone Bank has instituted a policy whereby she has the individual authority to approve loans up to $4,000,000. The president believes that this policy will allow flexibility to approve loans to valued clients much quicker than under the previous policy.

As an internal auditor of First Capone Bank, how would you respond to this change in policy?

E5-5

Internal controls

Objs 2, 3

One of the largest fraud losses in history involved a securities trader for the Singapore office of **Barings Bank**, a British merchant bank. The trader established an unauthorized account number that was used to hide $1.4 billion in losses. Even after Barings' internal auditors noted that the trader both executed trades and recorded them, management did not take action. As a result, a lone individual in a remote office bankrupted an internationally recognized firm overnight.

What general weaknesses in Barings' internal controls contributed to the occurrence and size of the fraud?

E5-6

Internal controls

Objs 2, 3

An employee of **JHT Holdings, Inc.**, a trucking company, was responsible for resolving roadway accident claims under $25,000. The employee created fake accident claims and wrote settlement checks of between $5,000 and $25,000 to friends or acquaintances acting as phony "victims." One friend recruited subordinates at his place of work to cash some of the checks. Beyond this, the JHT employee also recruited lawyers, who he paid to represent both the trucking company and the fake victims in the bogus accident settlements. When the lawyers cashed the checks, they allegedly split the money with the corrupt JHT employee. This fraud went undetected for two years.

Why would it take so long to discover such a fraud?

E5-7

Internal controls

Objs 2, 3

Quality Sound Co. discovered a fraud whereby one of its front office administrative employees used company funds to purchase goods, such as computers, digital cameras, compact disk players, and other electronic items for her own use. The fraud was discovered when employees noticed an increase in delivery frequency from vendors and the use of unusual vendors. After some investigation, it was discovered that the employee would alter the description or change the quantity on an invoice in order to explain the cost on the bill.

What general internal control weaknesses contributed to this fraud?

E5-8

Financial statement fraud

Objs 2, 3

A former chairman, CFO, and controller of **Donnkenny, Inc.**, an apparel company that makes sportswear for Pierre Cardin and Victoria Jones, pleaded guilty to financial statement fraud. These managers used false journal entries to record fictitious sales, hid inventory in public warehouses so that it could be recorded as "sold," and required sales orders to be backdated so that the sale could be moved back to an earlier period. The combined effect of these actions caused $25 million out of $40 million in quarterly sales to be phony.

a. Why might control procedures listed in this chapter be insufficient in stopping this type of fraud?
b. How could this type of fraud be stopped?

E5-9

Internal control of cash receipts

Objs 2, 3

The procedures used for over-the-counter receipts are as follows. At the close of each day's business, the sales clerks count the cash in their respective cash drawers, after which they determine the amount recorded by the cash register and prepare the memorandum cash form, noting any discrepancies. An employee from the cashier's office counts the cash, compares the total with the memorandum, and takes the cash to the cashier's office.

a. Indicate the weak link in internal control.
b. How can the weakness be corrected?

E5-10

Internal control of cash receipts

Objs 2, 3

Amber Meehan works at the drive-through window of Jackpot Burgers. Occasionally, when a drive-through customer orders, Amber fills the order and pockets the customer's money. She does not ring up the order on the cash register.

Identify the internal control weaknesses that exist at Jackpot Burgers, and discuss what can be done to prevent this theft.

E5-11

Internal control of cash receipts

Objs 2, 3

The mailroom employees send all remittances and remittance advices to the cashier. The cashier deposits the cash in the bank and forwards the remittance advices and duplicate deposit slips to the Accounting Department.

a. Indicate the weak link in internal control in the handling of cash receipts.
b. How can the weakness be corrected?

E5-12

Recording cash sales; cash short

Objs 2, 3

The actual cash received from cash sales was $21,099.75, and the amount indicated by the cash register total was $21,114.26.

a. What is the amount deposited in the bank for the day's sales?
b. What is the amount recorded for the day's sales?
c. How should the difference be recorded?
d. If a cashier is consistently over or short, what action should be taken?

E5-13

Recording cash sales; cash over

Objs 2, 3

The actual cash received from cash sales was $8,374.58, and the amount indicated by the cash register total was $8,351.14.

a. What is the amount deposited in the bank for the day's sales?
b. What is the amount recorded for the day's sales?
c. How should the difference be recorded?
d. If a cashier is consistently over or short, what action should be taken?

E5-14

Internal control of cash payments

Objs 2, 3

Paul's Rama Co. is a medium-size merchandising company. An investigation revealed that in spite of a sufficient bank balance, a significant amount of available cash discounts had been lost because of failure to make timely payments. In addition, it was discovered that the invoices for several purchases had been paid twice.

Outline procedures for the payment of vendors' invoices, so that the possibilities of losing available cash discounts and of paying an invoice a second time will be minimized.

E5-15

Internal control of cash payments

Objs 2, 3

Clear Voice Company, a communications equipment manufacturer, recently fell victim to a fraud scheme developed by one of its employees. To understand the scheme, it is necessary to review Clear Voice's procedures for the purchase of services.

The purchasing agent is responsible for ordering services (such as repairs to a photocopy machine or office cleaning) after receiving a service requisition from an authorized manager. However, since no tangible goods are delivered, a receiving report is not prepared. When the Accounting Department receives an invoice billing Clear Voice for a service call, the accounts payable clerk calls the manager who requested the service in order to verify that it was performed.

The fraud scheme involves Dana Foley, the manager of plant and facilities. Dana arranged for her uncle's company, Foley Industrial Supply and Service, to be placed on Clear Voice's approved vendor list. Dana did not disclose the family relationship.

On several occasions, Dana would submit a requisition for services to be provided by Foley Industrial Supply and Service. However, the service requested was really not needed, and it was never performed. Foley would bill Clear Voice for the service and then split the cash payment with Dana.

Explain what changes should be made to Clear Voice's procedures for ordering and paying for services in order to prevent such occurrences in the future.

E5-16

Bank reconciliation

Objs 4, 5

Identify each of the following reconciling items as: (a) an addition to the cash balance according to the bank statement, (b) a deduction from the cash balance according to the bank statement, (c) an addition to the cash balance according to the company's records, or (d) a deduction from the cash balance according to the company's records. (None of the transactions reported by bank debit and credit memoranda have been recorded by the company.)

1. Bank service charges, $48.
2. Outstanding checks, $8,125.50.
3. Deposit in transit, $12,200.
4. Note collected by bank, $8,750.
5. Check drawn by company for $150 but incorrectly recorded as $510.

6. Check for $200 incorrectly charged by bank as $2,000.
7. Check of a customer returned by bank to company because of insufficient funds, $1,200.

E5-17

Entries based on bank reconciliation

Objs 4, 5

Which of the reconciling items listed in Exercise 5-16 are required to be recorded in the company's accounts?

E5-18

Bank reconciliation

Objs 4, 5

✓ Adjusted balance: $8,506.50

The following data were accumulated for use in reconciling the bank account of Spectrum Co. for July:

a. Cash balance according to the company's records at July 31, $8,346.50.
b. Cash balance according to the bank statement at July 31, $9,066.35.
c. Checks outstanding, $3,175.25.
d. Deposit in transit, not recorded by bank, $2,615.40.
e. A check for $240 in payment of an account was erroneously recorded in the check register at $420.
f. Bank debit memorandum for service charges, $20.00.

Prepare a bank reconciliation, using the format shown in Exhibit 7.

E5-19

Records based on bank reconciliation

Objs 4, 5

Using the data presented in Exercise 5-18, record the effect on the accounts and financial statements of the company based upon the bank reconciliation.

E5-20

Recording note collected by bank

Objs 4, 5

Accompanying a bank statement for Bionics Company is a credit memorandum for $17,750, representing the principal ($15,000) and interest ($2,750) on a customer's note that had been collected by the bank. The depositor had been notified by the bank at the time of the collection, but had made no recording. Record the adjustment that should be made by the company to bring the accounting records up to date.

E5-21

Bank reconciliation

Objs 4, 5

✓ Adjusted balance: $15,175.60

An accounting clerk for Lock-It Co. prepared the following bank reconciliation:

LOCK-IT CO.
Bank Reconciliation
October 31, 2008

Cash balance according to company's records		$ 9,305.60
Add: Outstanding checks	$ 7,115.35	
Error by Lock-It Co. in recording Check No. 1007 as $4,715 instead of $4,175	540.00	
Note for $5,000 collected by bank, including interest	5,375.00	13,030.35
		$22,335.95
Deduct: Deposit in transit on October 31	$13,690.45	
Bank service charges	45.00	13,735.45
Cash balance according to bank statement		$ 8,600.50

a. From the data in the above bank reconciliation, prepare a new bank reconciliation for Lock-It Co., using the format shown in the illustrative problem.
b. If a balance sheet were prepared for Lock-It Co. on October 31, 2008, what amount should be reported for cash?

E5-22

Bank reconciliation

Objs 4, 5

✓ Corrected adjusted balance: $9,000.00

Identify the errors in the following bank reconciliation:

MKABE CO.
Bank Reconciliation
For the Month Ended June 30, 2008

Cash balance according to bank statement		$ 7,560.14
Add outstanding checks:		
No. 315	$ 717.42	
360	617.11	
364	906.15	
365	1,501.50	3,742.18
		$11,302.32
Deduct deposit of June 30, not recorded by bank		5,182.04
Adjusted balance		$ 7,120.28
Cash balance according to company's records		$ 3,735.70
Add: Proceeds of note collected by bank:		
Principal	$6,000.00	
Interest	180.00	$6,180.00
Service charges		27.00	6,207.00
		$ 9,942.70
Deduct: Check returned because of insufficient funds		$1,158.70
Error in recording June 15 deposit of $3,960 as $3,690		270.00	1,428.70
Adjusted balance		$ 8,514.00

E5-23

Using bank reconciliation to determine cash receipts stolen

Objs 4, 5

Argonaut Co. records all cash receipts on the basis of its cash register tapes. Argonaut Co. discovered during November 2008 that one of its sales clerks had stolen an undetermined amount of cash receipts when she took the daily deposits to the bank. The following data have been gathered for November:

Cash in bank according to the general ledger	$12,510.45
Cash according to the November 30, 2008, bank statement	22,060.65
Outstanding checks as of November 30, 2008	6,381.42
Bank service charge for November	35.00
Note receivable, including interest collected by bank in November	7,140.00

No deposits were in transit on November 30, which fell on a Sunday.

a. Using bank reconciliation, determine the amount of cash receipts stolen by the sales clerk.
b. What accounting controls would have prevented or detected this theft?

E5-24

Recording petty cash fund transactions

Obj 6

Illustrate the effect on the accounts and financial statements of the following transactions:

a. Established a petty cash fund of $1,000.
b. The amount of cash in the petty cash fund is now $261.59. Replenished the fund, based on the following summary of petty cash receipts: office supplies, $379.10; miscellaneous selling expense, $216.25; miscellaneous administrative expense, $143.06.

E5-25

Recording petty cash fund transactions

Obj 6

Illustrate the effect on the accounts and financial statements of the following transactions:

a. Established a petty cash fund of $800.
b. The amount of cash in the petty cash fund is now $140.70. Replenished the fund, based on the following summary of petty cash receipts: office supplies, $427.60; miscellaneous selling expense, $180.00; miscellaneous administrative expense, $51.70.

E5-26

Variation in cash flows

Obj 7

Mattel, Inc., designs, manufactures, and markets toy products worldwide. Mattel's toys include Barbie™ fashion dolls and accessories, Hot Wheels™, and Fisher-Price brands. For a recent year, Mattel reported the following net cash flows from operating activities (in millions):

First quarter ending March 31, 2006	$(290.1)
Second quarter ending June 30, 2006	(357.9)
Third quarter ending September 30, 2006	(367.7)
Year ending December 31, 2006	876.0

Explain how Mattel can report negative net cash flows from operating activities during the first three quarters yet report net positive cash flows on December 31.

Problems

P5-1

Evaluating internal control of cash

Objs 2, 3

The following procedures were recently installed by Sacha's Company:

a. The accounts payable clerk prepares a voucher for each disbursement. The voucher along with the supporting documentation is forwarded to the treasurer's office for approval.
b. After necessary approvals have been obtained for the payment of a voucher, the treasurer signs and mails the check. The treasurer then stamps the voucher and supporting documentation as paid and returns the voucher and supporting documentation to the accounts payable clerk for filing.
c. Along with petty cash expense receipts for postage, office supplies, etc., several postdated employee checks are in the petty cash fund.
d. At the end of the day, cash register clerks are required to use their own funds to make up any cash shortages in their registers.
e. All mail is opened by the mail clerk, who forwards all cash remittances to the cashier. The cashier prepares a listing of the cash receipts and forwards a copy of the list to the accounts receivable clerk for recording in the accounts.
f. At the end of each day, any deposited cash receipts are placed in the bank's night depository.
g. At the end of each day, an accounting clerk compares the duplicate copy of the daily cash deposit slip with the deposit receipt obtained from the bank.
h. The bank reconciliation is prepared by the cashier, who works under the supervision of the treasurer.

Instructions

Indicate whether each of the procedures of internal control over cash represents (1) a strength or (2) a weakness. For each weakness, indicate why it exists.

P5-2

Bank reconciliation

Objs 4, 5

SPREADSHEET

✓ 1. Adjusted balance: $12,110.30

The cash account for Bonita Medical Co. at September 30, 2008, indicated a balance of $5,335.30. The bank statement indicated a balance of $5,604.60 on September 30, 2008. Comparing the bank statement and the accompanying canceled checks and memoranda with the records revealed the following reconciling items:

a. Checks outstanding totaled $4,790.45.
b. A deposit of $9,226.15, representing receipts of September 30, had been made too late to appear on the bank statement.
c. The bank had collected for $7,725 on a note left for collection. The face of the note was $7,500.
d. A check for $4,315 returned with the statement had been incorrectly recorded by Bonita Medical Co. as $3,415. The check was for the payment of an obligation to Rowe Co. for the purchase of office equipment on account.
e. A check drawn for $230 had been erroneously charged by the bank as $2,300.
f. Bank service charges for September amounted to $50.

Instructions

1. Prepare a bank reconciliation.
2. Illustrate the effects on the accounts and financial statements of the bank reconciliation.

P5-3

Bank reconciliation

Objs 4, 5

SPREADSHEET

✓ 1. Adjusted balance: $9,175.15

The cash account for Cabrillo Co. at March 1, 2008, indicated a balance of $10,676.67. During March, the total cash deposited was $39,146.38, and checks written totaled $42,918.40. The bank statement indicated a balance of $10,960.06 on March 31. Comparing the bank statement, the canceled checks, and the accompanying memoranda with the records revealed the following reconciling items:

a. Checks outstanding totaled $11,008.25.
b. A deposit of $8,773.34, representing receipts of March 31, had been made too late to appear on the bank statement.
c. The bank had collected for Cabrillo Co. $3,710 on a note left for collection. The face of the note was $3,500.
d. A check for $380 returned with the statement had been incorrectly charged by the bank as $830.
e. A check for $419 returned with the statement had been recorded by Cabrillo Co. as $149. The check was for the payment of an obligation to Greaven Co. on account.
f. Bank service charges for March amounted to $40.
g. A check for $1,129.50 from Kene-Miller Co. was returned by the bank because of insufficient funds.

Instructions

1. Prepare a bank reconciliation as of March 31.
2. Illustrate the effects on the accounts and financial statements of the bank reconciliation.

P5-4

Bank reconciliation

Objs 4, 5

SPREADSHEET

✓ 1. Adjusted balance: $12,822.02

Pacific Furniture Company deposits all cash receipts each Wednesday and Friday in a night depository after banking hours. The data required to reconcile the bank statement as of June 30 have been taken from various documents and records and are reproduced as follows. The sources of the data are printed in capital letters. All checks were written for payments on account.

JUNE BANK STATEMENT:

```
                                    MEMBER FDIC              PAGE  1
 A
 NB   AMERICAN NATIONAL BANK          ACCOUNT NUMBER
      OF DETROIT                      FROM 6/01/20–   TO 6/30/20–
 DETROIT, MI 48201-2500  (313)933-8547   BALANCE          9,447.20

                                    9  DEPOSITS          8,691.77

                                   20  WITHDRAWALS       7,345.91

      PACIFIC FURNITURE COMPANY     4  OTHER DEBITS
                                       AND CREDITS       2,298.70CR

                                       NEW BALANCE      13,091.76
```

* – – – CHECKS AND OTHER DEBITS – – – *				– DEPOSITS – – *	– DATE – *	– – BALANCE– – *
No.731	162.15	No.738	251.40	690.25	6/01	9,723.90
No.739	60.55	No.740	237.50	1,080.50	6/02	10,506.35
No.741	495.15	No.742	501.90	854.17	6/04	10,363.47
No.743	671.30	No.744	506.88	840.50	6/09	10,025.79
No.745	117.25	No.746	298.66	MS 2,500.00	6/09	12,109.88
No.748	450.90	No.749	640.13	MS 125.00	6/09	11,143.85
No.750	276.77	No.751	299.37	896.61	6/11	11,464.32
No.752	537.01	No.753	380.95	882.95	6/16	11,429.31
No.754	449.75	No.756	113.95	1,606.74	6/18	12,472.35
No.757	407.95	No.760	486.39	897.34	6/23	12,475.35
				942.71	6/25	13,418.06
		NSF	291.90		6/28	13,126.16
		SC	34.40		6/30	13,091.76

```
      EC — ERROR CORRECTION          OD — OVERDRAFT
      MS — MISCELLANEOUS             PS — PAYMENT STOPPED
      NSF — NOT SUFFICIENT FUNDS     SC — SERVICE CHARGE
 * * *                        * * *                      * * *
      THE RECONCILEMENT OF THIS STATEMENT WITH YOUR RECORDS IS ESSENTIAL.
      ANY ERROR OR EXCEPTION SHOULD BE REPORTED IMMEDIATELY.
```

CASH ACCOUNT:
   Balance as of June 1 $9,317.40

CASH RECEIPTS FOR MONTH OF JUNE $9,565.31

DUPLICATE DEPOSIT TICKETS:
   Date and amount of each deposit in June:

Date	Amount	Date	Amount	Date	Amount
June 1	$1,080.50	June 10	$ 896.61	June 22	$ 897.34
3	854.17	15	882.95	24	942.71
8	840.50	17	1,660.47	30	1,510.06

(continued)

CHECKS WRITTEN:

Number and amount of each check issued in June:

Check No.	Amount	Check No.	Amount	Check No.	Amount
740	$237.50	747	Void	754	$ 449.75
741	495.15	748	$450.90	755	272.75
742	501.90	749	640.31	756	113.95
743	671.30	750	276.77	757	407.95
744	506.88	751	299.37	758	259.60
745	117.25	752	537.01	759	901.50
746	298.66	753	380.95	760	486.39
Total amount of checks issued in June					$8,305.84

BANK RECONCILIATION FOR PRECEDING MONTH:

PACIFIC FURNITURE COMPANY
Bank Reconciliation
May 31, 20—

Cash balance according to bank statement		$ 9,447.20
Add deposit for May 31, not recorded by bank		690.25
		$10,137.45
Deduct outstanding checks:		
No. 731	$162.15	
736	345.95	
738	251.40	
739	60.55	
Adjusted balance		820.05
		$ 9,317.40
Cash balance according to depositor's records		$ 9,352.50
Deduct service charges		35.10
Adjusted balance		$ 9,317.40

Instructions

1. Prepare a bank reconciliation as of June 30. If errors in recording deposits or checks are discovered, assume that the errors were made by the company. Assume that all deposits are from cash sales. All checks are written to satisfy accounts payable.
2. Illustrate the effects on the accounts and financial statements of the bank reconciliation.
3. What is the amount of Cash that should appear on the balance sheet as of June 30?
4. Assume that a canceled check for $390 has been incorrectly recorded by the bank as $930. Briefly explain how the error would be included in a bank reconciliation and how it should be corrected.

Activities

A5-1

Sarbanes-Oxley internal control report

Using the Web site **http://www.sec.gov,** click on "Search for Company Filings" and then click on "Search Company & Other Filers." Enter "Hershey" and then click on "47111 - Hershey Co." Find the 10-K filed on 2-23-2007, click on "htm," and click on "d10k.htm." Once the 10-K filing appears, find the "Management Report on Internal Control over Financial Reporting" by searching the document for the key words "internal control" using the Word "Find" command, and answer the following questions:

1. How many times is "internal control" mentioned in Hershey's 10-K?
2. Are there any recent changes in internal control over financial reporting?

3. What criteria were used by management to analyze and assess internal control as a basis for the "Management Report on Internal Control over Financial Reporting"?
4. Who signed the "Management Report on Internal Control over Financial Reporting" on behalf of Hershey's management?
5. Do Hershey's internal controls guarantee its financial reporting is complete and accurate?
6. Who is Hershey's independent public accounting firm?

A5-2

Ethics and professional conduct in business

ETHICS

During the preparation of the bank reconciliation for Colonial Co., Javier Frailey, the assistant controller, discovered that El Camino National Bank incorrectly recorded an $819 check written by Colonial Co. as $189. Javier has decided not to notify the bank but wait for the bank to detect the error. Javier plans to record the $630 error as Other Income if the bank fails to detect the error within the next three months.

Discuss whether Javier is behaving in a professional manner.

A5-3

Internal controls

The following is an excerpt from a conversation between two sales clerks, Fred Loya and Steph Gillespie. Both Fred and Steph are employed by Wireless Electronics, a locally owned and operated electronics retail store.

Fred: Did you hear the news?
Steph: What news?
Fred: Alice and John were both arrested this morning.
Steph: What? Arrested? You're putting me on!
Fred: No, really! The police arrested them first thing this morning. Put them in handcuffs, read them their rights—the whole works. It was unreal!
Steph: What did they do?
Fred: Well, apparently they were filling out merchandise refund forms for fictitious customers and then taking the cash.
Steph: I guess I never thought of that. How did they catch them?
Fred: The store manager noticed that returns were twice that of last year and seemed to be increasing. When he confronted Alice, she became flustered and admitted to taking the cash, apparently over $5,000 in just three months. They're going over the last six months' transactions to try to determine how much John stole. He apparently started stealing first.

Suggest appropriate control procedures that would have prevented or detected the theft of cash.

A5-4

Internal controls

The following is an excerpt from a conversation between the store manager of Trader Sam's Grocery Stores, Jennings Maloy, and Sam Burley, president of Trader Sam's Grocery Stores.

Sam: Jennings, I'm concerned about this new scanning system.
Jennings: What's the problem?
Sam: Well, how do we know the clerks are ringing up all the merchandise?
Jennings: That's one of the strong points about the system. The scanner automatically rings up each item, based on its bar code. We update the prices daily, so we're sure that the sale is rung up for the right price.
Sam: That's not my concern. What keeps a clerk from pretending to scan items and then simply not charging his friends? If his friends were buying 10-15 items, it would be easy for the clerk to pass through several items with his finger over the bar code or just pass the merchandise through the scanner with the wrong side showing. It would look normal for anyone observing. In the old days, we at least could hear the cash register ringing up each sale.
Jenning's: I see your point.

Suggest ways that Trader Sam's Grocery Stores could prevent or detect the theft of merchandise as described.

A5-5

Ethics and professional conduct in business

ETHICS

Pete Harsh and Sara Alper are both cash register clerks for Farmers' Markets. Gina Majed is the store manager for Farmers' Markets. The following is an excerpt of a conversation between Pete and Sara:

Pete: Sara, how long have you been working for Farmers' Markets?
Sara: Almost five years this July. You just started two weeks ago . . . right?
Pete: Yes. Do you mind if I ask you a question?
Sara: No, go ahead.
Pete: What I want to know is, have they always had this rule that if your cash register is short at the end of the day, you have to make up the shortage out of your own pocket?
Sara: Yes, as long as I've been working here.
Pete: Well, it's the pits. Last week I had to pay in almost $50.
Sara: It's not that big a deal. I just make sure that I'm not short at the end of the day.
Pete: How do you do that?
Sara: I just short-change a few customers early in the day. There are a few jerks that deserve it anyway. Most of the time, their attention is elsewhere and they don't think to check their change.
Pete: What happens if you're over at the end of the day?
Sara: Majed lets me keep it as long as it doesn't get to be too large. I've not been short in over a year. I usually clear about $50 to $80 extra per day.

Discuss this case from the viewpoint of proper controls and professional behavior.

A5-6

Bank reconciliation and internal control

The records of Filippi's Company indicate a March 31 cash balance of $10,806.05, which includes undeposited receipts for March 30 and 31. The cash balance on the bank statement as of March 31 is $7,004.95. This balance includes a note of $3,000 plus $120 interest collected by the bank but not recorded in the journal. Checks outstanding on March 31 were as follows: No. 670, $1,129.16; No. 679, $830; No. 690, $525.90; No. 2148, $127.40; No. 2149, $520; and No. 2151, $851.50.

On March 3, the cashier resigned, effective at the end of the month. Before leaving on March 31, the cashier prepared the following bank reconciliation:

Cash balance per books, March 31		$10,806.05
Add outstanding checks:		
No. 2148	$127.40	
2149	520.00	
2151	851.50	1,198.90
		$12,004.95
Less undeposited receipts		5,000.00
Cash balance per bank, March 31		$ 7,004.95
Deduct unrecorded note with interest		3,120.00
True cash, March 31		$ 3,884.95

Calculator Tape of Outstanding Checks:

0.00*
127.40+
520.00+
851.50+
1,198.90*

Subsequently, the owner of Filippi's Company discovered that the cashier had stolen an unknown amount of undeposited receipts, leaving only $5,000 to be deposited on March 31. The owner, a close family friend, has asked your help in determining the amount that the former cashier has stolen.

1. Determine the amount the cashier stole from Filippi's. Show your computations in good form.
2. How did the cashier attempt to conceal the theft?
3. a. Identify two major weaknesses in internal controls, which allowed the cashier to steal the undeposited cash receipts.
   b. Recommend improvements in internal controls, so that similar types of thefts of undeposited cash receipts can be prevented.

A5-7

Observe internal controls over cash

GROUP

Select a business in your community and observe its internal controls over cash receipts and cash payments. The business could be a bank or a bookstore, restaurant, department store, or other retailer. In groups of three or four, identify and discuss the similarities and differences in each business's cash internal controls.

Answers to Self-Examination Questions

1. **C** Compliance with laws and regulations (answer C) is an objective, not an element, of internal control. The control environment (answer A), monitoring (answer B), control procedures (answer D), risk assessment, and information and communication are the five elements of internal control.

2. **C** The error was made by the bank, so the cash balance according to the bank statement needs to be adjusted. Since the bank deducted $90 ($540.50 − $450.50) too little, the error of $90 should be deducted from the cash balance according to the bank statement (answer C).

3. **B** On any specific date, the cash account in a company's ledger may not agree with the account in the bank's ledger because of delays and/or errors by either party in recording transactions. The purpose of a bank reconciliation, therefore, is to determine the reasons for any differences between the two account balances. All errors should then be corrected by the company or the bank, as appropriate. In arriving at the adjusted cash balance according to the bank statement, outstanding checks must be deducted (answer B) to adjust for checks that have been written by the company but that have not yet been presented to the bank for payment.

4. **C** All reconciling items that are added to and deducted from the cash balance according to the company's records on the bank reconciliation (answer C) require that adjustments be recorded by the company to correct errors made in recording transactions or to bring the cash account up to date for delays in recording transactions.

5. **D** To avoid the delay, annoyance, and expense that is associated with paying all obligations by check, relatively small amounts (answer A) are paid from a petty cash fund. The fund is established by estimating the amount of cash needed to pay these small amounts during a specified period (answer B), and it is then reimbursed when the amount of money in the fund is reduced to a predetermined minimum amount (answer C).

Receivables and Inventories

Learning Objectives

After studying this chapter, you should be able to:

Obj 1
Describe the common classifications of receivables.

Obj 2
Describe the nature of and the accounting for uncollectible receivables.

Obj 3
Describe the direct write-off method of accounting for uncollectible receivables.

Obj 4
Describe the allowance method of accounting for uncollectible receivables.

Obj 5
Describe the common classifications of inventories.

Obj 6
Describe three inventory cost flow assumptions and how they impact the financial statements.

Obj 7
Compare and contrast the use of the three inventory costing methods.

Obj 8
Describe how receivables and inventory are reported on the financial statements.

What is the role of receivables in business? Unlike the individual consumer purchasing a DVD at **Wal-Mart** for cash or by **MasterCard** or **Visa**, a business normally purchases merchandise on account. That is, the seller records a receivable and invoices the buyer for payment at a later time. For example, **The Hershey Company** will record a receivable and invoice **Kroger** supermarkets for delivery of chocolate candy to various stores. Kroger will pay for the candy after delivery according to the terms of the invoice.

What is the role of inventory in business? From a consumer's perspective, inventory allows us to compare items, touch items, purchase on impulse, and take immediate delivery of a product on purchase. For example, at **Best Buy** you can inspect digital television sets before deciding which set best suits your needs and tastes. To support Wal-Mart's need for immediate product shipments, **Procter & Gamble** holds an inventory of Tide®. Inventory also provides protection against disruptions in production and transportation. For example, an unexpected strike by a supplier's employees can halt production for a manufacturer or cause lost sales for a merchandiser. Inventory also allows a business to meet unexpected increases in the demand for its product.

In this chapter, we discuss accounting and reporting issues related to receivables and inventories. Specifically, the effects on the financial statements of estimating uncollectible receivables and inventory cost flow assumptions are emphasized.

Classification of Receivables

Many companies sell on credit in order to sell more services or products. The receivables that result from such sales are normally classified as accounts receivable or notes receivable. The term **receivables** includes all money claims against other entities, including people, business firms, and other organizations. These receivables are usually a significant portion of the total current assets. For example, a recent annual report of **La-Z-Boy Chair Company** reported that receivables made up over 48% of La-Z-Boy's current assets.

Accounts Receivable

The most common transaction creating a receivable is selling merchandise or services on credit. The receivable is recorded as an increase to the accounts receivable account. Such **accounts receivable** are normally expected to be collected within a relatively short period, such as 30 or 60 days. They are classified on the balance sheet as a current asset.

Notes Receivable

A **note receivable**, or promissory note, is a written promise to pay a sum of money (face amount) on demand or at a definite time. It can be payable either to an individual or a business, or to the bearer or holder of the note. It is signed by the person or firm that makes the promise. The one to whose order the note is payable is called the *payee*, and the one making the promise is called the *maker*.

The date a note is to be paid is called the *due date* or *maturity date*. The period of time between the issuance date and the due date of a short-term note may be stated in days or months. When the term of a note is stated in days, the due date is the specified number of days after its issuance. To illustrate, the due date of a 90-day note dated March 16 is June 14, as shown below.

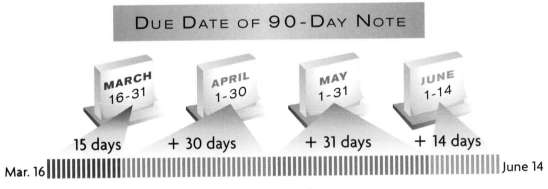

DUE DATE OF 90-DAY NOTE

MARCH 16-31   APRIL 1-30   MAY 1-31   JUNE 1-14

15 days   + 30 days   + 31 days   + 14 days

Mar. 16 |||||||||||||||||||||||||||||||||||||||||||||||||||||||||||||||||||||| June 14

Total of 90 days

The interest rate on notes is normally stated in terms of a year, regardless of the actual period of time involved. Thus, the interest on $2,000 for one year at 12% is $240 (12% × $2,000). The interest on $2,000 for 90 days at 12% is $60 ($2,000 × 12% × 90/360). To simplify computations, we will use 360 days per year. In practice, companies such as banks and mortgage companies use the exact number of days in a year, 365. The amount of interest is normally reported in the Other Income section of the income statement.

The amount that is due at the maturity or due date of a note receivable is its **maturity value**. The maturity value of a note is the sum of the face amount and the interest.

For example, the maturity value of a $25,000, 9%, 120-day note receivable is $25,750 [$25,000 + ($25,000 × 9% × 120/360)].

Notes may be used to settle a customer's account receivable. A claim supported by a note has some advantages over a claim in the form of an account receivable. By signing a note, the debtor recognizes the debt and agrees to pay it according to the terms listed. A note is thus a stronger legal claim.

Other Receivables

Other receivables are normally listed separately on the balance sheet. If they are expected to be collected within 1 year, they are classified as current assets. If collection is expected beyond 1 year, they are classified as noncurrent assets and reported under the caption *Investments*. *Other receivables* include interest receivable, taxes receivable, and receivables from officers or employees.

Describe the nature of and the accounting for uncollectible receivables.

Uncollectible Receivables

In prior chapters, we described and illustrated the accounting for transactions involving sales of merchandise or services on credit. A major issue that we have not yet discussed is that some customers will not pay their accounts. That is, some accounts receivable will be uncollectible.

Many retail businesses may shift the risk of uncollectible receivables to other companies. For example, some retailers do not accept sales on account, but will only accept cash or credit cards. Such policies shift the risk to the credit card companies.

Companies may also sell their receivables to other companies. This is often the case when a company issues its own credit card. For example, **Macy's**, **Sears**, and **JC Penney** issue their own credit cards. Selling receivables is called *factoring* the receivables, and the buyer of the receivables is called a *factor*. An advantage of factoring is that the company selling its receivables receives immediate cash for operating and other needs. In addition, depending upon the factoring agreement, some of the risk of uncollectible accounts may be shifted to the factor.

Regardless of the care used in granting credit and the collection procedures used, a part of the credit sales will not be collectible. The operating expense recorded from

HOW BUSINESSES MAKE MONEY

Coffee Anyone?

Starbucks' strategic goal is to establish the Starbucks name as the most recognized and respected brand in the world. To achieve this goal, the company focuses on two core areas of business: retail coffee stores and nonretail sales. When planning new retail stores, Starbucks focuses on high-traffic, high-visibility locations that offer convenient access for pedestrians and drivers. Starbucks varies the size and format of its stores to fit the location. As a result, you may find Starbucks in a variety of locations, including downtown and suburban retail centers, office buildings, and university campuses. The company's specialty operations further develop the Starbucks brand through alternative supply channels and new products. For example,

the company has recently expanded coffee sales to grocery stores, warehouse clubs, and restaurants. Other activities include joint ventures with companies, such as **PepsiCo Inc.** and **Dreyer's Grand Ice Cream**, to market food products such as Frappucino and Dreyer's Ice Cream under the Starbucks name. Finally, Starbucks has recently extended its brand-building activities to nonfood items by offering a Starbucks credit card in conjunction with **Chase** and music through the Starbucks Hear Music channel on XMSR.

Source: Starbucks Corporation Form 10-K filing with the Securities and Exchange Commission for the year ending October 3, 2004.

uncollectible receivables is called **bad debt expense**, *uncollectible accounts expense*, or *doubtful accounts expense*.

When does an account or a note become uncollectible? There is no general rule for determining when an account is uncollectible. Once a receivable is past due, a company should first notify the customer and try to collect the account. If after repeated attempts the customer doesn't pay, the company may turn the account over to a collection agency. After the collection agency attempts collection, any remaining balance in the account is considered worthless. One of the most significant indications of partial or complete uncollectibility occurs when the debtor goes into bankruptcy. Other indications include the closing of the customer's business and an inability to locate or contact the customer.

There are two methods of accounting for receivables that appear to be uncollectible: the direct write-off method and the allowance method. The **direct write-off method** records bad debt expense only when an account is judged to be worthless. The **allowance method** records bad debt expense by estimating uncollectible accounts at the end of the accounting period and recording an adjustment.

In the next sections of this chapter, we describe and illustrate the accounting for bad debt expense using the direct write-off method and the allowance method. We begin by describing and illustrating the direct write-off method since it is simpler and easier to understand. The direct write-off method is used by smaller companies and by companies with few receivables.[1] Generally accepted accounting principles, however, require companies with a large amount of receivables to use the allowance method.

Direct Write-Off Method for Uncollectible Accounts

Obj 3

Describe the direct write-off method of accounting for uncollectible receivables.

Under the direct write-off method, bad debt expense is not recorded until the customer's account is determined to be worthless. At that time, the customer's account receivable is written off. To illustrate, assume that a $4,200 account receivable from D. L. Ross has been determined to be uncollectible. The effect on the accounts and financial statements of writing off the account is as follows:

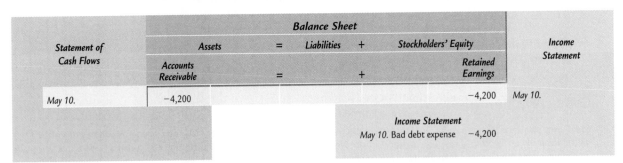

What happens if an account receivable that has been written off is later collected? In such cases, the account is reinstated by reversing the write-off. The cash received in payment is then recorded as a receipt on account.

To illustrate, assume that the D. L. Ross account of $4,200 written off on May 10 is later collected on November 21. The effect on the accounts and financial statements of the reinstatement and receipt of cash is as follows:

---

[1]The direct write-off method is also required for federal income tax purposes.

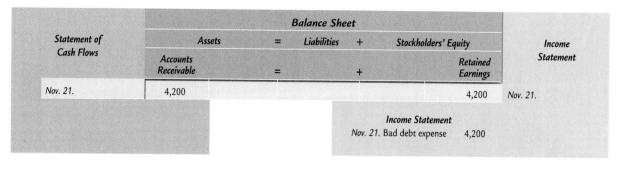

The direct write-off method is used by businesses that sell most of their goods or services for cash and accept only MasterCard or Visa, which are recorded as cash sales. In such cases, receivables are a small part of the current assets and any bad debt expense would be small. Examples of such businesses are a restaurant, a convenience store, and a small retail store.

Allowance Method for Uncollectible Accounts

Obj 4

Describe the allowance method of accounting for uncollectible receivables.

As we mentioned earlier, the allowance method is required by generally accepted accounting principles for companies with large accounts receivable. As a result, most well-known companies such as **General Electric**, PepsiCo Inc., **Intel**, and **FedEx** use the allowance method.

As discussed in the preceding section, the direct write-off method records bad debt expense only when an account is determined to be worthless. In contrast, the allowance method estimates the accounts receivable that will not be collected and records bad debt expense for this estimate at the end of each accounting period. Based upon this estimate, an adjustment for bad debt expense is then recorded.

To illustrate, assume that ExTone Company began operations in August and chose to use the calendar year as its fiscal year. As of December 31, 2008, ExTone Company has an accounts receivable balance of $1,000,000 that includes some accounts that are past due. However, ExTone doesn't know which customer accounts will be uncollectible. Based upon industry data, ExTone estimates that $40,000 of its accounts receivable will be uncollectible. Using this estimate, the effect on the accounts and financial statements of recording the adjustment on December 31 is shown at the top of page 212.

Since the $40,000 reduction in accounts receivable is an estimate, specific customer accounts cannot be reduced or adjusted. Instead, a contra asset account entitled **Allowance for Doubtful Accounts** is used.

As shown above, the preceding adjustment affects the balance sheet and income statement. First, the adjustment reduces the value of the receivables to the amount of cash expected to be realized in the future. This amount, $960,000 ($1,000,000 – $40,000),

Statement of Cash Flows	Balance Sheet					Income Statement
	Assets	=	Liabilities	+	Stockholders' Equity	
	Allow. for − Doubtful Acc'ts.	=		+	Retained Earnings	
Dec. 31.	−40,000				−40,000	Dec. 31.

	Income Statement	
	Dec. 31. Bad debt expense	−40,000

is called the **net realizable value** of the receivables. The net realizable value of the receivables is reported on the balance sheet. Second, the adjustment records $40,000 of bad debt expense, which will be matched against the related revenues of the period on the income statement and, thus, reduces retained earnings.

You should note that after the preceding adjustment has been recorded, Accounts Receivable still has a balance of $1,000,000. This balance represents the total owed by customers on account and is supported by the individual customer accounts.[2] The accounts receivable contra account, Allowance for Doubtful Accounts, has a negative balance of $40,000.

Write-Offs to the Allowance Account

When a customer's account is identified as uncollectible, it is written off against the allowance account. This requires the company to remove the specific accounts receivable and an equal amount from the allowance account. For example, the effect on the accounts and financial statements on January 21, 2009, of writing off John Parker's account of $6,000 with ExTone Company is as follows:

Statement of Cash Flows	Balance Sheet						Income Statement
	Assets		=	Liabilities	+	Stockholders' Equity	
	Accounts Receivables	− Allow. for Doubtful Acc'ts. =					
Jan. 21.	−6,000	6,000					

At the end of a period, the Allowance for Doubtful Accounts will normally have a balance. This is because the Allowance for Doubtful Accounts is based upon an estimate. As a result, the total write-offs to the allowance account during the period will rarely equal the balance of the account at the beginning of the period. The allowance account will have a negative balance at the end of the period if the write-offs during the period are less than the beginning balance. It will have a positive balance if the write-offs exceed the beginning balance. However, after the end-of-period adjustment is recorded, Allowance for Doubtful Accounts should always have a negative balance.

What happens if an account receivable that has been written off against the allowance account is later collected? Like the direct write-off method, the account is reinstated by reversing the write-off. The cash received in payment is then recorded as a receipt on account.

[2]The individual customer accounts are often maintained in a separate file or record called a *subsidiary ledger*. The sum of the individual customer accounts equals the balance of the accounts receivable reported in the balance sheet.

To illustrate, assume that Nancy Smith's account of $5,000 which was written off on April 2 is later collected on June 10. ExTone Company records the reinstatement and the collection is as follows:

Statement of Cash Flows	Balance Sheet						Income Statement
	Assets		=	**Liabilities**	+	**Stockholders' Equity**	
	Accounts Receivable	− Allow. for Doubtful Acc'ts. =					
June 10.	5,000	−5,000					

Statement of Cash Flows	Balance Sheet						Income Statement
	Assets		=	**Liabilities**	+	**Stockholders' Equity**	
	Cash	+ Accounts Receivable =					
June 10.	5,000	−5,000					

Statement of Cash Flows
June 10. Operating   5,000

Estimating Uncollectibles

As we indicated earlier in this section, the allowance method estimates bad debt expense at the end of the period. How is the amount of uncollectible accounts estimated? The estimate of uncollectibles at the end of a fiscal period is based on past experience and forecasts of the future. When the general economy is doing well, the estimate of bad debt expense is normally less than it would be when the economy is doing poorly.

Two methods are commonly used to estimate uncollectible accounts receivable at the end of the period. The estimate may be based upon (1) a percent of sales or (2) an analysis of the receivables. We describe and illustrate each method next.

Estimate Based on Percent of Sales   Since accounts receivable are created by credit sales, bad debt expense can be estimated as a percent of credit sales. To illustrate, assume that on December 31, 2009, the Allowance for Doubtful Accounts for ExTone Company has a negative balance of $3,250. In addition, ExTone estimates that 1½% of 2009 credit sales will be uncollectible. If credit sales for the year are $3,000,000, the effect of the adjustment of $45,000 ($3,000,000 × 0.015) on the accounts and financial statements on December 31 is as follows:

Statement of Cash Flows	Balance Sheet						Income Statement
	Assets		=	**Liabilities**	+	**Stockholders' Equity**	
	Allow. for −Doubtful Acc'ts.		=		+	Retained Earnings	
Dec. 31.	−45,000					−45,000	Dec. 31.

Income Statement
Dec. 31. Bad debt expense   −45,000

Estimate Based on Analysis of Receivables   The longer an account receivable is outstanding, the less likely that it will be collected. Thus, we can base the estimate of uncollectible accounts on how long specific accounts have been outstanding. For this purpose, we can use a process called **aging the receivables.**

Receivables are aged by preparing a schedule that classifies each customer's receivable by its due date. The number of days an account is past due is the number of days between the due date of the account and the date the aging schedule is prepared. To illustrate, assume that Rodriguez Company is preparing an aging schedule for its accounts receivable of $86,300 as of August 31, 2009. The $160 account receivable for Saxon Woods Company was due on May 29. As of August 31, Saxon's account is 94 days past due, as shown below.

Number of days past due in May	2 days (31 − 29)
Number of days past due in June	30 days
Number of days past due in July	31 days
Number of days past due in August	31 days
Total number of days past due	94 days

A portion of the aging schedule for Rodriguez Company is shown in Exhibit 1. The schedule shows the total amount of receivables in each aging class.

EXHIBIT 1   *Aging of Accounts Receivable*

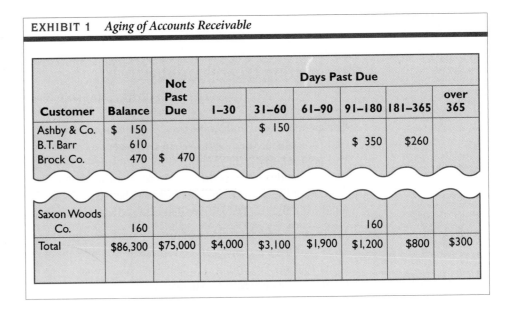

Customer	Balance	Not Past Due	Days Past Due					
			1–30	31–60	61–90	91–180	181–365	over 365
Ashby & Co.	$ 150			$ 150				
B.T. Barr	610					$ 350	$260	
Brock Co.	470	$ 470						
Saxon Woods Co.	160					160		
Total	$86,300	$75,000	$4,000	$3,100	$1,900	$1,200	$800	$300

Rodriguez Company uses a sliding scale of percentages, based on industry or company experience, to estimate the amount of uncollectibles in each aging class. As shown in Exhibit 2, the percent estimated as uncollectible increases the longer the account is past due. For accounts not past due, the percent is 2%, while for accounts over 365 days past due the percent is 80%. The total of these amounts is the desired end-of-period balance for the Allowance for Doubtful Accounts. For Rodriguez Company, the desired August 31 balance of the Allowance for Doubtful Accounts is a negative $3,390.

Comparing the estimate of $3,390 with the unadjusted balance of the allowance account determines the amount of the adjustment for bad debt expense. For example,

EXHIBIT 2 *Estimate of Uncollectible Accounts*

Age Interval	Balance	Estimated Uncollectible Accounts	
		Percent	Amount
Not past due	$75,000	2%	$1,500
1–30 days past due	4,000	5	200
31–60 days past due	3,100	10	310
61–90 days past due	1,900	20	380
91–180 days past due	1,200	30	360
181–365 days past due	800	50	400
Over 365 days past due	300	80	240
Total	$86,300		$3,390

assume that the unadjusted balance of the allowance account is a negative $510. The amount to be added to this balance is therefore $2,880 ($3,390 − $510), and the adjustment is recorded for $2,880 as shown below.

Statement of Cash Flows	Balance Sheet					Income Statement
	Assets	=	Liabilities	+	Stockholders' Equity	
	Allow. for −Doubtful Acc'ts.	=		+	Retained Earnings	
Aug. 31.	−2,880				−2,880	Aug. 31.

Income Statement
Aug. 31. Bad debt expense −2,880

After the adjustment is recorded, the Allowance for Doubtful Accounts will have a negative balance of $3,390.

If the unadjusted balance of the allowance account had been a positive balance of $300, the amount of the adjustment would have been $3,690 ($3,390 + $300). After the adjustment is recorded, the balance of the allowance account would still have been a negative $3,390 (−$3,690 + $300).

INTEGRITY, OBJECTIVITY, AND ETHICS IN BUSINESS

Receivables Fraud

Financial reporting frauds are often tied to accounts receivable, because receivables allow companies to record revenue before cash is received. Take, for example, the case of entrepreneur Michael Weinstein, who acquired **Coated Sales Inc.** with the dream of growing the small specialty company into a major corporation. To acquire funding that would facilitate this growth, Weinstein had to artificially boost the company's sales. He accomplished this by adding millions in false accounts receivable to existing customer accounts.

The company's auditors began to sense a problem when they called one of the company's customers to confirm a large order. When the customer denied placing the order, the auditors began to investigate the company's receivables more closely. Their analysis revealed a fraud which overstated profits by $55 million and forced the company into bankruptcy, costing investors and creditors over $160 million.

Source: Joseph T. Wells, "Follow Fraud to the Likely Perpetrator," *Journal of Accountancy,* March 2001.

Inventory Classification for Merchandisers and Manufacturers

In Chapter 4, we defined a merchandiser as a company that purchases products for resale, such as apparel, consumer electronics, hardware, or food items. We stated that the merchandise on hand (not sold) at the end of the period was a current asset called **merchandise inventory**. Inventory sold becomes the *cost of merchandise sold*. Merchandise inventory is a significant current asset for most merchandising companies, as illustrated for four well-known merchandising companies in Exhibit 3.

EXHIBIT 3	*Size of Merchandise Inventory for Merchandising Businesses*	
	Merchandise Inventory as a Percentage of Current Assets	*Merchandise Inventory as a Percentage of Total Assets*
Wal-Mart	72%	22%
Best Buy	44	30
Home Depot	71	25
Kroger	68	22

What costs should be included in merchandise inventory? As we illustrated in earlier chapters, the cost of merchandise is its purchase price, less any purchase discounts. These costs are usually the largest portion of the inventory cost. Merchandise inventory also includes other costs, such as transportation, import duties, property taxes, and insurance costs. The underlying accounting concept is that the inventory cost must include all the costs of ownership. For example, the CarMax division of ***Circuit City Stores Inc.***, states:

> Parts and labor used to recondition vehicles, as well as transportation and other incremental expenses associated with acquiring vehicles, are included in the CarMax Group's inventory.

In contrast, manufacturing companies convert raw materials into final products, which are often sold to merchandising businesses. A manufacturing company has three types of inventory, as illustrated in Exhibit 4.

Materials inventory consists of the cost of raw materials used in manufacturing a product. For example, The Hershey Company uses cocoa and sugar in making chocolate. The cost of cocoa and sugar held in the storage silos at the end of the period would be reported on the balance sheet as materials inventory.

Work in process inventory consists of the costs for partially completed product. These costs include the *direct materials*, which are a product's component materials that are introduced into the manufacturing process. For example, Hershey introduces cocoa and sugar in the process of making chocolate. Other costs are also added in the manufacturing process, such as direct labor and factory overhead costs. *Direct labor costs* are the wages of factory workers directly involved with making a product. *Factory overhead costs* are all factory costs other than direct labor and materials, such as equipment depreciation, supervisory salaries, and power costs. The balance sheet reports the work in process inventory at the end of the period as a current asset.

Finished goods inventory consists of the costs of direct materials, direct labor, and factory overhead for completed production. The finished goods inventory for Hershey is the cost of packaged chocolate held in a finished goods warehouse at the end of the period. When the finished goods are sold, the costs are transferred to the **cost of goods sold** or the *cost of merchandise sold* on the income statement.

EXHIBIT 4 *Manufacturing Inventories*

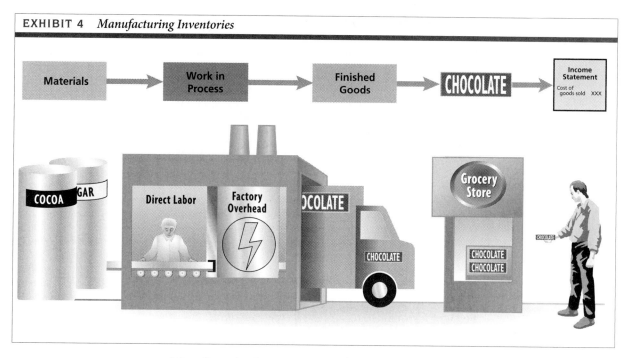

Manufacturing inventories are often disclosed in the footnotes to the financial statements of a manufacturer. For example, The Hershey Company reported inventories of $648,820,000 as follows:

Materials	$214,335,000
Work in process	94,740,000
Finished goods	339,745,000
Total inventories	$648,820,000

In this chapter, we will illustrate inventory accounting and analysis issues from the perspective of the merchandising business. However, many of the points apply equally well to a manufacturer. The accounting for manufacturing inventories is covered in a managerial accounting course.

HOW BUSINESSES MAKE MONEY

The Consumer Electronic Wars: Best Buy versus Circuit City

How does Best Buy compete against Circuit City Stores Inc. in the intensely competitive consumer electronics market? It doesn't just follow a "me too" method but approaches the market by trying to find a way to distinguish itself from Circuit City. First, a warmer color and lighting scheme, featuring light yellows, was chosen over Circuit City's darker color scheme. Second, it opened up bigger stores to provide extra space for the "software" of home electronics. Best Buy believes that more space devoted to CD music, DVD movies, and computer software creates customer foot traffic that eventually translates into other sales. Third, Best Buy introduced a "do-it-yourself" emphasis on the sales floor. Rather than using commissioned salespersons, Best Buy believes that noncommissioned sales personnel can support floor sales. That is, it believes that customers don't need an expert to sell them a product. As a result, the selling expenses as a percent of revenues are reduced. Has the emphasis worked? Over the last 5 years, Best Buy has grown from $15,189 million to $27,433 million in sales, an 81% increase, while Circuit City's sales have decreased by 1%.

Obj **6**

Describe three inventory
cost flow assumptions
and how they impact the
financial statements.

Inventory Cost Flow Assumptions

When you arrive in line to purchase a movie ticket, the tickets are sold on a first-in, first-out (fifo) order. That is, those who arrive first in line purchase their tickets before those who arrive later. In this section, we will see how this ordering concept is used to value inventory. This issue arises when identical units of merchandise are acquired at different unit costs during a period. When the company sells one of these identical items, it must determine a unit cost so that it can record the proper cost of sale. To illustrate, assume that three identical units of Item X are purchased during May, as shown below.

Item X		Units	Cost
May 10	Purchase	1	$ 9
18	Purchase	1	13
24	Purchase	1	14
Total		3	$36
Average cost per unit			$12

Assume that the company sells one unit on May 30 for $20. If this unit can be identified with a specific purchase, the *specific identification method* can be used to determine the cost of the unit sold. For example, if the unit sold was purchased on May 18, the cost assigned to the unit would be $13, and the gross profit would be $7 ($20 – $13). If, however, the unit sold was purchased on May 10, the cost assigned to the unit would be $9, and the gross profit would be $11 ($20 – $9). The specific identification method is normally used by companies that sell relatively expensive items, such as jewelry or automobiles. For example, **Oakwood Homes Corp.**, a manufacturer and seller of mobile homes, stated in the footnotes to its annual report:

> Inventories are valued at the lower of cost or market, with cost determined using the specific identification method for new and used manufactured homes.

The specific identification method is not practical unless each unit can be identified accurately. An automobile dealer, for example, may be able to use this method, since each automobile has a unique serial number. For many businesses, however, identical units cannot be separately identified, and a cost flow must be assumed. That is, which units have been sold and which units are still in inventory must be assumed.

Three common cost flow assumptions are used in business. Each of these assumptions is identified with an inventory costing method, as shown below.

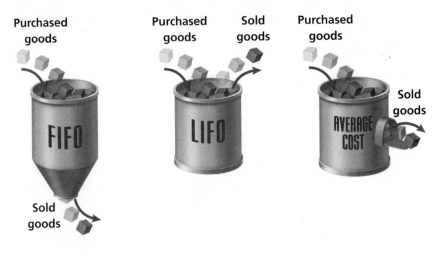

When the **first-in, first-out (fifo) method** is used, the ending inventory is made up of the most recent costs. When the **last-in, first-out (lifo) method** is used, the ending inventory is made up of the earliest costs. When the **average cost method** is used, the cost of the units in inventory is an average of the purchase costs.

To illustrate, we use the preceding example to prepare the income statement for May and the balance sheet as of May 31 for each of the cost flow methods. These financial statements are shown in Exhibit 5.

As you can see, selecting an inventory costing method can have a significant impact on the financial statements. For this reason, the selection has important implications for managers and others in analyzing and interpreting the financial statements. The chart in Exhibit 6, on page 220, shows the frequency with which fifo, lifo, and the average cost methods are used in practice for firms exceeding $1 billion in sales.

EXHIBIT 5   *Effect of Inventory Costing Methods on Financial Statements*

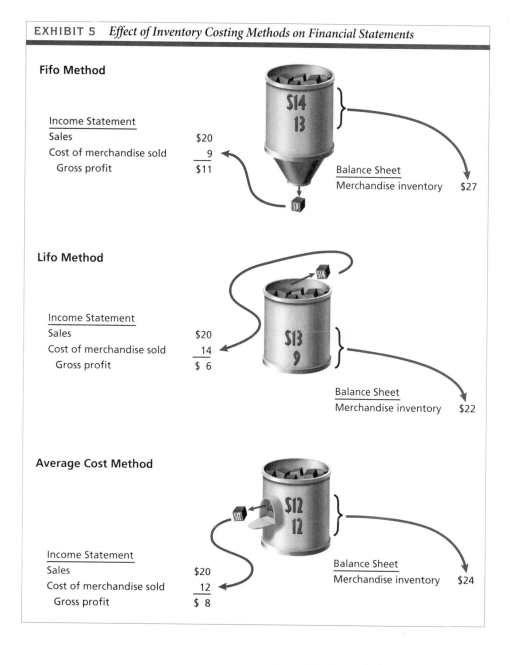

Fifo Method

Income Statement

Sales	$20
Cost of merchandise sold	9
Gross profit	$11

Balance Sheet
Merchandise inventory $27

Lifo Method

Income Statement

Sales	$20
Cost of merchandise sold	14
Gross profit	$ 6

Balance Sheet
Merchandise inventory $22

Average Cost Method

Income Statement

Sales	$20
Cost of merchandise sold	12
Gross profit	$ 8

Balance Sheet
Merchandise inventory $24

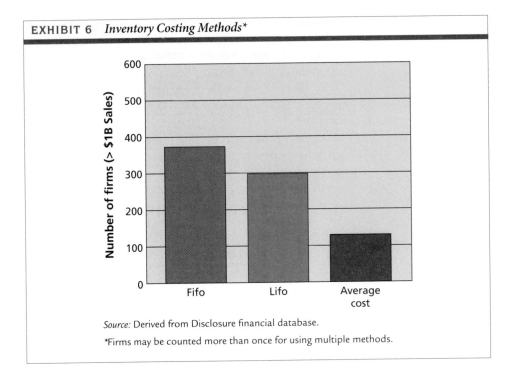

EXHIBIT 6   *Inventory Costing Methods**

Source: Derived from Disclosure financial database.

*Firms may be counted more than once for using multiple methods.

Comparing Inventory Costing Methods

Obj 7

Compare and contrast the use of the three inventory costing methods.

As we illustrated in Exhibit 5, when prices change, the different inventory costing methods affect the income statement and balance sheet differently. That is, the methods yield different amounts for (1) the cost of the merchandise sold for the period, (2) the gross profit (and net income) for the period, and (3) the ending inventory.

Use of the First-In, First-Out (Fifo) Method

When the fifo method is used during a period of inflation or rising prices, the earlier unit costs are lower than the more recent unit costs. Much of the benefit of the larger amount of gross profit is lost, however, because the inventory must be replaced at ever higher prices. In fact, the balance sheet will report the ending merchandise inventory at an amount that is about the same as its current replacement cost. When prices are

INTEGRITY, OBJECTIVITY, AND ETHICS IN BUSINESS

Facilitating Others

Best Buy is focusing on growing from within (based upon the strength of its employees) and building a strength-based company. Brad Anderson, chief executive officer and vice chairman of Best Buy, stated:

Being a leader is not so much what you do, but what you facilitate from others. . . . [Best Buy is

committed to] . . . show respect, humility and integrity; learn from challenge and change; have fun while being best and unleash the power of our people.

Source: Laura Heller, "Best Buy Chief Learns Valuable Lessons in First Year in Office," *Discount Store News*, Monday, July 7, 2003.

increasing, the larger gross profits that result from the fifo method are often called *inventory profits* or *illusory profits*. You should note that in a period of deflation or declining prices, the effect is just the opposite.

Use of the Last-In, First-Out (Lifo) Method

When the lifo method is used during a period of inflation or rising prices, the results are opposite those of the other two methods. The lifo method will yield a higher amount of cost of merchandise sold, a lower amount of gross profit, and a lower amount of inventory at the end of the period than will the other two methods. The reason for these effects is that the cost of the most recently acquired units is about the same as the cost of their replacement. In a period of inflation, the more recent unit costs are higher than the earlier unit costs. Thus, it can be argued that the lifo method more nearly matches current costs with current revenues earnings reports. For example, **DaimlerChrysler's** reason for changing from the fifo method to the lifo method was stated in the following note that accompanied its financial statements:

> DaimlerChrysler changed its method of accounting from first-in, first-out (fifo) to last-in, first-out (lifo) for substantially all of its domestic productive inventories. The change to lifo was made to more accurately match current costs with current revenues.

The rules used for external financial reporting need not be the same as those used for income tax reporting. One exception to this general rule is the use of lifo. If a firm elects to use lifo inventory valuation for tax purposes, then the business must also use lifo for external financial reporting. This is called the **lifo conformity rule**. Thus, in periods of rising prices, lifo offers an income tax savings because it reports the lowest amount of net income of the three methods. Many managers elect to use lifo because of the tax savings, even though the reported earnings will be lower.

The ending inventory on the balance sheet may be quite different from its current replacement cost (or fifo estimate).[3] In such cases, the financial statements will include a note that states the estimated difference between the lifo inventory and the inventory if fifo had been used. This difference is called the **lifo reserve**. An example of such a note for **Deere & Company** is shown below.

> Most inventories owned by (John) Deere & Company and its United States equipment subsidiaries are valued at cost, on the last-in, first-out (lifo) basis. . . . If all inventories had been valued on a fifo basis, estimated inventories by major classification at October 31 in millions of dollars would have been as follows:

	2006	2005
Raw materials and supplies	$ 712	$ 716
Work in process	372	425
Finished machines and parts	2,013	2,126
Total fifo value	$3,097	$3,267
Less (lifo reserve) adjustment to lifo value	1,140	1,132
Inventories	$1,957	$2,135

As shown above, the lifo reserve may be quite large for companies. For example, for Deere & Company the lifo reserve is over 37% ($1,140 ÷ $3,097) of the total fifo value.

---

[3]The fifo estimate is replacement cost, which is often similar to fifo.

The wide differences in the percent of lifo reserve to fifo are a result of two major factors: (1) price inflation of the inventory and (2) the age of the inventory. Generally, old lifo inventory combined with rapid price inflation will result in large lifo reserves, such as those seen in the natural resources industry.

If a business sells some of its old lifo inventory, the lifo reserve is said to be liquidated. Since old lifo inventory is normally at low prices, selling old lifo inventory will result in a lower cost of merchandise sold and a higher gross profit and net income.

Whenever lifo inventory is liquidated, investors and analysts should be careful in interpreting the income statement. In such cases, most investors and analysts will adjust earnings to what they would have been under fifo.

Use of the Average Cost Method

As you might have already reasoned, the average cost method is, in a sense, a compromise between fifo and lifo. The effect of price trends is averaged in determining the cost of merchandise sold and the ending inventory. For a series of purchases, the average cost will be the same, regardless of the direction of price trends. For example, reversing the sequence of unit costs presented in the preceding illustration would not affect the reported cost of merchandise sold, gross profit, or ending inventory.

Reporting Receivables and Inventory

Obj 8

Describe how receivables and inventory are reported on the financial statements.

Receivables and inventory are reported as current assets on the balance sheet, as shown in Exhibit 7. In addition, generally accepted accounting principles require that supplementary information concerning these accounts be reported in the footnotes accompanying the financial statements. In this section, we focus on both the financial statement and footnote reporting requirements for receivables and inventory.

EXHIBIT 7   *Receivables and Inventory in Balance Sheet*

	CRABTREE CO.	
	Balance Sheet	
	December 31, 20—	
Assets		
Current assets:		
Cash and cash equivalents		$119,500.00
Notes receivable		250,000.00
Accounts receivable	$445,000.00	
Less allowance for doubtful accounts	15,000.00	430,000.00
Interest receivable		14,500.00
Merchandise inventory—at lower of cost (first-in, first-out method) or market		216,300.00

Receivables

All receivables expected to be realized in cash within a year are presented in the Current Assets section of the balance sheet. These assets are normally listed in the order of their liquidity, that is, the order in which they are expected to be converted to cash during normal operations. The receivables are presented on Starbucks' balance sheet, as shown here.[4]

Assets (in millions)	Oct. 1, 2006	Oct. 2, 2005
Current assets:		
Cash and cash equivalents	$ 312.6	$ 173.8
Marketable securities	141.0	133.2
Accounts receivable, net of allowances of $3.8 and $3.1, respectively	224.3	190.8
Inventories	636.2	546.3
Prepaid expenses and other current assets	215.7	165.2
Total current assets	$1,529.8	$1,209.3

Starbucks reports net accounts receivable of $224.3 and $190.8. The allowances for doubtful accounts of $3.8 and $3.1 are subtracted from the total accounts receivable to arrive at the net receivables. Alternatively, the allowances for each year could be shown in a note to the financial statements.

Other disclosures related to receivables are presented either on the face of the financial statements or in the accompanying notes.[5] Such disclosures include the market (fair) value of the receivables if significantly different from the reported value. In addition, if unusual credit risks exist within the receivables, the nature of the risks should be disclosed. For example, if the majority of the receivables are due from one customer or are due from customers located in one area of the country or one industry, these facts should be disclosed.

Starbucks did not report any unusual credit risks related to its receivables. However, the following credit risk disclosure was adapted from the 2006 financial statements of Deere & Company:

> Trade accounts and notes receivable have significant concentrations of credit risk in the agricultural, commercial and consumer, and construction and forestry sectors. The portion of credit receivables related to the agricultural business was 54%, that related to commercial and consumer business was 23%, and that related to the construction and forestry business was 23%. On a geographic basis, there is not a disproportionate concentration of credit risk in any area.

Inventory

Merchandise inventory is usually presented in the Current Assets section of the balance sheet, following receivables. The method of determining the cost of the inventory (fifo, lifo, or average) should be shown. It is not unusual for large businesses with varied activities to use different costing methods for different segments of their inventories. The details may be disclosed in parentheses on the balance sheet or in a footnote to the financial statements.

---

[4]Adapted from Starbucks Corporation amended 10-K for the year ended October 1, 2006.
[5]*Statement of Financial Accounting Standards No. 105*, "Disclosures of Information about Financial Instruments with Off-Balance Sheet Risk and Financial Instruments with Concentrations of Credit Risk," and *No. 107*, "Disclosures about Fair Value of Financial Instruments" (Norwalk, CT: Financial Accounting Standards Board).

Inventory is valued at other than cost when (1) the cost of replacing items in inventory is below the recorded cost, and (2) the inventory is not salable at normal sales prices. This latter case may be due to imperfections, shop wear, style changes, or other causes. In either situation, the method of valuing the inventories (cost or lower of cost or market) should also be disclosed on the balance sheet.

Valuation at Lower of Cost or Market

If the cost of replacing an item in inventory is lower than the original purchase cost, the **lower-of-cost-or-market (LCM) method** is used to value the inventory. *Market*, as used in *lower of cost or market*, is the cost to replace the merchandise on the inventory date. This market value is based on quantities normally purchased from the usual source of supply. In businesses where inflation is the norm, market prices rarely decline. In businesses where technology changes rapidly (e.g., microcomputers and televisions), market declines are common. The primary advantage of the lower-of-cost-or-market method is that the gross profit (and net income) is reduced in the period in which the market decline occurred, rather than waiting until the inventory is sold.

In applying the lower-of-cost-or-market method, the cost and replacement cost can be determined in one of three ways. Cost and replacement cost can be determined for (1) each item in the inventory, (2) major classes or categories of inventory, or (3) the inventory as a whole. In practice, the cost and replacement cost of each item are usually determined.

To illustrate, assume that 400 identical units of Item A are in inventory, acquired at a unit cost of $10.25 each. If at the inventory date the item would cost $10.50 to replace, the cost price of $10.25 would be multiplied by 400 to determine the inventory value. On the other hand, if the item could be replaced at $9.50 a unit, the replacement cost of $9.50 would be used for valuation purposes.

Exhibit 8 illustrates a method of organizing inventory data and applying lower-of-cost-or-market to each inventory item. The amount of the market decline, $450 ($15,520 – $15,070), may be reported as a separate item on the income statement or included in the cost of merchandise sold. Regardless, net income will be reduced by the amount of the market decline.

EXHIBIT 8   *Determining Inventory at Lower of Cost or Market*

Commodity	Inventory Quantity	Unit Cost Price	Unit Market Price	Total Cost	Total Market	Lower of C or M
A	400	$10.25	$ 9.50	$ 4,100	$ 3,800	$ 3,800
B	120	22.50	24.10	2,700	2,892	2,700
C	600	8.00	7.75	4,800	4,650	4,650
D	280	14.00	14.75	3,920	4,130	3,920
Total				$15,520	$15,472	$15,070

Valuation at Net Realizable Value

As you would expect, merchandise that is out of date, spoiled, or damaged or that can be sold only at prices below cost should be written down. Such merchandise should be valued at net realizable value. Net realizable value is the estimated selling price less any direct cost of disposal, such as sales commissions. For example, assume that damaged merchandise costing $1,000 can be sold for only $800, and direct selling expenses are estimated to be $150. This inventory should be valued at $650 ($800 − $150), which is its net realizable value. For example, **Digital Theater Systems Inc.** provides digital entertainment technologies, products, and services to the motion picture, consumer electronics, and professional audio industries. In the notes to its recent financial statements, Digital Theater reported the following write-downs of its monochrome projector inventory:

> Inventories are stated at the lower of cost or market. Cost is determined using the first-in, first-out method. The Company evaluates its ending inventories for estimated excess quantities and obsolescence. The Company's evaluation includes the analysis of future sales demand by product, within specific time horizons. Inventories in excess of projected future demand are written down to net realizable value. In addition, the Company assesses the impact of changing technology on inventory balances and writes down inventories that are considered obsolete. The Company recorded an inventory write-down of $3,871 (thousands) related to its monochrome projector inventory . . . due to declines in future demand and technological obsolescence.

Key Points

1. **Describe the common classifications of receivables.**

   The term *receivables* includes all money claims against other entities, including people, business firms, and other organizations. Receivables are normally classified as accounts receivable, notes receivable, or other receivables.

2. **Describe the nature of and the accounting for uncollectible receivables.**

   The two methods of accounting for uncollectible receivables are the direct write-off method and the allowance method. The direct write-off method recognizes the expense only when the account is judged to be uncollectible. The allowance method provides in advance for uncollectible receivables.

3. **Describe the direct write-off method of accounting for uncollectible receivables.**

   Under the direct write-off method, writing off an account increases Bad Debt Expense and decreases Accounts Receivable. Neither an allowance account nor an adjustment is needed at the end of the period.

4. **Describe the allowance method of accounting for uncollectible receivables.**

   A year-end adjustment provides for (1) the reduction of the value of the receivables to the amount of cash expected to be realized from them in the future and (2) the allocation to the current period of the expected expense resulting from such reduction. The adjustment increases Bad Debt Expense and Allowance for Doubtful Accounts. When an account is believed to be uncollectible, it is written off against the allowance account.

   When the estimate of uncollectibles is based on the amount of sales for the period, the adjustment is made without regard to the balance of the allowance account. When the estimate of uncollectibles is based on the amount and the age of the receivable accounts at the end of the period, the adjustment is recorded so that the balance of the allowance account will equal the estimated uncollectibles at the end of the period.

   The allowance account, which will have a negative balance after the adjustment has been posted, is a contra asset account. The bad debt expense is generally reported on the income statement as an administrative expense.

5. **Describe the common classifications of inventories.**

The inventory of a merchandiser is called merchandise inventory. The cost of merchandise inventory that is sold is reported on the income statement. Manufacturers typically have three types of inventory: materials, work in process, and finished goods. When finished goods are sold, the cost is reported on the income statement as cost of goods sold.

6. **Describe three inventory cost flow assumptions and how they impact the financial statements.**

The three common cost flow assumptions used in business are the (1) first-in, first-out method, (2) last-in, first-out method, and (3) average cost method. Each method normally yields different amounts for the cost of merchandise sold and the ending merchandise inventory. Thus, the choice of a cost flow assumption directly affects the financial statements.

7. **Compare and contrast the use of the three inventory costing methods.**

The three inventory costing methods will normally yield different amounts for (1) the ending inventory, (2) the cost of the merchandise sold for the period, and (3) the gross profit (and net income) for the period. During periods of inflation, the fifo method yields the lowest amount for the cost of merchandise sold, the highest amount for gross profit (and net income), and the highest amount for the ending inventory. The lifo method yields the opposite results. During periods of deflation, the preceding effects are reversed. The average cost method yields results that are between those of fifo and lifo.

8. **Describe how receivables and inventory are reported on the financial statements.**

All receivables that are expected to be realized in cash within a year are presented in the Current Assets section of the balance sheet. It is normal to list the assets in the order of their liquidity, which is the order in which they can be converted to cash in normal operations. In addition to the allowance for doubtful accounts, additional receivable disclosures include the market (fair) value and unusual credit risks.

Inventory is normally presented in the Current Assets section of the balance sheet following receivables. If the market price of an item of inventory is lower than its cost, the lower market price is used to compute the value of the item. Market price is the cost to replace the merchandise on the inventory date. It is possible to apply the lower of cost or market to each item in the inventory, to major classes or categories, or to the inventory as a whole.

Merchandise that can be sold only at prices below cost should be valued at net realizable value, which is the estimated selling price less any direct costs of disposal.

Key Terms

Accounts receivable

Aging the receivables

Allowance for Doubtful Accounts

Allowance method

Average cost method

Bad debt expense

Cost of goods sold

Direct write-off method

Finished goods inventory

First-in, first-out (fifo) method

Last-in, first-out (lifo) method

Lifo conformity rule

Lifo reserve

Lower-of-cost-or-market (LCM) method

Materials inventory

Maturity value

Merchandise inventory

Net realizable value

Note receivable

Receivables

Work in process inventory

Illustrative Problem

Stewart Co. is a construction supply company that uses the allowance method of accounting for uncollectible accounts receivable. It is estimated that 3% of the credit sales of $1,375,000 for the year ended December 31 will be uncollectible. In addition, Stewart Co.'s beginning inventory and purchases during the year ended December 31, 2008, were as follows:

		Units	Unit Cost	Total Cost
January 1	Inventory	1,000	$50.00	$ 50,000
March 10	Purchase	1,200	52.50	63,000
August 30	Purchase	800	55.00	44,000
November 26	Purchase	2,000	56.00	112,000
Total		5,000		$269,000

Instructions

1. Determine the amount of the adjustment for uncollectible accounts as of December 31, 2008.
2. Illustrate the effects of the adjustment for uncollectible accounts on the accounts and financial statements of Stewart Co.
3. If the balance of Allowance for Doubtful Accounts was a negative $7,500, would the amount of adjustment determined in (1) change?
4. Assuming that 3,300 units were sold during the year, determine the cost of inventory on December 31, 2008, using each of the following inventory costing methods:
   a. first-in, first-out
   b. last-in, first-out
   c. average cost

Solution

1. $41,250 ($1,375,000 × 3%)
2.

Statement of Cash Flows		Balance Sheet					Income Statement
	Assets	=	**Liabilities**	+		**Stockholders' Equity**	
	Allow. for − Doubtful Acc'ts.	=		+		Retained Earnings	
Dec. 31.	−41,250					−41,250	Dec. 31.

Income Statement
Dec. 31. Bad debt expense −41,250

3. No. Under the percent of sales method the amount of the adjustment is determined without considering the balance of the Allowance for Doubtful Accounts. Under the analysis of receivables method, however, the balance of the Allowance for Doubtful Accounts does affect the amount of the adjustment.
4. a. First-in, first-out method: 1,700 units at $56 = $95,200
   b. Last-in, first-out method:

1,000 units at $50.00	$50,000
700 units at $52.50	36,750
1,700	$86,750

   c. Average cost method:
   Average cost per unit: $269,000 ÷ 5,000 units = $53.80
   Inventory, December 31, 2008: 1,700 units at $53.80 = $91,460

Self-Examination Questions　　*(Answers appear at end of chapter.)*

1. At the end of the fiscal year, before the accounts are adjusted, Accounts Receivable has a balance of $200,000 and Allowance for Doubtful Accounts has a negative balance of $2,500. If the estimate of uncollectible accounts determined by aging the receivables is $8,500, the amount of bad debt expense is:
   A. $2,500
   B. $6,000
   C. $8,500
   D. $11,000

2. At the end of the fiscal year, Accounts Receivable has a balance of $100,000 and Allowance for Doubtful Accounts has a negative balance of $7,000. The expected net realizable value of the accounts receivable is:
   A. $7,000
   B. $93,000
   C. $100,000
   D. $107,000

3. The direct labor cost should be recognized first in which inventory account?
   A. Materials Inventory
   B. Merchandise Inventory
   C. Finished Goods Inventory
   D. Work in Process Inventory

4. The following units of a particular item were available for sale during the period:

Beginning inventory	40 units at $20
First purchase	50 units at $21
Second purchase	50 units at $22
Third purchase	50 units at $23

   What is the unit cost of the 35 units on hand at the end of the period as determined under the fifo costing method?
   A. $20
   B. $21
   C. $22
   D. $23

5. If merchandise inventory is being valued at cost and the price level is steadily rising, the method of costing that will yield the highest net income is:
   A. lifo
   B. fifo
   C. average
   D. periodic

Class Discussion Questions

1. What are the three classifications of receivables?

2. What types of transactions give rise to accounts receivable?

3. In what section of the balance sheet should a note receivable be listed if its term is (a) 120 days, (b) 6 years?

4. Give two examples of other receivables.

5. Strommer's Hardware is a small hardware store in the rural township of Lewistown that rarely extends credit to its customers in the form of an account receivable. The few customers that are allowed to carry accounts receivable are long-time residents of Lewistown and have a history of doing business at Strommer's. What method of accounting for uncollectible receivables should Strommer's Hardware use? Why?

6. Which of the two methods of accounting for uncollectible accounts provides for the recognition of the expense at the earlier date?

7. What kind of an account (asset, liability, etc.) is Allowance for Doubtful Accounts?

8. After the accounts are adjusted at the end of the fiscal year, Accounts Receivable has a balance of $578,600 and Allowance for Doubtful Accounts has a negative balance of $16,850. Describe how the accounts receivable and the allowance for doubtful accounts are reported on the balance sheet.

9. A firm has consistently adjusted its allowance account at the end of the fiscal year by adding a fixed percent of the period's net sales on account. After

5 years, the balance in Allowance for Doubtful Accounts has become very large in relationship to the balance in Accounts Receivable. Give two possible explanations.

10. How are manufacturing inventories different from those of a merchandiser?

11. Do the terms *fifo* and *lifo* refer to techniques used in determining quantities of the various classes of merchandise on hand? Explain.

12. Does the term *last-in* in the lifo method mean that the items in the inventory are assumed to be the most recent (last) acquisitions? Explain.

13. If merchandise inventory is being valued at cost and the price level is steadily rising, which of the three methods of costing—fifo, lifo, or average cost—will yield (a) the highest inventory cost, (b) the lowest inventory cost, (c) the highest gross profit, (d) the lowest gross profit?

14. Which of the three methods of inventory costing—fifo, lifo, or average cost—will in general yield an inventory cost most nearly approximating current replacement cost?

15. If inventory is being valued at cost and the price level is steadily rising, which of the three methods of costing—fifo, lifo, or average cost—will yield the lowest annual income tax expense? Explain.

16. What is the lifo reserve, and why would an analyst be careful in interpreting the earnings of a company that has liquidated some of its lifo reserve?

17. Under what section should accounts receivable be reported on the balance sheet?

18. Because of imperfections, an item of merchandise cannot be sold at its normal selling price. How should this item be valued for financial statement purposes?

19. How is the method of determining the cost of inventory and the method of valuing it disclosed in the financial statements?

Exercises

E6-1

Classifications of receivables

Obj 1

The **Boeing Company** is one of the world's major aerospace firms, with operations involving commercial aircraft, military aircraft, missiles, satellite systems, and information and battle management systems. As of December 31, 2006, Boeing had $2,667 million of receivables involving U.S. government contracts and $1,423 million of receivables involving commercial aircraft customers, such as **Delta Air Lines** and **United Airlines**. Should Boeing report these receivables separately in the financial statements, or combine them into one overall accounts receivable amount? Explain.

E6-2

Determine the due date and interest on notes

Obj 1

SPREADSHEET

✓ a. May 5, $225

Determine the due date, the amount of interest due at maturity, and the maturity value on the following notes:

	Date of Note	Face Amount	Interest Rate	Term of Note
a.	March 6	$15,000	9%	60 days
b.	May 20	8,000	10	60 days
c.	June 2	5,000	12	90 days
d.	August 30	18,000	10	120 days
e.	October 1	10,500	12	60 days

E6-3

Nature of uncollectible accounts

Obj 2

✓ a. 19.9%

The MGM Mirage owns and operates casinos including the MGM Grand and the Bellagio in Las Vegas. As of December 31, 2006, the MGM Mirage reported accounts and notes receivable of $452,945,000 and allowance for doubtful accounts of $90,024,000. **Johnson & Johnson** manufactures and sells a wide range of health care products including Band-Aids and Tylenol. As of December 31, 2006, Johnson & Johnson reported accounts receivable of $8,872,000,000 and allowance for doubtful accounts of $160,000,000.

(continued)

a. Compute the percentage of the allowance for doubtful accounts to the total accounts and notes receivable as of December 31, 2006, for The MGM Mirage.
b. Compute the percentage of the allowance for doubtful accounts to the accounts receivable as of December 31, 2006, for Johnson & Johnson.
c. Discuss possible reasons for the difference in the two ratios computed in (a) and (b).

E6-4

Uncollectible accounts, using direct write-off method

Obj 3

Illustrate the effects on the accounts and financial statements of the following transactions in the accounts of Healthy Co., a hospital supply company that uses the direct write-off method of accounting for uncollectible receivables:

Mar. 3.   Received $5,000 from Dr. Ian Garrick on account and wrote off the remainder owed of $7,500 as uncollectible.

Aug. 30.   Reinstated the account of Dr. Ian Garrick that had been written off on March 3 and received $7,500 cash in full payment.

E6-5

Uncollectible receivables, using allowance method

Obj 4

Illustrate the effects on the accounts and financial statements of the following transactions in the accounts of Bamboo Garden Company, a restaurant supply company that uses the allowance method of accounting for uncollectible receivables:

Feb. 17.   Received $3,000 from Jessica Fowler on account and wrote off the remainder owed of $2,100 as uncollectible.

July 8.   Reinstated the account of Jessica Fowler that had been written off on February 17 and received $2,100 cash in full payment.

E6-6

Writing off accounts receivable

Objs 3, 4

Planet.com, a computer consulting firm, has decided to write off the $12,175 balance of an account owed by a customer. Illustrate the effects on the accounts and financial statements to record the write-off (a) assuming that the direct write-off method is used, and (b) assuming that the allowance method is used.

E6-7

Estimating doubtful accounts

Obj 4

Renegade Co. is a wholesaler of motorcycle supplies. An aging of the company's accounts receivable on December 31, 2008, and a historical analysis of the percentage of uncollectible accounts in each age category are as follows:

Age Interval	Balance	Percent Uncollectible
Not past due	$400,000	1%
1–30 days past due	80,000	2
31–60 days past due	18,000	5
61–90 days past due	12,500	10
91–180 days past due	6,000	70
Over 180 days past due	2,500	90
	$519,000	

Estimate what the proper balance of the allowance for doubtful accounts should be as of December 31, 2008.

E6-8

Entry for uncollectible accounts

Obj 4

Using the data in Exercise 6-7, assume that the allowance for doubtful accounts for Renegade Co. had a positive balance of $3,500 as of December 31, 2008.

Illustrate the effects of the adjustment for uncollectible accounts as of December 31, 2008, on the accounts and financial statements.

E6-9

Providing for doubtful accounts

Obj 4

✓ a. $13,750
b. $12,900

At the end of the current year, the accounts receivable account has a balance of $650,000, and net sales for the year total $5,500,000. Determine the amount of the adjustment for doubtful accounts under each of the following assumptions:

a. The allowance account before adjustment has a negative balance of $3,175. Bad debt expense is estimated at ¼ of 1% of net sales.
b. The allowance account before adjustment has a negative balance of $4,600. An aging of the accounts in the customer's ledger indicates estimated doubtful accounts of $17,500.
c. The allowance account before adjustment has a positive balance of $8,100. Bad debt expense is estimated at ½ of 1% of net sales.
d. The allowance account before adjustment has a positive balance of $8,100. An aging of the accounts in the customer's ledger indicates estimated doubtful accounts of $24,650.

E6-10

Effect of doubtful accounts on net income

Objs 3, 4

During its first year of operations, West Plumbing Supply Co. had net sales of $1,800,000, wrote off $51,000 of accounts as uncollectible using the direct write-off method, and reported net income of $125,000. Determine what the net income would have been if the allowance method had been used, and the company estimated that 3% of net sales would be uncollectible.

E6-11

Effect of doubtful accounts on net income

Objs 3, 4

✓ b. $7,500 negative balance

Using the data in Exercise 6-10, assume that during the second year of operations West Plumbing Supply Co. had net sales of $2,200,000, wrote off $61,500 of accounts as uncollectible using the direct write-off method, and reported net income of $143,500.

a. Determine what net income would have been in the second year if the allowance method (using 3% of net sales) had been used in both the first and second years.
b. Determine what the balance of the allowance for doubtful accounts would have been at the end of the second year if the allowance method had been used in both the first and second years.

E6-12

Manufacturing inventories

Obj 5

Qualcomm Incorporated is a leading developer and manufacturer of digital wireless telecommunications products and services. Qualcomm reported the following inventories on September 30, 2006, in the notes to its financial statements:

	(In millions) **September 30, 2006**
Raw materials	$ 30
Work in process	13
Finished goods	207
	$250

a. Why does Qualcomm report three different inventories?
b. What costs are included in each of the three classes of inventory?

E6-13

Television costs of Walt Disney Company

Obj 5

The Walt Disney Company shows "television costs" as an asset on its balance sheet. In the notes to its financial statements, the following television cost disclosure was made:

	Sept. 30, 2006
Television costs:	
Released, less amortization	$ 882
Completed, not released	210
In process	228
In development or preproduction	17
	$1,337

a. Interpret the four television cost asset categories.
b. How are these classifications similar or dissimilar to the inventory classifications used in a manufacturing firm?

E6-14

Inventory by three methods

Obj 6

✓ b. $1,410

The units of an item available for sale during the year were as follows:

Jan. 1	Inventory	18 units at $40
Feb. 26	Purchase	36 units at $46
June 18	Purchase	42 units at $52
Dec. 29	Purchase	24 units at $55

There are 33 units of the item in the physical inventory at December 31. The periodic inventory system is used. Determine the inventory cost by (a) the first-in, first-out method, (b) the last-in, first-out method, and (c) the average cost method.

E6-15

Inventory by three methods; cost of merchandise sold

SPREADSHEET

Obj 6

✓ a. Inventory, $9,760

The units of an item available for sale during the year were as follows:

Jan. 1	Inventory	168 units at $60
Apr. 15	Purchase	232 units at $65
Sept. 3	Purchase	80 units at $68
Nov. 23	Purchase	120 units at $70

There are 140 units of the item in the physical inventory at December 31. The periodic inventory system is used. Determine the inventory cost and the cost of merchandise sold by three methods, presenting your answers in the following form:

	Cost	
Inventory Method	**Merchandise Inventory**	**Merchandise Sold**
a. First-in, first-out	$	$
b. Last-in, first-out		
c. Average cost		

E6-16

Comparing inventory methods

Obj 7

Assume that a firm separately determined inventory under fifo and lifo and then compared the results.

1. In each space below, place the correct sign [less than (<), greater than (>), or equal (=)] for each comparison, assuming periods of rising prices.

a. Fifo inventory	_____	Lifo inventory
b. Fifo cost of goods sold	_____	Lifo cost of goods sold
c. Fifo net income	_____	Lifo net income
d. Fifo income tax	_____	Lifo income tax

2. Why would management prefer to use lifo over fifo in periods of rising prices?

E6-17

Receivables in the balance sheet

Obj 8

List any errors you can find in the following partial balance sheet.

MISHKIE COMPANY
Balance Sheet
December 31, 2008

Assets		
Current assets:		
Cash		$127,500
Notes receivable	$400,000	
Less interest receivable	24,000	376,000
Accounts receivable	$529,200	
Plus allowance for doubtful accounts	42,000	571,200

E6-18

Lower-of-cost-or-market inventory

Obj 8

SPREADSHEET

✓ LCM: $10,473

On the basis of the following data, determine the value of the inventory at the lower of cost or market. Assemble the data in the form illustrated in Exhibit 8.

Commodity	Inventory Quantity	Unit Cost Price	Unit Market Price
62CF3	10	$120	$131
41DH2	35	80	75
O3MQ3	10	275	260
23FH6	16	40	28
10KT4	40	90	94

E6-19

Merchandise inventory on the balance sheet

Obj 8

Based on the data in Exercise 6-18 and assuming that cost was determined by the fifo method, show how the merchandise inventory would appear on the balance sheet.

Problems

P6-1

Allowance method for doubtful accounts

Obj 4

SPREADSHEET

✓ 1. Estimate of doubtful accounts, $76,171

Steelhead Company supplies flies and fishing gear to sporting goods stores and outfitters throughout the western United States. The accounts receivable clerk for Steelhead prepared the following partially completed aging-of-receivables schedule as of the end of business on December 31, 2008.

	A	B	C	D	E	F	G	H	
			Not		Days Past Due				
			Past						
	Customer	Balance	Due	1–30	31–60	61–90	91–120	Over 120	
1	Alexandra Fishery	15,000	15,000						1
2	Cutthroat Sports	5,500			5,500				2
3									3
39	Yellowstone Sports	2,900		2,900					39
40	Totals	895,900	454,800	249,500	101,700	33,900	32,100	23,900	40

(continued)

Steelhead Company has a past history of uncollectible accounts by age category, as follows:

Age Class	Percent Uncollectible
Not past due	2%
1–30 days past due	5
31–60 days past due	10
61–90 days past due	25
91–120 days past due	45
Over 120 days past due	90

Instructions

1. Estimate the allowance for doubtful accounts, based on the aging-of-receivables schedule.
2. Assume that the allowance for doubtful accounts for Steelhead Company has a positive balance of $3,199 before adjustment on December 31, 2008. Illustrate the effect on the accounts and financial statements of the adjustment for uncollectible accounts.
3. Steelhead Company reported credit sales of $5,000,000 during 2008. Assume that instead of using the analysis of receivables method of estimating uncollectible accounts, Steelhead uses the percent of sales method and estimates that 1.75% of sales will be uncollectible. Illustrate the effect on the accounts and financial statements of the adjustment for uncollectible accounts using the percent of sales method.
4. Assume that on February 10, 2009, Steelhead wrote off the $9,000 account of Green River Outfitters as uncollectible. Illustrate the effect on the accounts and financial statements of the write-off of the Green River account.
5. Assume that on May 17, 2009, Green River Outfitters paid $9,000 on its account. Illustrate the effect on the accounts and financial statements of reinstating and collecting the Green River account.
6. If, instead of using the allowance method, Steelhead uses the direct write-off method, illustrate the effect on the accounts and financial statements of the following:
   a. The write-off of the Green River Outfitters account on February 10, 2009.
   b. The reinstatement and collection of the Green River Outfitters account on May 17, 2009.
7. Does *Amazon.com* use the direct write-off or allowance method of accounting for uncollectible accounts receivable? Explain.

P6-2

Estimate uncollectible accounts

Obj 4

✓ (a) 2005, $21,750

For several years, sales have been on a "cash only" basis. On January 1, 2005, however, Litespeed Co. began offering credit on terms of n/30. The amount of the adjusting entry to record the estimated uncollectible receivables at the end of each year has been ¼ of 1% of credit sales, which is the rate reported as the average for the industry. Credit sales and the year-end credit balances in Allowance for Doubtful Accounts for the past four years are as follows:

Year	Credit Sales	Allowance for Doubtful Accounts
2005	$8,160,000	$ 8,520
2006	8,400,000	15,840
2007	8,520,000	22,680
2008	8,700,000	32,820

Ursula Sykes, president of Litespeed Co., is concerned that the method used to account for and write off uncollectible receivables is unsatisfactory. She has asked for your advice in the analysis of past operations in this area and for recommendations for change.

Instructions

1. Determine the amount of (a) the addition to Allowance for Doubtful Accounts and (b) the accounts written off for each of the four years.

2. a. Advise Ursula Sykes as to whether the estimate of ¼ of 1% of credit sales appears reasonable.

   b. Assume that after discussing (a) with Ursula Sykes, she asked you what action might be taken to determine what the balance of Allowance for Doubtful Accounts should be at December 31, 2008, and what possible changes, if any, you might recommend in accounting for uncollectible receivables. How would you respond?

P6-3

Compare two methods of accounting for uncollectible receivables

Objs 3, 4

✓ 1. Year 4: Balance of allowance account, end of year, $17,150

Pegasus Company, a telephone service and supply company, has just completed its fourth year of operations. The direct write-off method of recording bad debt expense has been used during the entire period. Because of substantial increases in sales volume and the amount of uncollectible accounts, the firm is considering changing to the allowance method. Information is requested as to the effect that an annual provision of ¾% of sales would have had on the amount of bad debt expense reported for each of the past four years. It is also considered desirable to know what the balance of Allowance for Doubtful Accounts would have been at the end of each year. The following data have been obtained from the accounts:

Year	Sales	Uncollectible Accounts Written Off	Year of Origin of Accounts Receivable Written Off as Uncollectible			
			1st	2nd	3rd	4th
1st	$ 910,000	$ 3,500	$3,500			
2nd	1,064,000	4,130	2,660	$1,470		
3rd	1,330,000	7,980	980	5,600	$1,400	
4th	2,520,000	10,920		1,680	3,570	$5,670

Instructions

1. Assemble the desired data, using the following column headings:

	Bad Debt Expense			
Year	Expense Actually Reported	Expense Based on Estimate	Increase (Decrease) in Amount of Expense	Balance of Allowance Account, End of Year

2. Experience during the first four years of operations indicated that the receivables were either collected within two years or had to be written off as uncollectible. Does the estimate of ¾% of sales appear to be reasonably close to the actual experience with uncollectible accounts originating during the first two years? Explain.

P6-4

Inventory by three cost flow methods

Objs 6, 7

SPREADSHEET

✓ 1. $6,863

Del Mar Appliances uses the periodic inventory system. Details regarding the inventory of appliances at August 1, 2007, purchases invoices during the year, and the inventory count at July 31, 2008, are summarized as follows:

Model	Inventory, August 1	Purchases Invoices			Inventory Count, July 31
		1st	2nd	3rd	
T742	2 at $125	2 at $130	4 at $135	2 at $140	5
PM18	7 at 242	6 at 250	5 at 260	10 at 259	9
K21G	6 at 80	5 at 82	8 at 89	8 at 90	6
H60W	2 at 108	2 at 110	3 at 128	3 at 130	5
B153Z	8 at 88	4 at 79	3 at 85	6 at 92	8
J600T	5 at 160	4 at 170	4 at 175	7 at 180	8
C273W	—	4 at 75	4 at 100	4 at 101	5

(continued)

Instructions

1. Determine the cost of the inventory on July 31, 2008, by the first-in, first-out method. Present data in columnar form, using the following headings:

Model	Quantity	Unit Cost	Total Cost

    If the inventory of a particular model comprises one entire purchase plus a portion of another purchase acquired at a different unit cost, use a separate line for each purchase.
2. Determine the cost of the inventory on July 31, 2008, by the last-in, first-out method, following the procedures indicated in (1).
3. Determine the cost of the inventory on July 31, 2008, by the average cost method, using the columnar headings indicated in (1).
4. Discuss which method (fifo or lifo) would be preferred for income tax purposes in periods of (a) rising prices and (b) declining prices.

P6-5

Lower-of-cost-or-market inventory

Obj 8

SPREADSHEET

✓ Total LCM, $43,703

Data on the physical inventory of Exchange Company as of December 31, 2008, are presented below.

Description	Inventory Quantity	Unit Market Price
AC172	38	$ 56
BE43	18	180
CJ9	30	120
E34	125	26
F17	18	550
G68	60	15
K41	5	390
Q79	375	6
RZ13	90	18
S60	6	235
W21	140	18
XR90	15	745

Quantity and cost data from the last purchases invoice of the year and the next-to-the-last purchases invoice are summarized as follows:

Description	Last Purchases Invoice		Next-to-the-Last Purchases Invoice	
	Quantity Purchased	Unit Cost	Quantity Purchased	Unit Cost
AC172	25	$ 60	30	$ 58
BE43	35	175	20	180
CJ9	18	130	25	128
E34	150	25	100	24
F17	10	565	10	560
G68	100	15	100	14
K41	10	385	5	384
Q79	500	6	500	6
RZ13	80	22	50	21
S60	5	250	4	260
W21	100	20	75	19
XR90	9	750	9	740

Instructions

Determine the inventory at cost and also at the lower of cost or market, using the first-in, first-out method. Record the appropriate unit costs on an inventory sheet and complete the pricing of the inventory. When there are two different unit costs applicable to an item, proceed as follows:

1. Draw a line through the quantity, and insert the quantity and unit cost of the last purchase.
2. On the following line, insert the quantity and unit cost of the next-to-the-last purchase.
3. Total the cost and market columns and insert the lower of the two totals in the Lower of C or M column. The first item on the inventory sheet has been completed below as an example.

Inventory Sheet
December 31, 2008

| | | | | Total | | |
Description	Inventory Quantity	Unit Cost Price	Unit Market Price	Cost	Market	Lower of C or M
AC172	3̶8̶ 25	$60	$56	$1,500	$1,400	
	13	58		754	728	
				$2,254	$2,128	$2,128

Activities

A6-1

Ethics and professional conduct in business

ETHICS

Neka Kiser, vice president of operations for Mountain National Bank, has instructed the bank's computer programmer to use a 365-day year to compute interest on depository accounts (payables). Neka also instructed the programmer to use a 360-day year to compute interest on loans (receivables).

Discuss whether Neka is behaving in a professional manner.

A6-2

Collecting accounts receivable

The following is an excerpt from a conversation between the office manager, Santiago Surillo, and the president of Lighthouse Construction Supplies Co., Blanca Espinosa. Lighthouse sells building supplies to local contractors.

Santiago: Blanca, we're going to have to do something about these overdue accounts receivable. One-third of our accounts are over 60 days past due, and I've had accounts that have stayed open for almost a year!

Blanca: I didn't realize it was that bad. Any ideas?

Santiago: Well, we could stop giving credit. Make everyone pay with cash or a credit card. We accept MasterCard and Visa already, but only the walk-in customers use them. Almost all of the contractors put purchases on their bills.

Blanca: Yes, but we've been allowing credit for years. As far as I know, all of our competitors allow contractors credit. If we stopped giving credit, we'd lose many of our contractors. They'd just go elsewhere. You know, some of these guys run up bills as high as $40,000 or $50,000. There's no way they could put that kind of money on a credit card.

Santiago: That's a good point. But we've got to do something.

Blanca: How many of the contractor accounts do you actually end up writing off as uncollectible?

Santiago: Not many. Almost all eventually pay. It's just that they take so long!

Suggest one or more solutions to Lighthouse Construction Supplies Co.'s problem concerning the collection of accounts receivable.

A6-3

Ethics and professional conduct in business

Beeson Co. is experiencing a decrease in sales and operating income for the fiscal year ending December 31, 2008. Julia Faure, controller of Beeson Co., has suggested that all orders received before the end of the fiscal year be shipped by midnight, December 31, 2008, even if the shipping department must work overtime. Since Beeson Co. ships all merchandise FOB shipping point, it would record all such shipments as sales for the year ending December 31, 2008, thereby offsetting some of the decreases in sales and operating income.

Discuss whether Julia Faure is behaving in a professional manner.

A6-4

Lifo and inventory flow

The following is an excerpt from a conversation between Jack O'Brien, the warehouse manager for Murrieta Wholesale Co., and its accountant, Carole Timmons. Murrieta Wholesale operates a large regional warehouse that supplies produce and other grocery products to grocery stores in smaller communities.

Jack: Carole, can you explain what's going on here with these monthly statements?

Carole: Sure, Jack. How can I help you?

Jack: I don't understand this last-in, first-out inventory procedure. It just doesn't make sense.

Carole: Well, what it means is that we assume that the last goods we receive are the first ones sold. So the inventory is made up of the items we purchased first.

Jack: Yes, but that's my problem. It doesn't work that way! We always distribute the oldest produce first. Some of that produce is perishable! We can't keep any of it very long or it'll spoil.

Carole: Jack, you don't understand. We only *assume* that the products we distribute are the last ones received. We don't actually have to distribute the goods in this way.

Jack: I always thought that accounting was supposed to show what really happened. It all sounds like "make believe" to me! Why not report what really happens?

Respond to Jack's concerns.

Answers to Self-Examination Questions

1. **B** The estimate of uncollectible accounts, $8,500 (answer C), is the amount of the desired balance of Allowance for Doubtful Accounts after adjustment. The amount of the current provision to be made for bad debt expense is thus $6,000 (answer B), which is the amount that must be added to the Allowance for Doubtful Accounts negative balance of $2,500 (answer A), so that the account will have the desired balance of $8,500.

2. **B** The amount expected to be realized from accounts receivable is the balance of Accounts Receivable, $100,000, less the balance of Allowance for Doubtful Accounts, $7,000, or $93,000 (answer B).

3. **D** The direct labor costs are introduced into production initially as work in process. Once the units are completed, these costs are transferred to finished goods inventory (answer C). Materials inventory (answer A) includes only material costs, not direct labor cost. Merchandise inventory (answer B) is not used in a manufacturing setting, hence does not include direct labor cost.

4. **D** The fifo method of costing is based on the assumption that costs should be charged against revenue in the order in which they were incurred (first-in, first-out). Thus, the most recent costs are assigned to inventory. The 35 units would be assigned a unit cost of $23 (answer D).

5. **B** When the price level is steadily rising, the earlier unit costs are lower than recent unit costs. Under the fifo method (answer B), these earlier costs are matched against revenue to yield the highest possible net income. The periodic inventory system (answer D) is a system and not a method of costing.

CHAPTER 7

Fixed Assets and Intangible Assets

Learning Objectives

After studying this chapter, you should be able to:

Obj 1
Define, classify, and account for the cost of fixed assets.

Obj 2
Compute depreciation using the straight-line and double-declining-balance methods.

Obj 3
Describe the accounting for the disposal of fixed assets.

Obj 4
Describe the accounting for depletion of natural resources.

Obj 5
Describe the accounting for intangible assets.

Obj 6
Describe how depreciation expense is reported in an income statement, and prepare a balance sheet that includes fixed assets and intangible assets.

D o you remember purchasing your first car? You probably didn't buy your first car like you buy a CD. A used or new car is expensive and will affect your life for years to come. Typically, you would spend hours considering different makes and models, safety ratings, warranties, and operating costs before deciding on the final purchase.

Like buying her first car, Lovie Yancey spent a lot of time before deciding to open her first restaurant. In 1952, she created the biggest, juiciest hamburger anyone had ever seen. She called it a Fatburger. The restaurant initially started as a 24-hour operation to cater to the schedules of professional musicians. As a fan of popular music and the performers, Yancey played rhythm & blues, jazz, and blues recordings for her customers. Fatburger's popularity with entertainers was illustrated when its name was used in a 1992 rap by Ice Cube. "Two in the mornin' got the Fatburger," Cube said in "It Was A Good Day," a track on his "Predator" album.

The demand for this incredible burger was such that, in 1980, Ms. Yancey decided to offer Fatburger franchise opportunities. In 1990, with the goal of expanding Fatburger throughout the world, the Fatburger Corporation purchased the business from Ms. Yancey. Today, Fatburger has grown to a multi-restaurant chain with owners and investors such as talk show host Montel Williams, Cincinnati Bengals' tackle Willie Anderson, comedian David Spade, and musicians Cher, Janet Jackson, and Pharrell.

So, how much would it cost you to open a Fatburger restaurant? The total investment ranges from $491,500 to $818,000 per restaurant. Starting a Fatburger restaurant would require a significant investment that would affect your life for years to come. In this chapter, we discuss the accounting for investments in fixed assets such as those used to open a Fatburger restaurant. We also discuss how to determine the portion of the fixed asset that becomes an expense over time. Finally, we discuss the accounting for the disposal of fixed assets and accounting for intangible assets such as patents and copyrights.

Source: http://www.fatburger.net and Battinto Batts, "Pharrell's next meaty venture? Burgers," *The Virginian-Pilot,* August 8, 2005.

Nature of Fixed Assets

Businesses use a variety of fixed assets, such as equipment, furniture, tools, machinery, buildings, and land. **Fixed assets** are long-term or relatively permanent assets. They are *tangible assets* because they exist physically. They are owned and used by the business and are not offered for sale as part of normal operations. Other descriptive titles for these assets are *plant assets* or *property, plant, and equipment.*

The fixed assets of a business can be a significant part of the total assets. Exhibit 1 shows the percentage of fixed assets to total assets for some select companies, divided between service, manufacturing, and merchandising firms. As you can see, the fixed assets for most firms comprise a significant proportion of their total assets. In contrast, **CA (Computer Associates)** is a consulting firm that relies less on fixed assets to deliver value to customers.

EXHIBIT 1 *Fixed Assets as a Percentage of Total Assets—Selected Companies*	
	Fixed Assets as a Percentage of Total Assets
Service Firms	
Pacific Gas and Electric Co.	63%
Sprint Corporation	27%
CA (Computer Associates)	4%
Manufacturing Firms	
Sun Microsystems Inc.	12%
Boeing Co.	15%
E. I. duPont de Nemours & Co.	33%
Merchandising Firms	
Barnes & Noble Inc.	25%
Kroger Company	56%
Wal-Mart Stores Inc.	58%

Classifying Costs

Exhibit 2 displays questions that help classify costs. If the purchased item is long-lived, then it should be *capitalized,* which means it should appear on the balance sheet as an asset. Otherwise, the cost should be reported as an expense on the income statement. Capitalized costs are normally expected to last more than a year. If the asset is also used for a productive purpose, which involves a repeated use or benefit, then it should be classified as a fixed asset, such as land, buildings, or equipment. An asset need not actually be used on an ongoing basis or even often. For example, standby equipment for use in the event of a breakdown of regular equipment or for use only during peak periods is included in fixed assets. Fixed assets that have been abandoned or are no longer used should not be classified as a fixed asset.

Fixed assets are owned and used by the business and are not offered for resale. Long-lived assets held for resale are not classified as fixed assets, but should be listed

EXHIBIT 2   *Classifying Costs*

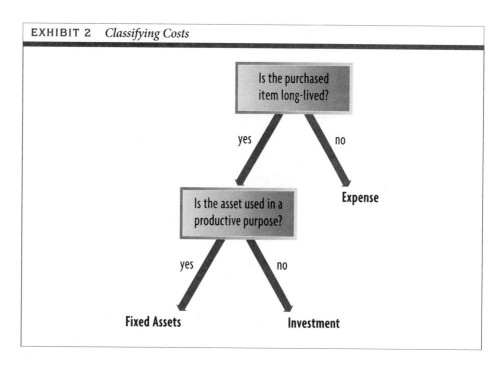

on the balance sheet in a section entitled *investments*. For example, undeveloped land acquired as an investment for resale would be classified as an investment, not land.

The Cost of Fixed Assets

The costs of acquiring fixed assets include all amounts spent to get the asset in place and ready for use. For example, freight costs and the costs of installing equipment are included as part of the asset's total cost. The direct costs associated with new construction, such as labor and materials, should increase a "construction in progress" asset account. When the construction is complete, the costs should be reclassified by decreasing the construction in progress account and increasing the appropriate fixed asset account. For growing companies, construction in progress can be significant. For example, **Intel Corporation** disclosed $2.7 billion of construction in progress, which was over 15% of its total fixed assets.

The details of fixed assets are disclosed on the face of the balance sheet or the notes to the financial statements. For example, **Marriott International Inc.** had the following fixed asset disclosures on a recent balance sheet:

	($ in millions)
Land	$ 316
Buildings	724
Furniture and equipment	888
Construction in progress	215
Total	$2,143

These categories are typical for a lodging company. Other types of companies would have categories to fit their particular business.

Exhibit 3 summarizes some of the common costs of acquiring fixed assets. These costs should be recorded by increasing the related fixed asset account, such as Land,[1] Building, Land Improvements, or Machinery and Equipment.

EXHIBIT 3   *Costs of Acquiring Fixed Assets*

Land

- Purchase price
- Sales taxes
- Permits from government agencies
- Broker's commissions
- Title fees
- Surveying fees
- Delinquent real estate taxes
- Razing or removing unwanted buildings, less any salvage
- Grading and leveling
- Paving a public street bordering the land

Building

- Architects' fees
- Engineers' fees
- Insurance costs incurred during construction
- Interest on money borrowed to finance construction
- Walkways to and around the building
- Sales taxes
- Repairs (purchase of existing building)
- Reconditioning (purchase of existing building)
- Modifying for use
- Permits from government agencies

Machinery & Equipment

- Sales taxes
- Freight
- Installation
- Repairs (purchase of used equipment)
- Reconditioning (purchase of used equipment)
- Insurance while in transit
- Assembly
- Modifying for use
- Testing for use
- Permits from government agencies

Land Improvements

- Trees and shrubs
- Fences
- Outdoor lighting
- Paved parking areas

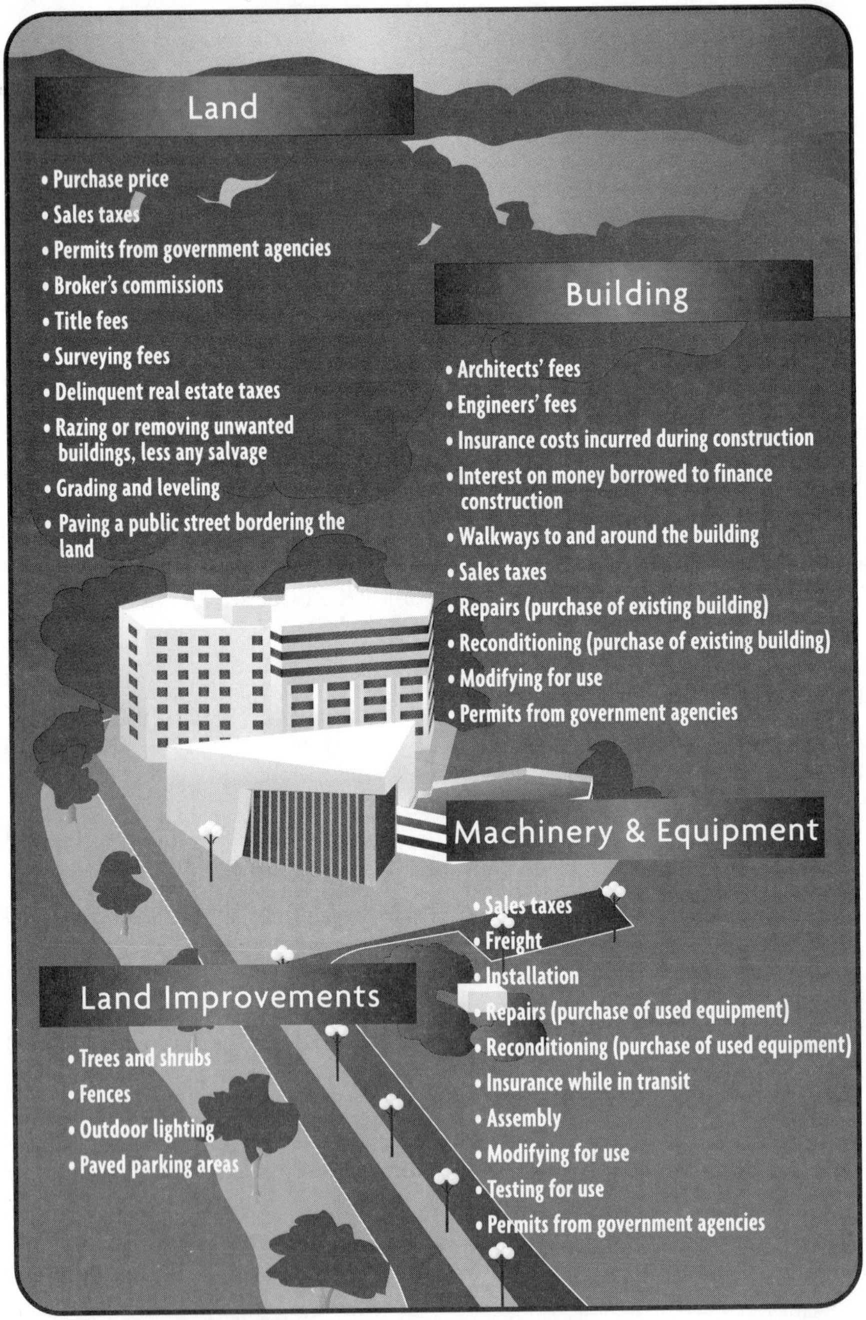

[1] As discussed here, land is assumed to be used only as a location or site and not for its mineral deposits or other natural resources.

Only costs necessary for preparing a long-lived asset for use should be included as a cost of the asset. Unnecessary costs that do not increase the asset's usefulness are recorded as an expense. For example, the following costs are included as an expense:

- Vandalism
- Mistakes in installation
- Uninsured theft
- Damage during unpacking and installing
- Fines for not obtaining proper permits from governmental agencies

Revenue and Capital Expenditures

Once a fixed asset has been acquired and placed in service, expenditures may be incurred for ordinary maintenance and repairs. In addition, expenditures may be incurred for improving an asset or for extraordinary repairs that extend the asset's useful life. Expenditures that benefit only the current period are called **revenue expenditures**. Expenditures that improve the asset or extend its useful life are **capital expenditures**. We discuss common revenue and capital expenditures in the following paragraphs.

Ordinary Maintenance and Repairs   Expenditures related to the ordinary maintenance and repairs of a fixed asset are recorded as an expense of the current period. Such expenditures are *revenue expenditures* and are recorded as increases to Repairs and Maintenance Expense. For example, $300 paid for a tune-up of a delivery truck would be recorded as an increase in Repairs and Maintenance Expense and a decrease in Cash by $300.

Asset Improvements   After a fixed asset has been placed in service, expenditures may be incurred to improve an asset. For example, the service value of a delivery truck might be improved by adding a $5,500 hydraulic lift, thus allowing easier and quicker loading of heavy cargo. Such expenditures are *capital expenditures* and are recorded as increases to the fixed asset account. In the case of the hydraulic lift, the expenditure is recorded as an increase in Delivery Truck and a decrease in Cash by $5,500. Because the cost of the delivery truck has increased, depreciation for the truck would also change over its remaining useful life.

Extraordinary Repairs   After a fixed asset has been placed in service, expenditures may be incurred to extend the asset's useful life. For example, the engine of a forklift that is near the end of its useful life may be overhauled at a cost of $4,500, thus extending the useful life of the forklift by eight years. Such expenditures are *capital expenditures* and are recorded as a decrease in the accumulated depreciation account. In the case of the forklift, the expenditure is recorded as a decrease in Accumulated Depreciation—Forklift and a decrease in Cash. Because the forklift's remaining useful life has changed, depreciation for the forklift would also change based on the new book value of the forklift.

The revenue and capital expenditures are summarized below.

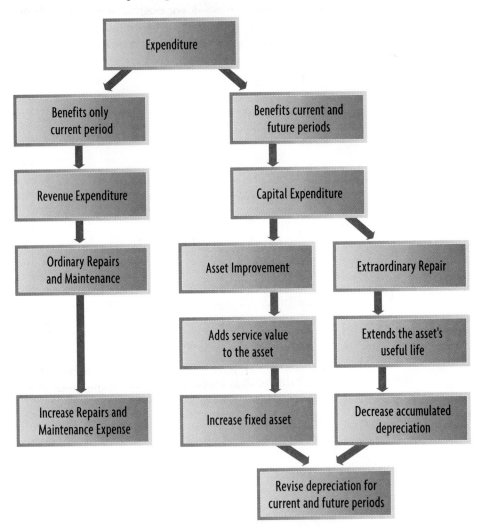

Obj 2

Compute depreciation using the straight-line and double-declining-balance methods.

Accounting for Depreciation

As we have discussed in earlier chapters, land has an unlimited life and therefore can provide unlimited services. On the other hand, other fixed assets such as equipment, buildings, and land improvements lose their ability, over time, to provide services. As a result, the costs of equipment, buildings, and land improvements should be transferred to expense accounts in a systematic manner during their expected useful lives. This periodic transfer of cost to expense is called **depreciation**.

The adjustment for depreciation is usually made at the end of each month or at the end of the year. This adjustment increases *Depreciation Expense* and the *contra asset* account entitled *Accumulated Depreciation* or *Allowance for Depreciation.* The use of a contra asset account allows the original cost to remain unchanged in the fixed asset account.

Factors that cause a decline in the ability of a fixed asset to provide services may be identified as physical depreciation or functional depreciation. **Physical depreciation** occurs from wear and tear while in use and from the action of the weather. *Functional* *depreciation* occurs when a fixed asset is no longer able to provide services at the level for which it was intended. For example, a personal computer made in the 1980s would not be able to provide an Internet connection. Advances in technology have made functional depreciation an increasingly important cause of depreciation.

The term *depreciation* as used in accounting is often misunderstood because the same term is also used in business to mean a decline in the market value of an asset. However, the amount of a fixed asset's unexpired cost reported in the balance sheet usually does not agree with the amount that could be realized from its sale. Fixed assets are held for use in a business rather than for sale. It is assumed that the business will continue as a going concern. Thus, a decision to dispose of a fixed asset is based mainly on the usefulness of the asset to the business and not on its market value.

Another common misunderstanding is that accounting for depreciation provides cash needed to replace fixed assets as they wear out. This misunderstanding probably occurs because depreciation, unlike most expenses, does not require an outlay of cash in the period in which it is recorded. The cash account is neither increased nor decreased by the periodic entries that transfer the cost of fixed assets to depreciation expense accounts.

Depreciation Expense

letermining the amount of depreciation expense to
e three factors are (1) the fixed asset's initial cost,
3) its estimated value at the end of its useful life.
lual value, scrap value, salvage value, or **trade-in**
nship among the three factors and the periodic

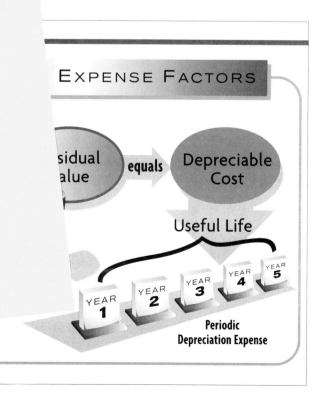

A fixed asset's **residual value** at the end of its expected useful life must be estimated at the time the asset is placed in service. If a fixed asset is expected to have little or no residual value when it is taken out of service, then its initial cost should be spread over its expected useful life as depreciation expense. If, however, a fixed asset is expected to have a significant residual value, the difference between its initial cost and its residual value, called the asset's **depreciable cost**, is the amount that is spread over the asset's useful life as depreciation expense.

A fixed asset's **expected useful life** must also be estimated at the time the asset is placed in service. Estimates of expected useful lives are available from various trade associations and other publications. For federal income tax purposes, the Internal Revenue Service has established guidelines for useful lives. These guidelines may also be helpful in determining depreciation for financial reporting purposes.

In practice, many businesses use the guideline that all assets placed in or taken out of service during the first half of a month are treated as if the event occurred on the first day of *that* month. That is, these businesses compute depreciation on these assets for the entire month. Likewise, all fixed asset additions and deductions during the second half of a month are treated as if the event occurred on the first day of the *next* month. We will follow this practice in this chapter.

It is not necessary that a business use a single method of computing depreciation for all its depreciable assets. The methods used in the accounts and financial statements may also differ from the methods used in determining income taxes and property taxes. The two methods commonly used are (1) straight-line and (2) double-declining-balance.

Straight-Line Method   The **straight-line method** provides for the same amount of depreciation expense for each year of the asset's useful life. For example, assume that the cost of a depreciable asset is $24,000, its estimated residual value is $2,000, and its estimated life is 5 years. The annual depreciation is computed as follows:

$$\frac{\$24{,}000 \text{ cost} - \$2{,}000 \text{ estimated residual value}}{5 \text{ years estimated life}} = \$4{,}400 \text{ annual depreciation}$$

When an asset is used for only part of a year, the annual depreciation is prorated. For example, assume that the fiscal year ends on December 31 and that the asset in the above example is placed in service on October 1. The depreciation for the first fiscal year of use would be $1,100 ($4,400 × 3/12).

For ease in applying the straight-line method, the annual depreciation may be converted to a percentage of the depreciable cost. This percentage is determined by dividing 100% by the number of years of useful life. For example, a useful life of 20 years converts to a 5% rate (100%/20), 8 years converts to a 12.5% rate (100%/8), and so on.[2] In the above example, the annual depreciation of $4,400 can be computed by multiplying the depreciable cost of $22,000 by 20% (100%/5).

The straight-line method is simple and is widely used. It provides a reasonable transfer of costs to periodic expense when the asset's use and the related revenues from its use are about the same from period to period.

Double-Declining-Balance Method   The **double-declining-balance method** provides for a declining periodic expense over the estimated useful life of the asset. To apply this method, the annual straight-line depreciation rate is doubled. For example, the

---

[2]The depreciation rate may also be expressed as a fraction. For example, the annual straight-line rate for an asset with a 3-year useful life is 1/3.

declining-balance rate for an asset with an estimated life of 5 years is 40%, which is double the straight-line rate of 20% (100%/5).

For the first year of use, the cost of the asset is multiplied by the double-declining-balance rate. After the first year, the declining **book value** (cost minus accumulated depreciation) of the asset is multiplied by this rate. To illustrate, the annual declining-balance depreciation for an asset with an estimated 5-year life and a cost of $24,000 is shown below.

Year	Cost	Accum. Depr. at Beginning of Year	Book Value at Beginning of Year		Rate	Depreciation for Year	Book Value at End of Year
1	$24,000		$24,000.00	×	40%	$9,600.00	$14,400.00
2	24,000	$ 9,600.00	14,400.00	×	40%	5,760.00	8,640.00
3	24,000	15,360.00	8,640.00	×	40%	3,456.00	5,184.00
4	24,000	18,816.00	5,184.00	×	40%	2,073.60	3,110.40
5	24,000	20,889.60	3,110.40		—	1,110.40	2,000.00

You should note that when the double-declining-balance method is used, the estimated residual value is *not* considered in determining the depreciation rate. It is also ignored in computing the periodic depreciation. However, the asset should not be depreciated below its estimated residual value. In the above example, the estimated residual value was $2,000. Therefore, the depreciation for the fifth year is $1,110.40 ($3,110.40 − $2,000.00) instead of $1,244.16 (40% × $3,110.40).

In the example above, we assumed that the first use of the asset occurred at the beginning of the fiscal year. This is normally not the case in practice, however, and depreciation for the first partial year of use must be computed. For example, assume that the asset above was in service at the end of the *third* month of the fiscal year. In this case, only a portion (9/12) of the first full year's depreciation of $9,600 is allocated to the first fiscal year. Thus, depreciation of $7,200 (9/12 × $9,600) is allocated to the first partial year of use. The depreciation for the second fiscal year would then be $6,720 [40% × ($24,000 − $7,200)].

Comparing Depreciation Methods

The straight-line method provides for the same periodic amounts of depreciation expense over the life of the asset. The double-declining-balance method provides for a higher depreciation amount in the first year of the asset's use, followed by a gradually declining amount. For this reason, the double-declining-balance method is called an **accelerated depreciation method**. It is most appropriate when the decline in an asset's productivity or earning power is greater in the early years of its use than in later years. Further, using this method is often justified because repairs tend to increase with the age of an asset. The reduced amounts of depreciation in later years are thus offset to some extent by increased repair expenses.

The periodic depreciation amounts for the straight-line method and the double-declining-balance method are compared in Exhibit 5. This comparison is based on an asset cost of $24,000, an estimated life of 5 years, and an estimated residual value of $2,000.

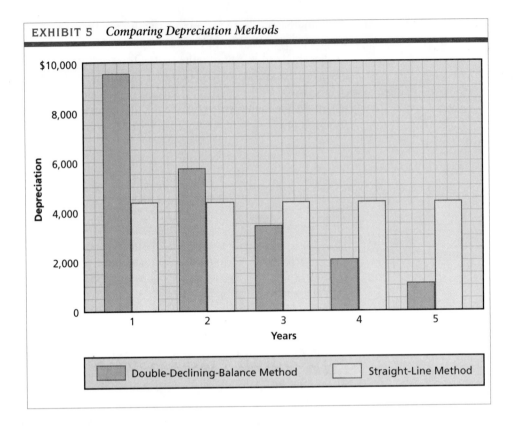

EXHIBIT 5 *Comparing Depreciation Methods*

Depreciation for Federal Income Tax

The Internal Revenue Code specifies the *Modified Accelerated Cost Recovery System (MACRS)* for use by businesses in computing depreciation for tax purposes. MACRS specifies eight classes of useful life and depreciation rates for each class. The two most common classes, other than real estate, are the 5-year class and the 7-year class.[3] The 5-year class includes automobiles and light-duty trucks, and the 7-year class includes most machinery and equipment. The depreciation deduction for these two classes is similar to that computed using the double-declining-balance method.

In using the MACRS rates, residual value is ignored, and all fixed assets are assumed to be put in and taken out of service in the middle of the year. For the 5-year-class assets, depreciation is spread over 6 years, as shown in the following MACRS schedule of depreciation rates:

Year	5-Year-Class Depreciation Rates
1	20.0%
2	32.0
3	19.2
4	11.5
5	11.5
6	5.8
	100.0%

[3]Real estate is in 27½-year classes and 31½-year classes and is depreciated by the straight-line method.

INTEGRITY, OBJECTIVITY, AND ETHICS IN BUSINESS

Capital Crime

One of the largest alleged accounting frauds in history involved the improper accounting for capital expenditures. *WorldCom Inc.,* the second-largest telecommunications company in the United States, improperly treated maintenance expenditures on its telecommunications network as capital expenditures. As a result, the company had to restate its prior years' earnings downward by nearly $4 billion to correct this error. The company declared bankruptcy within months of disclosing the error.

To simplify its record keeping, a business will sometimes use the MACRS method for both financial statement and tax purposes. This is acceptable if MACRS does not result in significantly different amounts than would have been reported using one of the two depreciation methods discussed earlier in this chapter.

Using MACRS for both financial statement and tax purposes may, however, hurt a business. In one case, a business that had used MACRS depreciation for its financial statements lost a $1 million order because its fixed assets had low book values. The bank viewed these low book values as inadequate, so it would not loan the business the amount needed to produce the order.

Obj **3**

Describe the accounting for the disposal of fixed assets.

Disposal of Fixed Assets

Fixed assets that are no longer useful may be discarded, sold, or traded[4] for other fixed assets. The details of how to record a disposal will vary. In all cases, however, the book value of the asset must be removed from the accounts. This is done by decreasing the asset's accumulated depreciation account for its balance on the date of disposal and decreasing the asset account for the cost of the asset.

A fixed asset should not be removed from the accounts only because it has been fully depreciated. If the asset is still used by the business, the cost and accumulated depreciation should remain in the ledger. This maintains accountability for the asset in the ledger. If the book value of the asset was removed from the ledger, the accounts would contain no evidence of the continued existence of the asset. In addition, the cost and the accumulated depreciation data on such assets are often needed for property tax and income tax reports.

Discarding Fixed Assets

When fixed assets are no longer useful to the business and have no residual or market value, they are discarded. To illustrate, assume that an item of equipment acquired at a cost of $25,000 is fully depreciated at December 31, the end of the preceding fiscal year. On February 14, the equipment is discarded. The effect on the accounts and financial statements is as follows:

Statement of Cash Flows	Balance Sheet					Income Statement
	Assets		=	Liabilities +	Stockholders' Equity	
	Equipment −	Acc. Dep.— Equip. =				
Feb. 14.	−25,000	25,000				

[4]Accounting for fixed asset exchanges (trades) is a topic covered in advanced accounting courses.

If an asset has not been fully depreciated, depreciation should be recorded prior to removing it from service and from the accounting records. To illustrate, assume that equipment costing $6,000 is depreciated at an annual straight-line rate of 10%. In addition, assume that on December 31 of the preceding fiscal year, the accumulated depreciation balance, after adjustments, is $4,750. Finally, assume that the asset is removed from service on the following March 24. The effect of recording the depreciation for the three months of the current period prior to the asset's removal from service is as follows:

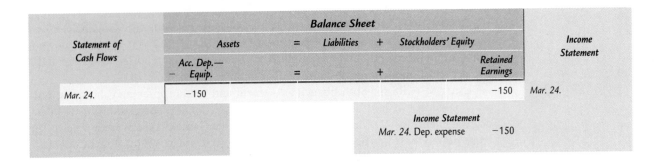

The effect of discarding of the equipment is as follows:

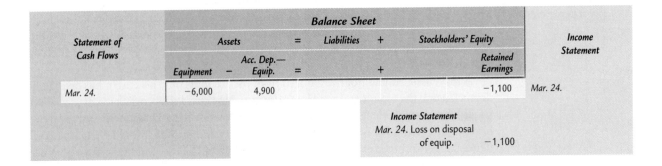

The loss of $1,100 is recorded because the balance of the accumulated depreciation account ($4,900) is less than the balance in the equipment account ($6,000). Losses on the discarding of fixed assets are nonoperating items and are normally reported in the Other Expense section of the income statement.

Selling Fixed Assets

Recording the sale of a fixed asset is similar to the previous illustration, except that the cash or other asset received must also be recorded. If the selling price is more than the book value of the asset, the transaction results in a gain. If the selling price is less than the book value, there is a loss.

To illustrate, assume that equipment is acquired at a cost of $10,000 and is depreciated at an annual straight-line rate of 10%. The equipment is sold for cash on October 12 of the eighth year of its use. The balance of the accumulated depreciation account as of the preceding December 31 is $7,000. The effect on the accounts and financial statements of updating the depreciation for the nine months of the current year is as follows:

Statement of Cash Flows	Balance Sheet						Income Statement
	Assets	**=**	**Liabilities**	**+**	**Stockholders' Equity**		
	Acc. Dep.— − Equip.	=		+		Retained Earnings	
Oct. 12.	−750					−750	Oct. 12.

Income Statement
Oct. 12. Dep. exp.—equip. −750

After the current depreciation is recorded, the book value of the asset is $2,250 ($10,000 − $7,750). The effect of the sale, assuming three different selling prices, is as follows:

Sold at book value, for $2,250. No gain or loss.

Statement of Cash Flows	Balance Sheet						Income Statement
	Assets			**=**	**Liabilities**	**+ Stockholders' Equity**	
	Cash	+ Equipment	− Acc. Dep.— Equip.	=			
Oct. 12.	2,250	−10,000	7,750				

Statement of Cash Flows
Oct. 12. Investing 2,250

Sold below book value, for $1,000. Loss of $1,250.

Statement of Cash Flows	Balance Sheet							Income Statement
	Assets			**=**	**Liabilities**	**+ Stockholders' Equity**		
	Cash	+ Equipment	− Acc. Dep.— Equip.	=		+	Retained Earnings	
Oct. 12.	1,000	−10,000	7,750				−1,250	Oct. 12.

Statement of Cash Flows
Oct. 12. Investing 1,000

Income Statement
Oct. 12. Loss on disposal of equip. −1,250

Sold above book value, for $2,800. Gain of $550.

Statement of Cash Flows	Balance Sheet							Income Statement
	Assets			**=**	**Liabilities**	**+ Stockholders' Equity**		
	Cash	+ Equipment	− Acc. Dep.— Equip.	=		+	Retained Earnings	
Oct. 12.	2,800	−10,000	7,750				550	Oct. 12.

Statement of Cash Flows
Oct. 12. Investing 2,800

Income Statement
Oct. 12. Gain on disposal of equip. 550

Obj 4

Describe the accounting
for depletion of natural
resources.

Natural Resources

The fixed assets of some businesses include timber, metal ores, minerals, or other natural resources. As these businesses harvest or mine and then sell these resources, a portion of the cost of acquiring them must increase an expense account. This process of transferring the cost of natural resources to an expense account is called **depletion**. The amount of depletion is determined by multiplying the quantity extracted during the period by the depletion rate. This rate is computed by dividing the cost of the mineral deposit by its estimated size.

To illustrate, assume that a business paid $400,000 for the mining rights to a mineral deposit estimated at 1,000,000 tons of ore. The depletion rate is $0.40 per ton ($400,000/1,000,000 tons). If 90,000 tons are mined during the year, the periodic depletion is $36,000 (90,000 tons × $0.40). The effect of the depletion on the accounts and financial statements is shown below.

Statement of Cash Flows	Balance Sheet					Income Statement
	Assets	=	Liabilities	+	Stockholders' Equity	
	− Acc. Depletion	=		+	Retained Earnings	
Dec. 31.	−36,000				−36,000	Dec. 31.

Income Statement
Dec. 31. Depletion exp.   −36,000

Like the accumulated depreciation account, Accumulated Depletion is a *contra asset* account. It is reported on the balance sheet as a deduction from the cost of the mineral deposit.

Obj 5

Describe the accounting for
intangible assets.

Intangible Assets

Patents, copyrights, trademarks, and goodwill are long-lived assets that are useful in the operations of a business and are not held for sale. These assets are called **intangible assets** because they do not exist physically.

The basic principles of accounting for intangible assets are like those described earlier for fixed assets. The major concerns are determining (1) the initial cost and (2) the **amortization**—the amount of cost to transfer to expense. Amortization results from the passage of time or a decline in the usefulness of the intangible asset.

Patents

Manufacturers may acquire exclusive rights to produce and sell goods with one or more unique features. Such rights are granted by **patents**, which the federal government issues to inventors. These rights continue in effect for 20 years. A business may purchase patent rights from others, or it may obtain patents developed by its own research and development efforts.

The initial cost of a purchased patent, including any related legal fees, is recorded by increasing an asset account. This cost is written off, or amortized, over the years of the patent's expected usefulness. This period of time may be less than the remaining legal life of the patent. The estimated useful life of the patent may also change as technology or consumer tastes change.

The straight-line method is normally used to determine the periodic amortization. Amortization is recorded by increasing an expense account and decreasing the patents account. A separate contra asset account is usually *not* used for intangible assets.

To illustrate, assume that at the beginning of its fiscal year, a business acquires patent rights for $100,000. The patent had been granted 6 years earlier by the Federal Patent Office. Although the patent will not expire for 14 years, its remaining useful life is estimated as 5 years. The effect of the amortization of the patent at the end of the fiscal year is as follows:

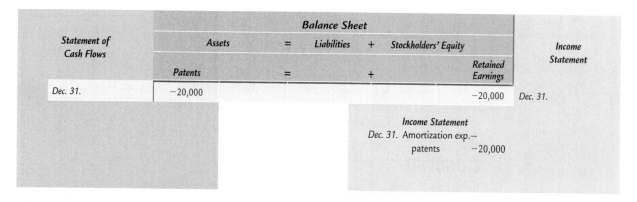

Rather than purchase patent rights, a business may incur significant costs in developing patents through its own research and development efforts. Such *research and development costs* are usually accounted for as current operating expenses in the period in which they are incurred. Expensing research and development costs is justified because the future benefits from research and development efforts are highly uncertain.

Copyrights and Trademarks

The exclusive right to publish and sell a literary, artistic, or musical composition is granted by a **copyright**. Copyrights are issued by the federal government and extend for 70 years beyond the author's death. The costs of a copyright include all costs of creating the work plus any administrative or legal costs of obtaining the copyright. A copyright that is purchased from another should be recorded at the price paid for it. Copyrights are amortized over their estimated useful lives. For example, **Sony Corporation** states the following amortization policy with respect to its artistic and music intangible assets:

> Intangibles, which mainly consist of artist contracts and music catalogs, are being amortized on a straight-line basis principally over 16 years and 21 years, respectively.

A **trademark** is a name, term, or symbol used to identify a business and its products. For example, the distinctive red-and-white **Coca-Cola** logo is an example of a trademark. Most businesses identify their trademarks with ® in their advertisements and on their products. Under federal law, businesses can protect against others using their trademarks by registering them for 10 years and renewing the registration for 10-year periods thereafter. Like a copyright, the legal costs of registering a trademark with the federal government are recorded as an asset. Thus, even though the Coca-Cola trademarks are extremely valuable, they are not shown on the balance sheet, because the legal costs for establishing these trademarks are immaterial. If, however, a trademark is purchased from another business, the cost of its purchase is recorded as an asset. The cost of a trademark is in most cases considered to have an indefinite useful life. Thus, trademarks are not amortized over a useful life, as are the previously discussed intangible assets.

INTEGRITY, OBJECTIVITY, AND ETHICS IN BUSINESS

21st-Century Pirates

Pirated software is a major concern of software companies. For example, during a recent global sweep, **Microsoft** seized nearly five million units of counterfeit Microsoft software with an estimated retail value of $1.7 billion. U.S. copyright laws and practices are sometimes ignored or disputed in other parts of the world.

Businesses must honor the copyrights held by software companies by eliminating pirated software from corporate computers. The **Business Software Alliance (BSA)** represents the largest software companies in campaigns to investigate illegal use of unlicensed software by businesses. The BSA estimates software industry losses of nearly $12 billion annually from software piracy. Employees using pirated software on business assets risk bringing legal penalties to themselves and their employers.

Rather, trademarks should be tested periodically for impaired value. When a trademark is impaired from competitive threats or other circumstances, the trademark should be written down and a loss recognized.

Goodwill

In business, **goodwill** refers to an intangible asset of a business that is created from such favorable factors as location, product quality, reputation, and managerial skill. Goodwill allows a business to earn a rate of return on its investment that is often in excess of the normal rate for other firms in the same business.

Generally accepted accounting principles permit goodwill to be recorded in the accounts only if it is objectively determined by a transaction. An example of such a transaction is the purchase of a business at a price in excess of the net assets (assets – liabilities) of the acquired business. The excess is recorded as goodwill and reported as an intangible asset. Unlike patents and copyrights, goodwill is not amortized. However, a loss should be recorded if the business prospects of the acquired firm become significantly impaired. This loss would normally be disclosed in the Other Expense section of the income statement. To illustrate, **Time Warner** recorded one of the largest losses in corporate history (nearly $54 billion) for the write-down of goodwill associated with the AOL and Time Warner merger. The effect on the accounts and financial statements is as follows:

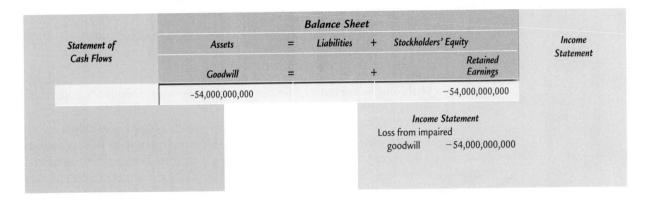

Exhibit 6 shows the frequency of intangible asset disclosures for a sample of 600 large firms. As you can see, goodwill is the most frequently reported intangible asset. This is because goodwill arises from merger transactions, which are very common.

EXHIBIT 6 *Frequency of Intangible Asset Disclosures for 600 Firms*

Intangible Asset Category	Number of Firms
Goodwill	522
Trademarks, brand names, and copyrights	271
Patents	149
Customer lists	243
Technology	140
Franchises and licenses	106
Other	79

Source: Accounting Trends & Techniques, 59th ed., American Institute of Certified Public Accountants, New York, 2006. Note: Some firms have multiple disclosures.

Financial Reporting for Fixed Assets and Intangible Assets

Obj 6

Describe how depreciation expense is reported in an income statement, and prepare a balance sheet that includes fixed assets and intangible assets.

How should fixed assets and intangible assets be reported in the financial statements? The amount of depreciation and amortization expense of a period should be reported separately in the income statement or disclosed in a note. A general description of the method or methods used in computing depreciation should also be reported.

The amount of each major class of fixed assets should be disclosed in the balance sheet or in notes. The related accumulated depreciation should also be disclosed, either by major class or in total. The fixed assets may be shown at their **book value** (cost less accumulated depreciation), which can also be described as their **net** amount. If there are too many classes of fixed assets, a single amount may be presented in the balance sheet, supported by a separate detailed listing. Fixed assets are normally presented under the more descriptive caption of **property, plant, and equipment**.

The cost of mineral rights or ore deposits is normally shown as part of the fixed assets section of the balance sheet. The related accumulated depletion should also be disclosed. In some cases, the mineral rights are shown net of depletion on the face of the balance sheet, accompanied by a note that discloses the amount of the accumulated depletion.

HOW BUSINESSES MAKE MONEY

Hub-and-Spoke or Point-to-Point?

Southwest Airlines uses a simple fare structure, featuring low, unrestricted, unlimited, everyday coach fares. These fares are possible by Southwest's use of a point-to-point, rather than hub-and-spoke, business approach. **United, Delta,** and **American** employ a hub-and-spoke approach in which an airline establishes major hubs that serve as connecting links to other cities. For example, Delta has established major connecting hubs in Atlanta, Cincinnati, and Salt Lake City. In contrast, Southwest focuses on point-to-point service between selected cities with over 300 one-way, nonstop city pairs with an average length of 500 miles and average flying time of 1.5 hours. As a result,

Southwest minimizes connections, delays, and total trip time. Southwest also focuses on serving conveniently located satellite or downtown airports, such as Dallas Love Field, Houston Hobby, and Chicago Midway. Because these airports are normally less congested than hub airports, Southwest is better able to maintain high employee productivity and reliable ontime performance. This operating approach permits the company to achieve high asset utilization of its fixed assets, such as its 737 aircraft. For example, aircraft are scheduled to spend only 25 minutes at the gate, thereby reducing the number of aircraft and gate facilities that would otherwise be required.

EXHIBIT 7   *Fixed Assets and Intangible Assets in the Balance Sheet*

DISCOVERY MINING CO.
Balance Sheet
December 31, 2008

Assets

Total current assets ... $ 462,500

Property, plant, and equipment:	Cost	Accum. Depr.	Book Value		
Land	$ 30,000	—	$ 30,000		
Buildings	110,000	$ 26,000	84,000		
Factory equipment	650,000	192,000	458,000		
Office equipment	120,000	13,000	107,000		
	$ 910,000	$ 231,000		$679,000	

Mineral deposits:	Cost	Accum. Depl.	Book Value		
Alaska deposit	$1,200,000	$ 800,000	$400,000		
Wyoming deposit	750,000	200,000	550,000		
	$1,950,000	$1,000,000		950,000	

Total property, plant, and equipment					1,629,000
Intangible assets:					
Patents				$ 75,000	
Goodwill				50,000	
Total intangible assets					125,000

Intangible assets are usually reported in the balance sheet in a separate section immediately following fixed assets. The balance of each major class of intangible assets should be disclosed at an amount net of amortization taken to date. Exhibit 7 is a partial balance sheet that shows the reporting of fixed assets and intangible assets.

Key Points

1. **Define, classify, and account for the cost of fixed assets.**

   Fixed assets are long-term tangible assets that are owned by the business and are used in the normal operations of the business. Examples of fixed assets are equipment, buildings, and land. The initial cost of a fixed asset includes all amounts spent to get the asset in place and ready for use. For example, sales tax, freight, insurance in transit, and installation costs are all included in the cost of a fixed asset. Once a fixed asset has been acquired and placed in service, revenue and capital expenditures may be incurred. Expenditures related to the ordinary maintenance and repairs

   of a fixed asset are revenue expenditures and are recorded as an expense of the current period. Expenditures to improve an asset are capital expenditures and are recorded as increases to the fixed asset account. Expenditures to extend the asset's useful life are capital expenditures and are recorded as a decrease in accumulated depreciation.

2. **Compute depreciation using the straight-line and double-declining-balance methods.**

   In computing depreciation, three factors need to be considered: (1) the fixed asset's initial cost, (2) the useful life of the asset, and (3) the residual value of the asset.

The straight-line method spreads the initial cost less the residual value equally over the useful life. The double-declining-balance method is applied by multiplying the declining book value of the asset by twice the straight-line rate.

3. Describe the accounting for the disposal of fixed assets.

The recording of disposals of fixed assets will vary. In all cases, however, any depreciation for the current period should be recorded, and the book value of the asset is then removed from the accounts. Removing the book value from the accounts decreases the asset's accumulated depreciation account and the asset account for the cost of the asset. For assets retired from service, a loss may be recorded for any remaining book value of the asset.

When a fixed asset is sold, the book value is removed and the cash or other asset received is also recorded. If the selling price is more than the book value of the asset, the transaction results in a gain. If the selling price is less than the book value, there is a loss.

4. Describe the accounting for depletion of natural resources.

The amount of periodic depletion is computed by multiplying the quantity of minerals extracted during the period by a depletion rate. The depletion rate is computed by dividing the cost of the mineral deposit by its estimated size. Recording depletion increases a depletion expense account and an accumulated depletion account.

5. Describe the accounting for intangible assets.

Long-term assets that are without physical attributes but are used in the business are classified as intangible assets. Examples of intangible assets are patents, copyrights, trademarks, and goodwill. The initial cost of an intangible asset should be recorded by increasing an asset account. For patents and copyrights, this cost should be written off, or amortized, over the years of the asset's expected usefulness by increasing an expense account and decreasing the intangible asset account. Trademarks and goodwill are not amortized, but are written down only on impairment.

6. Describe how depreciation expense is reported in an income statement, and prepare a balance sheet that includes fixed assets and intangible assets.

The amount of depreciation expense and the method or methods used in computing depreciation should be disclosed in the financial statements. In addition, each major class of fixed assets should be disclosed, along with the related accumulated depreciation. Intangible assets are usually presented in the balance sheet in a separate section immediately following fixed assets. Each major class of intangible assets should be disclosed at an amount net of the amortization recorded to date.

Key Terms

Accelerated depreciation method	Depreciation	Residual value
Amortization	Double-declining-balance method	Revenue expenditures
Book value	Fixed assets	Straight-line method
Capital expenditures	Goodwill	Trademark
Copyright	Intangible assets	
Depletion	Patents	

Illustrative Problem

McCollum Company, a furniture wholesaler, acquired new equipment at a cost of $150,000 at the beginning of the fiscal year. The equipment has an estimated life of 5 years and an estimated residual value of $12,000. Ellen McCollum, the president, has requested information regarding alternative depreciation methods.

(continued)

Instructions

Determine the annual depreciation for each of the 5 years of estimated useful life of the equipment, the accumulated depreciation at the end of each year, and the book value of the equipment at the end of each year by (a) the straight-line method and (b) the double-declining-balance method.

Solution

	Year	Depreciation Expense	Accumulated Depreciation, End of Year	Book Value, End of Year
a.	1	$27,600*	$ 27,600	$122,400
	2	27,600	55,200	94,800
	3	27,600	82,800	67,200
	4	27,600	110,400	39,600
	5	27,600	138,000	12,000

*$27,600 = ($150,000 − $12,000) ÷ 5

	Year	Depreciation Expense	Accumulated Depreciation, End of Year	Book Value, End of Year
b.	1	$60,000**	$ 60,000	$ 90,000
	2	36,000	96,000	54,000
	3	21,600	117,600	32,400
	4	12,960	130,560	19,440
	5	7,440***	138,000	12,000

**$60,000 = $150,000 × 40%
***The asset is not depreciated below the estimated residual value of $12,000.

Self-Examination Questions   *(Answers appear at end of chapter.)*

1. Which of the following expenditures incurred in connection with acquiring machinery is a proper addition to the asset account?
   A. Freight
   B. Installation costs
   C. Both A and B
   D. Neither A nor B

2. What is the amount of depreciation, using the double-declining-balance method (twice the straight-line rate) for the second year of use for equipment costing $9,000, with an estimated residual value of $600 and an estimated life of 3 years?
   A. $6,000
   B. $3,000
   C. $2,000
   D. $400

3. An example of an accelerated depreciation method is:
   A. Straight-line
   B. Double-declining-balance
   C. Units-of-production
   D. Depletion

4. Hyde Inc. purchased mineral rights estimated at 2,500,000 tons near Great Falls, Montana, for $3,600,000 on August 7, 2008. During the remainder of the year, Hyde mined 175,000 tons of ore. What is the depletion expense for 2008?
   A. $121,528
   B. $252,000
   C. $1,500,000
   D. $3,600,000

5. Which of the following is an example of an intangible asset?
   A. Patents
   B. Goodwill
   C. Copyrights
   D. All of the above

Class Discussion Questions

1. Which of the following qualities are characteristic of fixed assets? (a) tangible, (b) capable of repeated use in the operations of the business, (c) held for sale in the normal course of business, (d) used rarely in the operations of the business, (e) long-lived.

2. Office Outfitters Co. has a fleet of automobiles and trucks for use by salespersons and for delivery of office supplies and equipment. Westgate Auto Sales Co. has automobiles and trucks for sale. Under what caption would the automobiles and trucks be reported on the balance sheet of (a) Office Outfitters Co., (b) Westgate Auto Sales Co.?

3. Design Space Co. acquired an adjacent vacant lot with the hope of selling it in the future at a gain. The lot is not intended to be used in Design Space's business operations. Where should such real estate be listed in the balance sheet?

4. Triplent Company solicited bids from several contractors to construct an addition to its office building. The lowest bid received was for $750,000. Triplent Company decided to construct the addition itself at a cost of $590,000. What amount should be recorded in the building account?

5. Distinguish between the accounting for capital expenditures and revenue expenditures.

6. Immediately after a used truck is acquired, a new motor is installed and the tires are replaced at a total cost of $4,150. Is this a capital expenditure or a revenue expenditure?

7. Classify each of the following expenditures as either a revenue or capital expenditure: (a) installation of a video messaging system on a semitrailer, (b) changing oil in a delivery truck, (c) purchase of a color copier.

8. Are the amounts at which fixed assets are reported in the balance sheet their approximate market values as of the balance sheet date? Discuss.

9. a. Does the recognition of depreciation in the accounts provide a special cash fund for the replacement of fixed assets? Explain.
   b. Describe the nature of depreciation as the term is used in accounting.

10. Emporium Company purchased a machine that has a manufacturer's suggested life of 20 years. The company plans to use the machine on a special project that will last 13 years. At the completion of the project, the machine will be sold. Over how many years should the machine be depreciated?

11. Is it necessary for a business to use the same method of computing depreciation (a) for all classes of its depreciable assets, (b) in the financial statements and in determining income taxes?

12. a. Under what conditions is the use of an accelerated depreciation method most appropriate?
    b. Why is an accelerated depreciation method often used for income tax purposes?
    c. What is the Modified Accelerated Cost Recovery System (MACRS), and under what conditions is it used?

13. For some of the fixed assets of a business, the balance in Accumulated Depreciation is exactly equal to the cost of the asset. (a) Is it permissible to record additional depreciation on the assets if they are still useful to the business? Explain. (b) When should an entry be made to remove the cost and the accumulated depreciation from the accounts?

14. How is depletion determined?

15. a. Over what period of time should the cost of a patent acquired by purchase be amortized?
    b. In general, what is the required accounting treatment for research and development costs?
    c. How should goodwill be amortized?

Exercises

E7-1

Costs of acquiring fixed assets

Obj 1

Kelly Melnik owns and operates Aaladin Print Co. During July, Aaladin Print Co. incurred the following costs in acquiring two printing presses. One printing press was new, and the other was used by a business that recently filed for bankruptcy.

Costs related to new printing press:

1. Sales tax on purchase price
2. Insurance while in transit

(continued)

3. Freight
4. Special foundation
5. Fee paid to factory representative for installation
6. New parts to replace those damaged in unloading

Costs related to used printing press:

7. Fees paid to attorney to review purchase agreement
8. Installation
9. Repair of vandalism during installation
10. Replacement of worn-out parts
11. Freight
12. Repair of damage incurred in reconditioning the press

a. Indicate which costs incurred in acquiring the new printing press should be debited to the asset account.
b. Indicate which costs incurred in acquiring the used printing press should be debited to the asset account.

E7-2

Determine cost of land

Obj 1

Serenity Ski Co. has developed a tract of land into a ski resort. The company has cut the trees, cleared and graded the land and hills, and constructed ski lifts. (a) Should the tree cutting, land clearing, and grading costs of constructing the ski slopes increase be debited to the land account? (b) If such costs are debited to Land, should they be depreciated?

E7-3

Determine cost of land

Obj 1

✓ $224,650

Next Day Delivery Company acquired an adjacent lot to construct a new warehouse, paying $25,000 and giving a short-term note for $175,000. Legal fees paid were $1,200, delinquent taxes assumed were $10,850, and fees paid to remove an old building from the land were $15,000. Materials salvaged from the demolition of the building were sold for $2,400. A contractor was paid $760,000 to construct a new warehouse. Determine the cost of the land to be reported on the balance sheet.

E7-4

Capital and revenue expenditures

Obj 1

Thare Co. incurred the following costs related to trucks and vans used in operating its delivery service:

1. Change the oil and greased the joints of all the trucks and vans.
2. Installed security systems on four of the newer trucks.
3. Changed the radiator fluid on a truck that had been in service for the past four years.
4. Installed a hydraulic lift to a van.
5. Removed a two-way radio from one of the trucks and installed a new radio with a greater range of communication.
6. Overhauled the engine on one of the trucks that had been purchased three years ago.
7. Tinted the back and side windows of one of the vans to discourage theft of contents.
8. Repaired a flat tire on one of the vans.
9. Rebuilt the transmission on one of the vans that had been driven 40,000 miles. The van was no longer under warranty.
10. Replaced the trucks' suspension system with a new suspension system that allows for the delivery of heavier loads.

Classify each of the costs as a capital expenditure or a revenue expenditure.

E7-5

Capital and revenue expenditures

Obj 1

Felix Little owns and operates Big Sky Transport Co. During the past year, Felix incurred the following costs related to his 18-wheel truck.

1. Replaced a headlight that had burned out.
2. Replaced fog and cab light bulbs.
3. Installed a television in the sleeping compartment of the truck.
4. Removed the old CB radio and replaced it with a newer model with a greater range.
5. Replaced a shock absorber that had worn out.
6. Installed a wind deflector on top of the cab to increase fuel mileage.
7. Replaced the old radar detector with a newer model that detects the KA frequencies now used by many of the state patrol radar guns. The detector is wired directly into the cab, so that it is partially hidden. In addition, Felix fastened the detector to the truck with a locking device that prevents its removal.
8. Changed engine oil.
9. Replaced the hydraulic brake system that had begun to fail during his latest trip through the Rocky Mountains.
10. Modified the factory-installed turbo charger with a special-order kit designed to add 50 more horsepower to the engine performance.

Classify each of the costs as a capital expenditure or a revenue expenditure.

E7-6

Nature of depreciation

Obj 2

Armored Metal Co. reported $975,600 for equipment and $600,000 for accumulated depreciation—equipment on its balance sheet.

Does this mean (a) that the replacement cost of the equipment is $975,600 and (b) that $600,000 is set aside in a special fund for the replacement of the equipment? Explain.

E7-7

Straight-line depreciation rates

Obj 2

✓ a. 50%

Convert each of the following estimates of useful life to a straight-line depreciation rate, stated as a percentage, assuming that the residual value of the fixed asset is to be ignored: (a) 2 years, (b) 8 years, (c) 10 years, (d) 20 years, (e) 25 years, (f) 40 years, (g) 50 years.

E7-8

Straight-line depreciation

Obj 2

✓ $11,200

A refrigerator used by a meat processor has a cost of $198,500, an estimated residual value of $30,500, and an estimated useful life of 15 years. What is the amount of the annual depreciation computed by the straight-line method?

E7-9

Depreciation by two methods

Obj 2

✓ a. $2,800

A John Deere tractor acquired on January 5 at a cost of $44,800 has an estimated useful life of 16 years. Assuming that it will have no residual value, determine the depreciation for each of the first two years (a) by the straight-line method and (b) by the double-declining-balance method. Round to the nearest dollar.

E7-10

Depreciation by two methods

Obj 2

✓ a. $9,500

A storage tank acquired at the beginning of the fiscal year at a cost of $86,000 has an estimated residual value of $10,000 and an estimated useful life of eight years. Determine the following: (a) the amount of annual depreciation by the straight-line method and (b) the amount of depreciation for the first and second year computed by the double-declining-balance method.

E7-11

Partial-year depreciation

Obj 2

✓ a. First year, $1,250

Sandblasting equipment acquired at a cost of $68,000 has an estimated residual value of $18,000 and an estimated useful life of 10 years. It was placed in service on October 1 of the current fiscal year, which ends on December 31. Determine the depreciation for the current fiscal year and for the following fiscal year by (a) the straight-line method and (b) the double-declining-balance method.

E7-12

Book value of fixed assets

Obj 2

The following data were taken from recent annual reports of **Interstate Bakeries Corporation (IBC).** Interstate Bakeries produces, distributes, and sells fresh bakery products nationwide through supermarkets, convenience stores, and its 67 bakeries and 1,500 thrift stores.

	June 3, 2006	May 28, 2005
Land and buildings	$390,573,000	$ 440,164,000
Machinery and equipment	931,408,000	1,023,527,000
Accumulated depreciation	720,880,000	758,318,000

a. Compute the book value of the fixed assets for 2006 and 2005 and explain the differences, if any.
b. Would you normally expect the book value of fixed assets to increase or decrease during the year?

E7-13

Sale of asset

Obj 3

✓ a. $250,000

Equipment acquired on January 3, 2005, at a cost of $360,000, has an estimated useful life of 12 years, has an estimated residual value of $30,000, and is depreciated by the straight-line method.

a. What was the book value of the equipment at December 31, 2008, the end of the year?
b. Assuming that the equipment was sold on April 1, 2009, for $220,000, illustrate the effects on the accounts and financial statements of (1) depreciation for the three months until the sale date, and (2) the sale of the equipment.

E7-14

Disposal of fixed asset

Obj 3

✓ b. $98,750

Equipment acquired on January 3, 2005, at a cost of $147,500, has an estimated useful life of eight years and an estimated residual value of $17,500.

a. What was the annual amount of depreciation for the years 2005, 2006, and 2007, using the straight-line method of depreciation?
b. What was the book value of the equipment on January 1, 2008?
c. Assuming that the equipment was sold on January 2, 2008, for $95,000, illustrate the effects on the accounts and financial statements of the sale.
d. Assuming that the equipment had been sold on January 2, 2008, for $100,000 instead of $95,000, illustrate the effects on the accounts and financial statements of the sale.

E7-15

Recording depletion

Obj 4

✓ a. $4,500,000

Rainbow Mining Co. acquired mineral rights for $30,000,000. The mineral deposit is estimated at 75,000,000 tons. During the current year, 11,250,000 tons were mined and sold.

a. Determine the amount of depletion expense for the current year.
b. Illustrate the effects on the accounts and financial statements of the depletion expense.

E7-16

Recording amortization

Obj 5

✓ a. $52,850

Venture Company acquired patent rights on January 3, 2005, for $661,500. The patent has a useful life equal to its legal life of 15 years. On January 5, 2008, Venture successfully defended the patent in a lawsuit at a cost of $105,000.

a. Determine the patent amortization expense for the current year ended December 31, 2008.
b. Journalize the adjusting entry to recognize the amortization.

E7-17

Goodwill impairment

Obj 5

On January 1, 2005, StreetSmart Financial, Inc., purchased the assets of NIT Insurance Co. for $40,000,000, a price reflecting a $15,000,000 goodwill premium. On December 31, 2008, StreetSmart determined that the goodwill from the NIT acquisition was impaired and had a value of only $9,000,000.

a. Determine the book value of the goodwill on December 31, 2008, prior to making the impairment adjustment.
b. Illustrate the effects on the accounts and financial statements of the December 31, 2008, adjustment for the goodwill impairment.

E7-18

Book value of fixed assets

Obj 6

Apple Computer, Inc., designs, manufactures, and markets personal computers and related software. Apple also manufactures and distributes music players (Ipod) along with related accessories and service, including the online distribution of third-party music. The following information was taken from a recent annual report of Apple:

Property, Plant, and Equipment (in millions):

	2006	**2005**
Land and buildings	$626	$361
Machinery, equipment, and internal-use software	595	470
Office furniture and equipment	94	81
Other fixed assets related to leases	760	569
Accumulated depreciation and amortization	(794)	(664)

a. Compute the book value of the fixed assets for 2006 and 2005 and explain the differences, if any.
b. Would you normally expect the book value of fixed assets to increase or decrease during the year?

E7-19

Balance sheet presentation

Obj 6

List the errors you find in the following partial balance sheet:

PLANET BRONZE COMPANY
Balance Sheet
December 31, 2008
Assets

Total current assets			$ 478,000

	Replacement Cost	**Accumulated Depreciation**	**Book Value**
Property, plant, and equipment:			
Land	$ 80,000	$ 16,000	$ 64,000
Buildings	208,000	60,800	147,200
Factory equipment	440,000	233,600	206,400
Office equipment	96,000	64,000	32,000
Patents	64,000	—	64,000
Goodwill	36,000	4,000	32,000
Total property plant, and equipment	$924,000	$378,400	545,600

Problems

P7-1

Allocate payments and receipts to fixed asset accounts

Obj 1

SPREADSHEET

✓ 2. Land, $322,400

The following payments and receipts are related to land, land improvements, and buildings acquired for use in a wholesale apparel business. The receipts are identified by an asterisk.

a.	Finder's fee paid to real estate agency	$ 7,500
b.	Cost of real estate acquired as a plant site: Land	210,000
	Building	50,000
c.	Fee paid to attorney for title search	2,500
d.	Delinquent real estate taxes on property, assumed by purchaser	20,650
e.	Cost of razing and removing building	16,250
f.	Cost of filling and grading land	12,500
g.	Proceeds from sale of salvage materials from old building	5,000*
h.	Architect's and engineer's fees for plans and supervision	36,000
i.	Special assessment paid to city for extension of water main to the property	8,000
j.	Premium on one-year insurance policy during construction	3,600
k.	Money borrowed to pay building contractor	900,000*
l.	Cost of trees and shrubbery planted	18,000
m.	Cost of repairing windstorm damage during construction	3,000
n.	Cost of repairing vandalism damage during construction	4,200
o.	Cost of paving parking lot to be used by customers	15,000
p.	Proceeds from insurance company for windstorm and vandalism damage	7,000*
q.	Interest incurred on building loan during construction	54,000
r.	Payment to building contractor for new building	1,000,000
s.	Refund of premium on insurance policy (j) canceled after 10 months	600*

Instructions

1. Assign each payment and receipt to Land (unlimited life), Land Improvements (limited life), Building, or Other Accounts. Indicate receipts by an asterisk. Identify each item by letter and list the amounts in columnar form, as follows:

Item	Land	Land Improvements	Building	Other Accounts

2. Determine the amount increases to Land, Land Improvements, and Building.
3. The costs assigned to the land, which is used as a plant site, will not be depreciated, while the costs assigned to land improvements will be depreciated. Explain this seemingly contradictory application of the concept of depreciation.

P7-2

Compare two depreciation methods

Obj 2

✓ a. 2007: straight-line depreciation, $107,500

Seal Coatings Company purchased waterproofing equipment on January 2, 2007, for $475,000. The equipment was expected to have a useful life of 4 years, and a residual value of $45,000.

Instructions

Determine the amount of depreciation expense for the years ended December 31, 2007, 2008, 2009, and 2010, by (a) the straight-line method, and (b) the double-declining-balance method. Also determine the total depreciation expense for the 4 years by each method. The following columnar headings are suggested for recording the depreciation expense amounts:

	Depreciation Expense	
Year	Straight-Line Method	Double-Declining-Balance Method

P7-3

Depreciation by two methods; partial years

Obj 2

SPREADSHEET

✓ a. 2006, $1,255

Covershot Company purchased plastic laminating equipment on July 1, 2006, for $7,830. The equipment was expected to have a useful life of 3 years, and a residual value of $300.

Instructions

Determine the amount of depreciation expense for the years ended December 31, 2006, 2007, 2008, and 2009, by (a) the straight-line method, and (b) the double-declining-balance method.

P7-4

Depreciation by two methods; sale of fixed asset

Objs 2, 3

✓ 1. b. Year 1, $70,000 depreciation expense

New lithographic equipment, acquired at a cost of $175,000 at the beginning of a fiscal year, has an estimated useful life of five years and an estimated residual value of $15,000. The manager requested information regarding the effect of alternative methods on the amount of depreciation expense each year. On the basis of the data presented to the manager, the double-declining-balance method was selected. In the first week of the fifth year, the equipment was sold for $25,000.

Instructions

1. Determine the annual depreciation expense for each of the estimated five years of use, the accumulated depreciation at the end of each year, and the book value of the equipment at the end of each year by (a) the straight-line method and (b) the double-declining-balance method (at twice the straight-line rate). The following columnar headings are suggested for each schedule:

Year	Depreciation Expense	Accumulated Depreciation, End of Year	Book Value, End of Year

2. Illustrate the effects on the accounts and financial statements of the sale.
3. Illustrate the effects on the accounts and financial statements of the sale, assuming a sale price of $20,000 instead of $25,000.

P7-5

Amortization and depletion

Objs 4, 5

✓ 1. a. $216,000

Data related to the acquisition of timber rights and intangible assets during the current year ended December 31 are as follows:

a. Timber rights on a tract of land were purchased for $648,000 on July 5. The stand of timber is estimated at 3,600,000 board feet. During the current year, 1,200,000 board feet of timber were cut and sold.
b. Goodwill in the amount of $27,000,000 was purchased on January 7.
c. Governmental and legal costs of $780,000 were incurred on October 4 in obtaining a patent with an estimated economic life of 12 years. Amortization is to be for one-fourth year.

Instructions

1. Determine the amount of the amortization or depletion expense for the current year for each of the preceding items.
2. Illustrate the effects on the accounts and financial statements of the adjustments for the amortization or depletion expense for each item.

Activities

A7-1

Ethics and professional conduct in business

ETHICS

Leah Corbin, CPA, is an assistant to the controller of Beartooth Consulting Co. In her spare time, Leah also prepares tax returns and performs general accounting services for clients. Frequently, Leah performs these services after her normal working hours, using Beartooth Consulting Co.' s computers and laser printers. Occasionally, Leah's clients will call her at the office during regular working hours.

    Discuss whether Leah is performing in a professional manner.

A7-2

Financial vs. tax depreciation

The following is an excerpt from a conversation between two employees of Resource Technologies, Haley Eubanks and Clay Hamon. Haley is the accounts payable clerk, and Clay is the cashier.

Haley: Clay, could I get your opinion on something?
Clay: Sure, Haley.
Haley: Do you know Amber, the fixed assets clerk?
Clay: I know who she is, but I don't know her real well. Why?
Haley: Well, I was talking to her at lunch last Monday about how she liked her job, etc. You know, the usual . . . and she mentioned something about having to keep two sets of books . . . one for taxes and one for the financial statements. That can't be good accounting, can it? What do you think?
Clay: Two sets of books? It doesn't sound right.
Haley: It doesn't seem right to me either. I was always taught that you had to use generally accepted accounting principles. How can there be two sets of books? What can be the difference between the two?

How would you respond to Clay and Haley if you were Amber?

A7-3

Effect of depreciation on net income

Cowboy Construction Co. specializes in building replicas of historic houses. Tom Askew, president of Cowboy Construction, is considering the purchase of various items of equipment on July 1, 2006, for $150,000. The equipment would have a useful life of five years and no residual value. In the past, all equipment has been leased. For tax purposes, Tom is considering depreciating the equipment by the straight-line method. He discussed the matter with his CPA and learned that, although the straight-line method could be elected, it was to his advantage to use the Modified Accelerated Cost Recovery System (MACRS) for tax purposes. He asked for your advice as to which method to use for tax purposes.

1. Compute depreciation for each of the years (2006, 2007, 2008, 2009, 2010, and 2011) of useful life by (a) the straight-line method and (b) MACRS. In using the straight-line method, one-half year's depreciation should be computed for 2006 and 2011. Use the MACRS rates presented in the chapter.
2. Assuming that income before depreciation and income tax is estimated to be $300,000 uniformly per year and that the income tax rate is 30%, compute the net income for each of the years 2006, 2007, 2008, 2009, 2010, and 2011, if (a) the straight-line method is used and (b) MACRS is used.
3. What factors would you present for Tom's consideration in the selection of a depreciation method?

A7-4

Shopping for a delivery truck

GROUP

You are planning to acquire a delivery truck for use in your business for three years. In groups of three or four, explore a local dealer's purchase and leasing options for the truck. Summarize the costs of purchasing versus leasing, and list other factors that might help you decide whether to buy or lease the truck.

A7-5

Ethics and professional conduct in business

ETHICS

The following is an excerpt from a conversation between the chief executive officer, Harry Balmer, and the chief financial officer, Connie Kenner, of BKX Group Inc.:

Harry (CEO): Connie, as you know, the auditors are coming in to audit our year-end financial statements pretty soon. Do you see any problems on the horizon?

Connie (CFO): Well, you know about our "famous" Robert Company acquisition of a couple of years ago. We booked $5,000,000 of goodwill from that acquisition, and the accounting rules require us to recognize any impairment of goodwill.

Harry (CEO): Uh-oh.

Connie (CFO): Yeah right. We had to shut the old Robert Company operations down this year because those products were no longer selling. Thus, our auditor is going to insist that we write off the $5,000,000 of goodwill to reflect the impaired value.

Harry (CEO): We can't have that—at least not this year! Do everything you can to push back on this one. We just can't take that kind of a hit this year. The most we could stand is $3,000,000. Connie, keep the write-off to $3,000,000 and promise anything in the future. Then we'll deal with that when we get there.

How should Connie respond to the CEO?

A7-6

Applying for patents, copyrights, and trademarks

Go to the Internet and review the procedures for applying for a patent, a copyright, and a trademark. One Internet site that is useful for this purpose is **http://idresearch.com,** which is linked to the text's Web site at **academic.cengage.com/warren/survey4e.** Prepare a written summary of these procedures.

Answers to Self-Examination Questions

1.　**C**　All amounts spent to get a fixed asset (such as machinery) in place and ready for use are proper additions to the asset account. In the case of machinery acquired, the freight (answer A) and the installation costs (answer B) are both (answer C) proper charges to the machinery account.

2.　**C**　The periodic charge for depreciation under the double-declining-balance method for the second year is determined by first computing the depreciation charge for the first year. The depreciation for the first year of $6,000 (answer A) is computed by multiplying the cost of the equipment, $9,000, by ⅔ (the straight-line rate of ⅓ multiplied by 2). The depreciation for the second year of $2,000 (answer C) is then determined by multiplying the book value at the end of the first year, $3,000 (the cost of $9,000 minus the first-year depreciation of $6,000), by ⅔. The third year's depreciation is $400 (answer D). It is determined by multiplying the book value at the end of the second year, $1,000, by ⅔, thus yielding $667. However, the equipment cannot be depreciated below its residual value of $600; thus,

the third-year depreciation is $400 ($1,000 − $600).

3.　**B**　A depreciation method that provides for a higher depreciation amount in the first year of the use of an asset and a gradually declining periodic amount thereafter is called an accelerated depreciation method. The double-declining-balance method (answer B) is an example of such a method.

4.　**B**　$252,000. The depletion expense is determined by first computing a depletion rate. For Hyde Inc. the depletion rate is $1.44 per ton ($3,600,000/2,500,000 tons). The depletion rate of $1.44 per ton is then multiplied by the number of tons mined during the year, or 175,000 tons, to determine the depletion expense of $252,000 (175,000 tons × $1.44).

5.　**D**　Long-lived assets that are useful in operations, not held for sale, and without physical qualities are called intangible assets. Patents, goodwill, and copyrights are examples of intangible assets (answer D).

CHAPTER 8

Liabilities and Stockholders' Equity

Learning Objectives

After studying this chapter, you should be able to:

Obj 1
Describe how businesses finance their operations.

Obj 2
Describe and illustrate current liabilities, notes payable, taxes, contingencies, and payroll.

Obj 3
Describe and illustrate the financing of operations through issuance of bonds.

Obj 4
Describe and illustrate the financing of operations through issuance of stock.

Obj 5
Describe and illustrate the accounting for cash and stock dividends.

Obj 6
Describe the effects of stock splits on the financial statements.

Obj 7
Describe financial statement reporting of liabilities and stockholders' equity.

Obj 8
Analyze the impact of debt or equity financing on earnings per share.

Banks and other financial institutions provide loans, or credit, to finance purchases for immediate consumption, termed trade, and for purchases of fixed assets. Using credit is probably as old as commerce itself. The Babylonians were lending money as early as 1300 B.C., and the Bible indicates the use of debt in the time of Moses. The proper use of credit can provide an individual convenience and buying power. Credit cards provide individuals convenience by supporting Internet purchases, by eliminating the hassles of checks or cash, and by consolidating payments to a single credit card company. Credit also creates purchasing power by allowing individuals to purchase fixed assets, such as automobiles and houses, prior to having the total purchase price. Just imagine if you had to save the complete purchase price of a home prior to purchase. Most of us would only be able to buy a house by the time our families were grown and gone. Thus, credit allows us to purchase assets whose benefits are consumed in the long term, such as houses and cars, with obligations that match the time period. Thus, credit cards are appropriate uses of credit for near-term consumption, while a mortgage is appropriate for purchasing a home.

In the same way, the proper use of debt can help a business reach its business objectives. For example, *Barnes & Noble*, a major media superstore in the United States, uses short-term credit to purchase books, music, and DVDs from publishers and studios. As these items are sold, cash is generated to pay back the suppliers for these purchases. In addition, Barnes & Noble uses long-term debt to expand its business. As a result of Barnes & Noble's wise use of credit and continued success, it has become the number one retail brand for quality, sold over 500 million books annually, become the second-largest coffeehouse in the United States, and built a network of over 820 stores.

Businesses also finance operations by issuing stock. In this chapter, we describe and illustrate debt and stock financing.

Financing Operations

A business must finance its operations through either debt or equity. Debt financing includes all liabilities owed by a business, including both current and long-term liabilities. For example, most businesses maintain a normal amount of accounts payable due vendors and other suppliers. In effect, these vendors and suppliers are helping finance the business. A business may also issue notes or bonds to finance its operations. While accounts payable normally do not include interest payments, notes and bonds require that interest be paid periodically.

A business may also finance its operations through equity. A proprietorship or partnership obtains equity financing from investments by the owner(s). A corporation obtains its equity financing by issuing stock. Corporations can issue different classes of stock with different rights and privileges, such as rights to dividend payments.

Another way to think of how businesses finance their operations is to think of the accounting equation. In the preceding chapters, we focused primarily on the income statement and the asset side of the balance sheet. In this chapter, we are focusing on the right side of the accounting equation: the liabilities and stockholders' equity. We begin by describing current liabilities, including notes payable, deferred taxes, contingencies, and payroll. We then focus on bonds payable and stock financing.

Liabilities

Liabilities are debts owed to others. Liabilities due within a short time, usually 1 year, are current liabilities. Liabilities due beyond 1 year are classified as long-term liabilities. In addition, in some cases a business incurs a liability if certain events occur in the future. In this section, we describe and illustrate these various types of liabilities.

Current Liabilities

Your credit card balance is probably due within a short time, such as 30 days. Such liabilities that are to be paid out of current assets and are due within a short time, usually within 1 year, are called *current liabilities*. Most current liabilities arise from two basic transactions:

1. Receiving goods or services prior to making payment.
2. Receiving payment prior to delivering goods or services.

An example of the first type of transaction is an account payable arising from a purchase of merchandise for resale. An example of the second type of transaction is unearned rent arising from the receipt of rent in advance. We described and illustrated the accounting for accounts payable and unearned liabilities in earlier chapters. In the remainder of this section, we focus on notes payable, deferred liabilities, contingencies, and payroll-related liabilities.

Notes Payable

Notes can be issued to creditors to temporarily satisfy an account payable created earlier. They can also be issued when merchandise or other assets are purchased. For example, assume that a business issues a 90-day, 12% note for $1,000, dated August 1, 2008, to Murray Co. for a $1,000 overdue account. The effect on the accounts and financial statements of Murray Co. for issuing and paying the note follows.[1]

---

[1] The effect on the accounts and financial statements are shown for the issuer (borrower) of the note. The effects for the receiver (lender) of the note are exactly opposite those for the issuer.

Issuing a 90-day, 12% note on account on August 1.

Statement of Cash Flows	Balance Sheet					Income Statement
	Assets	=	Liabilities	+	Stockholders' Equity	
		=	Accounts Payable	+	Notes Payable	
Aug. 1.			−1,000		1,000	

Paying of note on October 30.

Statement of Cash Flows	Balance Sheet					Income Statement
	Assets	=	Liabilities	+	Stockholders' Equity	
	Cash	=	Notes Payable	+	Retained Earnings	
Oct. 30.	−1,030		−1,000		−30	Oct. 30.

Statement of Cash Flows		Income Statement	
Oct. 30. Operating	−1,030	Oct. 30. Interest expense	−30

The interest expense is reported in the Other Expense section of the income statement for the year ended December 31, 2008. If the accounting period ends before the maturity date of the note, interest expense to the end of the period should be recorded.

Income Taxes

Under the United States Tax Code, corporations are taxable entities that must pay federal income taxes. Depending on where it is located, a corporation may also be required to pay state and local income taxes. Although we limit our discussion to federal income taxes, the basic concepts also apply to other income taxes.

Most corporations are required to pay estimated federal income taxes in four installments throughout the year. For example, assume that a corporation with a calendar-year accounting period estimates its income tax expense for the year as $84,000. The effect on the accounts and the financial statements of the first of the four estimated tax payments of $21,000 (¼ of $84,000) is as follows:

Statement of Cash Flows	Balance Sheet					Income Statement
	Assets	=	Liabilities	+	Stockholders' Equity	
	Cash	=		+	Retained Earnings	
April 5.	−21,000				−21,000	April 5.

Statement of Cash Flows		Income Statement	
April 5. Operating	−21,000	Apr. 5. Income tax exp.	−21,000

At year-end, the actual taxable income and the related tax are determined. If additional taxes are owed, the additional liability is recorded. If the total estimated tax payments are more than the tax liability based on actual taxable income, the overpayment should increase Income Tax Receivable and decrease Income Tax Expense.

The **taxable income** of a corporation is determined according to the tax laws. It is often different from the income before income taxes reported in the income statement according to generally accepted accounting principles. As a result, the *income tax based on taxable income* usually differs from the *income tax based on income before taxes*. This difference may need to be allocated between various financial statement periods, depending on the nature of the items causing the differences.

Some differences between taxable income and income before income taxes are created because items are recognized in one period for tax purposes and in another period for income statement purposes. Such differences, called **temporary differences**, reverse or turn around in later years. For example, a company may use MACRS (Modified Accelerated Cost Recovery System) depreciation for tax purposes and the straight-line method for financial reporting purposes.

Since temporary differences reverse in later years, they do not change or reduce the total amount of taxable income over the life of a business. For example, MACRS recognizes more depreciation in the early years but less depreciation in the later years. However, the total depreciation expense is the same for MACRS and the straight-line method over the life of the asset.

Temporary differences affect only the timing of the recognition of revenues and expenses for tax purposes. As a result, the total amount of taxes paid does not change. Only the timing of the payment of taxes is affected. In most cases, managers use tax-planning techniques so that temporary differences delay or defer the payment of taxes to later years. As a result, at the end of each year the amount of the current tax liability and the postponed (deferred) liability must be recorded.

To illustrate, assume that at the end of the first year of operations, a corporation reports $300,000 income before income taxes on its income statement. If we assume an income tax rate of 40%, the income tax expense reported on the income statement is $120,000 ($300,000 × 0.40).[2] However, to reduce the amount owed for current income taxes, the corporation uses tax planning to reduce the taxable income to $100,000. Thus, the income tax actually due for the year is only $40,000 ($100,000 × 0.40). The $80,000 ($120,000 − $40,000) difference between the two tax amounts is created by timing differences. This amount is deferred to future years. The example is summarized here.

Income tax based on $300,000 reported income at 40%	$120,000
Income tax based on $100,000 taxable income at 40%	40,000
Income tax deferred to future years	$ 80,000

The effect of the deferral on the accounts and financial statements is shown as follows:

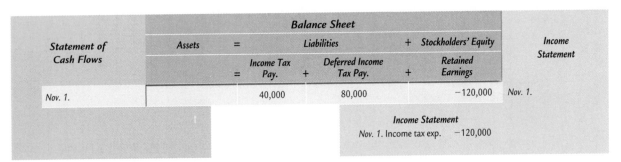

INTEGRITY, OBJECTIVITY, AND ETHICS IN BUSINESS

Today's Mistakes Can Be Tomorrow's Liability

Environmental and public health claims are quickly growing into some of the largest contingent liabilities facing companies. For example, tobacco, asbestos, and environmental cleanup claims have reached billions of dollars and have led to a number of corporate bankruptcies. Managers must be careful that today's decisions do not become tomorrow's nightmares.

The income tax expense reported on the income statement is the total tax, $120,000, expected to be paid on the income for the year. In future years, the $80,000 in *Deferred Income Tax Payable* will be transferred to *Income Tax Payable* as the timing differences reverse and the taxes become due.

The balance of Deferred Income Tax Payable at the end of a year is reported as a liability. The amount due within one year is classified as a current liability. The remainder is classified as a long-term liability or reported in the Deferred Liability section following the Long-Term Liabilities section.[3]

Contingent Liabilities

Some past transactions will result in liabilities if certain events occur in the future. These potential obligations are called **contingent liabilities**. For example, **Ford Motor Company** would have a contingent liability for the estimated costs associated with warranty work. The obligation is contingent on a future event, namely, a customer requiring warranty work on a vehicle. The obligation is the result of a past transaction, which is the original sale of the vehicle.

If the contingent liability is probable and the amount of the liability can be reasonably estimated, it should be recorded in the accounts. An example of such a liability is Ford Motor Company's vehicle warranties. These warranty costs are probable because it is known that warranty repairs will be required on some vehicles. In addition, the costs can be estimated from past warranty experience.

To illustrate, assume that during June a company sells a product for $60,000 that has a 36-month warranty for repairing defects. Past experience indicates that the average cost to repair defects is 5% of the sales price. Warranty expense of $3,000 (0.05 × $60,000) should be recorded along with an increase in estimated product warranty liabilities. By recording the warranty expense in June, revenues and expenses are properly matched in that warranty costs are recorded in the same period as the sales. When the defective product is repaired, the repair costs are recorded by decreasing the warranty liability account and decreasing cash, supplies, or other appropriate accounts.

Warranty Liability. Caterpillar Inc. designs, manufactures, markets, and sells construction, mining, and forestry machinery such as tractors and backhoe loaders. Caterpillar estimates its warranty liability using a historical average of actual warranty payments. Caterpillar disclosed the following warranty data in its 2006 annual report:

	2006	2005	2004
	(Millions of dollars)		
Warranty liability, January 1	$879	$785	$624
Payments	(745)	(712)	(571)
Provision for warranty	819	806	732
Warranty liability, December 31	$953	$879	$785

[3]In some cases, a deferred tax asset can arise for tax benefits to be received in the future. Such deferred tax assets are reported as either a current or long-term asset, depending on when the benefits are expected to be realized.

Payroll

The term **payroll** refers to the amount paid to employees for the services they provide during a period. Payroll can include either salaries or wages or both. *Salary* usually refers to payment for managerial, administrative, or similar services. The rate of salary is normally expressed in terms of a month or a year. The word *wages* usually refers to payment for manual labor, both skilled and unskilled. The rate of wages is normally stated on an hourly or weekly basis. Payroll and related payroll taxes have a significant effect on the net income of most businesses. Although the amount of such expenses varies widely, it is not unusual for a business's payroll and payroll-related expenses to equal nearly one-third of its revenue.

The total earnings of an employee for a payroll period, including bonuses and overtime pay, is called **gross pay**. From this amount is subtracted one or more deductions to arrive at the net pay. **Net pay** is the amount the employer must pay the employee. The deductions for federal taxes are usually the largest deduction. Deductions may also be required for state or local income taxes. Still other deductions may be made for FICA tax, medical insurance, contributions to pensions, and items authorized by individual employees.

The FICA tax withheld from employees contributes to two federal programs. The first program, called *social security*, is for old age, survivors, and disability insurance (OASDI). The second program, called *Medicare*, is health insurance for senior citizens. The FICA tax rate and the amounts subject to the tax are established annually by law.[4]

To illustrate recording payroll, assume that McDermott Co. had a gross payroll of $13,800 for the week ending April 11. Assume that the FICA tax was 7.5% of the gross payroll and that federal and state withholding was $1,655 and $280, respectively. The effect on the accounts and financial statements of McDermott Co. of recording the payroll follows:

Statement of Cash Flows	Balance Sheet					Income Statement
	Assets =	Liabilities			+ Stockholders' Equity	
	Cash =	FICA Tax Payable +	Employee Federal Income Tax Payable +	Employee State Income Tax Payable +	Retained Earnings	
April 11.	−10,830	1,035	1,655	280	−13,800	April 11.

Statement of Cash Flows		Income Statement	
April 11. Operating	−10,830	April 11. Wages and salary exp.	−13,800

The FICA, federal, and state taxes withheld from the employees' earnings are not expenses to the employer. Rather, these amounts are withheld on the behalf of employees. These amounts must be remitted periodically to the appropriate state and federal agencies.

In addition to amounts withheld on behalf of employees, most employers are also subject to federal and state payroll taxes based on the amount paid their employees. Such taxes are an operating expense of the business.

[4]The social security tax portion of the FICA tax is limited to a specific amount of the annual compensation for each individual. The 2007 limitation is $97,500. The Medicare portion is not subject to a limitation. Throughout this text, we will simplify by assuming that all compensation is within the social security limitation. By doing so, the social security and Medicare can be expressed as a single rate of 7.5%. The single rate for 2007 is 7.65%.

Employers are required to contribute to the social security and Medicare programs for each employee. The employer must match the employee's contribution to each program. In addition, most businesses must pay federal and state unemployment taxes.

The Federal Unemployment Tax Act (FUTA) provides for temporary payments to those who become unemployed as a result of layoffs due to economic causes beyond their control. Types of employment subject to this program are similar to those covered by FICA taxes. The FUTA tax rate and maximum earnings of each employee subject to the tax are established annually by law.

State Unemployment Tax Acts (SUTA) also provide for payments to unemployed workers. The amounts paid as benefits are obtained, for the most part, from a tax levied on employers only. The employment experience and the status of each employer's tax account are reviewed annually, and the tax rates are adjusted accordingly by each state.

The employer's payroll taxes become liabilities when the related payroll is *paid* to employees. The prior payroll information of McDermott Co. indicates that the amount of FICA tax withheld is $1,035 on April 11. Since the employer must match the employees' FICA contributions, the employer's social security payroll tax will also be $1,035. Furthermore, assume that the FUTA and SUTA taxes are $145 and $25, respectively. The effect on the accounts and financial statements of McDermott Co. of recording the payroll tax liabilities for the week follows.

Statement of Cash Flows		Balance Sheet						Income Statement
	Assets =		Liabilities			+	Stockholders' Equity	
	=	FICA Tax Payable +	FUTA Tax Payable +	SUTA Tax Payable +			Retained Earnings	
April 11.		1,035	145	25			−1,205	April 11.

Income Statement
April 11. Payroll tax exp.   −1,205

Payroll tax liabilities are paid to appropriate taxing authorities on a quarterly basis by decreasing cash and the related taxes payable.

Many companies provide their employees a variety of benefits in addition to salary and wages earned. Such **fringe benefits** can take many forms, including vacations, pension plans, and health, life, and disability insurance coverage. When the employer pays part or all of the cost of the fringe benefits, these costs must be recognized as expenses. To properly match revenues and expenses, the estimated cost of these benefits should be recorded as an expense during the period in which the employee earns the benefit. In recording the expense, the related liability is also recorded.

Bonds

Obj **3**

Describe and illustrate the financing of operations through issuance of bonds.

Many large corporations finance their operations through the issuance of bonds. A **bond** is simply a form of an interest-bearing note. Like a note, a bond requires periodic interest payments, and the face amount must be repaid at the maturity date.

A corporation that issues bonds enters into a contract, called a **bond indenture** or trust indenture, with the bondholders. A bond issue is normally divided into a number

INTEGRITY, OBJECTIVITY, AND ETHICS IN BUSINESS

Résumé Padding

Misrepresenting your accomplishments on your résumé could come back to haunt you. In one case, the Chief Financial Officer (CFO) of **Veritas Software** was forced to resign his position when it was discovered that he had lied about earning an MBA from Stanford University, when in actuality he had earned only an undergraduate degree from Idaho State University.

Source: Reuters News Service, October 4, 2002

of individual bonds. Usually the face value of each bond, called the *principal*, is $1,000 or a multiple of $1,000. The interest on bonds may be payable annually, semiannually, or quarterly. Most bonds pay interest semiannually.

The prices of bonds are quoted on bond exchanges as a percentage of the bonds' face value. Thus, investors could purchase or sell Time Warner bonds quoted at 109⅞ for $1,098.75. Likewise, bonds quoted at 110 could be purchased or sold for $1,100.

When a corporation issues bonds, the price that buyers are willing to pay for the bonds depends on these three factors:

1. The face amount of the bonds due at the maturity date.
2. The periodic interest to be paid on the bonds.
3. The market rate of interest.

The periodic interest to be paid on the bonds is identified in the bond indenture and is expressed as a percentage of the face amount of the bond. This percentage or rate of interest is called the **contract rate** or *coupon rate*. The **market rate of interest**, sometimes called the *effective rate of interest*, is determined by transactions between buyers and sellers of similar bonds. If the contract rate of interest is the same as the market rate of interest, the bonds sell for their face amount.

To illustrate, assume that on January 1 a corporation issues for cash $100,000 of 12%, 5-year bonds, with interest of $6,000 payable semiannually. The market rate of interest at the time the bonds are issued is 12%. Since the contract rate and the market rate of interest are the same, the bonds will sell at their face amount. The effect on the accounts and financial statements of issuing the bonds, paying the semiannual interest, and paying off the bonds at the maturity date is shown here.

Issuance of bonds payable at face amount on January 1.

Statement of Cash Flows			Balance Sheet				Income Statement
	Assets	=	Liabilities	+	Stockholders' Equity		
	Cash	=	Bonds Payable				
Jan. 1.	100,000		100,000				

Statement of Cash Flows	
Jan. 1. Financing	100,000

Payment of semiannual interest on June 30. (Interest: $100,000 \times 0.12 \times 1/_2 = $6,000)

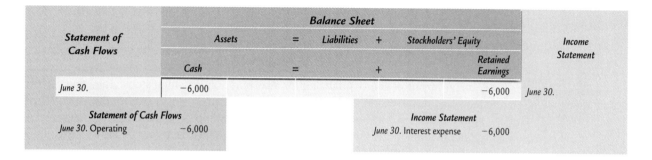

Statement of Cash Flows		Balance Sheet					Income Statement
	Assets	=	Liabilities	+	Stockholders' Equity		
	Cash	=		+	Retained Earnings		
June 30.	−6,000				−6,000		June 30.

Statement of Cash Flows		Income Statement	
June 30. Operating	−6,000	June 30. Interest expense	−6,000

Payment of face value of bonds at maturity.

Statement of Cash Flows		Balance Sheet				Income Statement
	Assets	=	Liabilities	+	Stockholders' Equity	
	Cash	=	Bonds Payable			
Dec. 31.	−100,000		−100,000			

Statement of Cash Flows	
Dec. 31. Financing	−100,000

What if the contract rate of interest differs from the market rate of interest at the time the bonds are issued? If the market rate of interest is higher than the contract rate, the sale is at a **discount on bonds payable**, or less than the face amount of the bonds. Why is this the case? Buyers are not willing to pay the face amount for bonds whose contract rate is lower than the market rate. The discount, in effect, represents the amount necessary to make up for the difference in the market and the contract rates of interest. For example, if the market rate of interest was 13%, the preceding bonds would sell for $96,406.[5] The $3,594 discount ($100,000 − $96,406) can be viewed as the amount that is needed to entice investors to accept a contract rate of interest that is below the market rate. In other words, you can think of the discount as the market's way of adjusting a bond's contract rate of interest to the higher market rate of interest.

If the market rate is lower than the contract rate, the sale is at a **premium on bonds payable**, or more than the face amount of the bonds. In this case, buyers are willing to pay more than the face amount for bonds whose contract rate is higher than the market rate. For example, if the market rate of interest is 11%, the preceding bonds would sell for $103,769.[6] The premium of $3,769 may be viewed as the amount investors are willing to pay above the face value of the bonds to purchase bonds paying an interest rate of 12% rather than the market interest rate of 11%.

[5]The proceeds of $96,406 can be computed using present value tables. Such computations, however, are beyond the scope of our discussion in this chapter.
[6]The proceeds of $103,769 can be computed using present value tables. Such computations, however, are beyond the scope of our discussion in this chapter.

Generally accepted accounting principles require that bond discounts and premiums be amortized to interest expense over the life of the bond. The amortization of a discount increases interest expense, and the amortization of a premium reduces interest expense.

Stock

Obj **4**

Describe and illustrate the financing of operations through issuance of stock.

A major means of equity financing for a corporation is issuing stock. The equity in the assets that results from issuing stock is called *paid-in capital* or *contributed capital*. Another major means of equity financing for a corporation's operations is through retaining net income in the business, called *retained earnings*. In this section, we discuss the financing of a corporation's operations through issuing stock.

The number of shares of stock that a corporation is authorized to issue is stated in its charter. The term *issued* refers to the shares issued to the stockholders. A corporation may, under circumstances we discuss later in this chapter, reacquire some of the stock that it has issued. The stock remaining in the hands of stockholders is then called **outstanding stock**. The relationship between authorized, issued, and outstanding stock is shown in the margin.

Shares of stock are often assigned a monetary amount, called **par**. Corporations can issue stock certificates to stockholders to document their ownership. Printed on a stock certificate is the par value of the stock, the name of the stockholder, and the number of shares owned. Stock can also be issued without par, in which case it is called *no-par stock*. Some states require the board of directors to assign a **stated value** to no-par stock.

Because corporations have limited liability, creditors have no claim against the personal assets of stockholders. However, some state laws require that corporations maintain a minimum stockholder contribution to protect creditors. This minimum amount is called *legal capital*. The amount of required legal capital varies among the states, but it usually includes the amount of par or stated value of the shares of stock issued.

Number of shares authorized, issued, and outstanding

The major rights that accompany ownership of a share of stock are as follows:

1. The right to vote in matters concerning the corporation.
2. The right to share in distributions of earnings.
3. The right to share in assets on liquidation.

Common and Preferred Stock

When only one class of stock is issued, it is called **common stock**. In this case, each share of common stock has equal rights. To appeal to a broader investment market, a corporation can issue one or more classes of stock with various preference rights. A common example of such a right is the preference to dividends. Such a stock is generally called a **preferred stock**.

The dividend rights of preferred stock are usually stated in monetary terms or as a percentage of par. For example, $4 preferred stock has a right to an annual $4-per-share dividend. If the par value of the preferred stock were $50, the same right to dividends could be stated as 8% ($4/$50) preferred stock.

The board of directors of a corporation has the sole authority to distribute dividends to the stockholders. When such action is taken, the directors are said to *declare a dividend*. Since dividends are normally based on earnings, a corporation cannot guarantee dividends even to preferred stockholders. However, because they have first rights to any dividends, the preferred stockholders have a better chance of receiving regular dividends than do the common stockholders.

Issuance of Stock

Because different classes of stock have different rights, a separate account is used for recording the amount of each class of stock issued to investors in a corporation. Stock is often issued by a corporation at a price other than its par. This happens because the par value of a stock is simply its legal capital. The price at which stock can be sold by a corporation depends on a variety of factors, such as these:

1. The financial condition, earnings record, and dividend record of the corporation.
2. Investor expectations of the corporation's potential earning power.
3. General business and economic conditions and prospects.

Normally, stock is issued for a price that is more than its par. In this case, it is sold at a **premium on stock**.[7] Thus, if stock with a par of $50 is issued for a price of $60, the stock is sold at a premium of $10. When stock is issued at a premium, Cash or another asset account is increased for the amount received. Common Stock or Preferred Stock is then increased for the par amount. The excess of the amount paid over par is a part of the total capital contributed by the stockholders of the corporation. This amount is usually recorded in an account entitled Paid-In Capital in Excess of Par.

To illustrate, assume that Caldwell Company issues 2,000 shares of $1 par common stock for cash at $55 on November 1. The effects on the accounts and financial statements follow:

Statement of Cash Flows		Balance Sheet						Income Statement
		Assets	=	Liabilities	+	Stockholders' Equity		
		Cash	=		+	Common Stock	+ Paid-In Capital in Excess of Par	
Nov. 1.		110,000				2,000	108,000	

Statement of Cash Flows	
Nov. 1. Financing	110,000

When stock is issued in exchange for assets other than cash, such as land, buildings, and equipment, the assets acquired should be recorded at their fair market value. If this value cannot be objectively determined, the fair market price of the stock issued may be used.

In most states, both preferred and common stock may be issued without a par value. When no-par stock is issued, the entire proceeds are recorded in the stock account. In some states, no-par stock may be assigned a stated value per share. The stated value is recorded like a par value, and the excess of the proceeds over the stated value is recorded in a paid-in capital in excess of stated value account, similar to the recording of a premium.

Reacquired Stock

A corporation may buy its own stock to provide shares for resale to employees, for reissuing as a bonus to employees, or for supporting the market price of the stock. For

---

[7]When stock is issued for a price that is less than its par, the stock is sold at a discount. Many states do not permit stock to be issued at a discount. In others, it may be done only under unusual conditions. For these reasons, we assume that stock is sold at par or at a premium in the remainder of this text.

example, ***General Motors*** bought back its common stock and stated that two primary uses of this stock would be for incentive compensation plans and employee savings plans. Stock that a corporation has once issued and then reacquires is called **treasury stock**.

The purchase of treasury stock increases Treasury Stock and decreases Cash by the cost of the repurchased shares. At the end of the year, the balance of the treasury stock account is reported as a reduction of stockholders' equity. When treasury stock is sold or reissued, Cash is increased by the proceeds from the sale and Treasury Stock is decreased by the cost of its repurchase. Any difference increases or decreases an account called Paid-In Capital from Treasury Stock.

Dividends

Obj **5**

Describe and illustrate the accounting for cash and stock dividends.

When a board of directors declares a cash dividend, it authorizes the distribution of a portion of the corporation's cash to stockholders. When a board of directors declares a stock dividend, it authorizes the distribution of a portion of its stock. In both cases, the declaration of a dividend reduces the corporation's retained earnings.

Cash Dividends

A cash distribution of earnings by a corporation to its shareholders is called a **cash dividend**. Although dividends may be paid in the form of other assets, cash dividends are the most common form.

There are usually three conditions that a corporation must meet to pay a cash dividend:

1. Sufficient retained earnings
2. Sufficient cash
3. Formal action by the board of directors

A large amount of retained earnings does not always mean that a corporation has cash available for paying dividends. Also, a corporation's board of directors is not required by law to declare dividends. This is true even if both retained earnings and cash are large enough to justify a dividend. However, most corporations try to maintain a stable dividend record to make their stock attractive to investors. Although dividends may be paid once a year or semiannually, most corporations pay dividends quarterly. In years of high profits, a corporation may declare a special or extra dividend.

You may have seen announcements of dividend declarations in financial newspapers or investor services. An example of such an announcement follows.

> On June 26, the board of directors of ***Campbell Soup Co.*** declared a quarterly cash dividend of $0.225 per common share to stockholders of record as of the close of business on July 8, payable on July 31.

This announcement includes three important dates: *the date of declaration* (June 26), *the date of record* (July 8), and *the date of payment* (July 31). During the period of time between the record date and the payment date, the stock price is usually quoted as selling *ex-dividends*. This means that since the date of record has passed, a new investor will not receive the dividend.

To illustrate, assume that on *December 1* Hiber Corporation's board of directors declares the following quarterly cash dividend. The date of record is *December 10,* and the date of payment is *January 2.*

	Dividend per Share	Total Dividends
Preferred stock, $100 par, 5,000 shares outstanding	$2.50	$12,500
Common stock, $10 par, 100,000 shares outstanding	$0.30	30,000
Total		$42,500

The effect of the declaration of the dividend on the accounts and financial statements is as follows:

Statement of Cash Flows	Balance Sheet					Income Statement
	Assets	=	Liabilities	+	Stockholders' Equity	
		=	Cash Dividends Payable	+	Retained Earnings	
Dec. 1.			42,500		−42,500	

Note that the date of record, December 10, does not affect the accounts or the financial statements since this date merely determines which stockholders will receive the dividend. The payment of the dividend on January 2 decreases cash and dividends payable.

If a corporation holding treasury stock declares a cash dividend, the dividends are not paid on the treasury shares. To do so would place the corporation in the position of earning income through dealing with itself. For example, if Hiber Corporation in the preceding illustration had held 5,000 shares of its own common stock, the cash dividends on the common stock would have been $28,500 [(100,000 − 5,000) × $0.30] instead of $30,000.

Stock Dividends

A distribution of shares of stock to stockholders is called a **stock dividend**. Usually, such distributions are in common stock and are issued to holders of common stock. Stock dividends are different from cash dividends in that there is no distribution of cash or other assets to stockholders.

The effect of a stock dividend on the stockholders' equity of the issuing corporation is to transfer retained earnings to paid-in capital. For public corporations, the amount transferred from the retained earnings account to the paid-in capital account is normally the fair value (market price) of the shares issued in the stock dividend.[8]

A stock dividend does not change the assets, liabilities, or total stockholders' equity of the corporation. Likewise, it does not change a stockholder's proportionate interest (equity) in the corporation. For example, if a stockholder owned 1,000 of a corporation's 10,000 shares outstanding, the stockholder owns 10% (1,000/10,000) of the corporation. After declaring a 6% stock dividend, the corporation will issue 600 additional shares (10,000 shares × 0.06), and the total shares outstanding will be 10,600. The stockholder of 1,000 shares will receive 60 additional shares and will then own 1,060 shares, which is still a 10% equity.

---

[8]The use of fair market value is justified as long as the number of shares issued for the stock dividend is small (less than 25% of the shares outstanding).

Stock Splits

Obj 6

Describe the effects of stock splits on the financial statements.

Corporations sometimes reduce the par or stated value of their common stock and issue a proportionate number of additional shares. When this is done, a corporation is said to have *split* its stock, and the process is called a **stock split**.

When stock is split, the reduction in par or stated value applies to all shares, including the unissued, issued, and treasury shares. A major objective of a stock split is to reduce the stock's market price per share. This, in turn, should attract more investors to enter the market for the stock and broaden the types and numbers of stockholders.

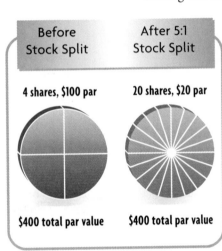

Before Stock Split	After 5:1 Stock Split
4 shares, $100 par	20 shares, $20 par
$400 total par value	$400 total par value

To illustrate a stock split, assume that Rojek Corporation has 10,000 shares of $100 par common stock outstanding with a current market price of $150 per share. The board of directors declares a 5-for-1 stock split, reduces the par to $20, and increases the number of shares to 50,000. The amount of common stock outstanding is $1,000,000 both before and after the stock split. Only the number of shares and the par value per share are changed. Each Rojek Corporation shareholder owns the same total par amount of stock before and after the stock split. For example, a stockholder who owned 4 shares of $100 par stock before the split (total par of $400) would own 20 shares of $20 par stock after the split (total par of $400).

Since there are more shares outstanding after the stock split, we would expect that the market price of the stock would fall. For example, in the preceding example, there would be 5 times as many shares outstanding after the split. Thus, we would expect the market price of the stock to fall from $150 to approximately $30 ($150/5).

Sometimes a firm will authorize a *reverse stock split* in which the number of shares outstanding is reduced to increase the market price of the stock. A common rationale for a reverse stock split is to increase the market value of the stock above minimum listing requirements for a stock exchange. For example, NASDAQ requires a minimum market price of $1 per share. Firms that drop below the $1 market price will sometimes authorize a reverse stock split to increase the market price above the minimum requirement. ***Iomega Corp.*** justified its reverse 1:5 stock split when shares were trading near $1, stating:

> a reverse split will boost shares to above $5 each. Getting it to $5 would make it more attractive to institutional investors.

Since a stock split changes only the par or stated value and the number of shares outstanding, it is not recorded by a journal entry. Although the accounts are not affected, the details of stock splits are normally disclosed in the notes to the financial statements.

Reporting Liabilities and Stockholders' Equity

Obj 7

Describe financial statement reporting of liabilities and stockholders' equity.

Liabilities that are expected to be paid within 1 year are presented in the Current Liabilities section of the balance sheet. Thus, any notes or bonds payable maturing within 1 year should be shown as current liabilities. However, if the notes or bonds are to be paid from noncurrent assets or if the notes or bonds are going to be refinanced, they should be reported as noncurrent liabilities. The detailed descriptions, including terms, due dates, and interest rates for notes or bonds, should be reported either on the balance sheet or in an accompanying footnote. Also, the fair market value of notes or bonds should be disclosed. Exhibit 1 illustrates the reporting of liabilities on the balance sheet.

EXHIBIT 1   *Partial Balance Sheet with Liabilities and Stockholders' Equity*

ESCOE CORPORATION
Balance Sheet
December 31, 2009

Liabilities

Current liabilities:

Accounts payable	$ 488,200	
Notes payable (9% due on March 1, 2010)	250,000	
Accrued interest payable	15,000	
Accrued salaries and wages payable	13,500	
Other accrued liabilities	9,850	
Total current liabilities		$ 776,550

Long-term liabilities:

Debenture 8% bonds payable, due December 31, 2023		
(Market value $950,000)		1,000,000
Total liabilities		$1,776,550

Stockholders' Equity

Paid-in capital:

Preferred 10% stock, $50 par		
(20,000 shares authorized and issued)	$1,000,000	
Common stock, $20 par (250,000 shares authorized,		
100,000 shares issued)	2,000,000	
Additional paid-in capital in excess of par	520,000	
Total paid-in capital	$3,520,000	
Retained earnings	4,580,500	
Total	$8,100,500	
Deduct treasury stock (1,000 shares at cost)	75,000	
Total stockholders' equity		8,025,500
Total liabilities and stockholders' equity		$9,802,050

As we discussed earlier in this chapter, some contingent liabilities are not reported on the balance sheet. Such liabilities that are probable but cannot be reasonably estimated or are only possible should be disclosed in the footnotes to the financial statements. To illustrate such a disclosure, a portion of the footnote taken from an annual report of **eBay Inc.**, is shown:

> eBay was served with a lawsuit . . . filed on behalf of a purported class of eBay users who purchased allegedly forged autographed sports memorabilia on eBay. The lawsuit claims eBay was negligent in permitting certain named (and other unnamed) defendants to sell allegedly forged autographed sports memorabilia on eBay. . . . Management believes that the ultimate resolution of these disputes will not have a material adverse impact on eBay's consolidated financial positions, results of operations, or cash flows.

Although stockholders' equity is reported on the balance sheet, significant changes in stockholders' equity during the year should also be disclosed. Changes in retained earnings are often presented in a separate retained earnings statement. Changes in paid-in capital during the year may be reported on the face of the balance sheet or in the accompanying footnotes. Some companies prepare a separate statement of stockholders' equity that includes changes in both paid-in capital and retained earnings. An example of a statement of stockholders' equity is shown in Exhibit 2.

EXHIBIT 2   *Statement of Stockholders' Equity*

TELEX INC.
Statement of Stockholders' Equity
For the Year Ended December 31, 2009

	Preferred Stock	Common Stock	Paid-In Capital in Excess of Par— Common Stock	Retained Earnings	Treasury (Common) Stock	Total
Balance, January 1	$5,000,000	$10,000,000	$3,000,000	$2,000,000	$(500,000)	$19,500,000
Net income				850,000		850,000
Dividends on preferred stock				(250,000)		(250,000)
Dividends on common stock				(400,000)		(400,000)
Issuance of additional common stock		500,000	50,000			550,000
Purchase of treasury stock					(30,000)	(30,000)
Balance, December 31	$5,000,000	$10,500,000	$3,050,000	$2,200,000	$(530,000)	$20,220,000

Obj **8**

Analyze the impact of debt or equity financing on earnings per share.

Earnings per Share

One of the many factors that influence the decision of whether to finance operations using debt or equity is the effect of each alternative on earnings per share. Earnings per share is a major profitability measure that is reported in the financial statements and is followed closely by the financial press. As a result, corporate managers closely monitor the impact of decisions on earnings per share.

If a corporation has issued only common stock, **earnings per share** is computed by dividing net income by the number of shares of common stock outstanding.[9] If preferred and common stock have been issued, the net income must first be reduced by the amount of preferred dividends. To illustrate, assume that Lincoln Corporation has 100,000 shares of 9%, $100 par preferred stock and 50,000 shares of $200 par common stock outstanding. The earnings per share is computed as shown on the top of the next page.

---

[9]Earnings per share is further discussed in Chapter 9, "Financial Statement Analysis."

	2009	2008
Net income	$91,000	$76,500
Preferred dividends	9,000	9,000
	$82,000	$67,500
Shares of common stock outstanding	50,000 shares	50,000 shares
Earnings per share of common stock	$1.64	$1.35

To illustrate the possible effects of debt and equity financing on earnings per share, assume that Martin Corporation is considering the following alternative plans for financing $4,000,000 of its operations:

Plan 1: 100% financing from issuing common stock, $10 par

Plan 2: 50% financing from issuing preferred 9% stock, $50 par
50% financing from issuing common stock, $10 par

Plan 3: 50% financing from issuing 12% bonds
25% financing from issuing preferred 9% stock, $50 par
25% financing from issuing common stock, $10 par

In each case, we assume that the stocks or bonds are issued at their par or face amount. The corporation is expecting to earn $800,000 annually before deducting interest on the bonds and income taxes estimated at 40% of income. Exhibit 3 shows the effect of the three plans on the income of the corporation and the earnings per share on common stock.

Exhibit 3 indicates that plan 3 yields the highest earnings per share on common stock and is thus the most attractive for common stockholders. If the estimated earnings are more than $800,000, the difference between the earnings per share to common stockholders under plan 1 and plan 3 is even greater.[10] However, if smaller earnings occur, plans 2 and 3 become less attractive to common stockholders.

EXHIBIT 3   *Effect of Alternative Financing Plans—$800,000 Earnings*

	Plan 1	Plan 2	Plan 3
12% bonds	—	—	$2,000,000
Preferred 9% stock, $50 par	—	$2,000,000	1,000,000
Common stock, $10 par	$4,000,000	2,000,000	1,000,000
Total	$4,000,000	$4,000,000	$4,000,000
Earnings before interest and income tax	$ 800,000	$ 800,000	$ 800,000
Deduct interest on bonds	—	—	240,000
Income before income tax	$ 800,000	$ 800,000	$ 560,000
Deduct income tax	320,000	320,000	224,000
Net income	$ 480,000	$ 480,000	$ 336,000
Dividends on preferred stock	—	180,000	90,000
Available for dividends on common stock	$ 480,000	$ 300,000	$ 246,000
Shares of common stock outstanding	÷ 400,000	÷ 200,000	÷ 100,000
Earnings per share on common stock	$ 1.20	$ 1.50	$ 2.46

[10]The higher earnings per share under plan 3 is due to a finance concept known as *leverage*. This concept is discussed further in Chapter 9, "Financial Statement Analysis."

Key Points

1. Describe how businesses finance their operations.

A business must finance its operations through either debt or equity. Debt financing includes all liabilities owed by a business, including both current and long-term liabilities. A corporation may also finance its operations by issuing stock. Corporations may issue different classes of stock that contain different rights and privileges, such as rights to dividend payments.

2. Describe and illustrate current liabilities, notes payable, taxes, contingencies, and payroll.

Liabilities that are to be paid out of current assets and are due within a short time, usually within 1 year, are called *current liabilities*. Most current liabilities arise from either receiving goods or services prior to making payment or receiving payment prior to delivering goods or services. Current liabilities can also arise from notes payable, taxes, contingencies, and payroll. Warranties are examples of liabilities arising from contingencies. Wages and salaries payable and employee and employer payroll taxes are examples of liabilities arising from payroll. Deferrred income taxes arise from temporary differences between taxable income and income before taxes as reported on the income statement.

3. Describe and illustrate the financing of operations through issuance of bonds.

Many large corporations finance their operations through the issuance of bonds. A bond is simply a form of an interest-bearing note that requires periodic interest payments and the repayment of the face amount at the maturity date. When the contract rate of interest differs from the market rate of interest, bonds are issued at discounts or premiums. The amortization of discounts and premiums affects interest expense.

4. Describe and illustrate the financing of operations through issuance of stock.

A corporation may finance its operations by issuing either preferred or common stock. Preferred stock has preferential rights, including the right to receive dividends ahead of the common stockholders. When stock is issued at a premium, Cash or another asset account is increased for the amount received. Common Stock or Preferred Stock is increased for the par amount. The excess of the amount paid over par is a part of the paid-in capital and is normally recorded in an account entitled Paid-In Capital in Excess of Par.

Stock that a corporation has once issued and then reacquires is called *treasury stock*. It decreases stockholders' equity.

5. Describe and illustrate the accounting for cash and stock dividends.

When a board of directors declares a cash dividend, it authorizes the distribution of a portion of the corporation's cash to stockholders. When a board of directors declares a stock dividend, it authorizes the distribution of a portion of the stock. In both cases, the declaration of a dividend reduces the retained earnings of the corporation.

6. Describe the effects of stock splits on the financial statements.

Corporations sometimes reduce the par or stated value of their common stock and issue a proportionate number of additional shares in what is called a *stock split*. Since a stock split changes only the par or stated value and the number of shares outstanding, it is not recorded. However, the details of stock splits are normally disclosed in the notes to the financial statements.

7. Describe financial statement reporting of liabilities and stockholders' equity.

Liabilities that are expected to be paid within 1 year are presented in the Current Liabilities section of the balance sheet. Notes or bonds payable not maturing within 1 year should be shown as noncurrent liabilities. The detailed descriptions including terms, due dates, and interest rates for notes or bonds should be reported either on the balance sheet or in an accompanying footnote. Also, the fair market value of notes or bonds should be disclosed. The notes should disclose any contingent liabilities that cannot be reasonably estimated or are only possible. Significant changes in stockholders' equity during the year should also be reported.

8. Analyze the impact of debt or equity financing on earnings per share.

One of the many factors that influence the decision of whether to finance operations using debt or equity is the effect of each alternative on earnings per share. If a corporation has issued only common stock, earnings per share is computed by dividing net income by the number of shares of common stock outstanding. If preferred and common stock have been issued, the net income must first be reduced by the amount of preferred dividends.

Key Terms

Bond	Fringe benefits	Premium on bonds payable
Bond indenture	Gross pay	Premium on stock
Cash dividend	Market rate of interest	Stated value
Common stock	Net pay	Stock dividend
Contingent liabilities	Outstanding stock	Stock split
Contract rate	Par	Taxable income
Discount on bonds payable	Payroll	Temporary differences
Earnings per share	Preferred stock	Treasury stock

Illustrative Problem

Differences between the accounting methods applied to accounts and financial reports and those used in determining taxable income yielded the following amounts for the first four years of a corporation's operations:

	First Year	Second Year	Third Year	Fourth Year
Income before income taxes	$400,000	$480,000	$600,000	$520,000
Taxable income	300,000	420,000	630,000	600,000

The income tax rate for each of the four years was 40% of taxable income, and each year's taxes were promptly paid.

Instructions

1. Determine for each year the amounts described by the following captions, presenting the information in the form indicated:

Year	Income Tax Deducted on Income Statement	Income Tax Payments for the Year	Deferred Income Tax Payable	
			Year's Addition (Deduction)	Year-End Balance

2. Total the first three amount columns.

Solution

1. and 2.

Year	Income Tax Deducted on Income Statement	Income Tax Payments for the Year	Deferred Income Tax Payable	
			Year's Addition (Deduction)	Year-End Balance
First	$160,000	$120,000	$40,000	$40,000
Second	192,000	168,000	24,000	64,000
Third	240,000	252,000	(12,000)	52,000
Fourth	208,000	240,000	(32,000)	20,000
Total	$800,000	$780,000	$20,000	

Self-Examination Questions   *(Answers appear at end of chapter.)*

1. A business issued a $5,000, 60-day, 12% note to the bank. The amount due at maturity is:
   A. $4,900
   B. $5,000
   C. $5,100
   D. $5,600

2. Which of the following taxes are employers usually not required to withhold from employees?
   A. Federal income tax
   B. Federal unemployment compensation tax
   C. FICA tax
   D. State and local income tax

3. Employers do not incur an expense for which of the following payroll taxes?
   A. FICA tax
   B. Federal unemployment compensation tax
   C. State unemployment compensation tax
   D. Employees' federal income tax

4. If a corporation plans to issue $1,000,000 of 12% bonds when the market rate for similar bonds is 10%, the bonds can be expected to sell at:
   A. Their face amount
   B. A premium
   C. A discount
   D. A price below their face amount

5. A corporation has issued 25,000 shares of $100 par common stock and holds 3,000 of these shares as treasury stock. If the corporation declares a $2 per share cash dividend, what amount will be recorded as cash dividends?
   A. $22,000
   B. $25,000
   C. $44,000
   D. $50,000

Class Discussion Questions

1. What two types of transactions cause most current liabilities?

2. When are short-term notes payable issued?

3. When should the liability associated with a product warranty be recorded? Discuss.

4. **Deere & Company,** a company well known for manufacturing farm equipment, reported more than $400 million of product warranties in recent financial statements. How would costs of repairing a defective product be recorded?

5. **Delta Air Lines'** SkyMiles program allows frequent flyers to earn credit toward free tickets and other amenities. (a) Does Delta Air Lines have a contingent liability for award redemption by its SkyMiles members? (b) When should a contingent liability be recorded?

6. For each of the following payroll-related taxes, indicate whether it generally applies to (1) employees only, (2) employers only, or (3) both employees and employers:
   a. Federal income tax
   b. Federal unemployment compensation tax
   c. Medicare tax
   d. Social security tax
   e. State unemployment compensation tax

7. To match revenues and expenses properly, should the expense for employee vacation pay be recorded in the period during which the vacation privilege is earned or during the period in which the vacation is taken? Discuss.

8. Identify the two distinct obligations incurred by a corporation when issuing bonds.

9. A corporation issues $18,000,000 of 6% bonds to yield an effective interest rate of 7%.
   a. Was the amount of cash received from the sale of the bonds more or less than $18,000,000?
   b. Identify the following amounts related to the bond issue: (1) face amount, (2) market rate of interest, (3) contract rate of interest, and (4) maturity amount.

10. The following data relate to a $2,000,000, 8% bond issue for a selected semiannual interest period:

Bond carrying amount at beginning of period	$2,125,000
Interest paid at end of period	160,000
Interest expense allocable to the period	148,750

   (a) Were the bonds issued at a discount or at a premium? (b) What expense account was decreased to amortize the discount or premium?

11. Of two corporations organized at approximately the same time and engaged in competing businesses, one issued $50 par common stock, and the other issued $1 par common stock. Do the par designations provide any indication as to which stock is preferable as an investment? Explain.

12. When a corporation issues stock at a premium, is the premium income? Explain.

13. a. In what respect does treasury stock differ from unissued stock?
    b. How should treasury stock be presented on the balance sheet?

14. A corporation reacquires 10,000 shares of its own $75 par common stock for $800,000, recording it at cost. (a) What effect does this transaction have on revenue or expense of the period? (b) What effect does it have on stockholders' equity?

15. The treasury stock in Question 14 is resold for $900,000. (a) What is the effect on the corporation's revenue of the period? (b) What is the effect on stockholders' equity?

16. A corporation with preferred stock and common stock outstanding has a substantial balance in its retained earnings account at the beginning of the current fiscal year. Although net income for the current year is sufficient to pay the preferred dividend of $40,000 each quarter and a common dividend of $100,000 each quarter, the board of directors declares dividends only on the preferred stock. Suggest possible reasons that the board passes the dividends on the common stock.

17. An owner of 100 shares of Mountain Spring Company common stock receives a stock dividend of 6 shares. (a) What is the effect of the stock dividend on the stockholder's proportionate interest (equity) in the corporation? (b) How does the total equity of 106 shares compare with the total equity of 100 shares before the stock dividend?

18. What is the primary purpose of a stock split?

Exercises

E8-1
Current liabilities
Objs 2, 7
✓ Total current liabilities, $348,250

Rock On Magazine Co. sold 11,400 annual subscriptions of *Rock On* for $35 during December 2008. These new subscribers will receive monthly issues, beginning in January 2009. In addition, the business had taxable income of $140,000 during the first calendar quarter of 2009. The federal tax rate is 35%. A quarterly tax payment will be made on April 7, 2009.
   Prepare the current liabilities section of the balance sheet for Rock On Magazine Co. on March 31, 2009.

E8-2
Recording notes payable
Obj 2

A business issued a 60-day, 7% note for $15,000 to a creditor on account. Illustrate the effects on the accounts and financial statements of recording (a) the issuance of the note and (b) the payment of the note at maturity, including interest.

E8-3
Recording income taxes
Obj 2

Illustrate the effects on the accounts and financial statements of recording the following selected transactions of Lone Star Leather Co.:

Apr. 15. Paid the first installment of the estimated income tax for the current fiscal year ending December 31, $90,000. No entry had been made to record the liability.
Dec. 31. Recorded the estimated income tax liability for the year just ended and the deferred income tax liability, based on the April 15 transaction and the following data:

Income tax rate	40%
Income before income tax	$950,000
Taxable income according to tax return	$800,000

Assume that the June 15 and September 15 installments of $90,000 were also paid.

E8-4
Deferred income taxes
Obj 2

Storage Systems Inc. recognized service revenue of $420,000 on its financial statements in 2007. Assume, however, that the tax code requires this amount to be recognized for tax purposes in 2008. The taxable income for 2007 and 2008 is $2,600,000 and $3,000,000, respectively. Assume a tax rate of 40%.

(continued)

Illustrate the effects on the accounts and financial statements of the tax expense, deferred taxes, and taxes payable for 2007 and 2008, respectively.

E8-5

Accrued product warranty

Obj 2

Digital Audio Works, Inc. warrants its products for 1 year. The estimated product warranty is 1½% of sales. Assume that sales were $975,000 for January. In February, a customer received warranty repairs requiring $5,280 of parts.

a.   Determine the warranty liability at January 31, the end of the first month of the current year.
b.   What accounts are decreased for the warranty work provided in February?

E8-6

Accrued product warranty

Obj 2

Ford Motor Company disclosed estimated product warranty payable for 2006 and 2005 as follows.

	December 31	
	2006	**2005**
	(in millions)	
Product warranty payable	$6,032	$6,243

Ford's sales were $153,474 million in 2005 and decreased to $143,307 million in 2006. Assume that the total paid on warranty claims during 2006 was $4,106 million.

a.   Illustrate the effects on the accounts and financial statements for the 2006 product warranty expense.
b.   Assuming $4,106 million in warranty claims paid during 2006, explain the $211 million decrease in the total warranty liability from 2005 to 2006.

E8-7

Contingent liabilities

Obj 2

Several months ago, Northwest Cover Paint Company experienced a hazardous materials spill at one of its plants. As a result, the Environmental Protection Agency (EPA) fined the company $750,000. The company is contesting the fine. In addition, an employee is seeking $1,000,000 damages related to the spill. Last, a homeowner has sued the company for $200,000. The homeowner lives 25 miles from the plant, but believes that the incident has reduced the home's resale value by $200,000.

Northwest Cover's legal counsel believes that it is probable that the EPA fine will stand. In addition, counsel indicates that an out-of-court settlement of $300,000 has recently been reached with the employee. The final papers will be signed next week. Counsel believes that the homeowner's case is much weaker and will be decided in favor of Northwest Cover. Other litigation related to the spill is possible, but the damage amounts are uncertain.

a.   Illustrate the effects of the contingent liabilities associated with the hazardous materials spill on the accounts and financial statements.
b.   Prepare a note disclosure relating to this incident.

E8-8

Contingent liabilities

Obj 2

The following note accompanied recent financial statements for **Goodyear Tire and Rubber Company:**

Goodyear is a defendant in numerous lawsuits involving approximately 62,000 claimants alleging various asbestos related personal injuries purported to result from exposure to asbestos in certain rubber coated products manufactured by Goodyear.

Goodyear has recorded liabilities aggregating $229.1 million for potential product liability and other (asbestos) tort claims, including related legal fees expected to be incurred, presently asserted against Goodyear.

The portion of the recorded liabilities for potential product liability and other tort claims relating to asbestos claims is based on pending claims. The amount recorded reflects an estimate of the cost of defending and resolving pending claims, based on available information and our experience in disposing of asbestos claims in the past.

a. Illustrate the effects on the accounts and financial statements of recording the contingent liability of $229,100,000.
b. Why was the contingent liability recorded?

E8-9

Calculate payroll

Obj 2

✓ b. Net pay, $883.25

An employee earns $22 per hour and 1½ times that rate for all hours in excess of 40 hours per week. Assume that the employee worked 50 hours during the week, and that the gross pay prior to the current week totaled $42,710. Assume further that the FICA tax rate was 7.5% (on earnings up to $100,000) and federal income tax to be withheld was $235.

a. Determine the gross pay for the week.
b. Determine the net pay for the week.

E8-10

Summary payroll data

Obj 2

✓ (3) Total earnings, $260,000

In the following summary of data for a payroll period, some amounts have been intentionally omitted:

Earnings:	
1. At regular rate	?
2. At overtime rate	$ 39,480
3. Total earnings	?
Deductions:	
4. Social security tax	15,250
5. Medicare tax	3,900
6. Income tax withheld	46,590
7. Medical insurance	7,775
8. Union dues	?
9. Total deductions	76,000
10. Net amount paid	184,000
Wages and Salaries Expense Accounts:	
11. Factory Wages	138,900
12. Sales Salaries	?
13. Office Salaries	59,200

Calculate the amounts omitted in lines (1), (3), (8), and (12).

E8-11

Recording payroll taxes

Obj 2

According to a summary of the payroll of Matrix Publishing Co., $380,000 was subject to the 7.5% FICA tax. Also, $16,000 was subject to state and federal unemployment taxes.

a. Calculate the employer's payroll taxes, using the following rates: state unemployment, 4.3%; federal unemployment, 0.8%.
b. Illustrate the effects on the accounts and financial statements of recording the accrual of payroll taxes.

E8-12

Accrued vacation pay

Obj 2

A business provides its employees with varying amounts of vacation per year, depending on the length of employment. The estimated amount of the current year's vacation pay is $246,000. Illustrate the effects on the accounts and financial statements of the adjustment required on January 31, the end of the first month of the current year, to record the accrued vacation pay.

E8-13

Bond price

Obj 3

Walt Disney 2.125% bonds due in 2023 were reported in *The Wall Street Journal* as selling for 103.536. Were the bonds selling at a premium or at a discount? Explain.

E8-14

Issuing bonds

Obj 3

Heritage Optics Inc. produces and distributes fiber optic cable for use by telecommunications companies. Heritage Optics Inc. issued $30,000,000 of 15-year, 6% bonds on May 1 of the current year, with interest payable on May 1 and November 1. The fiscal year of the company is the calendar year. Illustrate the effects on the accounts and financial statements of recording the following selected transactions for the current year:

May   1. Issued the bonds for cash at their face amount.

Nov.   1. Paid the interest on the bonds.

Dec. 31. Recorded accrued interest for two months.

E8-15

Dividends per share

Objs 4, 5

✓ Preferred stock, lst year: $0.80

Electro-Rad Inc., a developer of radiology equipment, has stock outstanding as follows: 50,000 shares of 2%, preferred stock of $50 par, and 100,000 shares of $25 par common. During its first four years of operations, the following amounts were distributed as dividends: first year, $40,000; second year, $98,000; third year, $120,000; fourth year, $195,000. Calculate the dividends per share on each class of stock for each of the four years.

E8-16

Dividends per share

Objs 4, 5

✓ Preferred stock, 3rd year: $0.10

CompuLead Inc., a software development firm, has stock outstanding as follows: 40,000 shares of 1%, preferred stock of $25 par, and 50,000 shares of $75 par common. During its first four years of operations, the following amounts were distributed as dividends: first year, $6,000; second year, $26,000; third year, $4,000; fourth year, $60,000. Calculate the dividends per share on each class of stock for each of the four years.

E8-17

Issuing par stock

Obj 4

On February 4, Cinderella Rocks Inc., a marble contractor, issued for cash 30,000 shares of $20 par common stock at $64, and on March 31, it issued for cash 18,000 shares of $75 par preferred stock at $90.

a.   Illustrate the effects on the accounts and financial statements of the February 4 and March 31 transactions.

b.   What is the total amount invested (total paid-in capital) by all stockholders as of March 31?

E8-18

Issuing stock for assets other than cash

Obj 4

On November 10, Craddock's Corporation, a wholesaler of hydraulic lifts, acquired land in exchange for 15,000 shares of $8 par common stock with a current market price of $32. Illustrate the effects on the accounts and financial statements of the purchase of the land.

E8-19

Treasury stock transactions

Obj 4

Mountain Springs Inc. bottles and distributes spring water. On May 2 of the current year, Mountain Springs reacquired 3,000 shares of its common stock at $72 per share.

a.   What is the balance of Treasury Stock on December 31 of the current year?

b.   Where will the balance of Treasury Stock be reported on the balance sheet?

c.   For what reasons might Mountain Springs have purchased the treasury stock?

E8-20

Treasury stock transactions

Obj 4

Azalea Gardens Inc. develops and produces spraying equipment for lawn maintenance and industrial uses. On September 9 of the current year, Azalea Gardens Inc. reacquired 12,000 shares of its common stock at $89 per share.

a.   What is the balance of Treasury Stock on December 31 of the current year?

b.   How will the balance in Treasury Stock be reported on the balance sheet?

E8-21

Treasury stock transactions

Obj 4

Tacoma Inc. bottles and distributes spring water. On June 12 of the current year, Tacoma Inc. reacquired 15,000 shares of its common stock at $48 per share.

a.   What is the balance of Treasury Stock on December 31 of the current year?

b.   Where will the balance of Treasury Stock be reported on the balance sheet?

c.   For what reasons might Tacoma Inc. have purchased the treasury stock?

E8-22

Cash dividends

Obj 5

The dates of importance in connection with a cash dividend of $95,000 on a corporation's common stock are April 9, May 9, and June 8. Illustrate the effects on the accounts and financial statements for each date.

E8-23

Effect of cash dividend and stock split

Objs 5, 6

Indicate whether the following actions would (+) increase, (−) decrease, or (0) not affect Indigo Inc.'s total assets, liabilities, and stockholders' equity:

	Assets	Liabilities	Stockholders' Equity
(1) Declaring a cash dividend	_____	_____	_____
(2) Paying the cash dividend declared in (1)	_____	_____	_____
(3) Authorizing and issuing stock certificates in a stock split	_____	_____	_____
(4) Declaring a stock dividend	_____	_____	_____
(5) Issuing stock certificates for the stock dividend declared in (4)	_____	_____	_____

E8-24

Effect of stock split

Obj 6

Rolling Pin Corporation wholesales ovens and ranges to restaurants throughout the Midwest. Rolling Pin Corporation, which had 50,000 shares of common stock outstanding, declared a 3-for-1 stock split (2 additional shares for each share issued).

a. What will be the number of shares outstanding after the split?
b. If the common stock had a market price of $180 per share before the stock split, what would be an approximate market price per share after the split?

E8-25

Stockholders' equity section of balance sheet

Obj 7

✓ Total stockholders' equity, $4,020,000

The following accounts and their balances appear in the ledger of Heart and Saul Inc. on April 30 of the current year:

Common Stock, $50 par	$ 900,000
Paid-In Capital in Excess of Par	110,000
Paid-In Capital from Sale of Treasury Stock	42,000
Retained Earnings	3,178,000
Treasury Stock	210,000

Prepare the Stockholders' Equity section of the balance sheet as of April 30. Twenty-five thousand shares of common stock are authorized, and 3,500 shares have been reacquired.

E8-26

Stockholders' equity section of balance sheet

Obj 7

✓ Total stockholders' equity, $4,726,500

Sports Car Inc. retails racing products for BMWs, Porsches, and Ferraris. The following accounts and their balances appear in the ledger of Sports Car Inc. on November 30, the end of the current year:

Common Stock, $5 par	$ 875,000
Paid-In Capital in Excess of Par—Common Stock	700,000
Paid-In Capital in Excess of Par—Preferred Stock	25,000
Paid-In Capital from Sale of Treasury Stock—Common	16,000
Preferred 3% Stock, $75 par	937,500
Retained Earnings	2,338,000
Treasury Stock—Common	165,000

Twenty thousand shares of preferred and 400,000 shares of common stock are authorized. There are 22,000 shares of common stock held as treasury stock.

Prepare the Stockholders' Equity section of the balance sheet as of November 30, the end of the current year.

E8-27

Effect of financing on earnings per share

Obj 8

✓ a. $0.68

Bliss Co., which produces and sells skiing equipment, is financed as follows:

Bonds payable, 6% (issued at face amount)	$4,000,000
Preferred $2 stock (nonparticipating), $25 par	4,000,000
Common stock, $20 par	4,000,000

Income tax is estimated at 40% of income.

Determine the earnings per share of common stock, assuming that the income before bond interest and income tax is (a) $1,000,000, (b) $1,800,000, and (c) $3,200,000.

E8-28

Evaluate alternative financing plans

Obj 8

Based upon the data in Exercise 8-27, discuss factors other than earnings per share that should be considered in evaluating such financing plans.

Problems

— see illustrated problem

P8-1

Income tax allocation

Obj 2

✓ 1. Year-end balance, 3rd year, $12,000

Differences between the accounting methods applied to accounts and financial reports and those used in determining taxable income yielded the following amounts for the first four years of a corporation's operations:

	First Year	Second Year	Third Year	Fourth Year
Income before income taxes	$250,000	$300,000	$500,000	$400,000
Taxable income	200,000	280,000	540,000	430,000

The income tax rate for each of the four years was 40% of taxable income, and each year's taxes were promptly paid.

Instructions

1. Determine for each year the amounts described by the following captions, presenting the information in the form indicated:

Year	Income Tax Deducted on Income Statement	Income Tax Payments for the Year	Deferred Income Tax Payable	
			Year's Addition (Deduction)	Year-End Balance

2. Total the first three amount columns.
3. Illustrate the effects of recording the current and deferred tax liabilities on the accounts and financial statements for the first year.

P8-2

See 276-7

Recording payroll and payroll taxes

Obj 2

✓ 1. $42,000

The following information about the payroll for the week ended January 31 was obtained from the records of Greenfield Co.:

Show Gross salary not from company

Salaries:		Deductions:	
Sales salaries	$320,000	Income tax withheld	$109,760
Warehouse salaries	84,500	U.S. savings bonds	16,400
Office salaries	155,500	Group insurance	24,690
	$560,000		

Tax rates assumed:
FICA tax, 7.5% of employee annual earnings
State unemployment (employer only), 4.2%
Federal unemployment (employer only), 0.8%

1—Combined

Instructions

1. For the January 31 payroll, determine the employee FICA tax payable.
2. Illustrate the effect on the accounts and financial statements of paying and recording the January 31 payroll.
3. Determine the following amounts for the employer payroll taxes related to the January 31 payroll: (a) FICA tax payable, (b) state unemployment tax payable, and (c) federal unemployment tax payable.
4. Illustrate the effect on the accounts and financial statements of recording the liability for the January 31 payroll taxes.

P8-3

Present value; bond premium; bonds payable transactions

Obj 3

Goodbody Vaults Corporation produces and sells burial vaults. On July 1, 2008, Goodbody Vaults Corporation issued $12,000,000 of 10-year, 8% bonds at par. Interest on the bonds is payable semi-annually on December 31 and June 30. The fiscal year of the company is the calendar year.

Instructions

1. Illustrate the effects of the issuance of the bonds on July 1, 2008, on the accounts and financial statements.
2. Illustrate the effects of the first semiannual interest payment on December 31, 2008, on the accounts and financial statements.
3. Illustrate the effects of the payment of the face value of bonds at maturity on the accounts and financial statements.
4. If the market rate of interest were 7% on July 1, 2008, would the bonds have sold at a discount or premium?

P8-4

Stock transactions for corporate expansion

Obj 4

On January 31 of the current year, the following accounts and their balances appear in the ledger of Gargantuan Corp., a meat processor:

Preferred 3% Stock, $25 par (50,000 shares authorized, 30,000 shares issued)	$ 750,000
Paid-In Capital in Excess of Par—Preferred Stock	90,000
Common Stock, $30 par (400,000 shares authorized, 120,000 shares issued)	3,600,000
Paid-In Capital in Excess of Par—Common Stock	300,000
Retained Earnings	5,794,000

At the annual stockholders' meeting on April 2, the board of directors presented a plan for modernizing and expanding plant operations at a cost of approximately $2,550,000. The plan provided (a) that a building, valued at $1,200,000, and the land on which it is located, valued at $300,000, be acquired in accordance with preliminary negotiations by the issuance of 45,000 shares of common stock, (b) that 15,000 shares of the unissued preferred stock be issued through an underwriter, and (c) that the corporation borrow $500,000. The plan was approved by the stockholders and accomplished by the following transactions:

June 6. Issued 45,000 shares of common stock in exchange for land and a building, according to the plan.
14. Issued 15,000 shares of preferred stock, receiving $36 per share in cash.
30. Borrowed $500,000 from Mt. Baker National Bank, giving a 7% mortgage note.

No other transactions occurred during June.

Instructions

Illustrate the effects on the accounts and financial statements of each of the preceding transactions.

P8-5

Dividends on preferred and common stock

Objs 4, 5

SPREADSHEET

✓ 1. Common dividends in 2004: $20,000

Olympic Theatre Inc. owns and operates movie theaters throughout Texas and California. Olympic Theatre has declared the following annual dividends over a six-year period: 2003, $21,000; 2004, $50,000; 2005, $15,000; 2006, $80,000; 2007, $90,000; and 2008, $140,000. During the entire period, the outstanding stock of the company was composed of 10,000 shares of 4% preferred stock, $75 par, and 100,000 shares of common stock, $10 par.

Instructions

1. Calculate the total dividends and the per-share dividends declared on each class of stock for each of the six years. Summarize the data in tabular form, using the following column headings:

Year	Total Dividends	Preferred Dividends		Common Dividends	
		Total	Per Share	Total	Per Share
2003	$21,000				
2004	50,000				
2005	15,000				
2006	80,000				
2007	90,000				
2008	140,000				

2. Calculate the average annual dividend per share for each class of stock for the six-year period.
3. Assuming that the preferred stock was sold at $80 and common stock was sold at par at the beginning of the six-year period, calculate the average annual percentage return on initial shareholders' investment, based on the average annual dividend per share (a) for preferred stock and (b) for common stock.

P8-6

Effect of financing on earnings per share

Obj 8

SPREADSHEET

✓ 1. Plan 3: $10.64

Three different plans for financing a $30,000,000 corporation are under consideration by its organizers. Under each of the following plans, the securities will be issued at their par or face amount, and the income tax rate is estimated at 40% of income.

	Plan 1	Plan 2	Plan 3
8% bonds	—	—	$20,000,000
Preferred $2 stock, $50 par	—	$20,000,000	10,000,000
Common stock, $10 par	$40,000,000	20,000,000	10,000,000
Total	$40,000,000	$40,000,000	$40,000,000

Instructions

1. Determine for each plan the earnings per share of common stock, assuming that the income before bond interest and income tax is $20,000,000.
2. Determine for each plan the earnings per share of common stock, assuming that the income before bond interest and income tax is $2,600,000.
3. Discuss the advantages and disadvantages of each plan.

Activities

A8-1

How businesses make money

GROUP

One reason that **PepsiCo®** purchased **Quaker Oats** in 2001 was to acquire rights to its sports drink, Gatorade. However, Gatorade is under increasing pressure from its competitors, including **Coca-Cola's** Powerade®. As a result, PepsiCo is initiating an aggressive advertising campaign to promote and grow sales of Gatorade.

In groups of three or four, answer the following questions:

1. Locate the Web site for Gatorade. (a) How and why was Gatorade developed? (b) What is Gatorade's share of the sports-drink market?
2. Drinks can be labeled as sports, lifestyle, or active thirst drinks. (a) How would you describe each of these drink labels? (b) Give an example of what you would label a sports, lifestyle, and active thirst drink.
3. Do you think PepsiCo's advertising campaign will focus on Gatorade as a sports, lifestyle, or active thirst drink? Explain.

A8-2

General Electric bond issuance

ETHICS

General Electric Capital, a division of **General Electric,** uses long-term debt extensively. In early 2002, GE Capital issued $11 billion in long-term debt to investors, then within days filed legal documents to prepare for another $50 billion long-term debt issue. As a result of the $50 billion filing, the price of the initial $11 billion offering declined (due to higher risk of more debt).

> *Bill Gross, a manager of a bond investment fund, "denounced a 'lack in candor' related to GE's recent debt deal. 'It was the most recent and most egregious example of how bondholders are mistreated.' Gross argued that GE was not forthright when GE Capital recently issued $11 billion in bonds, one of the largest issues ever from a U.S. corporation. What bothered Gross is that three days after the issue the company announced its intention to sell as much as $50 billion in additional debt, warrants, preferred stock, guarantees, letters of credit and promissory notes at some future date."*

In your opinion, did GE Capital act unethically by selling $11 billion of long-term debt without telling those investors that a few days later it would be filing documents to prepare for another $50 billion debt offering?

Source: Jennifer Ablan, "Gross Shakes the Bond Market; GE Calms It, a Bit," *Barron's,* March 25, 2002.

A8-3

Preferred stock vs. bonds

Fiestas Inc. has decided to expand its operations to owning and operating theme parks. The following is an excerpt from a conversation between the chief executive officer, Juan Laurenzo, and the vice-president of finance, Christina Jose.

Juan: Christina, have you given any thought to how we're going to finance the acquisition of Frightmare Corporation?

Christina: Well, the two basic options, as I see it, are to issue either preferred stock or bonds. The equity market is a little depressed right now. The rumor is that the Federal Reserve Bank's going to increase the interest rates either this month or next.

Juan: Yes, I've heard the rumor. The problem is that we can't wait around to see what's going to happen. We'll have to move on this next week if we want any chance to complete the acquisition of Frightmare.

Christina: Well, the bond market is strong right now. Maybe we should issue debt this time around.

(continued)

Juan: That's what I would have guessed as well. Frightmare's financial statements look pretty good, except for the volatility of its income and cash flows. But that's characteristic of the industry.

Discuss the advantages and disadvantages of issuing preferred stock versus bonds.

A8-4

Investing in bonds

GROUP

Select a bond from listings that appear daily in *The Wall Street Journal,* and summarize the information related to the bond you select. Include the following information in your summary:

1. Contract rate of interest
2. Year when the bond matures
3. Current yield (effective rate of interest)
4. Closing price of bond (indicate date)
5. Other information noted about the bond (see the Explanatory Notes to the listings)

In groups of three or four, share the information you developed about the bond you selected. As a group, select one bond to invest $100,000 in and prepare a justification for your choice for presentation to the class. For example, your justification should include a consideration of risk and return.

A8-5

Financing business expansion

You hold a 25% common stock interest in the family-owned business, a vending machine company. Your sister, who is the manager, has proposed an expansion of plant facilities at an expected cost of $5,000,000. Two alternative plans have been suggested as methods of financing the expansion. Each plan is briefly described as follows:

Plan 1. Issue $5,000,000 of 20-year, 7% bonds at face amount.
Plan 2. Issue an additional 87,500 shares of $5 par common stock at $20 per share, and $3,250,000 of 20-year, 7% bonds at face amount.

The balance sheet as of the end of the previous fiscal year is as follows:

VENDCO, INC.
Balance Sheet
December 31, 2008

Assets	
Current assets	$ 2,350,000
Property, plant, and equipment	5,150,000
Total assets	$ 7,500,000
Liabilities and Stockholders' Equity	
Liabilities	$ 2,000,000
Common stock, $5	800,000
Paid-in capital in excess of par	80,000
Retained earnings	4,620,000
Total liabilities and stockholders' equity	$ 7,500,000

Net income has remained relatively constant over the past several years. The expansion program is expected to increase yearly income before bond interest and income tax from $500,000 in the previous year to $700,000 for this year. Your sister has asked you, as the company treasurer, to prepare an analysis of each financing plan.

1. Prepare a table indicating the expected earnings per share on the common stock under each plan. Assume an income tax rate of 40%. Round to the nearest cent.
2. a. Discuss the factors that should be considered in evaluating the two plans.
   b. Which plan offers the greater benefit to the present stockholders? Give reasons for your opinion.

A8-6

Board of directors' actions

ETHICS

In early 2002, Bernie Ebbers, the CEO of **WorldCom Group,** a major telecommunications company, was having personal financial troubles. Ebbers pledged a large stake of his WorldCom stock as security for some personal loans. As the price of WorldCom stock sank, Ebbers' bankers threatened to sell his stock in order to protect their loans. To avoid having his stock sold, Ebbers asked the board of directors of WorldCom to loan him nearly $400 million of corporate assets at 2.5% interest to pay off his bankers. The board agreed to lend him the money.

Comment on the decision of the board of directors in this situation.

A8-7

Issuing stock

Las Animas Inc. began operations on January 2, 2008, with the issuance of 75,000 shares of $50 par common stock. The sole stockholders of Las Animas Inc. are Cindy Stern and Dr. Kassay Heyen, who organized Las Animas Inc. with the objective of developing a new flu vaccine. Dr. Heyen claims that the flu vaccine, which is nearing the final development stage, will protect individuals against 80% of the flu types that have been medically identified. To complete the project, Las Animas Inc. needs $5,000,000 of additional funds. The local banks have been unwilling to loan the funds because of the lack of sufficient collateral and the riskiness of the business.

The following is a conversation between Cindy Stern, the chief executive officer of Las Animas Inc., and Dr. Kassay Heyen, the leading researcher.

Stern: What are we going to do? The banks won't loan us any more money, and we've got to have $5 million to complete the project. We are so close! It would be a disaster to quit now. The only thing I can think of is to issue additional stock. Do you have any suggestions?

Heyen: I guess you're right. But if the banks won't loan us any more money, how do you think we can find any investors to buy stock?

Stern: I've been thinking about that. What if we issue investors 100,000 shares of common stock at $50 par and promise them that we will pay them 2% of net sales until they have received an amount equal to what they paid for the stock?

Heyen: What happens when we pay back the $5 million? Do the investors get to keep the stock? If they do, it'll dilute our ownership.

Stern: How about, if after we pay back the $5 million, we make them turn in their stock for $100 per share? That's twice what they paid for it, plus they would have already gotten all their money back. That's a $100 profit per share for the investors.

Heyen: It could work. We get our money, but don't have to pay any interest, dividends, or the 2% of net sales until we start generating net sales. At the same time, the investors could get their money back plus earn a nice profit.

Stern: We'll need current financial statements for the new investors. I'll get our accountant working on them and contact our attorney to draw up a legally binding contract for the new investors. Yes, this could work.

In late 2008, the attorney and the various regulatory authorities approved the new stock offering, and 100,000 shares of common stock were privately sold to new investors at the stock's par of $50.

In preparing financial statements for 2008, Cindy Stern and Debra Allen, the controller for Las Animas Inc., have the following conversation:

Allen: Cindy, I've got a problem.

Stern: What's that, Debra?

Allen: Issuing common stock to raise that additional $5 million was a great idea. But . . .

Stern: But what?

Allen: I've got to prepare the 2008 annual financial statements, and I am not sure how to classify the common stock.

Stern: What do you mean? It's common stock.

Allen: I'm not so sure. I called the auditor and explained how we are contractually obligated to pay the new stockholders 2% of net sales until $50 per share is paid. Then, we may be obligated to pay them $100 per share.

Stern: So . . .

(continued)

Allen: So the auditor thinks that we should classify the additional issuance of $5 million as debt, not stock! And, if we put the $5 million on the balance sheet as debt, we will violate our other loan agreements with the banks. And, if these agreements are violated, the banks may call in all our debt immediately. If they do that, we are in deep trouble. We'll probably have to file for bankruptcy. We just don't have the cash to pay off the banks.

1. Discuss the arguments for and against classifying the issuance of the $5 million of stock as debt.
2. What do you think might be a practical solution to this classification problem?

A8-8

Profiling a corporation

GROUP

Select a public corporation you are familiar with or which interests you. Using the Internet, your school library, and other sources, develop a short (two to five pages) profile of the corporation. Include in your profile the following information:

1. Name of the corporation
2. State of incorporation
3. Nature of its operations
4. Total assets for the most recent balance sheet
5. Total revenues for the most recent income statement
6. Net income for the most recent income statement
7. Classes of stock outstanding
8. Market price of the stock outstanding
9. High and low price of the stock for the past year
10. Dividends paid for each share of stock during the past year

In groups of three or four, discuss each corporate profile. Select one of the corporations, assuming that your group has $100,000 to invest in its stock. Summarize why your group selected the corporation it did and how financial accounting information may have affected your decision. Keep track of the performance of your corporation's stock for the remainder of the term.

Note: Most major corporations maintain home pages on the Internet. This home page provides a variety of information on the corporation and often includes the corporation's financial statements. In addition, the New York Stock Exchange website (**http://www.nyse.com**) includes links to the home pages of many listed companies. Financial statements can also be accessed using EDGAR, the electronic archives of financial statements filed with the Securities and Exchange Commission (SEC).

SEC documents can also be retrieved using the EdgarScan™ service from ***Pricewaterhouse Coopers*** at **http://edgarscan.pwcglobal.com**. To obtain annual report information, key in a company name in the appropriate space. EdgarScan will list the reports available to you for the company you've selected. Select the most recent annual report filing, identified as a 10-K or 10-K405. EdgarScan provides an outline of the report, including the separate financial statements, which can also be selected in an Excel® spreadsheet.

Answers to Self-Examination Questions

1.   C   The maturity value is $5,100, determined as follows:

Face amount of note	$5,000
Plus interest ($5,000 × 0.12 × 60/360)	100
Maturity value	$5,100

2.   B   Employers are usually required to withhold a portion of their employees' earnings for payment of federal income taxes (answer A), FICA tax (answer C), and state and local income taxes (answer D). Generally, federal unemployment compensation taxes (answer B) are levied against the employer only and thus are not deducted from employee earnings.

3.   D   The employer incurs an expense for FICA tax (answer A), federal unemployment compensation tax (answer B), and state unemployment compensation tax (answer C). The employees' federal income tax (answer D) is not an expense of the employer. It is withheld from the employees' earnings.

4.   B   Since the contract rate on the bonds is higher than the prevailing market rate, a rational investor would be willing to pay more than the face amount, or a premium (answer B), for the bonds. If the contract rate and the market rate were equal, the bonds could be expected to sell at their face amount (answer A). Likewise, if the market rate is higher than the contract rate, the bonds would sell at a price below their face amount (answer D) or at a discount (answer C).

5.   C   If a corporation that holds treasury stock declares a cash dividend, the dividends are not paid on the treasury shares. To do so would place the corporation in the position of earning income through dealing with itself. Thus, the corporation will record $44,000 (answer C) as cash dividends [(25,000 shares issued less 3,000 shares held as treasury stock) × $2 per share dividend].

CHAPTER 9

Financial Statement Analysis

Learning Objectives

After studying this chapter, you should be able to:

Obj 1
Describe basic financial statement analytical procedures.

Obj 2
Apply financial statement analysis to assess the solvency of a business.

Obj 3
Apply financial statement analysis to assess the profitability of a business.

Obj 4
Summarize the uses and limitations of analytical measures.

Obj 5
Describe the contents of corporate annual reports.

The Wall Street Journal reported that the common stock of **Microsoft Corporation** was selling for $26.15 per share. If you had funds to invest, would you invest in Microsoft common stock?

Microsoft is a well-known, international company. However, **United Airlines**, **WorldCom**, **Kmart**, **Polaroid**, and **Planet Hollywood** were also well-known companies. These latter companies share the common characteristic of having declared bankruptcy!

Obviously, being well known is not necessarily a good basis for investing. Knowledge that a company has a good product, by itself, may also be an inadequate basis for investing in the company. Even with a good product, a company may go bankrupt for a variety of reasons, such as inadequate financing. For example, Planet Hollywood sought bankruptcy protection, even though it was owned and promoted by such prominent Hollywood stars as Bruce Willis, Whoopi Goldberg, and Arnold Schwarzenegger.

How, then, does one decide on the companies in which to invest? This chapter describes and illustrates common financial data that can be analyzed to assist you in making investment decisions. In addition, the contents of corporate annual reports are discussed.

Basic Analytical Procedures

The basic financial statements provide much of the information users need to make economic decisions about businesses. In this chapter, we illustrate how to perform a complete analysis of these statements by integrating individual various measures.

Analytical procedures may be used to compare items on a current statement with related items on earlier statements. For example, cash of $150,000 on the current balance sheet may be compared with cash of $100,000 on the balance sheet of a year earlier. The current year's cash may be expressed as 1.5 or 150% of the earlier amount, or as an increase of 50% or $50,000.

Analytical procedures are also widely used to examine relationships within a financial statement. To illustrate, assume that cash of $50,000 and inventories of $250,000 are included in the total assets of $1,000,000 on a balance sheet. In relative terms, the cash balance is 5% of the total assets, and the inventories are 25% of the total assets.

In this chapter, we will illustrate a number of common analytical measures. The measures are not ends in themselves. They are only guides in evaluating financial and operating data. Many other factors, such as trends in the industry and general economic conditions, should also be considered.

Horizontal Analysis

The percentage analysis of increases and decreases in related items in comparative financial statements is called **horizontal analysis**. The amount of each item on the most recent statement is compared with the related item on one or more earlier statements. The amount of increase or decrease in the item is listed, along with the percent of increase or decrease.

Horizontal analysis may compare two statements. In this case, the earlier statement is used as the base. Horizontal analysis may also compare three or more statements. In this case, the earliest date or period may be used as the base for comparing all later dates or periods. Alternatively, each statement may be compared to the immediately preceding statement. Exhibit 1 is a condensed comparative balance sheet for 2 years for Lincoln Company, with horizontal analysis.

We cannot fully evaluate the significance of the various increases and decreases in the items shown in Exhibit 1 without additional information. Although total assets at the end of 2009 were $91,000 (7.4%) less than at the beginning of the year, liabilities were reduced by $133,000 (30%), and stockholders' equity increased $42,000 (5.3%). It appears that the reduction of $100,000 in long-term liabilities was achieved mostly through the sale of long-term investments.

The balance sheet in Exhibit 1 may be expanded to include the details of the various categories of assets and liabilities. An alternative is to present the details in separate schedules. Exhibit 2 is a supporting schedule with horizontal analysis.

The decrease in accounts receivable may be due to changes in credit terms or improved collection policies. Likewise, a decrease in inventories during a period of increased sales may indicate an improvement in the management of inventories.

The changes in the current assets in Exhibit 2 appear favorable. This assessment is supported by the 24.8% increase in net sales shown in Exhibit 3, on page 308.

An increase in net sales may not have a favorable effect on operating performance. The percentage increase in Lincoln Company's net sales is accompanied by a greater

---

EXHIBIT 1   *Comparative Balance Sheet—Horizontal Analysis*

LINCOLN COMPANY
COMPARATIVE BALANCE SHEET
DECEMBER 31, 2009 AND 2008

	2009	2008	INCREASE (DECREASE) AMOUNT	PERCENT
Assets				
Current assets	$ 550,000	$ 533,000	$ 17,000	3.2%
Long-term investments	95,000	177,500	(82,500)	(46.5)
Property, plant, and equipment (net)	444,500	470,000	(25,500)	(5.4)
Intangible assets	50,000	50,000	—	
Total assets	$1,139,500	$1,230,500	$ (91,000)	(7.4)
Liabilities				
Current liabilities	$ 210,000	$ 243,000	$ (33,000)	(13.6)
Long-term liabilities	100,000	200,000	(100,000)	(50.0)
Total liabilities	$ 310,000	$ 443,000	$(133,000)	(30.0)
Stockholders' Equity				
Preferred 6% stock, $100 par	$ 150,000	$ 150,000	—	—
Common stock, $10 par	500,000	500,000	—	—
Retained earnings	179,500	137,500	$ 42,000	30.5
Total stockholders' equity	$ 829,500	$ 787,500	$ 42,000	5.3
Total liabilities and stockholders' equity	$1,139,500	$1,230,500	$ (91,000)	(7.4)

EXHIBIT 2   *Comparative Schedule of Current Assets—Horizontal Analysis*

LINCOLN COMPANY
Comparative Schedule of Current Assets
December 31, 2009 and 2008

	2009	2008	Increase (Decrease) Amount	Percent
Cash	$ 90,500	$ 64,700	$ 25,800	39.9%
Marketable securities	75,000	60,000	15,000	25.0
Accounts receivable (net)	115,000	120,000	(5,000)	(4.2)
Inventories	264,000	283,000	(19,000)	(6.7)
Prepaid expenses	5,500	5,300	200	3.8
Total current assets	$550,000	$533,000	$ 17,000	3.2

percentage increase in the cost of goods (merchandise) sold.[1] This has the effect of reducing gross profit. Selling expenses increased significantly, and administrative expenses increased slightly. Overall, operating expenses increased by 20.7%, whereas gross profit increased by only 19.7%.

---

[1]The term *cost of goods sold* is often used in practice in place of *cost of merchandise sold*. Such usage is followed in this chapter.

EXHIBIT 3   *Comparative Income Statement—Horizontal Analysis*

LINCOLN COMPANY
Comparative Income Statement
For the Years Ended December 31, 2009 and 2008

			Increase (Decrease)	
	2009	*2008*	*Amount*	*Percent*
Sales	$1,530,500	$1,234,000	$296,500	24.0%
Sales returns and allowances	32,500	34,000	(1,500)	(4.4)
Net sales	$1,498,000	$1,200,000	$298,000	24.8
Cost of goods sold	1,043,000	820,000	223,000	27.2
Gross profit	$ 455,000	$ 380,000	$ 75,000	19.7
Selling expenses	$ 191,000	$ 147,000	$ 44,000	29.9
Administrative expenses	104,000	97,400	6,600	6.8
Total operating expenses	$ 295,000	$ 244,400	$ 50,600	20.7
Income from operations	$ 160,000	$ 135,600	$ 24,400	18.0
Other income	8,500	11,000	(2,500)	(22.7)
	$ 168,500	$ 146,600	$ 21,900	14.9
Other expense	6,000	12,000	(6,000)	(50.0)
Income before income tax	$ 162,500	$ 134,600	$ 27,900	20.7
Income tax expense	71,500	58,100	13,400	23.1
Net income	$ 91,000	$ 76,500	$ 14,500	19.0

The increase in income from operations and in net income is favorable. However, a study of the expenses and additional analyses and comparisons should be made before reaching a conclusion as to the cause.

Exhibit 4 illustrates a comparative retained earnings statement with horizontal analysis. It reveals that retained earnings increased 30.5% for the year. The increase is due to net income of $91,000 for the year, less dividends of $49,000.

Vertical Analysis

A percentage analysis may also be used to show the relationship of each component to the total within a single statement. This type of analysis is called **vertical analysis**.

EXHIBIT 4   *Comparative Retained Earnings Statement—Horizontal Analysis*

LINCOLN COMPANY
Comparative Retained Earnings Statement
December 31, 2009 and 2008

			Increase (Decrease)	
	2009	*2008*	*Amount*	*Percent*
Retained earnings, January 1	$137,500	$100,000	$37,500	37.5%
Net income for the year	91,000	76,500	14,500	19.0
Total	$228,500	$176,500	$52,000	29.5
Dividends:				
On preferred stock	$ 9,000	$ 9,000	—	—
On common stock	40,000	30,000	$10,000	33.3
Total	$ 49,000	$ 39,000	$10,000	25.6
Retained earnings, December 31	$179,500	$137,500	$42,000	30.5

Like horizontal analysis, the statements may be prepared in either detailed or condensed form. In the latter case, additional details of the changes in individual items may be presented in supporting schedules. In such schedules, the percentage analysis may be based on either the total of the schedule or the statement total. Although vertical analysis is limited to an individual statement, its significance may be improved by preparing comparative statements.

In vertical analysis of the balance sheet, each asset item is stated as a percent of the total assets. Each liability and stockholders' equity item is stated as a percent of the total liabilities and stockholders' equity. Exhibit 5 is a condensed comparative balance sheet with vertical analysis for Lincoln Company.

The major percentage changes in Lincoln Company's assets are in the current asset and long-term investment categories. In the Liabilities and Stockholders' Equity sections of the balance sheet, the greatest percentage changes are in long-term liabilities and retained earnings. Stockholders' equity increased from 64% to 72.8% of total liabilities and stockholders' equity in 2008. There is a comparable decrease in liabilities.

EXHIBIT 5 *Comparative Balance Sheet—Vertical Analysis*

LINCOLN COMPANY
Comparative Balance Sheet
December 31, 2009 and 2008

	2009		2008	
	Amount	*Percent*	*Amount*	*Percent*
Assets				
Current assets	$ 550,000	48.3%	$ 533,000	43.3%
Long-term investments	95,000	8.3	177,500	14.4
Property, plant, and equipment (net)	444,500	39.0	470,000	38.2
Intangible assets	50,000	4.4	50,000	4.1
Total assets	$1,139,500	100.0%	$1,230,500	100.0%
Liabilities				
Current liabilities	$ 210,000	18.4%	$ 243,000	19.7%
Long-term liabilities	100,000	8.8	200,000	16.3
Total liabilities	$ 310,000	27.2%	$ 443,000	36.0%
Stockholders' Equity				
Preferred 6% stock, $100 par	$ 150,000	13.2%	$ 150,000	12.2%
Common stock, $10 par	500,000	43.9	500,000	40.6
Retained earnings	179,500	15.7	137,500	11.2
Total stockholders' equity	$ 829,500	72.8%	$ 787,500	64.0%
Total liabilities and stockholders' equity	$1,139,500	100.0%	$1,230,500	100.0%

In a vertical analysis of the income statement, each item is stated as a percent of net sales. Exhibit 6 is a condensed comparative income statement with vertical analysis for Lincoln Company.

EXHIBIT 6   *Comparative Income Statement—Vertical Analysis*

LINCOLN COMPANY
Comparative Income Statement
For the Years Ended December 31, 2009 and 2008

	2009		2008	
	Amount	*Percent*	*Amount*	*Percent*
Sales	$1,530,500	102.2%	$1,234,000	102.8%
Sales returns and allowances	32,500	2.2	34,000	2.8
Net sales	$1,498,000	100.0%	$1,200,000	100.0%
Cost of goods sold	1,043,000	69.6	820,000	68.3
Gross profit	$ 455,000	30.4%	$ 380,000	31.7%
Selling expenses	$ 191,000	12.8%	$ 147,000	12.3%
Administrative expenses	104,000	6.9	97,400	8.1
Total operating expenses	$ 295,000	19.7%	$ 244,400	20.4%
Income from operations	$ 160,000	10.7%	$ 135,600	11.3%
Other income	8,500	0.6	11,000	0.9
	$ 168,500	11.3%	$ 146,600	12.2%
Other expense	6,000	0.4	12,000	1.0
Income before income tax	$ 162,500	10.9%	$ 134,600	11.2%
Income tax expense	71,500	4.8	58,100	4.8
Net income	$ 91,000	6.1%	$ 76,500	6.4%

We must be careful when judging the significance of differences between percentages for the 2 years. For example, the decline of the gross profit rate from 31.7% in 2008 to 30.4% in 2009 is only 1.3 percentage points. In terms of dollars of potential gross profit, however, it represents a decline of approximately $19,500 (1.3% × $1,498,000).

Common-Size Statements

Horizontal and vertical analyses with both dollar and percentage amounts are useful in assessing relationships and trends in financial conditions and operations of a business. Vertical analysis with both dollar and percentage amounts is also useful in comparing one company with another or with industry averages. Such comparisons are easier to make with the use of common-size statements. In a **common-size statement**, all items are expressed in percentages.

Common-size statements are useful in comparing the current period with prior periods, individual businesses, or one business with industry percentages. Industry data are often available from trade associations and financial information services. Exhibit 7 is a comparative common-size income statement for two businesses.

Exhibit 7 indicates that Lincoln Company has a slightly higher rate of gross profit than Madison Corporation. However, this advantage is more than offset by Lincoln Company's higher percentage of selling and administrative expenses. As a result, the income from operations of Lincoln Company is 10.7% of net sales, compared with 14.4% for Madison Corporation—an unfavorable difference of 3.7 percentage points.

EXHIBIT 7   *Common-Size Income Statement*

LINCOLN COMPANY AND MADISON CORPORATION
Condensed Common-Size Income Statement
For the Year Ended December 31, 2009

	Lincoln Company	Madison Corporation
Sales	102.2%	102.3%
Sales returns and allowances	2.2	2.3
Net sales	100.0%	100.0%
Cost of goods sold	69.6	70.0
Gross profit	30.4%	30.0%
Selling expenses	12.8%	11.5%
Administrative expenses	6.9	4.1
Total operating expenses	19.7%	15.6%
Income from operations	10.7%	14.4%
Other income	0.6	0.6
	11.3%	15.0%
Other expense	0.4	0.5
Income before income tax	10.9%	14.5%
Income tax expense	4.8	5.5
Net income	6.1%	9.0%

Other Analytical Measures

In addition to the preceding analyses, other relationships may be expressed in ratios and percentages. Often, these items are taken from the financial statements and thus are a type of vertical analysis. Comparing these items with items from earlier periods is a type of horizontal analysis.

Obj 2

Apply financial statement analysis to assess the solvency of a business.

Solvency Analysis

Some aspects of a business's financial condition and operations are of greater importance to some users than others. However, all users are interested in the ability of a business to pay its debts as they are due and to earn income. The ability of a business to meet its financial obligations (debts) is called **solvency**. The ability of a business to earn income is called **profitability**.

The factors of solvency and profitability are interrelated. A business that cannot pay its debts on a timely basis may experience difficulty in obtaining credit. A lack of available credit may, in turn, lead to a decline in the business's profitability. Eventually, the business may be forced into bankruptcy. Likewise, a business that is less profitable than its competitors is likely to be at a disadvantage in obtaining credit or new capital from stockholders.

In the following paragraphs, we discuss various types of financial analyses that are useful in evaluating the solvency of a business. In the next section, we discuss various types of profitability analyses. The examples in both sections are based on Lincoln

Company's financial statements presented earlier. In some cases, data from Lincoln Company's financial statements of the preceding year and from other sources are also used. These historical data are useful in assessing the past performance of a business and in forecasting its future performance. The results of financial analyses may be even more useful when they are compared with those of competing businesses and with industry averages.

Solvency analysis focuses on the ability of a business to pay or otherwise satisfy its current and noncurrent liabilities. It is normally assessed by examining balance sheet relationships, using the following major analyses:

1. Current position analysis
2. Accounts receivable analysis
3. Inventory analysis
4. The ratio of fixed assets to long-term liabilities
5. The ratio of liabilities to stockholders' equity
6. The number of times interest charges are earned

Current Position Analysis

To be useful in assessing solvency, a ratio or other financial measure must relate to a business's ability to pay or otherwise satisfy its liabilities. Using measures to assess a business's ability to pay its current liabilities is called *current position analysis*. Such analysis is of special interest to short-term creditors.

An analysis of a firm's current position normally includes determining the working capital, the current ratio, and the quick ratio. The current and quick ratios are most useful when analyzed together and compared to previous periods and other firms in the industry.

Working Capital   The excess of the current assets of a business over its current liabilities is called working capital. The working capital is often used in evaluating a company's ability to meet currently maturing debts. It is especially useful in making monthly or other period-to-period comparisons for a company. However, amounts of working capital are difficult to assess when comparing companies of different sizes or in comparing such amounts with industry figures. For example, working capital of $250,000 may be adequate for a small local hardware store, but it would be inadequate for all of **Home Depot**.

Current Ratio   Another means of expressing the relationship between current assets and current liabilities is the **current ratio**. This ratio is sometimes called the *working capital ratio* or *bankers' ratio*. The ratio is computed by dividing the total current assets by the total current liabilities. For Lincoln Company, working capital and the current ratio for 2009 and 2008 are as follows:

	2009	2008
Current assets	$550,000	$533,000
Current liabilities	210,000	243,000
Working capital	$340,000	$290,000
Current ratio	2.6	2.2

The current ratio is a more reliable indicator of solvency than is working capital. To illustrate, assume that as of December 31, 2009, the working capital of a competitor is much greater than $340,000, but its current ratio is only 1.3. Considering these facts alone, Lincoln Company, with its current ratio of 2.6, is in a more favorable position to obtain short-term credit than the competitor, which has the greater amount of working capital.

Quick Ratio The working capital and the current ratio do not consider the makeup of the current assets. To illustrate the importance of this consideration, the current position data for Lincoln Company and Jefferson Corporation as of December 31, 2009, are as follows:

	Lincoln Company	Jefferson Corporation
Current assets:		
Cash	$ 90,500	$ 45,500
Marketable securities	75,000	25,000
Accounts receivable (net)	115,000	90,000
Inventories	264,000	380,000
Prepaid expenses	5,500	9,500
Total current assets	$550,000	$550,000
Current liabilities	210,000	210,000
Working capital	$340,000	$340,000
Current ratio	2.6	2.6

Both companies have a working capital of $340,000 and a current ratio of 2.6. But the ability of each company to pay its current debts is significantly different. Jefferson Corporation has more of its current assets in inventories. Some of these inventories must be sold and the receivables collected before the current liabilities can be paid in full. Thus, a large amount of time may be necessary to convert these inventories into cash. Declines in market prices and a reduction in demand could also impair its ability to pay current liabilities. In contrast, Lincoln Company has cash and current assets (marketable securities and accounts receivable) that can generally be converted to cash rather quickly to meet its current liabilities.

A ratio that measures the "instant" debt-paying ability of a company is called the **quick ratio** or *acid-test ratio*. It is the ratio of the total quick assets to the total current liabilities. **Quick assets** are cash and other current assets that can be quickly converted to cash. Quick assets normally include cash, marketable securities, and receivables. The quick ratio data for Lincoln Company are as follows:

	2009	2008
Quick assets:		
Cash	$ 90,500	$ 64,700
Marketable equity securities	75,000	60,000
Accounts receivable (net)	115,000	120,000
Total quick assets	$280,500	$244,700
Current liabilities	$210,000	$243,000
Quick ratio	1.3	1.0

Accounts Receivable Analysis

The size and makeup of accounts receivable change constantly during business operations. Sales on account increase accounts receivable, whereas collections from customers decrease accounts receivable. Firms that grant long credit terms usually have larger accounts receivable balances than those granting short credit terms. Increases or decreases in the volume of sales also affect the balance of accounts receivable.

It is desirable to collect receivables as promptly as possible. The cash collected from receivables improves solvency. In addition, the cash generated by prompt collections from customers may be used in operations for such purposes as purchasing merchandise in large quantities at lower prices. The cash may also be used for payment of dividends to stockholders or for other investing or financing purposes. Prompt collection also lessens the risk of loss from uncollectible accounts.

Accounts Receivable Turnover   The relationship between sales and accounts receivable may be stated as the **accounts receivable turnover**. This ratio is computed by dividing net sales by the average net accounts receivable.[2] It is desirable to base the average on monthly balances, which allows for seasonal changes in sales. When such data are not available, it may be necessary to use the average of the accounts receivable balance at the beginning and the end of the year. If there are trade notes receivable as well as accounts, the two may be combined. The accounts receivable turnover data for Lincoln Company are as follows:

	2009	*2008*
Net sales	$1,498,000	$1,200,000
Accounts receivable (net):		
Beginning of year	$ 120,000	$ 140,000
End of year	115,000	120,000
Total	$ 235,000	$ 260,000
Average (Total ÷ 2)	$ 117,500	$ 130,000
Accounts receivable turnover	12.7	9.2

The increase in the accounts receivable turnover for 2009 indicates that there has been an improvement in the collection of receivables. This may be due to a change in the granting of credit or in collection practices or both.

Number of Days' Sales in Receivables   Another measure of the relationship between sales and accounts receivable is the **number of days' sales in receivables**. This ratio is computed by dividing the average accounts receivable by the average daily sales. Average daily sales is determined by dividing net sales by 365 days. The number of days' sales in receivables is computed for Lincoln Company as follows:

	2009	*2008*
Average accounts receivable (net), end of year	$117,500	$130,000
Net sales	$1,498,000	$1,200,000
Average daily sales (Net sales ÷ 365)	$4,104	$3,288
Number of days' sales in receivables	28.6*	39.5*

*Average accounts receivable ÷ Average daily sales

[2]If known, credit sales should be used in the numerator. Because credit sales are not normally known by external users, we use net sales in the numerator.

The number of days' sales in receivables is an estimate of the length of time (in days) the accounts receivable have been outstanding. Comparing this measure with the credit terms provides information on the efficiency in collecting receivables. For example, assume that the number of days' sales in receivables for Grant Inc. is 40. If Grant Inc's credit terms are n/45, then its collection process appears to be efficient. On the other hand, if Grant Inc's credit terms are n/30, its collection process does not appear to be efficient. A comparison with other firms in the same industry and with prior years also provides useful information. Such comparisons may indicate efficiency of collection procedures and trends in credit management.

Inventory Analysis

A business should keep enough inventory on hand to meet the needs of its customers and its operations. At the same time, however, an excessive amount of inventory reduces solvency by tying up funds. Excess inventories also increase insurance expense, property taxes, storage costs, and other related expenses. These expenses further reduce funds that could be used elsewhere to improve operations. Finally, excess inventory also increases the risk of losses because of price declines or obsolescence of the inventory. Two measures that are useful for evaluating the management of inventory are the inventory turnover and the number of days' sales in inventory.

Inventory Turnover   The relationship between the volume of goods (merchandise) sold and inventory may be stated as the **inventory turnover**. It is computed by dividing the cost of goods sold by the average inventory. If monthly data are not available, the average of the inventories at the beginning and the end of the year may be used. The inventory turnover for Lincoln Company is computed as follows:

	2009	2008
Cost of goods sold	$1,043,000	$820,000
Inventories:		
Beginning of year	$ 283,000	$311,000
End of year	264,000	283,000
Total	$ 547,000	$594,000
Average (Total ÷ 2)	$ 273,500	$297,000
Inventory turnover	3.8	2.8

The inventory turnover improved for Lincoln Company because of an increase in the cost of goods sold and a decrease in the average inventories. Differences across inventories, companies, and industries are too great to allow a general statement on what is a good inventory turnover. For example, a firm selling food should have a higher turnover than a firm selling furniture or jewelry. Likewise, the perishable foods department of a supermarket should have a higher turnover than the soaps and cleansers department. However, for each business or each department within a business, there is a reasonable turnover rate. A turnover lower than this rate could mean that inventory is not being managed properly.

Number of Days' Sales in Inventory   Another measure of the relationship between the cost of goods sold and inventory is the **number of days' sales in inventory**. This measure is computed by dividing the average inventory by the average daily cost of goods sold (cost of goods sold divided by 365). The number of days' sales in inventory for Lincoln Company is computed as follows:

	2009	2008
Average inventories	$273,500	$297,000
Cost of goods sold (COGS)	$1,043,000	$820,000
Average daily cost of goods sold (COGS ÷ 365 days)	$2,858	$2,247
Number of days' sales in inventory	95.7*	132.2*

*Average inventory ÷ Average daily cost of goods sold

The number of days' sales in inventory is a rough measure of the length of time it takes to acquire, sell, and replace the inventory. For Lincoln Company, there is a major improvement in the number of days' sales in inventory during 2009. However, a comparison with earlier years and similar firms would be useful in assessing Lincoln Company's overall inventory management.

Ratio of Fixed Assets to Long-Term Liabilities

Long-term notes and bonds are often secured by mortgages on fixed assets. The **ratio of fixed assets to long-term liabilities** is a solvency measure that indicates the margin of safety of the noteholders or bondholders. It also indicates the ability of the business to borrow additional funds on a long-term basis. The ratio of fixed assets to long-term liabilities for Lincoln Company is as follows:

	2009	2008
Fixed assets (net)	$444,500	$470,000
Long-term liabilities	$100,000	$200,000
Ratio of fixed assets to long-term liabilities	4.4	2.4

The major increase in this ratio at the end of 2009 is mainly due to liquidating one-half of Lincoln Company's long-term liabilities. If the company needs to borrow additional funds on a long-term basis in the future, it is in a strong position to do so.

Ratio of Liabilities to Stockholders' Equity

Claims against the total assets of a business are divided into two groups: (1) claims of creditors and (2) claims of owners. The relationship between the total claims of the creditors and owners—the **ratio of liabilities to stockholders' equity**—is a solvency measure that indicates the margin of safety for creditors. It also indicates the ability of the business to withstand adverse business conditions. When the claims of creditors are large in relation to the equity of the stockholders, there are usually significant interest payments. If earnings decline to the point where the company is unable to meet its interest payments, the business may be taken over by the creditors.

The relationship between creditor and stockholder equity is shown in the vertical analysis of the balance sheet. For example, the balance sheet of Lincoln Company in Exhibit 5 indicates that on December 31, 2009, liabilities represented 27.2% and stockholders' equity represented 72.8% of the total liabilities and stockholders' equity (100.0%). Instead of expressing each item as a percent of the total, this relationship may be expressed as a ratio of one to the other, as follows:

	2009	2008
Total liabilities	$310,000	$443,000
Total stockholders' equity	$829,500	$787,500
Ratio of liabilities to stockholders' equity	0.37	0.56

The balance sheet of Lincoln Company shows that the major factor affecting the change in the ratio was the $100,000 decrease in long-term liabilities during 2009. The ratio at the end of both years shows a large margin of safety for the creditors.

Number of Times Interest Charges Earned

Corporations in some industries, such as airlines, normally have high ratios of debt to stockholders' equity. For such corporations, the relative risk of the debtholders is normally measured as the **number of times interest charges are earned**, sometimes called

Sarbanes-Oxley Act

The Sarbanes-Oxley Act became law on June 30, 2002, in response to widespread concerns about conflicts of interest between auditors and their clients, perceived weaknesses in corporate governance, and inadequate financial disclosure. Thus, Sarbanes-Oxley provided reforms in three main areas: the accounting profession, corporate governance, and financial disclosure.

Accounting Profession: A new provision in Sarbanes-Oxley prevents the independent auditor from providing other non-aligned services to a client, such as bookkeeping or internal auditing services. Providing tax services to an audit client is still acceptable. In addition, the act established a new Public Company Accounting Oversight Board (PCAOB), consisting of five members responsible for establishing and overseeing auditing, quality control, ethics, and independence standards related to preparing audit reports.

Corporate Governance: Corporate governance refers to methods for aligning the behavior of corporate managers with the interests of shareholders. Sarbanes-Oxley added important requirements to the audit committee of the board of directors. The audit committee must be members of the board of directors and independent of management. In addition, the audit committee is required to be responsible for appointment, compensation, and oversight of the independent auditors. In addition, Sarbanes-Oxley requires the CEO and CFO to certify the fairness of financial statements and the effectiveness of the internal controls. For example, an excerpt from the certification of a recent quarterly report of **Bank of America** by its CEO, Kenneth D. Lewis, is shown as follows:

I, Kenneth D. Lewis, certify that:

I have reviewed this quarterly report of Bank of America Corporation;

Based on my knowledge, the financial statements, and other financial information included in this quarterly report, fairly present in all material respects the financial condition, results of operations and cash flows of the (company) as of, and for, the periods presented in this quarterly report;

The . . . officers and I have disclosed, based on our most recent evaluation, to (the company's) auditors and the audit committee . . . :

- *all significant deficiencies in the design or operation of internal controls which could adversely affect (the company's) ability to record, process, summarize and report financial data and have identified for the (company's) auditors any material weaknesses in internal controls; and*

- *any fraud, whether or not material, that involves management or other employees who have a significant role in the (company's) internal controls; . . .*

/s/ Kenneth D. Lewis

Financial Disclosure: Sarbanes-Oxley also requires new or enhanced financial disclosures of transactions between related parties. These disclosures are prompted by a concern that such transactions are subject to a higher risk of self-dealing. In addition, the act requires material off-balance-sheet arrangements to be disclosed, such as the complex partnership transactions that led to the **Enron** failure.

the *fixed charge coverage ratio,* during the year. The higher the ratio, the lower the risk that interest payments will not be made if earnings decrease. In other words, the higher the ratio, the greater the assurance that interest payments will be made on a continuing basis. This measure also indicates the general financial strength of the business, which is of interest to stockholders and employees as well as creditors.

The amount available to meet interest charges is not affected by taxes on income. This is because interest is deductible in determining taxable income. Thus, the number of times interest charges are earned is computed as shown below.

	2009	2008
Income before income tax	$ 900,000	$ 800,000
Add interest expense	300,000	250,000
Amount available to meet interest charges	$1,200,000	$1,050,000
Number of times interest charges earned	4	4.2

Analysis such as this can also be applied to dividends on preferred stock. In such a case, net income is divided by the amount of preferred dividends to yield the *number of times preferred dividends are earned.* This measure indicates the risk that dividends to preferred stockholders may not be paid.

Profitability Analysis

Obj 3

Apply financial statement analysis to assess the profitability of a business.

The ability of a business to earn profits depends on the effectiveness and efficiency of its operations as well as the resources available to it. Profitability analysis, therefore, focuses primarily on the relationship between operating results as reported in the income statement and resources available to the business as reported in the balance sheet. Major analyses used in assessing profitability include the following:

1. Ratio of net sales to assets
2. Rate earned on total assets
3. Rate earned on stockholders' equity
4. Rate earned on common stockholders' equity
5. Earnings per share on common stock
6. Price-earnings ratio
7. Dividends per share
8. Dividend yield

Ratio of Net Sales to Assets

The ratio of net sales to assets is a profitability measure that shows how effectively a firm utilizes its assets. For example, two competing businesses have equal amounts of assets. If the sales of one are twice the sales of the other, the business with the higher sales is making better use of its assets.

In computing the ratio of net sales to assets, any long-term investments are excluded from total assets, because such investments are unrelated to normal operations involving the sale of goods or services. Assets may be measured as the total at the end of the year, the average at the beginning and end of the year, or the average of monthly totals. The basic data and the computation of this ratio for Lincoln Company are as follows:

	2009	2008
Net sales	$1,498,000	$1,200,000
Total assets (excluding long-term investments):		
Beginning of year	$1,053,000	$1,010,000
End of year	1,044,500	1,053,000
Total	$2,097,500	$2,063,000
Average (Total ÷ 2)	$1,048,750	$1,031,500
Ratio of net sales to assets	1.4	1.2

This ratio improved during 2009, primarily due to an increase in sales volume. A comparison with similar companies or industry averages would be helpful in assessing the effectiveness of Lincoln Company's use of its assets.

Rate Earned on Total Assets

The **rate earned on total assets** measures the profitability of total assets, without considering how the assets are financed. This rate is therefore not affected by whether the assets are financed primarily by creditors or stockholders.

The rate earned on total assets is computed by adding interest expense to net income and dividing this sum by the average total assets. Adding interest expense to net income eliminates the effect of whether the assets are financed by debt or equity. The rate earned by Lincoln Company on total assets is computed as follows:

	2009	2008
Net income	$ 91,000	$ 76,500
Plus interest expense	6,000	12,000
Total	$ 97,000	$ 88,500
Total assets:		
Beginning of year	$1,230,500	$1,187,500
End of year	1,139,500	1,230,500
Total	$2,370,000	$2,418,000
Average (Total ÷ 2)	$1,185,000	$1,209,000
Rate earned on total assets	8.2%	7.3%

The rate earned on total assets of Lincoln Company during 2009 improved over that of 2008. A comparison with similar companies and industry averages would be useful in evaluating Lincoln Company's profitability on total assets.

Sometimes it may be desirable to compute the *rate of income from operations to total assets.* This is especially true if significant amounts of nonoperating income and expense are reported on the income statement. In this case, any assets related to the nonoperating income and expense items should be excluded from total assets in computing the rate. In addition, using income from operations (which is before tax) has the advantage of eliminating the effects of any changes in the tax structure on the rate of earnings. When evaluating published data on rates earned on assets, you should be careful to determine the exact nature of the measure that is reported.

Rate Earned on Stockholders' Equity

Another measure of profitability is the **rate earned on stockholders' equity**. It is computed by dividing net income by average total stockholders' equity. In contrast to the rate earned on total assets, this measure emphasizes the rate of income earned on the amount invested by the stockholders.

The total stockholders' equity may vary throughout a period. For example, a business may issue or retire stock, pay dividends, and earn net income. If monthly amounts are not available, the average of the stockholders' equity at the beginning and the end of the year is normally used to compute this rate. For Lincoln Company, the rate earned on stockholders' equity is computed as follows:

	2009	2008
Net income	$ 91,000	$ 76,500
Stockholders' equity:		
Beginning of year	$ 787,500	$ 750,000
End of year	829,500	787,500
Total	$1,617,000	$1,537,500
Average (Total ÷ 2)	$ 808,500	$ 768,750
Rate earned on stockholders' equity	11.3%	10.0%

The rate earned by a business on the equity of its stockholders is usually higher than the rate earned on total assets. This occurs when the amount earned on assets acquired with creditors' funds is more than the interest paid to creditors. This difference in the rate on stockholders' equity and the rate on total assets is called **leverage**.

Lincoln Company's rate earned on stockholders' equity for 2009, 11.3%, is greater than the rate of 8.2% earned on total assets. The leverage of 3.1% (11.3% − 8.2%) for 2009 compares favorably with the 2.7% (10.0% − 7.3%) leverage for 2008. Exhibit 8 shows the 2009 and 2008 leverages for Lincoln Company.

EXHIBIT 8 *Leverage*

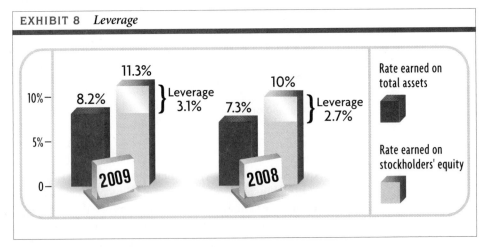

Rate Earned on Common Stockholders' Equity

A corporation may have both preferred and common stock outstanding. In this case, the common stockholders have the residual claim on earnings. The **rate earned on common stockholders' equity** focuses only on the rate of profits earned on the amount invested by the common stockholders. It is computed by subtracting preferred dividend requirements from the net income and dividing by the average common stockholders' equity.

Lincoln Company has $150,000 of 6% preferred stock outstanding on December 31, 2009 and 2008. Thus, the annual preferred dividend requirement is $9,000 ($150,000 × 6%). The common stockholders' equity equals the total stockholders' equity, including retained earnings, less the par of the preferred stock ($150,000). The basic data and the rate earned on common stockholders' equity for Lincoln Company are as follows:

	2009	2008
Net income	$ 91,000	$ 76,500
Preferred dividends	9,000	9,000
Remainder—identified with common stock	$ 82,000	$ 67,500
Common stockholders' equity:		
Beginning of year	$ 637,500	$ 600,000
End of year	679,500	637,500
Total	$1,317,000	$1,237,500
Average (Total ÷ 2)	$ 658,500	$ 618,750
Rate earned on common stockholders' equity	12.5%	10.9%

The rate earned on common stockholders' equity differs from the rates earned by Lincoln Company on total assets and total stockholders' equity. This occurs if there are borrowed funds and also preferred stock outstanding, which rank ahead of the common shares in their claim on earnings. Thus, the concept of leverage, as we discussed in the preceding section, can also be applied to the use of funds from the sale of preferred stock as well as borrowing. Funds from both sources can be used in an attempt to increase the return on common stockholders' equity.

Earnings per Share on Common Stock

One of the profitability measures often quoted by the financial press is **earnings per share (EPS) on common stock**. It is also normally reported in the income statement in corporate annual reports. If a company has issued only one class of stock, the earnings per share is computed by dividing net income by the number of shares of stock outstanding. If preferred and common stock are outstanding, the net income is first reduced by the amount of preferred dividend requirements.[3]

The data on the earnings per share of common stock for Lincoln Company are as follows:

	2009	2008
Net income	$91,000	$76,500
Preferred dividends	9,000	9,000
Remainder—identified with common stock	$82,000	$67,500
Shares of common stock outstanding	50,000	50,000
Earnings per share on common stock	$1.64	$1.35

[3]Additional details related to earnings per share were discussed in a previous chapter.

Price-Earnings Ratio

Another profitability measure quoted by the financial press is the **price-earnings (P/E) ratio** on common stock. The price-earnings ratio is an indicator of a firm's future earnings prospects. It is computed by dividing the market price per share of common stock at a specific date by the annual earnings per share. To illustrate, assume that the market prices per common share are 41 at the end of 2009 and 27 at the end of 2008. The price-earnings ratio on common stock of Lincoln Company is computed as follows:

	2009	2008
Market price per share of common stock	$41.00	$27.00
Earnings per share on common stock	÷ 1.64	÷ 1.35
Price-earnings ratio on common stock	25	20

The price-earnings ratio indicates that a share of common stock of Lincoln Company was selling for 20 times the amount of earnings per share at the end of 2008. At the end of 2009, the common stock was selling for 25 times the amount of earnings per share.

Dividends per Share and Dividend Yield

Since the primary basis for dividends is earnings, dividends per share and earnings per share on common stock are commonly used by investors in assessing alternative stock investments. The dividends per share for Lincoln Company were $0.80 ($40,000 ÷ 50,000 shares) for 2009 and $0.60 ($30,000 ÷ 50,000 shares) for 2008.

Dividends per share can be reported with earnings per share to indicate the relationship between dividends and earnings. Comparing these two per-share amounts indicates the extent to which the corporation is retaining its earnings for use in operations. Exhibit 9 shows these relationships for Lincoln Company.

The **dividend yield** on common stock is a profitability measure that shows the rate of return to common stockholders in terms of cash dividends. It is of special interest

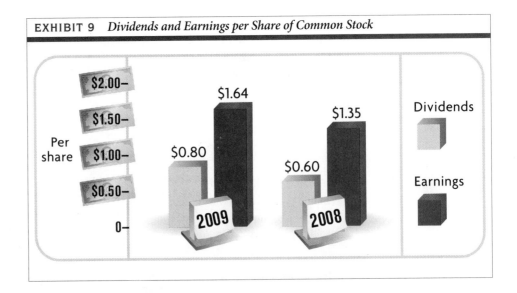

EXHIBIT 9 *Dividends and Earnings per Share of Common Stock*

to investors whose main investment objective is to receive current returns (dividends) on an investment rather than an increase in the market price of the investment. The dividend yield is computed by dividing the annual dividends paid per share of common stock by the market price per share on a specific date. To illustrate, assume that the market price was 41 at the end of 2009 and 27 at the end of 2008. The dividend yield on common stock of Lincoln Company is as follows:

	2009	2008
Dividends per share of common stock	$ 0.80	$ 0.60
Market price per share of common stock	÷ 41.00	÷ 27.00
Dividend yield on common stock	1.95%	2.22%

Summary of Analytical Measures

Obj 4

Summarize the uses and limitations of analytical measures.

Exhibit 10 presents a summary of the analytical measures that we have discussed. These measures can be computed for most medium-sized businesses. Depending on the specific business being analyzed, some measures might be omitted or additional measures could be developed. The type of industry, the capital structure, and the diversity of the business's operations usually affect the measures used. For example, analysis for an airline might include revenue per passenger mile and cost per available seat as measures. Likewise, analysis for a hotel might focus on occupancy rates.

Percentage analyses, ratios, turnovers, and other measures of financial position and operating results are useful analytical measures. They are helpful in assessing a business's past performance and predicting its future. They are not, however, a substitute for sound judgment. In selecting and interpreting analytical measures, conditions peculiar to a business or its industry should be considered. In addition, the influence of the general economic and business environment should be considered.

In determining trends, the interrelationship of the measures used in assessing a business should be carefully studied. Comparable indexes of earlier periods should also be studied. Data from competing businesses may be useful in assessing the efficiency of operations for the firm under analysis. In making such comparisons, however, the effects of differences in the accounting methods used by the businesses should be considered.

Corporate Annual Reports

Obj 5

Describe the contents of corporate annual reports.

Corporations normally issue annual reports to their stockholders and other interested parties. Such reports summarize the corporation's operating activities for the past year and plans for the future. There are many variations in the order and form for presenting the major sections of annual reports. However, one section of the annual report is devoted to the financial statements, including the accompanying notes. In addition, annual reports usually include a Management Discussion and Analysis (MDA) and an independent auditors' report.

EXHIBIT 10   *Summary of Analytical Measures*

	Method of Computation	*Use*
Solvency measures:		
Working capital	Current assets − Current liabilities	To indicate the ability to meet currently maturing obligations
Current ratio	$\dfrac{\text{Current assets}}{\text{Current liabilities}}$	
Quick ratio	$\dfrac{\text{Quick assets}}{\text{Current liabilities}}$	To indicate instant debt-paying ability
Accounts receivable turnover	$\dfrac{\text{Net sales}}{\text{Average accounts receivable}}$	To assess the efficiency in collecting receivables and in the management of credit
Number of days' sales in receivables	$\dfrac{\text{Average accounts receivable}}{\text{Average daily sales}}$	
Inventory turnover	$\dfrac{\text{Cost of goods sold}}{\text{Average inventory}}$	To assess the efficiency in the management of inventory
Number of days' sales in inventory	$\dfrac{\text{Average inventory}}{\text{Average daily cost of goods sold}}$	
Ratio of fixed assets to long-term liabilities	$\dfrac{\text{Fixed assets (net)}}{\text{Long-term liabilities}}$	To indicate the margin of safety to long-term creditors
Ratio of liabilities to stockholders' equity	$\dfrac{\text{Total liabilities}}{\text{Total stockholders' equity}}$	To indicate the margin of safety to creditors
Number of times interest charges earned	$\dfrac{\text{Income before income tax + Interest expense}}{\text{Interest expense}}$	To assess the risk to debtholders in terms of number of times interest charges were earned
Profitability measures:		
Ratio of net sales to assets	$\dfrac{\text{Net sales}}{\text{Average total assets (excluding long-term investments)}}$	To assess the effectiveness in the use of assets
Rate earned on total assets	$\dfrac{\text{Net income + Interest expense}}{\text{Average total assets}}$	To assess the profitability of the assets
Rate earned on stockholders' equity	$\dfrac{\text{Net income}}{\text{Average total stockholders' equity}}$	To assess the profitability of the investment by stockholders
Rate earned on common stockholders' equity	$\dfrac{\text{Net income − Preferred dividends}}{\text{Average common stockholders' equity}}$	To assess the profitability of the investment by common stockholders
Earnings per share on common stock	$\dfrac{\text{Net income − Preferred dividends}}{\text{Shares of common stock outstanding}}$	
Price-earnings ratio	$\dfrac{\text{Market price per share of common stock}}{\text{Earnings per share of common stock}}$	To indicate future earnings prospects, based on the relationship between market value of common stock and earnings
Dividends per share of common stock	$\dfrac{\text{Dividends}}{\text{Shares of common stock outstanding}}$	To indicate the extent to which earnings are being distributed to common stockholders
Dividend yield	$\dfrac{\text{Dividends per share of common stock}}{\text{Market price per share of common stock}}$	To indicate the rate of return to common stockholders in terms of dividends

INTEGRITY, OBJECTIVITY, AND ETHICS IN BUSINESS

Do You Swear . . .

The Sarbanes-Oxley Act of 2002 was enacted in response to the perceived abuses in accounting, corporate responsibility, and public disclosure in the early part of this decade. One of the provisions of this act is to require the principal executive and financial officers to certify under oath and penalty of law that the financial statements have been personally reviewed, contain no material omissions, and present fairly the financial condition and results of operations.

Management Discussion and Analysis

A required disclosure in the annual report filed with the Securities and Exchange Commission is the **Management Discussion and Analysis (MDA)**. The MDA provides critical information in interpreting the financial statements and assessing the future of the company.

The MDA includes an analysis of the results of operations and discusses management's opinion about future performance. It compares the prior year's income statement with the current year's to explain changes in sales, significant expenses, gross profit, and income from operations. For example, an increase in sales may be explained by referring to higher shipment volume or stronger prices.

The MDA also includes an analysis of the company's financial condition. It compares significant balance sheet items between successive years to explain changes in liquidity and capital resources. In addition, the MDA discusses significant risk exposure.

INTEGRITY, OBJECTIVITY, AND ETHICS IN BUSINESS

One Bad Apple

A recent survey by *CFO* magazine reported that 17% of the chief financial officers were pressured by their chief executive officer to misrepresent financial results, while only 5% admitted to knowingly violating generally accepted accounting principles.

Independent Auditors' Report

Before issuing annual statements, all publicly held corporations are required to have an independent audit (examination) of their financial statements. For the financial statements of most companies, the CPAs who conduct the audit render an opinion on the fairness of the statements.

In addition, since 2004, the Sarbanes-Oxley Act has required the independent auditor to provide an additional report attesting to management's assessment of internal control. This report expresses the auditor's opinion on the accuracy of management's internal control assertion.[4]

[4]Final reporting guidelines were formulated by appropriate professional and regulatory bodies, including the SEC, AICPA, and PCAOB.

HOW BUSINESSES MAKE MONEY

Investing Strategies

How does one decide in which companies to invest? As with any other significant purchase, you would need to do some research to guide your investment decision, and that research should stem from your overall investment philosophy. If you were buying a car for performance, you would research performance characteristics, but if you were purchasing for economy, then you would research economy characteristics. You should research investment alternatives in the same way. There are four different investment philosophies that match different investment preferences: value, growth, income, and technical investing.

Value Investing

The value investor attempts to determine the intrinsic value of a business and then compare this value to the stock price. The investor is normally searching for undervalued stocks. That is, the investor attempts to discover stocks with an intrinsic value that is greater than the stock price. Value investors often look for quiet, out-of-favor, "boring" companies that have excellent financial performance. Investing in such stocks assumes that the stock price will eventually rise to match the intrinsic value. This method of investing was popularized by Benjamin Graham and is used by one of the most successful investors in the world, Warren Buffett. As stated by one author, "Graham's conviction rested on certain assumptions. First, he believed that the market frequently mispriced stocks. This mispricing was most often caused by human emotions of fear and greed. At the height of optimism, greed moved stocks beyond their intrinsic value, creating an overpriced market. At other times, fear moved prices below intrinsic value, creating an undervalued market."* Naturally, the key to successful value investing is to accurately determine a stock's intrinsic value. This will often include analyzing company financial ratios, as discussed in this chapter, relative to target ratios and industry norms.

Growth Investing

The growth investor tries to identify companies that are growing sales and earnings through new products, markets, or opportunities. Growth companies are often young companies that are still unproven but that possess unique technologies or capabilities. Investors hope to "ride the wave" of growth by purchasing these companies before their potential becomes obvious. Unlike value investors, growth investors will often purchase companies that are the "Ferraris" of the stock market. Growth investing carries the risk that the growth may not occur. Any moderation in growth can lead to severe price declines. Growth investors use many of the ratios discussed in this chapter to identify high-potential growth companies.

Income Investing

Income investors purchase common stocks for their dividend stream. High-dividend-paying companies are often in low-growth and stable industries. The stock price of such companies is usually not very volatile. Thus, the majority of the investment return comes from dividends. Many of the ratios discussed in this chapter can help identify companies with financial strength and high dividends.

Technical Investing

Investors who use technical analysis do not concern themselves with the fundamental financial strength and performance of the business but, instead, attempt to find clues of future performance from past performance. Technical investors often use charts of the historical prices in order to discover recurring price patterns that will help them determine if the stock price is near a top (signal to sell) or near a bottom (signal to buy). Technical analysts believe that the recurring patterns provide clues into market psychology and can be used to develop buy-and-sell rules. These rules are as varied as the number of investors developing them. Naturally, if everyone agreed upon a technical rule that actually predicted the future, then everyone would use the rule and it would eventually cease to work.

*Robert G. Hagstrom, *The Warren Buffett Way*.

Key Points

1. Describe basic financial statement analytical procedures.

The analysis of percentage increases and decreases in related items in comparative financial statements is called horizontal analysis. The analysis of percentages of component parts to the total in a single statement is called vertical analysis. Financial statements in which all amounts are expressed in percentages for purposes of analysis are called common-size statements.

2. **Apply financial statement analysis to assess the solvency of a business.**

    The primary focus of financial statement analysis is the assessment of solvency and profitability. All users are interested in the ability of a business to pay its debts as they come due (solvency) and to earn income (profitability). Solvency analysis is normally assessed by examining the following balance sheet relationships: (1) current position analysis, (2) accounts receivable analysis, (3) inventory analysis, (4) the ratio of fixed assets to long-term liabilities, (5) the ratio of liabilities to stockholders' equity, and (6) the number of times interest charges are earned.

3. **Apply financial statement analysis to assess the profitability of a business.**

    Profitability analysis focuses mainly on the relationship between operating results (income statement) and resources available (balance sheet). Major analyses used in assessing profitability include (1) the ratio of net sales to assets, (2) the rate earned on total assets, (3) the rate earned on stockholders' equity, (4) the rate earned on common stockholders' equity, (5) earnings per share on common stock, (6) the price-earnings ratio, (7) dividends per share, and (8) dividend yield.

4. **Summarize the uses and limitations of analytical measures.**

    In selecting and interpreting analytical measures, conditions peculiar to a business or its industry should be considered. For example, the type of industry, capital structure, and diversity of the business's operations affect the measures used. In addition, the influence of the general economic and business environment should be considered.

5. **Describe the contents of corporate annual reports.**

    Corporate annual reports normally include financial statements and the accompanying notes, the Management Discussion and Analysis, and the Independent Auditors' Report.

Key Terms

Accounts receivable turnover

Common-size statement

Current ratio

Dividend yield

Earnings per share (EPS) on common stock

Horizontal analysis

Inventory turnover

Leverage

Management Discussion and Analysis (MDA)

Number of days' sales in inventory

Number of days' sales in receivables

Number of times interest charges are earned

Price-earnings (P/E) ratio

Profitability

Quick assets

Quick ratio

Rate earned on common stockholders' equity

Rate earned on stockholders' equity

Rate earned on total assets

Ratio of fixed assets to long-term liabilities

Ratio of liabilities to stockholders' equity

Solvency

Vertical analysis

Illustrative Problem

Rainbow Paint Co.'s comparative financial statements for the years ending December 31, 2009 and 2008, are as follows. The market price of Rainbow Paint Co.'s common stock was $30 on December 31, 2008, and $25 on December 31, 2009.

(continued)

RAINBOW PAINT CO.
Comparative Income Statement
For the Years Ended December 31, 2009 and 2008

	2009	2008
Sales	$5,125,000	$3,257,600
Sales returns and allowances	125,000	57,600
Net sales	$5,000,000	$3,200,000
Cost of goods sold	3,400,000	2,080,000
Gross profit	$1,600,000	$1,120,000
Selling expenses	$ 650,000	$ 464,000
Administrative expenses	325,000	224,000
Total operating expenses	$ 975,000	$ 688,000
Income from operations	$ 625,000	$ 432,000
Other income	25,000	19,200
	$ 650,000	$ 451,200
Other expense (interest)	105,000	64,000
Income before income tax	$ 545,000	$ 387,200
Income tax expense	300,000	176,000
Net income	$ 245,000	$ 211,200

RAINBOW PAINT CO.
Comparative Retained Earnings Statement
For the Years Ended December 31, 2009 and 2008

	2009	2008
Retained earnings, January 1	$723,000	$581,800
Add net income for year	245,000	211,200
Total	$968,000	$793,000
Deduct dividends:		
On preferred stock	$ 40,000	$ 40,000
On common stock	45,000	30,000
Total	$ 85,000	$ 70,000
Retained earnings, December 31	$883,000	$723,000

RAINBOW PAINT CO.
Comparative Balance Sheet
December 31, 2009 and 2008

	2009	2008
Assets		
Current assets:		
Cash	$ 175,000	$ 125,000
Marketable securities	150,000	50,000
Accounts receivable (net)	425,000	325,000
Inventories	720,000	480,000
Prepaid expenses	30,000	20,000
Total current assets	$1,500,000	$1,000,000
Long-term investments	250,000	225,000
Property, plant, and equipment (net)	2,093,000	1,948,000
Total assets	$3,843,000	$3,173,000

	2009	2008
Liabilities		
Current liabilities	$ 750,000	$ 650,000
Long-term liabilities:		
Mortgage note payable, 10%, due 2012	$ 410,000	—
Bonds payable, 8%, due 2015	800,000	$ 800,000
Total long-term liabilities	$1,210,000	$ 800,000
Total liabilities	$1,960,000	$1,450,000
Stockholders' Equity		
Preferred 8% stock, $100 par	$ 500,000	$ 500,000
Common stock, $10 par	500,000	500,000
Retained earnings	883,000	723,000
Total stockholders' equity	$1,883,000	$1,723,000
Total liabilities and stockholders' equity	$3,843,000	$3,173,000

Instructions

Determine the following measures for 2009:

1. Working capital
2. Current ratio
3. Quick ratio
4. Accounts receivable turnover
5. Number of days' sales in receivables
6. Inventory turnover
7. Number of days' sales in inventory
8. Ratio of fixed assets to long-term liabilities
9. Ratio of liabilities to stockholders' equity
10. Number of times interest charges earned
11. Number of times preferred dividends earned
12. Ratio of net sales to assets
13. Rate earned on total assets
14. Rate earned on stockholders' equity
15. Rate earned on common stockholders' equity
16. Earnings per share on common stock
17. Price-earnings ratio
18. Dividends per share of common stock
19. Dividend yield

Solution

(Ratios are rounded to the nearest single digit after the decimal point.)

1. Working capital: $750,000
   $1,500,000 − $750,000

2. Current ratio: 2.0
   $1,500,000/$750,000

3. Quick ratio: 1.0
   $750,000/$750,000

4. Accounts receivable turnover: 13.3
   $5,000,000/[($425,000 + $325,000)/2]

5. Number of days' sales in receivables: 27.4 days
   $5,000,000/365 = $13,699
   $375,000/$13,699

6. Inventory turnover: 5.7
   $3,400,000/[($720,000 + $480,000)/2]

(continued)

7. Number of days' sales in inventory: 64.4 days
   $3,400,000/365 = $9,315
   $600,000/$9,315

8. Ratio of fixed assets to long-term liabilities: 1.7
   $2,093,000/$1,210,000

9. Ratio of liabilities to stockholders' equity: 1.0
   $1,960,000/$1,883,000

10. Number of times interest charges earned: 6.2
    ($545,000 + $105,000)/$105,000

11. Number of times preferred dividends earned: 6.1
    $245,000/$40,000

12. Ratio of net sales to assets: 1.5
    $5,000,000/[($3,593,000 + $2,948,000)/2]

13. Rate earned on total assets: 10.0%
    ($245,000 + $105,000)/[($3,843,000 + $3,173,000)/2]

14. Rate earned on stockholders' equity: 13.6%
    $245,000/[($1,883,000 + $1,723,000)/2]

15. Rate earned on common stockholders' equity: 15.7%
    ($245,000 − $40,000)/[($1,383,000 + $1,223,000)/2]

16. Earnings per share on common stock: $4.10
    ($245,000 − $40,000)/50,000

17. Price-earnings ratio: 6.1
    $25/$4.10

18. Dividends per share of common stock: $0.90
    $45,000/50,000 shares

19. Dividend yield: 3.6%
    $0.90/$25

Self-Examination Questions   *(Answers appear at end of chapter.)*

1. What type of analysis is indicated by the following?

	Amount	*Percent*
Current assets	$100,000	20%
Property, plant, and equipment	400,000	80
Total assets	$500,000	100%

   A. Vertical analysis
   B. Horizontal analysis
   C. Profitability analysis
   D. Contribution margin analysis

2. Which of the following measures indicates the ability of a firm to pay its current liabilities?
   A. Working capital
   B. Current ratio
   C. Quick ratio
   D. All of the above

3. The ratio determined by dividing total current assets by total current liabilities is:
   A. current ratio.
   B. working capital ratio.
   C. bankers' ratio.
   D. all of the above.

4. The ratio of the quick assets to current liabilities, which indicates the "instant" debt-paying ability of a firm, is the:
   A. current ratio.
   B. working capital ratio.
   C. quick ratio.
   D. bankers' ratio.

5. A measure useful in evaluating efficiency in the management of inventories is the:
   A. working capital ratio.
   B. quick ratio.
   C. number of days' sales in inventory.
   D. ratio of fixed assets to long-term liabilities.

Class Discussion Questions

1. What is the difference between horizontal and vertical analysis of financial statements?

2. What is the advantage of using comparative statements for financial analysis rather than statements for a single date or period?

3. The current year's amount of net income (after income tax) is 20% larger than that of the preceding year. Does this indicate an improved operating performance? Discuss.

4. How would you respond to a horizontal analysis that showed an expense increasing by over 80%?

5. How would the current and quick ratios of a service business compare?

6. For Lindsay Corporation, the working capital at the end of the current year is $8,000 less than the working capital at the end of the preceding year, reported as follows:

	Current Year	Preceding Year
Current assets:		
Cash, marketable securities, and receivables	$35,000	$36,000
Inventories	55,000	42,000
Total current assets	$90,000	$78,000
Current liabilities	50,000	30,000
Working capital	$40,000	$48,000

Has the current position improved? Explain.

7. Why would the accounts receivable turnover ratio be different between *Wal-Mart* and *Procter & Gamble*?

8. A company that grants terms of n/45 on all sales has a yearly accounts receivable turnover, based on monthly averages, of 5. Is this a satisfactory turnover? Discuss.

9. a. Why is it advantageous to have a high inventory turnover?
   b. Is it possible for the inventory turnover to be too high? Discuss.
   c. Is it possible to have a high inventory turnover and a high number of days' sales in inventory? Discuss.

10. What do the following data taken from a comparative balance sheet indicate about the company's ability to borrow additional funds on a long-term basis in the current year as compared to the preceding year?

	Current Year	Preceding Year
Fixed assets (net)	$300,000	$300,000
Total long-term liabilities	100,000	120,000

11. a. How does the rate earned on total assets differ from the rate earned on stockholders' equity?
    b. Which ratio is normally higher? Explain.

12. a. Why is the rate earned on stockholders' equity by a thriving business ordinarily higher than the rate earned on total assets?
    b. Should the rate earned on common stockholders' equity normally be higher or lower than the rate earned on total stockholders' equity? Explain.

13. The net income (after income tax) of Choi Inc. was $15 per common share in the latest year and $60 per common share for the preceding year. At the beginning of the latest year, the number of shares outstanding was doubled by a stock split. There were no other changes in the amount of stock outstanding. What were the earnings per share in the preceding year, adjusted for comparison with the latest year?

14. The price-earnings ratio for the common stock of Cotter Company was 10 at December 31, the end of the current fiscal year. What does the ratio indicate about the selling price of the common stock in relation to current earnings?

15. Why would the dividend yield differ significantly from the rate earned on common stockholders' equity?

16. Favorable business conditions may bring about certain seemingly unfavorable ratios, and unfavorable business operations may result in apparently favorable ratios. For example, Trivec Company increased its sales and net income substantially for the current year, yet the current ratio at the end of the year is lower than at the beginning of the year. Discuss some possible causes of the apparent weakening of the current position, while sales and net income have increased substantially.

Exercises

Revenue and expense data for Jazz-Tech Communications Co. are as follows:

	2008	2007
Sales	$750,000	$600,000
Cost of goods sold	450,000	312,000
Selling expenses	120,000	126,000
Administrative expenses	105,000	84,000
Income tax expense	37,500	30,000

a. Prepare an income statement in comparative form, stating each item for both 2008 and 2007 as a percent of sales. Round to one decimal place.
b. Comment on the significant changes disclosed by the comparative income statement.

The following comparative income statement (in thousands of dollars) for two recent years was adapted from the annual report of **Speedway Motorsports, Inc.**, owner and operator of several major motor speedways, such as the Atlanta, Texas, and Las Vegas Motor Speedways.

	Year 2	Year 1
Revenues:		
Admissions	$156,718	$150,253
Event-related revenue	137,074	127,055
NASCAR broadcasting revenue	110,016	90,682
Other operating revenue	42,711	36,539
Total revenue	$446,519	$404,529
Expenses and other:		
Direct expense of events	$ 81,432	$ 77,962
NASCAR purse and sanction fees	78,473	69,691
Other direct expenses	102,053	101,408
General and administrative	65,152	58,698
Total expenses and other	$327,110	$307,759
Income from continuing operations	$119,409	$ 96,770

a. Prepare a comparative income statement for Years 1 and 2 in vertical form, stating each item as a percent of revenues. Round to one decimal place.
b. Comment on the significant changes.

Revenue and expense data for the current calendar year for Jaribo Communications Company and for the communications industry are as follows. The Jaribo Communications Company data are expressed in dollars. The communications industry averages are expressed in percentages.

	Jaribo Communications Company	Communications Industry Average
Sales	$1,265,000	101.0%
Sales returns and allowances	15,000	1.0
Cost of goods sold	450,000	41.0
Selling expenses	525,000	38.0
Administrative expenses	143,750	10.5
Other income	22,500	1.2
Other expense (interest)	18,750	1.7
Income tax expense	50,000	4.0

a. Prepare a common-size income statement comparing the results of operations for Jaribo Communications Company with the industry average. Round to one decimal place.
b. As far as the data permit, comment on significant relationships revealed by the comparisons.

E9-4

Vertical analysis of balance sheet

Obj 1

SPREADSHEET

✓ Retained earnings, Dec. 31, 2008, 47.5%

Balance sheet data for the Dover Hot Tub Company on December 31, the end of the fiscal year, are as follows:

	2008	2007
Current assets	$768,000	$250,000
Property, plant, and equipment	336,000	650,000
Intangible assets	96,000	100,000
Current liabilities	270,000	175,000
Long-term liabilities	300,000	255,000
Common stock	60,000	70,000
Retained earnings	570,000	500,000

Prepare a comparative balance sheet for 2008 and 2007, stating each asset as a percent of total assets and each liability and stockholders' equity item as a percent of the total liabilities and stockholders' equity. Round to one decimal place.

E9-5

Horizontal analysis of the income statement

Obj 1

SPREADSHEET

✓ a. Net income decrease, 53.3%

Income statement data for Web-pics Company for the year ended December 31, 2008 and 2007, are as follows:

	2008	2007
Sales	$117,000	$150,000
Cost of goods sold	56,000	70,000
Gross profit	$ 61,000	$ 80,000
Selling expenses	$ 36,000	$ 37,500
Administrative expenses	12,500	10,000
Total operating expenses	$ 48,500	$ 47,500
Income before income tax	$ 12,500	$ 32,500
Income tax expense	2,000	10,000
Net income	$ 10,500	$ 22,500

a. Prepare a comparative income statement with horizontal analysis, indicating the increase (decrease) for 2008 when compared with 2007. Round to one decimal place.
b. What conclusions can be drawn from the horizontal analysis?

E9-6

Current position analysis

Obj 2

✓ a. 2008 working capital, $1,265,000

The following data were taken from the balance sheet of Outdoor Supplier Company:

	Dec. 31, 2008	Dec. 31, 2007
Cash	$325,000	$300,000
Marketable securities	270,000	256,000
Accounts and notes receivable (net)	440,000	430,000
Inventories	675,000	557,000
Prepaid expenses	130,000	81,000
Accounts and notes payable (short-term)	425,000	450,000
Accrued liabilities	150,000	130,000

a. Determine for each year (1) the working capital, (2) the current ratio, and (3) the quick ratio. Round ratios to one decimal place.
b. What conclusions can be drawn from these data as to the company's ability to meet its currently maturing debts?

E9-7

Current position analysis

Obj 2

✓ a. (1) Year 1, current ratio, 1.2

PepsiCo, Inc., the parent company of Frito-Lay snack foods and Pepsi beverages, had the following current assets and current liabilities at the end of two recent years:

	Year 2 (in millions)	Year 1 (in millions)
Cash and cash equivalents	$1,716	$1,280
Short-term investments, at cost	3,166	2,165
Accounts and notes receivable (net)	3,261	2,999
Inventories	1,693	1,541
Prepaid expenses and other current assets	618	654
Short-term obligations	2,889	1,054
Accounts payable and other current liabilities	5,971	5,999
Income taxes payable	546	99

a. Determine the (1) current ratio and (2) quick ratio for both years. Round to one decimal place.
b. What conclusions can you draw from these data?

E9-8

Current position analysis

Obj 2

The bond indenture for the 20-year, 11% debenture bonds dated January 2, 2007, required working capital of $560,000, a current ratio of 1.5, and a quick ratio of 1.2, at the end of each calendar year until the bonds mature. At December 31, 2008, the three measures were computed as follows:

1. Current assets:

Cash	$190,000	
Marketable securities	95,000	
Accounts and notes receivable (net)	171,000	
Inventories	20,000	
Prepaid expenses	4,500	
Intangible assets	55,000	
Property, plant, and equipment	65,000	
Total current assets (net)		$600,500
Current liabilities:		
Accounts and short-term notes payable	$250,000	
Accrued liabilities	150,000	
Total current liabilities		400,000
Working capital		$200,500

2. Current ratio = 1.50 ($600,500/$400,000)
3. Quick ratio = 2.04 ($511,000/$250,000)

a. List the errors in the determination of the three measures of current position analysis.
b. Is the company satisfying the terms of the bond indenture?

E9-9

Accounts receivable analysis

Obj 2

✓ a. Accounts receivable turnover, 2008, 6.9

The following data are taken from the financial statements of Creekside Technology Inc. Terms of all sales are 2/10, n/60.

	2008	2007	2006
Accounts receivable, end of year	$ 75,452	$ 85,500	$81,624
Monthly average accounts receivable (net)	78,261	80,645	—
Net sales	540,000	500,000	—

a. Determine for each year (1) the accounts receivable turnover and (2) the number of days' sales in receivables. Round to nearest dollar and one decimal place.
b. What conclusions can be drawn from these data concerning accounts receivable and credit policies?

Polo Ralph Lauren Corporation designs, markets, and distributes a variety of apparel, home decor, accessory, and fragrance products. The company's products include such brands as Polo by Ralph Lauren, Ralph Lauren Purple Label, Ralph Lauren Polo Jeans Co., and Chaps. Polo Ralph Lauren reported the following (in thousands):

	For the Period Ending	
	March 31, 2007	**April 1, 2006**
Net Sales	$4,295,400	$3,746,300
Accounts receivable	511,900	516,600

Assume that accounts receivable (in millions) were $530,503 at the beginning of the 2006 fiscal year.

a. Compute the accounts receivable turnover for 2007 and 2006. Round to one decimal place.
b. Compute the days' sales in receivables for 2007 and 2006. Round to one decimal place.
c. What conclusions can be drawn from these analyses regarding Ralph Lauren's efficiency in collecting receivables?

The following data were extracted from the income statement of Clear View Systems Inc.:

	Current Year	**Preceding**
Sales	$756,000	$950,760
Beginning inventories	67,200	44,000
Cost of goods sold	492,000	528,200
Ending inventories	64,000	67,200

a. Determine for each year (1) the inventory turnover and (2) the number of days' sales in inventory. Round to nearest dollar and one decimal place.
b. What conclusions can be drawn from these data concerning the inventories?

Dell Inc. and **Hewlett-Packard Company (HP)** compete with each other in the personal computer market. Dell's strategy is to assemble computers to customer orders, rather than for inventory. Thus, for example, Dell will build and deliver a computer within four days of a customer entering an order on a Web page. Hewlett-Packard, on the other hand, builds some computers prior to receiving an order, then sells from this inventory once an order is received. Below is selected financial information for both companies from a recent year's financial statements (in millions):

	Dell Inc.	**Hewlett-Packard Company**
Sales	$55,908	$86,696
Cost of goods sold	45,620	66,440
Inventory, beginning of period	459	7,071
Inventory, end of period	576	6,877

a. Determine for both companies (1) the inventory turnover and (2) the number of days' sales in inventory. Round to one decimal place.
b. Interpret the inventory ratios by considering Dell's and Hewlett-Packard's operating strategies.

The following data were taken from the financial statements of Quality Construction Inc. for December 31, 2008 and 2007:

	December 31, 2008	**December 31, 2007**
Accounts payable	$ 240,000	$ 224,000
Current maturities of serial bonds payable	320,000	320,000
Serial bonds payable, 10%, issued 2004, due 2014	1,600,000	1,920,000
Common stock, $1 par value	160,000	160,000
Paid-in capital in excess of par	800,000	800,000
Retained earnings	3,404,800	2,560,000

(continued)

The income before income tax was $844,800 and $537,600 for the years 2008 and 2007, respectively.

a. Determine the ratio of liabilities to stockholders' equity at the end of each year. Round to one decimal place.
b. Determine the number of times the bond interest charges are earned during the year for both years. Round to one decimal place.
c. What conclusions can be drawn from these data as to the company's ability to meet its currently maturing debts?

E9-14

Ratio of liabilities to stock-holders' equity and number of times interest charges earned

Obj 2

✓ a. Hasbro, 1.0

Hasbro and *Mattel Inc.,* are the two largest toy companies in North America. Condensed liabilities and stockholders' equity from a recent balance sheet are shown for each company as follows:

	Hasbro	Mattel, Inc.
Current liabilities	$1,148,611,000	$1,727,171,000
Long-term debt	302,698,000	400,000,000
Deferred liabilities	149,627,000	243,509,000
Total liabilities	$1,600,936,000	$2,370,680,000
Shareholders' equity:		
Common stock, $0.50 par value	$ 104,847,000	$ 441,369,000
Additional paid-in capital	380,745,000	1,594,332,000
Retained earnings	1,721,209,000	1,093,288,000
Accumulated other comprehensive loss and other equity items	82,290,000	(269,828,000)
Treasury stock, at cost	(649,367,000)	(473,349,000)
Total stockholders' equity	$1,639,724,000	$2,385,812,000
Total liabilities and stockholders' equity	$3,240,660,000	$4,756,492,000

The income from operations and interest expense from the income statement for both companies were as follows:

	Hasbro	Mattel, Inc.
Income from operations	$293,012,000	$730,817,000
Interest expense	31,698,000	77,764,000

a. Determine the ratio of liabilities to stockholders' equity for both companies. Round to one decimal place.
b. Determine the number of times interest charges are earned for both companies. Round to one decimal place.
c. Interpret the ratio differences between the two companies.

E9-15

Ratio of liabilities to stock-holders' equity and ratio of fixed assets to long-term liabilities

Obj 2

✓ a. H.J. Heinz, 3.1

Recent balance sheet information for two companies in the food industry, *H.J. Heinz Company* and *The Hershey Company*, are as follows (in thousands of dollars):

	H.J. Heinz	Hershey
Net property, plant, and equipment	$2,163,938	$1,659,138
Current liabilities	2,587,068	1,518,223
Long-term debt	4,121,984	942,755
Other liabilities (pensions, deferred taxes)	1,266,093	813,182
Stockholders' equity	2,602,573	1,021,076

a. Determine the ratio of liabilities to stockholders' equity for both companies. Round to one decimal place.

b. Determine the ratio of fixed assets to long-term liabilities for both companies. Round to one decimal place.
c. Interpret the ratio differences between the two companies.

E9-16

Ratio of net sales to assets

Obj 3

✓ a. YRC Worldwide, 1.9

Three major segments of the transportation industry are motor carriers, such as **YRC Worldwide;** railroads, such as **Union Pacific**; and transportation arrangement services, such as **C.H. Robinson Worldwide Inc.** Recent financial statement information for these three companies is shown as follows (in thousands of dollars):

	YRC Worldwide	Union Pacific	C.H. Robinson Worldwide
Net sales	$6,767,485	$12,215,000	$4,341,538
Average total assets	3,545,199	34,041,500	994,423

a. Determine the ratio of net sales to assets for all three companies. Round to one decimal place.
b. Assume that the ratio of net sales to assets for each company represents their respective industry segment. Interpret the differences in the ratio of net sales to assets in terms of the operating characteristics of each of the respective segments.

E9-17

Profitability ratios

Obj 3

✓ a. Rate earned on total assets, 2008, 11.6%

The following selected data were taken from the financial statements of Berry Group Inc. for December 31, 2008, 2007, and 2006:

	December 31, 2008	December 31, 2007	December 31, 2006
Total assets	$1,160,000	$1,040,000	$880,000
Notes payable (10% interest)	150,000	150,000	150,000
Common stock	360,000	360,000	360,000
Preferred $8 stock, $100 par (no change during year)	160,000	160,000	160,000
Retained earnings	426,900	327,200	205,000

The 2008 net income was $112,500, and the 2007 net income was $135,000. No dividends on common stock were declared between 2006 and 2008.

a. Determine the rate earned on total assets, the rate earned on stockholders' equity, and the rate earned on common stockholders' equity for the years 2007 and 2008. Round to one decimal place.
b. What conclusions can be drawn from these data as to the company's profitability?

E9-18

Profitability ratios

Obj 3

✓ a. Year 2 rate earned on total assets, 6.0%

Ann Taylor Retail, Inc., sells professional women's apparel through company-owned retail stores. Recent financial information for Ann Taylor is provided below (all numbers in thousands):

	Year 2	Year 1
Net income	$81,872	$63,276
Interest expense	2,083	3,641

End of year...	Year 2	Year 1	Year 0
Total assets	$1,492,906	$1,327,338	$1,256,397
Total stockholders' equity	1,034,482	926,744	818,856

Assume the apparel industry average rate earned on total assets is 8.2%, and the average rate earned on stockholders' equity is 16.7% for Year 1.

a. Determine the rate earned on total assets for Ann Taylor for Year 2 and Year 1. Round to one digit after the decimal place.

(continued)

b. Determine the rate earned on stockholders' equity for Ann Taylor for Year 2 and Year 1. Round to one decimal place.

c. Evaluate the two-year trend for the profitability ratios determined in (a) and (b).

d. Evaluate Ann Taylor's profit performance relative to the industry.

E9-19

Six measures of solvency or profitability

Objs 2, 3

✓ c. Ratio of net sales to assets, 1.5

The following data were taken from the financial statements of Bendax Enterprises Inc. for the current fiscal year. Assuming that long-term investments totaled $240,000 throughout the year and that total assets were $2,525,000 at the beginning of the year, determine the following: (a) ratio of fixed assets to long-term liabilities, (b) ratio of liabilities to stockholders' equity, (c) ratio of net sales to assets, (d) rate earned on total assets, (e) rate earned on stockholders' equity, and (f) rate earned on common stockholders' equity. Round to one decimal place.

Property, plant, and equipment (net)			$1,200,000
Liabilities:			
Current liabilities		$ 60,000	
Mortgage note payable, 8%, issued 1997, due 2013		825,000	
Total liabilities			$ 885,000
Stockholders' equity:			
Preferred $9 stock, $100 par (no change during year)			$ 250,000
Common stock, $20 par (no change during year)			800,000
Retained earnings:			
Balance, beginning of year	$600,000		
Net income	216,000	$816,000	
Preferred dividends	$ 22,500		
Common dividends	57,600	80,100	
Balance, end of year			735,900
Total stockholders' equity			$1,785,900
Net sales			$3,600,000
Interest expense			$ 66,000

E9-20

Six measures of solvency or profitability

Objs 2, 3

✓ d. Price-earnings ratio, 16.1

The balance sheet for Chaney Resources Inc. at the end of the current fiscal year indicated the following:

Bonds payable, 10% (issued in 1995, due in 2015)	$2,250,000
Preferred $25 stock, $200 par	500,000
Common stock, $10 par	2,500,000

Income before income tax was $625,000, and income taxes were $175,000 for the current year. Cash dividends paid on common stock during the current year totaled $125,000. The common stock was selling for $25 per share at the end of the year. Determine each of the following: (a) number of times bond interest charges are earned, (b) number of times preferred dividends are earned, (c) earnings per share on common stock, (d) price-earnings ratio, (e) dividends per share of common stock, and (f) dividend yield. Round to one decimal place except earnings per share, which should be rounded to two decimal places.

E9-21

Earnings per share, price-earnings ratio, dividend yield

Obj 3

✓ b. Price-earnings ratio, 14.8

The following information was taken from the financial statements of Royer Medical Inc. for December 31 of the current fiscal year:

Common stock, $5 par value (no change during the year)	$1,500,000
Preferred $5 stock, $50 par (no change during year)	450,000

The net income was $450,000, and the declared dividends on the common stock were $75,000 for the current year. The market price of the common stock is $20 per share.

For the common stock, determine (a) the earnings per share, (b) the price-earnings ratio, (c) the dividends per share, and (d) the dividend yield. Round to one decimal place except earnings per share, which should be rounded to two decimal places.

E9-22

Earnings per share

Obj 3

✓ b. Earnings per share on common stock, $3.00

The net income reported on the income statement of Ground Hog Co. was $1,250,000. There were 250,000 shares of $40 par common stock and 50,000 shares of $10 preferred stock outstanding throughout the current year. The income statement included two extraordinary items: a $360,000 gain from condemnation of land and a $235,000 loss arising from flood damage, both after applicable income tax. Determine the per share figures for common stock for (a) income before extraordinary items and (b) net income.

E9-23

Price-earnings ratio; dividend yield

Obj 3

The table below shows the stock price, earnings per share, and dividends per share for three companies:

	Price	Earnings per Share	Dividends per Share
Bank of America Corporation	$44.47	$4.15	$2.00
eBay Inc.	41.60	0.78	0.00
The Coca-Cola Company	41.19	2.04	1.12

a. Determine the price-earnings ratio and dividend yield for the three companies. Round to one decimal place.
b. Explain the differences in these ratios across the three companies.

Problems

P9-1

Horizontal analysis for income statement

Obj 1

SPREADSHEET

✓ 1. Net sales, 25.1% increase

For 2008, Doane Inc. reported its most significant increase in net income in years. At the end of the year, Jeff Newton, the president, is presented with the following condensed comparative income statement:

DOANE INC.
Comparative Income Statement
For the Years Ended December 31, 2008 and 2007

	2008	2007
Sales	$91,500	$73,200
Sales returns and allowances	1,440	1,200
Net sales	$90,060	$72,000
Cost of goods sold	50,400	42,000
Gross profit	$39,660	$30,000
Selling expenses	$16,560	$14,400
Administrative expenses	10,800	9,600
Total operating expenses	$27,360	$24,000
Income from operations	$12,300	$ 6,000
Other income	600	600
Income before income tax	$12,900	$ 6,600
Income tax expense	2,880	1,440
Net income	$10,020	$ 5,160

Instructions

1. Prepare a comparative income statement with horizontal analysis for the two-year period, using 2007 as the base year. Round to one decimal place.

(continued)

2. To the extent the data permit, comment on the significant relationships revealed by the horizontal analysis prepared in (1).

P9-2

Vertical analysis for income statement

Obj 1

SPREADSHEET

✓ 1. Net income, 2007, 8.0%

For 2008, Dusan Water Supplies Inc. initiated a sales promotion campaign that included the expenditure of an additional $21,000 for advertising. At the end of the year, Ivana Novatna, the president, is presented with the following condensed comparative income statement:

DUSAN WATER SUPPLIES INC.
Comparative Income Statement
For the Years Ended December 31, 2008 and 2007

	2008	2007
Sales	$255,000	$214,000
Sales returns and allowances	5,000	4,000
Net sales	$250,000	$210,000
Cost of goods sold	142,500	121,800
Gross profit	$107,500	$ 88,200
Selling expenses	$100,000	$ 50,400
Administrative expenses	20,000	16,800
Total operating expenses	$120,000	$ 67,200
Income from operations	$ (12,500)	$ 21,000
Other income	6,250	4,200
Income before income tax	$ (6,250)	$ 25,200
Income tax expense (benefit)	(2,500)	8,400
Net income (loss)	$ (3,750)	$ 16,800

Instructions

1. Prepare a comparative income statement for the two-year period, presenting an analysis of each item in relationship to net sales for each of the years. Round to one decimal place.
2. To the extent the data permit, comment on the significant relationships revealed by the vertical analysis prepared in (1).

P9-3

Effect of transactions on current position analysis

Obj 2

SPREADSHEET

✓ 1. c. Quick ratio, 1.4

Data pertaining to the current position of Tsali Industries, Inc., are as follows:

Cash	$195,000
Marketable securities	92,500
Accounts and notes receivable (net)	293,000
Inventories	357,500
Prepaid expenses	15,000
Accounts payable	295,000
Notes payable (short-term)	92,000
Accrued expenses	42,500

Instructions

1. Compute (a) the working capital, (b) the current ratio, and (c) the quick ratio. Round to one decimal place.
2. List the following captions on a sheet of paper:

Transaction	Working Capital	Current Ratio	Quick Ratio

Compute the working capital, the current ratio, and the quick ratio after each of the following transactions, and record the results in the appropriate columns. Consider each transaction separately and assume that only that transaction affects the data given above. Round to one decimal point.

a. Sold marketable securities at no gain or loss, $37,500.
b. Paid accounts payable, $84,000.
c. Purchased goods on account, $55,000.
d. Paid notes payable, $32,500.
e. Declared a cash dividend, $38,000.
f. Declared a common stock dividend on common stock, $21,500.
g. Borrowed cash from bank on a long-term note, $185,000.
h. Received cash on account, $93,500.
i. Issued additional shares of stock for cash, $175,000.
j. Paid cash for prepaid expenses, $15,000.

P9-4

*Nineteen measures of sol-
vency and profitability*

Objs 2, 3

SPREADSHEET

✓ 9. Ratio of liabilities
to stockholders'
equity, 0.5

The comparative financial statements of Triad Images Inc. are as follows. The market price of Triad Images Inc. common stock was $55 on December 31, 2008.

TRIAD IMAGES INC.
Comparative Retained Earnings Statement
For the Years Ended December 31, 2008 and 2007

	Dec. 31, 2008	Dec. 31, 2007
Retained earnings, January 1	$1,006,500	$ 781,500
Add net income for year	430,000	277,500
Total	$1,436,500	$1,059,000
Deduct dividends:		
On preferred stock	$ 12,500	$ 12,500
On common stock	40,000	40,000
Total	$ 52,500	$ 52,500
Retained earnings, December 31	$1,384,000	$1,006,500

TRIAD IMAGES INC.
Comparative Income Statement
For the Years Ended December 31, 2008 and 2007

	2008	2007
Sales	$3,395,000	$ 3,062,500
Sales returns and allowances	35,000	22,500
Net sales	$3,360,000	$ 3,040,000
Cost of goods sold	1,500,000	1,437,500
Gross profit	$1,860,000	$ 1,602,500
Selling expenses	$ 726,000	$ 718,750
Administrative expenses	486,000	475,000
Total operating expenses	$1,212,000	$ 1,193,750
Income from operations	$ 648,000	$ 408,750
Other income	48,000	37,500
	$ 696,000	$ 446,250
Other expense (interest)	98,000	50,000
Income before income tax	$ 598,000	$ 396,250
Income tax expense	168,000	118,750
Net income	$ 430,000	$ 227,500

(continued)

TRIAD IMAGES INC.
Comparative Balance Sheet
December 31, 2008 and 2007

	Dec. 31, 2008	Dec. 31, 2007
Assets		
Current assets:		
Cash	$ 132,000	$ 120,000
Marketable securities	387,000	157,500
Accounts receivable (net)	260,000	196,500
Inventories	425,000	332,500
Prepaid expenses	27,500	35,000
Total current assets	$1,231,500	$ 841,500
Long-term investments	319,500	250,000
Property, plant, and equipment (net)	2,575,000	2,000,000
Total assets	$4,126,000	$3,091,500
Liabilities		
Current liabilities	$ 342,000	$ 285,000
Long-term liabilities:		
Mortgage note payable, 8%, due 2013	$ 600,000	—
Bonds payable, 10%, due 2017	500,000	$ 500,000
Total long-term liabilities	$1,100,000	$ 500,000
Total liabilities	$1,442,000	$ 785,000
Stockholders' Equity		
Preferred $2.50 stock, $100 par	$ 500,000	$ 500,000
Common stock, $20 par	800,000	800,000
Retained earnings	1,384,000	1,006,500
Total stockholders' equity	$2,684,000	$2,306,500
Total liabilities and stockholders' equity	$4,126,000	$3,091,500

Instructions

Determine the following measures for 2008, rounding to one decimal place:

1. Working capital
2. Current ratio
3. Quick ratio
4. Accounts receivable turnover
5. Number of days' sales in receivables
6. Inventory turnover
7. Number of days' sales in inventory
8. Ratio of fixed assets to long-term liabilities
9. Ratio of liabilities to stockholders' equity
10. Number of times interest charges earned
11. Number of times preferred dividends earned
12. Ratio of net sales to assets
13. Rate earned on total assets
14. Rate earned on stockholders' equity
15. Rate earned on common stockholders' equity
16. Earnings per share on common stock
17. Price-earnings ratio
18. Dividends per share of common stock
19. Dividend yield

P9-5

Solvency and profitability trend analysis

Objs 2, 3

Shore Company has provided the following comparative information:

	2008	2007	2006	2005	2004
Net income	$ 42,000	$ 70,000	$ 140,000	$ 210,000	$ 210,000
Interest expense	142,800	133,000	119,000	112,000	105,000
Income tax expense	12,600	21,000	42,000	63,000	63,000
Total assets (ending balance)	2,240,000	2,100,000	1,890,000	1,680,000	1,400,000
Total stockholders' equity (ending balance)	812,000	770,000	700,000	560,000	350,000
Average total assets	2,170,000	1,995,000	1,785,000	1,540,000	1,260,000
Average stockholders' equity	791,000	735,000	630,000	455,000	315,000

You have been asked to evaluate the historical performance of the company over the last five years.

Selected industry ratios have remained relatively steady at the following levels for the last five years:

	2004–2008
Rate earned on total assets	14%
Rate earned on stockholders' equity	20%
Number of times interest charges earned	3.0
Ratio of liabilities to stockholders' equity	2.0

Instructions

1. Prepare four line graphs with the ratio on the vertical axis and the years on the horizontal axis for the following four ratios (rounded to one decimal place):
   a. Rate earned on total assets
   b. Rate earned on stockholders' equity
   c. Number of times interest charges earned
   d. Ratio of liabilities to stockholders' equity
   Display both the company ratio and the industry benchmark on each graph. That is, each graph should have two lines.
2. Prepare an analysis of the graphs in (1).

Activities

A9-1

Analysis of financing corporate growth

Assume that the president of Ice Mountain Brewery made the following statement in the Annual Report to Shareholders:

"The founding family and majority shareholders of the company do not believe in using debt to finance future growth. The founding family learned from hard experience during Prohibition and the Great Depression that debt can cause loss of flexibility and eventual loss of corporate control. The company will not place itself at such risk. As such, all future growth will be financed either by stock sales to the public or by internally generated resources."

As a public shareholder of this company, how would you respond to this policy?

A9-2

*Receivables and inventory
turnover*

Roan Mountain Fitness Company has completed its fiscal year on December 31, 2008. The auditor, Steve Berry, has approached the CFO, Tony Brubaker, regarding the year-end receivables and inventory levels of Roan Mountain Fitness. The following conversation takes place:

Steve: We are beginning our audit of Roan Mountain Fitness and have prepared ratio analyses to determine if there have been significant changes in operations or financial position. This helps us guide the audit process. This analysis indicates that the inventory turnover has decreased from 4.5 to 2.1, while the accounts receivable turnover has decreased from 10 to 6. I was wondering if you could explain this change in operations.

Tony: There is little need for concern. The inventory represents computers that we were unable to sell during the holiday buying season. We are confident, however, that we will be able to sell these computers as we move into the next fiscal year.

Steve: What gives you this confidence?

Tony: We will increase our advertising and provide some very attractive price concessions to move these machines. We have no choice. Newer technology is already out there, and we have to unload this inventory.

Steve: . . . and the receivables?

Tony: As you may be aware, the company is under tremendous pressure to expand sales and profits. As a result, we lowered our credit standards to our commercial customers so that we would be able to sell products to a broader customer base. As a result of this policy change, we have been able to expand sales by 35%.

Steve: Your responses have not been reassuring to me.

Tony: I'm a little confused. Assets are good, right? Why don't you look at our current ratio? It has improved, hasn't it? I would think that you would view that very favorably.

Why is Steve concerned about the inventory and accounts receivable turnover ratios and Tony's responses to them? What action may Steve need to take? How would you respond to Tony's last comment?

A9-3

Vertical analysis

The condensed income statements through income from operations for **Dell Inc.** and **Apple Computer, Inc.**, are reproduced below for recent fiscal years (numbers in millions of dollars).

	Dell Inc.	Apple Computer, Inc.
Sales (net)	$55,908	$13,931
Cost of sales	45,958	9,888
	$ 9,950	$ 4,043

The following information is available for three recent years (in millions except per-share amounts):

	Year 3	Year 2	Year 1
Net income (loss)	$2,024	$3,487	$495
Preferred dividends	$0	$0	$0
Shares outstanding for computing earnings per share	1,846	1,830	1,832
Cash dividend per share	$0.40	$0.40	$0.40
Average total assets	$287,669	$308,032	$293,678
Average stockholders' equity	$14,501	$13,848	$8,532
Average stock price per share	$11.22	$14.98	$11.95

1. Calculate the following ratios for each year:
   a. Rate earned on total assets
   b. Rate earned on stockholders' equity
   c. Earnings per share
   d. Dividend yield
   e. Price-earnings ratio
2. What is the ratio of average liabilities to average stockholders' equity for Year 3?
3. Why does Ford have so much leverage?
4. Explain the direction of the dividend yield and price-earnings ratio in light of Ford's profitability trend.

A9-5

Comprehensive profitability and solvency analysis

Marriott International, Inc., and ***Hilton Hotels Corporation*** are two major owners and managers of lodging and resort properties in the United States. Abstracted income statement information for the two companies is as follows for a recent year:

	Marriott *(in millions)*	Hilton *(in millions)*
Operating profit before other expenses and interest	$477	$658
Other income (expenses)	318	(19)
Interest expense	(99)	(274)
Income before income taxes	$696	$365
Income tax expense	100	127
Net income	$596	$238

Balance sheet information is as follows:

	Marriott *(in millions)*	Hilton *(in millions)*
Total liabilities	$4,587	$5,674
Total stockholders' equity	4,081	2,568
Total liabilities and stockholders' equity	$8,668	$8,242

The average liabilities, stockholders' equity, and total assets were as follows:

	Marriott	Hilton
Average total liabilities	$4,210	$5,809
Average total stockholders' equity	3,960	2,404
Average total assets	8,423	8,213

(continued)

1. Determine the following ratios for both companies (round to one decimal place after the whole percent):
   a. Rate earned on total assets
   b. Rate earned on total stockholders' equity
   c. Number of times interest charges are earned
   d. Ratio of liabilities to stockholders' equity
2. Analyze and compare the two companies, using the information in (1).

Answers to Self-Examination Questions

1. **A**   Percentage analysis indicating the relationship of the component parts to the total in a financial statement, such as the relationship of current assets to total assets (20% to 100%) in the question, is called vertical analysis (answer A). Percentage analysis of increases and decreases in corresponding items in comparative financial statements is called horizontal analysis (answer B). An example of horizontal analysis would be the presentation of the amount of current assets in the preceding balance sheet, along with the amount of current assets at the end of the current year, with the increase or decrease in current assets between the periods expressed as a percentage. Profitability analysis (answer C) is the analysis of a firm's ability to earn income. Contribution margin analysis (answer D) is discussed in a later managerial accounting chapter.

2. **D**   Various solvency measures, categorized as current position analysis, indicate a firm's ability to meet currently maturing obligations,

and the quick ratio (answer C) is the ratio of the sum of cash, receivables, and marketable securities to current liabilities.

3. **D**   The ratio of current assets to current liabilities is usually called the current ratio (answer A). It is sometimes called the working capital ratio (answer B) or bankers' ratio (answer C).

4. **C**   The ratio of the sum of cash, receivables, and marketable securities (sometimes called quick assets) to current liabilities is called the quick ratio (answer C) or acid-test ratio. The current ratio (answer A), working capital ratio (answer B), and bankers' ratio (answer D) are terms that describe the ratio of current assets to current liabilities.

5. **C**   The number of days' sales in inventory (answer C), which is determined by dividing the average inventory by the average daily cost of goods sold, expresses the relationship between the cost of goods sold and inventory. It indicates the efficiency in the management of

CHAPTER 10

Accounting Systems for Manufacturing Businesses

Learning Objectives

After studying this chapter, you should be able to:

Obj 1
Distinguish the activities of a manufacturing business from those of a merchandising or service business.

Obj 2

Obj 5
Use job order cost information for decision making.

Obj 6
Diagram the flow of costs for a service business that uses a job

S uppose you go down to the local *Starbucks* and buy a bagel and coffee before class. How much should Starbucks charge you? The purchase price must be greater than the costs of producing and serving the bagel and coffee. Moreover, Starbucks needs to be able to answer additional questions, such as:

• How many bagels must be sold in a given month and at what given prices to cover costs?

• How should the price for a single bagel differ from the price for a dozen bagels?

• How many employees should be in the shop at different times of the day?

• Should the shop stay open 24 hours per day?

Starbucks can answer all of these questions with the aid of cost information. In this chapter, you will be introduced to cost concepts used in managerial accounting that help answer questions like those above. In addition, we will see how cost information is developed and used when work is performed on a specified quantity of product.

We will begin this chapter by describing the nature of manufacturing businesses. We then introduce basic cost terms and describe accounting systems for manufacturing businesses. Using this as a basis, we describe and illustrate a job order cost accounting system. We conclude this chapter by focusing on recent trends in manufacturing and the design of manufacturing accounting systems.

Nature of Manufacturing Businesses

Distinguish the activities of a manufacturing business from those of a merchandising or service business.

In Chapters 2 and 3, we described and illustrated accounting systems for service businesses. In Chapter 4, we described and illustrated accounting systems for merchandising businesses. In this chapter, we focus on manufacturing businesses. Examples of manufacturing businesses include **General Motors** and **Intel Corporation**.

The revenue activities of a service business involve providing services to customers. The revenue activities of a merchandising business involve the buying and selling of merchandise. In contrast, manufacturing businesses must first produce the products they sell. A manufacturing business converts materials into finished products through the use of machinery and labor.

Like merchandising businesses, a manufacturing business reports sales from selling its products. The cost of the products sold is normally reported as **cost of goods sold**, whereas a merchandising business reports these costs as cost of merchandise sold. The subtraction of the cost of goods sold from sales is reported as gross profit. Operating expenses are deducted from gross profit to arrive at net income.

Materials, products in the process of being manufactured, and finished products are reported on the manufacturer's balance sheet as inventories. Like merchandise inventory, these inventories are reported as current assets.

Manufacturing Cost Terms

Define and illustrate materials, factory labor, and factory overhead costs.

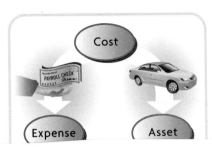

Managers rely on managerial accountants to provide useful *cost* information to support decision making. What is a cost? A **cost** is a payment of cash or its equivalent or the commitment to pay cash in the future for the purpose of generating revenues. A cost provides a benefit that is used immediately or deferred to a future period of time. If the benefit is used immediately, then the cost is an expense, such as salary expense. If the benefit is deferred, then the cost is an asset, such as equipment. As the asset is used, an expense, such as depreciation expense, is recognized.

In this section, we will illustrate manufacturing costs for Legend Guitars, a manufacturing firm. A *manufacturing business* converts materials into a finished product through the use of machinery and labor.

manufacturer.

EXHIBIT 1   *Guitar Making Operations of Legend Guitars*

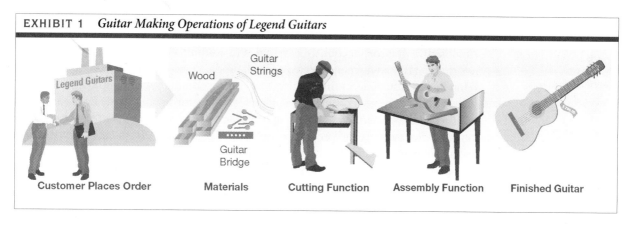

Customer Places Order — Materials — Cutting Function — Assembly Function — Finished Guitar

EXAMPLES OF DIRECT MATERIALS

Television Manufacturer

Furniture Manufacturer

Automobile Manufacturer

The costs of materials that are not a significant portion of the total product cost are termed *indirect materials*. Indirect materials are considered a part of factory overhead, which we discuss later. For Legend Guitars, the cost of glue is classified as indirect materials.

Factory Labor

The cost of wages of employees who are directly involved in converting materials into the manufactured product is classified as **direct labor cost**. The direct labor cost of Legend Guitars includes the wages of the employees who operate the saws and cutting machines and assemble the guitars. Other examples of direct labor costs are carpenters' wages for a construction contractor, mechanics' wages in an automotive repair shop, machine operators' wages in a tool manufacturing plant, and assemblers' wages in a microcomputer assembly plant.

As a practical matter, a direct labor cost must not only be an integral part of the finished product, but it must also be a significant portion of the total cost of the product. For Legend Guitars, the wages of the saw and cutting machine operators and the guitar assemblers are a significant portion of the total cost of each guitar. Labor costs that do not enter directly into the manufacture of a product are termed *indirect labor* and are recorded as factory overhead. Indirect labor for Legend Guitars might include the salaries of maintenance, plant management, and quality control personnel.

Factory Overhead Cost

Costs other than direct materials cost and direct labor cost incurred in the manufacturing process are classified as **factory overhead cost**. Factory overhead is sometimes called *manufacturing overhead* or *factory burden*. Examples of factory overhead costs, in addition to indirect materials and indirect labor, are machine depreciation, factory utilities, factory supplies, and factory insurance. In addition, payments to employees for overtime and nonproductive time (such as idle time) are considered factory overhead. For many industries, factory overhead costs are becoming a larger portion of the costs of a product as manufacturing processes become more automated.

The direct materials, direct labor, and factory overhead costs are considered **product costs**, because they are associated with making a product. The costs of converting the materials into finished products consist of direct labor and factory overhead costs, which are commonly called **conversion costs**.

Cost Accounting System Overview

An objective of a **cost accounting system** is to accumulate product costs. Product cost information is used by managers to establish product prices, control operations, and develop financial statements. In addition, the cost accounting system improves control by supplying data on the costs incurred by each manufacturing department or process.

There are two main types of cost accounting systems for manufacturing operations: job order cost systems and process cost systems. Each of the two systems is widely used, and any one manufacturer may use more than one type. In this chapter, we will illustrate the job order cost system. In the next chapter, we will illustrate the process cost system.

A **job order cost system** provides a separate record for the cost of each quantity of product that passes through the factory. A particular quantity of product is termed a *job*. A job order cost system is best suited to industries that manufacture custom goods to fill special orders from customers or that produce a high variety of products for stock. Manufacturers that use a job order cost system are sometimes called *job shops*. An example of a job shop would be an apparel manufacturer, such as **Levi Strauss**.

Many service firms also use job order cost systems to accumulate the costs associated with providing client services. For example, an accounting firm will accumulate all of the costs associated with a particular client engagement, such as accountant time, copying charges, and travel costs. Recording costs in this manner helps the accounting firm control costs during a client engagement and determines client billing and profitability.

Under a **process cost system**, costs are accumulated for each of the departments or processes within the factory. A process system is best suited for manufacturers of units of product that are not distinguishable from each other during a continuous production process. Examples would be oil refineries, paper producers, chemical processors, aluminum smelters, and food processors.

We describe and illustrate only job order cost systems in this chapter because they are often used by service as well as manufacturing businesses. However, we will introduce many manufacturing terms and concepts that also apply to process cost systems.[1]

Job Order Cost Systems for Manufacturing Businesses

[1]Process cost accounting systems are described and illustrated in Appendix 2.

EXHIBIT 2   *Flow of Manufacturing Costs*

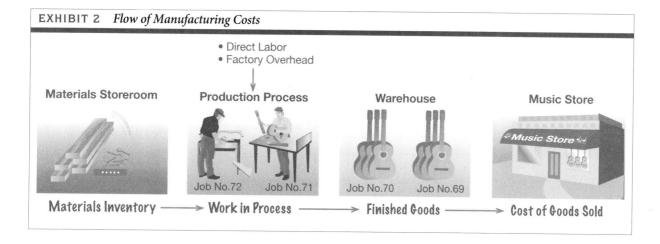

The *cost of goods sold* for a manufacturer is comparable to the *cost of merchandise sold* for a merchandising business.

In a job order cost accounting system, perpetual inventory records are maintained for materials, work in process, and finished goods inventories. For example, materials inventory is supported by subsidiary inventory accounts that record the increase, decrease, and amount on hand for each type of material. These subsidiary materials accounts are kept in a ledger, called a *subsidiary ledger*. The sum of the subsidiary ledger accounts equals the balance of the materials account, called the *controlling account*.[2]

Materials

The procedures used to purchase, store, and issue materials to production often differ among manufacturers. Exhibit 3 shows the basic information and cost flows for the wood received and issued to production by Legend Guitars.

Purchased materials are first received and inspected by the Receiving Department. The Receiving Department personnel prepare a **receiving report**, showing the quantity

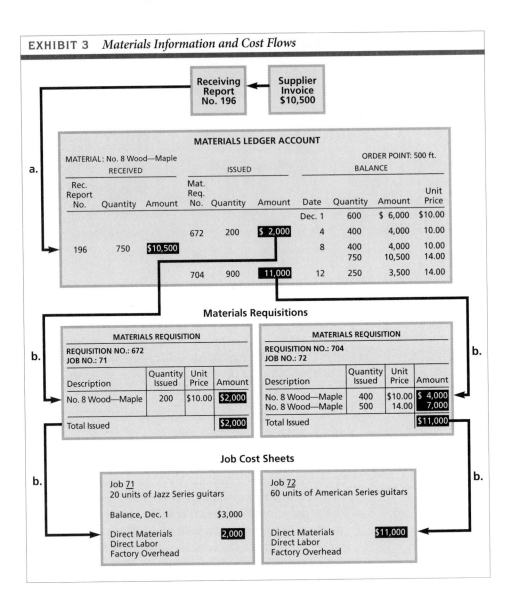

EXHIBIT 3 *Materials Information and Cost Flows*

The materials account is a controlling account. A separate account for each type of material is maintained in a subsidiary **materials ledger**. Details as to the quantity and cost of materials received are recorded in the materials ledger on the basis of the receiving reports. A typical form of a materials ledger account is illustrated in Exhibit 3.

Materials are released from the storeroom to the factory in response to **materials requisitions** from the Production Department. An illustration of a materials requisition is in Exhibit 3. The completed requisition for each job serves as the basis for posting quantities and dollar data to the job cost sheets in the case of direct materials or to factory overhead in the case of indirect materials. **Job cost sheets**, which are illustrated in Exhibit 3, show the work in process subsidiary ledger. For Legend Guitars, Job 71 is for 20 units of Jazz Series guitars, while Job 72 is for 60 units of American Series guitars.

In Exhibit 3, the first-in, first-out costing method is used. A summary of the materials requisitions completed during the month is the basis for transferring the cost of the direct materials from the materials account to the account for work in process. The flow

INTEGRITY, OBJECTIVITY, AND ETHICS IN BUSINESS

Phony Invoice Scams

A popular method for defrauding a company is to issue a phony invoice. The scam begins by initially contacting the target firm to discover details of key business contacts, business operations, and products. The swindler then uses this information to create a fictitious invoice. The invoice will include names, figures, and other details to give it the appearance of legitimacy. This type of scam can be avoided if invoices are matched with receiving documents prior to issuing a check.

of materials from the materials storeroom to production ($2,000 + $11,000) increases Work in Process and decreases Materials Inventory. The effect on the accounts and financial statements is shown below.

Statement of Cash Flows	Balance Sheet						Income Statement
	Assets		=	Liabilities	+	Stockholders' Equity	
	Materials	+	Work in Process	=			
b.	−13,000		13,000				

Many organizations are using computerized information processes that account for the flow of materials. In a computerized setting, the storeroom manager would record the release of materials into a computer, which would automatically update the subsidiary materials records.

Factory Labor

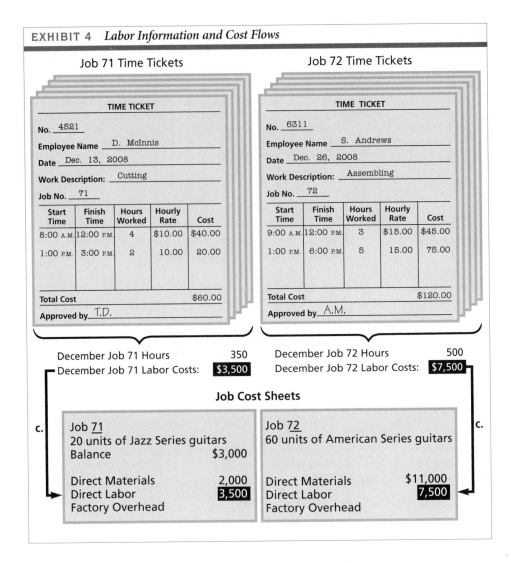

EXHIBIT 4   *Labor Information and Cost Flows*

Job 71 Time Tickets

TIME TICKET

No. 4521

Employee Name   D. McInnis

Date   Dec. 13, 2008

Work Description: Cutting

Job No.   71

Start Time	Finish Time	Hours Worked	Hourly Rate	Cost
8:00 A.M.	12:00 P.M.	4	$10.00	$40.00
1:00 P.M.	3:00 P.M.	2	10.00	20.00

Total Cost $60.00

Approved by   T.D.

Job 72 Time Tickets

TIME TICKET

No. 6311

Employee Name   S. Andrews

Date   Dec. 26, 2008

Work Description: Assembling

Job No.   72

Start Time	Finish Time	Hours Worked	Hourly Rate	Cost
9:00 A.M.	12:00 P.M.	3	$15.00	$45.00
1:00 P.M.	6:00 P.M.	5	15.00	75.00

Total Cost $120.00

Approved by   A.M.

December Job 71 Hours   350
December Job 71 Labor Costs: $3,500

December Job 72 Hours   500
December Job 72 Labor Costs: $7,500

Job Cost Sheets

Job 71
20 units of Jazz Series guitars
Balance $3,000

Direct Materials   2,000
Direct Labor   3,500
Factory Overhead

Job 72
60 units of American Series guitars

Direct Materials $11,000
Direct Labor   7,500
Factory Overhead

Job 72. The direct labor costs that flow into production increase Work in Process and Wages Payable. The effect on the accounts and financial statements is shown below.

Statement of Cash Flows	Balance Sheet				Income Statement
	Assets	=	Liabilities	+ Stockholders' Equity	
	Work in Process	=	Wages Payable		
c.	11,000		11,000		

As with recording direct materials, many organizations are automating the labor recording process. Employees may log their time directly into computer terminals at their workstations. Alternatively, employees may be issued magnetic cards, much like credit cards, to log in and out of work assignments that are spread across a wide geographical area. For example, **Shell Oil Company** uses a magnetic card system to track the work of maintenance crews in its refinery operations.

Factory Overhead Cost

Factory overhead includes all manufacturing costs except direct materials and direct labor. Increases in Factory Overhead come from various sources, such as indirect materials, indirect labor, factory power, and factory depreciation. For example, the factory overhead of $4,600 incurred in December for Legend Guitars affects the accounts and financial statements as shown below.

Statement of Cash Flows	Balance Sheet							Income Statement
	Assets			=	Liabilities		+ Stockholders' Equity	
	Materials +	Factory Overhead −	Accumulated Depreciation =		Wages Payable +	Utilities Payable		
d.	−500	4,600	−1,200		2,000	900		

Allocating Factory Overhead

Factory overhead is much different from direct labor and direct materials because it is indirectly related to the jobs. How, then, do the jobs get assigned a portion of

To illustrate calculating a predetermined overhead rate, assume that Legend Guitars estimates the total factory overhead cost to be $50,000 for the year and the activity base to be 10,000 direct labor hours. The predetermined factory overhead rate would be calculated as $5 per direct labor hour, as follows:

$$\text{Predetermined factory overhead rate} = \frac{\text{Estimated total factory overhead costs}}{\text{Estimated activity base}}$$

$$\text{Predetermined factory overhead rate} = \frac{\$50,000}{10,000 \text{ direct labor hours}} = \$5 \text{ per direct labor hour}$$

Why is the predetermined overhead rate calculated from estimated numbers at the beginning of the period? The answer is to ensure timely information. If a company waited until the end of an accounting period when all overhead costs are known, the allocated factory overhead would be accurate but not timely. If the cost system is to have maximum usefulness, cost data should be available as each job is completed, even though there may be a small sacrifice in accuracy. Only through timely reporting can management make needed adjustments in pricing or in manufacturing methods and achieve the best possible combination of revenue and cost on future jobs.

A number of companies are using a new product-costing approach called activity-based costing. **Activity-based costing** is a method of accumulating and allocating factory overhead costs to products, using many overhead rates. Each rate is related to separate factory activities, such as inspecting, moving, and machining. Activity-based costing is discussed and illustrated at the end of this chapter.

Applying Factory Overhead to Work in Process

As factory overhead costs are incurred, they increase the factory overhead account, as shown previously in transaction (d). For Legend Guitars, factory overhead costs are applied to production at the rate of $5 per direct labor hour. The amount of factory overhead applied to each job would be recorded in the job cost sheets as shown in Exhibit 5. For example, the 850 direct labor hours used in Legend Guitars' December operations would all be traced to individual jobs. Job 71 used 350 labor hours, so $1,750 (350 × $5) of factory overhead would be applied to Job 71. Similarly, $2,500 (500 × $5) of factory overhead would be applied to Job 72.

The factory overhead costs applied to production increase the work in process account and decrease the factory overhead account. The effects of applying the $4,250 ($1,750 + $2,500) of factory overhead to production on the accounts and financial statements for Legend Guitars are shown below.

Statement of Cash Flows	Balance Sheet					Income Statement
	Assets		=	Liabilities	+	Stockholders' Equity	
	Work in Process	+	Factory Overhead	=			
e.	4,250		−4,250				

EXHIBIT 5   *Assigning Factory Overhead to Jobs*

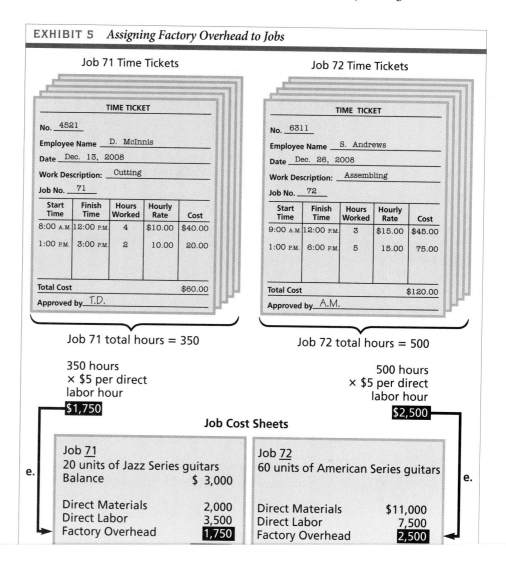

Disposal of Factory Overhead Balance

The balance in the factory overhead account is carried forward from month to month on interim balance sheets as a positive or negative balance. This balance should not be carried over to the next year, however, since it applies to the operations of the year just ended.

One approach for disposing of the balance of factory overhead at the end of the year is to transfer the entire balance to the cost of goods sold account.[4] To illustrate, the effect on the accounts and financial statements of eliminating an underapplied overhead balance of $150 at the end of the year for Legend Guitars would be as follows:

Statement of Cash Flows	Balance Sheet					Income Statement
	Assets	=	Liabilities	+	Stockholders' Equity	
	Factory Overhead	=		+	Retained Earnings	
f.	−150				−150	f.

Income Statement	
f. Cost of goods sold	−150

Work in Process

Costs incurred for the various jobs increase Work in Process. Legend Guitars' job costs described in the preceding sections may be summarized as follows:

- **Direct materials, $13,000**—Work in Process increased and Materials decreased (transaction b); data obtained from summary of materials requisitions.
- **Direct labor, $11,000**—Work in Process increased and Wages Payable increased (transaction c); data obtained from summary of time tickets.
- **Factory overhead, $4,250**—Work in Process increased and Factory Overhead decreased (transaction e); data obtained from summary of time tickets.

The details concerning the costs incurred on each job order are accumulated in the job cost sheets. Exhibit 6 illustrates the relationship between the job cost sheets and the work in process controlling account.

In this example, Job 71 was started in November and completed in December. The beginning December balance for Job 71 represents the costs carried over from the end of November. Job 72 was started in December but was not yet completed at the end of the month. Thus, the balance of the incomplete Job 72, or $21,000, will be shown on the balance sheet on December 31 as work in process inventory.

When Job 71 was completed, the direct materials costs, the direct labor costs, and the factory overhead costs were totaled and divided by the number of units produced to determine the cost per unit. If we assume that 20 units of Jazz Series guitars were produced for Job 71, then the unit cost would be $512,50 ($10,250 ÷ 20 units).

---

[4]Alternatively, the balance may be allocated among the work in process, finished goods, and cost of goods sold balances. This approach brings the accounts into agreement with the costs actually incurred. Since this approach is a more complex calculation that adds little additional accuracy, it will not be used in this text.

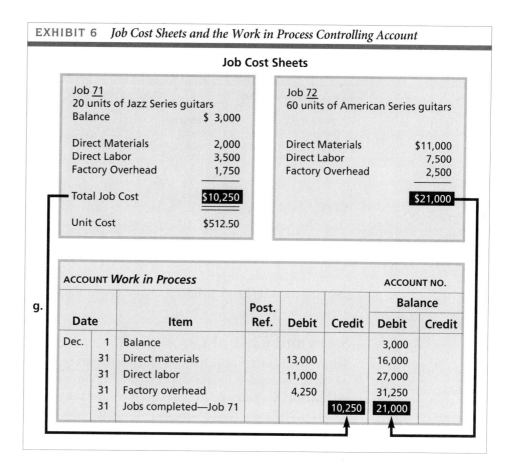

EXHIBIT 6 *Job Cost Sheets and the Work in Process Controlling Account*

Job Cost Sheets

Job 71
20 units of Jazz Series guitars

Balance	$ 3,000
Direct Materials	2,000
Direct Labor	3,500
Factory Overhead	1,750
Total Job Cost	$10,250
Unit Cost	$512.50

Job 72
60 units of American Series guitars

Direct Materials	$11,000
Direct Labor	7,500
Factory Overhead	2,500
	$21,000

ACCOUNT **Work in Process**   ACCOUNT NO.

g.

Date		Item	Post. Ref.	Debit	Credit	Balance Debit	Balance Credit
Dec.	1	Balance				3,000	
	31	Direct materials		13,000		16,000	
	31	Direct labor		11,000		27,000	
	31	Factory overhead		4,250		31,250	
	31	Jobs completed—Job 71			10,250	21,000	

Upon completing Job 71, the job cost sheet was removed from the cost ledger and filed for future reference. At the end of the accounting period (December), the total costs for all completed jobs during the period are determined. These costs are then transferred

EXHIBIT 7   Finished Goods Ledger Account

ITEM: *Jazz Series guitars*

Manufactured			Shipped			Balance			
Job Order No.	Quantity	Amount	Ship Order No.	Quantity	Amount	Date	Quantity	Amount	Unit Cost
						Dec. 1	40	$20,000	$500.00
			643	40	$20,000	9	—	—	—
71	20	$10,250				31	20	10,250	512.50

sold, and units on hand. Exhibit 7, shown above, illustrates an account in the finished goods ledger for Legend Guitars.

Sales and Cost of Goods Sold

Sales for a manufacturing business and a merchandising business have the same effect on the accounts and financial statements. To illustrate, assume that Legend Guitars sold the 40 Jazz Series guitars during December for $850 per unit. These guitars have a cost of $500 per unit. The cost data can be obtained from the finished goods ledger. The effect of selling the 40 Jazz guitars on the accounts and financial statements is as follows:

Statement of Cash Flows	Balance Sheet						Income Statement
	Assets		=	Liabilities	+	Stockholders' Equity	
	Accounts Receivable +	Finished Goods =			+	Retained Earnings	
h.	34,000	−20,000				14,000	h.

	Income Statement	
h. Sales		34,000
Cost of goods sold		−20,000
Net income		14,000

Period Costs

In addition to product costs (direct materials, direct labor, and factory overhead), businesses have period costs. **Period costs** are expenses that are used in generating revenue during the current period and are not involved in the manufacturing process. Period costs are generally classified into two categories: selling and administrative. *Selling expenses* are incurred in marketing the product and delivering the sold product to customers. *Administrative expenses* are incurred in the administration of the business and are not related to the manufacturing or selling functions. Examples of administrative expenses include office supplies and depreciation of office equipment. Assuming Legend

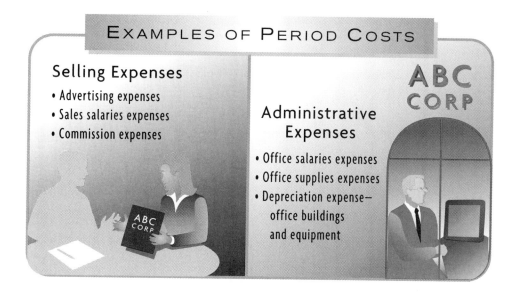

EXAMPLES OF PERIOD COSTS

Selling Expenses

- Advertising expenses
- Sales salaries expenses
- Commission expenses

Administrative Expenses

- Office salaries expenses
- Office supplies expenses
- Depreciation expense— office buildings and equipment

ABC CORP

Guitars incurred sales salaries of $2,000 and office salaries of $1,500, the effect on the accounts and financial statements is as follows:

Statement of Cash Flows		Assets	=	Liabilities	+	Stockholders' Equity		Income Statement
				Salaries Payable	+		**Retained Earnings**	
i.			=	3,500			−3,500	*i.*

Balance Sheet

	Income Statement	
i.	Sales salaries exp.	−2,000
	Office salaries exp.	−1,500

EXHIBIT 8 *Flow of Manufacturing Costs for Legend Guitars*

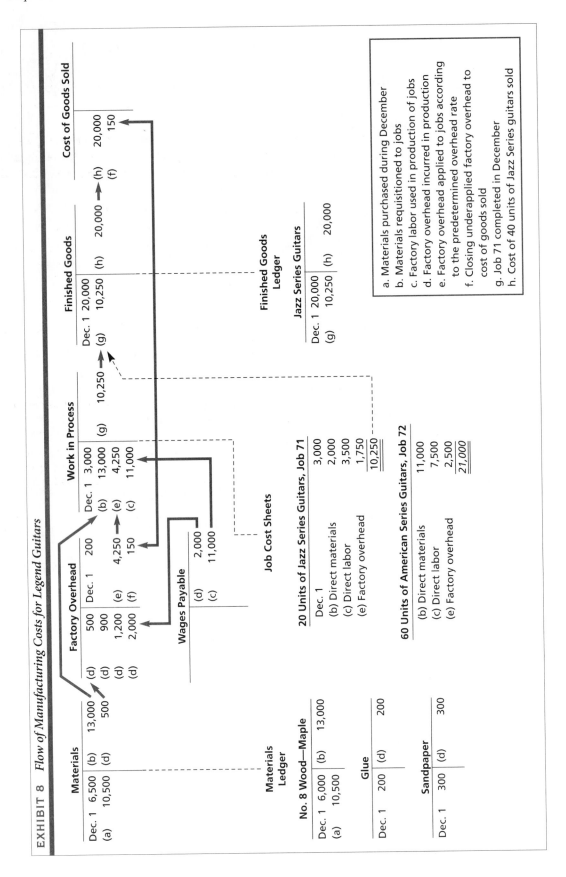

Materials

Dec. 1	6,500	(b)	13,000
(a)	10,500	(d)	500

Factory Overhead

Dec. 1	500	(d)	200
(d)	900		
(e)	1,200	(e)	4,250
(f)	2,000	(f)	150

Work in Process

Dec. 1	3,000	(g)	10,250
(b)	13,000		
(e)	4,250		
(c)	11,000		

Finished Goods

Dec. 1	20,000	(h)	20,000
(g)	10,250		

Cost of Goods Sold

(h)	20,000		
(f)	150		

Wages Payable

		(d)	2,000
		(c)	11,000

Materials Ledger

No. 8 Wood—Maple

Dec. 1	6,000	(b)	13,000
(a)	10,500		

Glue

Dec. 1	200	(d)	200

Sandpaper

Dec. 1	300	(d)	300

Job Cost Sheets

20 Units of Jazz Series Guitars, Job 71

Dec. 1	3,000
(b) Direct materials	2,000
(c) Direct labor	3,500
(e) Factory overhead	1,750
	10,250

60 Units of American Series Guitars, Job 72

(b) Direct materials	11,000
(c) Direct labor	7,500
(e) Factory overhead	2,500
	21,000

Finished Goods Ledger

Jazz Series Guitars

Dec. 1	20,000	(h)	20,000
(g)	10,250		

a. Materials purchased during December
b. Materials requisitioned to jobs
c. Factory labor used in production of jobs
d. Factory overhead incurred in production
e. Factory overhead applied to jobs according to the predetermined overhead rate
f. Closing underapplied factory overhead to cost of goods sold
g. Job 71 completed in December
h. Cost of 40 units of Jazz Series guitars sold

EXHIBIT 9   *Income Statement of Legend Guitars*

LEGEND GUITARS
Income Statement
For the Month Ended December 31, 2008

Sales		$34,000
Cost of goods sold		20,150
Gross profit		$13,850
Selling and administrative expenses:		
Sales salaries expense	$2,000	
Office salaries expense	1,500	
Total selling and administrative expenses		3,500
Income from operations		$10,350

Obj **5**

Use job order cost information for decision making.

Job Order Costing for Decision Making

The job order cost system that we developed in the previous sections can be used to evaluate an organization's cost performance. The unit costs for similar jobs can be compared over time to determine if costs are staying within expected ranges. If costs increase for some unexpected reason, the details in the job cost sheets can help discover the reasons.

To illustrate, Exhibit 10 shows the direct materials on the job cost sheets for Jobs 54 and 63 for Legend Guitars. The wood used in manufacturing guitars is measured in board feet. Since both job cost sheets refer to the same type and number of guitars, the direct materials cost per unit should be about the same. However, the materials cost per guitar for Job 54 is $100, while for Job 63 it is $125. The materials costs have increased since the guitars were produced for Job 54.

EXHIBIT 10   *Comparing Data from Job Cost Sheets*

Job cost sheets can be used to investigate possible reasons for the increased cost. First, you should note that the price for direct materials did not change. Thus, the cost increase is not related to increasing prices. What about the wood consumption? This tells us a different story. The quantity of wood used to produce 40 guitars in Job 54 is 400 board feet. However, Job 63 required 500 board feet for the same number of guitars. How can this be explained? Any one of the following explanations is possible and could be investigated further:

1. There was a new employee that was not adequately trained for cutting the wood for guitars. As a result, the employee improperly cut and scrapped many pieces.
2. The lumber was of poor quality. As a result, the cutting operator ended up using and scrapping additional pieces of lumber.
3. The cutting tools were in need of repair. As a result, the cutting operators miscut and scrapped many pieces of wood.
4. The operator was careless. As a result of poor work, many pieces of cut wood had to be scrapped.
5. The instructions attached to the job were incorrect. The operator cut wood according to the instructions but discovered that the pieces would not fit. As a result, many pieces had to be scrapped.

You should note that many of these explanations are not necessarily related to operator error. Poor cost performance may be the result of root causes that are outside the control of the operator.

HOW BUSINESSES MAKE MONEY

Defense Contract Acquisitions

The aerospace and defense industry uses job orders to account for program costs and revenues. Such defense programs (or contracts) are awarded by the U.S. government for various defense needs. The financial disclosures for **Northrop Grumman Corp.,** a major defense contractor, include a section on contract acquisitions. Contract acquisitions are the dollar amount of contracts awarded for defense products or services for a given year. These are not the same as revenues, because some of the awarded contracts may still be unperformed, or backlogged. However, contract acquisitions do provide a means of evaluating a defense contractor's revenue potential. A partial listing of Northrop's recent contract acquisitions showed the following:

Aerospace electronic systems	$1,339,000,000
Air combat systems	1,594,000,000
Airborne early warning/electronic warfare	601,000,000
Airborne ground surveillance/battle management	446,000,000
Ship surface combatants	3,042,000,000

Additional disclosures indicate the aerospace electronic systems includes funding of $255 million for the Wedgetail program and $148 million for the BAT program. Air combat systems includes a $30 million increase in the F-18 program. Airborne early warning includes $231 million funding for the multiyear electronic warfare system purchase for 25 E-2C aircraft. Airborne ground surveillance includes orders for one Joint STARS aircraft, while surface combatants includes a $370 million contract award for an Aegis-class large destroyer.

Each of these programs, such as the Aegis destroyer program, is treated as a separate master program. The master program will be divided into smaller segments or jobs in what is termed a work breakdown structure. Costs will be accumulated by job and closed out to cost of goods sold and matched to revenue earned as contracts are completed.

Job Order Cost Systems for Professional Service Businesses

Obj 6

Diagram the flow of costs for a service business that uses a job order cost accounting system.

A job order cost accounting system may be useful to the management of a professional service business in planning and controlling operations. For example, an advertising agency, an attorney, and a physician all share the common characteristic of providing services to individual customers, clients, or patients. In such cases, the customer, client, or patient can be viewed as an individual job for which costs are accumulated.

Since the "product" of a service business is service, management's focus is on direct labor and overhead costs. The cost of any materials or supplies used in rendering services for a client is usually small and is normally included as part of the overhead.

The direct labor and overhead costs of rendering services to clients are accumulated in a work in process account. This account is supported by a cost ledger. A job cost sheet is used to accumulate the costs for each client's job. When a job is completed and the client is billed, the costs are transferred to a cost of services account. This account is similar to the cost of merchandise sold account for a merchandising business or the cost of goods sold account for a manufacturing business. A finished goods account and related finished goods ledger are not necessary, since the revenues associated with the services are recorded after the services have been provided. The flow of costs through a service business using a job order cost accounting system is shown in Exhibit 11.

EXHIBIT 11   *Flow of Costs through a Service Business*

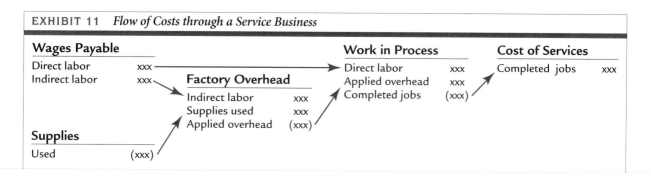

Exhibit 12 lists some of the just-in-time manufacturing principles and the traditional manufacturing principles. In the following paragraphs, we briefly discuss each of the just-in-time principles.

EXHIBIT 12 *Operating Principles of Just-in-Time versus Traditional Manufacturing*

Issue	Just-in-Time Manufacturing	Traditional Manufacturing
Inventory	Reduces inventory.	Increases inventory to "buffer" or protect against process problems.
Lead time	Reduces lead time.	Increases lead time as a buffer against uncertainty.
Setup time	Reduces setup time.	Disregards setup time as an improvement priority.
Production layout	Emphasizes product-oriented layout.	Emphasizes process-oriented layout.
Role of the employee	Emphasizes team-oriented employee involvement.	Emphasizes work of individuals, following manager instructions.
Production scheduling policy	Emphasizes pull manufacturing.	Emphasizes push manufacturing.
Quality	Emphasizes zero defects.	Tolerates defects.
Suppliers	Emphasizes supplier partnering.	Treats suppliers as "arm's-length," independent entities.

Reducing Inventory

Supporters of just-in-time manufacturing view inventory as wasteful and unnecessary. They argue that inventory can hide underlying production problems. For example, they point out that inventory is often used to maintain sales and production levels during various production interruptions, such as machine breakdowns, manufacturing schedule changes, transportation delays, and unexpected scrap and rework. An important focus in just-in-time manufacturing is to remove these production problems so that the materials, work in process, and finished goods inventory levels can be reduced or eliminated.

The role of inventory can be explained by referring to a river. Inventory is the water in a river, while the rocks at the bottom of the river are the production problems. When the water level is high, all the rocks at the bottom of the river are hidden. In other words, inventory hides the production problems. However, as the water level drops, the rocks become exposed, one by one. Reducing inventory reveals production problems. Once these problems are fixed, the "water level" can be reduced even further to expose more "rocks" for elimination until an efficient, effective production process is achieved.

Reducing Lead Times

Lead time, sometimes called *throughput time,* is a measure of the time that elapses between starting a unit of product into the beginning of a process and completing the unit of product. If a product begins the process at 1:00 p.m. and is completed at 5:00 p.m., the lead time is four hours.

Reducing lead times can be an objective for products manufactured in the plant or any other item that is produced through a process. For example, lead times could be reduced for processing sales orders, invoices, insurance applications, or hospital patients.

The total lead time can be divided into value-added and nonvalue-added time portions. **Value-added lead time** is the time required to actually manufacture a unit of a product. It is the conversion time for a unit. For example, value-added lead time includes the time to drill and pack parts for shipment. **Nonvalue-added lead time** is the time that a unit of product sits in inventories or moves unnecessarily. Nonvalue-added lead time occurs in poor production processes. In a well-functioning process, the product should spend very little time waiting in inventory because inventory is at a minimum. The product should also spend little time moving because operations are sequenced closely.

Just-in-time manufacturing attempts to make the nonvalue-added lead time very small, thereby reducing the cost and improving the speed of production. Reducing nonvalue-added lead time is often directly related to reducing inventory. Organizations that use many work in process inventory locations could discover that the percentage of nonvalue-added lead time can often approach 90% of the total lead time. Just-in-time concepts have allowed **Boeing Company** to slash the time it takes to deliver a commercial plane from $1^1/_2$ years to 10 months.

Reducing Setup Time

A **setup** is the effort required to prepare an operation for a new production run. For example, a beverage company's bottling line would need to be cleaned between flavor changes. If setups are long and expensive, the production run (*batch*) must be large to recover the setup cost. Large batches increase inventory, and larger inventories add to lead time.

Emphasizing Product-Oriented Layout

Organizing work around products is called a **product-oriented layout** (or *product cells*)

Emphasizing Employee Involvement

Employee involvement is a management approach that grants employees the responsibility and authority to make decisions about operations rather than relying solely on management instructions. This decision-making authority requires accounting and other information to be made available to all employees.

Employee involvement uses teams organized in product cells rather than just the efforts of isolated, individual employees. Such employee teams can be *cross-trained* to perform any operation within the product cell. For example, employees learn how to operate several different machines within their product cell. Moreover, team members are trained to perform functions traditionally handled by centralized service departments. For example, direct labor employees are able to perform their own maintenance, quality control, housekeeping, and production improvement work. When direct labor employees perform such indirect functions, the distinction between direct and indirect labor cost becomes less important.

Emphasizing Pull Manufacturing

Another important just-in-time principle is to produce items only as they are needed by the customer. This principle is called **pull manufacturing** (or *make to order*). In pull manufacturing, the status of the next operation determines when products are moved or produced. If the next operation is busy, production stops so that material does not pile up in front of the busy operation. If the next operation is ready, product can be produced or moved to that operation.

The system that accomplishes pull manufacturing is often called *kanban,* which is Japanese for "cards." Electronic cards or containers signal production quantities to be filled by the feeder operation. The cards link the customer back through each stage of production. When a consumer purchases a product, a card triggers assembly of a replacement product, which in turn triggers cards to manufacture the components required for the assembly. This creates a flow of parts and products that move to the drumbeat of customer demand.

In contrast, the traditional approach is to schedule production based on forecasted customer requirements. This principle is called **push manufacturing** (or *make to stock*). In push manufacturing, product is released for manufacturing without reference to line status but according to a production schedule. The schedule "pushes" product to inventory ahead of known customer demand. As a result, manufacturers using push manufacturing generally have more inventory than do manufacturers using pull manufacturing. As stated by one consultant, "If your manufacturing operations are still set up around guessing demand, you will forever be in a loop of producing and holding the wrong items and not having enough of what the customer actually wants."[5]

Kenney Manufacturing Company, a manufacturer of window shades, estimated that 50% of its window shade process was nonvalue-added. By using pull manufacturing and changing the line layout, Kenney was able to reduce inventory by 82% and lead time by 84%.

Emphasizing Zero Defects

Just-in-time manufacturing practices strive to eliminate poor quality. Poor quality results in an increased need for inspection, more production interruptions, an increased

---

[5]Jennifer Shah, "E-biz Requires Leaner Operation, More Integration," *Electronic Buyers News,* July 31, 2000, quoting David Rucker of TBM Institute.

need for rework, additional recordkeeping for scrap, a higher cost from scrap, and additional warranty costs. Thus, one of the primary objectives of just-in-time manufacturing is to improve the process so that products are made right the first time.

Emphasizing Supply Chain Management

Supply chain management is the coordination and control of materials, services, information, and finances as they move in a process from the supplier, through the manufacturer, wholesaler, and retailer to the consumer. Supply chain management involves developing long-term customer/supplier agreements with supply chain partners. Such partnering encourages supply chain partners to commit to delivering products with the right quality, at the right cost, at the right time. Supply chain management often involves improving partner operations by employing just-in-time principles. Thus, the just-in-time approach does not stop within the four walls of the factory but extends to the supply chain partner operations as well. ***Toyota Motor*** is famous for its willingness to work with supply chain partners in developing its just-in-time capabilities.

Supply chains that embrace just-in-time principles use electronic data interchange, radio frequency identification devices (RFID), and the Internet to improve the information flows between suppliers and customers. **Electronic data interchange (EDI)** is a method of using computers to electronically communicate orders, relay information, and make or receive payments from one organization to another. **Radio frequency identification devices (RFID)** are electronic tags (chips) placed on or embedded within products that can be read by radio waves that allow instant monitoring of product location. The Internet allows customers and suppliers to link their business planning and control systems through enterprise resource planning systems. **Enterprise resource planning (ERP)** systems are integrated business and information systems used by companies to plan and control both internal and supply chain operations. The result is an effective and efficient supply chain that operates from raw materials to the final consumer.

Obj **8**

Describe and illustrate the use of activity-based

Activity-Based Costing

In today's complex manufacturing systems, product costs can be distorted if inappropriate factory overhead rates are used. One way to avoid this distortion is by using the

pathological testing, dietary, and laundry. Each activity cost pool has an estimated activity base measuring the output of the activity. The cost of activities is allocated to patients by multiplying the activity rate by the number of activity-base usage quantities consumed by each patient. Exhibit 13 illustrates the activity-based costing method for Hopewell Hospital.

Each activity rate shown in Exhibit 13 is determined by dividing the budgeted activity cost pool by the estimated activity-base quantity. To illustrate, assume that the radiological testing activity cost pool budget is $960,000, and the total estimated activity-base quantity is 3,000 images. The activity rate of $320 per image is calculated as follows:

$$\text{Radiological testing activity rate} = \frac{\$960,000}{3,000 \text{ images}} = \$320 \text{ per image}$$

EXHIBIT 13   *Activity-Based Costing Method—Hopewell Hospital*

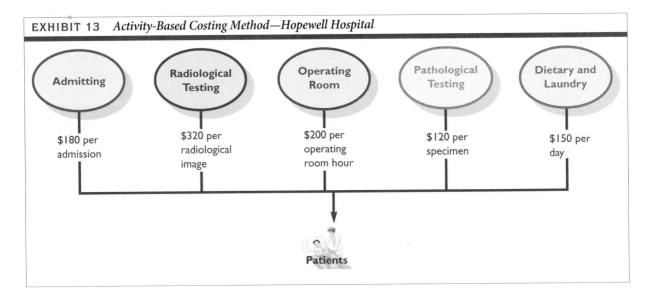

The activity rates for the other activities are determined in a similar manner. These activity rates are used to allocate costs to patients. To illustrate, assume that Mary Wilson was a patient of the hospital. The hospital overhead cost associated with services (activities) performed for Mary Wilson is determined by multiplying the activity-base quantity for Mary Wilson's stay in the hospital by the activity rate. The sum of the costs across the activities is the total hospital overhead cost of services performed for Mary Wilson. These calculations follow.

Patient Name: Mary Wilson

Activity	Activity-Base Usage	×	Activity Rate	=	Activity Cost
Admitting	1 admission	×	$180 per admission	=	$ 180
Radiological testing	2 images	×	320 per image	=	640
Operating room	4 hours	×	200 per hour	=	800
Pathological testing	1 specimen	×	120 per specimen	=	120
Dietary and laundry	7 days	×	150 per day	=	1,050
Total					$2,790

EXHIBIT 14   *Customer Profitability Report*

HOPEWELL HOSPITAL
Customer (Patient) Profitability Report
For the Period Ended December 31, 2009

	Adcock, Kim	Birini, Brian	Conway, Don		Wilson, Mary
Revenues	$9,500	$21,400	$5,050		$3,300
Less patient costs:					
Drugs and supplies	$ 400	$ 1,000	$ 300		$ 200
Admitting	180	180	180		180
Radiological testing	1,280	2,560	1,280		640
Operating room	2,400	6,400	1,600		800
Pathological testing	240	600	120		120
Dietary and laundry	4,200	14,700	1,050		1,050
Total patient costs	$8,700	$25,440	$4,530		$2,990
Income from operations	$ 800	$ (4,040)	$ 520		$ 310

The patient activity costs can be combined with the direct costs, such as drugs and supplies, and are reported with the revenues earned for each patient in a customer profitability report. A partial customer profitability report for Hopewell Hospital is shown in Exhibit 14 above.

HOW BUSINESSES MAKE MONEY

Making a Movie without a Set (or Even Actors)

Movie making is a high-risk venture. The movie must be completely shot and marketed before one dollar is received from the box office. If the movie is a hit, then all is well; but if it's a bomb, money will be lost. This is termed a "blockbuster" business emphasis and is common to businesses that have large up-front costs in the face of uncertain follow-on revenues, such as pharmaceuticals, video games, and publishing.

The blockbuster emphasis assumes that not all movies will be hits. Indeed, very few movie studios make money on all of their releases. Rather, the studio hopes to have enough hits to overcome the losses from the bombs and to make money in the end. Studios must continually create a few hits to overcome their "misses."

As the cost of movie making has increased, the risk of losing money has heightened as well. That is, the movie must become an even bigger blockbuster just to break even, much less contribute to the losses of other movies. One important approach to reining in costs is *CGI,* or *computer-generated imagery.* CGI got an important start from George Lucas, creator of the *Star Wars* movies, when he realized that he wouldn't be able to afford the miniatures and models for his original *Star Wars* trilogy. Lucas decided that he would have to turn to computers to create his futuristic world.

Thus was born **Industrial Light & Magic**, his digital imaging company, which is the undisputed leader in the industry. CGI has come a long way. In the early 1980s, it took a Cray computer 15 to 20 minutes to render one frame on *The Last Starfighter.* In the 2000s, CGI was used in over 95% of Lucas's *Attack of the Clones.* Today, an average four-second digital effect costs between $25,000 and $125,000.

Not only has CGI played a huge role in conventional movie making, but it is also transforming animated films. The traditional method of hand drawing individual frames, or cells, for an animated feature is giving way to digital animation from companies such as **Pixar Animation** (*Toy Story, Monsters, Inc.,* and *Finding Nemo*). The superiority of computer-aided animation drove **Fox Film Entertainment** to shut down its cell-animation unit and focus exclusively on CGI.

Looking to the future of movie making, it's becoming more and more difficult to distinguish between the "real" and the "digital." As Lucas was walking the set of a two-mile re-creation of downtown Manhattan for another movie, he wondered why this wasn't being re-created digitally at lower cost inside the technical studios of Industrial Light & Magic. This type of question will be asked more and more by Hollywood producers.

The report in Exhibit 14 can be used by the administrators to guide decisions on pricing or service delivery. For example, there was a large loss on services provided to Brian Birini. Further investigation could reveal that services provided to Birini were out of line with what would be allowed for reimbursement by the insurance company. As a result, future losses could be avoided by lobbying for a higher insurance reimbursement or aligning the services closer to the revenues allowed by the insurance company.

Key Points

1. **Distinguish the activities of a manufacturing business from those of a merchandising or service business.**

A manufacturing business must first produce the products it sells. A manufacturing business converts materials into a finished product through the use of machinery and labor. Materials, products in the process of being manufactured, and finished products are reported on the balance sheet as inventories under the Current Assets caption.

2. **Define and illustrate materials, factory labor, and factory overhead costs.**

A manufacturer converts materials into a finished product by using machinery and labor. The cost of materials that are an integral part of the manufactured product is direct materials cost. The cost of wages of employees who are involved in converting materials into the manufactured product is direct labor cost. Costs other than direct materials and direct labor costs are factory overhead costs, including indirect materials and labor. Direct labor and factory overhead are termed conversion costs. Direct materials, direct labor, and factory overhead costs are associated with products and are called product costs.

3. **Describe accounting systems used by manufacturing businesses.**

A cost accounting system accumulates product costs. The cost accounting system is used by management to determine the proper product cost for inventory valuation on the financial statements, to support product pricing decisions, and to identify opportunities for cost reduction and improved production efficiency. The two primary cost accounting systems are job order and process cost systems.

4. **Describe and illustrate a job order cost accounting system.**

A job order cost system provides for a separate record of the cost of each particular quantity of product that passes through the factory. Direct materials, direct labor, and factory overhead costs are accumulated in a subsidiary cost ledger, in which each account is represented by a job cost sheet. Work in Process is the controlling account for the cost ledger. As a job is finished, its costs are transferred to the finished goods ledger, for which Finished Goods is the controlling account.

5. **Use job order cost information for decision making.**

Job order cost information can support pricing and cost analysis. Managers can use job cost information to identify unusual trends and areas for cost improvement.

6. **Diagram the flow of costs for a service business that uses a job order cost accounting system.**

A cost flow diagram for a service business using a job order cost accounting system is shown in Exhibit 11. For a service business, the cost of materials or supplies used is normally included as part of the overhead. The direct labor and overhead costs of rendering services are accumulated in a work in process account. When a job is completed and the client is billed, the costs are transferred to a cost of services account.

7. **Describe just-in-time manufacturing.**

The just-in-time manufacturing philosophy uses different principles than do traditional manufacturing methods. Just-in-time attempts to reduce lead time while traditional methods attempt to lengthen lead time to provide a time buffer for uncertainty. Just-in-time emphasizes a product-oriented production layout rather than a process-oriented layout. Just-in-time emphasizes a team-oriented work environment; the traditional approach is more individual oriented. Just-in-time views setup time reduction as a high-priority item. With reduced setup times, just-in-time manufacturers can emphasize pull manufacturing rather than push manufacturing. Just-in-time manufacturers must emphasize high quality since there is very little inventory to protect production against quality problems. Finally, just-in-time manufacturers emphasize supplier partnering to improve the quality and delivery of incoming materials.

8. **Describe and illustrate the use of activity-based costing in a service business.**

Activity-based costing can be applied in service settings to determine the cost of individual service offerings. Service costs are determined by multiplying activity rates by the amount of activity-base quantities consumed by the customer using the service offering. Such information can support service pricing and profitability analysis.

Key Terms

Activity base	Finished goods ledger	Process-oriented layout
Activity-based costing	Job cost sheet	Product costs
Activity cost pools	Job order cost system	Product-oriented layout
Conversion costs	Just-in-time (JIT) manufacturing	Pull manufacturing
Cost	Lead time	Push manufacturing
Cost accounting system	Managerial accounting	Receiving report
Cost allocation	Materials inventory	Setup
Cost of goods sold	Materials ledger	Supply chain management
Direct labor cost	Materials requisitions	Time tickets
Direct materials cost	Nonvalue-added lead time	Underapplied factory overhead
Electronic data interchange (EDI)	Overapplied factory overhead	Value-added lead time
Employee involvement	Period costs	Work in process inventory
Factory overhead cost	Predetermined factory overhead rate	
Finished goods inventory	Process cost system	

Illustrative Problem

Derby Music Company specializes in producing and packaging compact discs (CDs) for the music recording industry. Derby uses a job order cost system. The following data summarize the operations related to production for March, the first month of operations:

a. Materials purchased on account, $15,500.
b. Materials requisitioned and labor used:

	Materials	Factory Labor
Job No. 100	$2,650	$1,770
Job No. 101	1,240	650
Job No. 102	980	420
Job No. 103	3,420	1,900
Job No. 104	1,000	500
Job No. 105	2,100	1,760
For general factory use	450	650

(continued)

c.   Factory overhead costs incurred on account, $2,700.
d.   Depreciation of machinery, $1,750.
e.   Factory overhead is applied at a rate of 70% of direct labor cost.
f.   Jobs completed: Nos. 100, 101, 102, 104.
g.   Jobs 100, 101, and 102 were shipped, and customers were billed for $8,100, $3,800, and
     $3,500, respectively.

Instructions

1.   Prepare a schedule summarizing manufacturing costs by job during the month. Use the
     following form:

Job	Direct Materials	Direct Labaor	Factory Overhead	Total

2.   Prepare a schedule of jobs finished.
3.   Prepare a schedule of jobs sold.
4.   Prepare a schedule of completed jobs on hand at the end of the month.
5.   Prepare a schedule of unfinished jobs at the end of the month.

Solution

1.   Schedule of manufacturing costs incurred during month:

Job	Direct Materials	Direct Labor	Factory Overhead	Total
Job No. 100	$ 2,650	$1,770	$1,239	$ 5,659
Job No. 101	1,240	650	455	2,345
Job No. 102	980	420	294	1,694
Job No. 103	3,420	1,900	1,330	6,650
Job No. 104	1,000	500	350	1,850
Job No. 105	2,100	1,760	1,232	5,092
	$11,390	$7,000	$4,900	$23,290

2.   Schedule of the cost of jobs finished:

Job	Direct Materials	Direct Labor	Factory Overhead	Total
Job No. 100	$2,650	$1,770	$1,239	$ 5,659
Job No. 101	1,240	650	455	2,345
Job No. 102	980	420	294	1,694
Job No. 104	1,000	500	350	1,850
				$11,548

3.   Schedule of the cost of jobs sold:

Job No. 100	$5,659
Job No. 101	2,345
Job No. 102	1,694
	$9,698

4.
Schedule of Completed Jobs	
Job No. 104:	
Direct materials	$1,000
Direct labor	500
Factory overhead	350
Balance of Finished Goods, March, 31	$1,850

5.
	Schedule of Unfinished Jobs			
Job	Direct Materials	Direct Labor	Factory Overhead	Total
Job No. 103	$3,420	$1,900	$1,330	$ 6,650
Job No. 105	2,100	1,760	1,232	5,092
Balance of Work in Process, March 31				$11,742

Self-Examination Questions   *(Answers appear at end of chapter.)*

1. Which of the following is *not* considered a cost of manufacturing a product?
   A. Direct materials cost   C. Sales salaries
   B. Factory overhead cost   D. Direct labor cost

2. Which of the following costs would be included as part of the factory overhead costs of a computer manufacturer?
   A. The cost of memory chips
   B. Depreciation of testing equipment
   C. Wages of computer assemblers
   D. The cost of disk drives

3. A company estimated $420,000 of factory overhead cost and 16,000 direct labor hours for the period. During the period, a job was completed with $4,500 of direct materials and $3,000 of direct labor. The

   direct labor rate was $15 per hour. What is the factory overhead applied to this job?
   A. $2,100   C. $78,750
   B. $5,250   D. $420,000

4. If the factory overhead account has a negative balance, factory overhead is said to be:
   A. underapplied.   C. underabsorbed.
   B. overapplied.   D. in error.

5. Which of the following is *not* a characteristic of the just-in-time philosophy?
   A. Product-oriented layout
   B. Push manufacturing (make to stock)
   C. Short lead times
   D. Reducing setup time as a critical improvement priority

Class Discussion Questions

1. For a company that produces desktop computers, would memory chips be considered a direct or an indirect materials cost of each computer produced?

2. How is product cost information used by managers?

3. a. Name two principal types of cost accounting systems.
   b. Which system provides for a separate record of each particular quantity of product that passes through the factory?
   c. Which system accumulates the costs for each department or process within the factory?

4. What kind of firm would use a job order cost system?

5. *Hewlett-Packard Company* assembles ink jet printers in which a high volume of standardized units are assembled and tested. Is the job order cost system appropriate in this situation?

6. How does the use of the materials requisition help control the issuance of materials from the storeroom?

7. a. Differentiate between the clock card and the time ticket.
   b. Why should the total time reported on an employee's time tickets for a payroll period be compared with the time reported on the employee's clock cards for the same period?

8. Describe the source of the data for increasing Work in Process for (a) direct materials, (b) direct labor, and (c) factory overhead.

9. Discuss how the predetermined factory overhead rate can be used in job order cost accounting to assist management in pricing jobs.

10. a. How is a predetermined factory overhead rate calculated?
    b. Name three common bases used in calculating the rate.

11. a. What is (1) overapplied factory overhead and (2) underapplied factory overhead?
    b. If the factory overhead account has a positive balance, was factory overhead underapplied or overapplied?

12. At the end of the fiscal year, there was a relatively minor balance in the factory overhead account. What procedure can be used for disposing of the balance in the account?

13. What is the difference between a product cost and a period cost?

14. How can job cost information be used to identify cost improvement opportunities?

15. Describe how a job order cost system can be used for professional service businesses.

16. What is the benefit of just-in-time processing?

17. What are some examples of nonvalue-added lead time?

18. Why do just-in-time manufacturers favor pull or make-to-order manufacturing?

19. Why would a just-in-time manufacturer strive to produce zero defects?

20. How is supplier partnering different from traditional supplier relationships?

21. How can activity-based costing be used in service companies?

Exercises

E10-1

Classify costs as materials, labor, or factory overhead

Obj 2

Indicate whether each of the following costs of an airplane manufacturer would be classified as direct materials cost, direct labor cost, or factory overhead cost:

a. Steel used in landing gear
b. Controls for flight deck
c. Welding machinery lubricants
d. Salary of test pilot

e. Wages of assembly line worker
f. Tires
g. Aircraft engines
h. Depreciation of welding equipment

E10-2

Classifying costs as materials, labor, or factory overhead

Obj 2

Indicate whether the following costs of **Colgate-Palmolive Company** would be classified as direct materials cost, direct labor cost, or factory overhead cost:

a. Packaging materials
b. Depreciation on production machinery
c. Salary of process engineers
d. Depreciation on the Clarksville, Indiana, soap plant
e. Scents and fragrances

f. Wages of manufacturing employees
g. Resins for soap and shampoo products
h. Plant manager salary for the Morristown, Tennessee, toothpaste plant
i. Maintenance supplies
j. Wages paid to Packaging Department employees

E10-3

Classifying costs as factory overhead

Obj 2

Which of the following items are properly classified as part of factory overhead for **Caterpillar**?

a. Vice president of finance's salary
b. Interest expense on debt
c. Plant manager's salary at Aurora, Illinois, manufacturing plant
d. Consultant fees for a study of production line employee productivity
e. Factory supplies used in the Morganton, North Carolina, engine parts plant

f. Amortization of patents on new assembly process
g. Steel plate
h. Depreciation on Peoria, Illinois, headquarters building
i. Property taxes on the Danville, Kentucky, tractor tread plant
j. Sales incentive fees to dealers

E10-4

Classifying costs as product or period costs

Objs 2, 4

For apparel manufacturer ***Ann Taylor, Inc.***, classify each of the following costs as either a product cost or a period cost:

a. Factory janitorial supplies
b. Depreciation on office equipment
c. Advertising expenses
d. Fabric used during production
e. Depreciation on sewing machines
f. Property taxes on factory building and equipment
g. Sales commissions
h. Wages of sewing machine operators
i. Repairs and maintenance costs for sewing machines

j. Salary of production quality control supervisor
k. Factory supervisors' salaries
l. Oil used to lubricate sewing machines
m. Travel costs of salespersons
n. Corporate controller's salary
o. Utility costs for office building
p. Research and development costs
q. Salaries of distribution center personnel

E10-5

Concepts and terminology

Objs 2, 4

From the choices presented in the parentheses, choose the appropriate term for completing each of the following sentences:

a. Materials that are an integral part of the manufactured product are classified as (direct materials, materials inventory).
b. An example of factory overhead is (plant depreciation, sales office depreciation).
c. Direct labor costs combined with factory overhead costs are called (product, conversion) costs.
d. Implementing automatic factory robotics equipment normally (increases, decreases) the factory overhead component of product costs.

e. The wages of an assembly worker are normally considered a (period, product) cost.
f. Payments of cash or its equivalent or the commitment to pay cash in the future for the purpose of generating revenues are (costs, expenses).
g. Advertising expenses are usually viewed as (period, product) costs.
h. The balance sheet of a manufacturer would include an account for (cost of goods sold, work in process inventory).

E10-6

Transactions in a job order cost system

Obj 4

Five selected transactions for the current month are indicated by letters in the following accounts in a job order cost accounting system:

Materials	
(a) decrease	

Work in Process	
(a) increase	
(b) increase	
(c) increase	
(d) decrease	

Wages Payable	
(b) increase	

Finished Goods	
(d) increase	
(e) decrease	

Factory Overhead	
(a) increase	
(b) increase	
(c) decrease	

Cost of Goods Sold	
(e) increase	

Describe each of the five transactions.

E10-7

Cost flow relationships

Obj 4

✓ c. $271,500

The following information is available for the first month of operations of Korv Inc., a manufacturer of art and craft items:

Sales	$775,000
Gross profit	265,000
Indirect labor	63,000
Indirect materials	32,000
Other factory overhead	17,500
Materials purchased	303,000
Total manufacturing costs for the period	620,000
Materials inventory, end of period	35,000

Using the above information, determine the following missing amounts:

a. Cost of goods sold
b. Direct materials cost
c. Direct labor cost

E10-8

Cost of materials issuances by fifo method

Obj 4

SPREADSHEET

✓ b. $2,400

An incomplete subsidiary ledger of wire cable for August is as follows:

RECEIVED			ISSUED			BALANCE			
Receiving Report Number	*Quantity*	*Unit Price*	*Materials Requisition Number*	*Quantity*	*Amount*	*Date*	*Quantity*	*Amount*	*Unit Price*
						Aug. 1	200	$3,200	$16.00
110	240	$18.00				Aug. 3			
			108	300		Aug. 5			
139	160	20.00				Aug. 19			
			120	180		Aug. 25			

a. Complete the materials issuances and balances for the wire cable subsidiary ledger under fifo.
b. Determine the balance of wire cable at the end of August.
c. Determine the total amount of materials transferred to work in process for August.
d. Explain how the materials ledger might be used as an aid in maintaining inventory quantities on hand.

E10-9

Recording issuing of materials

Obj 4

Materials issued for the current month are as follows:

Requisition No.	Material	Job No.	Amount
811	Aluminium	511	$10,400
812	Steel	514	18,650
813	Plastic	526	875
814	Abrasives	Indirect	325
815	Titanium alloy	533	42,300

a. Determine the amount of materials transferred to Work in Process and Factory Overhead for the current month.
b. Illustrate the effect on the accounts and financial statements of the materials transferred in (a).

E10-10

Entries for materials

Obj 4

✓ c. fabric, $31,700

Combes Furniture Company manufactures furniture. Combes uses a job order cost system. Balances on November 1 from the materials ledger are as follows:

Fabric	$ 33,500
Polyester filling	8,100
Lumber	107,400
Glue	1,600

The materials purchased during November are summarized from the receiving reports as follows:

Fabric	$549,900
Polyester filling	104,200
Lumber	969,500
Glue	14,200

Materials were requisitioned to individual jobs as follows:

	Fabric	Polyester Filling	Lumber	Glue	Total
Job 11	$362,200	$64,500	$611,300		$1,038,000
Job 12	121,700	13,900	198,600		334,200
Job 13	67,800	10,300	182,400		260,500
Factory overhead—indirect materials				$11,700	11,700
Total	$551,700	$88,700	$992,300	$11,700	$1,644,400

The glue is not a significant cost, so it is treated as indirect materials (factory overhead).

a. Determine the total purchase of materials in November.
b. Determine the amounts of materials transferred to Work in Process and Factory Overhead for the requisition of materials in November.
c. Determine the November 30 balances that would be shown in the materials ledger accounts.

E10-11

Recording factory labor costs

Obj 4

A summary of the time tickets for the current month follows:

Job No.	Amount	Job No.	Amount
101	$1,620	141	$ 1,780
122	1,590	Indirect labor	13,400
133	760	143	3,330
139	5,210	147	1,080

a. Determine the amounts of factory labor costs transferred to Work in Process and Factory Overhead for the current month.
b. Illustrate the effects on the accounts and financial statements of the factory labor costs transferred in (a).

E10-12

Recording factory labor costs

Obj 4

The weekly time tickets indicate the following distribution of labor hours for three direct labor employees:

	Hours			
	Job 111	Job 112	Job 113	Process Improvement
Johnny Daniels	18	10	5	7
Jack Walker	7	8	23	2
Jim Morgan	8	12	16	4

(continued)

The direct labor rate earned by the three employees is as follows:

Daniels	$11.40
Walker	13.50
Morgan	11.75

The process improvement category includes training, quality improvement, housekeeping, and other indirect tasks.

a. Determine the amounts of factory labor costs transferred to Work in Process and Factory Overhead for the week.

b. Assume that Jobs 111 and 112 were completed but not sold during the week and that Job 113 remained incomplete at the end of the week. How would the direct labor costs for all three jobs be reflected on the financial statements at the end of the week?

E10-13

Recording direct labor and factory overhead

Obj 4

Chasse Homes Inc. manufactures mobile homes. Chasse uses a job order cost system. The time tickets from October jobs are summarized below.

Job 502	$2,352
Job 503	1,440
Job 504	960
Job 505	1,320
Factory supervision	2,760

Factory overhead is applied to jobs on the basis of a predetermined overhead rate of $20 per direct labor hour. The direct labor rate is $12 per hour.

a. Determine the total factory labor costs transferred to Work in Process and Factory Overhead for October.

b. Determine the amount of factory overhead applied to production for October.

c. Illustrate the effects of the factory overhead applied in (b) on the accounts and financial statements.

E10-14

Factory overhead rates and account balances

Obj 4

✓ b. $13.00 per direct labor hour

Staten Island Turbine operates two factories. The company applies factory overhead to jobs on the basis of machine hours in Factory 1 and on the basis of direct labor hours in Factory 2. Estimated factory overhead costs, direct labor hours, and machine hours are as follows:

	Factory 1	*Factory 2*
Estimated factory overhead cost for fiscal year beginning May 1	$236,800	$118,300
Estimated direct labor hours for year		9,100
Estimated machine hours for year	12,800	
Actual factory overhead costs for May	$23,200	$11,625
Actual direct labor hours for May		885
Actual machine hours for May	1,270	

a. Determine the factory overhead rate for Factory 1.

b. Determine the factory overhead rate for Factory 2.

c. Determine the factory overhead applied to production in each factory for May.

d. Determine the balances of the factory accounts for each factory as of May 31, and indicate whether the amounts represent overapplied or underapplied factory overhead.

E10-15

Predetermined factory overhead rate

Obj 4

The Engine Shop uses a job order cost system to determine the cost of performing engine repair work. Estimated costs and expenses for the coming period are as follows:

Engine parts	$ 650,750
Shop direct labor	520,625
Shop and repair equipment depreciation	12,800
Shop supervisor salaries	93,125
Shop property tax	22,300
Shop supplies	12,650
Advertising expense	18,100
Administrative office salaries	61,600
Administrative office depreciation expense	8,050
Total costs and expenses	$1,400,000

The average shop direct labor rate is $17 per hour.
Determine the predetermined shop overhead rate per direct labor hour.

E10-16

Predetermined factory overhead rate

Obj 4

✓ a. $175 per hour

San Jose Medical Center has a single operating room that is used by local physicians to perform surgical procedures. The cost of using the operating room is accumulated by each patient procedure and includes the direct materials costs (drugs and medical devices), physician surgical time, and operating room overhead. On August 1 of the current year, the annual operating room overhead is estimated to be:

Disposable supplies	$116,700
Depreciation expense	18,000
Utilities	11,200
Nurse salaries	164,000
Technician wages	57,600
Total operating room overhead	$367,500

The overhead costs will be assigned to procedures based on the number of surgical room hours. The Medical Center expects to use the operating room an average of seven hours per day, six days per week. In addition, the operating room will be shut down two weeks per year for general repairs.

a. Determine the predetermined operating room overhead rate for the year.
b. Allison Mann had a 5-hour procedure on August 10. How much operating room overhead would be charged to her procedure, using the rate determined in part (a)?
c. During August, the operating room was used 182 hours. The actual overhead costs incurred for August were $30,700. Determine the overhead under- or overapplied for the period.

E10-17

Recording jobs completed; cost of unfinished jobs

Obj 4

✓ b. $5,800

The following account appears in the ledger after only part of the postings have been completed for January:

Work in Process	
Balance, January 1	$15,500
Direct materials	86,200
Direct labor	64,300
Factory overhead	93,700

Jobs finished during January are summarized as follows:

Job 320	$57,600	Job 327	$26,100
Job 326	75,400	Job 350	94,800

a. Determine the cost of jobs completed.
b. Determine the cost of the unfinished jobs at January 31.

E10-18

Entries for factory costs and jobs completed

Obj 4

✓ d. $ 18,340

Tobias Printing Inc. began printing operations on July 1. Jobs 101 and 102 were completed during the month, and all costs applicable to them were recorded on the related cost sheets. Jobs 103 and 104 are still in process at the end of the month, and all applicable costs except factory overhead have been recorded on the related cost sheets. In addition to the materials and labor charged directly to the jobs, $725 of indirect materials and $6,380 of indirect labor were used during the month. The cost sheets for the four jobs entering production during the month are as follows, in summary form:

Job 101	
Direct materials	6,800
Direct labor	1,560
Factory overhead	3,900
Total	12,260

Job 102	
Direct materials	3,000
Direct labor	880
Factory overhead	2,200
Total	6,080

Job 103	
Direct materials	8,700
Direct labor	1,350
Factory overhead	

Job 104	
Direct materials	1,500
Direct labor	500
Factory overhead	

Determine each of the following for July:

a. Direct and indirect materials used.
b. Direct and indirect labor used.
c. Factory overhead applied (a single overhead rate is used based on direct labor *cost*).
d. Cost of completed Jobs 101 and 102.

E10-19

Financial statements of a manufacturing firm

Obj 4

SPREADSHEET

✓ a. Income from operations, $47,600

The following events took place for Wreckin Ronnie Inc. during July 2008, the first month of operations, as a producer of road bikes:

- Purchased $165,800 of materials.
- Used $147,600 of direct materials in production.
- Incurred $96,250 of direct labor wages.
- Applied factory overhead at a rate of 80% of direct labor cost.
- Transferred $302,900 of work in process to finished goods.
- Sold goods with a cost of $301,300.
- Sold goods for $520,000.
- Incurred $119,000 of selling expenses.
- Incurred $52,100 of administrative expenses.

a. Prepare the July income statement for Wreckin Ronnie. Assume that Wreckin Ronnie uses the perpetual inventory method.
b. Determine the inventory balances at the end of the first month of operations.

E10-20

Decision making with job order costs

Obj 5

Bronx Machinery Inc. is a job shop. The management of Bronx Machinery uses the cost information from the job sheets to assess its cost performance. Information on the total cost, product type, and quantity of items produced is as follows:

Date	*Job No.*	*Quantity*	*Product*	*Amount*
Jan. 2	101	450	105X	$10,350
Jan. 24	125	1,500	205B	16,500
Feb. 18	144	750	205B	9,000
Mar. 4	162	500	105X	10,000

Date	Job No.	Quantity	Product	Amount
Mar. 28	173	1,100	120T	6,600
May 20	190	1,250	120T	11,250
June 10	201	450	105X	6,750
Aug. 9	210	1,900	120T	22,800
Sept. 16	215	500	205B	5,500
Nov. 11	227	650	105X	7,800
Dec. 9	238	1,050	120T	16,800

a. Develop a graph for *each* product (three graphs), with Job No. (in date order) on the horizontal axis and unit cost on the vertical axis. Use this information to determine Bronx Machinery's cost performance over time for the three products.

b. What additional information would you require to investigate Bronx Machinery's cost performance more precisely?

E10-21

Decision making with job order costs

Obj 5

Sharp Trophies Inc. uses a job order cost system for determining the cost to manufacture award products (plaques and trophies). Among the company's products is an engraved plaque that is awarded to participants who complete an executive education program at a local university. The company sells the plaque to the university for $75 each.

Each plaque has a brass plate engraved with the name of the participant. Engraving requires approximately 6 minutes per name. Improperly engraved names must be redone. The plate is screwed to a walnut backboard. This assembly takes approximately 3 minutes per unit. Improper assembly must be redone using a new walnut backboard.

During the first half of the year, the university had two separate executive education classes. The job cost sheets for the two separate jobs indicated the following information:

Job 103 March 4

	Cost per Unit	Units	Job Cost
Direct materials:			
Wood	$20.00/unit	30 units	$ 600.00
Brass	18.00/unit	30 units	540.00
Engraving labor	40.00/hr.	3 hrs.	120.00
Assembly labor	28.00/hr.	1.5 hrs.	42.00
Factory overhead	30.00/hr.	6 hrs.	180.00
			$1,482.00
Plaques shipped			÷ 30
Cost per plaque			$ 49.40

Job 116 April 15

	Cost per Unit	Units	Job Cost
Direct materials:			
Wood	$ 20.00/unit	25 units	$ 500.00
Brass	18.00/unit	25 units	450.00
Engraving labor	40.00/hr.	4 hrs.	160.00
Assembly labor	28.00/hr.	2 hrs.	56.00
Factory overhead	30.00/hr.	4 hrs.	120.00
			$1,286.00
Plaques shipped			÷ 20
Cost per plaque			$ 64.30

a. Why did the cost per plaque increase from $49.40 to $64.30?

b. What improvements would you recommend for Sharp Trophies Inc.?

E10-22

Job order cost accounting entries for a service business

Obj 6

✓ d. Cost of Services Completed, $609,800

Tec Trends Inc. provides advertising services for clients across the nation. Tec Trends is presently working on four projects, each for a different client. Tec Trends accumulates costs for each account (client) on the basis of both direct costs and allocated indirect costs. The direct costs include the charged time of professional personnel and media purchases (air time and ad space). Overhead is allocated to each project as a percentage of media purchases. The predetermined overhead rate is 40% of media purchases.

On July 1, the four advertising projects had the following accumulated costs:

	July 1 Balances
Spitzer Hotel	$120,000
Gonzalez Bank	15,000
Gulliani Beverage	66,000
Koch Rentals	18,000

During July, Tec Trends Inc. incurred the following direct labor and media purchase costs related to preparing advertising for each of the four accounts:

	Direct Labor	Media Purchases
Spitzer Hotel	$ 42,000	$154,000
Gonzalez Bank	17,000	143,000
Gulliani Beverage	81,000	128,000
Koch Rentals	107,000	83,000
Total	$247,000	$508,000

At the end of July, both the Spitzer Hotel and Gonzalez Bank campaigns were completed. The costs of completed campaigns are debited to the cost of services account.

Determine each of the following for the month:

a. Direct labor costs.
b. Media purchases.
c. Overhead applied.
d. Completion of Spitzer Hotel and Gonzalez Bank campaigns.

E10-23

Just-in-time principles

Obj 7

The chief executive officer (CEO) of Lordsland Inc. has just returned from a management seminar describing the benefits of the just-in-time philosophy. The CEO issued the following statement after returning from the conference:

> This company will become a just-in-time manufacturing company. Presently, we have too much inventory. To become just-in-time we need to eliminate the excess inventory. Therefore, I want all employees to begin reducing inventories until we are just-in-time. Thank you for your cooperation.

How would you respond to the CEO's statement?

E10-24

Just-in-time as a strategy

Obj 7

The American apparel (textile) industry has moved much of its operations offshore in the pursuit of lower labor costs. Apparel imports rose from 2% of all production in 1962 to over 60% in 2006. Offshore manufacturers make long runs of standard mass-market apparel items. These are then brought to the United States in container ships, requiring significant time between original order and delivery. As a result, retail customers must accurately forecast market demands for imported apparel items.

Assuming that you work for a U.S.-based apparel company, how would you recommend responding to the low-cost imports?

E10-25

Lead time reduction— service company

Obj 7

Homeguard Insurance Company takes ten days to make payments on insurance claims. Claims are processed through three departments: Data Input, Claims Audit, and Claims Adjustment. The three departments are on different floors, approximately one hour apart from each other. Claims are processed in batches of 100. Each batch of 100 claims moves through the three departments on a wheeled cart. Management is concerned about customer dissatisfaction caused by the long lead time for claim payments.

How might this process be changed so that the lead time could be reduced significantly?

E10-26

Just-in-time principles

Obj 7

Celestial Shirt Company manufactures various styles of men's casual wear. Shirts are cut and assembled by a workforce that is paid by piece rate. This means that they are paid according to the amount of work completed during a period of time. To illustrate, if the piece rate is $0.10 per sleeve assembled, and the worker assembles 700 sleeves during the day, then the worker would be paid $70 (700 × $0.10) for the day's work.

The company is considering adopting a just-in-time manufacturing philosophy by organizing work cells around various types of products and employing pull manufacturing. However, no change is expected in the compensation policy. On this point, the manufacturing manager stated the following:

> *"Piecework compensation provides an incentive to work fast. Without it, the workers will just goof off and expect a full day's pay. We can't pay straight hourly wages—at least not in this industry."*

How would you respond to the manufacturing manager's comments?

E10-27

Supply chain management

Obj 7

The following is an excerpt from a recent article discussing supplier relationships with the Big Three North American automakers.

> *"The Big Three select suppliers on the basis of lowest price and annual price reductions," said Neil De Koker, president of the Original Equipment Suppliers Association. "They look globally for the lowest parts prices from the lowest cost countries," De Koker said. "There is little trust and respect. Collaboration is missing." Japanese auto makers want long-term supplier relationships. They select suppliers as a person would a mate. The Big Three are quick to beat down prices with methods such as electronic auctions or rebidding work to a competitor. The Japanese are equally tough on price but are committed to maintaining supplier continuity. "They work with you to arrive at a competitive price, and they are willing to pay because they want long-term partnering," said Carl Code, a vice president at Ernie Green Industries. "They [**Honda** and **Toyota**] want suppliers to make enough money to stay in business, grow and bring them innovation." The Big Three's supply chain model is not much different from the one set by Henry Ford. In 1913, he set up the system of independent supplier firms operating at arm's length on short-term contracts. One consequence of the Big Three's low-price-at-all-costs mentality is that suppliers are reluctant to offer them their cutting-edge technology out of fear the contract will be resourced before the research and development costs are recouped.*

a. Contrast the Japanese supply chain model with that of the Big Three.
b. Why might a supplier prefer the Japanese model?
c. What benefits might accrue to the Big Three by adopting the Japanese supply chain practices?

Source: Robert Sherefkin and Amy Wilson, "Suppliers Prefer Japanese Business Model," *Rubber & Plastics News,* March 17, 2003, Vol. 24, No. 11.

E10-28

Employee involvement

Obj 7

Quickie Designs Inc. uses teams in the manufacture of lightweight wheelchairs. Two features of its team approach are team hiring and peer reviews. Under team hiring, the team recruits, interviews, and hires new team members from within the organization. Using peer reviews, the team evaluates each member of the team with regard to quality, knowledge, teamwork, goal performance, attendance, and safety. These reviews provide feedback to the team member for improvement.

How do these two team approaches differ from using managers to hire and evaluate employees?

E10-29

Activity-based costing for a hospital

Obj 8

SPREADSHEET

✓ a. Patient Malone,
$6,495

Mercy Hospital plans to use activity-based costing to assign hospital indirect costs to the care of patients. The hospital has identified the following activities and activity rates for the hospital indirect costs:

Activity	Activity Rate
Room and meals	$165 per day
Radiology	$250 per image
Pharmacy	$45 per physician order
Chemistry lab	$85 per test
Operating room	$680 per operating room hour

The records of two representative patients were analyzed, using the activity rates. The activity information associated with the two patients is as follows:

	Patient Malone	Patient Talbot
Number of days	8 days	4 days
Number of images	5 images	3 images
Number of physician orders	6 orders	2 orders
Number of tests	7 tests	3 tests
Number of operating room hours	4.5 hours	2 hours

a. Determine the activity cost associated with each patient.
b. Why is the total activity cost different for the two patients?

E10-30

Activity-based costing in an insurance company

Obj 8

SPREADSHEET

✓ a. Auto, $840,375

Sentinel Insurance Company carries three major lines of insurance: auto, workers' compensation, and homeowners. The company has prepared the following report for 2009:

SENTINEL INSURANCE COMPANY
Product Profitability Report
For the Year Ended December 31, 2009

	Auto	Workers' Compensation	Homeowners
Premium revenue	$6,000,000	$5,000,000	$7,000,000
Less estimated claims	4,200,000	3,500,000	4,900,000
Underwriting income	$1,800,000	$1,500,000	$2,100,000
Underwriting income as a percent of premium revenue	30%	30%	30%

Management is concerned that the administrative expenses may make some of the insurance lines unprofitable. However, the administrative expenses have not been allocated to the insurance lines. The controller has suggested that the administrative expenses could be assigned to the insurance lines using activity-based costing. The administrative expenses are comprised of five activities. The activities and their rates are as follows:

	Activity Rates
New policy processing	$170 per new policy
Cancellation processing	$260 per cancellation
Claim audits	$550 per claim audit
Claim disbursements processing	$115 per disbursement
Premium collection processing	$50 per premium collected

Activity base usage data for each line of insurance were retrieved from the corporate records and are shown below.

	Auto	Workers' Comp.	Homeowners
Number of new policies	1,200	1,400	3,100
Number of canceled policies	500	180	1,650
Number of audited claims	350	120	710
Number of claim disbursements	375	150	740
Number of premiums collected	7,800	1,600	12,000

a. Complete the product profitability report through the administrative activities. Determine the income from operations as a percent of premium revenue, rounded to one decimal place.
b. Interpret the report.

Problems

P10-1

Classifying costs

Objs 2, 4

The following is a list of costs that were incurred in the production and sale of boats:

a. Commissions to sales representatives, based upon the number of boats sold.
b. Cost of boat for "grand prize" promotion in local bass tournament.
c. Memberships for key executives in the Bass World Association.
d. Cost of electrical wiring for boats.
e. Cost of normal scrap from defective hulls.
f. Cost of metal hardware for boats, such as ornaments and tie-down grasps.
g. Cost of paving the employee parking lot.
h. Hourly wages of assembly line workers.
i. Annual bonus paid to top executives of the company.
j. Straight-line depreciation on factory equipment.
k. Wood paneling for use in interior boat trim.
l. Steering wheels.
m. Special advertising campaign in *Bass World*.
n. Masks for use by sanders in smoothing boat hulls.
o. Power used by sanding equipment.
p. Yearly cost maintenance contract for robotic equipment.
q. Oil to lubricate factory equipment.
r. Canvas top for boats.
s. Executive end-of-year bonuses.
t. Salary of shop supervisor.
u. Decals.
v. Annual fee to pro-fisherman Jim Bo Wilks to promote the boats.
w. Paint for boats.
x. Legal department costs for the year.
y. Fiberglass for producing the boat hull.
z. Salary of president of company.

Instructions

Classify each cost as either a product cost or a period cost. Indicate whether each product cost is a direct materials cost, a direct labor cost, or a factory overhead cost. Indicate whether each period cost is a selling expense or an administrative expense. Use the following tabular headings for your answer, placing an "X" in the appropriate column.

	Product Costs			Period Costs	
Cost	Direct Materials Cost	Direct Labor Cost	Factory Overhead Expense	Selling Expense	Administrative Expense

P10-2

Entries and schedules for unfinished jobs and completed jobs

Obj 4

SPREADSHEET

✓ 5. Work in Process balance, $131,975

Godwin Fixtures Co. uses a job order cost system. The following data summarize the operations related to production for April 2008, the first month of operations:

a. Materials purchased on account, $137,000.
b. Materials requisitioned and factory labor used:

Job	Materials	Factory Labor
No. 601	$18,100	$17,000
No. 602	20,000	25,500
No. 603	13,050	9,700
No. 604	34,500	33,550
No. 605	15,700	14,800
No. 606	17,800	18,300
For general factory use	6,600	47,000

(continued)

c.   Factory overhead costs incurred on account, $60,000.
d.   Depreciation of machinery and equipment, $14,500.
e.   The factory overhead rate is $53 per machine hour. Machine hours used:

Job	Machine Hours
No. 601	215
No. 602	230
No. 603	175
No. 604	300
No. 605	198
No. 606	225
Total	1,343

f.   Jobs completed: 601, 602, 603, and 605.
g.   Jobs were shipped and customers were billed as follows: Job 601, $72,750; Job 602, $88,780; Job 605, $74,500.

Instructions

1.   Prepare a schedule summarizing manufacturing costs by job for April. Use the following form:

Job	Direct Materials	Direct Labor	Factory Overhead	Total

2.   Prepare a schedule of jobs finished in April.
3.   Prepare a schedule of jobs sold in April. What account does this schedule support for the month of April?
4.   Prepare a schedule of completed jobs on hand as of April 30, 2008. What account does this schedule support?
5.   Prepare a schedule of unfinished jobs as of April 30, 2008. What account does this schedule support?

P10-3

Job order cost sheet

Objs 4, 5

Nu-Life Furniture Company refinishes and reupholsters furniture. Nu-Life uses a job order cost system. When a prospective customer asks for a price quote on a job, the estimated cost data are inserted on an unnumbered job cost sheet. If the offer is accepted, a number is assigned to the job, and the costs incurred are recorded in the usual manner on the job cost sheet. After the job is completed, reasons for the variances between the estimated and actual costs are noted on the sheet. The data are then available to management in evaluating the efficiency of operations and in preparing quotes on future jobs. On July 1, 2008, an estimate of $1,512.64 for reupholstering two chairs and a couch was given to Ed Douthett. The estimate was based on the following data:

Estimated direct materials:	
17 meters at $23 per meter	$ 391.00
Estimated direct labor:	
24 hours at $14 per hour	336.00
Estimated factory overhead (65% of direct labor cost)	218.40
Total estimated costs	$ 945.40
Markup (60% of production costs)	567.24
Total estimate	$1,512.64

On July 4, the chairs and couch were picked up from the residence of Ed Douthett, 411 Austin Lane, Alexandria, with a commitment to return them on September 13. The job was completed on September 10.

The related materials requisitions and time tickets are summarized as follows:

Materials Requisition No.	Description	Amount
3480	7 meters at $23	$161
3492	11 meters at $23	253

Time Ticket No.	Description	Amount
H143	13 hours at $14	$182
H151	15 hours at $14	210

Instructions

1. Prepare a job order cost sheet showing the estimate given to the customer. Use the format shown below.
2. Assign number 00-10-23 to the job, record the costs incurred, and complete the job order cost sheet. Comment on the reasons for the variances between actual costs and estimated costs. For this purpose, assume that two meters of materials were spoiled, the factory overhead rate has been proved to be satisfactory, and an inexperienced employee performed the work.

JOB ORDER COST SHEET

Customer _____   Date _____

Address _____   Date wanted _____

_____   Date completed _____

Item _____   Job No. _____

ESTIMATE

Direct Materials		Direct Labor		Summary	
	Amount		Amount		Amount
___ meter at $___	_____	___ hours at $___	_____	Direct materials	_____
___ meter at $___	_____	___ hours at $___	_____	Direct labor	_____
___ meter at $___	_____	___ hours at $___	_____	Factory overhead	_____
___ meter at $___	_____	___ hours at $___	_____	Total cost	_____
Total	_____	Total	_____		

ACTUAL

Mat. Req. No.	Direct Materials Description	Amount	Mat. Req. No.	Direct Labor Description	Amount	Summary Item	Amount
___	_____	_____	___	_____	_____	Direct materials	_____
___	_____	_____	___	_____	_____	Direct labor	_____
___	_____	_____	___	_____	_____	Factory overhead	_____
___	_____	_____	___	_____	_____	Total cost	_____
Total		_____	Total		_____		

P10-4

Analyzing manufacturing cost accounts

Obj 4

SPREADSHEET

✓ G. $245,250

Dupont Fishing Equipment Company manufactures fishing rods in a wide variety of lengths and weights. The following incomplete ledger accounts refer to transactions that are summarized for November:

Materials

Nov.	1	Balance	10,000
	30	Purchases	120,000
	30	Requisitions	(A)

Work in Process

Nov.	1	Balance	(B)
	30	Materials	(C)
	30	Direct labor	(D)
	30	Factory overhead applied	(E)
	30	Completed jobs	(F)

Finished Goods

Nov.	1	Balance	0
	30	Completed jobs	(F)
	30	Cost of goods sold	(G)

Wages Payable

Nov.	30	Wages incurred	130,000

Factory Overhead

Nov.	1	Balance	2,500
	30	Indirect labor	(H)
	30	Indirect materials	3,000
	30	Other overhead	60,000
	30	Factory overhead applied	(E)

In addition, the following information is available:

a. Materials and direct labor were applied to six jobs in November.

Job No.	Style	Quantity	Direct Materials	Direct Labor
No. 111	DL-8	70	$ 15,000	$ 12,000
No. 112	DL-18	100	23,000	18,000
No. 113	DL-11	120	27,500	25,000
No. 114	SL-101	100	11,000	12,500
No. 115	SL-110	175	28,000	27,500
No. 116	DL-14	80	15,000	14,500
Total		645	$119,500	$109,500

b. Factory overhead is applied to each job at a rate of 75% of direct labor cost.
c. The November 1 Work in Process balance consisted of two jobs, as follows:

Job No.	Style	Work in Process, November 1
Job 111	DL-8	$20,000
Job 112	DL-18	30,000
Total		$50,000

d. Customer jobs completed and units sold in November were as follows:

Job No.	Style	Completed in November	Units Sold in November
Job 111	DL-8	X	60
Job 112	DL-18	X	100
Job 113	DL-11	X	80
Job 114	SL-101		0
Job 115	SL-110	X	150
Job 116	DL-14		0

Instructions

1. Determine the missing amounts associated with each letter. Provide supporting calculations by completing a table with the following headings:

Job No.	Quantity	Nov. 1 Work in Process	Direct Materials	Direct Labor	Factory Overhead	Total Cost	Unit Cost	Units Sold	Cost of Goods Sold

2. Determine the November 30 balances for each of the inventory accounts and factory overhead.

P10-5

Flow of costs and income statement

Obj 4

SPREADSHEET

✓ 1. Income from operations, $2,998,000

Outdoor Software Inc. is a designer, manufacturer, and distributor of software for microcomputers. A new product, *Landscape 2008,* was released for production and distribution in early 2008. In January, $700,000 was spent to design print advertisement. For the first six months of 2008, the company spent $2,500,000 promoting *Landscape 2008* in trade magazines. The product was ready for manufacture on January 10, 2008.

Outdoor uses a job order cost system to accumulate costs associated with each software title. Direct materials unit costs are:

Blank CD	$ 4.50
Packaging	8.00
Manual	11.00
Total	$23.50

The actual production process for the software product is fairly straightforward. First, blank CDs are brought to a CD copying machine. The copying machine requires 1 hour per 1,500 CDs.

After the program is copied onto the CD, the CD is brought to assembly, where assembly personnel pack the CD and manual for shipping. The direct labor cost for this work is $0.75 per unit.

The completed packages are then sold to retail outlets through a sales force. The sales force is compensated by a 10% commission on the wholesale price for all sales.

Total completed production was 45,000 units during the year. Other information is as follows:

Number of software units sold in 2008	40,000
Wholesale price per unit	$200

Factory overhead cost is applied to jobs at the rate of $1,200 per copy machine hour. There were an additional 1,000 copied CDs, packaging, and manuals waiting to be assembled on December 31, 2008.

(continued)

Instructions

1. Prepare an annual income statement for the *Landscape 2008* product, including supporting calculations, from the given information.
2. Determine the balances in the finished goods and work in process inventory for the *Landscape 2008* product on December 31, 2008.

Activities

A10-1

Ethics and professional conduct in business

ETHICS

Farrar Manufacturing Company allows employees to purchase, at cost, manufacturing materials, such as metal and lumber, for personal use. To purchase materials for personal use, an employee must complete a materials requisition form, which must then be approved by the employee's immediate supervisor. Peggy Carron, an assistant cost accountant, charges the employee an amount based on Farrar's net purchase cost.

Peggy Carron is in the process of replacing a deck on her home and has requisitioned lumber for personal use, which has been approved in accordance with company policy. In computing the cost of the lumber, Peggy reviewed all the purchase invoices for the past year. She then used the lowest price to compute the amount due the company for the lumber.

Discuss whether Peggy behaved in an ethical manner.

A10-2

Financial vs. managerial accounting

The following statement was made by the vice president of finance of Haberman Inc.: "The managers of a company should use the same information as the shareholders of the firm. When managers use the same information in guiding their internal operations as shareholders use in evaluating their investments, the managers will be aligned with the stockholders' profit objectives."

Respond to the vice president's statement.

A10-3

Classifying costs

On-Time Computer Repairs provides computer repair services for the community. Laurie Estes's computer was not working, and she called On-Time for a home repair visit. The On-Time technician arrived at 2:00 P.M. to begin work. By 4:00 P.M. the problem was diagnosed as a failed circuit board. Unfortunately, the technician did not have a new circuit board in the truck, since the technician's previous customer had the same problem, and a board was used on that visit. Replacement boards were available back at the On-Time shop. Therefore, the technician drove back to the shop to retrieve a replacement board. From 4:00 to 5:00 P.M., the On-Time technician drove the round trip to retrieve the replacement board from the shop.

At 5:00 P.M. the technician was back on the job at Laurie's home. The replacement procedure is somewhat complex, since a variety of tests must be performed once the board is installed. The job was completed at 6:00 P.M.

Laurie's repair bill showed the following:

Circuit board	$ 80
Labor charges	190
Total	$270

Laurie was surprised at the size of the bill and asked for some greater detail supporting the calculations. On-Time responded with the following explanations:

Cost of materials:	
Purchase price of circuit board	$60
Markup on purchase price to cover storage and handling	20
Total materials charge	$80

The labor charge per hour is detailed as follows:

2:00–3:00 P.M.	$ 40
3:00–4:00 P.M.	35
4:00–5:00 P.M.	45
5:00–6:00 P.M.	70
Total labor charge	$190

Further explanations in the differences in the hourly rates are as follows:

First hour:

Base labor rate	$20
Fringe benefits	7
Overhead (other than storage and handling)	8
Total base labor rate	$35
Additional charge for first hour of any job to cover the cost of vehicle depreciation, fuel, and employee time in transit. A 30-minute transit time is assumed.	5
	$40

Third hour:

Base labor rate	$35
The trip back to the shop includes vehicle depreciation and fuel; therefore, a charge was added to the hourly rate to cover these costs. The round trip took an hour.	10
	$45

Fourth hour:

Base labor rate	$35
Overtime premium for time worked in excess of an eight-hour day (starting at 5:00 P.M.) is equal to the base rate.	35
	$70

1. If you were in Laurie's position, how would you respond to the bill? Are there parts of the bill that appear incorrect to you? If so, what argument would you employ to convince On-Time that the bill is too high?

2. Use the headings below to construct a table. Fill in the table by first listing the costs identified in the activity in the left-hand column. For each cost, place a check mark in the appropriate column identifying the correct cost classification. Assume that each service call is a job.

Cost	Direct Materials	Direct Labor	Overhead

A10-4

Managerial analysis

The controller of the plant of Commercial Plumbing Supplies prepared a graph of the unit costs from the job cost reports for Product QQQ. The graph appeared as follows:

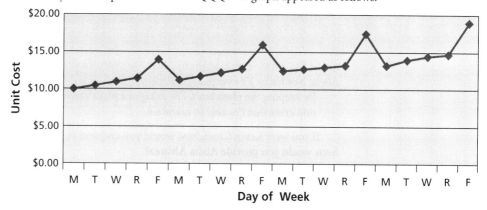

How would you interpret this information? What further information would you request?

A10-5

Factory overhead rate

Machine-Tech Inc., a specialized tool manufacturer, uses a job order costing system. The overhead is allocated to jobs on the basis of direct labor hours. The overhead rate is now $1,500 per direct labor hour. The design engineer thinks that this is illogical. The design engineer has stated the following:

> Our accounting system doesn't make any sense to me. It tells me that every labor hour carries an additional burden of $1,500. This means that direct labor makes up only 5% of our total product cost, yet it drives all our costs. In addition, these rates give my design engineers incentives to "design out" direct labor by using machine technology. Yet, over the past years as we have had less and less direct labor, the overhead rate keeps going up and up. I won't be surprised if next year the rate is $2,000 per direct labor hour. I'm also concerned because small errors in our estimates of the direct labor content can have a large impact on our estimated costs. Just a 30-minute error in our estimate of assembly time is worth $750. Small mistakes in our direct labor time estimates really swing our bids around. I think this puts us at a disadvantage when we are going after business.

1. What is the engineer's concern about the overhead rate going "up and up"?
2. What did the engineer mean about the large overhead rate being a disadvantage when placing bids and seeking new business?
3. What do you think is a possible solution?

A10-6

Classifying costs

GROUP

With a group of students, visit a local copy and graphics shop or a pizza restaurant. As you observe the operation, consider the costs associated with running the business. As a group, identify as many costs as you can and classify them according to the following table headings:

Cost	Direct Materials	Direct Labor	Overhead	Selling Expense

A10-7

Just-in-time principles

Winter Comfort Inc. manufactures electric space heaters. While the CEO, Kevin Cross, is visiting the production facility, the following conversation takes place with the plant manager, Alicia Alvarez:

Kevin: As I walk around the facility, I can't help noticing all the materials inventories. What's going on?

Alicia: I have found our suppliers to be very unreliable in meeting their delivery commitments. Thus, I keep a lot of materials on hand so as to not risk running out and shutting down production.

Kevin: Not only do I see a lot of materials inventory, but there also seems to be a lot of finished goods inventory on hand. Why is this?

Alicia: As you know, I am evaluated on maintaining a low cost per unit. The one way that I am able to reduce my unit costs is by producing as many space heaters as possible. This allows me to spread my fixed costs over a larger base. When orders are down, the excess production builds up as inventory, as we are seeing now. But don't worry—I'm really keeping our costs down this way.

Kevin: I'm not so sure. It seems that this inventory must cost us something.

Alicia: Not really. I'll eventually use the materials and we'll eventually sell the finished goods. By keeping the plant busy, I'm using our plant assets wisely. This is reflected in the low unit costs that I'm able to maintain.

If you were Kevin Cross, how would you respond to Alicia Alvarez? What recommendations would you provide Alicia Alvarez?

Answers to Self-Examination Questions

1. **C** Sales salaries (answer C) is a selling expense and is not considered a cost of manufacturing a product. Direct materials cost (answer A), factory overhead cost (answer B), and direct labor cost (answer D) are costs of manufacturing a product.

2. **B** Depreciation of testing equipment (answer B) is included as part of the factory overhead costs of the computer manufacturer. The cost of memory chips (answer A) and the cost of disk drives (answer D) are both considered a part of direct materials cost. The wages of computer assemblers (answer C) are part of direct labor costs.

3. **B**

$$\text{Predetermined factory overhead rate} = \frac{\text{Estimated total factory overhead costs}}{\text{Estimated activity base}}$$

$$\text{Predetermined factory overhead rate} = \frac{\$420,000}{16,000 \text{ dlh}} = \$26.25$$

$$\text{Hours applied to the job:} \frac{\$3,000}{\$15 \text{ per hour}} = 200 \text{ hours}$$

Factory overhead applied to the job:

$$200 \text{ hours} \times \$26.25 = \$5,250$$

4. **B** If the amount of factory overhead applied during a particular period exceeds the actual overhead costs, the factory overhead account will have a negative balance and is said to be overapplied (answer B) or overabsorbed. If the amount applied is less than the actual costs, the account will have a positive balance and is said to be underapplied (answer A) or underabsorbed (answer C). Since an "estimated" predetermined overhead rate is used to apply overhead, a negative balance does not necessarily represent an error (answer D).

5. **B** The just-in-time philosophy embraces a product-oriented layout (answer A), making lead times short (answer C) and reducing setup times (answer D). Pull manufacturing, the opposite of push manufacturing (answer B), is also a just-in-time principle.

Cost Behavior and Cost-Volume-Profit Analysis

Learning Objectives

After studying this chapter, you should be able to:

Obj 1
Classify costs by their behavior as variable costs, fixed costs, or mixed costs.

Obj 2
Compute the contribution margin, the contribution margin ratio, and the unit contribution margin, and explain how they may be useful to managers.

Obj 3
Using the unit contribution margin, determine the break-even point and the volume necessary to achieve a target profit.

Obj 4
Using a cost-volume-profit chart and a profit-volume chart, determine the break-even point and the volume necessary to achieve a target profit.

Obj 5
Calculate the break-even point for a business selling more than one product.

Obj 6
Compute the operating leverage and the margin of safety, and explain how managers use these concepts.

Obj 7
List the assumptions underlying cost-volume-profit analysis.

What are the costs of operating your car? You will normally pay a license plate (tag) fee once a year. This cost does not change, regardless of the number of miles you drive. On the other hand, the total amount you spend on gasoline during the year changes on a day-to-day basis as you drive. The more you drive, the more you spend on gasoline.

How does such operating cost information affect you? Information on how your car's operating costs behave could be relevant in planning a summer vacation. For example, you might be trying to decide between taking an airline flight or driving your car to your vacation destination. In this case, your license plate fee and annual car insurance costs will not change, regardless of whether you drive your car or fly. Thus, these costs would not affect your decision. However, the estimated cost of gasoline and routine maintenance would affect your decision.

As in operating your car, all of the costs of operating a business do not behave in the same way. In this chapter, we discuss commonly used methods for classifying costs according to how they change. We also discuss how management uses cost-volume-profit analysis as a tool in making decisions.

Obj 1

Classify costs by their
behavior as variable costs,
fixed costs, or mixed costs.

Cost Behavior

Knowing how costs behave is useful to management for a variety of purposes. For example, knowing how costs behave allows managers to predict profits as sales and production volumes change. Knowing how costs behave is also useful for estimating costs. Estimated costs, in turn, affect a variety of management decisions, such as whether to use excess machine capacity to produce and sell a product at a reduced price.

Cost behavior refers to the manner in which a cost changes as a related activity changes. To understand cost behavior, two factors must be considered. First, we must identify the activities that are thought to relate to the cost incurred. Such activities are called **activity bases** (or *activity drivers*). Second, we must specify the range of activity over which the changes in the cost are of interest. This range of activity is called the **relevant range**.

To illustrate, hospital administrators must plan and control hospital food costs. To fully understand why food costs change, the activity that causes cost to be incurred must be identified. In the case of food costs, the feeding of patients is a major cause of these costs. The number of patients *treated* by the hospital would not be a good activity base, since some patients are outpatients who do not stay in the hospital. The number of patients who *stay* in the hospital, however, is a good activity base for studying food costs. Once the proper activity base is identified, food costs can then be analyzed over the range of the number of patients who normally stay in the hospital (the relevant range).

Three of the most common classifications of cost behavior are variable costs, fixed costs, and mixed costs.

Variable Costs

When the level of activity is measured in units produced, direct materials and direct labor costs are generally classified as variable costs. **Variable costs** are costs that vary in proportion to changes in the level of activity. For example, assume that Jason Inc. produces stereo sound systems under the brand name of J-Sound. The parts for the stereo systems are purchased from outside suppliers for $10 per unit and are assembled in Jason Inc.'s Waterloo plant. The direct materials costs for Model JS-12 for the relevant range of 5,000 to 30,000 units of production are as follows:

Number of Units of Model JS-12 Produced	Direct Materials Cost per Unit	Total Direct Materials Cost
5,000 units	$10	$ 50,000
10,000	10	100,000
15,000	10	150,000
20,000	10	200,000
25,000	10	250,000
30,000	10	300,000

Variable costs are the same per unit, while the total variable cost changes in proportion to changes in the activity base. For Model JS-12, for example, the direct materials cost for 10,000 units ($100,000) is twice the direct materials cost for 5,000 units ($50,000). The total direct materials cost varies in proportion to the number of units produced because the direct materials cost per unit ($10) is the same for all levels of production. Thus, producing 20,000 additional units of JS-12 will increase the direct materials cost by $200,000 (20,000 × $10), producing 25,000 additional units will increase the materials cost by $250,000, and so on.

Exhibit 1 illustrates how the variable costs for direct materials for Model JS-12 behave in total and on a per-unit basis as production changes.

EXHIBIT 1 *Variable Cost Graphs*

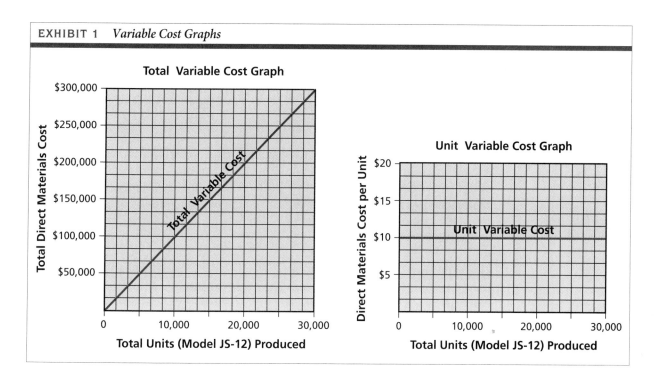

Managers use a variety of activity bases for evaluating cost behavior. The following list provides some examples of variable costs, along with their related activity bases for various types of businesses.

Type of Business	Cost	Activity Base
University	Instructor salaries	Number of classes
Passenger airline	Fuel	Number of miles flown
Manufacturing	Direct materials	Number of units produced
Hospital	Nurse wages	Number of patients
Hotel	Maid wages	Number of guests
Bank	Teller wages	Number of banking transactions

Fixed Costs

Fixed costs are costs that remain the same in total dollar amount as the level of activity changes. To illustrate, assume that Minton Inc. manufactures, bottles, and distributes La Fleur Perfume at its Los Angeles plant. The production supervisor at the Los Angeles plant is Jane Sovissi, who is paid a salary of $75,000 per year. The relevant range of activity for a year is 50,000 to 300,000 bottles of perfume. Sovissi's salary is a fixed cost that does not vary with the number of units produced. Regardless of the number of bottles produced within the range of 50,000 to 300,000 bottles, Sovissi receives a salary of $75,000.

Although the total fixed cost remains the same as the number of bottles produced changes, the fixed cost per bottle changes. As more bottles are produced, the total fixed costs are spread over a larger number of bottles, and thus the fixed cost per bottle decreases. This relationship is shown below for Jane Sovissi's $75,000 salary.

Number of Bottles of Perfume Produced	Total Salary for Jane Sovissi	Salary per Bottle of Perfume Produced
50,000 bottles	$75,000	$1.500
100,000	75,000	0.750
150,000	75,000	0.500
200,000	75,000	0.375
250,000	75,000	0.300
300,000	75,000	0.250

Exhibit 2 illustrates how the fixed cost of Jane Sovissi's salary behaves in total and on a per-unit basis as production changes. When units produced is the measure of activity, examples of fixed costs include straight-line depreciation of factory equipment, insurance on factory plant and equipment, and salaries of factory supervisors. Other examples of fixed costs and their activity bases for a variety of businesses are as follows:

Type of Business	Fixed Cost	Activity Base
University	Building depreciation	Number of students
Passenger airline	Airplane depreciation	Number of miles flown
Manufacturing	Plant manager salary	Number of units produced
Hospital	Property insurance	Number of patients
Hotel	Property taxes	Number of guests
Bank	Branch manager salary	Number of customer accounts

EXHIBIT 2 *Fixed Cost Graphs*

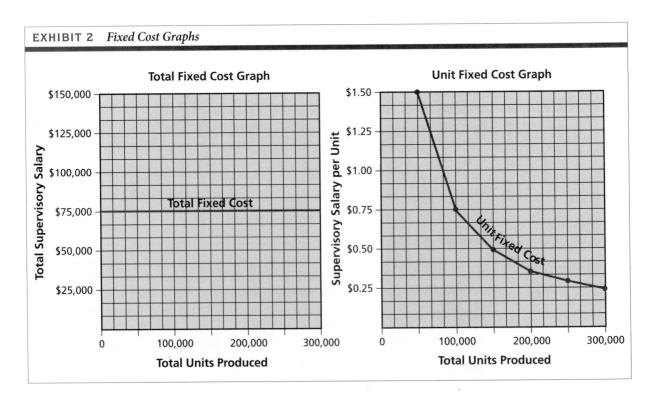

Mixed Costs

A **mixed cost** has characteristics of both a variable and a fixed cost. For example, over one range of activity, the total mixed cost may remain the same. It thus behaves as a fixed cost. Over another range of activity, the mixed cost may change in proportion to changes in the level of activity. It thus behaves as a variable cost. Mixed costs are sometimes called *semivariable* or *semifixed* costs.

To illustrate, assume that Simpson Inc. manufactures sails, using rented machinery. The rental charges are $15,000 per year, plus $1 for each machine hour used over 10,000 hours. If the machinery is used 8,000 hours, the total rental charge is $15,000. If the machinery is used 20,000 hours, the total rental charge is $25,000 [$15,000 + (10,000 hours × $1)], and so on. Thus, if the level of activity is measured in machine hours and the relevant range is 0 to 40,000 hours, the rental charges are a fixed cost up to 10,000 hours and a variable cost thereafter. This mixed cost behavior is shown graphically in Exhibit 3.

EXHIBIT 3   *Mixed Costs*

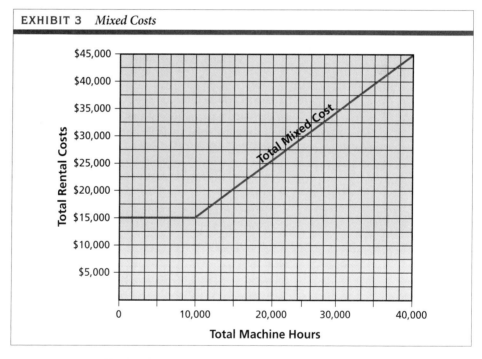

In analyses, mixed costs are usually separated into their fixed and variable components. The **high-low method** is a cost estimation technique that may be used for this purpose.[1] The high-low method uses the highest and lowest activity levels and their related costs to estimate the variable cost per unit and the fixed cost component of mixed costs.

To illustrate, assume that the Equipment Maintenance Department of Kason Inc. incurred the following costs during the past five months:

	Production	Total Cost
June	1,000 units	$45,550
July	1,500	52,000
August	2,100	61,500
September	1,800	57,500
October	750	41,250

[1]Other methods of estimating costs, such as the scattergraph method and the least squared method, are discussed in cost accounting textbooks.

The number of units produced is the measure of activity, and the number of units produced between June and October is the relevant range of production. For Kason Inc., the difference between the number of units produced and the difference between the total cost at the highest and lowest levels of production are as follows:

	Production	Total Cost
Highest level	2,100 units	$61,500
Lowest level	750	41,250
Difference	1,350 units	$20,250

Since the total fixed cost does not change with changes in volume of production, the $20,250 difference in the total cost is the change in the total variable cost. Hence, dividing the difference in the total cost by the difference in production provides an estimate of the variable cost per unit. For Kason Inc., this estimate is $15, as shown below.

$$\text{Variable cost per unit} = \frac{\text{Difference in total cost}}{\text{Difference in production}}$$

$$\text{Variable cost per unit} = \frac{\$20,250}{1,350 \text{ units}} = \$15$$

The fixed cost will be the same at both the highest and the lowest levels of production. Thus, the fixed cost can be estimated at either of these levels. This is done by subtracting the estimated total variable cost from the total cost, using the following total cost equation:

Total cost = (Variable cost per unit × Units of production) + Fixed cost

Highest level:
$61,500	= ($15 × 2,100 units) + Fixed cost
$61,500	= $31,500 + Fixed cost
$30,000	= Fixed cost

Lowest level:
$41,250	= ($15 × 750 units) + Fixed cost
$41,250	= $11,250 + Fixed cost
$30,000	= Fixed cost

The total equipment maintenance cost for Kason Inc. can thus be analyzed as a $30,000 fixed cost and a $15-per-unit variable cost. Using these amounts in the total cost equation, the total equipment maintenance cost at other levels of production can be estimated.

Summary of Cost Behavior Concepts

The following table summarizes the cost behavior attributes of variable costs and fixed costs:

Cost	Effect of Changing Activity Level	
	Total Amount	Per-Unit Amount
Variable	Increases and decreases proportionately with activity level.	Remains the same regardless of activity level.
Fixed	Remains the same regardless of activity level.	Increases and decreases inversely with activity level.

Examples of common variable, fixed, and mixed costs when the number of units produced is the activity base are:

Variable Cost	Fixed Cost	Mixed Cost
Direct materials	Depreciation expense	Quality Control Department salaries
Direct labor	Property taxes	Purchasing Department salaries
Electricity expense	Officer salaries	Maintenance expenses
Sales commissions	Insurance expense	Warehouse expenses

Mixed costs contain a fixed cost component that is incurred even if nothing is produced. For analyses, the fixed and variable cost components of mixed costs should be separated. Separating costs into their variable and fixed components for reporting purposes can be useful for decision making. One method of reporting variable and fixed costs is called **variable costing** or *direct costing*. Under variable costing, only the variable manufacturing costs (direct materials, direct labor, and variable factory overhead) are included in the product cost. The fixed factory overhead is an expense of the period in which it is incurred.

 Obj 2

Cost-Volume-Profit Relationships

Compute the contribution margin, the contribution margin ratio, and the unit contribution margin, and explain how they may be useful to managers.

After costs have been classified as fixed and variable, their effect on revenues, volume, and profits can be studied by using cost-volume-profit analysis. **Cost-volume-profit analysis** is the systematic examination of the relationships among selling prices, sales and production volume, costs, expenses, and profits.

Cost-volume-profit analysis provides management with useful information for decision making. For example, cost-volume-profit analysis may be used in setting selling prices, selecting the mix of products to sell, choosing among marketing strategies, and analyzing the effects of changes in costs on profits. In today's business environment, management must make such decisions quickly and accurately. As a result, the importance of cost-volume-profit analysis has increased in recent years.

Contribution Margin Concept

One relationship among cost, volume, and profit is the contribution margin. The **contribution margin** is the excess of sales revenues over variable costs. The contribution margin concept is especially useful in business planning because it gives insight into the profit potential of a firm. To illustrate, the income statement of Lambert Inc. in Exhibit 4 has been prepared in a contribution margin format.

EXHIBIT 4   *Contribution Margin Income Statement*

Sales	$1,000,000
Variable costs	600,000
Contribution margin	$ 400,000
Fixed costs	300,000
Income from operations	$ 100,000

The contribution margin of $400,000 is available to cover the fixed costs of $300,000. Once the fixed costs are covered, any remaining amount adds directly to the income

Contribution Margin

Income from Operations

FIXED COSTS

from operations of the company. Consider the graphic to the left. The fixed costs are a bucket and the contribution margin is water filling the bucket. Once the bucket is filled, the overflow represents income from operations. Up until the point of overflow, however, the contribution margin contributes to fixed costs (filling the bucket).

Contribution Margin Ratio The contribution margin can also be expressed as a percentage. The **contribution margin ratio**, sometimes called the *profit-volume ratio*, indicates the percentage of each sales dollar available to cover the fixed costs and to provide income from operations. For Lambert Inc., the contribution margin ratio is 40%, as computed below.

$$\text{Contribution margin ratio} = \frac{\text{Sales} - \text{Variable costs}}{\text{Sales}}$$

$$\text{Contribution margin ratio} = \frac{\$1,000,000 - \$600,000}{\$1,000,000} = 40\%$$

The contribution margin ratio measures the effect of an increase or a decrease in sales volume on income from operations. For example, assume that the management of Lambert Inc. is studying the effect of adding $80,000 in sales orders. Multiplying the contribution margin ratio (40%) by the change in sales volume ($80,000) indicates that income from operations will increase $32,000 if the additional orders are obtained. The validity of this analysis is illustrated by the following contribution margin income statement of Lambert Inc.:

Sales	$1,080,000
Variable costs ($1,080,000 × 60%)	648,000
Contribution margin ($1,080,000 × 40%)	$ 432,000
Fixed costs	300,000
Income from operations	$ 132,000

Variable costs as a percentage of sales are equal to 100% minus the contribution margin ratio. Thus, in the above income statement, the variable costs are 60% (100% − 40%) of sales, or $648,000 ($1,080,000 × 60%). The total contribution margin, $432,000, can also be computed directly by multiplying the sales by the contribution margin ratio ($1,080,000 × 40%).

In using the contribution margin ratio in analysis, factors other than sales volume, such as variable cost per unit and sales price, are assumed to remain constant. If such factors change, their effect must be considered.

The contribution margin ratio is also useful in setting business policy. For example, if the contribution margin ratio of a firm is large and production is at a level below 100% capacity, a large increase in income from operations can be expected from an increase in sales volume. A firm in such a position might decide to devote more effort to sales promotion because of the large change in income from operations that will result from changes in sales volume. In contrast, a firm with a small contribution margin ratio will probably want to give more attention to reducing costs before attempting to promote sales.

Unit Contribution Margin The unit contribution margin is also useful for analyzing the profit potential of proposed projects. The **unit contribution margin** is the sales price less the variable cost per unit. For example, if Lambert Inc.'s unit selling price is $20 and its unit variable cost is $12, the unit contribution margin is $8 ($20 – $12).

The *contribution margin ratio* is most useful when the increase or decrease in sales volume is measured in sales *dollars*. The *unit contribution margin* is most useful when the increase or decrease in sales volume is measured in sales *units* (quantities). To illustrate, assume that Lambert Inc. sold 50,000 units. Its income from operations is $100,000, as shown in the following contribution margin income statement:

Sales (50,000 units × $20)	$1,000,000
Variable costs (50,000 units × $12)	600,000
Contribution margin (50,000 units × $8)	$ 400,000
Fixed costs	300,000
Income from operations	$ 100,000

If Lambert Inc.'s sales could be increased by 15,000 units, from 50,000 units to 65,000 units, its income from operations would increase by $120,000 (15,000 units × $8), as shown below.

Sales (65,000 units × $20)	$1,300,000
Variable costs (65,000 units × $12)	780,000
Contribution margin (65,000 units × $8)	$ 520,000
Fixed costs	300,000
Income from operations	$ 220,000

Unit contribution margin analyses can provide useful information for managers. The preceding illustration indicates, for example, that Lambert could spend up to $120,000 for special advertising or other product promotions to increase sales by 15,000 units.

Mathematical Approach to Cost-Volume-Profit Analysis

Obj 3

Using the unit contribution margin, determine the break-even point and the volume necessary to achieve a target profit.

Accountants use various approaches for expressing the relationship of costs, sales (volume), and income from operations (operating profit). The mathematical approach is one approach that is used often in practice.

The mathematical approach to cost-volume-profit analysis uses equations (1) to determine the units of sales necessary to achieve the break-even point in operations or (2) to determine the units of sales necessary to achieve a target or desired profit. We will next describe and illustrate these equations and their use by management in profit planning.

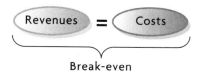

Break-Even Point

The **break-even point** is the level of operations at which a business's revenues and expired costs are exactly equal. At break-even, a business will have neither an income nor a loss from operations. The break-even point is useful in business planning, especially when expanding or decreasing operations.

To illustrate the computation of the break-even point, assume that the fixed costs for Barker Corporation are estimated to be $90,000. The unit selling price, unit variable cost, and unit contribution margin for Barker Corporation are as follows:

Unit selling price	$25
Unit variable cost	15
Unit contribution margin	$10

The break-even point is 9,000 units, which can be computed by using the following equation:

$$\text{Break-even sales (units)} = \frac{\text{Fixed costs}}{\text{Unit contribution margin}}$$

$$\text{Break-even sales (units)} = \frac{\$90,000}{\$10} = 9,000 \text{ units}$$

The following income statement verifies the preceding computation:

Sales (9,000 units × $25)	$225,000
Variable costs (9,000 units × $15)	135,000
Contribution margin	$ 90,000
Fixed costs	90,000
Income from operations	$ 0

The break-even point is affected by changes in the fixed costs, unit variable costs, and the unit selling price. Next, we will briefly describe the effect of each of these factors on the break-even point.

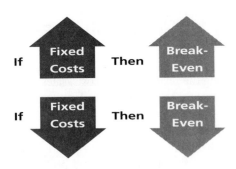

Effect of Changes in Fixed Costs Although fixed costs do not change in total with changes in the level of activity, they may change because of other factors. For example, changes in property tax rates or factory supervisors' salaries change fixed costs. Increases in fixed costs will raise the break-even point. Likewise, decreases in fixed costs will lower the break-even point.

To illustrate, assume that Bishop Co. is evaluating a proposal to budget an additional $100,000 for advertising. Fixed costs before the additional advertising are estimated at $600,000, and the unit contribution margin is $20. The break-even point before the additional expense is 30,000 units, computed as follows:

$$\text{Break-even sales (units)} = \frac{\text{Fixed costs}}{\text{Unit contribution margin}}$$

$$\text{Break-even sales (units)} = \frac{\$600,000}{\$20} = 30,000 \text{ units}$$

If the additional amount is spent, the fixed costs will increase by $100,000 and the break-even point will increase to 35,000 units, computed as follows:

$$\text{Break-even sales (units)} = \frac{\text{Fixed costs}}{\text{Unit contribution margin}}$$

$$\text{Break-even sales (units)} = \frac{\$700,000}{\$20} = 35,000 \text{ units}$$

The $100,000 increase in the fixed costs requires an additional 5,000 units ($100,000 ÷ $20) of sales to break even. In other words, an increase in sales of 5,000 units is required in order to generate an additional $100,000 of total contribution margin (5,000 units × $20) to cover the increased fixed costs.

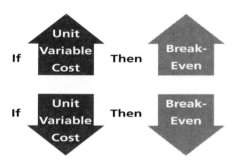

Effect of Changes in Unit Variable Costs Although unit variable costs are not affected by changes in volume of activity, they may be affected by other factors. For example, changes in the price of direct materials and the wages for factory workers providing direct labor will change unit variable costs. Increases in unit variable costs will raise the break-even point. Likewise, decreases in unit variable costs will lower the break-even point. For example, when fuel prices rise or decline, there is a direct impact on the break-even freight load for the ***Union Pacific*** railroad.

To illustrate, assume that Park Co. is evaluating a proposal to pay an additional 2% commission on sales to its salespeople as an incentive to increase sales. Fixed costs are estimated at $840,000, and the unit selling price, unit variable cost, and unit contribution margin before the additional 2% commission are as follows:

Unit selling price	$250
Unit variable cost	145
Unit contribution margin	$105

The break-even point is 8,000 units, computed as follows:

$$\text{Break-even sales (units)} = \frac{\text{Fixed costs}}{\text{Unit contribution margin}}$$

$$\text{Break-even sales (units)} = \frac{\$840,000}{\$105} = 8,000 \text{ units}$$

If the sales commission proposal is adopted, variable costs will increase by $5 per unit ($250 × 2%). This increase in the variable costs will decrease the unit contribution margin by $5 (from $105 to $100). Thus, the break-even point is raised to 8,400 units, computed as follows:

$$\text{Break-even sales (units)} = \frac{\text{Fixed costs}}{\text{Unit contribution margin}}$$

$$\text{Break-even sales (units)} = \frac{\$840,000}{\$100} = 8,400 \text{ units}$$

At the original break-even point of 8,000 units, the new unit contribution margin of $100 would provide only $800,000 to cover fixed costs of $840,000. Thus, an additional 400 units of sales will be required in order to provide the additional $40,000 (400 units × $100) contribution margin necessary to break even.

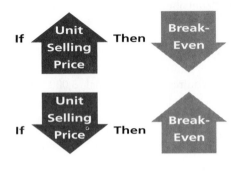

Effect of Changes in the Unit Selling Price   Increases in the unit selling price will lower the break-even point, while decreases in the unit selling price will raise the break-even point. To illustrate, assume that Graham Co. is evaluating a proposal to increase the unit selling price of its product from $50 to $60. The following data have been gathered:

	Current	*Proposed*
Unit selling price	$50	$60
Unit variable cost	30	30
Unit contribution margin	$20	$30
Total fixed costs	$600,000	$600,000

The break-even point based on the current selling price is 30,000 units, computed as follows:

$$\text{Break-even sales (units)} = \frac{\text{Fixed costs}}{\text{Unit contribution margin}}$$

$$\text{Break-even sales (units)} = \frac{\$600,000}{\$20} = 30,000 \text{ units}$$

If the selling price is increased by $10 per unit, the break-even point is decreased to 20,000 units, computed as follows:

$$\text{Break-even sales (units)} = \frac{\text{Fixed costs}}{\text{Unit contribution margin}}$$

$$\text{Break-even sales (units)} = \frac{\$600,000}{\$30} = 20,000 \text{ units}$$

The increase of $10 per unit in the selling price increases the unit contribution margin by $10. Thus, the break-even point decreases by 10,000 units (from 30,000 units to 20,000 units).

Summary of Effects of Changes on Break-Even Point   The break-even point in sales (units) moves in the same direction as changes in the variable cost per unit and fixed costs. In contrast, the break-even point in sales (units) moves in the opposite direction to changes in the sales price per unit. A summary of the impact of these changes on the break-even point in sales (units) is shown below.

Type of Change	*Direction of Change*	*Effect of Change on Break-Even Sales (Units)*
Fixed cost	Increase	Increase
	Decrease	Decrease
Variable cost per unit	Increase	Increase
	Decrease	Decrease
Unit sales price	Increase	Decrease
	Decrease	Increase

Target Profit

At the break-even point, sales and costs are exactly equal. However, the break-even point is not the goal of most businesses. Rather, managers seek to maximize profits. By modifying the break-even equation, the sales volume required to earn a target or desired amount of profit may be estimated. For this purpose, target profit is added to the break-even equation as shown below.

$$\text{Sales (units)} = \frac{\text{Fixed costs + Target profit}}{\text{Unit contribution margin}}$$

To illustrate, assume that fixed costs are estimated at $200,000, and the desired profit is $100,000. The unit selling price, unit variable cost, and unit contribution margin are as follows:

Unit selling price	$75
Unit variable cost	45
Unit contribution margin	$30

The sales volume necessary to earn the target profit of $100,000 is 10,000 units, computed as follows:

$$\text{Sales (units)} = \frac{\text{Fixed costs + \textbf{Target profit}}}{\text{Unit contribution margin}}$$

$$\text{Sales (units)} = \frac{\$200,000 + \mathbf{\$100,000}}{\$30} = 10,000 \text{ units}$$

The following income statement verifies this computation:

Sales (10,000 units × $75)	$750,000
Variable costs (10,000 units × $45)	450,000
Contribution margin (10,000 units × $30)	$300,000
Fixed costs	200,000
Income from operations	$100,000	← Target profit

INTEGRITY, OBJECTIVITY, AND ETHICS IN BUSINESS

Predicting Break-Even

The SEC requires management to provide forward-looking statements about known trends, events, or uncertainties impacting their business. These disclosures are required as part of the management discussion and analysis portion of the SEC annual report (10-K). Often, as part of these disclosures, companies operating with losses will predict when they anticipate to break even. For example, **Ford Motor Co.** stated in its 2001 annual report that "based on these [*vehicle demand assumptions*] and other assumptions (e.g., assumptions regarding marketing costs, which are expected to be higher in 2002), we expect 2002 earnings (excluding unusual items) to be about break even." (Emphasis added.)

Graphic Approach to Cost-Volume-Profit Analysis

Obj 4

Using a cost-volume-profit chart and a profit-volume chart, determine the break-even point and the volume necessary to achieve a target profit.

Cost-volume-profit analysis can be presented graphically as well as in equation form. Many managers prefer the graphic format because the income or loss from operations (operating profit or loss) for different levels of sales can readily be determined. Next, we describe two graphic approaches that managers find useful.

Cost-Volume-Profit (Break-Even) Chart

A **cost-volume-profit chart**, sometimes called a *break-even chart*, may assist management in understanding relationships among costs, sales, and operating profit or loss. To illustrate, the cost-volume-profit chart in Exhibit 5 is based on the following data:

Unit selling price	$50
Unit variable cost	30
Unit contribution margin	$20
Total fixed costs	$100,000

We constructed the cost-volume-profit chart in Exhibit 5 as follows:

A. Volume expressed in units of sales is indicated along the horizontal axis. The range of volume shown on the horizontal axis should reflect the *relevant range* in which the business expects to operate. Dollar amounts representing total sales and costs are indicated along the vertical axis.

B. A sales line is plotted by beginning at zero on the left corner of the graph. A second point is determined by multiplying any units of sales on the horizontal axis by the unit sales price of $50. For example, for 10,000 units of sales, the total

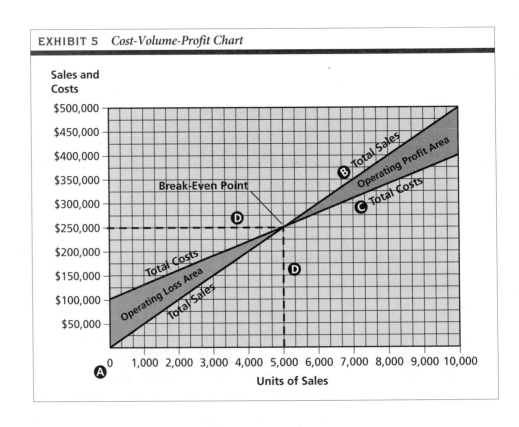

EXHIBIT 5 *Cost-Volume-Profit Chart*

sales would be $500,000 (10,000 units × $50). The sales line is drawn upward to the right from zero through the $500,000 point.

C. A cost line is plotted by beginning with total fixed costs, $100,000, on the vertical axis. A second point is determined by multiplying any units of sales on the horizontal axis by the unit variable costs and adding the fixed costs. For example, for 10,000 units of sales, the total estimated costs would be $400,000 [(10,000 units × $30) + $100,000]. The cost line is drawn upward to the right from $100,000 on the vertical axis through the $400,000 point.

D. Horizontal and vertical lines are drawn at the intersection point of the sales and cost lines, which is the break-even point, and the areas representing operating profit and operating loss are identified.

In Exhibit 5, the dotted lines drawn from the intersection point of the total sales line and the total cost line identify the break-even point in total sales dollars and units. The break-even point is $250,000 of sales, which represents a sales volume of 5,000 units. Operating profits will be earned when sales levels are to the right of the break-even point (operating profit area). Operating losses will be incurred when sales levels are to the left of the break-even point (operating loss area).

Changes in the unit selling price, total fixed costs, and unit variable costs can be analyzed by using a cost-volume-profit chart. Using the data in Exhibit 5, assume that a proposal to reduce fixed costs by $20,000 is to be evaluated. In this case, the total fixed costs would be $80,000 ($100,000 – $20,000). As shown in Exhibit 6, the total cost line should be redrawn, starting at the $80,000 point (total fixed costs) on the vertical axis. A second point is determined by multiplying any units of sales on the horizontal axis by the unit variable costs and adding the fixed costs. For example, for 10,000 units of sales, the total estimated costs would be $380,000 [(10,000 units × $30) + $80,000]. The cost line is drawn upward to the right from $80,000 on the vertical axis through the $380,000

EXHIBIT 6   *Revised Cost-Volume-Profit Chart*

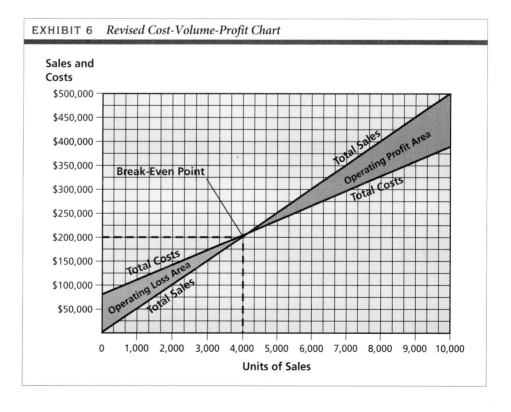

point. The revised cost-volume-profit chart in Exhibit 6 indicates that the break-even point decreases to $200,000 or 4,000 units of sales.

Profit-Volume Chart

Another graphic approach to cost-volume-profit analysis, the **profit-volume chart**, focuses on profits. This is in contrast to the cost-volume-profit chart, which focuses on sales and costs. The profit-volume chart plots only the difference between total sales and total costs (or profits). In this way, the profit-volume chart allows managers to determine the operating profit (or loss) for various levels of operations.

To illustrate, assume that the profit-volume chart in Exhibit 7 is based on the same data as used in Exhibit 5. These data are as follows:

Unit selling price	$50
Unit variable cost	30
Unit contribution margin	$20
Total fixed costs	$100,000

The maximum operating loss is equal to the fixed costs of $100,000. Assuming that the maximum unit sales within the relevant range is 10,000 units, the maximum operating profit is $100,000, computed as follows:

Sales (10,000 units × $50)	$500,000
Variable costs (10,000 units × $30)	300,000
Contribution margin (10,000 units × $20)	$200,000
Fixed costs	100,000
Operating profit	$100,000	← Maximum profit

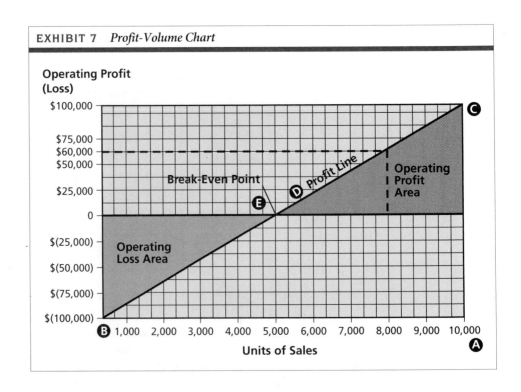

EXHIBIT 7   *Profit-Volume Chart*

We constructed the profit-volume chart in Exhibit 7 as follows:

A. Volume expressed in units of sales is indicated along the horizontal axis. The range of volume shown on the horizontal axis should reflect the *relevant range* in which the business expects to operate. In this illustration, the maximum number of sales units within the relevant range is assumed to be 10,000 units. Dollar amounts indicating operating profits and losses are shown along the vertical axis.

B. A point representing the maximum operating loss is plotted on the vertical axis at the left. This loss is equal to the total fixed costs at the zero level of sales.

C. A point representing the maximum operating profit within the relevant range is plotted on the right.

D. A diagonal profit line is drawn connecting the maximum operating loss point with the maximum operating profit point.

E. The profit line intersects the horizontal zero operating profit line at the break-even point expressed in units of sales, and the areas indicating operating profit and loss are identified.

In Exhibit 7, the break-even point is 5,000 units of sales, which is equal to total sales of $250,000 (5,000 units × $50). Operating profit will be earned when sales levels are to the right of the break-even point (operating profit area). Operating losses will be incurred when sales levels are to the left of the break-even point (operating loss area). For example, at sales of 8,000 units, an operating profit of $60,000 will be earned, as shown in Exhibit 7.

The effect of changes in the unit selling price, total fixed costs, and unit variable costs on profit can be analyzed using a profit-volume chart. To illustrate, using the data in Exhibit 7, we will evaluate the effect on profit of an increase of $20,000 in fixed costs. In this case, the total fixed costs would be $120,000 ($100,000 + $20,000), and the maximum operating loss would also be $120,000. If the maximum sales within the relevant range is 10,000 units, the maximum operating profit would be $80,000, computed as follows:

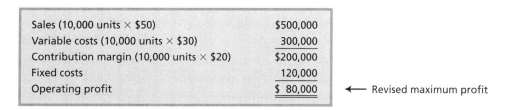

Sales (10,000 units × $50)	$500,000
Variable costs (10,000 units × $30)	300,000
Contribution margin (10,000 units × $20)	$200,000
Fixed costs	120,000
Operating profit	$ 80,000

⟵ Revised maximum profit

A revised profit-volume chart is constructed by plotting the maximum operating loss and maximum operating profit points and drawing the revised profit line. The original and the revised profit-volume charts are shown in Exhibit 8.

The revised profit-volume chart indicates that the break-even point is 6,000 units of sales. This is equal to total sales of $300,000 (6,000 units × $50). The operating loss area of the chart has increased, while the operating profit area has decreased under the proposed change in fixed costs.

Use of Computers in Cost-Volume-Profit Analysis

With computers, the graphic approach and the mathematical approach to cost-volume-profit analysis are easy to use. Managers can vary assumptions regarding selling prices, costs, and volume and can immediately see the effects of each change on the break-even point and profit. Such an analysis is called a *"what if"* analysis or *sensitivity analysis*.

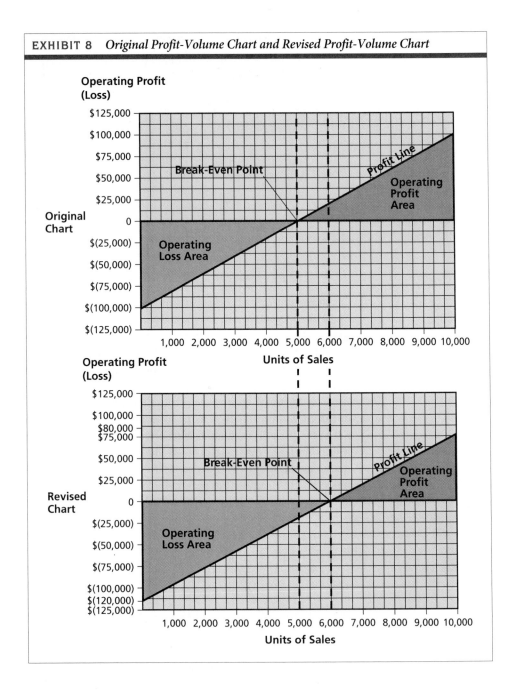

EXHIBIT 8   *Original Profit-Volume Chart and Revised Profit-Volume Chart*

Sales Mix Considerations

Obj 5

Calculate the break-even point for a business selling more than one product.

In most businesses, more than one product is sold at varying selling prices. In addition, the products often have different unit variable costs, and each product makes a different contribution to profits. Thus, the sales volume necessary to break even or to earn a target profit for a business selling two or more products depends upon the sales mix. The **sales mix** is the relative distribution of sales among the various products sold by a business.

To illustrate the calculation of the break-even point for a company that sells more than one product, assume that Cascade Company sold 8,000 units of Product A and

2,000 units of Product B during the past year. The sales mix for products A and B can be expressed as percentages (80% and 20%) or as a ratio (80:20).

Cascade Company's fixed costs are $200,000. The unit selling prices, unit variable costs, and unit contribution margins for products A and B are as follows:

20%
Product
B

80%
Product
A

Sales Mix

Product	Unit Selling Price	Unit Variable Cost	Unit Contribution Margin
A	$ 90	$70	$20
B	140	95	45

In computing the break-even point, it is useful to think of the individual products as components of one overall enterprise product. For Cascade Company, this overall enterprise product is called E. We can think of the unit selling price of E as equal to the total of the unit selling prices of products A and B, multiplied by their sales mix percentages. Likewise, we can think of the unit variable cost and unit contribution margin of E as equal to the total of the unit variable costs and unit contribution margins of products A and B, multiplied by the sales mix percentages. These computations are as follows:

Unit selling price of E: ($90 × 0.8) + ($140 × 0.2) = $100
Unit variable cost of E: ($70 × 0.8) + ($ 95 × 0.2) = $ 75
Unit contribution margin of E: ($20 × 0.8) + ($ 45 × 0.2) = $ 25

The break-even point of 8,000 units of E can be determined in the normal manner as follows:

$$\text{Break-even sales (units)} = \frac{\text{Fixed costs}}{\text{Unit contribution margin}}$$

$$\text{Break-even sales (units)} = \frac{\$200,000}{\$25} = 8,000 \text{ units}$$

Since the sales mix for products A and B is 80% and 20%, the break-even quantity of A is 6,400 units (8,000 units × 80%) and B is 1,600 units (8,000 units × 20%). This analysis can be verified in the following income statement:

	Product A	Product B	Total
Sales:			
6,400 units × $90	$576,000		$576,000
1,600 units × $140		$224,000	224,000
Total sales	$576,000	$224,000	$800,000
Variable costs:			
6,400 units × $70	$448,000		$448,000
1,600 units × $95		$152,000	152,000
Total variable costs	$448,000	$152,000	$600,000
Contribution margin	$128,000	$ 72,000	$200,000
Fixed costs			200,000
Income from operations			$ 0	← Break-even point

The effects of changes in the sales mix on the break-even point can be determined by repeating this analysis, assuming a different sales mix.

Obj **6**

Compute the operating leverage and the margin of safety, and explain how managers use these concepts.

Special Cost-Volume-Profit Relationships

Some additional relationships useful to managers can be developed from cost-volume-profit data. Two of these relationships are the operating leverage and the margin of safety.

Operating Leverage

The relative mix of a business's variable costs and fixed costs is measured by the **operating leverage**. It is computed as follows:

$$\text{Operating leverage} = \frac{\text{Contribution margin}}{\text{Income from operations}}$$

Since the difference between contribution margin and income from operations is fixed costs, companies with large amounts of fixed costs will generally have a high operating leverage. Thus, companies in capital-intensive industries, such as the airline and automotive industries, will generally have a high operating leverage. A low operating leverage is normal for companies in industries that are labor-intensive, such as professional services.

Managers can use operating leverage to measure the impact of changes in sales on income from operations. A high operating leverage indicates that a small increase in sales will yield a large percentage increase in income from operations. In contrast, a low operating leverage indicates that a large increase in sales is necessary to significantly increase income from operations. To illustrate, assume the following operating data for Jones Inc. and Wilson Inc.:

	Jones Inc.	Wilson Inc.
Sales	$400,000	$400,000
Variable costs	300,000	300,000
Contribution margin	$100,000	$100,000
Fixed costs	80,000	50,000
Income from operations	$ 20,000	$ 50,000

Both companies have the same sales, the same variable costs, and the same contribution margin. Jones Inc. has larger fixed costs than Wilson Inc. and, as a result, a lower income from operations and a higher operating leverage. The operating leverage for each company is computed as follows:

Jones Inc.	*Wilson Inc.*
$\text{Operating leverage} = \dfrac{\$100,000}{\$20,000} = 5$	$\text{Operating leverage} = \dfrac{\$100,000}{\$50,000} = 2$

Jones Inc.'s operating leverage indicates that, for each percentage point change in sales, income from operations will change five times that percentage. In contrast, for each percentage point change in sales, the income from operations of Wilson Inc. will change only two times that percentage. For example, if sales increased by 10% ($40,000) for each company, income from operations will increase by 50% (10% × 5), or $10,000 (50% × $20,000), for Jones Inc. The sales increase of $40,000 will increase income from operations by only 20% (10% × 2), or $10,000 (20% × $50,000), for Wilson Inc. The validity of this analysis is shown as follows:

	Jones Inc.	Wilson Inc.
Sales	$440,000	$440,000
Variable costs	330,000	330,000
Contribution margin	$110,000	$110,000
Fixed costs	80,000	50,000
Income from operations	$ 30,000	$ 60,000

For Jones Inc., even a small increase in sales will generate a large percentage increase in income from operations. Thus, Jones's managers may be motivated to think of ways to increase sales. In contrast, Wilson's managers might attempt to increase operating leverage by reducing variable costs and thereby change the cost structure.

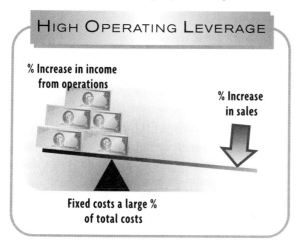

HIGH OPERATING LEVERAGE

% Increase in income from operations

% Increase in sales

Fixed costs a large % of total costs

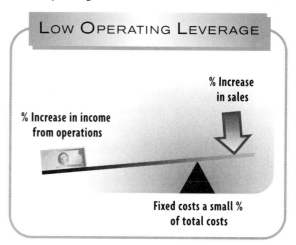

LOW OPERATING LEVERAGE

% Increase in sales

% Increase in income from operations

Fixed costs a small % of total costs

Operating Leverage in the Airline Industry

The commercial airline industry has high operating leverage. The annual fixed costs of the airplanes, ground facilities, and service network are high relative to the variable costs, such as fuel. Thus, when this industry operates above break-even, it is very profitable; however, at below break-even, the industry generates large losses. To help assess the break-even point, **Delta Air Lines Inc.** provided the following disclosure in its annual report to the Securities and Exchange Commission (10-K):

	2006	*2005*
Passenger load factor	78.5%	76.5%
Break-even passenger load factor	78.2%	87.0%

As can be seen from the preceding data, Delta's passenger load factor increased slightly from 2005 to 2006. In addition, the break-even passenger load factor decreased from 87.0% to 78.2%, a decrease of 8.8%. This decrease was caused by Delta's cost cutting efforts and fare increases.

Margin of Safety

The difference between the current sales revenue and the sales at break-even point is called the **margin of safety**. It indicates the possible decrease in sales that may occur before an operating loss results. For example, if the margin of safety is low, even a small decline in sales revenue may result in an operating loss.

If sales are $250,000, the unit selling price is $25, and sales at the break-even point are $200,000, the margin of safety is 20%, computed as follows:

$$\text{Margin of safety} = \frac{\text{Sales} - \text{Sales at break-even point}}{\text{Sales}}$$

$$\text{Margin of safety} = \frac{\$250,000 - \$200,000}{\$250,000} = 20\%$$

The margin of safety may also be stated in terms of units. In this illustration, for example, the margin of safety of 20% is equivalent to $50,000 ($250,000 × 20%). In units, the margin of safety is 2,000 units ($50,000 ÷ $25). Thus, the current sales of $250,000 may decline $50,000 or 2,000 units before an operating loss occurs.

Assumptions of Cost-Volume-Profit Analysis

Obj **7**

List the assumptions underlying cost-volume-profit analysis.

The reliability of cost-volume-profit analysis depends upon the validity of several assumptions. The primary assumptions are as follows:

1. Total sales and total costs can be represented by straight lines.
2. Within the relevant range of operating activity, the efficiency of operations does not change.
3. Costs can be accurately divided into fixed and variable components.
4. The sales mix is constant.
5. There is no change in the inventory quantities during the period.

These assumptions simplify cost-volume-profit analysis. Since they are often valid for the relevant range of operations, cost-volume-profit analysis is useful to decision making.[2]

HOW BUSINESSES MAKE MONEY

Managing the Power Stack

Electric utility companies, such as ***Duke Energy Corporation***, generate electricity by using a variety of means, such as nuclear, coal, and oil/gas generating facilities. Power companies manage their various power generation resources to match the demand for power, using what is termed the "power stack." The power stack matches demand for power by arranging generating facilities in the order of cost per kilowatt-hour. The least cost per kilowatt-hour facilities satisfy initial demand at the bottom of the stack, while the highest cost per kilowatt-hour power sources are placed at the top of the stack for peak loads, as illustrated below.

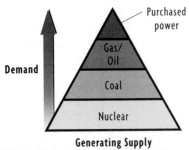

Generating Supply

The lowest cost facilities form what is termed "base load." If the power company uses nuclear power facilities,

these will often be placed in base load. Nuclear power plants have a high fixed cost but a low variable fuel cost. These facilities are very efficient at high utilization levels; thus, they form the base of the power stack. As demand increases, power generation facilities with lower fixed costs and higher variable fuel costs are switched on. Coal plants are usually next in the stack, followed by gas- or oil-fired turbines. Last, during the peak demands of summer, the power company may be required to purchase electricity in the power market. This power is usually the most expensive power available, but it is also the most flexible because it requires no fixed costs.

Managing power generating resources in this way gives management the ability to price electricity to customers according to the time of day they demand power. For example, a factory willing to run during the night can receive a price discount because power generated during the lower-demand night hours comes from lower in the power stack. Likewise, when a power company sells electricity in the power market, management must know the stack location for the power sales in order to remain profitable.

As the U.S. power market becomes more deregulated, a company's understanding of its power stack will become critical to business success.

---

[2]The impact of violating these assumptions is discussed in advanced accounting texts.

Key Points

1. **Classify costs by their behavior as variable costs, fixed costs, or mixed costs.**

   Cost behavior refers to the manner in which a cost changes as a related activity changes. Variable costs are costs that vary in total in proportion to changes in the level of activity. Fixed costs are costs that remain the same in total dollar amount as the level of activity changes. A mixed cost has attributes of both a variable and a fixed cost.

2. **Compute the contribution margin, the contribution margin ratio, and the unit contribution margin, and explain how they may be useful to managers.**

   The contribution margin concept is useful in business planning because it gives insight into the profit potential of a firm. The contribution margin is the excess of sales revenues over variable costs. The contribution margin ratio is computed as follows:

   $$\textbf{Contribution margin ratio} = \frac{\textbf{Sales} - \textbf{Variable costs}}{\textbf{Sales}}$$

   The unit contribution margin is the excess of the unit selling price over the unit variable cost.

3. **Using the unit contribution margin, determine the break-even point and the volume necessary to achieve a target profit.**

   The mathematical approach to cost-volume-profit analysis uses the unit contribution margin concept and the following equations to determine the break-even point and the volume necessary to achieve a target profit for a business:

   $$\textbf{Break-even sales (units)} = \frac{\textbf{Fixed costs}}{\textbf{Unit contribution margin}}$$

   $$\textbf{Sales (units)} = \frac{\textbf{Fixed costs} + \textbf{Target profit}}{\textbf{Unit contribution margin}}$$

4. **Using a cost-volume-profit chart and a profit-volume chart, determine the break-even point and the volume necessary to achieve a target profit.**

   A cost-volume-profit chart focuses on the relationships among costs, sales, and operating profit or loss. Preparing and using a cost-volume-profit chart to determine the break-even point and the volume

necessary to achieve a target profit are illustrated in this chapter.

   The profit-volume chart focuses on profits rather than on revenues and costs. Preparing and using a profit-volume chart to determine the break-even point and the volume necessary to achieve a target profit are illustrated in this chapter.

5. **Calculate the break-even point for a business selling more than one product.**

   Calculating the break-even point for a business selling two or more products is based on a specified sales mix. Given the sales mix, the break-even point can be computed, using the methods illustrated for Cascade Company in this chapter.

6. **Compute the operating leverage and the margin of safety, and explain how managers use these concepts.**

   Operating leverage is computed as follows:

   $$\textbf{Operating leverage} = \frac{\textbf{Contribution margin}}{\textbf{Income from operations}}$$

   Operating leverage is useful in measuring the impact of changes in sales on income from operations without preparing formal income statements. For example, a high operating leverage indicates that a small increase in sales will yield a large percentage increase in income from operations.

   The margin of safety as a percentage of current sales is computed as follows:

   $$\textbf{Margin of safety} = \frac{\textbf{Sales} - \textbf{Sales at break-even point}}{\textbf{Sales}}$$

   The margin of safety is useful in evaluating past operations and in planning future operations. For example, if the margin of safety is low, even a small decline in sales revenue will result in an operating loss.

7. **List the assumptions underlying cost-volume-profit analysis.**

   The primary assumptions underlying cost-volume-profit analysis are as follows:

   1. Total sales and total costs can be represented by straight lines.
   2. Within the relevant range of operating activity, the efficiency of operations does not change.

3. Costs can be accurately divided into fixed and variable components.
4. The sales mix is constant.

5. There is no change in the inventory quantities during the period.

Key Terms

Activity bases (drivers)

Break-even point

Contribution margin

Contribution margin ratio

Cost behavior

Cost-volume-profit analysis

Cost-volume-profit chart

Fixed costs

High-low method

Margin of safety

Mixed cost

Operating leverage

Profit-volume chart

Relevant range

Sales mix

Unit contribution margin

Variable costing

Variable costs

Illustrative Problem

Wyatt Inc. expects to maintain the same inventories at the end of the year as at the beginning of the year. The estimated fixed costs for the year are $288,000, and the estimated variable costs per unit are $14. It is expected that 60,000 units will be sold at a price of $20 per unit. Maximum sales within the relevant range are 70,000 units.

Instructions

1. What is (a) the contribution margin ratio and (b) the unit contribution margin?
2. Determine the break-even point in units.
3. Construct a cost-volume-profit chart, indicating the break-even point.
4. Construct a profit-volume chart, indicating the break-even point.
5. What is the margin of safety?

Solution

1. a. $\text{Contribution margin ratio} = \dfrac{\text{Sales} - \text{Variable costs}}{\text{Sales}}$

$$\text{Contribution margin ratio} = \dfrac{(60{,}000 \text{ units} \times \$20) - (60{,}000 \text{ units} \times \$14)}{(60{,}000 \text{ units} \times \$20)}$$

$$\text{Contribution margin ratio} = \dfrac{\$1{,}200{,}000 - \$840{,}000}{\$1{,}200{,}000} = \dfrac{\$360{,}000}{\$1{,}200{,}000}$$

$\text{Contribution margin ratio} = 30\%$

   b. Unit contribution margin = Unit selling price − Unit variable costs

   Unit contribution margin = $20 − $14 = $6

2. $\text{Break-even sales (units)} = \dfrac{\text{Fixed costs}}{\text{Unit contribution margin}}$

$$\text{Break-even sales (units)} = \dfrac{\$288{,}000}{\$6} = 48{,}000 \text{ units}$$

3. **Sales and Costs**

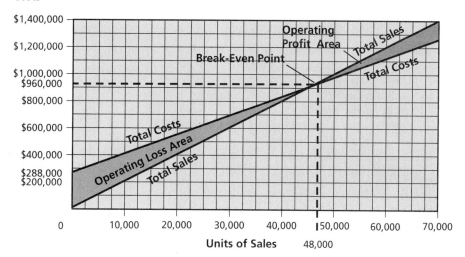

4. **Operating Profit (Loss)**

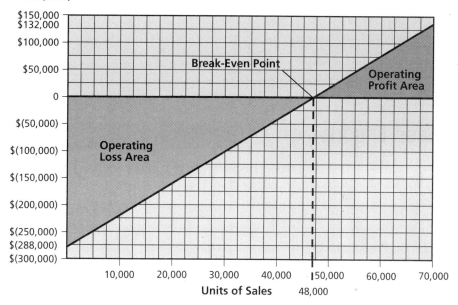

5. Margin of safety:

Expected sales (60,000 units × $20)	$1,200,000
Break-even point (48,000 units × $20)	960,000
Margin of safety	$ 240,000

or

$$\text{Margin of safety} = \frac{\text{Sales} - \text{Sales at break-even point}}{\text{Sales}}$$

$$\text{Margin of safety} = \frac{\$240,000}{\$1,200,000} = 20\%$$

Self-Examination Questions   *(Answers appear at end of chapter.)*

1. Which of the following statements describes variable costs?
   A. Costs that vary on a per-unit basis as the level of activity changes.
   B. Costs that vary in total in direct proportion to changes in the level of activity.
   C. Costs that remain the same in total dollar amount as the level of activity changes.
   D. Costs that vary on a per-unit basis, but remain the same in total as the level of activity changes.

2. If sales are $500,000, variable costs are $200,000, and fixed costs are $240,000, what is the contribution margin ratio?
   A. 40%   C. 52%
   B. 48%   D. 60%

3. If the unit selling price is $16, the unit variable cost is $12, and fixed costs are $160,000, what are the break-even sales (units)?

   A. 5,714 units   C. 13,333 units
   B. 10,000 units   D. 40,000 units

4. Based on the data presented in Question 3, how many units of sales would be required to realize income from operations of $20,000?
   A. 11,250 units   C. 40,000 units
   B. 35,000 units   D. 45,000 units

5. Based on the following operating data, what is the operating leverage?

Sales	$600,000
Variable costs	240,000
Contribution margin	$360,000
Fixed costs	160,000
Income from operations	$200,000

   A. 0.8   C. 1.8
   B. 1.2   D. 4.0

Class Discussion Questions

1. Describe how total variable costs and unit variable costs behave with changes in the level of activity.

2. How would each of the following costs be classified if units produced is the activity base?
   a. Direct labor costs
   b. Direct materials cost
   c. Electricity costs of $0.20 per kilowatt-hour

3. Describe the behavior of (a) total fixed costs and (b) unit fixed costs as the level of activity increases.

4. How would each of the following costs be classified if units produced is the activity base?
   a. Straight-line depreciation of plant and equipment
   b. Salary of factory supervisor ($80,000 per year)
   c. Property insurance premiums of $5,000 per month on plant and equipment

5. In cost analyses, how are mixed costs treated?

6. Which of the following graphs illustrates how total variable costs behave with changes in total units produced?

(a)

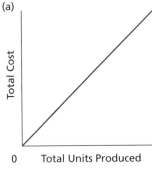

(b)

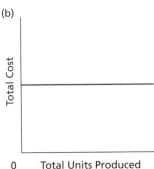

7. Which of the following graphs illustrates how unit variable costs behave with changes in total units produced?

(a)

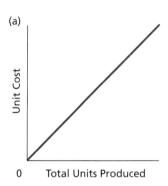

0   Total Units Produced

(b)

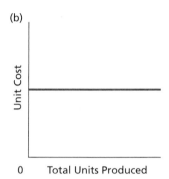

0   Total Units Produced

8. Which of the following graphs best illustrates fixed costs per unit as the activity base changes?

(a)

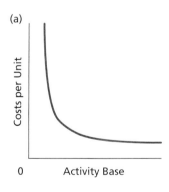

0   Activity Base

(b)

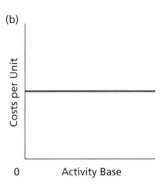

0   Activity Base

9. In applying the high-low method of cost estimation, how is the total fixed cost estimated?

10. If fixed costs increase, what would be the impact on the (a) contribution margin? (b) income from operations?

11. An examination of the accounting records of Hudson Company disclosed a high contribution margin ratio and production at a level below maximum capacity. Based on this information, suggest a likely means of improving income from operations. Explain.

12. If the unit cost of direct materials is decreased, what effect will this change have on the break-even point?

13. If insurance rates are increased, what effect will this change in fixed costs have on the break-even point?

14. Both Stratton Company and Callahan Company had the same sales, total costs, and income from operations for the current fiscal year; yet Stratton Company had a lower break-even point than Callahan Company. Explain the reason for this difference in break-even points.

15. How does the sales mix affect the calculation of the break-even point?

16. What does operating leverage measure, and how is it computed?

17. The reliability of cost-volume-profit (CVP) analysis depends upon several key assumptions. What are those primary assumptions?

Exercises

E11-1

Classify costs

Obj 1

Following is a list of various costs incurred in producing frozen pizzas. With respect to the production and sale of frozen pizzas, classify each cost as either variable, fixed, or mixed.

1. Property insurance premiums, $1,500 per month plus $0.005 for each dollar of property over $3,000,000
2. Packaging
3. Hourly wages of inspectors

(continued)

4. Pension cost, $0.50 per employee hour on the job
5. Hourly wages of machine operators
6. Rent on warehouse, $5,000 per month plus $5 per square foot of storage used
7. Refrigerant used in refrigeration equipment
8. Pepperoni
9. Dough
10. Tomato paste
11. Property taxes, $50,000 per year on factory building and equipment
12. Electricity costs, $0.08 per kilowatt-hour
13. Salary of plant manager
14. Straight-line depreciation on the production equipment
15. Janitorial costs, $3,000 per month

E11-2

Identify cost graphs

Obj 1

The following cost graphs illustrate various types of cost behavior:

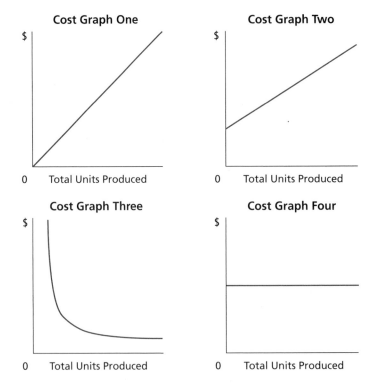

For each of the following costs, identify the cost graph that best illustrates its cost behavior as the number of units produced increases.

a. Per-unit direct labor cost
b. Salary of quality control supervisor, $5,000 per month
c. Total direct materials cost
d. Electricity costs of $3,000 per month plus $0.05 per kilowatt-hour
e. Per-unit cost of straight-line depreciation on factory equipment

E11-3

Identify activity bases

Obj 1

For a major university, match each cost in the following table with the activity base most appropriate to it. An activity base may be used more than once, or not used at all.

Cost:	Activity Base:
1. Financial aid office salaries	a. Number of enrolled students and alumni
2. Instructor salaries	b. Student credit hours
3. Housing personnel wages	c. Number of student/athletes
4. Admissions office salaries	d. Number of enrollment applications
5. School supplies	e. Number of students living on campus
6. Record office salaries	f. Number of financial aid applications

E11-4

Identify activity bases

Obj 1

From the following list of activity bases for an automobile dealership, select the base that would be most appropriate for each of these costs: (1) preparation costs (cleaning, oil, and gasoline costs) for each car received, (2) salespersons' commission of 3% of the sales price for each car sold, and (3) administrative costs for ordering cars.

a. Dollar amount of cars on hand	e. Number of cars ordered
b. Dollar amount of cars received	f. Number of cars sold
c. Dollar amount of cars sold	g. Number of cars on hand
d. Dollar amount of cars ordered	h. Number of cars received

E11-5

Identify fixed and variable costs

Obj 1

Intuit Inc. develops and sells software products for the personal finance market, including popular titles such as Quicken® and TurboTax®. Classify each of the following costs and expenses for this company as either variable or fixed to the number of units produced and sold:

a. Straight-line depreciation of computer equipment
b. Sales commissions
c. Television advertising campaign
d. Packaging costs
e. CDs
f. Shipping expenses
g. Salaries of customer support personnel
h. Salaries of software developers
i. Wages of telephone order assistants
j. User's guides
k. President's salary
l. Property taxes on general offices

E11-6

Relevant range and fixed and variable costs

Obj 1

✓ a. $0.40

Laser Tex Inc. manufactures low-end computer components within a relevant range of 100,000 to 140,000 disks per year. Within this range, the following partially completed manufacturing cost schedule has been prepared:

CDs produced	100,000	120,000	140,000
Total costs:			
Total variable costs	$ 40,000	(d)	(j)
Total fixed costs	84,000	(e)	(k)
Total costs	$124,000	(f)	(l)
Cost per unit:			
Variable cost per unit	(a)	(g)	(m)
Fixed cost per unit	(b)	(h)	(n)
Total cost per unit	(c)	(i)	(o)

Complete the cost schedule, identifying each cost by the appropriate letter (a) through (o).

E11-7

High-low method

Obj 1

✓ a. $10.00 per unit

[handwritten: TC = FC + VC]

W & O Inc. has decided to use the high-low method to estimate the total cost and the fixed and variable cost components of the total cost. The data for various levels of production are as follows:

Units Produced	Total Costs
10,000	$750,000
22,500	845,000
30,000	950,000

[handwritten: low - VC = 950,000 - 750,000 / 30,000 - 10,000 = 10; high]

a. Determine the variable cost per unit and the fixed cost.
b. Based on part (a), estimate the total cost for 25,000 units of production.

E11-8

High-low method for service company

Obj 1

✓ Fixed cost, $250,000

Great Plains Railroad decided to use the high-low method and operating data from the past six months to estimate the fixed and variable components of transportation costs. The activity base used by Great Plains Railroad is a measure of railroad operating activity, termed "gross-ton miles," which is the total number of tons multiplied by the miles moved.

	Transportation Costs	Gross-Ton Miles
January	$1,050,000	285,000
February	1,150,000	325,000
March	1,350,000	400,000
April	1,000,000	250,000
May	1,225,000	375,000
June	1,600,000	450,000

Determine the variable cost per gross-ton mile and the fixed cost.

E11-9

Contribution margin ratio

Obj 2

✓ a. 55%

a. Spock Company budgets sales of $840,000, fixed costs of $378,000, and variable costs of $378,000. What is the contribution margin ratio for Spock Company?
b. If the contribution margin ratio for Kirk Company is 34%, sales were $600,000, and fixed costs were $175,000, what was the income from operations?

E11-10

Contribution margin and contribution margin ratio

Obj 2

✓ b. 34.00%

For a recent year, *McDonald's* had the following sales and expenses (in millions):

Sales	$15,352
Food and packaging	$ 5,204
Payroll	4,040
Occupancy (rent, depreciation, etc.)	1,022
General, selling, and administrative expenses	2,220
	$12,486
Income from operations	$ 2,866

Assume that the variable costs consist of food and packaging, payroll, and 40% of the general, selling, and administrative expenses.

a. What is McDonald's contribution margin? Round to the nearest million.
b. What is McDonald's contribution margin ratio? Round to two decimal places.
c. How much would income from operations increase if same-store sales increased by $450 million for the coming year, with no change in the contribution margin ratio or fixed costs?

E11-11

Break-even sales and sales to realize income from operations

Obj 3

✓ b. 20,435 units

For the current year ending March 31, Zing Company expects fixed costs of $425,750, a unit variable cost of $40, and a unit selling price of $65.

a. Compute the anticipated break-even sales (units).
b. Compute the sales (units) required to realize income from operations of $85,125.

E11-12

Break-even sales

Obj 3

✓ a. 74,884,566 barrels

Anheuser-Busch Companies, Inc., reported the following operating information for a recent year (in millions):

Net sales	$14,935
Cost of goods sold	$ 8,983
Marketing and distribution	2,590
	$11,573
Income from operations	$ 3,362*

*Before special items

In addition, Anheuser-Busch sold 136 million barrels of beer during the year. Assume that variable costs were 70% of the cost of goods sold and 45% of marketing and distribution expenses. Assume that the remaining costs are fixed. For the following year, assume that Anheuser-Busch expects pricing, variable costs per barrel, and fixed costs to remain constant, except that new distribution and general office facilities are expected to increase fixed costs by $133 million.

Rounding to the nearest cent:

a. Compute the break-even sales (barrels) for the current year.
b. Compute the anticipated break-even sales (barrels) for the following year.

E11-13

Break-even sales

Obj 3

✓ a. 9,600 units

Currently, the unit selling price of a product is $300, the unit variable cost is $225, and the total fixed costs are $720,000. A proposal is being evaluated to increase the unit selling price to $345.

a. Compute the current break-even sales (units).
b. Compute the anticipated break-even sales (units), assuming that the unit selling price is increased and all costs remain constant.

E11-14

Break-even analysis

Obj 3

The Junior League of Tampa, Florida, collected recipes from members and published a cookbook entitled *Life of the Party*. The book will sell for $22 per copy. The chairwoman of the cookbook development committee estimated that the league needed to sell 16,000 books to break even on its $140,000 investment. What is the variable cost per unit assumed in the Junior League's analysis? Round to the nearest cent.

E11-15

Break-even analysis

Obj 3

The America Online division of **Time Warner** has fueled its growth by using aggressive promotion strategies. One of these strategies is to send compact disk software to potential customers, offering free AOL service for a period of time. Assume that during a given promotional campaign, AOL mailed 3,200,000 disks to potential customers, offering three months' free service. In addition, assume the following information:

Cost per disk (including mailing)	$1.50
Number of months an average new customer stays with the service (including the three free months)	30 months
Revenue per month per customer account	$10.00
Variable cost per month per customer account	$1.00

Determine the number of new customer accounts needed to break even on the cost of the promotional campaign. In forming your answer, (1) treat the cost of mailing the disk as a fixed cost, and (2) treat the revenue less variable cost per account for the service period as the unit contribution margin.

E11-16

Break-even analysis

Obj 3

`SPREADSHEET`

Sprint Nextel is one of the largest digital wireless service providers in the United States. In a recent year, it had 39.7 million direct subscribers (accounts) that generated revenue of $14,647 million. Costs and expenses for the year were as follows (in millions):

Cost of revenue	$6,091
Selling, general, and administrative expenses	4,411
Depreciation	2,557

Assume that 70% of the cost of revenue and 40% of the selling, general, and administrative expenses are variable to the number of direct subscribers (accounts).

a.   What is Sprint Nextel's break-even number of accounts, using the data and assumptions above? Round units to the nearest million.
b.   How much revenue per account would be sufficient for Sprint Nextel to break even if the number of accounts remained constant?

E11-17

Cost-volume-profit chart

Obj 4

✓ b. $500,000

For the coming year, Knight Inc. anticipates fixed costs of $200,000, a unit variable cost of $15, and a unit selling price of $25. The maximum sales within the relevant range are $1,000,000.

a.   Construct a cost-volume-profit chart.
b.   Estimate the break-even sales (dollars) by using the cost-volume-profit chart constructed in part (a).
c.   What is the main advantage of presenting the cost-volume-profit analysis in graphic form rather than equation form?

E11-18

Profit-volume chart

Obj 4

✓ b. $200,000

Using the data for Knight Inc. in Exercise 11-17, (a) determine the maximum possible operating loss, (b) compute the maximum possible income from operations, (c) construct a profit-volume chart, and (d) estimate the break-even sales (units) by using the profit-volume chart constructed in part (c).

E11-19

Break-even chart

Obj 4

Name the following chart, and identify the items represented by the letters (a) through (f).

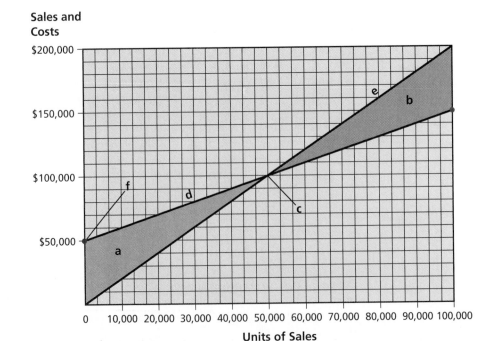

E11-20

Break-even chart

Obj 4

Name the following chart, and identify the items represented by the letters (a) through (f).

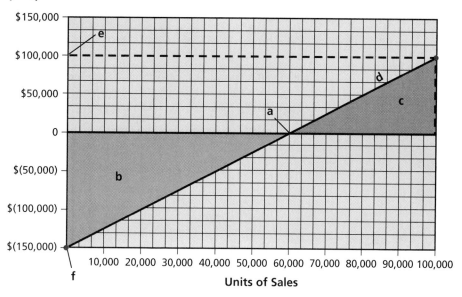

Operating Profit (Loss)

E11-21

Sales mix and break-even sales

Obj 5

✓ a. 280,000 units

Candies Inc. manufactures and sells two products, marshmallow bunnies and jelly beans. The fixed costs are $350,000, and the sales mix is 70% marshmallow bunnies and 30% jelly beans. The unit selling price and the unit variable cost for each product are as follows:

Products	Unit Selling Price	Unit Variable Cost
Marshmallow bunnies	$2.40	$1.00
Jelly beans	1.80	0.90

a. Compute the break-even sales (units) for the overall product, E.
b. How many units of each product, marshmallow bunnies and jelly beans, would be sold at the break-even point?

E11-22

Break-even sales and sales mix for a service company

Obj 5

✓ a. 65 seats

Fly-by-Night Airways provides air transportation services between New York and Miami. A single New York to Miami round-trip flight has the following operating statistics:

Fuel	$3,540
Flight crew salaries	7,310
Airplane depreciation	2,995
Variable cost per passenger—business class	45
Variable cost per passenger—tourist class	35
Round-trip ticket price—business class	350
Round-trip ticket price—tourist class	225

It is assumed that the fuel, crew salaries, and airplane depreciation are fixed, regardless of the number of seats sold for the round-trip flight.

a. Compute the break-even number of seats sold on a single round-trip flight for the overall product. Assume that the overall product is 20% business class and 80% tourist class tickets.
b. How many business class and tourist class seats would be sold at the break-even point?

E11-23

Margin of safety

Obj 6

✓ a. (2) 10%

a. If Larker Company, with a break-even point at $450,000 of sales, has actual sales of $500,000, what is the margin of safety expressed (1) in dollars and (2) as a percentage of sales?

b. If the margin of safety for Porter Company was 20%, fixed costs were $600,000, and variable costs were 70% of sales, what was the amount of actual sales (dollars)? (*Hint:* Determine the break-even in sales dollars first.)

E11-24

Break-even and margin of safety relationships

Obj 6

At a recent staff meeting, the management of Hom Technology Products was considering discontinuing the Hercules line of laptop computers from the product line. The chief financial analyst reported the following current monthly data for the Hercules:

Units of sales	32,000
Break-even units	36,800
Margin of safety in units	4,800

For what reason would you question the validity of these data?

E11-25

Operating leverage

Obj 6

✓ a. Juras, 3.00

Juras Inc. and Hinson Inc. have the following operating data:

	Juras	Hinson
Sales	$160,000	$215,000
Variable costs	130,000	115,000
Contribution margin	$ 30,000	$100,000
Fixed costs	20,000	75,000
Income from operations	$ 10,000	$ 25,000

a. Compute the operating leverage for Juras Inc. and Hinson Inc.

b. How much would income from operations increase for each company if the sales of each increased by 10%?

c. Why is there a difference in the increase in income from operations for the two companies? Explain.

Problems

P11-1

Classify costs

Obj 1

New Age Furniture Company manufactures sofas for distribution to several major retail chains. The following costs are incurred in the production and sale of sofas:

a. Springs

b. Consulting fee of $25,000 paid to efficiency specialists

c. Sewing supplies

d. Electricity costs of $0.10 per kilowatt-hour

e. Fabric for sofa coverings

f. Salary of production vice president

g. Salesperson's salary, $20,000 plus 5% of the selling price of each sofa sold

h. Janitorial supplies, $15 for each sofa produced

i. Employer's FICA taxes on controller's salary of $150,000

j. Rent on experimental equipment, $35 for every sofa produced

k. Wood for framing the sofas

l. Insurance premiums on property, plant, and equipment, $10,000 per year plus $15 per $10,000 of insured value over $15,000,000

m. Hourly wages of sewing machine operators

n. Salary of designers
o. Property taxes on property, plant, and equipment
p. Legal fees paid to attorneys in defense of the company in a patent infringement suit, $15,000 plus $175 per hour
q. Cartons used to ship sofas
r. Rental costs of warehouse, $15,000 per month
s. Straight-line depreciation on factory equipment
t. Foam rubber for cushion fillings

Instructions

Classify the preceding costs as either fixed, variable, or mixed. Use the following tabular headings and place an "X" in the appropriate column. Identify each cost by letter in the cost column.

Cost	Fixed Cost	Variable Cost	Mixed Cost

P11-2

Break-even sales under present and proposed conditions

Objs 2, 3

✓ 3. 13,250 units

French Board Inc., operating at full capacity, sold 25,125 units at a price of $75 per unit during 2008. Its income statement for 2008 is as follows:

Sales		$1,884,375
Cost of goods sold		1,100,000
Gross profit		$ 784,375
Expenses:		
Selling expenses	$125,000	
Administrative expenses	125,000	
Total expenses		250,000
Income from operations		$ 534,375

The division of costs between fixed and variable is as follows:

	Fixed	Variable
Cost of sales	40%	60%
Selling expenses	50%	50%
Administrative expenses	75%	25%

Management is considering a plant expansion program that will permit an increase of $487,500 in yearly sales. The expansion will increase fixed costs by $135,000, but will not affect the relationship between sales and variable costs.

Instructions

1. Determine for 2008 the total fixed costs and the total variable costs.
2. Determine for 2008 (a) the unit variable cost and (b) the unit contribution margin.
3. Compute the break-even sales (units) for 2008.
4. Compute the break-even sales (units) under the proposed program.
5. Determine the amount of sales (units) that would be necessary under the proposed program to realize the $534,375 of income from operations that was earned in 2008.
6. Determine the maximum income from operations possible with the expanded plant.
7. If the proposal is accepted and sales remain at the 2008 level, what will the income or loss from operations be for 2009?
8. Based on the data given, would you recommend accepting the proposal? Explain.

P11-3

Break-even sales and cost-volume-profit chart

Objs 3, 4

✓ 1. 17,500 units

For the coming year, Wisconsin Products Inc. anticipates a unit selling price of $72, a unit variable cost of $34, and fixed costs of $665,000.

Instructions

1. Compute the anticipated break-even sales (units).
2. Compute the sales (units) required to realize income from operations of $95,000.
3. Construct a cost-volume-profit chart, assuming maximum sales of 40,000 units within the relevant range.
4. Determine the probable income (loss) from operations if sales total 29,000 units.

P11-4

Break-even sales and cost-volume-profit chart

Objs 3, 4

✓ 1. 1,500 units

Last year, Pocket PC Co. had sales of $430,000, based on a unit selling price of $215. The variable cost per unit was $155, and fixed costs were $90,000. The maximum sales within Pocket PC's relevant range are 3,000 units. Pocket PC is considering a proposal to spend an additional $24,000 on billboard advertising during the current year in an attempt to increase sales and utilize unused capacity.

Instructions

1. Construct a cost-volume-profit chart indicating the break-even sales for last year. Verify your answer, using the break-even equation.
2. Using the cost-volume-profit chart prepared in part (1), determine (a) the income from operations for last year and (b) the maximum income from operations that could have been realized during the year. Verify your answers arithmetically.
3. Construct a cost-volume-profit chart indicating the break-even sales for the current year, assuming that a noncancelable contract is signed for the additional billboard advertising. No changes are expected in the selling price or other costs. Verify your answer, using the break-even equation.
4. Using the cost-volume-profit chart prepared in (3), determine (a) the income from operations if sales total 2,500 units and (b) the maximum income from operations that could be realized during the year. Verify your answers arithmetically.

P11-5

Sales mix and break-even sales

Obj 5

SPREADSHEET

✓ 1. 52,200 units

Data related to the expected sales of two types of decorative flower pots for Boyeva Flower Pots, Inc. for the current year, which is typical of recent years, are as follows:

Products	Unit Selling Price	Unit Variable Cost	Sales Mix
Decorative Indoor Flower Pot	$ 9.00	$3.60	25%
Rugged Outdoor Flower Pot	12.00	5.40	75%

The estimated fixed costs for the current year are $328,860.

Instructions

1. Determine the estimated units of sales of the overall product necessary to reach the break-even point for the current year.
2. Based on the break-even sales (units) in part (1), determine the unit sales of both the Decorative Indoor Flower Pot and Rugged Outdoor Flower Pot for the current year.
3. Assume that the sales mix was 50% Decorative Indoor Flower Pot and 50% Rugged Outdoor Flower Pot. Compare the break-even point with that in part (1). Why is it so different?

P11-6

Contribution margin, break-even sales, cost-volume-profit chart, margin of safety, and operating leverage

Objs 2, 3, 4, 6

SPREADSHEET

✓ 2. 40.0%

Aspen Co. expects to maintain the same inventories at the end of 2008 as at the beginning of the year. The total of all production costs for the year is therefore assumed to be equal to the cost of goods sold. With this in mind, the various department heads were asked to submit estimates of the costs for their departments during 2008. A summary report of these estimates is as follows:

	Estimated Fixed Cost	Estimated Variable Cost (per unit sold)
Production costs:		
Direct materials	—	$ 8.90
Direct labor	—	3.80
Factory overhead	$ 80,200	2.10
Selling expenses:		
Sales salaries and commissions	41,200	1.70
Advertising	13,200	—
Travel	2,700	—
Miscellaneous selling expense	5,400	1.50
Administrative expenses:		
Office and officers' salaries	81,500	—
Supplies	4,700	0.70
Miscellaneous administrative expense	10,500	2.30
Total	$239,400	$21.00

It is expected that 19,000 units will be sold at a price of $35 a unit. Maximum sales within the relevant range are 30,000 units.

Instructions

1. Prepare an estimated income statement for 2008.
2. What is the expected contribution margin ratio?
3. Determine the break-even sales in units.
4. Construct a cost-volume-profit chart indicating the break-even sales.
5. What is the expected margin of safety?
6. Determine the operating leverage.

Activities

A11-1

Ethics and professional conduct in business

ETHICS

Paul Hambel is a financial consultant to Tecau Properties Inc., a real estate syndicate. Tecau Properties Inc. finances and develops commercial real estate (office buildings). The completed projects are then sold as limited partnership interests to individual investors. The syndicate makes a profit on the sale of these partnership interests. Paul provides financial information for the offering prospectus, which is a document that provides the financial and legal details of the limited partnership offerings. In one of the projects, the bank has financed the construction of a commercial office building at a rate of 7% for the first four years, after which time the rate jumps to 12% for the remaining 21 years of the mortgage. The interest costs are one of the major ongoing costs of a real estate project. Paul has reported prominently in the prospectus that the break-even occupancy for the first four years is 70%. This is the amount of office space that must be leased to cover the interest and general upkeep costs over the first four years. The 70% break-even is very low and thus communicates a low risk to potential investors. Paul uses the 70% break-even rate as a major marketing tool in selling the limited partnership interests. Buried in the fine print of the prospectus is additional information that would allow an astute investor to determine that the break-even occupancy will jump to 90% after the fourth year because of the contracted increase in the mortgage interest rate. Paul believes prospective investors are adequately informed as to the risk of the investment.

Comment on the ethical considerations of this situation.

A11-2
*Break-even sales,
contribution margin*

"For a student, a grade of 65 percent is nothing to write home about. But for the airline . . . [industry], filling 65 percent of the seats . . . is the difference between profit and loss.

"The [economy] might be just strong enough to sustain all the carriers on a cash basis, but not strong enough to bring any significant profitability to the industry. . . . For the airlines . . . , the emphasis will be on trying to consolidate routes and raise ticket prices. . . ."

The airline industry is notorious for boom and bust cycles. Why is airline profitability very sensitive to these cycles? Do you think that during a down cycle the strategy to consolidate routes and raise ticket prices is reasonable? What would make this strategy succeed or fail? Why?

Source: Edwin McDowell, "Empty Seats, Empty Beds, Empty Pockets," *The New York Times,* January 6, 1992, p. C3.

A11-3
Break-even analysis

Southern Video Games Inc. has finished a new video game, *Olympic Competition Bobsledding.* Management is now considering its marketing strategies. The following information is available:

Anticipated sales price per unit	$30
Variable cost per unit*	$15
Anticipated volume	500,000
Production costs	$5,000,000
Anticipated advertising	$2,500,000

*The cost of the video game, packaging, and copying costs.

Two managers, Molly Smith and Alex Clarke, had the following discussion of ways to increase the profitability of this new offering.

Molly: I think we need to think of some way to increase our profitability. Do you have any ideas?
Alex: Well, I think the best strategy would be to become aggressive on price.
Molly: How aggressive?
Alex: If we drop the price to $22 per unit and maintain our advertising budget at $2,500,000, I think we will generate sales of 1,400,000 units.
Molly: I think that's the wrong way to go. You're giving too much up on price. Instead, I think we need to follow an aggressive advertising strategy.
Alex: How aggressive?
Molly: If we increase our advertising to a total of $5,000,000, we should be able to increase sales volume to 1,250,000 units without any change in price.
Alex: I don't think that's reasonable. We'll never cover the increased advertising costs.

Which strategy is best: Do nothing? Follow the advice of Alex Clarke? Or follow Molly Smith's strategy?

A11-4
*Variable costs and activity
bases in decision making*

The owner of Banner-Tech, a printing company, is planning direct labor needs for the upcoming year. The owner has provided you with the following information for next year's plans:

	One Color	Two Color	Three Color	Four Color	Total
Number of banners	100	150	200	400	850

Each color on the banner must be printed one at a time. Thus, for example, a four-color banner will need to be run through the printing operation four separate times. The total production volume last year was 425 banners, as shown below.

	One Color	Two Color	Three Color	Total
Number of banners	100	125	200	425

As you can see, the four-color banner is a new product offering for the upcoming year. The owner believes that the expected 425-unit increase in volume from last year means that direct labor expenses should increase by 100% (425/425). What do you think?

A11-5

Variable costs and activity bases in decision making

Sales volume has been dropping at Winona Publishing Company. During this time, however, the Shipping Department manager has been under severe financial constraints. The manager knows that most of the Shipping Department's effort is related to pulling inventory from the warehouse for each order and performing the paperwork. The paperwork involves preparing shipping documents for each order. Thus, the pulling and paperwork effort associated with each sales order is essentially the same, regardless of the size of the order. The Shipping Department manager has discussed the financial situation with senior management. Senior management has responded by pointing out that sales volume has been dropping, so that the amount of work in the Shipping Department should be dropping. Thus, senior management told the Shipping Department manager that costs should be decreasing in the department.

The Shipping Department manager prepared the following information:

Month	Sales Volume	Number of Customer Orders	Sales Volume per Order
January	$152,000	800	$190
February	147,600	820	180
March	144,500	850	170
April	144,000	960	150
May	143,550	990	145
June	136,000	1,000	136
July	130,650	1,005	130
August	128,000	1,024	125

Given this information, how would you respond to senior management?

A11-6

Break-even analysis

GROUP

Break-even analysis is one of the most fundamental tools for managing any kind of business unit. Consider the management of your school. In a group, brainstorm some applications of break-even analysis at your school. Identify three areas where break-even analysis might be used. For each area, identify the revenues, variable costs, and fixed costs that would be used in the calculation.

Answers to Self-Examination Questions

1. **B** Variable costs vary in total in direct proportion to changes in the level of activity (answer B). Costs that vary on a per-unit basis as the level of activity changes (answer A) or remain constant in total dollar amount as the level of activity changes (answer C), or both (answer D), are fixed costs.

2. **D** The contribution margin ratio indicates the percentage of each sales dollar available to cover the fixed costs and provide income from operations and is determined as follows:

$$\text{Contribution margin ratio} = \frac{\text{Sales} - \text{Variable costs}}{\text{Sales}}$$

$$\text{Contribution margin ratio} = \frac{\$500,000 - \$200,000}{\$500,000}$$

$$= 60\%$$

3. **D** The break-even sales of 40,000 units (answer D) is computed as follows:

$$\text{Break-even sales (units)} = \frac{\text{Fixed costs}}{\text{Unit contribution margin}}$$

$$\text{Break-even sales (units)} = \frac{\$160,000}{\$4} = 40,000 \text{ units}$$

4. **D** Sales of 45,000 units are required to realize income from operations of $20,000, computed as follows:

$$\text{Sales (units)} = \frac{\text{Fixed costs} + \text{Target profit}}{\text{Unit contribution margin}}$$

$$\text{Sales (units)} = \frac{\$160,000 + \$20,000}{\$4} = 45,000 \text{ units}$$

5. **C** The operating leverage is 1.8, computed as follows:

$$\text{Operating leverage} = \frac{\text{Contribution margin}}{\text{Income from operations}}$$

$$\text{Operating leverage} = \frac{\$360,000}{\$200,000} = 1.8$$

CHAPTER 12

Differential Analysis and Product Pricing

Learning Objectives

After studying this chapter, you should be able to:

Obj 1

Prepare a differential analysis report for decisions involving leasing or selling equipment, discontinuing an unprofitable segment, manufacturing or purchasing a needed part, replacing usable fixed assets, processing further or selling an intermediate product, or accepting additional business at a special price.

Obj 2

Determine the selling price of a product, using the total cost, product cost, and variable cost concepts.

Obj 3

Calculate the relative profitability of products in bottleneck production environments.

Many of the decisions that you make depend on comparing the estimated costs of alternatives. The payoff from such comparisons is described in the following report from a University of Michigan study.

Richard Nisbett and two colleagues quizzed Michigan faculty members and university seniors on such questions as how often they walk out on a bad movie, refuse to finish a bad meal, start over on a weak term paper, or abandon a research project that no longer looks promising. They believe that people who cut their losses this way are following sound economic rules: calculating the net benefits of alternative courses of action, writing off past costs that can't be recovered, and weighing the opportunity to use future time and effort more profitably elsewhere.

They find that among faculty members, those who use cost-benefit reasoning in this fashion—being more likely to give up on research that isn't getting anywhere or using labor-saving devices as often as possible—have higher salaries relative to their age and departments. Not surprisingly, economists are more likely to apply the approach than professors of humanities or biology.

Among students, those who have learned to use cost-benefit analysis frequently are apt to have far better grades than their Scholastic Aptitude Test scores would have predicted. Again, the more economics courses the students have, the more likely they are to apply cost-benefit analysis outside the classroom.

Dr. Nisbett concedes that for many Americans, cost-benefit rules often appear to conflict with such traditional principles as "never give up" and "waste not, want not."

Managers must also consider the effects of alternative decisions on their businesses. In this chapter, we discuss differential analysis, which reports the effects of alternative decisions on total revenues and costs. We also describe and illustrate practical approaches to setting product prices. Finally, we discuss how production bottlenecks influence product mix and pricing decisions.

Source: Alan L. Otten, "Economic Perspective Produces Steady Yields," from People Patterns, *The Wall Street Journal,* March 31, 1992, p. B1.

Obj **1**

Prepare a differential
analysis report for decisions
involving leasing or selling
equipment, discontinuing
an unprofitable segment,
manufacturing or purcha-
sing a needed part,
replacing usable fixed
assets, processing further
or selling an intermediate
product, or accepting
additional business at a
special price.

Differential Analysis

Planning for future operations involves decision making. For some decisions, revenue
and cost data from the accounting records may be useful. However, the revenue and cost
data for use in evaluating courses of future operations or choosing among competing
alternatives are often not available in the accounting records and must be estimated.

Consider:

- The decision by **General Motors** to purchase on-board communications products
  from **Delphi Automotive Systems** instead of making them internally.
- The decision by **Marriott** hotels to accept a special price from a bid placed on
  Priceline.com.
- The decision by **United Airlines** to discontinue service to New Zealand.

In each of these decisions, the estimated revenues and costs were relevant. The relevant
revenues and costs focus on the differences between each alternative. Costs that have been
incurred in the past are not relevant to the decision. These costs are called **sunk costs**.

Differential revenue is the amount of increase or decrease in revenue expected from
a course of action as compared with an alternative. To illustrate, assume that certain
equipment is being used to manufacture calculators, which are expected to generate
revenue of $150,000. If the equipment could be used to make digital clocks, which would
generate revenue of $175,000, the differential revenue from making and selling digital
clocks is $25,000.

Differential cost is the amount of increase or decrease in cost that is expected from a
course of action as compared with an alternative. For example, if an increase in advertising expenditures from $100,000 to $150,000 is being considered, the differential cost of
the action is $50,000.

Differential income or loss is the difference between the differential revenue and
the differential costs. Differential income indicates that a particular decision is expected
to be profitable, while a differential loss indicates the opposite.

Differential analysis focuses on the effect of alternative courses of action on the
relevant revenues and costs. For example, if a manager must decide between two alternatives, differential analysis would involve comparing the differential revenues of the two
alternatives with the differential costs.

In this chapter, we will discuss the use of differential analysis in analyzing the following alternatives:

1. Leasing or selling equipment.
2. Discontinuing an unprofitable segment.
3. Manufacturing or purchasing a needed part.
4. Replacing usable fixed assets.
5. Processing further or selling an intermediate product.
6. Accepting additional business at a special price.

Lease or Sell

Management may have a choice between leasing or selling a piece of equipment that is
no longer needed in the business. In deciding which option is best, management may
use differential analysis. To illustrate, assume that Marcus Company is considering disposing of equipment that cost $200,000 and has $120,000 of accumulated depreciation
to date. Marcus Company can sell the equipment through a broker for $100,000 less
a 6% commission. Alternatively, Potamkin Company (the lessee) has offered to lease

Marcus Company

MARCUS COMPANY

Sell Equipment to   OR   Lease Equipment to

POTAMKIN CO

Broker

Potamkin Company

the equipment for 5 years for a total of $160,000. At the end of the fifth year of the lease, the equipment is expected to have no residual value. During the period of the lease, Marcus Company (the lessor) will incur repair, insurance, and property tax expenses estimated at $35,000. Exhibit 1 shows Marcus Company's analysis of whether to lease or sell the equipment.

Note that in Exhibit 1, the $80,000 book value ($200,000 − $120,000) of the equipment is a sunk cost and is not considered in the analysis. The $80,000 is a cost that resulted from a previous decision. It is not affected by the alternatives now being considered in leasing or selling the equipment. The relevant factors to be considered are the differential revenues and differential costs associated with the lease or sell decision. This analysis is verified by the traditional analysis in Exhibit 2.

The alternatives presented in Exhibits 1 and 2 were relatively simple. However, regardless of the complexity, the approach to differential analysis is basically the same. Two additional factors that often need to be considered are (1) differential revenue from investing the funds generated by the alternatives and (2) any income tax differential. In Exhibit 1, there could be differential interest revenue related to investing the cash flows from the two alternatives. Any income tax differential would

---

EXHIBIT 1   *Differential Analysis Report—Lease or Sell*

Proposal to Lease or Sell Equipment
June 22, 2009

Differential revenue from alternatives:		
Revenue from lease	$160,000	
Revenue from sale	100,000	
Differential revenue from lease		$60,000
Differential cost of alternatives:		
Repair, insurance, and property tax expenses	$ 35,000	
Commission expense on sale	6,000	
Differential cost of lease		29,000
Net differential income from the lease alternative		**$31,000**

EXHIBIT 2   *Traditional Analysis*

Lease or Sell

Lease alternative:		
Revenue from lease		$160,000
Depreciation expense for remaining 5 years	$80,000	
Repair, insurance, and property tax expenses	35,000	115,000
Net gain		$45,000
Sell alternative:		
Sales price		$100,000
Book value of equipment	$80,000	
Commission expense	6,000	86,000
Net gain		14,000
Net differential income from the lease alternative		**$31,000**

be related to the differences in the timing of the income from the alternatives and the differences in the amount of investment income.

Discontinue a Segment or Product

When a product or a department, branch, territory, or other segment of a business is generating losses, management may consider eliminating the product or segment. It is often assumed, sometimes in error, that the total income from operations of a business would be increased if the operating loss could be eliminated. Discontinuing the product or segment usually eliminates all of the product or segment's variable costs (direct materials, direct labor, sales commissions, and so on). However, if the product or segment is a relatively small part of the business, the fixed costs (depreciation, insurance, property taxes, and so on) may not be decreased by discontinuing it. It is possible in this case for the total operating income of a company to decrease rather than increase by eliminating the product or segment. To illustrate, the income statement for Battle Creek Cereal Co. presented in Exhibit 3 is for a normal year ending August 31, 2009.

EXHIBIT 3   *Income (Loss) by Product*

BATTLE CREEK CEREAL CO.
Condensed Income Statement
For the Year Ended August 31, 2009

	Corn Flakes	Toasted Oats	Bran Flakes	Total
Sales	$500,000	$400,000	$100,000	$1,000,000
Cost of goods sold:				
Variable costs	$220,000	$200,000	$ 60,000	$ 480,000
Fixed costs	120,000	80,000	20,000	220,000
Total cost of goods sold	$340,000	$280,000	$ 80,000	$ 700,000
Gross profit	$160,000	$120,000	$ 20,000	$ 300,000
Operating expenses:				
Variable expenses	$ 95,000	$ 60,000	$ 25,000	$ 180,000
Fixed expenses	25,000	20,000	6,000	51,000
Total operating expenses	$120,000	$ 80,000	$ 31,000	$ 231,000
Income (loss) from operations	$ 40,000	$ 40,000	$ (11,000)	$ 69,000

Because Bran Flakes incurs annual losses, management is considering discontinuing it. Total annual operating income of $80,000 ($40,000 Toasted Oats + $40,000 Corn Flakes) might seem to be indicated by the income statement in Exhibit 3 if Bran Flakes is discontinued.

Discontinuing Bran Flakes, however, would actually decrease operating income by $15,000, to $54,000 ($69,000 − $15,000). This is shown by the differential analysis report in Exhibit 4, in which we assume that discontinuing Bran Flakes would have no effect on fixed costs and expenses. The traditional analysis in Exhibit 5 verifies the differential analysis in Exhibit 4.

In Exhibit 5, only the short-term (1 year) effects of discontinuing Bran Flakes are considered. When eliminating a product or segment, management may also consider the long-term effects. For example, the plant capacity made available by discontinuing Bran Flakes might be eliminated. This could reduce fixed costs. Some employees may

EXHIBIT 4   *Differential Analysis Report—Discontinue an Unprofitable Segment*

Proposal to Discontinue Bran Flakes September 29, 2009		
Differential revenue from annual sales of Bran Flakes:		
Revenue from sales		$100,000
Differential cost of annual sales of Bran Flakes:		
Variable cost of goods sold	$60,000	
Variable operating expenses	25,000	85,000
Annual differential income from sales of Bran Flakes		**$ 15,000**

EXHIBIT 5   *Traditional Analysis*

Proposal to Discontinue Bran Flakes September 29, 2009			
	Bran Flakes, Toasted Oats, and Corn Flakes	*Discontinue Bran Flakes**	*Toasted Oats and Corn Flakes*
Sales	$1,000,000	$100,000	$900,000
Cost of goods sold:			
Variable costs	$ 480,000	$ 60,000	$420,000
Fixed costs	220,000	—	220,000
Total cost of goods sold	$ 700,000	$ 60,000	$640,000
Gross profit	$ 300,000	$ 40,000	$260,000
Operating expenses:			
Variable expenses	$ 180,000	$ 25,000	$155,000
Fixed expenses	51,000	—	51,000
Total operating expenses	$ 231,000	$ 25,000	$206,000
Income (loss) from operations	**$ 69,000**	**$ 15,000**	**$ 54,000**

*Fixed costs are assumed to remain unchanged with the discontinuance of Bran Flakes.

have to be laid off, and others may have to be relocated and retrained. Further, there may be a related decrease in sales of more profitable products to those customers who were attracted by the discontinued product.

Make or Buy

The assembly of many parts is often a major element in manufacturing some products, such as automobiles. These parts may be made by the product's manufacturer, or they may be purchased. For example, some of the parts for an automobile, such as the motor, may be produced by the automobile manufacturer. Other parts, such as tires, may be purchased from other manufacturers. In addition, in manufacturing motors, such items as spark plugs and nuts and bolts may be acquired from suppliers.

Management uses differential costs to decide whether to make or buy a part. For example, if a part is purchased, management has concluded that it is less costly to buy the part than to manufacture it. Make or buy options often arise when a manufacturer has excess productive capacity in the form of unused equipment, space, and labor.

The differential analysis is similar, whether management is considering making a part that is currently being purchased or purchasing a part that is currently being

made. To illustrate, assume that an automobile manufacturer has been purchasing instrument panels for $240 a unit. The factory is currently operating at 80% of capacity, and no major increase in production is expected in the near future. The cost per unit of manufacturing an instrument panel internally, including fixed costs, is estimated as follows:

Direct materials	$ 80
Direct labor	80
Variable factory overhead	52
Fixed factory overhead	68
Total cost per unit	$280

If the *make* price of $280 is simply compared with the *buy* price of $240, the decision is to buy the instrument panel. However, if unused capacity could be used in manufacturing the part, there would be no increase in the total amount of fixed factory overhead costs. Thus, only the variable factory overhead costs need to be considered. The relevant costs are summarized in the differential report in Exhibit 6.

EXHIBIT 6   *Differential Analysis Report—Make or Buy*

Proposal to Manufacture Instrument Panels
February 15, 2009

Purchase price of an instrument panel		$240.00
Differential cost to manufacture:		
Direct materials	$80.00	
Direct labor	80.00	
Variable factory overhead	52.00	212.00
Cost savings from manufacturing an instrument panel		**$ 28.00**

HOW BUSINESSES MAKE MONEY

Mattel Inc.

Mattel Inc., the largest U.S. toy manufacturer, reported the following domestic operating segment information for a recent year:

	Girls	Boys	Infant & Preschool
Revenues	$1,380,208	$766,073	$1,282,221
Operating income	389,788	110,004	187,009
Depreciation	42,338	33,505	28,054

Mattel segments its business by type of customer. The Girls segment includes sales of Barbie®, the Boys segment includes sales of Hot Wheels® and Matchbox®, and the Infant segment includes sales of Fisher-Price® toys. All the segments are profitable. The contribution margin (revenues less operating income and depreciation) in each segment is high. The Girls segment is the most profitable per sales dollar (28.2%), and the Boys and Infant segments are about equal in their profitability per sales dollar (14.4% and 14.6%, respectively). The discontinuance of any of these segments would cause Mattel's overall corporate income to decline.

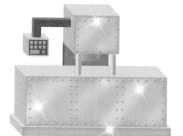

Other possible effects of a decision to manufacture the instrument panel should also be considered. For example, capacity committed to the instrument panel may not be available for more production opportunities in the future. This decision may affect employees. It may also affect future business relations with the instrument panel supplier, who may provide other essential parts. The company's decision to manufacture instrument panels might jeopardize the timely delivery of these other parts.

Replace Equipment

The usefulness of fixed assets may be reduced long before they are considered to be worn out. For example, equipment may no longer be efficient for the purpose for which it is used. On the other hand, the equipment may not have reached the point of complete inadequacy. Decisions to replace usable fixed assets should be based on relevant costs. The relevant costs are the future costs of continuing to use the equipment versus replacement. The book values of the fixed assets being replaced are sunk costs and are irrelevant.

To illustrate, assume that a business is considering the disposal of several identical machines having a total book value of $100,000 and an estimated remaining life of 5 years. The old machines can be sold for $25,000. They can be replaced by a single high-speed machine at a cost of $250,000. The new machine has an estimated useful life of 5 years and no residual value. Analyses indicate an estimated annual reduction in variable manufacturing costs from $225,000 with the old machine to $150,000 with the new machine. No other changes in the manufacturing costs or the operating expenses are expected. The relevant costs are summarized in the differential report in Exhibit 7.

Other factors are often important in equipment replacement decisions. For example, differences between the remaining useful life of the old equipment and the estimated life of the new equipment could exist. In addition, the new equipment might improve the overall quality of the product, resulting in an increase in sales volume. Additional factors could include the time value of money and other uses for the cash needed to purchase the new equipment.[1]

INTEGRITY, OBJECTIVITY, AND ETHICS IN BUSINESS

Related-Party Transactions

The make-or-buy decision can be complicated if the purchase (buy) is being made by a related party. A related party is one in which there is direct or indirect control of one party over another or the presence of a family member in a transaction. Such dependence or familiarity may interfere with the appropriateness of the business transaction. One investor has said, "Related parties are akin to steroids used by athletes. If you're an athlete and you can cut the mustard, you don't need steroids to make yourself stronger

or faster. By the same token, if you're a good company, you don't need related parties or deals that don't make sense." While related-party transactions are legal, GAAP (FASB Statement No. 56) and the Sarbanes-Oxley Act require that they must be disclosed under the presumption that such transactions are less than arm's length.

Source: Herb Greenburg, "Poor Relations: The Problem with Related-Party Transactions," *Fortune Advisor* (February 5, 2001), p. 198.

[1]The importance of the time value of money in equipment replacement decisions is discussed in Chapter 15.

EXHIBIT 7   *Differential Analysis Report—Replace Equipment*

	Proposal to Replace Equipment ***November 28, 2009***	
Annual variable costs—present equipment	$225,000	
Annual variable costs—new equipment	150,000	
Annual differential decrease in cost	$ 75,000	
Number of years applicable	× 5	
Total differential decrease in cost	$375,000	
Proceeds from sale of present equipment	25,000	$ 400,000
Cost of new equipment		250,000
Net differential decrease in cost, 5-year total		$150,000
Annual net differential decrease in cost—new equipment		$ 30,000

The amount of income that is forgone from an alternative use of an asset, such as cash, is called an **opportunity cost**. For example, your opportunity cost of attending school is the income forgone from lost work hours. Although the opportunity cost does not appear as a part of historical accounting data, it is useful in analyzing alternative courses of action. To illustrate, assume that the cash outlay of $250,000 for the new equipment, less the $25,000 proceeds from the sale of the present equipment, could be invested to yield a 10% return. Thus, the annual opportunity cost related to the purchase of the new equipment is $22,500 (10% × $225,000).

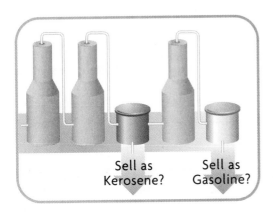

Sell as Kerosene?   Sell as Gasoline?

Process or Sell

When a product is manufactured, it progresses through various stages of production. Often a product can be sold at an intermediate stage of production, or it can be processed further and then sold. In deciding whether to sell a product at an intermediate stage or to process it further, differential analysis is useful. The differential revenues from further processing are compared to the differential costs of further processing. The costs of producing the intermediate product do not change, regardless of whether the intermediate product is sold or processed further. Thus, these costs are not differential costs and are irrelevant to the decision to process further.

To illustrate, assume that a business produces kerosene in batches of 4,000 gallons. Standard quantities of 4,000 gallons of direct materials are processed, which cost $0.60 per gallon. Kerosene can be sold without further processing for $0.80 per gallon. It can be processed further to yield gasoline, which can be sold for $1.25 per gallon. Gasoline requires additional processing costs of $650 per batch, and 20% of the gallons of kerosene will evaporate during production. Exhibit 8 summarizes the differential revenues and costs in deciding whether to process kerosene to produce gasoline.

The differential income from further processing kerosene into gasoline is $150 per batch. The initial cost of producing the intermediate kerosene, $2,400 (4,000 gallons × $0.60), is not considered in deciding whether to process kerosene further. This initial cost will be incurred, regardless of whether gasoline is produced.

EXHIBIT 8	*Differential Analysis Report—Process or Sell*

Proposal to Process Kerosene Further **October 1, 2009**		
Differential revenue from further processing per batch:		
Revenue from sale of gasoline [(4,000 gallons − 800 gallons evaporation) × $1.25]	$4,000	
Revenue from sale of kerosene (4,000 gallons × $0.80)	3,200	
Differential revenue		$800
Differential cost per batch:		
Additional cost of producing gasoline		650
Differential income from further processing gasoline per batch		**$150**

Accept Business at a Special Price

Differential analysis is also useful in deciding whether to accept additional business at a special price. The differential revenue that would be provided from the additional business is compared to the differential costs of producing and delivering the product to the customer. If the company is operating at full capacity, any additional production will increase both fixed and variable production costs. If, however, the normal production of the company is below full capacity, additional business may be undertaken without increasing fixed production costs. In this case, the differential costs of the additional production are the variable manufacturing costs. If operating expenses increase because of the additional business, these expenses should also be considered.

To illustrate, assume that the monthly capacity of a sporting goods business is 12,500 basketballs. Current sales and production are averaging 10,000 basketballs per month. The current manufacturing cost of $20 per unit consists of variable costs of $12.50 and fixed costs of $7.50. The normal selling price of the product in the domestic market is $30. The manufacturer receives from an exporter an offer for 5,000 basketballs at $18 each. Production can be spread over a three-month period without interfering with normal production or incurring overtime costs. Pricing policies in the domestic market will not be affected. Simply comparing the sales price of $18 with the present unit manufacturing cost of $20 indicates that the offer should be rejected. However, by focusing only on the differential cost, which in this case is the variable cost, the decision is different. Exhibit 9 shows the differential analysis report for this decision.

EXHIBIT 9	*Differential Analysis Report—Sell at Special Price*

Proposal to Sell Basketballs to Exporter **March 10, 2009**	
Differential revenue from accepting offer:	
Revenue from sale of 5,000 additional units at $18	$90,000
Differential cost of accepting offer:	
Variable costs of 5,000 additional units at $12.50	62,500
Differential income from accepting offer	**$27,500**

Proposals to sell a product in the domestic market at prices lower than the normal price may require additional considerations. For example, it may be unwise to increase sales volume in one territory by price reductions if sales volume is lost in other areas. Manufacturers must also conform to the Robinson-Patman Act, which prohibits price discrimination within the United States unless differences in prices can be justified by different costs of serving different customers.

Setting Normal Product Selling Prices

Obj **2**

Determine the selling price of a product, using the total cost, product cost, and variable cost concepts.

Differential analysis may be useful in deciding to lower selling prices for special short-run decisions, such as whether to accept business at a price lower than the normal price. In such cases, the minimum short-run price is set high enough to cover all variable costs. Any price above this minimum price will improve profits in the short run. In the long run, however, the normal selling price must be set high enough to cover all costs and expenses (both fixed and variable) and provide a reasonable profit. Otherwise, the business may not survive.

The normal selling price can be viewed as the target selling price to be achieved in the long run. The basic approaches to setting this price are as follows:

Market Methods	*Cost-Plus Methods*
1.　Demand-based methods	1.　Total cost concept
2.　Competition-based methods	2.　Product cost concept
	3.　Variable cost concept

Managers using the market methods refer to the external market to determine the price. Demand-based methods set the price according to the demand for the product. If there is high demand for the product, then the price may be set high, while lower demand may require the price to be set low. An example of setting different prices according to the demand for the product is found in the telecommunications industry, with low weekend rates and high business day rates for long-distance telephone calls.

Competition-based methods set the price according to the price offered by competitors. For example, if a competitor reduces the price, then management may be required to adjust the price to meet the competition. The market-based pricing approaches are discussed in greater detail in marketing courses, so we will not expand upon them here.

Managers using the cost-plus methods price the product in order to achieve a target profit. Managers add to the cost an amount called a **markup**, so that all costs plus a profit are included in the selling price. In the following paragraphs, we describe and illustrate the three cost concepts often used in applying the cost-plus approach: (1) total cost, (2) product cost, and (3) variable cost. A cost reduction method that uses market-method pricing, called target costing, is discussed later in this section.

Total Cost Concept

Using the **total cost concept**, all costs of manufacturing a product plus the selling and administrative expenses are included in the cost amount to which the markup is added. Since all costs and expenses are included in the cost amount, the dollar amount of the markup equals the desired profit.

The first step in applying the total cost concept is to determine the total cost of manufacturing the product. This cost includes the costs of direct materials, direct labor,

TOTAL COST CONCEPT

DESIRED SELLING PRICE

MARKUP:
Desired Profit

TOTAL COST:
Manufacturing Cost
+
Administrative
Expense
+
Selling Expense

and factory overhead and should be available from the accounting records. The next step is to add the estimated selling and administrative expenses to the total cost of manufacturing the product. The cost amount per unit is then computed by dividing the total costs by the total units expected to be produced and sold.

After the cost amount per unit has been determined, the dollar amount of the markup is determined. For this purpose, the markup is expressed as a percentage of cost. This percentage is then multiplied by the cost amount per unit. The dollar amount of the markup is then added to the cost amount per unit to arrive at the selling price.

The markup percentage for the total cost concept is determined by applying the following formula:

$$\text{Markup percentage} = \frac{\text{Desired profit}}{\text{Total costs}}$$

The numerator of the formula is only the desired profit. This is because all costs and expenses are included in the cost amount to which the markup is added. The denominator of the formula is the total costs.

To illustrate, assume that the costs for calculators of Digital Solutions Inc. are as follows:

Variable costs:	
Direct materials	$ 3.00 per unit
Direct labor	10.00
Factory overhead	1.50
Selling and administrative expenses	1.50
Total	$ 16.00 per unit
Fixed costs:	
Factory overhead	$50,000
Selling and administrative expenses	20,000

Digital Solutions Inc. desires a profit equal to a 20% rate of return on assets, $800,000 of assets are devoted to producing calculators, and 100,000 units are expected to be produced and sold. The calculators' total cost is $1,670,000, or $16.70 per unit, computed as follows:

Variable costs ($16.00 × 100,000 units)		$1,600,000
Fixed costs:		
Factory overhead	$50,000	
Selling and administrative expenses	20,000	70,000
Total costs		$1,670,000
Total cost per calculator ($1,670,000 ÷ 100,000 units)		$ 16.70

The desired profit is $160,000 (20% × $800,000), and the markup percentage for a calculator is 9.6%, computed as follows:

$$\textbf{Markup percentage} = \frac{\textbf{Desired profit}}{\textbf{Total costs}}$$

$$\text{Markup percentage} = \frac{\$160,000}{\$1,670,000} = 9.6\%$$

Based on the total cost per unit and the markup percentage for a calculator, Digital Solutions Inc. would price each calculator at $18.30 per unit, as shown below.

Total cost per calculator	$16.70
Markup ($16.70 × 9.6%)	1.60
Selling price	$18.30

The ability of the selling price of $18.30 to generate the desired profit of $160,000 is shown by the following income statement:

DIGITAL SOLUTIONS INC.
Income Statement
For the Year Ended December 31, 2009

Sales (100,000 units × $18.30)		$1,830,000
Expenses:		
Variable (100,000 units × $16.00)	$1,600,000	
Fixed ($50,000 + $20,000)	70,000	1,670,000
Income from operations		$ 160,000

The total cost concept of applying the cost-plus approach to product pricing is often used by contractors who sell products to government agencies. In many cases, government contractors are required by law to be reimbursed for their products on a total-cost-plus-profit basis.

Product Cost Concept

Using the **product cost concept**, only the costs of manufacturing the product, termed the product cost, are included in the cost amount to which the markup is added. Estimated

---

INTEGRITY, OBJECTIVITY, AND ETHICS IN BUSINESS

Price Fixing

Federal law prevents companies competing in similar markets from sharing cost and price information, or what is commonly termed "price fixing." For example, the Federal Trade Commission brought a suit against the major record labels and music retailers for conspiring to set CD prices at a minimum level, or MAP (minimum advertised price). In settling the suit, the major labels ceased their MAP policies and provided $143 million in cash and CDs for consumers.

PRODUCT COST CONCEPT

DESIRED SELLING PRICE

MARKUP:
Administrative Expense
+
Selling Expense
+
Desired Profit

PRODUCT COST:
Manufacturing Cost

selling expenses, administrative expenses, and profit are included in the markup. The markup percentage is determined by applying the following formula:

$$\text{Markup percentage} = \frac{\text{Desired profit} + \text{Total selling and administrative expenses}}{\text{Total manufacturing costs}}$$

The numerator of the markup percentage formula is the desired profit plus the total selling and administrative expenses. These expenses must be included in the markup, since they are not included in the cost amount to which the markup is added. The denominator of the formula includes the costs of direct materials, direct labor, and factory overhead.

To illustrate, assume the same data used in the preceding illustration. The manufacturing cost for Digital Solutions Inc.'s calculator is $1,500,000, or $15 per unit, computed as follows:

Direct materials ($3 × 100,000 units)		$ 300,000
Direct labor ($10 × 100,000 units)		1,000,000
Factory overhead:		
Variable ($1.50 × 100,000 units)	$150,000	
Fixed	50,000	200,000
Total manufacturing costs		$1,500,000
Manufacturing cost per calculator ($1,500,000 ÷ 100,000 units)		$15

The desired profit is $160,000 (20% × $800,000), and the total selling and administrative expenses are $170,000 [(100,000 units × $1.50 per unit) + $20,000]. The markup percentage for a calculator is 22%, computed as follows:

$$\text{Markup percentage} = \frac{\text{Desired profit} + \text{Total selling and administrative expenses}}{\text{Total manufacturing costs}}$$

$$\text{Markup percentage} = \frac{\$160,000 + \$170,000}{\$1,500,000}$$

$$\text{Markup percentage} = \frac{\$330,000}{\$1,500,000} = 22\%$$

Based on the manufacturing cost per calculator and the markup percentage, Digital Solutions Inc. would price each calculator at $18.30 per unit, as shown below.

Manufacturing cost per calculator	$15.00
Markup ($15 × 22%)	3.30
Selling price	$18.30

Variable Cost Concept

The **variable cost concept** emphasizes the distinction between variable and fixed costs in product pricing. Using the variable cost concept, only variable costs are included in the

VARIABLE COST CONCEPT

DESIRED SELLING PRICE

MARKUP:
Total Fixed Costs
+
Desired Profit

VARIABLE COST:
Variable
Manufacturing Cost
+
Variable
Administrative and
Selling Expenses

cost amount to which the markup is added. All variable manufacturing costs, as well as variable selling and administrative expenses, are included in the cost amount. Fixed manufacturing costs, fixed selling and administrative expenses, and profit are included in the markup.

The markup percentage is determined by applying the following formula:

$$\text{Markup percentage} = \frac{\text{Desired profit + Total fixed costs}}{\text{Total variable costs}}$$

The numerator of the markup percentage formula is the desired profit plus the total fixed manufacturing costs and the total fixed selling and administrative expenses. These costs and expenses must be included in the markup, since they are not included in the cost amount to which the markup is added. The denominator of the formula includes the total variable costs.

To illustrate, assume the same data used in the two preceding illustrations. The calculator variable cost is $1,600,000, or $16.00 per unit, computed as follows:

Variable costs:	
Direct materials ($3 × 100,000 units)	$ 300,000
Direct labor ($10 × 100,000 units)	1,000,000
Factory overhead ($1.50 × 100,000 units)	150,000
Selling and administrative expenses ($1.50 × 100,000 units)	150,000
Total variable costs	$1,600,000
Variable cost per calculator ($1,600,000 ÷ 100,000 units)	$16.00

The desired profit is $160,000 (20% × $800,000), the total fixed manufacturing costs are $50,000, and the total fixed selling and administrative expenses are $20,000. The markup percentage for a calculator is 14.4%, computed as follows:

$$\text{Markup percentage} = \frac{\text{Desired profit + Total fixed costs}}{\text{Total variable costs}}$$

$$\text{Markup percentage} = \frac{\$160,000 + \$50,000 + \$20,000}{\$1,600,000}$$

$$\text{Markup percentage} = \frac{\$230,000}{\$1,600,000} = 14.4\%$$

Based on the variable cost per calculator and the markup percentage, Digital Solutions Inc. would price each calculator at $18.30 per unit, as shown below.

Variable cost per calculator	$16.00
Markup ($16.00 × 14.4%)	2.30
Selling price	$18.30

Choosing a Cost-Plus Approach Cost Concept

All three cost concepts produced the same selling price ($18.30) for Digital Solutions Inc. In practice, however, the three cost concepts are usually not viewed as alternatives. Each cost concept requires different estimates of costs and expenses. This difficulty and the complexity of the manufacturing operations should be considered in choosing a cost concept.

To reduce the costs of gathering data, estimated (standard) costs rather than actual costs may be used with any of the three cost concepts. However, management should exercise caution when using estimated costs in applying the cost-plus approach. The estimates should be based on normal (attainable) operating levels and not theoretical (ideal) levels of performance. In product pricing, the use of estimates based on ideal- or maximum-capacity operating levels might lead to setting product prices too low. In this case, the costs of such factors as normal spoilage or normal periods of idle time might not be considered.

The decision-making needs of management are also an important factor in selecting a cost concept for product pricing. For example, managers who often make special pricing decisions are more likely to use the variable cost concept. In contrast, a government defense contractor would be more likely to use the total cost concept.

Activity-Based Costing

As illustrated in the preceding paragraphs, costs are an important consideration in setting product prices. To more accurately measure the costs of producing and selling products, some companies use activity-based costing. **Activity-based costing (ABC)** identifies and traces activities to specific products.

Activity-based costing may be useful in making product pricing decisions where manufacturing operations involve large amounts of factory overhead. In such cases, traditional overhead allocation using activity bases such as units produced or machine hours may yield inaccurate cost allocations. This, in turn, may result in distorted product costs and product prices. By providing more accurate product cost allocations, activity-based costing aids in setting product prices that will cover costs and expenses.

Target Costing

A method that combines market-based pricing with a cost reduction emphasis is **target costing**. Under target costing, a future selling price is anticipated, using the demand-based methods or the competition-based methods discussed previously. The targeted cost is determined by *subtracting* a desired profit from the expected selling price. In contrast, the three cost-plus concepts discussed previously begin with a given cost and *add* a markup to determine the selling price.

Target costing is used to motivate cost reduction as shown in Exhibit 10. The bar at the left in Exhibit 10 shows the actual cost and profit that can be earned during the present time period for a particular product. The bar at the right shows that the market price is expected to decline in the future. Thus, to earn a profit, a target cost is estimated as the difference between the expected market price and the desired profit. This target cost establishes a product cost objective that will maintain competitiveness and profitability.

Since the target cost is less than the current cost, managers must plan and remove cost from the design and manufacture of the product. The planned cost reduction is sometimes

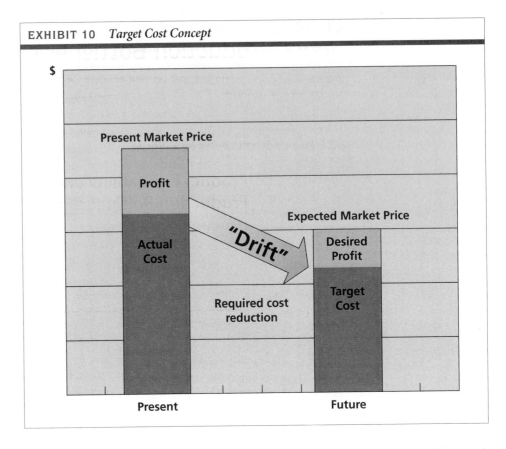

EXHIBIT 10   *Target Cost Concept*

referred to as the cost "drift." Cost can be removed from a product in a variety of ways, such as by simplifying the design, reducing the cost of direct materials, reducing the direct labor content, or eliminating waste from manufacturing operations. Using the target cost concept in this way provides managers with a road map for making improvements and gauging the success of their efforts over time. Target costing is especially useful in highly competitive markets that require continual product cost reductions to remain competitive.

HOW BUSINESSES MAKE MONEY

What Is a Product?

A product is often thought of in terms beyond just its physical attributes. For example, why a customer buys a product usually impacts how a business markets the product. Other considerations, such as warranty needs, servicing needs, and perceived quality, also affect business strategies.

Consider the four different types of products listed below. For these products, the frequency of purchase, the profit per unit, and the number of retailers differ. As a result, the sales and marketing approach for each product differs.

Product	Type of Product	Frequency of Purchase	Profit per Unit	Number of Retailers	Sales/Marketing Approach
Snickers®	Convenience	Often	Low	Many	Mass advertising
Sony® TV	Shopping	Occasional	Moderate	Many	Mass advertising; personal selling
Diamond ring	Specialty	Seldom	High	Few	Personal selling
Prearranged funeral	Unsought	Rare	High	Few	Aggressive selling

Obj **3**

Calculate the relative profitability of products in bottleneck production environments.

Product Profitability and Pricing under Production Bottlenecks

An important consideration influencing production volumes and prices is production bottlenecks. A production **bottleneck** (or **constraint**) occurs at the point in the process where the demand for the company's product exceeds the ability to produce the product. The **theory of constraints (TOC)** is a manufacturing strategy that focuses on reducing the influence of bottlenecks on a process.

The sand in the hourglass can pass only as fast as the narrowest point in the glass will allow.

Bottleneck

Product Profitability under Production Bottlenecks

When a company has a bottleneck in its production process, it should attempt to maximize its profitability, subject to the influence of the bottleneck. To illustrate, assume that Snapp-Off Tool Company makes three types of wrenches: small, medium, and large. All three products are processed through a heat treatment operation, which hardens the steel tools. Snapp-Off Tool's heat treatment process is operating at full capacity and is a production bottleneck. The product contribution margin per unit and the number of hours of heat treatment used by each type of wrench are as follows:

	Small Wrench	Medium Wrench	Large Wrench
Sales price per unit	$130	$140	$160
Variable cost per unit	40	40	40
Contribution margin per unit	$ 90	$100	$120
Heat treatment hours per unit	1	4	8

The large wrench appears to be the most profitable product because its contribution margin per unit is the greatest. However, the contribution margin per unit can be a misleading indicator of profitability in a bottleneck operation. The correct measure of performance is the value of each bottleneck hour, or the contribution margin per bottleneck hour. Using this measure, each product has a much different profitability when compared to the contribution margin per unit information, as shown in Exhibit 11.

EXHIBIT 11 *Contribution Margin per Bottleneck Hour*

	Small Wrench	Medium Wrench	Large Wrench
Sales price	$130	$140	$160
Variable cost per unit	40	40	40
Contribution margin per unit	$ 90	$100	$120
Bottleneck (heat treatment) hours per unit	÷ 1	÷ 4	÷ 8
Contribution margin per bottleneck hour	$ 90	$ 25	$ 15

The small wrench produces the most contribution margin per bottleneck (heat treatment) hour used, while the large wrench produces the smallest profit per bottleneck hour. Thus, the small wrench is the most profitable product. This information is the opposite of that implied by the unit contribution margin profit.

Product Pricing under Production Bottlenecks

Each hour of a bottleneck delivers profit to the company. When a company has a production bottleneck, the contribution margin per hour of bottleneck provides a measure of the product's relative profitability. This information can also be used to adjust the product price to better reflect the value of the product's use of a bottleneck. Products that use a large number of bottleneck hours per unit require more contribution margin than products that use few bottleneck hours per unit. For example, Snapp-Off Tool Company should increase the price of the large wrench in order to deliver more contribution margin per bottleneck hour.

To determine the price of the large wrench that would equate its profitability to the small wrench, we need to solve the following equation:

$$\text{Contribution margin per bottleneck hour per small wrench} = \frac{\text{Revised price of large wrench} - \text{Variable cost per large wrench}}{\text{Bottleneck hours per large wrench}}$$

$$\$90 = \frac{\text{Revised price of large wrench} - \$40}{8}$$

$$\$720 = \text{Revised price of large wrench} - \$40$$

$$\$760 = \text{Revised price of large wrench}$$

The large wrench's price would need to be increased to $760 in order to deliver the same contribution margin per bottleneck hour as does the small wrench, as verified below.

Revised price of large wrench	$760
Less: Variable cost per unit of large wrench	40
Contribution margin per unit of large wrench	$720
Bottleneck hours per unit of large wrench	÷ 8
Revised contribution margin per bottleneck hour	$ 90

At a price of $760, the company would be indifferent between producing and selling the small wrench or the large wrench, all else being equal. This analysis assumes that there is unlimited demand for the products. If the market were unwilling to purchase the large wrench at this price, then the company should produce the small wrench.

HOW BUSINESSES MAKE MONEY

Alternative Pricing Approaches

At various times, a business may use alternative pricing approaches, often as a supplement to the traditional cost-plus pricing of products. Some of these alternative approaches are described below.

- **Price skimming** is normally short term in nature and is used when a business has a new product that is unique in the marketplace. Because of the lack of competing products, the business sets the price at an artificially high level. It anticipates that it will have to lower the price once competitors enter the market. In the meantime, however, it will be able to earn high profits that can be used to cover the costs of developing the product. For example, *Samsung* initially set the price for its video cell phones at around $600. Eventually, as technology matured and competitors entered the market, the price for these phones fell.

- **Psychological pricing** is based on two behavioral tendencies of customers. First, customers often assume that the higher the price of a product, the higher the quality. Thus, for a special occasion, a novice wine buyer might be more inclined to purchase a higher-priced bottle of wine than a lower-priced bottle. Second, consumers are more likely to purchase a product priced just below the next whole number. For example, retailers often price products at $899 or $895, rather than $900. This type of pricing, called *odd-even pricing*, is used to imply bargains, even though the price difference between the odd and even number is insignificant.

- **Bundle pricing** involves grouping two related products together and pricing them as a single product. For example, appliance retailers often bundle a clothes washer and dryer together at a price that is less than the sum of the prices of the washer and dryer separately. Other examples of bundle pricing include "value meals" in fast-food restaurants and software bundled with PCs. Bundling products at a slightly reduced total price is intended to generate additional sales that otherwise might not have been made.

- **Dynamic pricing** is used when the price of a product changes depending upon supply, demand, time of day, season, weather conditions, and other factors. An example is the pricing of airline tickets. The price often depends on when the reservation is made, the degree of competition in the local market, number of seats already sold, and the time of day. Thus, the price of a ticket to fly between two cities can vary greatly. A business executive requiring an immediate one-day ahead round-trip ticket that departs in the morning and arrives back home in the evening will be charged a premium price. Another traveler with the same city-to-city destination can save money by reserving a ticket weeks ahead and flying during the off-peak midday hours.

Key Points

1. **Prepare a differential analysis report for decisions involving leasing or selling equipment, discontinuing an unprofitable segment, manufacturing or purchasing a needed part, replacing usable fixed assets, processing further or selling an intermediate product, or accepting additional business at a special price.**

   Differential analysis reports for leasing or selling, discontinuing a segment or product, making or buying, replacing equipment, processing or selling, and accepting business at a special price are illustrated in the text. Each analysis focuses on the differential revenues and/or costs of the alternative courses of action.

2. **Determine the selling price of a product, using the total cost, product cost, and variable cost concepts.**

   The three cost concepts commonly used in applying the cost-plus approach to product pricing are summarized as follows.

Cost Concept	Covered in Cost Amount	Covered in Markup
Total cost	Total costs	Desired profit
Product cost	Total manufacturing costs	Desired profit + Total selling and administrative expenses
Variable cost	Total variable costs	Desired profit + Total fixed costs

The markup percentages used in applying each cost concept are as follows:

Total cost concept:

$$\text{Markup percentage} = \frac{\text{Desired profit}}{\text{Total costs}}$$

Product cost concept:

$$\text{Markup percentage} = \frac{\text{Desired profit} + \text{Total selling and admin. expenses}}{\text{Total manufacturing costs}}$$

Variable cost concept:

$$\text{Markup percentage} = \frac{\text{Desired profit} + \text{Total fixed costs}}{\text{Total variable costs}}$$

Activity-based costing can be used to provide more accurate cost information in applying cost-plus concepts when indirect costs are insignificant. Target costing combines market-based methods with a cost-reduction emphasis.

3. **Calculate the relative profitability of products in bottleneck production environments.**

The profitability of a product in a bottleneck production environment may not be accurately shown in the contribution margin product report. Instead, the best measure of profitability is determined by dividing the contribution margin per unit by the bottleneck hours per unit. The resulting measure indicates the product's profitability per hour of bottleneck use. This information can be used to support product pricing decisions.

Key Terms

Activity-based costing (ABC)	Markup	Theory of constraints (TOC)
Bottleneck	Opportunity cost	Total cost concept
Differential analysis	Product cost concept	Variable cost concept
Differential cost	Sunk cost	
Differential revenue	Target costing	

Illustrative Problem

Inez Company recently began production of a new product, M, which required the investment of $1,600,000 in assets. The costs of producing and selling 80,000 units of Product M are estimated as follows:

Variable costs:	
Direct materials	$ 10.00 per unit
Direct labor	6.00
Factory overhead	4.00
Selling and administrative expenses	5.00
Total	$ 25.00 per unit
Fixed costs:	
Factory overhead	$800,000
Selling and administrative expenses	400,000

Inez Company is currently considering establishing a selling price for Product M. The president of Inez Company has decided to use the cost-plus approach to product pricing and has indicated that Product M must earn a 10% rate of return on invested assets.

Instructions

1. Determine the amount of desired profit from the production and sale of Product M.
2. Assuming that the total cost concept is used, determine (a) the cost amount per unit, (b) the markup percentage, and (c) the selling price of Product M.
3. Assuming that the product cost concept is used, determine (a) the cost amount per unit, (b) the markup percentage, and (c) the selling price of Product M.

4. Assuming that the variable cost concept is used, determine (a) the cost amount per unit, (b) the markup percentage, and (c) the selling price of Product M.
5. Assume that for the current year, the selling price of Product M was $42 per unit. To date, 60,000 units have been produced and sold, and analysis of the domestic market indicates that 15,000 additional units are expected to be sold during the remainder of the year. Recently, Inez Company received an offer from Wong Inc. for 4,000 units of Product M at $28 each. Wong Inc. will market the units in Korea under its own brand name, and no additional selling and administrative expenses associated with the sale will be incurred by Inez Company. The additional business is not expected to affect the domestic sales of Product M, and the additional units could be produced during the current year, using existing capacity. (a) Prepare a differential analysis report of the proposed sale to Wong Inc. (b) Based on the differential analysis report in (a), should the proposal be accepted?

Solution

1. **$160,000 ($1,600,000 × 10%)**

2. a. Total costs:

Variable ($25 × 80,000 units)	$2,000,000
Fixed ($800,000 + $400,000)	1,200,000
Total	$3,200,000

   Cost amount per unit: **$3,200,000 ÷ 80,000 units = $40.00**

   b. $$\text{Markup percentage} = \frac{\text{Desired profit}}{\text{Total costs}}$$

   $$\text{Markup percentage} = \frac{\$160,000}{\$3,200,000} = 5\%$$

   c.
Cost amount per unit	$40.00
Markup ($40 × 5%)	2.00
Selling price	$42.00

3. a. Total manufacturing costs:

Variable ($20 × 80,000 units)	$1,600,000
Fixed factory overhead	800,000
Total	$2,400,000

   Cost amount per unit: **$2,400,000 ÷ 80,000 units = $30.00**

   b. $$\text{Markup percentage} = \frac{\text{Desired profit} + \text{Total selling and administrative expenses}}{\text{Total manufacturing costs}}$$

   $$\text{Markup percentage} = \frac{\$160,000 + \$400,000 + (\$5 \times 80,000 \text{ units})}{\$2,400,000}$$

   $$\text{Markup percentage} = \frac{\$160,000 + \$400,000 + \$400,000}{\$2,400,000}$$

   $$\text{Markup percentage} = \frac{\$960,000}{\$2,400,000} = 40\%$$

   c.
Cost amount per unit	$30.00
Markup ($30 × 40%)	12.00
Selling price	$42.00

4. a. Variable cost amount per unit: $25
   Total variable costs: **$25 × 80,000 units = $2,000,000**

   b. $$\text{Markup percentage} = \frac{\text{Desired profit} + \text{Total fixed costs}}{\text{Total variable costs}}$$

(continued)

$$\text{Markup percentage} = \frac{\$160,000 + \$800,000 + \$400,000}{\$2,000,000}$$

$$\text{Markup percentage} = \frac{\$1,360,000}{\$2,000,000} = 68\%$$

c.
Cost amount per unit	$25.00
Markup ($25 × 68%)	17.00
Selling price	**$42.00**

5. a. ***Proposal to Sell to Wong Inc.***

Differential revenue from accepting offer:	
Revenue from sale of 4,000 additional units at $28	$112,000
Differential cost from accepting offer:	
Variable production costs of 4,000 additional units at $20	80,000
Differential income from accepting offer	$ 32,000

b. The proposal should be accepted.

Self-Examination Questions *(Answers appear at end of chapter.)*

1. Marlo Company is considering discontinuing a product. The costs of the product consist of $20,000 fixed costs and $15,000 variable costs. The variable operating expenses related to the product total $4,000. What is the differential cost?
   A. $19,000   C. $35,000
   B. $15,000   D. $39,000

2. Victor Company is considering disposing of equipment that was originally purchased for $200,000 and has $150,000 of accumulated depreciation to date. The same equipment would cost $310,000 to replace. What is the sunk cost?
   A. $50,000   C. $200,000
   B. $150,000   D. $310,000

3. Henry Company is considering spending $100,000 for a new grinding machine. This amount could be invested to yield a 12% return. What is the opportunity cost?
   A. $112,000   C. $12,000
   B. $88,000   D. $100,000

4. For which cost concept used in applying the cost-plus approach to product pricing are fixed manufacturing costs, fixed selling and administrative expenses, and desired profit allowed for in determining the markup?
   A. Total cost   C. Variable cost
   B. Product cost   D. Standard cost

5. Mendosa Company produces three products. All the products use a furnace operation, which is a production bottleneck. The following information is available:

	Product 1	Product 2	Product 3
Unit volume—March	1,000	1,500	1,000
Per-unit information:			
Sales price	$35	$33	$29
Variable cost	15	15	15
Contribution margin	$20	$18	$14
Furnace hours	4	3	2

From a profitability perspective, which product should be emphasized in April's advertising campaign?
A. Product 1   C. Product 3
B. Product 2   D. All three

Class Discussion Questions

1. Explain the meaning of (a) differential revenue, (b) differential cost, and (c) differential income.

2. It was reported that ***Exabyte***, a fast-growing (100-fold in 4 years) Colorado marketer of tape drives, has decided to purchase key components of its product from others. For example, ***Sony*** provides Exabyte with mechanical decks, and ***Solectron*** provides circuit boards. Exabyte's chief executive officer, Peter Behrendt, states, "If we'd tried to build our own plants, we could never have grown that fast or maybe survived." The decision to purchase key product components is an example of what type of decision illustrated in this chapter?

3. In the long run, the normal selling price must be set high enough to cover what factors?

4. A company could sell a building for $250,000 or lease it for $2,500 per month. What would need to be considered in determining if the lease option would be preferred?

5. A chemical company has a commodity-grade and a premium-grade product. Why might the company elect to process the commodity-grade product further to the premium-grade product?

6. A company accepts incremental business at a special price that exceeds the variable cost. What other issues must the company consider in deciding whether to accept the business?

7. A company fabricates a component at a cost of $6.00. A supplier offers to supply the same component for $5.50. Under what circumstances is it reasonable to purchase from the supplier?

8. Many fast-food restaurant chains, such as **McDonald's**, will occasionally discontinue restaurants in their system. What are some financial considerations in deciding to eliminate a store?

9. Why might the use of ideal standards in applying the cost-plus approach to product pricing lead to setting product prices that are too low?

10. Although the cost-plus approach to product pricing may be used by management as a general guideline, what are some examples of other factors that managers should also consider in setting product prices?

11. What method of determining product cost may be appropriate in settings where the manufacturing process is complex?

12. How does the target cost concept differ from cost-plus approaches?

13. Under what circumstances is it appropriate to use the target cost concept?

14. What is a production bottleneck?

15. What is the appropriate measure of a product's value when a firm is operating under production bottlenecks?

Exercises

E12-1

Lease or sell decision

Obj 1

SPREADSHEET

✓ a. Differential revenue from lease, $30,000

Vanderhoff Construction Company is considering selling excess machinery with a book value of $260,000 (original cost of $380,000 less accumulated depreciation of $120,000) for $210,000, less a 4% brokerage commission. Alternatively, the machinery can be leased for a total of $240,000 for five years, after which it is expected to have no residual value. During the period of the lease, Vanderhoff Construction Company's cost of repairs, insurance, and property tax expenses are expected to be $28,000.

a. Prepare a differential analysis report, dated January 3, 2008, for the lease or sell decision.
b. On the basis of the data presented, would it be advisable to lease or sell the machinery? Explain.

E12-2

Differential analysis report for a discontinued product

Obj 1

✓ a. Differential cost of annual sales, $299,400

A condensed income statement by product line for Canadian Beverage Inc. indicated the following for Lemon Mist for the past year:

Sales	$362,000
Cost of goods sold	185,000
Gross profit	$177,000
Operating expenses	215,000
Loss from operations	$ (38,000)

It is estimated that 23% of the cost of goods sold represents fixed factory overhead costs and that 27% of the operating expenses are fixed. Since Lemon Mist is only one of many products, the fixed costs will not be materially affected if the product is discontinued.

a. Prepare a differential analysis report, dated January 3, 2008, for the proposed discontinuance of Lemon Mist.
b. Should Lemon Mist be retained? Explain.

E12-3

Differential analysis report for a discontinued product

Obj 1

SPREADSHEET

✓ a. Differential income: bowls, $46,450

The condensed product-line income statement for Country Ceramics Company for the current year is as follows:

COUNTRY CERAMICS COMPANY
Product-Line Income Statement
For the Year Ended December 31, 2008

	Bowls	*Plates*	*Cups*
Sales	$132,000	$108,000	$83,000
Cost of goods sold	71,000	55,000	49,000
Gross profit	$ 61,000	$ 53,000	$34,000
Selling and administrative expenses	35,000	24,000	38,000
Income from operations	$ 26,000	$ 29,000	$(4,000)

Fixed costs are 15% of the cost of goods sold and 28% of the selling and administrative expenses. Country Ceramics assumes that fixed costs would not be materially affected if the Cups line were discontinued.

a. Prepare a differential analysis report for all three products for 2008.
b. Should the Cups line be retained? Explain.

E12-4

Segment analysis

Obj 1

The **Charles Schwab Corporation** is one of the more innovative brokerage and financial service companies in the United States. The company recently provided information about its major business segments as follows (in millions):

	Individual Investor	*Institutional Investor*	*U.S. Trust*
Revenues	$2,742	$803	$832
Income from operations	758	317	103
Depreciation	145	29	33

a. How do you believe Schwab defines the difference between the "Individual Investor" and "Institutional Investor" segments?
b. Provide a specific example of a variable and fixed cost in the "Individual Investor" segment.
c. Estimate the contribution margin for each segment.
d. If Schwab decided to sell its "Institutional Investor" accounts to another company, estimate how much operating income would decline.

E12-5

Decision to discontinue a product

Obj 1

On the basis of the following data, the general manager of Feet to Go Inc. decided to discontinue Children's Shoes because it reduced income from operations by $26,000. What is the flaw in this decision?

FEET TO GO INC.
Product-Line Income Statement
For the Year Ended August 31, 2008

	Children's Shoes	*Men's Shoes*	*Women's Shoes*	*Total*
Sales	$ 150,000	$300,000	$500,000	$950,000
Costs of goods sold:				
Variable costs	$ 90,000	$150,000	$220,000	$460,000
Fixed costs	40,000	60,000	120,000	220,000
Total cost of goods sold	$130,000	$210,000	$340,000	$680,000
Gross profit	$ 20,000	$ 90,000	$160,000	$270,000
Selling and administrative expenses:				
Variable selling and admin. expenses	$ 30,000	$ 45,000	$ 95,000	$170,000
Fixed selling and admin. expenses	16,000	20,000	25,000	61,000
Total selling and admin. expenses	$ 46,000	$ 65,000	$120,000	$231,000
Income (loss) from operations	$(26,000)	$ 25,000	$ 40,000	$ 39,000

E12-6
Make-or-buy decision

Obj 1

SPREADSHEET

✓ a. Cost savings from making, $3.00 per case

Hart Computer Company has been purchasing carrying cases for its portable computers at a delivered cost of $68 per unit. The company, which is currently operating below full capacity, charges factory overhead to production at the rate of 35% of direct labor cost. The fully absorbed unit costs to produce comparable carrying cases are expected to be:

Direct materials	$25.00
Direct labor	32.00
Factory overhead (35% of direct labor)	11.20
Total cost per unit	$68.20

If Hart Computer Company manufactures the carrying cases, fixed factory overhead costs will not increase and variable factory overhead costs associated with the cases are expected to be 25% of the direct labor costs.

a. Prepare a differential analysis report, dated June 5, 2008, for the make-or-buy decision.
b. On the basis of the data presented, would it be advisable to make the carrying cases or to continue buying them? Explain.

E12-7
Make-or-buy decision

Obj 1

SPREADSHEET

The Association of Retired Educators (ARE) employs five people in its Publication Department. These people lay out pages for pamphlets, brochures, and other publications for the ARE membership. The pages are delivered to an outside company for printing. The company is considering an outside publication service for the layout work. The outside service is quoting a price of $18 per layout page. The budget for the Publication Department for 2008 is as follows:

Salaries	$225,000
Benefits	38,000
Supplies	32,000
Office expenses	25,000
Office depreciation	22,000
Computer depreciation	30,000
Total	$372,000

The department expects to lay out 17,500 pages for 2008. The computers used by the department have an estimated salvage value of $5,000. The Publication Department office space would be used for future administrative needs, if the department's function were purchased from the outside.

a. Prepare a differential analysis report, dated December 15, 2007, for the make-or-buy decision, considering the 2008 differential revenues and costs.
b. On the basis of your analysis in part (a), should the page layout work be purchased from an outside company?
c. What additional considerations might factor into the decision making?

E12-8
Machine replacement decision

Obj 1

✓ a. Annual differential income, $12,250

A company is considering replacing an old piece of machinery, which cost $560,000 and has $320,000 of accumulated depreciation to date, with a new machine that costs $460,000. The old equipment could be sold for $78,000. The variable production costs associated with the old machine are estimated to be $170,000 for eight years. The variable production costs for the new machine are estimated to be $110,000 for eight years.

a. Determine the total and annualized differential income or loss anticipated from replacing the old machine.
b. What is the sunk cost in this situation?

E12-9

Differential analysis report for machine replacement

Obj 1

SPREADSHEET

✓ a. Annual differential increase in costs, $2,500

Bay Area Electronics Company assembles circuit boards by using a manually operated machine to insert electronic components. The original cost of the machine is $140,000, the accumulated depreciation is $110,000, its remaining useful life is 15 years, and its salvage value is negligible. On January 20, 2008, a proposal was made to replace the present manufacturing procedure with a fully automatic machine that will cost $270,000. The automatic machine has an estimated useful life of 15 years and no significant salvage value. For use in evaluating the proposal, the accountant accumulated the following annual data on present and proposed operations:

	Present Operations	Proposed Operations
Sales	$275,000	$275,000
Direct materials	$ 80,000	$ 80,000
Direct labor	45,000	—
Power and maintenance	7,500	32,000
Taxes, insurance, etc.	3,500	8,500
Selling and administrative expenses	80,000	80,000
Total expenses	$216,000	$200,500

a. Prepare a differential analysis report for the proposal to replace the machine. Include in the analysis both the net differential change in costs anticipated over the 15 years and the net annual differential change in costs anticipated.
b. Based only on the data presented, should the proposal be accepted?
c. What are some of the other factors that should be considered before a final decision is made?

E12-10

Sell or process further

Obj 1

✓ a. $225

Oregon Lumber Company incurs a cost of $465 per hundred board feet in processing certain "rough-cut" lumber, which it sells for $625 per hundred board feet. An alternative is to produce a "finished cut" at a total processing cost of $545 per hundred board feet, which can be sold for $850 per hundred board feet. What is the amount of (a) the differential revenue, (b) differential cost, and (c) differential income for processing rough-cut lumber into finished cut?

E12-11

Sell or process further

Obj 1

SPREADSHEET

Golden Roast Coffee Company produces Colombian coffee in batches of 7,700 pounds. The standard quantity of materials required in the process is 7,700 pounds, which cost $5.00 per pound. Colombian coffee can be sold without further processing for $8.90 per pound. Colombian coffee can also be processed further to yield Decaf Colombian, which can be sold for $11.60 per pound. The processing into Decaf Colombian requires additional processing costs of $18,326 per batch. The additional processing will also cause a 6% loss of product due to evaporation.

a. Prepare a differential analysis report for the decision to sell or process further.
b. Should Golden Roast sell Colombian coffee or process further and sell Decaf Colombian?
c. Determine the price of Decaf Colombian that would cause neither an advantage or disadvantage for processing further and selling Decaf Colombian.

E12-12

Decision on accepting additional business

Obj 1

✓ a. Differential income, $112,000

Workman's Denim Co. has an annual plant capacity of 65,000 units, and current production is 45,000 units. Monthly fixed costs are $40,000, and variable costs are $24 per unit. The present selling price is $36 per unit. On January 18, 2008, the company received an offer from Marshall Company for 16,000 units of the product at $31 each. Marshall Company will market the units in a foreign country under its own brand name. The additional business is not expected to affect the domestic selling price or quantity of sales of Workman's Denim Co.

a. Prepare a differential analysis report for the proposed sale to Marshall Company.
b. Briefly explain the reason why accepting this additional business will increase operating income.
c. What is the minimum price per unit that would produce a contribution margin?

E12-13

Accepting business at a special price

Obj 1

Jupiter Company expects to operate at 90% of productive capacity during May. The total manufacturing costs for May for the production of 25,000 batteries are budgeted as follows:

Direct materials	$272,000
Direct labor	96,000
Variable factory overhead	32,000
Fixed factory overhead	54,000
Total manufacturing costs	$454,000

The company has an opportunity to submit a bid for 1,000 batteries to be delivered by May 31 to a government agency. If the contract is obtained, it is anticipated that the additional activity will not interfere with normal production during May or increase the selling or administrative expenses. What is the unit cost below which Jupiter Company should not go in bidding on the government contract?

E12-14

Decision on accepting additional business

Obj 1

SPREADSHEET

✓ a. Differential revenue, $1,500,000

Sure-Grip Tire and Rubber Company has capacity to produce 170,000 tires. Sure-Grip presently produces and sells 130,000 tires for the North American market at a price of $90 per tire. Sure-Grip is evaluating a special order from a European automobile company, Continental Motors. Continental is offering to buy 25,000 tires for $60 per tire. Sure-Grip's accounting system indicates that the total cost per tire is as follows:

Direct materials	$26
Direct labor	9
Factory overhead (35% variable)	22
Selling and administrative expenses (40% variable)	18
Total	$75

Sure-Grip pays a selling commission equal to 5% of the selling price on North American orders, which is included in the variable portion of the selling and administrative expenses. However, this special order would not have a sales commission. If the order was accepted, the tires would be shipped overseas for an additional shipping cost of $6.00 per tire. In addition, Continental has made the order conditional on receiving European safety certification. Sure-Grip estimates that this certification would cost $110,000.

a. Prepare a differential analysis report dated August 4, 2008, for the proposed sale to Continental Motors.
b. What is the minimum price per unit that would be financially acceptable to Sure-Grip?

E12-15

Total cost concept of product costing

Obj 2

✓ d. $340

Sirrus Phone Company uses the total cost concept of applying the cost-plus approach to product pricing. The costs of producing and selling 3,500 units of mobile phones are as follows:

Variable costs:		Fixed costs:	
Direct materials	$130.00 per unit	Factory overhead	$175,000
Direct labor	50.00	Selling and adm. exp.	70,000
Factory overhead	35.00		
Selling and adm. exp.	25.00		
Total	$240.00 per unit		

(continued)

Sirrus desires a profit equal to a 30% rate of return on invested assets of $350,000.

a. Determine the amount of desired profit from the production and sale of mobile phones.
b. Determine the total costs and the cost amount per unit for the production and sale of 3,500 units of mobile phones.
c. Determine the markup percentage (rounded to two decimals places) for mobile phones.
d. Determine the selling price of mobile phones. Round to the nearest dollar.

E12-16

Product cost concept of product pricing

Obj 2

✓ b. 28.30%

Based on the data presented in Exercise 12-15, assume that Sirrus Phone Company uses the product cost concept of applying the cost-plus approach to product pricing.

a. Determine the total manufacturing costs and the cost amount per unit for the production and sale of 3,500 units of mobile phones.
b. Determine the markup percentage (rounded to two decimals places) for mobile phones.
c. Determine the selling price of mobile phones. Round to the nearest dollar.

E12-17

Variable cost concept of product pricing

Obj 2

✓ b. 41.67%

Based on the data presented in Exercise 12-15, assume that Sirrus Phone Company uses the variable cost concept of applying the cost-plus approach to product pricing.

a. Determine the variable costs and the cost amount per unit for the production and sale of 3,500 units of mobile phones.
b. Determine the markup percentage (rounded to two decimals places) for mobile phones.
c. Determine the selling price of mobile phones. Round to the nearest dollar.

E12-18

Target costing

Obj 2

TC = desired profit - selling price

Toyota Motor Corporation uses target costing. Assume that Toyota marketing personnel estimate that the competitive selling price for the Camry in the upcoming model year will need to be $34,000. Assume further that the Camry's total manufacturing cost for the upcoming model year is estimated to be $28,500 and that Toyota requires a 20% profit margin on selling price (which is equivalent to a 25% markup on product cost).

a. What price will Toyota establish for the Camry for the upcoming model year?
b. What impact will target costing have on Toyota, given the assumed information?

E12-19

Target costing

Obj 2

✓ b. $25

Spectrum Imaging Company manufactures color laser printers. Model A200 presently sells for $300 and has a total product cost of $250, as follows:

Direct materials	$170
Direct labor	50
Factory overhead	30
Total	$250

It is estimated that the competitive selling price for color laser printers of this type will drop to $270 next year. Spectrum Imaging has established a target cost to maintain its historical markup percentage on product cost. Engineers have provided the following cost reduction ideas:

1. Purchase a plastic printer cover with snap-on assembly. This will reduce the amount of direct labor by six minutes per unit.
2. Add an inspection step that will add three minutes per unit direct labor but reduce the materials cost by $6 per unit.
3. Decrease the cycle time of the injection molding machine from four minutes to three minutes per part. Thirty percent of the direct labor and 42% of the factory overhead is related to running injection molding machines.

The direct labor rate is $32 per hour.

a.   Determine the target cost for Model A200 assuming that the historical markup on product cost is maintained.

b.   Determine the required cost reduction.

c.   Evaluate the three engineering improvements to determine if the required cost reduction (drift) can be achieved.

E12-20

Product decisions under bottlenecked operations

Obj 3

Samson Metals Inc. has three grades of metal product, Type 5, Type 10, and Type 20. Financial data for the three grades are as follows:

	Type 5	*Type 10*	*Type 20*
Revenues	$16,000	$20,800	$12,000
Variable cost	$ 6,000	$ 8,000	$ 5,000
Fixed cost	4,000	4,000	4,000
Total cost	$10,000	$12,000	$ 9,000
Income from operations	$ 6,000	$ 8,800	$ 3,000
Number of units	÷ 4,000	÷ 4,000	÷ 4,000
Income from operations per unit	$ 1.50	$ 2.20	$ 0.75

Samson's operations require all three grades to be melted in a furnace before being formed. The furnace runs 24 hours a day, 7 days a week, and is a production bottleneck. The furnace hours required per unit of each product are as follows:

Type 5:   5 hours
Type 10: 10 hours
Type 20:   5 hours

The Marketing Department is considering a new marketing and sales campaign.

Which product should be emphasized in the marketing and sales campaign in order to maximize profitability?

E12-21

Product decisions under bottlenecked operations

Obj 3

✓ a. Total income from operations, $115,000

Gannett Glass Company manufactures three types of safety plate glass: large, medium, and small. All three products have high demand. Thus, Gannett Glass is able to sell all the safety glass that it can make. The production process includes an autoclave operation, which is a pressurized heat treatment. The autoclave is a production bottleneck. Total fixed costs are $550,000. In addition, the following information is available about the three products:

	Large	*Medium*	*Small*
Unit selling price	$240	$180	$120
Unit variable cost	126	80	68
Unit contribution margin	$114	$100	$ 52
Autoclave hours per unit	6	10	4
Total process hours per unit	20	16	12
Budgeted units of production	2,500	2,500	2,500

a.   Determine the contribution margin by glass type and the total company income from operations for the budgeted units of production.

b.   Prepare an analysis showing which product is the most profitable per bottleneck hour.

E12-22

Product pricing under bottlenecked operations

Obj 3

✓ Medium, $270

Based on the data presented in Exercise 12-21, assume that Gannett Glass wanted to price all products so that they produced the same profit potential as the highest profit product. Thus, determine the prices for each of the products so that they would produce a profit equal to the highest profit product.

Problems

P12-1

Differential analysis report involving opportunity costs

Obj 1

SPREADSHEET

✓ 1. Differential loss from operating store, $100,00

On July 1, Daybreak Stores Inc. is considering selling a building and purchasing the necessary equipment to operate a retail store. Alternatively, the company could use the funds to invest in $280,000 of 5% U.S. Treasury bonds that mature in 20 years. The bonds could be purchased at face value. The following data have been assembled:

Cost of store equipment	$280,000
Life of store equipment	20 years
Estimated residual value of store equipment	$20,000
Yearly costs to operate the store, excluding	
depreciation of store equipment	$70,000
Yearly expected revenues—years 1–10	$88,000
Yearly expected revenues—years 11–20	$96,000

Instructions

1. Prepare a report as of July 1, 2008, presenting a differential analysis of the proposed operation of the store for the 20 years as compared with present conditions.
2. Based on the results disclosed by the differential analysis, should the proposal be accepted?
3. If the proposal is accepted, what would be the total estimated income from operations of the store for the 20 years?

P12-2

Differential analysis report for machine replacement proposal

Obj 1

SPREADSHEET

Quebec Printing Company is considering replacing a machine that has been used in its factory for four years. Relevant data associated with the operations of the old machine and the new machine, neither of which has any estimated residual value, are as follows:

Old Machine	
Cost of machine, 10-year life	$360,000
Annual depreciation (straight-line)	36,000
Annual manufacturing costs, excluding depreciation	325,000
Annual nonmanufacturing operating expenses	215,000
Annual revenue	740,000
Current estimated selling price of machine	210,000

New Machine	
Cost of machine, 6-year life	$410,000
Annual depreciation (straight-line)	68,333
Estimated annual manufacturing costs, exclusive of depreciation	284,000

Annual nonmanufacturing operating expenses and revenue are not expected to be affected by purchase of the new machine.

Instructions

1. Prepare a differential analysis report as of October 13, 2008, comparing operations utilizing the new machine with operations using the present equipment. The analysis should indicate the total differential income that would result over the 6-year period if the new machine is acquired.
2. List other factors that should be considered before a final decision is reached.

P12-3

Differential analysis report for sales promotion proposal

Obj 1

SPREADSHEET

✓ 1. Differential income, moisturizer, $163,000

Cleopatra Cosmetics Company is planning a one-month campaign for May to promote sales of one of its two cosmetics products. A total of $110,000 has been budgeted for advertising, contests, redeemable coupons, and other promotional activities. The following data have been assembled for their possible usefulness in deciding which of the products to select for the campaign:

	Moisturizer	Perfume
Until selling price	$56	$75
Until production costs:		
Direct materials	$10	$14
Direct labor	5	8
Variable factory overhead	3	5
Fixed factory overhead	8	8
Total unit production costs	$26	$35
Unit variable selling expenses	12	18
Unit fixed selling expenses	4	2
Total unit costs	$42	$55
Operating income per unit	$14	$20

No increase in facilities would be necessary to produce and sell the increased output. It is anticipated that 10,500 additional units of moisturizer or 8,000 additional units of perfume could be sold without changing the unit selling price of either product.

Instructions

1. Prepare a differential analysis report as of April 15, 2008, presenting the additional revenue and additional costs anticipated from the promotion of moisturizer and perfume.
2. The sales manager had tentatively decided to promote perfume, estimating that operating income would be increased by $50,000 ($20 operating income per unit for 8,000 units, less promotion expenses of $110,000). The manager also believed that the selection of moisturizer would have less of an impact on operating income, $37,000 ($14 operating income per unit for 10,500 units, less promotion expenses of $110,000). State briefly your reasons for supporting or opposing the tentative decision.

P12-4

Differential analysis report for further processing

Obj 1

✓ 1. Differential revenue, $9,800

The management of Delta Sugar Company is considering whether to process further raw sugar into refined sugar. Refined sugar can be sold for $1.75 per pound, and raw sugar can be sold without further processing for $1.05 per pound. Raw sugar is produced in batches of 24,000 pounds by processing 90,000 pounds of sugar cane, which costs $0.25 per pound. Refined sugar will require additional processing costs of $0.36 per pound of raw sugar, and 1.2 pounds of raw sugar will produce 1 pound of refined sugar.

Instructions

1. Prepare a report as of August 30, 2008, presenting a differential analysis of the further processing of raw sugar to produce refined sugar.
2. Briefly report your recommendations.

illustrative problem

P12-5

Product pricing using the cost-plus approach concepts; differential analysis report for accepting additional business

Objs 1, 2

✓ 2. b. Markup percentage, 6%

Plasma Labs Inc. recently began production of a new product, flat panel displays, which required the investment of $3,000,000 in assets. The costs of producing and selling 20,000 units of flat panel displays are estimated as follows:

Variable costs per unit:		Fixed costs:	
Direct materials	$150	Factory overhead	$2,000,000
Direct labor	30	Selling and	
Factory overhead	50	administration	
Selling and administrative		expenses	1,000,000
expenses	20		
Total	$250		*150*

Plasma Labs Inc. is currently considering establishing a selling price for flat panel display. The president of Plasma Labs has decided to use the cost-plus approach to product pricing and has indicated that the displays must earn a 16% rate of return on invested assets.

Instructions

1. Determine the amount of desired profit from the production and sale of flat panel displays.
2. Assuming that the total cost concept is used, determine (a) the cost amount per unit, (b) the markup percentage, and (c) the selling price of flat panel displays.
3. Assuming that the product cost concept is used, determine (a) the cost amount per unit, (b) the markup percentage (rounded to two decimal places), and (c) the selling price of flat panel displays (rounded to nearest whole dollar).
4. Assuming that the variable cost concept is used, determine (a) the cost amount per unit, (b) the markup percentage, and (c) the selling price of flat panel displays.
5. Comment on any additional considerations that could influence establishing the selling price for flat panel displays.
6. Assume that as of September 1, 2008, 13,000 units of flat panel displays have been produced and sold during the current year. Analysis of the domestic market indicates that 4,400 additional units are expected to be sold during the remainder of the year at the normal product price determined under the total cost concept. On September 3, Plasma Labs Inc. received an offer from Vision Systems Inc. for 2,600 units of flat panel displays at $255 each. Vision Systems Inc. will market the units in Canada under its own brand name, and no selling and administrative expenses associated with the sale will be incurred by Plasma Labs Inc. The additional business is not expected to affect the domestic sales of flat panel displays, and the additional units could be produced using existing capacity.
   a. Prepare a differential analysis report of the proposed sale to Vision Systems Inc.
   b. Based upon the differential analysis report in part (a), should the proposal be accepted?

P12-6

Product pricing and profit analysis with bottleneck operations

Objs 1, 3

SPREADSHEET

✓ 1. High Grade, $125

Atlas Steel Company produces three grades of steel: high, good, and regular grade. Each of these products (grades) has high demand in the market, and Atlas is able to sell as much as it can produce of all three. The furnace operation is a bottleneck in the process and is running at 100% of capacity. Atlas wants to improve steel operation profitability. The variable conversion cost is $6 per process hour. The fixed cost is $1,530,000. In addition, the cost analyst was able to determine the following information about the three products:

	High Grade	Good Grade	Regular Grade
Budgeted units produced	6,000	6,000	6,000
Total process hours per unit	15	15	12
Furnace hours per unit	5	3	2
Unit selling price	$375	$350	$320
Direct materials cost per unit	$160	$140	$130

The furnace operation is part of the total process for each of these three products. Thus, for example, 5 of the 15 hours required to process High Grade steel are associated with the furnace.

Instructions

1. Determine the unit contribution margin for each product.
2. Provide an analysis to determine the relative product profitabilities, assuming that the furnace is a bottleneck.
3. Assume that management wishes to improve profitability by increasing prices on selected products. At what price would High and Good grades need to be offered in order to produce the same relative profitability as Regular Grade steel?

Activities

A12-1

Product pricing

ETHICS

Marcia Martinez is a cost accountant for Ascend Inc. Marcus Todd, vice president of marketing, has asked Marcia to meet with representatives of Ascend's major competitor to discuss product cost data. Marcus indicates that the sharing of these data will enable Ascend to determine a fair and equitable price for its products.

Would it be ethical for Marcia to attend the meeting and share the relevant cost data?

A12-2

Decision on accepting additional business

A manager of Back Tee Sporting Goods Company is considering accepting an order from an overseas customer. This customer has requested an order for 20,000 dozen golf balls at a price of $20.00 per dozen. The variable cost to manufacture a dozen golf balls is $17.00 per dozen. The full cost is $23.00 per dozen. Back Tee has a normal selling price of $28.00 per dozen. Back Tee's plant has just enough excess capacity on the second shift to make the overseas order.

What are some considerations in accepting or rejecting this order?

A12-3

Accept business at a special price

If you are not familiar with **Priceline.com Inc.**, go to its Web site. Assume that an individual bids $60 on Priceline.com for a room in Dallas, Texas, on August 24. Assume that August 24 is a Saturday, with low expected room demand in Dallas at a **Marriott International, Inc.**, hotel, so there is excess room capacity. The fully allocated cost per room per day is assumed from hotel records as follows:

Housekeeping labor cost*	$30
Hotel depreciation expense	42
Cost of room supplies (soap, paper, etc.)	5
Laundry labor and material cost*	10
Cost of desk staff	5
Utility cost (mostly air conditioning)	3
Total cost per room per day	$95

* Both housekeeping and laundry staff include many part-time workers, so that the workload is variable to demand.

Should Marriott accept the customer bid for a night in Dallas on August 24 at a price of $60?

A12-4

Make-or-buy decision

The president of Monarch Materials Inc., Todd Bentley, asked the controller, Megan Mayfield, to provide an analysis of a make vs. buy decision for material TS-101. The material is presently processed in Monarch's Roanoke facility. TS-101 is used in processing of final products in the facility. Megan determined the following unit production costs for the material as of March 15, 2008:

Direct materials	$ 7.50
Direct labor	2.70
Variable factory overhead	1.20
Fixed factory overhead	2.00
Total production costs per unit	$13.40

In addition, material TS-101 requires special hazardous material handling. This special handling adds an additional cost of $1.60 for each unit produced.

Material TS-101 can be purchased from an overseas supplier. The supplier does not presently do business with Monarch Materials. This supplier promises monthly delivery of the material at a price of $10.10 per unit, plus transportation cost of $0.40 per unit. In addition, Monarch would need to incur additional administrative costs to satisfy import regulations for hazardous material. These additional administrative costs are estimated to be $0.80 per purchased unit. Each purchased unit would also require special hazardous material handling of $1.60 per unit.

a. Prepare a differential analysis report to support Megan's recommendation on whether to continue making material TS-101 or whether to purchase the material from the overseas supplier.
b. What additional considerations should Megan address in the recommendation?

A12-5

Cost-plus and target costing concepts

The following conversation took place between Theo James, vice president of marketing, and Lee Corso, controller of Astor Computer Company:

Theo: I am really excited about our new computer coming out. I think it will be a real market success.

Lee: I'm really glad you think so. I know that our price is one variable that will determine if it's a success. If our price is too high, our competitors will be the ones with the market success.

Theo: Don't worry about it. We'll just mark our product cost up by 25% and it will all work out. I know we'll make money at those markups. By the way, what does the estimated product cost look like?

Lee: Well, there's the rub. The product cost looks as if it's going to come in at around $2,400. With a 25% markup, that will give us a selling price of $3,000.

Theo: I see your concern. That's a little high. Our research indicates that computer prices are dropping by about 20% per year and that this type of computer should be selling for around $2,500 when we release it to the market.

Lee: I'm not sure what to do.

Theo: Let me see if I can help. How much of the $2,400 is fixed cost?

Lee: About $400.

Theo: There you go. The fixed cost is sunk. We don't need to consider it in our pricing decision. If we reduce the product cost by $400, the new price with a 25% markup would be right at $2,500. Boy, I was really worried for a minute there. I knew something wasn't right.

a. If you were Lee, how would you respond to Theo's solution to the pricing problem?
b. How might target costing be used to help solve this pricing dilemma?

A12-6

Internet marketing

Many businesses are offering their products and services over the Internet. Some of these companies and their Internet addresses are listed below.

Company Name	Internet Address (URL)	Product
Delta Air Lines	http://www.delta.com	airline tickets
Amazon.com	http://www.amazon.com	books
Dell Inc.	http://www.dell.com	personal computers

a. In groups of three, assign each person in your group to one of the Internet sites listed above. For each site, determine the following:

1. A product (or service) description.
2. A product price.
3. A list of costs that are required to produce and sell the product selected in part (1) as listed in the annual report on SEC form 10-K.
4. Whether the costs identified in part (3) are fixed costs or variable costs.

b. Which of the three products do you believe has the largest markup on variable cost?

Answers to Self-Examination Questions

1. **A** Differential cost is the amount of increase or decrease in cost that is expected from a particular course of action compared with an alternative. For Marlo Company, the differential cost is $19,000 (answer A). This is the total of the variable product costs ($15,000) and the variable operating expenses ($4,000), which would not be incurred if the product is discontinued.

2. **A** A sunk cost is not affected by later decisions. For Victor Company, the sunk cost is the $50,000 (answer A) book value of the equipment, which is equal to the original cost of $200,000 (answer C) less the accumulated depreciation of $150,000 (answer B).

3. **C** The amount of income that could have been earned from the best available alternative to a proposed use of cash is the opportunity cost. For Henry Company, the opportunity cost is 12% of $100,000, or $12,000 (answer C).

4. **C** Under the variable cost concept of product pricing (answer C), fixed manufacturing costs, fixed administrative and selling expenses, and desired profit are allowed for in determining the markup. Only desired profit is allowed for in the markup under the total cost concept (answer A). Under the product cost concept (answer B), total selling and administrative expenses and desired profit are allowed for in determining the markup. Standard cost (answer D) can be used under any of the cost-plus approaches to product pricing.

5. **C** Product 3 has the highest unit contribution margin per bottleneck hour ($14/2 = $7). Product 1 (answer A) has the largest contribution margin per unit, but the lowest unit contribution per bottleneck hour ($20/4 = $5), so it is the least profitable product in the constrained environment. Product 2 (answer B) has the highest total profitability in March (1,500 units $\times$ $18), but this does not suggest that it has the highest profit potential. Product 2's unit contribution per bottleneck hour ($18/3 = $6) is between Products 1 and 3. Answer D is not true, since the products all have different profit potential in terms of unit contribution margin per bottleneck hour.

CHAPTER 13

Budgeting and Standard Cost Systems

Learning Objectives

After studying this chapter, you should be able to:

Obj 1
Describe the nature and objectives of budgeting.

Obj 2
Describe the master budget for a manufacturing business.

Obj 3
Describe the nature and use of standards.

Obj 4
Explain and illustrate how standards are used in budgeting.

Obj 5
Calculate and interpret the basic variances for direct materials and direct labor.

Obj 6
Explain how standards can be used for nonmanufacturing expenses.

Obj 7
Explain and provide examples of nonfinancial performance measures.

You may have financial goals for your life. To achieve these goals, it is necessary to plan for future expenses. For example, you may consider taking a part-time job to save money for school expenses for the coming school year. How much money would you need to earn and save in order to pay these expenses? One way to answer this question would be to prepare a budget. For example, a budget would show an estimate of your expenses associated with school, such as tuition, fees, and books. In addition, you would have expenses for day-to-day living, such as rent, food, and clothing. You might also have expenses for travel and entertainment. Once the school year begins, you can use the budget as a tool for guiding your spending priorities during the year.

The budget is used in businesses in much the same way as it can be used in personal life. For example, *DaimlerChrysler* uses budgeting to determine the number of cars to be produced, number of shifts to operate, number of people to be employed, and amount of material to be purchased. The budget provides the company a "game plan" for the year. In this chapter, you will see how budgets can be used for financial planning and control. We conclude this chapter by describing and illustrating standard cost systems.

Describe the nature and
objectives of budgeting.

Nature and Objectives of Budgeting

If you were driving across the country, you might plan your trip with the aid of a road map. The road map would lay out your route across the country, identify stopovers, and reduce your chances of getting lost. In the same way, a **budget** charts a course for a business by outlining the plans of the business in financial terms. Like the road map, the budget can help a company navigate through the year and reduce negative outcomes.

Although budgets are normally associated with profit-making businesses, they also play an important role in operating most units of government. For example, budgets are important in managing rural school districts and small villages as well as agencies of the federal government. Budgets are also important for managing the operations of churches, hospitals, and other nonprofit institutions. Individuals and families also use budgeting techniques in managing their financial affairs. In this chapter, we emphasize the principles of budgeting in the context of a business organized for profit.

The chart below shows the estimated portion of your total monthly income that should be budgeted for various living expenses.

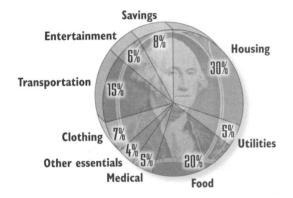

Source: Consumer Credit Counseling Service.

Objectives of Budgeting

Budgeting involves (1) establishing specific goals, (2) executing plans to achieve the goals, and (3) periodically comparing actual results with the goals. These goals include both the overall business goals as well as the specific goals for the individual units within the business. Establishing specific goals for future operations is part of the *planning* function of management, while executing actions to meet the goals is the *directing* function of management. Periodically comparing actual results with these goals and taking appropriate action is the *controlling* function of management. The relationships of these functions are illustrated in Exhibit 1.

Human Behavior and Budgeting

In the budgeting process, business, team, and individual goals are established. Human behavior problems can arise if (1) the budget goal is unachievable (too tight), (2) the budget goal is very easy to achieve (too loose), or (3) the budget goals of the business conflict with the objectives of employees (goal conflict).

Setting Budget Goals Too Tightly   People can become discouraged if performance expectations are set too high. For example, would you be inspired or discouraged by a guitar instructor expecting you to play like Eric Clapton after only a few lessons? You'd probably be discouraged. This same kind of problem can occur in businesses if employees view budget goals as unrealistic or unachievable. In such a case, the budget discourages employees from achieving the goals. On the other hand, aggressive but attainable goals are likely to inspire employees to achieve the goals. Therefore, it is important that employees (managers and nonmanagers) be involved in establishing reasonable budget estimates.

EXHIBIT 1 *Planning, Directing, and Controlling*

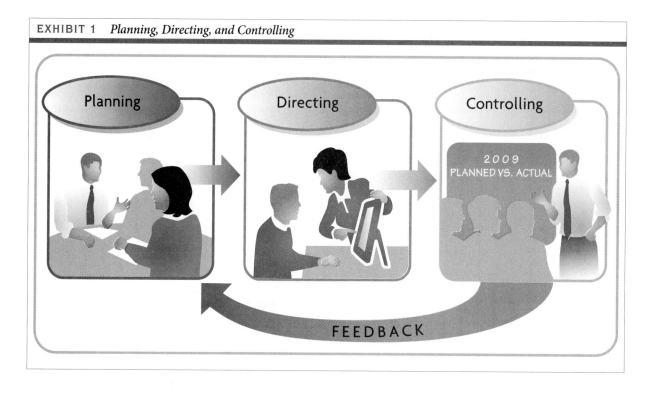

Involving all employees encourages cooperation both within and among departments. It also increases awareness of each department's importance to the overall objectives of the company. Employees view budgeting more positively when they have an opportunity to participate in the budget-setting process. This is because employees with a greater sense of control over the budget process will have a greater commitment to achieving its goals. In such cases, budgets are valuable planning tools that increase the possibility of achieving business goals.

Setting Budget Goals Too Loosely   Although it is desirable to establish attainable goals, it is undesirable to plan lower goals than may be possible. Such budget "padding" is termed **budgetary slack**. An example of budgetary slack is including spare employees in the plan. Managers may plan slack in the budget in order to provide a "cushion" for unexpected events or improve the appearance of operations. Budgetary slack can be avoided if lower- and mid-level managers are required to support their spending requirements with operational plans.

Slack budgets can cause employees to develop a "spend it or lose it" mentality. This often occurs at the end of the budget period when actual spending is less than the budget. Employees may attempt to spend the remaining budget (purchase equipment, hire consultants, purchase supplies) in order to avoid having the budget cut next period.

Setting Conflicting Budget Goals   **Goal conflict** occurs when individual self-interest differs from business objectives. This can happen when management establishes individual goals that conflict with overall business objectives. Often, such conflicts are subtle. For example, the Sales Department manager may be given a sales goal, while the Manufacturing Department manager may be given a cost reduction goal. It is

INTEGRITY, OBJECTIVITY, AND ETHICS IN BUSINESS

Budget Games

The budgeting system is designed to plan and control a business. However, it is common for the budget to be "gamed" by its participants. For example, cost center managers may pad their budgets with excess resources. In this way, the managers have additional resources for unexpected events during the period. If the budget is being used to establish the incentive plan, then sales managers have incentives to understate the sales potential of a territory in order to ensure hitting their quotas. Other times, managers engage in "land grabbing," which occurs when they overstate the sales potential of a territory in order to guarantee access to resources. If cost center managers believe that unspent resources will not roll over to future periods, then they may be encouraged to "spend it or lose it," causing wasteful expenditures. These types of problems can be partially overcome by separating the budget into planning and incentive components. This is why many organizations have parallel budget processes, one for resource planning and another, more challenging budget for motivating managers.

possible for both goals to conflict. The Sales Department may increase sales by promising customers small product deviations that are difficult and unprofitable to make. This would increase sales at the expense of Manufacturing's expense reduction goal and impact the overall profitability objectives of the firm. Likewise, Manufacturing may schedule the plant for maximum manufacturing efficiency with little regard for actual customer product demand. This would reduce manufacturing costs at the expense of the sales goal and reduce the overall profitability of the firm. Goal conflict can be avoided if budget goals are carefully designed for consistency across all areas of the organization.

Budgeting Systems

Budgeting systems vary among businesses because of such factors as organizational structure, complexity of operations, and management philosophy. Differences in budget systems are even more significant among different types of businesses, such as manufacturers and service businesses. The details of a budgeting system used by an automobile manufacturer such as **Ford** would obviously differ from those of a service company such as **American Airlines**. However, the basic budgeting concepts illustrated in the following paragraphs apply to all types of businesses and organizations.

The budgetary period for operating activities normally includes the fiscal year of a business. A year is short enough that future operations can be estimated fairly accurately, yet long enough that the future can be viewed in a broad context. However, to achieve effective control, the annual budgets are usually subdivided into shorter time periods, such as quarters of the year, months, or weeks.

A variation of fiscal-year budgeting, called **continuous budgeting**, maintains a 12-month projection into the future. The 12-month budget is continually revised by removing the data for the period just ended and adding estimated budget data for the same period next year, as shown in Exhibit 2.

Developing budgets for the next fiscal year usually begins several months prior to the end of the current year. This responsibility is normally assigned to a budget committee. Such a committee often consists of the budget director and such high-level executives as the controller, the treasurer, the production manager, and the sales manager. Once the budget has been approved, the budget process is monitored and summarized by the Accounting Department, which reports to the committee.

EXHIBIT 2

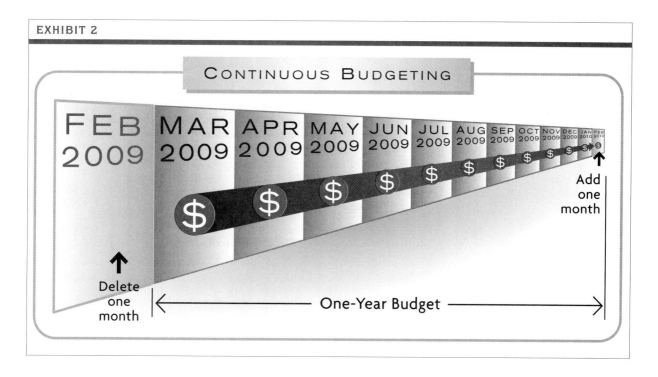

CONTINUOUS BUDGETING

FEB 2009 · MAR 2009 · APR 2009 · MAY 2009 · JUN 2009 · JUL 2009 · AUG 2009 · SEP 2009 · OCT 2009 · NOV 2009 · DEC 2009 · JAN 2010 · FEB 2010

Delete one month

One-Year Budget

Add one month

There are several methods of developing budget estimates. One method, termed **zero-based budgeting**, requires managers to estimate sales, production, and other operating data as though operations are being started for the first time. This approach has the benefit of taking a fresh view of operations each year. A more common approach is to start with last year's budget and revise it for actual results and expected changes for the coming year. Two major budgets using this approach are the static budget and the flexible budget.

Static Budget   A **static budget** shows the expected results of a responsibility center for only one activity level. Once the budget has been determined, it is not changed, even if the activity changes. Static budgeting is used by many service companies and for some administrative functions of manufacturing companies, such as purchasing, engineering, and accounting. For example, the Assembly Department manager for Colter Manufacturing Company prepared the static budget for the upcoming year, shown in Exhibit 3.

EXHIBIT 3   *Static Budget*

COLTER MANUFACTURING COMPANY
Assembly Department Budget
For the Year Ended July 31, 2009

Direct labor	$40,000
Electric power	5,000
Supervisor salaries	15,000
Total department costs	$60,000

Nashville's Budget By law, government entities must provide budget information to their citizens. This information can often be found on the government entity's Web site. For example, excerpts from the budget for Nashville, Tennessee, are as follows:

City of Nashville Budget (General Fund)

Revenues	
Property taxes	$246,488,785
Sales taxes	79,509,853
Licenses	64,295,575
Federal and state transfers	81,373,539
Other	105,618,371
Total revenues	$577,286,123
Expenses	
General government	$ 97,086,083
Fiscal administration	21,359,829
Administration of justice	42,890,268
Law enforcement	164,953,968
Fire prevention	27,927,212
Public health and welfare	53,667,025
Public works, highways, and streets	44,828,934
Recreation and community support	72,341,443
Other	52,231,361
Total expenses	$577,286,123

This budget shows the source of city revenues and where the dollars are spent. Property taxes are the greatest revenue source, and law enforcement is the largest expense of the General Fund (excluding schools). Note that as for most city and state governments, the revenue and expense budgets must balance. Each of the line items in the General Fund budget has greater detail at a lower level. For example, the Nashville city budget indicates that the "Fiscal Administration" is comprised of four line items, as follows:

Fiscal Administration

Finance	$ 9,282,120
Assessor of property	6,574,521
Trustee	2,018,973
County clerk	3,484,215
Total fiscal administration	$21,359,829

A disadvantage of static budgets is that they do not adjust for changes in activity levels. For example, assume that the actual amounts spent by the Assembly Department of Colter Manufacturing totaled $72,000, which is $12,000 or 20% ($12,000 ÷ $60,000) more than budgeted. Is this good news or bad news? At first you might think that this is a bad result. However, this conclusion may not be valid, since static budget results may be difficult to interpret. To illustrate, assume that the assembly manager constructed the budget based on plans to assemble *8,000* units during the year. However, if *10,000* units were actually produced, should the additional $12,000 in spending in excess of the budget be considered "bad news"? Maybe not. The Assembly Department provided 25% (2,000 units ÷ 8,000 units) more output for only 20% more cost.

Flexible Budget Unlike static budgets, **flexible budgets** show the expected results of a responsibility center for several activity levels. You can think of a flexible budget as a series of static budgets for different levels of activity. Such budgets are especially useful in estimating and controlling factory costs and operating expenses. Exhibit 4 is a flexible budget for the annual manufacturing expense in the Assembly Department of Colter Manufacturing Company.

When constructing a flexible budget, we first identify the relevant activity levels. In Exhibit 4, there are 8,000, 9,000, and 10,000 units of production. Alternative activity bases, such as machine hours or direct labor hours, may be used in measuring the volume of activity. Second, we identify the fixed and variable cost components of the costs

EXHIBIT 4   *Flexible Budget*

COLTER MANUFACTURING COMPANY
Assembly Department Budget
For the Year Ended July 31, 2009

Units of production	8,000	9,000	10,000
Variable cost:			
Direct labor ($5 per unit)	$40,000	$45,000	$50,000
Electric power ($0.50 per unit)	4,000	4,500	5,000
Total variable cost	$44,000	$49,500	$55,000
Fixed cost:			
Electric power	$ 1,000	$ 1,000	$ 1,000
Supervisor salaries	15,000	15,000	15,000
Total fixed cost	$16,000	$16,000	$16,000
Total department costs	$60,000	$65,500	$71,000

being budgeted. For example, in Exhibit 4, the electric power cost is separated into its fixed cost ($1,000 per month) and variable cost ($0.50 per unit). Last, we prepare the budget for each activity level by multiplying the variable cost per unit by the activity level and then adding the monthly fixed cost.

With a flexible budget, the department manager can be evaluated by comparing actual expenses to the budgeted amount for actual activity. For example, if Colter Manufacturing Company's Assembly Department actually spent $72,000 to produce 10,000 units, the manager would be considered over budget by $1,000 ($72,000 – $71,000). Under the static budget in Exhibit 3, the department was $12,000 over budget. This comparison is illustrated in Exhibit 5. The flexible budget for the Assembly

EXHIBIT 5

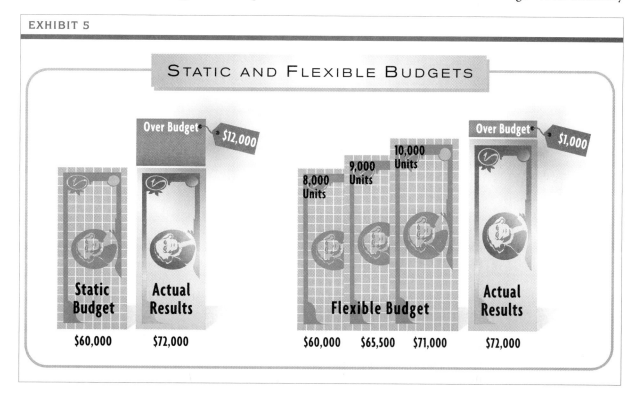

Department is much more accurate than the static budget, because budget amounts adjust for changes in activity.

Computerized Budgeting Systems In developing budgets, many firms use computerized budgeting systems. Such systems speed up and reduce the cost of preparing the budget. This is especially true when large quantities of data need to be processed. Computers are also useful in continuous budgeting. Reports that compare actual results with amounts budgeted can also be prepared on a timely basis through the use of computerized systems. For example, ***Fujitsu*** used Enterprise Resource Planning (ERP) software to streamline its budgeting process from six to eight weeks down to 10 to 15 days.

Managers often use computer spreadsheets or simulation models to represent the operating and budget relationships. By using computer simulation models, the impact of various operating alternatives on the budget can be assessed. For example, the budget can be revised to show the impact of a proposed change in indirect labor wage rates. Likewise, the budgetary effect of a proposed product line can be determined.

A common objective of using computer-based budgeting is to tie all the budgets of the organization together. The newest budgeting and planning (B&P) systems are accomplishing this by using Web-based applications to tie thousands of employees together. In the next section, we will illustrate how a company ties its budgets together to develop a complete plan.

Master Budget

Obj **2**

Describe the master budget for a manufacturing business.

Manufacturing operations require a series of budgets that are linked together in a **master budget**. The major parts of the master budget are as follows:

Budgeted Income Statement	*Budgeted Balance Sheet*
Sales budget	Cash budget
Cost of goods sold budget:	Capital expenditures budget
Production budget	
Direct materials purchases budget	
Direct labor cost budget	
Factory overhead cost budget	
Selling and administrative expenses budget	

Exhibit 6 shows the relationship among the income statement budgets. The budget process begins by estimating sales. The sales information is then provided to the various units for estimating the production and selling and administrative expenses budgets. The production budgets are used to prepare the direct materials purchases, direct labor cost, and factory overhead cost budgets. These three budgets are used to develop the cost of goods sold budget. Once these budgets and the selling and administrative expenses budget have been completed, the budgeted income statement can be prepared, as we illustrate in the following section.

After the budgeted income statement has been developed, the budgeted balance sheet can be prepared. Two major budgets comprising the budgeted balance sheet are the cash budget and the capital expenditures budget, which we illustrate later in the chapter.

EXHIBIT 6 *Income Statement Budgets*

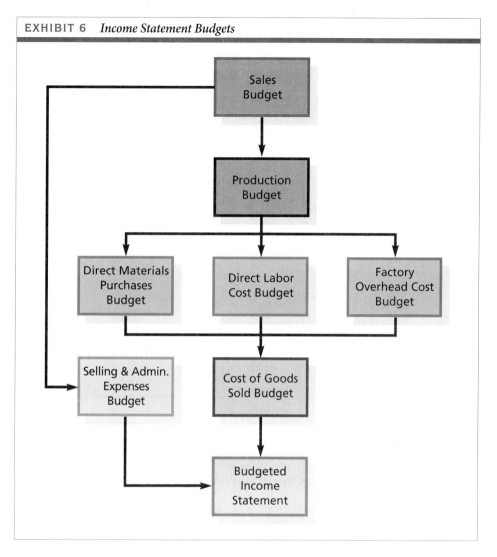

Income Statement Budgets

In the following sections, we will illustrate the major elements of the income statement budget. We will use a small manufacturing business, Elite Accessories Inc., as the basis for our illustration.

Sales Budget The **sales budget** normally indicates for each product (1) the quantity of estimated sales and (2) the expected unit selling price. These data are often reported by regions or by sales representatives.

In estimating the quantity of sales for each product, past sales volumes are often used as a starting point. These amounts are revised for factors that are expected to affect future sales, such as the following:

- Backlog of unfilled sales orders
- Planned advertising and promotion
- Expected industry and general economic conditions
- Productive capacity
- Projected pricing policy
- Findings of market research studies

Once an estimate of the sales volume is obtained, the expected sales revenue can be determined by multiplying the volume by the expected unit sales price. Exhibit 7 is the sales budget for Elite Accessories Inc.

EXHIBIT 7 *Sales Budget*

ELITE ACCESSORIES INC.
Sales Budget
For the Year Ended December 31, 2009

Product and Region	Unit Sales Volume	Unit Selling Price	Total Sales
Wallet:			
East	287,000	$12.00	$ 3,444,000
West	241,000	12.00	2,892,000
Total	528,000		$ 6,336,000
Handbag:			
East	156,400	$25.00	$ 3,910,000
West	123,600	25.00	3,090,000
Total	280,000		$ 7,000,000
Total revenue from sales			$13,336,000

For control purposes, management can compare actual sales and budgeted sales by product, region, or sales representative. Management would investigate any significant differences and take possible corrective actions.

Production Budget Production should be carefully coordinated with the sales budget to ensure that production and sales are kept in balance during the period. The number of units to be manufactured to meet budgeted sales and inventory needs for each product is set forth in the **production budget**. The budgeted volume of production is determined as follows:

> Expected units to be sold
> \+ Desired units in ending inventory
> − Estimated units in beginning inventory
> **Total units to be produced**

Exhibit 8 is the production budget for Elite Accessories Inc.

Direct Materials Purchases Budget The production budget is the starting point for determining the estimated quantities of direct materials to be purchased. Multiplying these quantities by the expected unit purchase price determines the total cost of direct materials to be purchased.

> Materials required for production
> \+ Desired ending materials inventory
> − Estimated beginning materials inventory
> **Direct materials to be purchased**

EXHIBIT 8   *Production Budget*

ELITE ACCESSORIES INC.
Production Budget
For the Year Ended December 31, 2009

	Units	
	Wallet	*Handbag*
Expected units to be sold (from Exhibit 7)	528,000	280,000
Plus desired ending inventory, December 31, 2009	80,000	60,000
Total	608,000	340,000
Less estimated beginning inventory, January 1, 2009	88,000	48,000
Total units to be produced	520,000	292,000

In Elite Accessories Inc.'s production operations, leather and lining are required for wallets and handbags. The quantity of direct materials expected to be used for each unit of product is as follows:

Wallet	*Handbag*
Leather: 0.30 square yard per unit	Leather: 1.25 square yards per unit
Lining: 0.10 square yard per unit	Lining: 0.50 square yard per unit

Based on these data and the production budget, the **direct materials purchases budget** is prepared. As shown in the budget in Exhibit 9, for Elite Accessories Inc. to produce 520,000 wallets, 156,000 square yards (520,000 units × 0.30 square yard per unit) of leather are needed. Likewise, to produce 292,000 handbags, 365,000 square yards (292,000 units × 1.25 square yards per unit) of leather are needed. We can compute the

EXHIBIT 9   *Direct Materials Purchases Budget*

ELITE ACCESSORIES INC.
Direct Materials Purchases Budget
For the Year Ended December 31, 2009

	Direct Materials		
	Leather	*Lining*	*Total*
Square yards required for production:			
Wallet (Note A)	156,000	52,000	
Handbag (Note B)	365,000	146,000	
Plus desired inventory, December 31, 2009	20,000	12,000	
Total	541,000	210,000	
Less estimated inventory, January 1, 2009	18,000	15,000	
Total square yards to be purchased	523,000	195,000	
Unit price (per square yard)	× $4.50	× $1.20	
Total direct materials to be purchased	$2,353,500	$234,000	$2,587,500

Note A: Leather: 520,000 units × 0.30 square yard per unit = 156,000 square yards
          Lining: 520,000 units × 0.10 square yard per unit = 52,000 square yards

Note B: Leather: 292,000 units × 1.25 square yards per unit = 365,000 square yards
          Lining: 292,000 units × 0.50 square yard per unit = 146,000 square yards

needs for lining in a similar manner. Then adding the desired ending inventory for each material and deducting the estimated beginning inventory determines the amount of each material to be purchased. Multiplying these amounts by the estimated cost per square yard yields the total materials purchase cost.

The direct materials purchases budget helps management maintain inventory levels within reasonable limits. For this purpose, the timing of the direct materials purchases should be coordinated between the purchasing and production departments.

Direct Labor Cost Budget The production budget also provides the starting point for preparing the direct labor cost budget. For Elite Accessories Inc., the labor requirements for each unit of product are estimated as follows:

Wallet	Handbag
Cutting Department: 0.10 hour per unit	Cutting Department: 0.15 hour per unit
Sewing Department: 0.25 hour per unit	Sewing Department: 0.40 hour per unit

Based on these data and the production budget, Elite Accessories Inc. prepares the direct labor budget. As shown in the budget in Exhibit 10, for Elite Accessories Inc. to produce 520,000 wallets, 52,000 hours (520,000 units × 0.10 hour per unit) of labor in the Cutting Department are required. Likewise, to produce 292,000 handbags, 43,800 hours (292,000 units × 0.15 hour per unit) of labor in the Cutting Department are required. In a similar manner, we can determine the direct labor hours needed in the Sewing Department to meet the budgeted production. Multiplying the direct labor hours for each department by the estimated department hourly rate yields the total direct labor cost for each department.

EXHIBIT 10 *Direct Labor Cost Budget*

ELITE ACCESSORIES INC.
Direct Labor Cost Budget
For the Year Ended December 31, 2009

	Cutting	Sewing	Total
Hours required for production:			
Wallet (Note A)	52,000	130,000	
Handbag (Note B)	43,800	116,800	
Total	95,800	246,800	
Hourly rate	× $12.00	× $15.00	
Total direct labor cost	$1,149,600	$3,702,000	$4,851,600

Note A: Cutting Department: 520,000 units × 0.10 hour per unit = 52,000 hours
Sewing Department: 520,000 units × 0.25 hour per unit = 130,000 hours

Note B: Cutting Department: 292,000 units × 0.15 hour per unit = 43,800 hours
Sewing Department: 292,000 units × 0.40 hour per unit = 116,800 hours

The direct labor needs should be coordinated between the production and personnel departments. This ensures that there will be enough labor available for production.

Factory Overhead Cost Budget The estimated factory overhead costs necessary for production make up the factory overhead cost budget. This budget usually includes the total estimated cost for each item of factory overhead, as shown in Exhibit 11.

EXHIBIT 11   *Factory Overhead Cost Budget*

ELITE ACCESSORIES INC.
Factory Overhead Cost Budget
For the Year Ended December 31, 2009

Indirect factory wages	$ 732,800
Supervisor salaries	360,000
Power and light	306,000
Depreciation of plant and equipment	288,000
Indirect materials	182,800
Maintenance	140,280
Insurance and property taxes	79,200
Total factory overhead cost	$2,089,080

A business may prepare supporting departmental schedules, in which the factory overhead costs are separated into their fixed and variable cost elements. Such schedules enable department managers to direct their attention to those costs for which they are responsible and to evaluate performance.

Cost of Goods Sold Budget   The direct materials purchases budget, direct labor cost budget, and factory overhead cost budget are the starting point for preparing the **cost of goods sold budget**. To illustrate, these data are combined with the desired ending inventory and the estimated beginning inventory data below to determine the budgeted cost of goods sold shown in Exhibit 12.

Estimated inventories on January 1, 2009		*Desired inventories on December 31, 2009*	
Finished goods	$1,095,600	Finished goods	$1,565,000
Work in process	214,400	Work in process	220,000

Selling and Administrative Expenses Budget   The sales budget is often used as the starting point for estimating the selling and administrative expenses. For example, a budgeted increase in sales may require more advertising. Exhibit 13 is a selling and administrative expenses budget for Elite Accessories Inc.

Detailed supporting schedules are often prepared for major items in the selling and administrative expenses budget. For example, an advertising expense schedule for the Marketing Department should include the advertising media to be used (newspaper, direct mail, television), quantities (column inches, number of pieces, minutes), and the cost per unit. Attention to such details results in realistic budgets. Effective control results from assigning responsibility for achieving the budget to department supervisors.

Budgeted Income Statement   The budgets for sales, cost of goods sold, and selling and administrative expenses, combined with the data on other income, other expense, and income tax, are used to prepare the budgeted income statement. Exhibit 14 is a budgeted income statement for Elite Accessories Inc.

The budgeted income statement summarizes the estimates of all phases of operations. This allows management to assess the effects of the individual budgets on profits for the year. If the budgeted net income is too low, management could review and revise operating plans in an attempt to improve income.

EXHIBIT 12 *Cost of Goods Sold Budget*

ELITE ACCESSORIES INC.
Cost of Goods Sold Budget
For the Year Ended December 31, 2009

Finished goods inventory, January 1, 2009			$ 1,095,600
Work in process inventory, January 1, 2009		$ 214,400	
Direct materials:			
Direct materials inventory,			
January 1, 2009 (Note A)	$ 99,000		
Direct materials purchases (from Exhibit 9)	2,587,500 ◄		
Cost of direct materials available for use	$2,686,500		
Less direct materials inventory,			
December 31, 2009 (Note B)	104,400		
Cost of direct materials placed			
in production	$2,582,100		
Direct labor (from Exhibit 10)	4,851,600 ◄		
Factory overhead (from Exhibit 11)	2,089,080 ◄		
Total manufacturing costs		9,522,780	
Total work in process during period		$9,737,180	
Less work in process inventory,			
December 31, 2009		220,000	
Cost of goods manufactured			9,517,180
Cost of finished goods available for sale			$10,612,780
Less finished goods inventory,			
December 31, 2009			1,565,000
Cost of goods sold			$ 9,047,780

Direct materials purchases budget

Direct labor cost budget

Factory overhead cost budget

Note A: Leather:	18,000 sq. yds. × $4.50 per sq. yd.	$ 81,000
Lining:	15,000 sq. yds. × $1.20 per sq. yd.	18,000
Direct materials inventory,		
January 1, 2009		$ 99,000
Note B: Leather:	20,000 sq. yds. × $4.50 per sq. yd.	$ 90,000
Lining:	12,000 sq. yds. × $1.20 per sq. yd.	14,400
Direct materials inventory,		
December 31, 2009		$104,400

Balance Sheet Budgets

Balance sheet budgets are used by managers to plan financing, investing, and cash objectives for the firm. The balance sheet budgets illustrated for Elite Accessories Inc. in the following sections are the cash budget and the capital expenditures budget.

Cash Budget   The **cash budget** is one of the most important elements of the budgeted balance sheet. The cash budget presents the expected receipts (inflows) and payments (outflows) of cash for a period of time.

    Information from the various operating budgets, such as the sales budget, the direct materials purchases budget, and the selling and administrative expenses budget, affects

EXHIBIT 13 *Selling and Administrative Expenses Budget*

ELITE ACCESSORIES INC.
Selling and Administrative Expenses Budget
For the Month Ended December 31, 2009

Selling expenses:		
Sales salaries expense	$715,000	
Advertising expense	360,000	
Travel expense	115,000	
Total selling expenses		$1,190,000
Administrative expenses:		
Officers' salaries expense	$360,000	
Office salaries expense	258,000	
Office rent expense	34,500	
Office supplies expense	17,500	
Miscellaneous administrative expenses	25,000	
Total administrative expenses		695,000
Total selling and administrative expenses		$1,885,000

EXHIBIT 14 *Budgeted Income Statement*

ELITE ACCESSORIES INC.
Budgeted Income Statement
For the Year Ended December 31, 2009

Revenue from sales (from Exhibit 7)		$13,336,000	← Sales budget
Cost of goods sold (from Exhibit 12)		9,047,780	← Cost of goods
Gross profit		4,288,220	sold budget
Selling and administrative expenses:			
Selling expenses (from Exhibit 13)	$1,190,000		← Selling and administrative expenses budget
Administrative expenses (from Exhibit 13)	695,000		
Total selling and administrative expenses		1,885,000	
Income from operations		$ 2,403,220	
Other income:			
Interest revenue	$ 98,000		
Other expense:			
Interest expense	90,000	8,000	
Income before income tax		$ 2,411,220	
Income tax		600,000	
Net income		$ 1,811,220	

the cash budget. In addition, the capital expenditures budget, dividend policies, and plans for equity or long-term debt financing affect the cash budget.

We illustrate the monthly cash budget for January, February, and March 2009, for Elite Accessories Inc. We begin by developing the estimated cash receipts and estimated cash payments portion of the cash budget.

Estimated Cash Receipts.   Estimated cash receipts are planned additions to cash from sales and other sources, such as issuing securities or collecting interest. A supporting schedule can be used in determining the collections from sales. To illustrate this schedule, assume the following information for Elite Accessories Inc.:

	Accounts receivable, January 1, 2009		$370,000
	January	*February*	*March*
Budgeted sales	$1,080,000	$1,240,000	$970,000

Elite Accessories Inc. expects to sell 10% of its merchandise for cash. Of the remaining 90% of the sales on account, 60% are expected to be collected in the month of the sale and the remainder in the next month.

Using this information, we prepare the schedule of collections from sales, shown in Exhibit 15. The cash receipts from sales on account are determined by adding the amounts collected from credit sales earned in the current period (60%) and the amounts accrued from sales in the previous period as accounts receivable (40%).

EXHIBIT 15   *Schedule of Collections from Sales*

ELITE ACCESSORIES INC.
Schedule of Collections from Sales
For the Three Months Ended March 31, 2009

	January	*February*	*March*
Receipts from cash sales:			
Cash sales (10% × current month's sales— Note A)	$108,000	$ 124,000	$ 97,000
Receipts from sales on account:			
Collections from prior month's sales (40% of previous month's credit sales— Note B)	$370,000	$ 388,800	$446,400
Collections from current month's sales (60% of current month's credit sales— Note C)	583,200	669,600	523,800
Total receipts from sales on account	$953,200	$1,058,400	$970,200

Note A: $108,000 = $1,080,000 × 10%
          $124,000 = $1,240,000 × 10%
          $ 97,000 = $ 970,000 × 10%

Note B: $370,000, given as January 1, 2009, Accounts Receivable balance
          $388,800 = $1,080,000 × 90% × 40%
          $446,400 = $1,240,000 × 90% × 40%

Note C: $583,200 = $1,080,000 × 90% × 60%
          $669,600 = $1,240,000 × 90% × 60%
          $523,800 = $ 970,000 × 90% × 60%

Estimated Cash Payments.   Estimated cash payments are planned reductions in cash from manufacturing costs, selling and administrative expenses, capital expenditures, and other sources, such as buying securities or paying interest or dividends. A supporting schedule can be used in estimating the cash payments for manufacturing costs. To illustrate, the schedule shown in Exhibit 16 is based on the following information for Elite Accessories:

Accounts payable, January 1, 2009		$190,000	
	January	*February*	*March*
Manufacturing costs	$840,000	$780,000	$812,000

Depreciation expense on machines is estimated to be $24,000 per month and is included in the manufacturing costs. The accounts payable were incurred for manufacturing costs. Elite Accessories Inc. expects to pay 75% of the manufacturing costs in the month in which they are incurred and the balance in the next month.

In Exhibit 16, the cash payments are determined by adding the amounts paid from costs incurred in the current period (75%) and the amounts accrued as a liability from costs in the previous period (25%). The $24,000 of depreciation must be excluded from all calculations, since depreciation is a noncash expense that should not be included in the cash budget.

EXHIBIT 16   *Schedule of Payments for Manufacturing Costs*

ELITE ACCESSORIES INC.
Schedule of Payments for Manufacturing Costs
For the Three Months Ended March 31, 2009

	January	*February*	*March*
Payments of prior month's manufacturing costs {[25% × previous month's manufacturing costs (less depreciation)]—Note A}	$190,000	$204,000	$189,000
Payments of current month's manufacturing costs {[75% × current month's manufacturing costs (less depreciation)]—Note B}	612,000	567,000	591,000
Total payments	$802,000	$771,000	$780,000

Note A: $190,000, given as January 1, 2009, Accounts Payable balance
       $204,000 = ($840,000 − $24,000) × 25%
       $189,000 = ($780,000 − $24,000) × 25%

Note B: $612,000 = ($840,000 − $24,000) × 75%
       $567,000 = ($780,000 − $24,000) × 75%
       $591,000 = ($812,000 − $24,000) × 75%

Completing the Cash Budget.   To complete the cash budget for Elite Accessories Inc., as shown in Exhibit 17, assume that Elite Accessories Inc. is expecting the following:

Cash balance on January 1	$280,000
Quarterly taxes paid on March 31	150,000
Quarterly interest expense paid on January 10	22,500
Quarterly interest revenue received on March 21	24,500
Sewing equipment purchased in February	274,000

EXHIBIT 17   *Cash Budget*

ELITE ACCESSORIES INC.
Cash Budget
For the Three Months Ended March 31, 2009

	January	February	March	
Estimated cash receipts from:				
Cash sales (from Exhibit 15)	$ 108,000	$ 124,000	$ 97,000	→ Schedule of collections from sales
Collections of accounts receivable				
(from Exhibit 15)	953,200	1,058,400	970,200	
Interest revenue			24,500	
Total cash receipts	$1,061,200	$1,182,400	$1,091,700	
Estimated cash payments for:				
Manufacturing costs (from Exhibit 16)	$ 802,000	$ 771,000	$ 780,000	→ Schedule of cash payments for manufacturing costs
Selling and administrative expenses	160,000	165,000	145,000	
Capital additions		274,000		
Interest expense	22,500			
Income taxes			150,000	
Total cash payments	$ 984,500	$1,210,000	$1,075,000	
Cash increase (decrease)	$ 76,700	$ (27,600)	$ 16,700	
Cash balance at beginning of month	280,000	356,700	329,100	
Cash balance at end of month	$ 356,700	$ 329,100	$ 345,800	
Minimum cash balance	340,000	340,000	340,000	
Excess (deficiency)	$ 16,700	$ (10,900)	$ 5,800	

In addition, monthly selling and administrative expenses, which are paid in the month incurred, are estimated as follows:

	January	February	March
Selling and administrative expenses	$160,000	$165,000	$145,000

We can compare the estimated cash balance at the end of the period with the minimum balance required by operations. Assuming that the minimum cash balance for Elite Accessories Inc. is $340,000, we can determine any expected excess or deficiency.

The minimum cash balance protects against variations in estimates and for unexpected cash emergencies. For effective cash management, much of the minimum cash balance should be deposited in income-producing securities that can be readily converted to cash. U.S. Treasury Bills or Notes are examples of such securities.

Capital Expenditures Budget   The **capital expenditures budget** summarizes plans for acquiring fixed assets. Such expenditures are necessary as machinery and other fixed assets wear out, become obsolete, or for other reasons need to be replaced. In addition, expanding plant facilities may be necessary to meet increasing demand for a company's product.

The useful life of many fixed assets extends over long periods of time. In addition, the amount of the expenditures for such assets may vary from year to year. It is normal to project the plans for a number of periods into the future in preparing the capital expenditures budget. Exhibit 18 is a 5-year capital expenditures budget for Elite Accessories Inc.

The capital expenditures budget should be considered in preparing the other operating budgets. For example, the estimated depreciation of new equipment affects the factory overhead cost budget and the selling and administrative expenses budget. The plans for financing the capital expenditures may also affect the cash budget.

EXHIBIT 18   *Capital Expenditures Budget*

ELITE ACCESSORIES INC.
Capital Expenditures Budget
For the 5 Years Ended December 31, 2013

Item	2009	2010	2011	2012	2013
Machinery—Cutting Department	$400,000			$280,000	$360,000
Machinery—Sewing Department	274,000	$260,000	$560,000	200,000	
Office equipment		90,000			60,000
Total	$674,000	$350,000	$560,000	$480,000	$420,000

Budgeted Balance Sheet   The budgeted balance sheet estimates the financial condition at the end of a budget period. The budgeted balance sheet assumes that all operating budgets and financing plans are met. It is similar to a balance sheet based on actual data in the accounts. For this reason, we do not illustrate a budgeted balance sheet for Elite Accessories Inc. If the budgeted balance sheet indicates a weakness in financial position, revising the financing plans or other plans may be necessary. For example, a large amount of long-term debt in relation to stockholders' equity might require revising financing plans for capital expenditures. Such revisions might include issuing equity rather than debt.

Standards

Obj **3**

Describe the nature and use of standards.

What are standards? *Standards* are performance goals. Service, merchandising, and manufacturing businesses may all use standards to evaluate and control operations. For example, long-haul drivers for **United Parcel Service** are expected to drive a standard distance per day. Salespersons for *The Limited* are expected to meet sales standards.

Manufacturers normally use standard costs for each of the three manufacturing costs: direct materials, direct labor, and factory overhead. Accounting systems that use standards for these costs are called **standard cost systems**. These systems enable management to determine how much a product should cost (**standard cost**), how much it does cost (actual cost), and the causes of any difference (**cost variances**). When actual costs are compared with standard costs, only the exceptions or variances are reported for cost control. This reporting by the *principle of exceptions* allows management to focus on correcting the variances. Thus, using standard costs assists management in controlling costs and in motivating employees to focus on costs.

Standard cost systems are commonly used with job order and process systems. Automated manufacturing operations may also integrate standard cost data with the computerized system that directs operations. Such systems detect and report variances automatically and make adjustments to operations in progress.

Setting Standards

Setting standards is both an art and a science. The standard-setting process normally requires the joint efforts of accountants, engineers, and other management personnel. The accountant plays an essential role by expressing in dollars and cents the results of judgments and studies. Engineers contribute to the standard-setting process by identifying the materials, labor, and machine requirements needed to produce the product. For example, engineers determine the direct materials requirements by studying the materials specifications for products and estimating normal spoilage in production. Time and motion studies may be used to determine the length of time required for each manufacturing operation. Engineering studies may also be used to determine standards for factory overhead, such as the amount of power needed to operate machinery.

Setting standards often begins with analyzing past operations. However, standards are not just an extension of past costs, and caution must be used in relying on past cost data. For example, inefficiencies may be contained within past costs. In addition, changes in technology, machinery, or production methods may make past costs irrelevant for future operations.

Types of Standards

Standards imply an acceptable level of production efficiency. One of the major objectives in setting standards is to motivate workers to achieve efficient operations.

Like the budgets we discussed earlier, tight, unrealistic standards may have a negative impact on performance. This is because workers may become frustrated with an inability to meet the standards and may give up trying to do their best. Such standards can be achieved only under perfect operating conditions, such as no idle time, no machine breakdowns, and no materials spoilage. These standards are called **ideal standards** or *theoretical standards*. Although ideal standards are not widely used, a few firms use ideal standards to motivate changes and improvement. Such an approach is termed "Kaizen costing." *Kaizen* is a Japanese term meaning "continuous improvement."

Standards that are too loose might not motivate employees to perform at their best. This is because the standard level of performance can be reached too easily. As a result, operating performance may be lower than what could be achieved.

Most companies use **currently attainable standards** (sometimes called *normal standards*). These standards can be attained with reasonable effort. Such standards allow for normal production difficulties and mistakes, such as materials spoilage and machine breakdowns. When reasonable standards are used, employees become more focused on cost and are more likely to put forth their best efforts.

An example from the game of golf illustrates the distinction between ideal and normal standards. In golf, "par" is an *ideal* standard for most players. Each player's USGA (United States Golf Association) handicap is the player's *normal* standard. The motivation of average players is to beat their handicaps because they may view beating par as unrealistic. Normal and ideal standards are illustrated as follows:

Currently
attainable
(personal best)

Ideal
(world record)

Reviewing and Revising Standards

Standard costs should be continuously reviewed and should be revised when they no longer reflect operating conditions. Inaccurate standards may distort management decision making and may weaken management's ability to plan and control operations.

Standards should not be revised, however, just because they differ from actual costs. They should be revised only when they no longer reflect the operating conditions that they were intended to measure. For example, the direct labor standard would not be revised simply because workers were unable to meet properly determined standards. On the other hand, standards should be revised when prices, product designs, labor rates, or manufacturing methods change. For example, when aluminum beverage cans were redesigned to taper slightly at the top of the can, manufacturers reduced the standard amount of aluminum per can because less aluminum was required for the top piece of the tapered can.

Support and Criticism of Standards

Standards are used to value inventory and to plan and control costs. Companies are also using standards to assess performance at lower levels of the organization, for shorter accounting periods, and for an increasing number of costs.

Using standards for performance evaluation has been criticized by some. For example, critics assert that standards limit improvement of operations by discouraging improvement beyond the standard. Regardless of this criticism, standards are widely used. Most managers strongly support standard cost systems and regard standards as critical for running large businesses efficiently.

Obj 4

Explain and illustrate how standards are used in budgeting.

Budgetary Performance Evaluation

As we discussed earlier in this chapter, the master budget assists a company in planning, directing, and controlling performance. In the remainder of this chapter, we will discuss using the master budget for control purposes. The control function, or budgetary performance evaluation, compares the actual performance against the budget.

We illustrate budget performance evaluation using Western Rider Inc., a manufacturer of blue jeans. Western Rider Inc. uses standard manufacturing costs in its budgets. The standards for direct materials, direct labor, and factory overhead are separated into two components: (1) a price standard and (2) a quantity standard. Multiplying these two elements together yields the standard cost per unit for a given manufacturing cost category, as shown for style XL jeans in Exhibit 19.

EXHIBIT 19   *Standard Cost for XL Jeans*

Manufacturing Costs	Standard Price	×	Standard Quantity per Pair	=	Standard Cost per Pair of XL Jeans
Direct materials	$5 per square yard		1.50 square yards		$ 7.50
Direct labor	$9 per hour		0.80 hour per pair		7.20
Factory overhead	$6 per hour		0.80 hour per pair		4.80
Total standard cost per pair					$19.50

The standard price and quantity are separated because the means of controlling them are normally different. For example, the direct materials price per square yard is controlled by the Purchasing Department, and the direct materials quantity per pair is controlled by the Production Department.

As we illustrated earlier, the budgeted costs at planned volumes are included in the master budget at the beginning of the period. The standard amounts budgeted for materials purchases, direct labor, and factory overhead are determined by multiplying the standard costs per unit by the *planned* level of production. At the end of the month, the standard costs per unit are multiplied by the *actual* production and compared to the actual costs. To illustrate, assume that Western Rider produced and sold 5,000 pairs of XL jeans. It incurred direct materials costs of $40,150, direct labor costs of $38,500, and factory overhead costs of $22,400. The **budget performance report** shown in Exhibit 20 summarizes the actual costs, the standard amounts for the actual level of production achieved, and the differences between the two amounts. These differences are called *cost variances*. A *favorable* cost variance occurs when the actual cost is less than the standard cost (at actual volumes). An *unfavorable* variance occurs when the actual cost exceeds the standard cost (at actual volumes).

EXHIBIT 20   *Budget Performance Report*

WESTERN RIDER INC.			
Budget Performance Report			
For the Month Ended June 30, 2009			
Manufacturing Costs	**Actual Costs**	**Standard Cost at Actual Volume (5,000 pairs of XL Jeans)***	**Cost Variance— (Favorable) Unfavorable**
Direct materials	$ 40,150	$37,500	$ 2,650
Direct labor	38,500	36,000	2,500
Factory overhead	22,400	24,000	(1,600)
Total manufacturing costs	$101,050	$97,500	$ 3,550

*5,000 pairs × $7.50 per pair = $37,500
5,000 pairs × $7.20 per pair = $36,000
5,000 pairs × $4.80 per pair = $24,000

Based on the information in the budget performance report, management can investigate major differences and take corrective action. In Exhibit 20, for example, the direct materials cost variance is an unfavorable $2,650. There are two possible explanations for this variance: (1) the amount of blue denim used per pair of blue jeans was different than expected, and/or (2) the purchase price of blue denim was different than expected. In the next sections, we will illustrate how to separate and analyze these variances for direct materials and direct labor.

Variances from Standards

Obj 5

Calculate and interpret the basic variances for direct materials and direct labor.

The total difference between actual costs and standard costs for a period is normally made up of several variances, some of which can be favorable and some unfavorable. There can be variances from standards in direct materials costs, in direct labor costs, and in factory overhead costs. The relationship of these variances to the total manufacturing cost variance is shown here. Illustrations and analyses of these variances for Western Rider Inc. are presented in the following paragraphs.[1]

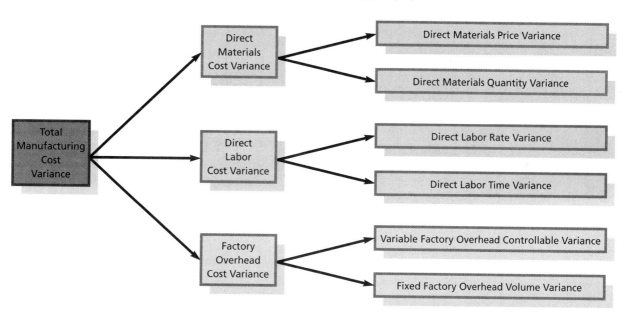

Direct Materials Variances

What caused Western Rider Inc.'s unfavorable materials variance of $2,650? Recall that the direct materials standards from Exhibit 19 are as follows:

Price standard: $5.00 per square yard
Quantity standard: 1.5 square yards per pair of XL jeans

To determine the number of standard square yards of denim budgeted, multiply the actual production for June 2009 (5,000 pairs) by the quantity standard (1.5 square yards per pair). Then multiply the standard square yards by the standard price per

[1]Factory overhead variances are described and illustrated in the Appendix at the end of this chapter.

square yard ($5.00) to determine the *standard* budgeted cost at the actual volume. The calculation is shown as follows:

Standard square yards per pair of jeans	1.5 sq. yards
Actual units produced	× 5,000 pairs of jeans
Standard square yards of denim budgeted for actual production	7,500 sq. yards
Standard price per square yard	× $5.00
Standard direct materials cost at actual production (same as Exhibit 20)	$37,500

This calculation assumes that there is no change in the beginning and ending materials inventories. Thus, the amount of materials budgeted for production equals the amount purchased.

Assume that the *actual* total cost for denim used during June 2009 was as follows:

Actual quantity of denim used in production	7,300 sq. yards
Actual price per square yard	× $5.50
Total actual direct materials cost (same as Exhibit 20)	$40,150

The total unfavorable cost variance of $2,650 ($40,150 − $37,500) results from an excess price per square yard of $0.50 and using 200 fewer square yards of denim. These two reasons can be reported as two separate variances, as shown in the next sections.

Direct Materials Price Variance The **direct materials price variance** is the difference between the actual price per unit ($5.50) and the standard price per unit ($5.00), multiplied by the actual quantity used (7,300 square yards). If the actual price per unit exceeds the standard price per unit, the variance is unfavorable, as shown for Western Rider Inc. If the actual price per unit is less than the standard price per unit, the variance is favorable. The calculation for Western Rider Inc. is as follows:

Price variance:	
Actual price per unit	$5.50 per square yard
Standard price per unit	5.00 per square yard
Price variance—unfavorable	$0.50 per square yard × actual qty., 7,300 sq. yds.
	= $3,650 U

Direct Materials Quantity Variance The **direct materials quantity variance** is the difference between the actual quantity used (7,300 square yards) and the standard quantity at actual production (7,500 square yards), multiplied by the standard price per unit ($5.00). If the actual quantity of materials used exceeds the standard quantity budgeted, the variance is unfavorable. If the actual quantity of materials used is less than the standard quantity, the variance is favorable, as shown for Western Rider Inc.:

Quantity variance:	
Actual quantity	7,300 square yards
Standard quantity at actual production	7,500
Quantity variance—favorable	(200) sq. yds. × standard price, $5.00 = ($1,000) F

Direct Materials Variance Relationships The direct materials variances can be illustrated by making the three calculations shown in Exhibit 21.

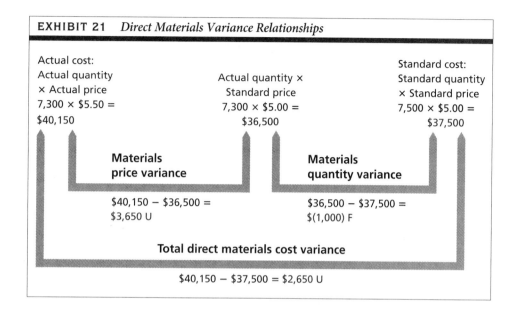

EXHIBIT 21 *Direct Materials Variance Relationships*

Reporting Direct Materials Variances The direct materials quantity variance should be reported to the proper operating management level for corrective action. For example, an unfavorable quantity variance might have been caused by malfunctioning equipment that has not been properly maintained or operated. However, unfavorable materials quantity variances are not always caused by operating departments. For example, the excess materials usage may be caused by purchasing inferior raw materials. In this case, the Purchasing Department should be held responsible for the variance.

The materials price variance should normally be reported to the Purchasing Department, which may or may not be able to control this variance. If materials of the same quality could have been purchased from another supplier at the standard price, the variance was controllable. On the other hand, if the variance resulted from a marketwide price increase, the variance may not be controllable.

Direct Labor Variances

Western Rider Inc.'s direct labor cost variance can also be separated into two parts. Recall that the direct labor standards from Exhibit 19 are as follows:

Rate standard: $9.00 per hour
Time standard: 0.80 hour per pair of XL jeans

The actual production (5,000 pairs) is multiplied by the time standard (0.80 hour per pair) to determine the number of standard direct labor hours budgeted. The standard direct labor hours are then multiplied by the standard rate per hour ($9.00) to determine the *standard* direct labor cost at actual volumes. These calculations are as follows.

Standard direct labor hours per pair of XL jeans	0.80	direct labor hours
Actual units produced	× 5,000	pairs of jeans
Standard direct labor hours budgeted for actual production	4,000	direct labor hours
Standard rate per direct labor hour	× $9.00	
Standard direct labor cost at actual production (same as Exhibit 20)	$36,000	

Assume that the actual total cost for direct labor during June 2009 was as follows:

Actual direct labor hours used in production	3,850 direct labor hours
Actual rate per direct labor hour	×$10.00
Total actual direct labor cost (same as Exhibit 20)	$ 38,500

The total unfavorable cost variance $2,500 ($38,500 – $36,000) results from an excess rate of $1.00 per direct labor hour and using 150 fewer direct labor hours. These two reasons can be reported as two separate variances, as we discuss next.

Direct Labor Rate Variance The **direct labor rate variance** is the difference between the actual rate per hour ($10.00) and the standard rate per hour ($9.00), multiplied by the actual hours worked (3,850 hours). If the actual rate per hour is less than the standard rate per hour, the variance is favorable. If the actual rate per hour exceeds the standard rate per hour, the variance is unfavorable, as shown below for Western Rider Inc.

Rate variance:		
Actual rate	$10.00	per hour
Standard rate	9.00	
Rate variance—unfavorable	$ 1.00	per hour × actual time, 3,850 hours = $3,850 U

Direct Labor Time Variance The **direct labor time variance** is the difference between the actual hours worked (3,850 hours) and the standard hours at actual production (4,000 hours), multiplied by the standard rate per hour ($9.00). If the actual hours worked exceed the standard hours, the variance is unfavorable. If the actual hours worked are less than the standard hours, the variance is favorable, as shown below for Western Rider Inc.

Time variance:		
Actual hours	3,850 direct labor hours	
Standard hours at actual production	4,000	
Time variance—favorable	(150) direct labor hours × standard rate, $9.00 = ($1,350) F	

Direct Labor Variance Relationships The direct labor variances can be illustrated by making the three calculations shown in Exhibit 22.

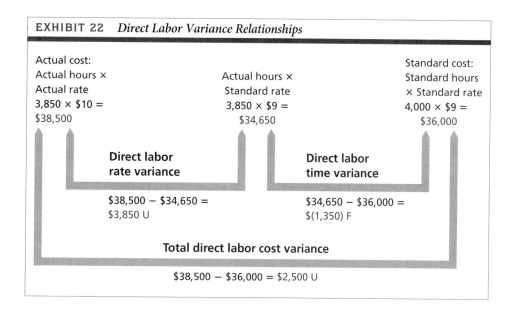

EXHIBIT 22 *Direct Labor Variance Relationships*

Actual cost:
Actual hours ×
Actual rate
3,850 × $10 =
$38,500

Actual hours ×
Standard rate
3,850 × $9 =
$34,650

Standard cost:
Standard hours
× Standard rate
4,000 × $9 =
$36,000

Direct labor rate variance

$38,500 − $34,650 =
$3,850 U

Direct labor time variance

$34,650 − $36,000 =
$(1,350) F

Total direct labor cost variance

$38,500 − $36,000 = $2,500 U

Reporting Direct Labor Variances   Controlling direct labor cost is normally the responsibility of the production supervisors. To aid them, reports analyzing the cause of any direct labor variance may be prepared. Differences between standard direct labor hours and actual direct labor hours can be investigated. For example, a time variance may be incurred because of the shortage of skilled workers. Such variances may be uncontrollable unless they are related to high turnover rates among employees, in which case the cause of the high turnover should be investigated.

Likewise, differences between the rates paid for direct labor and the standard rates can be investigated. For example, unfavorable rate variances may be caused by the improper scheduling and use of workers. In such cases, skilled, highly paid workers may be used in jobs that are normally performed by unskilled, lower-paid workers. In this case, the unfavorable rate variance should be reported for corrective action to the managers who schedule work assignments.

Standards for Nonmanufacturing Expenses

Obj 6

Explain how standards can be used for nonmanufacturing expenses.

Using standards for nonmanufacturing expenses, such as service, selling, and administrative expenses, is not as common as using standards for manufacturing costs. This is often due to many nonmanufacturing expenses not directly relating to a unit of output or other measure of activity. For example, the administrative expenses associated with the work of the office manager are not easily related to a measurable output. In these cases, nonmanufacturing expenses are normally controlled by using static budgets.

However, when nonmanufacturing activities are repetitive and produce a common output, standards can be applied. In these cases, the use of standards is similar to that described for a manufactured product. For example, standards can be applied to the work of customer service personnel who process sales orders. A standard cost for processing a sales order (the output) could be developed. The variance between the actual cost of processing a sales order and the standard cost could then be used to control sales order processing costs.

Obj **7**

Explain and provide
examples of nonfinancial
performance measures.

Nonfinancial Performance Measures

Many managers believe that financial performance measures, such as variances from standard, should be supplemented with nonfinancial measures of performance. Measuring both financial and nonfinancial performance helps employees consider multiple, and sometimes conflicting, performance objectives. For example, one company had a machining operation that was measured according to a direct labor time standard. Employees did their work quickly in order to create favorable direct labor time variances. Unfortunately, the fast work resulted in poor quality that, in turn, created difficulty in the assembly operation. The company decided to use both a labor time standard *and* a quality standard in order to encourage employees to consider both the speed and quality of their work.

In the preceding example, nonfinancial performance measures brought additional perspectives, such as quality of work, to evaluating performance. Some additional examples of nonfinancial performance measures are as follows:

Nonfinancial Performance Measures

Inventory turnover
On-time delivery
Elapsed time between a customer order and product delivery
Customer preference rankings compared to competitors
Response time to a service call
Time to develop new products
Employee satisfaction
Number of customer complaints

Nonfinancial measures can be linked to either the inputs or outputs of an activity or process. A **process** is a sequence of activities linked together for performing a particular task. For example, the procurement process consists of the "create purchase order" and "select vendor" activities that are performed in procuring materials. The relationship between a process or activity and its inputs and outputs is shown as follows:

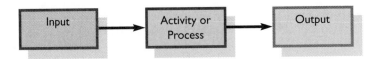

To illustrate nonfinancial measures for a single activity, consider the counter service activity of a fast-food restaurant. The following input/output relationship could be identified:

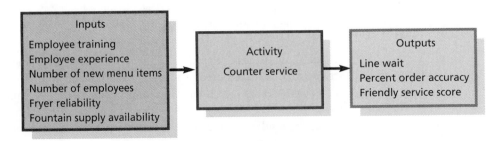

The outputs of the counter service activity include the customer line wait, order accuracy, and service experience. The inputs that impact these outputs include the number of employees, level of employee experience and training, reliability of the french fryer, menu complexity, fountain drink supply, and the like. Also, note that the inputs for one activity could be the outputs of another. For example, fryer reliability is an input to the counter service activity, but is an output of the french frying activity. Moving back, fryer maintenance would be an input to the french frying activity. Thus, a chain of inputs and outputs can be developed between a set of connected activities or processes. The fast-food restaurant can develop a set of linked nonfinancial performance measures across the chain of inputs and outputs. The output measures tell management how the activity is performing, such as keeping the line wait to a minimum. The input measures are the *levers* that impact the activity's performance. Thus, if the fast-food restaurant line wait is too long, then the input measures might indicate a need for more training, more employees, or better fryer reliability.

HOW BUSINESSES MAKE MONEY

Aligning the Budgeting System with Strategy

A business unit of a company can adopt either a build strategy or a harvest strategy. A *build* strategy is one where the business is designing, launching, and growing new products and markets. Build strategies often require short-term profit sacrifice in order to grow market share. HDTVs are an example of a product managed under a build strategy. A *harvest* strategy is often employed for business units with mature products enjoying high market share in low-growth industries. Harvest strategies maximize short-term earnings and cash flow, sometimes at the expense of market share. Often the term "cash cow" is used to describe a product managed under a harvest strategy. Tobacco is an example of such a product. Compared to the harvest strategy, a build strategy often has greater uncertainty, unpredictability, and change. Build strategies are usually employed in evolving product/market segments; thus, the competitive battle for market share is often fierce and unpredictable. The differences between build and harvest strategies imply different budgeting approaches. That is, the budget approach is contingent upon the strategy.

The build strategy should employ a budget approach that is flexible to the inherent uncertainty of the business. Thus, budgets should adapt to changing conditions by allowing periodic revisions and flexible targets. Often the managers controlled by the budget will participate in setting budget targets, so that all uncertainties are considered. In addition, the budget will complement other, more subjective, evaluation criteria. Overall, the budget serves as a short-term planning tool to guide management in executing an uncertain and evolving product market strategy.

Under the harvest strategy, the business is often much more stable and is managed to maximize profitability and cash flow. Cost control is much more important in a harvest strategy; thus, the budget is used to restrict the actions of managers. The budget is established with ambitious cost reduction targets, allowing little room for negotiation or revision. In addition, the managers controlled by the budget often do not participate in its development. Rather, the budget is imposed. In a harvest business, the budget is the major control tool and is often not supplemented with other, more subjective performance measures.

The descriptions above provide the extreme ends of a continuum. Real-world budget systems will blend tight versus loose, objective versus subjective, short-term versus long-term, programmed versus interactive, and mechanistic versus flexible characteristics to fit the strategy. Budgeting systems are not "one size fits all" solutions but must adapt to the underlying business conditions.

Appendix   Factory Overhead Variances

Factory overhead costs are more difficult to manage than are direct labor and materials costs. This is because the relationship between production volume and indirect costs is not easy to determine. For example, when production is increased, the direct materials will increase. But what about the Engineering Department overhead? The relationship between production volume and cost is less clear for the Engineering Department. Companies normally respond to this difficulty by separating factory overhead into variable and fixed costs. For example, manufacturing supplies are considered variable to production volume, whereas straight-line plant depreciation is considered fixed. In the following sections, we discuss the approaches used to budget and control factory overhead by separating overhead into fixed and variable components.

The Factory Overhead Flexible Budget

A flexible budget may be used to determine the impact of changing production on fixed and variable factory overhead costs. The standard overhead rate is determined by dividing the budgeted factory overhead costs by the standard amount of productive activity, such as direct labor hours. Exhibit 23 is a flexible factory overhead budget for Western Rider Inc.

In Exhibit 23, the standard factory overhead cost rate is $6.00. It is determined by dividing the total budgeted cost of 100% of normal capacity by the standard hours required at 100% of normal capacity, or $30,000 ÷ 5,000 hours = $6.00 per hour. This

---

EXHIBIT 23   *Factory Overhead Cost Budget Indicating Standard Factory Overhead Rate*

WESTERN RIDER INC.
Factory Overhead Cost Budget
For the Month Ended June 30, 2009

	80%	90%	100%	110%
Percent of normal capacity	80%	90%	100%	110%
Units produced	5,000	5,625	6,250	6,875
Direct labor hours (0.80 hour per unit)	4,000	4,500	5,000	5,500
Budgeted factory overhead:				
Variable costs:				
Indirect factory wages	$ 8,000	$ 9,000	$10,000	$11,000
Power and light	4,000	4,500	5,000	5,500
Indirect materials	2,400	2,700	3,000	3,300
Total variable cost	$14,400	$16,200	$18,000	$19,800
Fixed costs:				
Supervisory salaries	$ 5,500	$ 5,500	$ 5,500	$ 5,500
Depreciation of plant and equipment	4,500	4,500	4,500	4,500
Insurance and property taxes	2,000	2,000	2,000	2,000
Total fixed cost	$12,000	$12,000	$12,000	$12,000
Total factory overhead cost	$26,400	$28,200	$30,000	$31,800

Factory overhead rate per direct labor hour, $30,000 ÷ 5,000 hours = $6.00

rate can be subdivided into $3.60 per hour for variable factory overhead ($18,000 ÷ 5,000 hours) and $2.40 per hour for fixed factory overhead ($12,000 ÷ 5,000 hours).

Variances from standard for factory overhead cost result from:

1. Actual variable factory overhead cost greater or less than budgeted variable factory overhead for actual production.
2. Actual production at a level above or below 100% of normal capacity.

The first factor results in the controllable variance for variable overhead costs. The second factor results in a volume variance for fixed overhead costs. We will discuss each of these variances next.

Variable Factory Overhead Controllable Variance

The variable factory overhead **controllable variance** is the difference between the actual variable overhead incurred and the budgeted variable overhead for actual production. The controllable variance measures the *efficiency* of using variable overhead resources. Thus, if the actual variable overhead is less than the budgeted variable overhead, the variance is favorable. If the actual variable overhead exceeds the budgeted variable overhead, the variance is unfavorable.

To illustrate, recall that Western Rider Inc. produced 5,000 pairs of XL jeans in June. Each pair requires 0.80 standard labor hour for production. As a result, Western Rider Inc. had 4,000 standard hours at actual production (5,000 jeans × 0.80 hour). This represents 80% of normal productive capacity (4,000 hours ÷ 5,000 hours). The standard variable overhead at 4,000 hours worked, according to the budget in Exhibit 23, was $14,400 (4,000 direct labor hours × $3.60). The following actual factory overhead costs were incurred in June:

Actual costs:	
Variable factory overhead	$10,400
Fixed factory overhead	12,000
Total actual factory overhead	$22,400

The controllable variance can be calculated as follows:

Controllable variance:	
Actual variable factory overhead	$ 10,400
Budgeted variable factory overhead for actual amount produced (4,000 hrs. × $3.60)	14,400
Variance—favorable	$ (4,000) F

The variable factory overhead controllable variance indicates management's ability to keep the factory overhead costs within the budget limits. Since variable factory overhead costs are normally controllable at the department level, responsibility for controlling this variance usually rests with department supervisors.

Fixed Factory Overhead Volume Variance

Using currently attainable standards, Western Rider Inc. set its budgeted normal capacity at 5,000 direct labor hours. This is the amount of expected capacity that management believes will be used under normal business conditions. You should note that this amount may be much less than the total available capacity if management believes demand will be low.

The fixed factory overhead *volume variance* is the difference between the budgeted fixed overhead at 100% of normal capacity and the standard fixed overhead for the actual production achieved during the period. The volume variance measures the use of fixed overhead resources. If the standard fixed overhead exceeds the budgeted overhead at 100% of normal capacity, the variance is favorable. Thus, the firm used its plant and equipment more than would be expected under normal operating conditions. If the standard fixed overhead is less than the budgeted overhead at 100% of normal capacity, the variance is unfavorable. Thus, the company used its plant and equipment less than would be expected under normal operating conditions.

The volume variance for Western Rider Inc. is shown in the following calculation:

100% of normal capacity	5,000	direct labor hours
Standard hours at actual production	4,000	
Capacity not used	1,000	direct labor hours
Standard fixed overhead rate	× $2.40	
Volume variance—unfavorable	$ 2,400	U

Exhibit 24 illustrates the volume variance graphically. For Western Rider Inc., the budgeted fixed overhead is $12,000 at all levels. The standard fixed overhead at 5,000 hours is also $12,000. This is the point at which the standard fixed overhead line

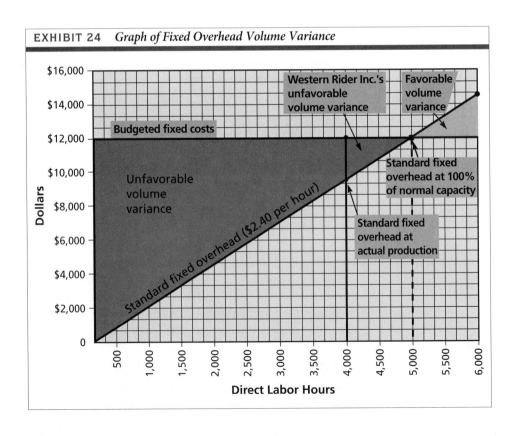

EXHIBIT 24   *Graph of Fixed Overhead Volume Variance*

intersects the budgeted fixed cost line. For actual volume greater than 100% of normal capacity, the volume variance is favorable. For volume at less than 100% of normal volume, the volume variance is unfavorable. For Western Rider Inc., the volume variance is unfavorable because the actual production is 4,000 standard hours, or 80% of normal volume. The amount of the volume variance, $2,400, can be viewed as the cost of the unused capacity (1,000 hours).

An unfavorable volume variance may be due to such factors as failure to maintain an even flow of work, machine breakdowns, repairs causing work stoppages, and failure to obtain enough sales orders to keep the factory operating at normal capacity. Management should determine the causes of the unfavorable variance and consider taking corrective action. A volume variance caused by an uneven flow of work, for example, can be remedied by changing operating procedures. Volume variances caused by lack of sales orders may be corrected through increased advertising or other sales effort.

Volume variances tend to encourage manufacturing managers to run the factory above the normal capacity. This is favorable when the additional production can be sold. However, if the additional production cannot be sold and must be stored as inventory, favorable volume variances may actually be harmful. For example, one paper company ran paper machines above normal volume in order to create favorable volume variances. Unfortunately, this created a six months' supply of finished goods inventory that had to be stored in public warehouses. The "savings" from the favorable volume variances were exceeded by the additional inventory carrying costs. By creating incentives for manufacturing managers to overproduce, the volume variances produced *goal conflicts*, as we described earlier in this chapter.

Reporting Factory Overhead Variances

The total factory overhead cost variance is the difference between the actual factory overhead and the total overhead applied to production. This calculation is as follows:

Total actual factory overhead	$22,400
Factory overhead applied (4,000 hours × $6.00 per hour)	24,000
Total factory overhead cost variance—favorable	$(1,600) F

The factory overhead cost variance may be broken down by each variable factory overhead cost and fixed factory overhead cost element in a *factory overhead cost variance report*. Such a report, which is useful to management in controlling costs, is shown in Exhibit 25. The report indicates both the controllable variance and the volume variance.

Factory Overhead Variances and the Factory Overhead Account

At the end of the period, the factory overhead account normally has a balance. As we discussed in an earlier chapter, a positive balance in Factory Overhead is underapplied overhead, while a negative balance is overapplied overhead. This end-of-period balance, which represents the difference between actual overhead incurred and applied overhead,

EXHIBIT 25   *Factory Overhead Cost Variance Report*

WESTERN RIDER INC.
Factory Overhead Cost Variance Report
For the Month Ended June 30, 2009

Productive capacity for the month (100% of normal)	5,000 hours			
Actual production for the month	4,000 hours			

	Budget (at Actual Production)	Actual	Variances Favorable	Variances Unfavorable
Variable factory overhead costs:				
Indirect factory wages	$ 8,000	$ 5,100	$2,900	
Power and light	4,000	4,200		$ 200
Indirect materials	2,400	1,100	1,300	
Total variable factory overhead cost	$14,400	$10,400		
Fixed factory overhead costs:				
Supervisory salaries	$ 5,500	$ 5,500		
Depreciation of plant and equipment	4,500	4,500		
Insurance and property taxes	2,000	2,000		
Total fixed factory overhead cost	$12,000	$12,000		
Total factory overhead cost	$26,400	$22,400		
Total controllable variances			$4,200	$ 200
Net controllable variance—favorable				$4,000
Volume variance—unfavorable:				
Capacity not used at the standard rate for fixed factory overhead—1,000 × $2.40				2,400
Total factory overhead cost variance—favorable				$1,600

is also the total factory overhead variance for the period. A positive balance, underapplied overhead, represents an unfavorable total factory overhead variance, while a negative balance, overapplied overhead, is a favorable variance.

To illustrate, the factory overhead account for Western Rider Inc. for the month ending June 30, 2009, is shown below.

Factory Overhead Account	
Actual factory overhead ($10,400 + $12,000)	$ 22,400
Less applied factory overhead (4,000 hours × $6.00 per hour)	24,000
Balance, overapplied factory overhead, June 30	$ (1,600)

The $1,600 overapplied factory overhead is the favorable total factory cost variance shown in Exhibit 25. The variable factory overhead controllable variance and the volume variance can be computed using the factory overhead account and comparing it with the budgeted total overhead for the actual amount produced. As shown on the next page, the difference between the actual overhead incurred and the budgeted overhead is the controllable variance. The difference between the applied overhead and the budgeted overhead is the volume variance.

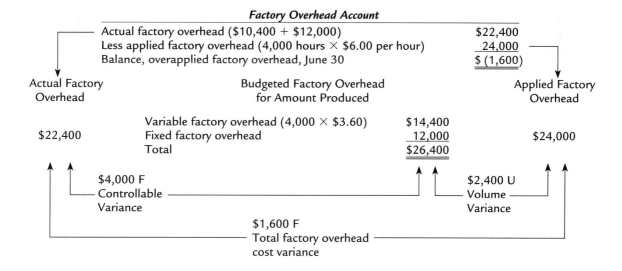

If the actual factory overhead exceeds (is less than) the budgeted factory overhead, the controllable variance is unfavorable (favorable). In contrast, if the applied factory overhead is less than (exceeds) the budgeted factory overhead, the volume variance is unfavorable (favorable). This is because, when the applied overhead is less than the budgeted overhead, the company has operated at less than normal capacity, and thus the volume variance is unfavorable.

It is also possible to break down many of the individual factory overhead cost variances into quantity and price variances, similar to direct materials and direct labor. For example, the indirect factory wages variance may include both time and rate variances. Likewise, the indirect materials variance may include both a quantity variance and a price variance. Such variances are illustrated in advanced textbooks.

Key Points

1. **Describe the nature and objectives of budgeting.**

   Budgeting involves (1) establishing specific goals, (2) executing plans to achieve the goals, and (3) periodically comparing actual results with these goals. In addition, budget goals should be established to avoid problems in human behavior. Thus, budgets should not be set too tightly, too loosely, or to cause goal conflict. Budgeting systems can use fiscal-year budgeting, continuous budgeting, or zero-based budgeting. Two major types of budgets are the static budget and the flexible budget. The static budget does not adjust with changes in activity while the flexible budget does adjust with changes in activity. Computers can be useful in speeding the budgetary process and in preparing timely budget performance reports. In addition,

   simulation models can be used to determine the impact of operating alternatives on various budgets.

2. **Describe the master budget for a manufacturing business.**

   The master budget consists of the budgeted income statement and budgeted balance sheet. These two budgets are developed from detailed supporting budgets. The income statement supporting budgets are the sales budget, production budget, direct materials purchases budget, direct labor cost budget, factory overhead cost budget, cost of goods sold budget, and selling and administrative expenses budget. Both the cash budget and the capital expenditures budget support the budgeted balance sheet. The cash budget consists of budgeted cash receipts and budgeted cash payments.

The capital expenditures budget is an important tool for planning expenditures for fixed assets.

3. Describe the nature and use of standards.

Standards represent performance benchmarks that can be compared to actual results in evaluating performance. Standards are developed, reviewed, and revised by accountants and engineers based on studies of operations. Standards are established so that they are neither too high nor too low but are attainable.

4. Explain and illustrate how standards are used in budgeting.

Budgets are prepared by multiplying the standard cost per unit by the planned production. To measure performance, the standard cost per unit is multiplied by the actual number of units produced, and the actual results are compared with the standard cost at actual volumes (cost variance).

5. Calculate and interpret the basic variances for direct materials and direct labor.

The direct materials cost variance can be separated into a direct materials price and a quantity variance. The direct materials price variance is calculated by multiplying the actual quantity by the difference between the actual and standard price. The direct materials quantity variance is calculated by multiplying the standard price by the difference between the actual materials used and the standard materials at actual volumes.

The direct labor cost variance can be separated into a direct labor rate and time variance. The direct labor rate variance is calculated by multiplying the actual hours worked by the difference between the actual labor rate and the standard labor rate. The direct labor time variance is calculated by multiplying the standard labor rate by the difference between the actual labor hours worked and the standard labor hours at actual volumes.

6. Explain how standards can be used for nonmanufacturing expenses.

Standards may be used for nonmanufacturing expenses when nonmanufacturing activities are repetitive and related to an activity base. Such standards may be useful to managers in planning, directing, and controlling nonmanufacturing expenses.

7. Explain and provide examples of nonfinancial performance measures.

Many companies use a combination of financial and nonfinancial measures in order for multiple perspectives to be incorporated in evaluating performance. Combining financial and nonfinancial measures helps employees balance cost efficiency with quality and customer service performance. Nonfinancial measures are often used in conjunction with the inputs or outputs of a process or activity.

Key Terms

Budget

Budget performance report

Budgetary slack

Capital expenditures budget

Cash budget

Continuous budgeting

Controllable variance

Cost of goods sold budget

Cost variances

Currently attainable standards

Direct labor rate variance

Direct labor time variance

Direct materials price variance

Direct materials purchases budget

Direct materials quantity variance

Flexible budget

Goal conflict

Ideal standards

Master budget

Process

Production budget

Sales budget

Standard cost

Standard cost systems

Static budget

Zero-based budgeting

Illustrative Problem

Hawley Inc. manufactures Product S for national distribution. The standard costs for the manufacture of Product S were as follows:

	Standard Costs	**Actual Costs**
Direct materials	1,500 pounds at $35	1,600 pounds at $32
Direct labor	4,800 hours at $11	4,500 hours at $11.80
Factory overhead	Rates per labor hour, based on 100% of normal capacity of 5,500 labor hours:	
	Variable cost, $2.40	$12,300 variable cost
	Fixed cost, $3.50	$19,250 fixed cost

Instructions

1. Determine the quantity variance, price variance, and total direct materials cost variance for Product S.
2. Determine the time variance, rate variance, and total direct labor cost variance for Product S.
3. Appendix: Determine the controllable variance, volume variance, and total factory overhead cost variance for Product S.

Solution

1.

	Direct Materials Cost Variance		
Quantity variance:			
Actual quantity	1,600 pounds		
Standard quantity	1,500		
Variance—unfavorable	100 pounds × standard price, $35		$ 3,500
Price variance:			
Actual price	$32.00 per pound		
Standard price	35.00		
Variance—favorable	$ (3.00) per pound × actual quantity, 1,600		(4,800)
Total direct materials cost variance—favorable			$(1,300)

2.

	Direct Labor Cost Variance		
Time variance:			
Actual time	4,500 hours		
Standard time	4,800 hours		
Variance—favorable	(300) hours × standard rate, $11		$(3,300)
Rate variance:			
Actual rate	$11.80		
Standard rate	11.00		
Variance—unfavorable	$ 0.80 per hour × actual time, 4,500 hrs.		3,600
Total direct labor cost variance—unfavorable			$ 300

3. Appendix

Factory Overhead Cost Variance

Variable factory overhead—controllable variance:		
Actual variable factory overhead cost incurred	$12,300	
Budgeted variable factory overhead for 4,800 hours	11,520*	
Variance—unfavorable		$ 780
Fixed factory overhead—volume variance:		
Budgeted hours at 100% of normal capacity	5,500 hours	
Standard hours for actual production	4,800	
Productive capacity not used	700 hours	
Standard fixed factory overhead cost rate	× $3.50	
Variance—unfavorable		2,450
Total factory overhead cost variance—unfavorable		$3,230

*4,800 hrs. × $2.40 = $11,520

OR

Factory Overhead Account

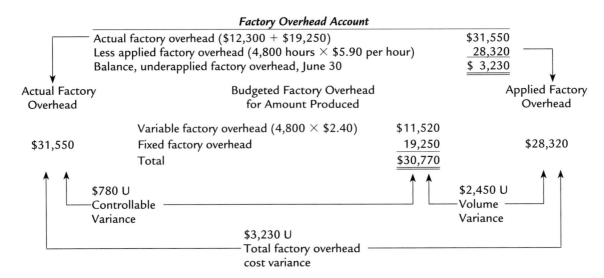

Actual factory overhead ($12,300 + $19,250)	$31,550	
Less applied factory overhead (4,800 hours × $5.90 per hour)	28,320	
Balance, underapplied factory overhead, June 30	$ 3,230	

Actual Factory Overhead   Budgeted Factory Overhead for Amount Produced   Applied Factory Overhead

	Variable factory overhead (4,800 × $2.40)	$11,520	
$31,550	Fixed factory overhead	19,250	$28,320
	Total	$30,770	

$780 U
Controllable Variance

$2,450 U
Volume Variance

$3,230 U
Total factory overhead cost variance

Self-Examination Questions   *(Answers appear at end of chapter.)*

1. Static budgets are often used by:
   A. production departments
   B. administrative departments
   C. responsibility centers
   D. capital projects

2. The total estimated sales for the coming year is 250,000 units. The estimated inventory at the beginning of the year is 22,500 units, and the desired inventory at the end of the year is 30,000 units. The total production indicated in the production budget is:

   A. 242,500 units   C. 280,000 units
   B. 257,500 units   D. 302,500 units

3. Dixon Company expects $650,000 of credit sales in March and $800,000 of credit sales in April. Dixon historically collects 70% of its sales in the month of sale and 30% in the following month. How much cash does Dixon expect to collect in April?
   A. $800,000   C. $755,000
   B. $560,000   D. $1,015,000

4. The actual and standard direct materials costs for producing a specified quantity of product are as follows:

Actual:	51,000 pounds at $5.05	$257,550
Standard:	50,000 pounds at $5.00	$250,000

The direct materials price variance is:

A. $50 unfavorable   C. $2,550 unfavorable
B. $2,500 unfavorable   D. $7,550 unfavorable

5. Bower Company produced 4,000 units of product. Each unit requires 0.5 standard hour. The standard labor rate is $12 per hour. Actual direct labor for the period was $22,000 (2,200 hours × $10 per hour). The direct labor time variance is:

A. 200 hours unfavorable
B. $2,000 unfavorable
C. $4,000 favorable
D. $2,400 unfavorable

Class Discussion Questions

1. Briefly describe the type of human behavior problems that might arise if budget goals are set too tightly.

2. Why should all levels of management and all departments participate in preparing and submitting budget estimates?

3. What behavioral problems are associated with setting a budget too loosely?

4. What behavioral problems are associated with establishing conflicting goals within the budget?

5. When would a company use zero-based budgeting?

6. Under what circumstances would a static budget be appropriate?

7. How do computerized budgeting systems aid firms in the budgeting process?

8. What is the first step in preparing a master budget?

9. Why should the production requirements set forth in the production budget be carefully coordinated with the sales budget?

10. Why should the timing of direct materials purchases be closely coordinated with the production budget?

11. In preparing the budget for the cost of goods sold, what are the three budgets from which data on relevant estimates of quantities and costs are combined with data on estimated inventories?

12. a. Discuss the purpose of the cash budget.
    b. If the cash for the first quarter of the fiscal year indicates excess cash at the end of each of the first two months, how might the excess cash be used?

13. Give an example of how the capital expenditures budget affects other operating budgets.

14. How are standards used in budgetary performance evaluation?

15. a. What are the two variances between the actual cost and the standard cost for direct materials?
    b. Discuss some possible causes of these variances.

16. The materials cost variance report for Nickols Inc. indicates a large favorable materials price variance and a significant unfavorable materials quantity variance. What might have caused these offsetting variances?

17. a. What are the two variances between the actual cost and the standard cost for direct labor?
    b. Who generally has control over the direct labor cost?

18. A new assistant controller recently was heard to remark: "All the assembly workers in this plant are covered by union contracts, so there should be no labor variances." Was the controller's remark correct? Discuss.

19. Would the use of standards be appropriate in a non-manufacturing setting, such as a fast-food restaurant?

20. Briefly explain why firms might use nonfinancial performance measures.

Exercises

E13-1

Flexible budget for selling and administrative expenses

Objs 1,2

SPREADSHEET

✓ Total selling and administrative expenses at $140,000 sales, $65,550

Master Electronics Company uses flexible budgets that are based on the following data:

Sales commissions	7% of sales
Advertising expense	18% of sales
Miscellaneous selling expense	$1,750 plus 4% of sales
Office salaries expense	$12,000 per month
Office supplies expense	5% of sales
Miscellaneous administrative expense	$1,400 per month plus 2% of sales

Prepare a flexible selling and administrative expenses budget for January 2008 for sales volumes of $100,000, $120,000, and $140,000. (Use Exhibit 4 as a model.)

E13-2

Flexible budget for Fabrication Department

Obj 2

SPREADSHEET

✓ Total department cost at 12,000 units, $957,600

Steelcase Inc. is one of the largest manufacturers of office furniture in the United States. In Grand Rapids, Michigan, it produces filing cabinets in two departments: Fabrication and Trim Assembly. Assume the following information for the Fabrication Department:

Steel per filing cabinet	50 pounds
Direct labor per filing cabinet	18 minutes
Supervisor salaries	$130,000 per month
Depreciation	$20,000 per month
Direct labor rate	$16 per hour
Steel cost	$1.25 per pound

Prepare a flexible budget for 12,000, 15,000, and 18,000 filing cabinets for the month of October 2008, similar to Exhibit 4, assuming that inventories are not significant.

E13-3

Sales and production budgets

Obj 2

SPREADSHEET

✓ b. Model DL total production, 7,420 units

Melody Audio Company manufactures two models of speakers, DL and XL. Based on the following production and sales data for September 2007, prepare (a) a sales budget and (b) a production budget.

	DL	XL
Estimated inventory (units), September 1	380	140
Desired inventory (units), September 30	450	110
Expected sales volume (units):		
East Region	4,400	3,200
West Region	2,950	2,100
Unit sales price	$120.00	$170.00

E13-4

Professional fees budget

Obj 2

SPREADSHEET

✓ Total professional fees, $13,956,000

Kimble and Sanchez, CPAs, offer three types of services to clients: auditing, tax, and small business accounting. Based on experience and projected growth, the following billable hours have been estimated for the year ending December 31, 2008:

	Billable Hours
Audit Department:	
Staff	34,500
Partners	5,200
Tax Department:	
Staff	27,700
Partners	4,150
Small Business Accounting Department:	
Staff	22,800
Partners	6,300

The average billing rate for staff is $120 per hour, and the average billing rate for partners is $240 per hour. Prepare a professional fees earned budget for Kimble and Sanchez, CPAs, for the year ending December 31, 2008, using the following column headings and showing the estimated professional fees by type of service rendered:

Billable Hours	Hourly Rate	Total Revenue

E13-5

Professional labor cost budget

Obj 2

SPREADSHEET

✓ Staff total labor cost, $6,375,000

Based on the data in Exercise 13-4 and assuming that the average compensation per hour for staff is $75 and for partners is $140, prepare a professional labor cost budget for Kimble and Sanchez, CPAs, for the year ending December 31, 2008. Use the following column headings:

Staff	Partners

E13-6

Direct materials purchases budget

Obj 2

SPREADSHEET

✓ Total cheese purchases, $131,813

Roma Frozen Pizza Inc. has determined from its production budget the following estimated production volumes for 12″ and 16″ frozen pizzas for November 2008:

	Units	
	12″ Pizza	16″ Pizza
Budgeted production volume	16,400	25,600

There are three direct materials used in producing the two types of pizza. The quantities of direct materials expected to be used for each pizza are as follows:

	12″ Pizza	16″ Pizza
Direct materials:		
Dough	1.00 lb. per unit	1.50 lbs. per unit
Tomato	0.60	0.90
Cheese	0.80	1.30

In addition, Roma has determined the following information about each material:

	Dough	Tomato	Cheese
Estimated inventory, November 1, 2008	675 lbs.	190 lbs.	525 lbs.
Desired inventory, November 30, 2008	480 lbs.	250 lbs.	375 lbs.
Price per pound	$1.20	$2.40	$2.85

Prepare November's direct materials purchases budget for Roma Frozen Pizza Inc.

E13-7

Direct materials purchases budget

Obj 2

SPREADSHEET

✓ Concentrate budgeted purchases, $90,900

Coca-Cola Enterprises is the largest bottler of Coca-Cola® in North America. The company purchases Coke® and Sprite® concentrate from *The Coca-Cola Company*, dilutes and mixes the concentrate with carbonated water, and then fills the blended beverage into cans or plastic two-liter bottles. Assume that the estimated production for Coke and Sprite two-liter bottles at the Chattanooga, Tennessee, bottling plant are as follows for the month of June:

Coke	192,000 two-liter bottles
Sprite	148,000 two-liter bottles

In addition, assume that the concentrate costs $75 per pound for both Coke and Sprite and is used at a rate of 0.2 pound per 100 liters of carbonated water in blending Coke and 0.15 pound per 100 liters of carbonated water in blending Sprite. Assume that two-liter bottles cost $0.07 per bottle and carbonated water costs $0.05 per liter.

Prepare a direct materials purchases budget for June 2008, assuming no changes between beginning and ending inventories for all three materials.

E13-8

Direct labor cost budget

Obj 2

SPREADSHEET

✓ Total direct labor cost, Assembly, $186,225

Match Point Racket Company manufactures two types of tennis rackets, the Junior and Pro Striker models. The production budget for March for the two rackets is as follows:

	Junior	Pro Striker
Production budget	7,300 units	18,400 units

Both rackets are produced in two departments, Forming and Assembly. The direct labor hours required for each racket are estimated as follows:

	Forming Department	Assembly Department
Junior	0.25 hour per unit	0.45 hour per unit
Pro Striker	0.40 hour per unit	0.60 hour per unit

The direct labor rate for each department is as follows:

Forming Department	$18.00 per hour
Assembly Department	$13.00 per hour

Prepare the direct labor cost budget for March 2008.

E13-9

Production and direct labor cost budgets

Obj 2

SPREADSHEET

✓ a. Total production of 501 Jeans, 47,000

Levi Strauss & Co. manufactures slacks and jeans under a variety of brand names, such as Dockers® and 501 Jeans®. Slacks and jeans are assembled by a variety of different sewing operations. Assume that the sales budget for Dockers and 501 Jeans shows estimated sales of 23,800 and 46,200 pairs, respectively, for March 2008. The finished goods inventory is assumed as follows:

	Dockers	501 Jeans
March 1 estimated inventory	320	1,230
March 31 desired inventory	520	2,030

Assume the following direct labor data per 10 pairs of Dockers and 501 Jeans for four different sewing operations:

	Direct Labor per 10 Pairs	
	Dockers	*501 Jeans*
Inseam	18 minutes	12 minutes
Outerseam	22	15
Pockets	7	9
Zipper	10	6
Total	57 minutes	42 minutes

a. Prepare a production budget for March. Prepare the budget in two columns: Dockers® and 501 Jeans®.
b. Prepare the March direct labor cost budget for the four sewing operations, assuming a $12 wage per hour for the inseam and outerseam sewing operations and a $14 wage per hour for the pocket and zipper sewing operations. Prepare the direct labor cost budget in four columns: inseam, outerseam, pockets, and zipper.

E13-10

Factory overhead cost budget

Obj 2

SPREADSHEET

✓ Total variable factory overhead costs, $243,000

Fresh Mint Candy Company budgeted the following costs for anticipated production for July 2008:

Advertising expenses	$275,000	Production supervisor wages	$125,000
Manufacturing supplies	14,000	Production control salaries	33,000
Power and light	42,000	Executive officer salaries	205,000
Sales commissions	290,000	Materials management salaries	29,000
Factory insurance	23,000	Factory depreciation	17,000

Prepare a factory overhead cost budget, separating variable and fixed costs. Assume that factory insurance and depreciation are the only factory fixed costs.

E13-11

Cost of goods sold budget

Obj 2

SPREADSHEET

✓ Cost of goods sold, $397,320

The controller of Moravian Ceramics Inc. wishes to prepare a cost of goods sold budget for April. The controller assembled the following information for constructing the cost of goods sold budget:

Direct materials:	Enamel	Paint	Porcelain	Total
Total direct materials purchases budgeted for April	$32,450	$4,730	$114,240	$151,420
Estimated inventory, April 1, 2008	1,150	2,800	4,330	8,280
Desired inventory, April 30, 2008	2,500	2,050	6,000	10,550

Direct labor cost:	Kiln Department	Decorating Department	Total
Total direct labor cost budgeted for April	$37,500	$134,400	$171,900

Finished goods inventories:	Dish	Bowl	Figurine	Total
Estimated inventory, April 1, 2008	$4,280	$2,970	$2,470	$ 9,720
Desired inventory, April 30, 2008	3,350	4,150	3,700	11,200

Work in process inventories:	
Estimated inventory, April 1, 2008	$2,800
Desired inventory, April 30, 2008	1,750

(continued)

Budgeted factory overhead costs for April:

Indirect factory wages	$55,500
Depreciation of plant and equipment	12,600
Power and light	4,900
Indirect materials	3,700
Total	$76,700

Use the preceding information to prepare a cost of goods sold budget for April 2008.

E13-12

Schedule of cash collections of accounts receivable

Obj 2

SPREADSHEET

✓ Total cash collected in May, $535,700

Happy Tails Wholesale Inc., a pet wholesale supplier, was organized on March 1, 2008. Projected sales for each of the first three months of operations are as follows:

March	$450,000
April	520,000
May	560,000

The company expects to sell 10% of its merchandise for cash. Of sales on account, 50% are expected to be collected in the month of the sale, 40% in the month following the sale, and the remainder in the second month following the sale.

Prepare a schedule indicating cash collections from sales for March, April, and May.

E13-13

Schedule of cash collections of accounts receivable

Obj 2

SPREADSHEET

✓ Total cash collected in January, $307,600

Office Warehouse Supplies Inc. has "cash and carry" customers and credit customers. Office Warehouse estimates that 40% of monthly sales are to cash customers, while the remaining sales are to credit customers. Of the credit customers, 30% pay their accounts in the month of sale, while the remaining 70% pay their accounts in the month following the month of sale. Projected sales for the first three months of 2008 are as follows:

January	$220,000
February	275,000
March	260,000

The Accounts Receivable balance on December 31, 2007, was $180,000.

Prepare a schedule of cash collections from sales for January, February, and March.

E13-14

Schedule of cash payments

Obj 2

SPREADSHEET

✓ Total cash payments in August, $107,875

A+ Learning Systems Inc. was organized on May 31, 2009. Projected selling and administrative expenses for each of the first three months of operations are as follows:

June	$114,800
July	124,500
August	129,000

Depreciation, insurance, and property taxes represent $20,000 of the estimated monthly expenses. The annual insurance premium was paid on May 31, and property taxes for the year will be paid in December. Three-fourths of the remainder of the expenses are expected to be paid in the month in which they are incurred, with the balance to be paid in the following month.

Prepare a schedule indicating cash payments for selling and administrative expenses for June, July, and August.

E13-15

Schedule of cash payments

Obj 2

SPREADSHEET

✓ Total cash payments in December, $128,720

Total Flex Physical Therapy Inc. is planning its cash payments for operations for the fourth quarter (October–December), 2009. The Accrued Expenses Payable balance on October 1 is $22,600. The budgeted expenses for the next three months are as follows:

	October	November	December
Salaries	$ 58,200	$ 63,500	$ 74,500
Utilities	5,300	5,600	7,100
Other operating expenses	44,700	52,800	62,700
Total	$108,200	$121,900	$144,300

Other operating expenses include $10,500 of monthly depreciation expense and $600 of monthly insurance expense that was prepaid for the year on March 1 of the current year. Of the remaining expenses, 80% are paid in the month in which they are incurred, with the remainder paid in the following month. The Accrued Expenses Payable balance on October 1 relates to the expenses incurred in September.

Prepare a schedule of cash payments for operations for October, November, and December.

E13-16

Capital expenditures budget

Obj 2

SPREADSHEET

✓ Total capital expenditures in 2008, $7,000,000

On January 1, 2008, the controller of Garden Master Tools Inc. is planning capital expenditures for the years 2008–2011. The following interviews helped the controller collect the necessary information for the capital expenditures budget.

Director of Facilities: A construction contract was signed in late 2007 for the construction of a new factory building at a contract cost of $12,000,000. The construction is scheduled to begin in 2008 and be completed in 2009.

Vice President of Manufacturing: Once the new factory building is finished, we plan to purchase $1.5 million in equipment in late 2009. I expect that an additional $300,000 will be needed early in the following year (2010) to test and install the equipment before we can begin production. If sales continue to grow, I expect we'll need to invest another million in equipment in 2011.

Vice President of Marketing: We have really been growing lately. I wouldn't be surprised if we need to expand the size of our new factory building in 2011 by at least 40%. Fortunately, we expect inflation to have minimal impact on construction costs over the next four years.

Director of Information Systems: We need to upgrade our information systems to wireless network technology. It doesn't make sense to do this until after the new factory building is completed and producing product. During 2010, once the factory is up and running, we should equip the whole facility with wireless technology. I think it would cost us $1,600,000 today to install the technology. However, prices have been dropping by 25% per year, so it should be less expensive at a later date.

President: I am excited about our long-term prospects. My only short-term concern is financing the $7,000,000 of construction costs on the portion of the new factory building scheduled to be completed in 2008.

Use the interview information above to prepare a capital expenditures budget for Garden Master Tools Inc. for the years 2008–2011.

E13-17

Standard product cost

Obj 3

Carolina Furniture Company manufactures unfinished oak furniture. Carolina uses a standard cost system. The direct labor, direct materials, and factory overhead standards for an unfinished dining room table are as follows:

(continued)

Direct labor:	standard rate	$17.00 per hour
	standard time per unit	3 hours
Direct materials (oak):	standard price	$8.60 per board foot
	standard quantity	16 board feet
Variable factory overhead:	standard rate	$2.60 per direct labor hour
Fixed factory overhead:	standard rate	$1.20 per direct labor hour

Determine the standard cost per dining room table.

E13-18

Budget performance report

Obj 4

SPREADSHEET

✓ b. Direct labor cost variance, $120 F

Vernon Bottle Company (VBC) manufactures plastic two-liter bottles for the beverage industry. The cost standards per 100 two-liter bottles are as follows:

Cost Category	Standard Cost per 100 Two-Liter Bottles
Direct labor	$1.28
Direct materials	5.21
Factory overhead	0.42
Total	$6.91

At the beginning of August, VBC management planned to produce 620,000 bottles. The actual number of bottles produced for August was 650,000 bottles. The actual costs for August of the current year were as follows:

Cost Category	Actual Cost for the Month Ended August 31, 2008
Direct labor	$ 8,200
Direct materials	34,500
Factory overhead	2,800
Total	$45,500

a. Prepare the August manufacturing standard cost budget (direct labor, direct materials, and factory overhead) for VBC, assuming planned production.
b. Prepare a budget performance report for manufacturing costs, showing the total cost variances for direct materials, direct labor, and factory overhead for August.
c. Interpret the budget performance report.

E13-19

Direct materials variances

Obj 5

✓ a. Price variance, $26,048 F

The following data relate to the direct materials cost for the production of 4,000 automobile tires:

Actual:	130,240 pounds at $1.65	$214,896
Standard:	128,760 pounds at $1.85	$238,206

a. Determine the price variance, quantity variance, and total direct materials cost variance.
b. To whom should the variances be reported for analysis and control?

E13-20

Standard direct materials cost per unit from variance data

Obj 5

The following data relating to direct materials cost for March of the current year are taken from the records of Top Toys Inc., a manufacturer of plastic toys:

Quantity of direct materials used	40,000 pounds
Actual unit price of direct materials	$1.48 per pound
Units of finished product manufactured	7,600 units
Standard direct materials per unit of finished product	5 pounds
Direct materials quantity variance—unfavorable	$2,700
Direct materials price variance—unfavorable	$5,200

Determine the standard direct materials cost per unit of finished product, assuming that there was no inventory of work in process at either the beginning or the end of the month.

E13-21

Standard product cost, direct materials variance

Obj 5

✓ a. $1 per pound

H.J. Heinz Company uses standards to control its materials costs. Assume that a batch of ketchup (1,500 pounds) has the following standards:

	Standard Quantity	Standard Price
Whole tomatoes	2,400 pounds	$0.40 per pound
Vinegar	130 gallons	2.50 per gallon
Corn syrup	10 gallons	8.00 per gallon
Salt	54 pounds	2.50 per pound

The actual materials in a batch may vary from the standard due to tomato characteristics. Assume that the actual quantities of materials for batch W196 were as follows:

2,500 pounds of tomatoes
115 gallons of vinegar
13 gallons of corn syrup
53 pounds of salt

a. Determine the standard unit materials cost per pound for a standard batch.
b. Determine the direct materials quantity variance for batch W196.

E13-22

Direct labor variances

Obj 5

✓ a. Rate variance, $2,040 U

The following data relate to labor cost for production of 12,500 cellular telephones:

Actual:	13,600 hours at $16.15	$219,640
Standard:	13,725 hours at $16.00	$219,600

a. Determine the rate variance, time variance, and total direct labor cost variance.
b. Discuss what might have caused these variances.

E13-23

Direct labor variances

Obj 5

✓ a. Time variance, $1,281 F

Blue Ridge Bicycle Company manufactures mountain bikes. The following data for May of the current year are available:

Quantity of direct labor used	1,400 hours
Actual rate for direct labor	$16.15 per hour
Bicycles completed in May	280
Standard direct labor per bicycle	5.30 hours
Standard rate for direct labor	$15.25 per hour
Planned bicycles for May	210

a. Determine the direct labor rate and time variances.
b. How much direct labor should be debited to Work in Process?

E13-24

Direct materials and direct labor variances

Obj 5

✓ Direct materials quantity variance, $400 F

At the beginning of July, Commercial Printers Company budgeted 14,000 books to be printed in July at standard direct materials and direct labor costs as follows:

Direct materials	$28,000
Direct labor	24,500
Total	$52,500

The standard materials price is $0.80 per pound. The standard direct labor rate is $14 per hour. At the end of July, the actual direct materials and direct labor costs were as follows:

Actual direct materials	$31,200
Actual direct labor	28,400
Total	$59,600

There were no direct materials price or direct labor rate variances for July. In addition, assume no changes in the direct materials inventory balances in July. Commercial Printers Company actually produced 15,800 units during July.

Determine the direct materials quantity and direct labor time variances.

E13-25

Standards for nonmanufacturing expenses

Obj 6

✓ a. $2,520

Midlands Hospital began using standards to evaluate its Admissions Department. The standard was broken into two types of admissions as follows:

Type of Admission	Standard Time to Complete Admission Record
Unscheduled admission	60 minutes
Scheduled admission	40 minutes

The unscheduled admission took longer, since name, address, and insurance information needed to be determined at the time of admission. Information was collected on scheduled admissions prior to the admissions, which was less time consuming.

The Admissions Department employs three full-time people (40 productive hours per week, with no overtime) at $21 per hour. For the most recent week, the department handled 48 unscheduled and 150 scheduled admissions.

a. How much was actually spent on labor for the week?
b. What are the standard hours for the actual volume for the week? Round to one decimal place.
c. Calculate a time variance, and report how well the department performed for the week.

E13-26

Nonfinancial performance measures

Obj 7

Rocky Mountain College wishes to monitor the efficiency and quality of its course registration process.

a. Identify three input and three output measures for this process.
b. Why would Rocky Mountain College use nonfinancial measures for monitoring this process?

13-27

...cial performance

Windytrail.com is an Internet retailer of sporting good products. Customers order sporting goods from the company, using an online catalog. The company processes these orders and delivers the requested product from its warehouse. The company wants to provide customers with an excellent purchase experience in order to expand the business through favorable word-of-mouth advertising and to drive repeat business. To help monitor performance, the company developed a set of performance measures for its order placement and delivery process.

Average computer response time to customer "clicks"
Dollar amount of returned goods
Elapsed time between customer order and product delivery
Maintenance dollars divided by hardware investment
Number of customer complaints divided by the number of orders
Number of misfilled orders
Number of orders per warehouse employee
Number of page faults or errors due to software programming errors
Server (computer) downtime
System capacity divided by customer demands
Training dollars per programmer

Identify the input and output measures related to the "order placement and delivery" process.

E13-28

Factory overhead cost variances

APP

SPREADSHEET

✓ Volume variance, $28,080 U

The following data relate to factory overhead cost for the production of 25,000 computers:

Actual:	Variable factory overhead	$650,000
	Fixed factory overhead	78,000
Standard:	32,000 hours at $21	672,000

If productive capacity of 100% was 50,000 hours and the factory overhead cost budgeted at the level of 32,000 standard hours was $700,080, determine the variable factory overhead controllable variance, fixed factory overhead volume variance, and total factory overhead cost variance. The fixed factory overhead rate was $1.56 per hour.

E13-29

Factory overhead cost variances

APP

SPREADSHEET

✓ a. $4,850 F

Banner Textiles Corporation began January with a budget for 28,000 hours of production in the Weaving Department. The department has a full capacity of 36,000 hours under normal business conditions. The budgeted overhead at the planned volumes at the beginning of January was as follows:

Variable overhead	$ 78,400
Fixed overhead	54,000
Total	$132,400

The actual factory overhead was $135,250 for January. The actual fixed factory overhead was as budgeted. During January, the Weaving Department had standard hours at actual production volume of 30,750 hours.

a. Determine the variable factory overhead controllable variance.
b. Determine the fixed factory overhead volume variance.

E13-30

Factory overhead cost variance report

APP

SPREADSHEET

✓ Net controllable variance, $450 U

Form Fit Molded Products Inc. prepared the following factory overhead cost budget for the Trim Department for October 2008, during which it expected to use 20,000 hours for production:

(continu

Variable overhead cost:		
Indirect factory labor	$49,000	
Power and light	12,000	
Indirect materials	32,000	
Total variable cost		$ 93,000
Fixed overhead cost:		
Supervisory salaries	$35,000	
Depreciation of plant and equipment	28,400	
Insurance and property taxes	21,600	
Total fixed cost		85,000
Total factory overhead cost		$178,000

Form Fit Molded Products has available 34,000 hours of monthly productive capacity in the Trim Department under normal business conditions. During October, the Trim Department actually used 24,000 hours for production. The actual fixed costs were as budgeted. The actual variable overhead for October was as follows:

Actual variable factory overhead cost:	
Indirect factory labor	$ 58,300
Power and light	15,000
Indirect materials	38,750
Total variable cost	$112,050

Construct a factory overhead cost variance report for the Trim Department for October.

Problems

P13-1

Sales, production, direct materials purchases, and direct labor cost budgets

Obj 2

SPREADSHEET

✓ 3. Total direct materials purchases, $9,806,650

The budget director of Outdoor Chef Grill Company requests estimates of sales, production, and other operating data from the various administrative units every month. Selected information concerning sales and production for October 2008 is summarized as follows:

a. Estimated sales for October by sales territory:

Maine:
Backyard Chef	4,500 units at $800 per unit
Master Chef	1,600 units at $1,600 per unit

Vermont:
Backyard Chef	3,800 units at $900 per unit
Master Chef	1,700 units at $1,450 per unit

New Hampshire:
Backyard Chef	4,200 units at $850 per unit
Master Chef	1,800 units at $1,700 per unit

b. Estimated inventories at October 1:

Direct materials:		Finished products:	
Grates	1,200 units	Backyard Chef	1,600 units
Stainless steel	2,300 lbs.	Master Chef	500 units
Burner subassemblies	650 units		
Shelves	500 units		

c. Desired inventories at October 31:

Direct materials:		Finished products:	
Grates	900 units	Backyard Chef	1,300 units
Stainless steel	2,000 lbs.	Master Chef	600 units
Burner subassemblies	800 units		
Shelves	450 units		

d. Direct materials used in production:

In manufacture of Backyard Chef:
Grates	3 units per unit of product
Stainless steel	25 lbs. per unit of product
Burner subassemblies	2 units per unit of product
Shelves	5 units per unit of product

In manufacture of Master Chef:
Grates	6 units per unit of product
Stainless steel	50 lbs. per unit of product
Burner subassemblies	4 units per unit of product
Shelves	6 units per unit of product

e. Anticipated purchase price for direct materials:

Grates	$18 per unit	Burner subassemblies	$115 per unit
Stainless steel	$5 per lb.	Shelves	$6 per unit

f. Direct labor requirements:

Backyard Chef:
Stamping Department	0.60 hour at $15 per hour
Forming Department	0.80 hour at $12 per hour
Assembly Department	1.50 hours at $9 per hour

Master Chef:
Stamping Department	0.80 hour at $15 per hour
Forming Department	1.60 hours at $12 per hour
Assembly Department	2.50 hours at $9 per hour

Instructions

1. Prepare a sales budget for October.
2. Prepare a production budget for October.
3. Prepare a direct materials purchases budget for October.
4. Prepare a direct labor cost budget for October.

P13-2

Budgeted income statement and supporting budgets

Obj 2

SPREADSHEET

✓ 4. Total direct labor cost in Fabrication Dept., $282,170

The budget director of Backyard Habitat Inc., with the assistance of the controller, treasurer, production manager, and sales manager, has gathered the following data for use in developing the budgeted income statement for December 2008:

a. Estimated sales for December:

Bird House	34,500 units at $40 per unit
Bird Feeder	25,800 units at $70 per unit

(continu

b. Estimated inventories at December 1:

Direct materials:		Finished products:	
Wood	2,600 ft.	Bird House	4,900 units at $25 per unit
Plastic	3,200 lbs.	Bird Feeder	2,500 units at $35 per unit

c. Desired inventories at December 31:

Direct materials:		Finished products:	
Wood	3,500 ft.	Bird House	5,300 units at $24 per unit
Plastic	2,800 lbs.	Bird Feeder	2,100 units at $36 per unit

d. Direct materials used in production:

In manufacture of Bird House:		In manufacture of Bird Feeder:	
Wood 0.80 ft. per unit of product		Wood 1.20 ft. per unit of product	
Plastic 0.50 lb. per unit of product		Plastic 0.75 lb. per unit of product	

e. Anticipated cost of purchases and beginning and ending inventory of direct materials:

Wood $6.50 per ft.   Plastic $0.90 per lb.

f. Direct labor requirements:

Bird House:	
Fabrication Department	0.25 hour at $14 per hour
Assembly Department	0.30 hour at $10 per hour
Bird Feeder:	
Fabrication Department	0.45 hour at $14 per hour
Assembly Department	0.35 hour at $10 per hour

g. Estimated factory overhead costs for December:

Indirect factory wages	$650,000	Power and light	$42,000
Depreciation of		Insurance and property tax	15,400
plant and equipment	165,000		

h. Estimated operating expenses for December:

Sales salaries expense	$675,000
Advertising expense	148,600
Office salaries expense	214,800
Depreciation expense—office equipment	4,900
Telephone expense—selling	5,200
Telephone expense—administrative	1,700
Travel expense—selling	39,200
Office supplies expense	3,500
Miscellaneous administrative expense	5,000

i. Estimated other income and expense for December:

Interest revenue	$16,900
Interest expense	10,600

j. Estimated tax rate: 35%

Instructions

1. Prepare a sales budget for December.
2. Prepare a production budget for December.
3. Prepare a direct materials purchases budget for December.
4. Prepare a direct labor cost budget for December.
5. Prepare a factory overhead cost budget for December.
6. Prepare a cost of goods sold budget for December. Work in process at the beginning of December is estimated to be $27,000, and work in process at the end of December is estimated to be $32,400.
7. Prepare a selling and administrative expenses budget for December.
8. Prepare a budgeted income statement for December.

P13-3

Cash budget

Obj 2

SPREADSHEET

✓ 1. October deficiency, $64,500

The controller of Santa Fe Housewares Inc. instructs you to prepare a monthly cash budget for the next three months. You are presented with the following budget information:

	August	September	October
Sales	$630,000	$715,000	$845,000
Manufacturing costs	350,000	360,000	410,000
Selling and administrative expenses	170,000	205,000	235,000
Capital expenditures			150,000

The company expects to sell about 10% of its merchandise for cash. Of sales on account, 70% are expected to be collected in full in the month following the sale and the remainder in the following month. Depreciation, insurance, and property tax expense represent $25,000 of the estimated monthly manufacturing costs. The annual insurance premium is paid in July, and the annual property taxes are paid in November. Of the remainder of the manufacturing costs, 80% are expected to be paid in the month in which they are incurred and the balance in the following month.

Current assets as of August 1 include cash of $50,000, marketable securities of $85,000, and accounts receivable of $635,000 ($500,000 from July sales and $135,000 from June sales). Sales on account for June and July were $450,000 and $500,000, respectively. Current liabilities as of August 1 include a $100,000, 15%, 90-day note payable due October 20 and $65,000 of accounts payable incurred in July for manufacturing costs. All selling and administrative expenses are paid in cash in the period they are incurred. It is expected that $1,800 in dividends will be received in August. An estimated income tax payment of $39,000 will be made in September. Santa Fe's regular quarterly dividend of $12,000 is expected to be declared in September and paid in October. Management desires to maintain a minimum cash balance of $40,000.

Instructions

1. Prepare a monthly cash budget and supporting schedules for August, September, and October.
2. On the basis of the cash budget prepared in part (1), what recommendation should be made to the controller?

P13-4

Direct materials and direct labor variance analysis

Obj 5

✓ c. Rate variance, $48 U

Dresses by Melissa Inc. manufactures dresses in a small manufacturing facility. Manufacturing has 15 employees. Each employee presently provides 32 hours of productive labor per week. Information about a production week is as follows:

(continu

Standard wage per hour	$10.40
Standard labor time per dress	15 minutes
Standard number of yards of fabric per dress	4.2 yards
Standard price per yard of fabric	$2.65
Actual price per yard of fabric	$2.70
Actual yards of fabric used during the week	7,200 yards
Number of dresses produced during the week	1,900
Actual wage per hour	$10.50
Actual hours per week	480 hours

Instructions

Determine (a) the standard cost per dress for direct materials and direct labor; (b) the price variance, quantity variance, and total direct materials cost variance; and (c) the rate variance, time variance, and total direct labor cost variance.

P13-5

Direct materials, direct labor, and factory overhead cost variance analysis

Obj 5

SPREADSHEET

✓ 3. Controllable variance, $155 F

Gulf Coast Resins Company processes a base chemical into plastic. Standard costs and actual costs for direct materials, direct labor, and factory overhead incurred for the manufacture of 2,600 units of product were as follows:

	Standard Costs	*Actual Costs*
Direct materials	6,850 pounds at $6.40	7,000 pounds at $6.35
Direct labor	2,050 hours at $19.80	2,100 hours at $20.20
Factory overhead	Rates per direct labor hour, based on 100% of normal capacity of 1,950 direct labor hours:	
	Variable cost, $2.50	$4,970 variable cost
	Fixed cost, $4.50	$8,775 fixed cost

Each unit requires 0.6 hour of direct labor.

Instructions

1. Determine the price variance, quantity variance, and total direct materials cost variance.
2. Determine the rate variance, time variance, and total direct labor cost variance.
3. Appendix: Determine the variable factory overhead controllable variance, the fixed factory overhead volume variance, and total factory overhead cost variance.

P13-6

Standards for nonmanufacturing expenses

Obj 7

3. $640 U

Elite Technologies Inc. does software development. One important activity in software development is writing software code. The manager of the WritePro Development Team determined that the average software programmer could write 45 lines of code in an hour. The plan for the first week in May called for 6,840 lines of code to be written on the WritePro product. The WritePro Team has four programmers. Each programmer is hired from an employment firm that requires temporary employees to be hired for a minimum of a 40-hour week. Programmers are paid $32.00 per hour. The manager offered a bonus if the team could generate more than 7,200 lines for the week, without overtime. Due to a project emergency, the programmers wrote more code in the first week of May than planned. The actual amount of code written in the first week of May was 7,650 lines, without overtime. As a result, the bonus caused the average programmer's hourly rate to increase to $36.00 per hour during the first week in May.

Instructions

1. If the team typed 6,840 lines of code according to the original plan, what would have been the labor time variance?
2. What was the actual labor time variance as a result of generating 7,650 lines of code?
3. What was the labor rate variance as a result of the bonus?
4. The manager is trying to determine if a better decision would have been to hire a temporary programmer to meet the higher programming demand in the first week of May, rather than paying out the bonus. If another employee was hired from the employment firm, what would have been the labor time variance in the first week?
5. Which decision is better, paying the bonus or hiring another programmer?
6. Are there any performance-related issues that the labor time and rate variances fail to consider? Explain.

P13-7

Standard factory overhead variance report

App

SPREADSHEET

✓ Controllable variance, $300 F

Power Equipment Inc., a manufacturer of construction equipment, prepared the following factory overhead cost budget for the Welding Department for July 2008. The company expected to operate the department at 100% of normal capacity of 4,800 hours.

Variable costs:		
Indirect factory wages	$14,160	
Power and light	7,680	
Indirect materials	8,880	
Total variable cost		$30,720
Fixed costs:		
Supervisory salaries	$16,000	
Depreciation of plant and equipment	43,500	
Insurance and property taxes	6,740	
Total fixed cost		66,240
Total factory overhead cost		$96,960

During July, the department operated at 5,000 hours, and the factory overhead costs incurred were indirect factory wages, $14,000; power and light, $9,250; indirect materials, $8,450; supervisory salaries, $16,000; depreciation of plant and equipment, $43,500; and insurance and property taxes, $6,740.

Instructions

Prepare a factory overhead cost variance report for July. To be useful for cost control, the budgeted amounts should be based on 5,000 hours.

Activities

A13-1

Ethics and professional conduct in business

ETHICS

The director of marketing for Livingston Computer Co., Jon Halls, had the following discussion with the company controller, Meredith Lomas, on August 29 of the current year:

Jon: Meredith, it looks like I'm going to spend much less than indicated on my August budget.
Meredith: I'm glad to hear it.
Jon: Well, I'm not so sure it's good news. I'm concerned that the president will see that I'm under budget and reduce my budget in the future. The only reason that I look good is that we've delayed an advertising campaign. Once the campaign hits in November, I'm sure my actual expenditures will go up. You see, we are also having our sales convention in November.

(contin[ued]

Having the advertising campaign and the convention at the same time is going to kill my November numbers.

Meredith: I don't think that's anything to worry about. We all expect some variation in actual spending month to month. What's really important is staying within the budgeted targets for the year. Does that look as if it's going to be a problem?

Jon: I don't think so, but just the same, I'd like to be on the safe side.

Meredith: What do you mean?

Jon: Well, this is what I'd like to do. I want to pay the convention-related costs in advance this month. I'll pay the hotel for room and convention space and purchase the airline tickets in advance. In this way, I can charge all these expenditures to August's budget. This would cause my actual expenses to come close to budget for August. Moreover, when the big advertising campaign hits in November, I won't have to worry about expenditures for the convention on my November budget as well. The convention costs will already be paid. Thus, my November expenses should be pretty close to budget.

Meredith: I can't tell you when to make your convention purchases, but I'm not too sure that it should be expensed on August's budget.

Jon: What's the problem? It looks like "no harm, no foul" to me. I can't see that there's anything wrong with this—it's just smart management.

How should Meredith Lomas respond to Jon Halls' request to expense the advanced payments for convention-related costs against August's budget?

A13-2

Evaluating budgeting systems

Children's Hospital of the King's Daughter in Norfolk, Virginia, introduced a new budgeting method that allowed the hospital's annual plan to be updated for changes in operating plans. For example, if the budget was based on 400 patient-days and the actual count rose to 450 patient-days, the variable costs of staffing, lab work, and medication costs could be adjusted to reflect this change. The budget manager stated, "I work with hospital directors to turn data into meaningful information and effect change before the month ends."

a. What budgeting methods are being used under the new approach?
b. Why are these methods superior to the former approaches?

A13-3

Service company static decision making

A bank manager of Citizens Bank Inc. uses the managerial accounting system to track the costs of operating the various departments within the bank. The departments include Cash Management, Trust Commercial Loans, Mortgage Loans, Operations, Credit Card, and Branch Services. The budget and actual results for the Operations Department are as follows:

Resources	Budget	Actual
Salaries	$150,000	$150,000
Benefits	30,000	30,000
Supplies	45,000	42,000
Travel	20,000	30,000
Training	25,000	35,000
Overtime	25,000	20,000
Total	$295,000	$307,000
Excess of actual over budget	$ 12,000	

a. What information is provided by the budget? Specifically, what questions can the bank manager ask of the Operations Department manager?
b. What information does the budget fail to provide? Specifically, could the budget information be presented differently to provide even more insight for the bank manager?

A13-4

Objectives of the master budget

Domino's Inc. operates pizza delivery and carryout restaurants. The annual report describes its business as follows:

> We offer a focused menu of high-quality, value priced pizza with three types of crust (Hand-Tossed, Thin Crust, and Deep Dish), along with buffalo wings, bread sticks, cheesy bread, CinnaStix®, and Coca-Cola® products. Our hand-tossed pizza is made from fresh dough produced in our regional distribution centers. We prepare every pizza using real cheese, pizza sauce made from fresh tomatoes, and a choice of high-quality meat and vegetable toppings in generous portions. Our focused menu and use of premium ingredients enable us to consistently and efficiently produce the highest-quality pizza.
>
> Over the 41 years since our founding, we have developed a simple, cost-efficient model. We offer a limited menu, our stores are designed for delivery and carry-out, and we do not generally offer dine-in service. As a result, our stores require relatively small, lower-rent locations and limited capital expenditures.

How would a master budget support planning, directing, and control for Domino's?

A13-5

Integrity and evaluating budgeting systems

The city of Westwood has an annual budget cycle that begins on July 1 and ends on June 30. At the beginning of each budget year, an annual budget is established for each department. The annual budget is divided by 12 months to provide a constant monthly static budget. On June 30, all unspent budgeted monies for the budget year from the various city departments must be "returned" to the General Fund. Thus, if department heads fail to use their budget by year-end, they will lose it. A budget analyst prepared a chart of the difference between the monthly actual and budgeted amounts for the recent fiscal year. The chart was as follows:

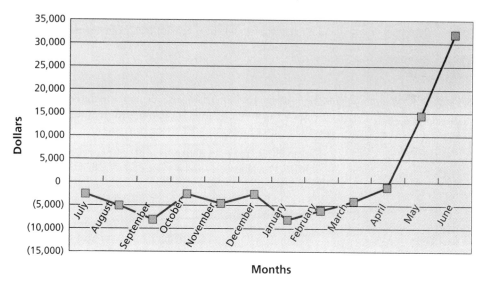

a. Interpret the chart.
b. Suggest an improvement in the budget system.

A13-6

Ethics and professional conduct in business using non-manufacturing standards

ETHICS

Trey McIntyre is a cost analyst with Global Insurance Company. Global is applying standards to its claims payment operation. Claims payment is a repetitive operation that could be evaluated with standards. Trey used time and motion studies to identify an ideal standard of 36 claims processed per hour. The Claims Processing Department manager, Carol Mann, has rejected this standard and has argued that the standard should be 30 claims processed per hour. Carol and Trey were unable to agree, so they decided to discuss this matter openly at a joint meeting with the vice president of operations, who would arbitrate a final decision. Prior to the meeting, Trey wrote the following memo to the VP.

(continued)

To: T. J. Logan, Vice President of Operations
From: Trey McIntyre
Re: Standards in the Claims Processing Department

As you know, Carol and I are scheduled to meet with you to discuss our disagreement with respect to the appropriate standards for the Claims Processing Department. I have conducted time and motion studies and have determined that the ideal standard is 36 claims processed per hour. Carol argues that 30 claims processed per hour would be more appropriate. I believe she is trying to "pad" the budget with some slack. I'm not sure what she is trying to get away with, but I believe a tight standard will drive efficiency up in her area. I hope you will agree when we meet with you next week.

Discuss the ethical and professional issues in this situation.

A13-7

Nonfinancial performance measures

The senior management of Lannigan Company has proposed the following three performance measures for the company:

1. Net income as a percent of stockholders' equity
2. Revenue growth
3. Employee satisfaction

Management believes these three measures combine both financial and nonfinancial measures and are thus superior to using just financial measures.

What advice would you give Lannigan Company for improving on its performance measurement system?

A13-8

Nonfinancial performance measures

At the Soladyne Division of **Rogers Corporation**, the controller used a number of measures to provide managers information about the performance of a just-in-time (JIT) manufacturing operation. Three measures used by the company are:

- Scrap Index: The sales dollar value of scrap for the period.
- Orders Past Due: Sales dollar value of orders that were scheduled for shipment, but were not shipped during the period.
- Buyer's Misery Index: Number of different customers that have orders that are late (scheduled for shipment, but not shipped).

1. Why do you think the scrap index is measured at sales dollar value, rather than at cost?
2. How is the "orders past due" measure different from the "buyer's misery index," or are the two measures just measuring the same thing?

A13-9

Variance interpretation

Sound Sensation Inc. is a small manufacturer of electronic musical instruments. The plant manager received the following variable factory overhead report for the period:

	Actual	Budgeted Variable Factory Overhead at Actual Production
Supplies	$28,000	$26,520
Power and light	35,000	33,990
Indirect factory wages	26,112	20,400
Total	$89,112	$80,910

Actual units produced: 10,200 (85% of practical capacity)

The plant manager is not pleased with the $8,202 unfavorable variable factory overhead controllable variance and has come to discuss the matter with the controller. The following discussion occurred:

Plant Manager: I just received this factory report for the latest month of operation. I'm not very pleased with these figures. Before these numbers go to headquarters, you and I will need to reach an understanding.

Controller: Go ahead, what's the problem?

Plant Manager: What's the problem? Well, everything. Look at the variance. It's too large. If I understand the accounting approach being used here, you are assuming that my costs are variable to the units produced. Thus, as the production volume declines, so should these costs. Well, I don't believe that these costs are variable at all. I think they are fixed costs. As a result, when we operate below capacity, the costs really don't go down at all. I'm being penalized for costs I have no control over at all. I need this report to be redone to reflect this fact. If anything, the difference between actual and budget is essentially a volume variance. Listen, I know that you're a team player. You really need to reconsider your assumptions on this one.

If you were in the controller's position, how would you respond to the plant manager?

Answers to Self-Examination Questions

1. B Administrative departments (answer B), such as Purchasing or Human Resources, will often use static budgeting. Production departments (answer A) frequently use flexible budgets. Responsibility centers (answer C) can use either static or flexible budgeting. Capital expenditure budgets are used to plan capital projects (answer D).

2. B The total production indicated in the production budget is 257,500 units (answer B), which is computed as follows:

Sales	250,000 units
Plus desired ending inventory	30,000 units
Total	280,000 units
Less estimated beginning inventory	22,500 units
Total production	257,500 units

3. C Dixon expects to collect 70% of April sales ($560,000) plus 30% of the March sales ($195,000) in April, for a total of $755,000 (answer C). Answer A is 100% of April sales. Answer B is 70% of April sales. Answer D adds 70% of both March and April sales.

4. C The unfavorable direct materials price variance of $2,550 is determined as follows:

Actual price	$5.05 per pound
Standard price	5.00
Price variance—unfavorable	$0.05 per pound

$0.05 × 51,000 actual pounds = $2,550

5. D The unfavorable direct labor time variance of $2,400 is determined as follows:

Actual direct labor time	2,200
Standard direct labor time	2,000
Direct labor time variance—unfavorable	200 × $12 standard rate = $2,400

CHAPTER 14

Performance Evaluation for Decentralized Operations

Learning Objectives

After studying this chapter, you should be able to:

Obj 1

List and explain the advantages and disadvantages of decentralized operations.

Obj 2

Prepare a responsibility accounting report for a cost center.

Obj 3

Prepare responsibility accounting reports for a profit center.

Obj 4

Compute and interpret the rate of return on investment, the residual income, and the balanced scorecard for an investment center.

Obj 5

Explain how the market price, negotiated price, and cost price approaches to transfer pricing may be used by decentralized segments of a business.

H ave you ever wondered if there is an economic reason why large retail stores, such as *JC Penney Co*. and *Sears*, are divided into departments? Typically, these stores include a Men's Department, Women's Department, Cosmetics Department, Gift Department, and Furnishings Department. Each department usually has a manager who is responsible for the financial performance of the department. The store may be the responsibility of a store manager, and a group of stores within a particular geographic area may be the responsibility of a division or district manager. If you were to be hired by a department store chain, you would probably begin your career in a department. Running a department would be a valuable experience before becoming responsible for a complete store. Likewise, responsibility for a complete store provides excellent training for other management positions.

In this chapter, we will focus on the role of accounting in assisting managers in planning and controlling organizational units, such as divisions, stores, and departments.

Obj 1

List and explain the advantages and disadvantages of decentralized operations.

Centralized and Decentralized Operations

A *centralized* business is one in which all major planning and operating decisions are made by top management. For example, a one-person, owner/manager-operated business is centralized because all plans and decisions are made by one person. In a small owner/manager-operated business, centralization may be desirable. This is because the owner/manager's close supervision ensures that the business will be operated in the way the owner/manager wishes.

Separating a business into **divisions** or operating units and delegating responsibility to unit managers is called **decentralization**. In a decentralized business, the unit managers are responsible for planning and controlling the operations of their units.

Divisions are often structured around common functions, products, customers, or regions. For example, **Delta Air Lines** is organized around *functions*, such as the Flight Operations Division. The **Procter & Gamble Company** is organized around common *products*, such as the Soap Division, which sells a wide array of cleaning products. The **Norfolk Southern Corporation** decentralizes its railroad operations into Eastern, Western, and Northern regional divisions.

There is no one best amount of decentralization for all businesses. In some companies, division managers have authority over all operations, including fixed asset acquisitions and retirements. In other companies, division managers have authority over profits but not fixed asset acquisitions and retirements. The proper amount of decentralization for a company depends on its advantages and disadvantages for the company's unique circumstances.

Advantages of Decentralization

As a business grows, it becomes more difficult for top management to maintain close daily contact with all operations. In such cases, delegating authority to managers closest to the operations usually results in better decisions. These managers often anticipate and react to operating data more quickly than could top management. In addition, as a company expands into a wide range of products and services, it becomes more difficult for top management to maintain operating expertise in all product lines and services. Decentralization allows managers to focus on acquiring expertise in their areas of responsibility. For example, in a company that maintains operations in insurance, banking, and health care, managers could become "experts" in their area of operation and responsibility.

Decentralized decision making also provides excellent training for managers. This may be a factor in helping a company retain quality managers. Since the art of management is best acquired through experience, delegating responsibility allows managers to acquire and develop managerial expertise early in their careers.

Businesses that work closely with customers, such as hotels, are often decentralized. This helps managers create good customer relations by responding quickly to customers' needs. In addition, because managers of decentralized operations tend to identify with customers and with operations, they are often more creative in suggesting operating and product improvements.

Disadvantages of Decentralization

A primary disadvantage of decentralized operations is that decisions made by one manager may negatively affect the profitability of the entire company. For example, the Pizza

Hut chain added chicken to its menu and ended up taking business away from KFC. Then KFC retaliated with a blistering ad campaign against Pizza Hut. This happened even though both chains are part of the same company, ***Yum Brands, Inc.!***

Another potential disadvantage of decentralized operations is duplicating assets and costs in operating divisions. For example, each manager of a product line might have a separate sales force and administrative office staff. Centralizing these personnel could save money. For example, ***McDonald's Corporation*** recently reduced the number of operating divisions in the United States from five to three in order to cut administrative expenses.

Responsibility Accounting

In a decentralized business, an important function of accounting is to assist unit managers in evaluating and controlling their areas of responsibility, called *responsibility centers*. **Responsibility accounting** is the process of measuring and reporting operating data by responsibility center. Three common types of responsibility centers are cost centers, profit centers, and investment centers. These three responsibility centers differ in their scope of responsibility, as shown below.

Cost Center	*Profit Center*	*Investment Center*
	Revenue	Revenue
Cost	− Cost	− Cost
	Profit	Profit
		Investment in assets

Responsibility Accounting for Cost Centers

Prepare a responsibility accounting report for a cost center.

In a **cost center**, the unit manager has responsibility and authority for controlling the costs incurred. For example, the supervisor of the Power Department has responsibility for the costs incurred in providing power. A cost center manager does not make decisions concerning sales or the amount of fixed assets invested in the center.

Since managers of cost centers have responsibility and authority over costs, responsibility accounting for cost centers focuses on costs. To illustrate, the budget performance reports in Exhibit 1 are part of a responsibility accounting system. These reports aid the managers in controlling costs.

In Exhibit 1, the reports prepared for the department supervisors show the budgeted and actual manufacturing costs for their departments. The supervisors can use these reports to focus on areas of significant difference, such as the difference between the budgeted and actual materials cost. The supervisor of Department 1 in Plant A may use additional information from a scrap report to determine why materials are over budget. Such a report might show that materials were scrapped as a result of machine malfunctions, improper use of machines by employees, or low-quality materials.

For higher levels of management, responsibility accounting reports are usually more summarized than for lower levels of management. In Exhibit 1, for example, the budget performance report for the plant manager summarizes budget and actual cost data for

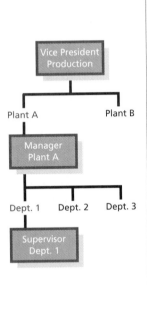

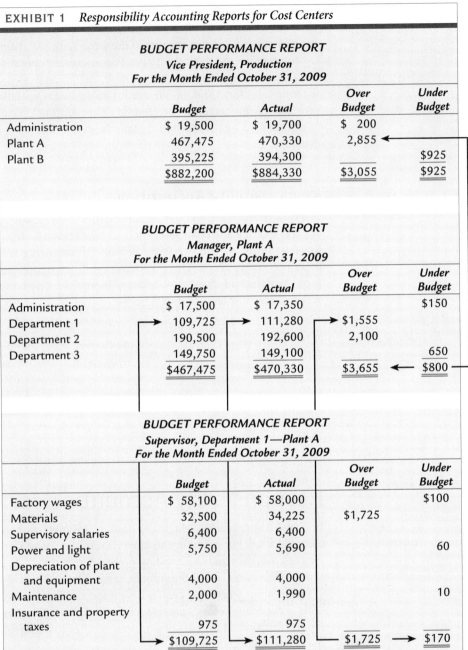

EXHIBIT 1   *Responsibility Accounting Reports for Cost Centers*

BUDGET PERFORMANCE REPORT
Vice President, Production
For the Month Ended October 31, 2009

	Budget	Actual	Over Budget	Under Budget
Administration	$ 19,500	$ 19,700	$ 200	
Plant A	467,475	470,330	2,855	
Plant B	395,225	394,300		$925
	$882,200	$884,330	$3,055	$925

BUDGET PERFORMANCE REPORT
Manager, Plant A
For the Month Ended October 31, 2009

	Budget	Actual	Over Budget	Under Budget
Administration	$ 17,500	$ 17,350		$150
Department 1	109,725	111,280	$1,555	
Department 2	190,500	192,600	2,100	
Department 3	149,750	149,100		650
	$467,475	$470,330	$3,655	$800

BUDGET PERFORMANCE REPORT
Supervisor, Department 1—Plant A
For the Month Ended October 31, 2009

	Budget	Actual	Over Budget	Under Budget
Factory wages	$ 58,100	$ 58,000		$100
Materials	32,500	34,225	$1,725	
Supervisory salaries	6,400	6,400		
Power and light	5,750	5,690		60
Depreciation of plant and equipment	4,000	4,000		
Maintenance	2,000	1,990		10
Insurance and property taxes	975	975		
	$109,725	$111,280	$1,725	$170

the departments under the manager's supervision. This report enables the plant manager to identify the department supervisors responsible for major differences. Likewise, the report for the vice president of production summarizes the cost data for each plant. The plant managers can thus be held responsible for major differences in budgeted and actual costs in their plants.

Cost centers may vary in size from a small department to an entire manufacturing plant. In addition, cost centers may exist within other cost centers. For example, we could view an entire university as a cost center, and each college and department within the university could also be a cost center, as shown in Exhibit 2.

EXHIBIT 2 *Cost Centers*

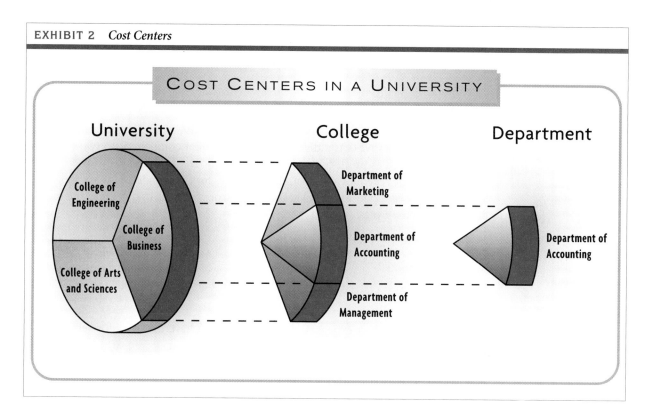

COST CENTERS IN A UNIVERSITY

University — College — Department

College of Engineering / College of Business / College of Arts and Sciences

Department of Marketing / Department of Accounting / Department of Management

Department of Accounting

Responsibility Accounting for Profit Centers

Obj 3

Prepare responsibility accounting reports for a profit center.

In a **profit center**, the unit manager has the responsibility and the authority to make decisions that affect both costs and revenues (and thus profits). Profit centers may be divisions, departments, or products. For example, a consumer products company might organize its brands (product lines) as divisional profit centers. The manager of each brand could have responsibility for product cost and decisions regarding revenues, such as setting sales prices. The manager of a profit center does not make decisions concerning the fixed assets invested in the center. For example, the brand manager of a consumer products company does not make the decision to expand the plant capacity for the brand.

Profit centers are often viewed as an excellent training assignment for new managers. For example, Lester B. Korn, Chairman and Chief Executive Officer of ***Korn/Ferry International***, offered the following strategy for young executives en route to top management positions:

> Get Profit-Center Responsibility—Obtain a position where you can prove yourself as both a specialist with particular expertise and a generalist who can exercise leadership, authority, and inspire enthusiasm among colleagues and subordinates.

Responsibility accounting reports usually show the revenues, expenses, and income from operations for the profit center. The profit center income statement should include only revenues and expenses that are controlled by the manager. *Controllable revenues* are revenues earned by the profit center. **Controllable expenses** are costs that can be influenced (controlled) by the decisions of profit center managers. For example, the manager of the Men's Department at **Nordstrom** most likely controls the salaries of department personnel, but does not control the property taxes of the store.

Service Department Charges

We will illustrate profit center income reporting for the Nova Entertainment Group (NEG). Assume that NEG is a diversified entertainment company with two operating divisions organized as profit centers: the Theme Park Division and the Movie Production Division. The revenues and operating expenses for the two divisions are shown below. The operating expenses consist of the direct expenses, such as the wages and salaries of a division's employees.

	Theme Park Division	*Movie Production Division*
Revenues	$6,000,000	$2,500,000
Operating expenses	2,495,000	405,000

In addition to direct expenses, divisions may also have expenses for services provided by internal centralized *service departments*. These service departments are often more efficient at providing service than are outside service providers. Examples of such service departments include the following:

- Research and Development
- Government Relations
- Telecommunications
- Publications and Graphics
- Facilities Management
- Purchasing
- Information Systems
- Payroll Accounting
- Transportation
- Personnel Administration

A profit center's income from operations should reflect the cost of any internal services used by the center. To illustrate, assume that NEG established a Payroll Accounting Department. The costs of the payroll services, called **service department charges**, are charged to NEG's profit centers, as shown in Exhibit 3.

Service department charges are *indirect expenses* to a profit center. They are similar to the expenses that would be incurred if the profit center had purchased the services from a source outside the company. A profit center manager has control over such expenses if the manager is free to choose *how much* service is used from the service department.

To illustrate service department charges, assume that NEG has two other service departments—Purchasing and Legal—in addition to Payroll Accounting. The

---

EXHIBIT 3 *Payroll Accounting Department Charges to NEG's Theme Park and Movie Production Divisions*

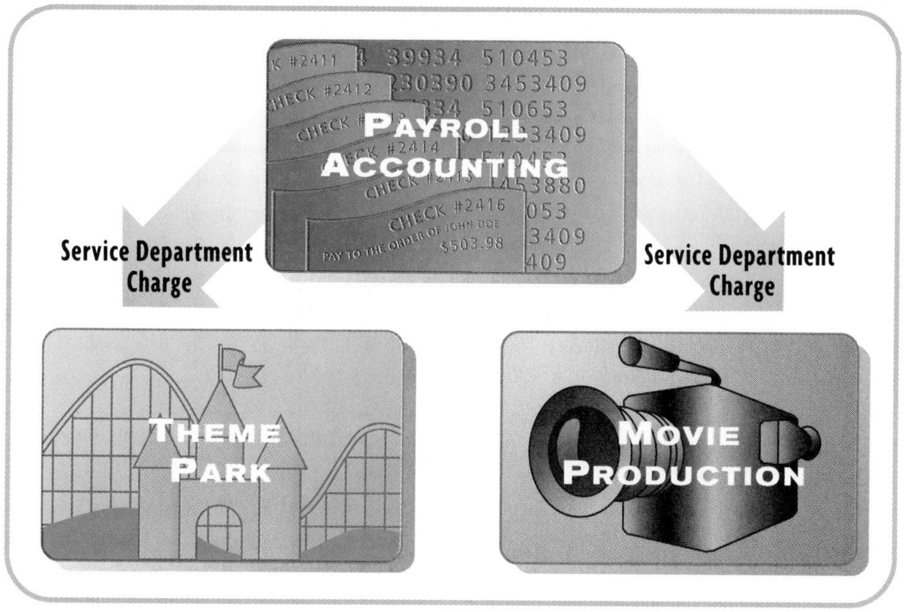

expenses for the year ended December 31, 2009, for each service department are as follows:

Purchasing	$400,000
Payroll Accounting	255,000
Legal	250,000
Total	$905,000

An *activity base* for each service department is used to charge service department expenses to the Theme Park and Movie Production Divisions. The activity base for each service department is a measure of the services performed. For NEG, the service department activity bases are as follows:

Department	Activity Base
Purchasing	Number of purchase requisitions
Payroll Accounting	Number of payroll checks
Legal	Number of billed hours

The use of services by the Theme Park and Movie Production Divisions is as follows:

	Service Usage		
	Purchasing	*Payroll Accounting*	*Legal*
Theme Park Division	25,000 purchase requisitions	12,000 payroll checks	100 billed hrs.
Movie Production Division	15,000	3,000	900
Total	40,000 purchase requisitions	15,000 payroll checks	1,000 billed hrs.

The rates at which services are charged to each division are called *service department charge rates*. These rates are determined by dividing each service department's expenses by the total service usage as follows:

$$\text{Purchasing: } \frac{\$400,000}{40,000 \text{ purchase requisitions}} = \$10 \text{ per purchase requisition}$$

$$\text{Payroll Accounting: } \frac{\$255,000}{15,000 \text{ payroll checks}} = \$17 \text{ per payroll check}$$

$$\text{Legal: } \frac{\$250,000}{1,000 \text{ hours}} = \$250 \text{ per hour}$$

The use of services by the Theme Park and Movie Production Divisions is multiplied by the service department charge rates to determine the charges to each division, as shown in Exhibit 4.

EXHIBIT 4   *Service Department Charges to NEG Divisions*

NOVA ENTERTAINMENT GROUP
Service Department Charges to NEG Divisions
For the Year Ended December 31, 2009

Service Department	Theme Park Division	Movie Production Division
Purchasing (Note A)	$250,000	$150,000
Payroll Accounting (Note B)	204,000	51,000
Legal (Note C)	25,000	225,000
Total service department charges	$479,000	$426,000

Note A:
25,000 purchase requisitions × $10 per purchase requisition = $250,000
15,000 purchase requisitions × $10 per purchase requisition = $150,000

Note B:
12,000 payroll checks × $17 per check = $204,000
3,000 payroll checks × $17 per check = $51,000

Note C:
100 hours × $250 per hour = $25,000
900 hours × $250 per hour = $225,000

The Theme Park Division employs many temporary and part-time employees who are paid weekly. This is in contrast to the Movie Production Division, which has a more permanent payroll that is paid on a monthly basis. As a result, the Theme Park Division requires 12,000 payroll checks. This results in a large service charge from Payroll Accounting to the Theme Park Division. In contrast, the Movie Production Division uses many legal services for contract negotiations. Thus, there is a large service charge from Legal to the Movie Production Division.

Profit Center Reporting

The divisional income statements for NEG are presented in Exhibit 5. These statements show the service department charges to the divisions.

EXHIBIT 5   *Divisional Income Statements—NEG*

NOVA ENTERTAINMENT GROUP
Divisional Income Statements
For the Year Ended December 31, 2009

	Theme Park Division	Movie Production Division
Revenues*	$6,000,000	$2,500,000
Operating expenses	2,495,000	405,000
Income from operations before service department charges	$3,505,000	$2,095,000
Less service department charges:		
Purchasing	$ 250,000	$ 150,000
Payroll Accounting	204,000	51,000
Legal	25,000	225,000
Total service department charges	$ 479,000	$ 426,000
Income from operations	$3,026,000	$1,669,000

*For a profit center that sells products, the income statement would show Net sales − Cost of goods sold = Gross profit. The operating expenses would be deducted from the gross profit to get the income from operations before service department charges.

The **income from operations** is a measure of a manager's performance. In evaluating the profit center manager, the income from operations should be compared over time to a budget. It should not be compared across profit centers, since the profit centers are usually different in terms of size, products, and customers.

Responsibility Accounting for Investment Centers

Obj 4

Compute and interpret the rate of return on investment, the residual income, and the balanced scorecard for an investment center.

In an **investment center**, the unit manager has the responsibility and the authority to make decisions that affect not only costs and revenues but also the assets invested in the center. Investment centers are widely used in highly diversified companies organized by divisions.

The manager of an investment center has more authority and responsibility than the manager of a cost center or a profit center. The manager of an investment center occupies a position similar to that of a chief operating officer or president of a company and is evaluated in much the same way.

Since investment center managers have responsibility for revenues and expenses, income from operations is an important part of investment center reporting. In addition, because the manager has responsibility for the assets invested in the center, two additional measures of performance are often used. These measures are the rate of return on investment and residual income. Top management often compares these measures across investment centers to reward performance and assess investment in the centers.

To illustrate, assume that DataLink Inc. is a cellular phone company that has three regional divisions, Northern, Central, and Southern. Condensed divisional income statements for the investment centers are shown in Exhibit 6.

EXHIBIT 6   *Divisional Income Statements—DataLink Inc.*

DATALINK INC.
Divisional Income Statements
For the Year Ended December 31, 2009

	Northern Division	Central Division	Southern Division
Revenues	$560,000	$672,000	$750,000
Operating expenses	336,000	470,400	562,500
Income from operations before service department charges	$224,000	$201,600	$187,500
Service department charges	154,000	117,600	112,500
Income from operations	$ 70,000	$ 84,000	$ 75,000

Using only income from operations, the Central Division is the most profitable division. However, income from operations does not reflect the amount of assets invested in each center. For example, if the amount of assets invested in the Central Division is twice that of the other divisions, then the Central Division would be the least profitable in terms of the rate of return on these assets.

Rate of Return on Investment

Since investment center managers also control the amount of assets invested in their centers, they should be held accountable for the use of these assets. One measure that considers the amount of assets invested is the **rate of return on investment (ROI)** or *rate of return on assets*. It is one of the most widely used measures for investment centers and is computed as follows:

$$\text{Rate of return on investment (ROI)} = \frac{\textbf{Income from operations}}{\textbf{Invested assets}}$$

The rate of return on investment is useful because the three factors subject to control by divisional managers (revenues, expenses, and invested assets) are used in its computation. By measuring profitability relative to the amount of assets invested in each division, the rate of return on investment can be used to compare divisions. The higher the rate of return on investment, the better the division utilizes its assets to generate income. To illustrate, the rate of return on investment for each division of DataLink Inc., based on the book value of invested assets, is as follows:

	Northern Division	Central Division	Southern Division
Income from operations	$ 70,000	$ 84,000	$ 75,000
Invested assets	$350,000	$700,000	$500,000
Rate of return on investment	20%	12%	15%

Although the Central Division generated the largest income from operations, its rate of return on investment (12%) is the lowest. Hence, relative to the assets invested,

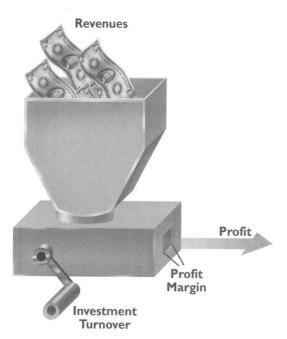

Revenues

Profit

Profit Margin

Investment Turnover

the Central Division is the least profitable division. In comparison, the rate of return on investment of the Northern Division is 20% and the Southern Division is 15%. One way to analyze these differences is by using an expanded formula, called the DuPont formula, for the rate of return on investment. The **DuPont formula**, created by a financial executive of *E. I. DuPont de Nemours & Co.* in 1919, states that the rate earned on total assets is the product of two factors.

The first factor is the ratio of income from operations to sales, often called the **profit margin**. The second factor is the ratio of sales to invested assets, often called the **investment turnover**. In the illustration at the left, profits can be earned by either increasing the investment turnover (turning the crank faster), by increasing the profit margin (increasing the size of the opening), or both.

Using the DuPont formula yields the same rate of return on investment for the Northern Division, 20%, as computed previously.

$$\text{Rate of return on investment (ROI)} = \text{Profit margin} \times \text{Investment turnover}$$

$$\text{Rate of return on investment (ROI)} = \frac{\text{Income from operations}}{\text{Sales}} \times \frac{\text{Sales}}{\text{Invested assets}}$$

$$\text{ROI} = \frac{\$70,000}{\$560,000} \times \frac{\$560,000}{\$350,000}$$

$$\text{ROI} = 12.5\% \times 1.6$$

$$\text{ROI} = 20\%$$

The DuPont formula for the rate of return on investment is useful in evaluating and controlling divisions. This is because the profit margin and the investment turnover focus on the underlying operating relationships of each division.

The profit margin component focuses on profitability by indicating the rate of profit earned on each sales dollar. If a division's profit margin increases, and all other factors remain the same, the division's rate of return on investment formula will increase. For example, a division might add more profitable products to its sales mix and thereby increase its overall profit margin and rate of return on investment.

The investment turnover component focuses on efficiency in using assets and indicates the rate at which sales are generated for each dollar of invested assets. The more sales per dollar invested, the greater the efficiency in using the assets. If a division's investment turnover increases, and all other factors remain the same, the division's rate of return on investment will increase. For example, a division might attempt to increase sales through special sales promotions or reduce inventory assets by using just-in-time principles, either of which would increase investment turnover.

The rate of return on investment, using the DuPont formula for each division of DataLink Inc., is summarized as follows:

$$\text{Rate of return on investment (ROI)} = \frac{\text{Income from operations}}{\text{Sales}} \times \frac{\text{Sales}}{\text{Invested assets}}$$

$$\text{Northern Division (ROI)} = \frac{\$70,000}{\$560,000} \times \frac{\$560,000}{\$350,000}$$

$$\text{ROI} = 12.5\% \times 1.6$$

$$\text{ROI} = 20\%$$

$$\text{Central Division (ROI)} = \frac{\$84,000}{\$672,000} \times \frac{\$672,000}{\$700,000}$$

$$\text{ROI} = 12.5\% \times 0.96$$

$$\text{ROI} = 12\%$$

$$\text{Southern Division (ROI)} = \frac{\$75,000}{\$750,000} \times \frac{\$750,000}{\$500,000}$$

$$\text{ROI} = 10\% \times 1.5$$

$$\text{ROI} = 15\%$$

Although the Northern and Central Divisions have the same profit margins, the Northern Division investment turnover (1.6) is larger than that of the Central Division (0.96). Thus, by using its invested assets more efficiently, the Northern Division's rate of return on investment is higher than the Central Division's. The Southern Division's profit margin of 10% and investment turnover of 1.5 are lower than those of the Northern Division. The product of these factors results in a return on investment of 15% for the Southern Division, compared to 20% for the Northern Division.

To determine possible ways of increasing the rate of return on investment, the profit margin and investment turnover for a division may be analyzed. For example, if the Northern Division is in a highly competitive industry in which the profit margin cannot be easily increased, the division manager might focus on increasing the investment turnover. To illustrate, assume that the revenues of the Northern Division could be increased by $56,000 through increasing operating expenses, such as advertising, to $385,000. The Northern Division's income from operations will increase from $70,000 to $77,000, as shown below.

Revenues ($560,000 + $56,000)	$616,000
Operating expenses	385,000
Income from operations before service department charges	$231,000
Service department charges	154,000
Income from operations	$ 77,000

The rate of return on investment for the Northern Division, using the DuPont formula, is recomputed as follows:

$$\text{Rate of return on investment (ROI)} = \frac{\text{Income from operations}}{\text{Sales}} \times \frac{\text{Sales}}{\text{Invested assets}}$$

$$\text{Northern Division revised (ROI)} = \frac{\$77,000}{\$616,000} \times \frac{\$616,000}{\$350,000}$$

$$\text{ROI} = 12.5\% \times 1.76$$

$$\text{ROI} = 22\%$$

Although the Northern Division's profit margin remains the same (12.5%), the investment turnover has increased from 1.6 to 1.76, an increase of 10% (0.16 ÷ 1.6). The 10% increase in investment turnover also increases the rate of return on investment by 10% (from 20% to 22%).

In addition to using it as a performance measure, the rate of return on investment may assist management in other ways. For example, in considering a decision to expand the operations of DataLink Inc., management might consider giving priority to the Northern Division because it earns the highest rate of return on investment. If the current rates of return on investment are maintained in the future, an investment in the Northern Division will return 20 cents (20%) on each dollar invested. In contrast, investments in the Central Division will earn only 12 cents per dollar invested, and investments in the Southern Division will return only 15 cents per dollar.

A disadvantage of the rate of return on investment as a performance measure is that it may lead divisional managers to reject new investments that could be profitable for the company as a whole. For example, the Northern Division of DataLink Inc. has an overall rate of return on investment of 20%. The minimum acceptable rate of return on investment for DataLink Inc. is 10%. The manager of the Northern Division has the opportunity of investing in a new project that is estimated will earn a 17% rate of return. If the manager of the Northern Division invests in the project, however, the

---

Time Warner The annual report of public companies must provide segment disclosure information identifying revenues, income from operations, and total assets. This information can be used with the DuPont formula to calculate the return on investment (ROI) for the segments of a company. For example, *Time Warner Inc.* operates three major segments:

1. *Cable:* Cable television systems, such as TWI Cable.

2. *Filmed Entertainment:* Warner Bros. and New Line Cinema studios and television production.

3. Networks: Cable television and broadcast network programming, such as Turner Networks, Home Box Office, and the WB.

The DuPont formulas for these three segments, as derived from a recent annual report, are as follows:

	Profit Margin ×	*Investment Turnover* =	*Return on Investment*
Cable	−2.4%	0.11	−0.3%
Filmed Entertainment	3.2%	0.42	1.3%
Networks	9.6%	0.27	2.6%

As can be seen from these data, Time Warner's three segments all have very low investment turnovers, at less than 0.50. The Cable segment has a strikingly low investment turnover at 0.11. The profit margins for Cable are negative, while the Filmed Entertainment segment has a weak profit margin of 3.2%. The Networks boasted the best margins at nearly 10%. Multiplying the profit margin by the investment turnover yields the ROI. The ROI is weak for all three segments. This information indicates that the Cable segment's profit margins and investment turnover must be improved. Expanding the number of subscribers or services, such as high-speed Internet services, could help improve both the profit margin and investment turnover of this segment. The Filmed Entertainment segment could improve profit margins and investment turnover by producing more blockbuster hits, such as *Lord of the Rings*. The Networks segment is very sensitive to advertising revenue. Advertising revenues were depressed from an industry slowdown. However, as the advertising cycle returns to health, the Networks segment should benefit.

Northern Division's overall rate of return will decrease from 20%. Thus, the division manager might decide to reject the project, even though the investment would exceed DataLink's minimum acceptable rate of return on investment. The CFO of **Millennium Chemicals Inc.** referred to a similar situation by stating: "We had too many divisional executives who failed to spend money on capital projects with more than satisfactory returns because those projects would have lowered the average return on assets of their particular business."

Residual Income

An additional measure of evaluating divisional performance—residual income—is useful in overcoming some of the disadvantages associated with the rate of return on investment. **Residual income**[1] is the excess of income from operations over a minimum acceptable income from operations, as illustrated below.

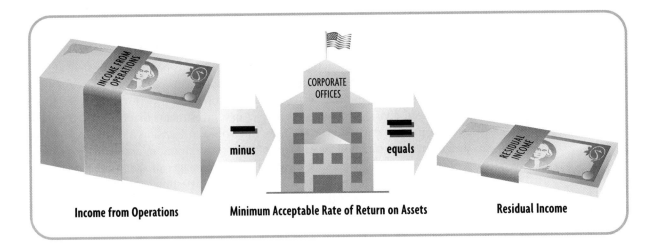

| Income from Operations | Minimum Acceptable Rate of Return on Assets | Residual Income |

The minimum acceptable income from operations is normally computed by multiplying a minimum rate of return by the amount of divisional assets. The minimum rate is set by top management, based on such factors as the cost of financing the business operations. To illustrate, assume that DataLink Inc. has established 10% as the minimum acceptable rate of return on divisional assets. The residual incomes for the three divisions are as follows:

	Northern Division	Central Division	Southern Division
Income from operations	$70,000	$84,000	$75,000
Minimum acceptable income from operations as a percent of assets:			
$350,000 × 10%	35,000		
$700,000 × 10%		70,000	
$500,000 × 10%			50,000
Residual income	$35,000	$14,000	$25,000

[1]Another popular term for residual income is Economic Value Added (EVA), which has been trademarked by the consulting firm Stern Stewart & Co.

The Northern Division has more residual income than the other divisions, even though it has the least amount of income from operations. This is because the assets on which to earn a minimum acceptable rate of return are less for the Northern Division than for the other divisions.

The major advantage of residual income as a performance measure is that it considers both the minimum acceptable rate of return and the total amount of the income from operations earned by each division. Residual income encourages division managers to maximize income from operations in excess of the minimum. This provides an incentive to accept any project that is expected to have a rate of return in excess of the minimum. Thus, the residual income number supports both divisional and overall company objectives.

The Balanced Scorecard[2]

In addition to financial divisional performance measures, many companies are also relying on nonfinancial divisional measures. One popular evaluation approach is the **balanced scorecard**. The balanced scorecard is a set of financial and nonfinancial measures that reflect multiple performance dimensions of a business. A common balanced scorecard design measures performance in the innovation and learning, customer, internal, and financial dimensions of a business. These four areas can be diagrammed as shown in Exhibit 7.

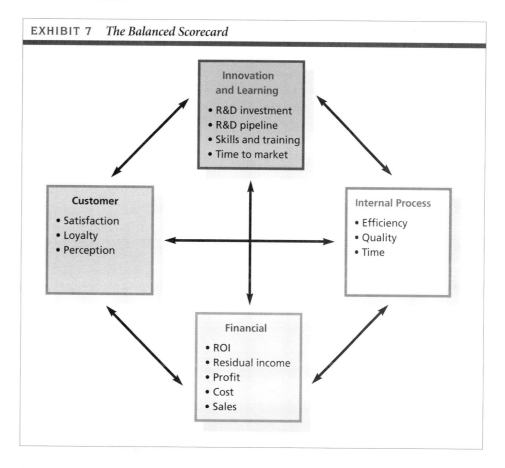

EXHIBIT 7   *The Balanced Scorecard*

[2]The balanced scorecard was developed by R. S. Kaplan and D. P. Norton and explained in *The Balanced Scorecard: Translating Strategy into Action* (Cambridge: Harvard Business School Press, 1996).

The *innovation and learning* perspective measures the amount of innovation in an organization. For example, a drug company, such as **Merck,** would measure the number of drugs in its FDA (Food and Drug Administration) approval pipeline, the amount of research and development (R&D) spending per period, and the length of time it takes to turn ideas into marketable products. Managing the performance of its R&D processes is critical to Merck's longer-term prospects and thus would be an additional performance perspective beyond the financial numbers. The *customer* perspective would measure customer satisfaction, loyalty, and perceptions. For example, **Amazon.com** measures the number of repeat visitors to its Web site as a measure of customer loyalty. Amazon.com needs repeat business because the costs to acquire a new customer are very high. The *internal process* perspective measures the effectiveness and efficiency of internal business processes. For example, **DaimlerChrysler** measures quality by the average warranty claims per automobile, measures efficiency by the average labor hours per automobile, and measures the average time to assemble each automobile. The *financial* perspective measures the economic performance of the responsibility center as we have illustrated in the previous sections of this chapter. All companies will use financial measures. The measures most commonly used are income from operations as a percent of sales and rate of return on investment.

The balanced scorecard is designed to reveal the underlying nonfinancial drivers, or causes, of financial performance. For example, if a business improves customer satisfaction, this will likely lead to improved financial performance. In addition, the balanced scorecard helps managers consider trade-offs between short- and long-term performance. For example, additional investment in research and development (R&D) would penalize the short-term financial perspective, because R&D is an expense that reduces income from operations. However, the innovation perspective would measure additional R&D expenditures favorably, because current R&D expenditures will lead to future profits from new products. The balanced scorecard will motivate the manager to invest in new R&D, even though it is recognized as a current period expense. A survey by Bain & Co., a consulting firm, indicated that 62% of large companies use the balanced scorecard.[3] Thus, the balanced scorecard is gaining acceptance because of its ability to reveal the underlying causes of financial performance, while helping managers consider the short- and long-term implications of their decisions.

Transfer Pricing

Obj 5

Explain how the market price, negotiated price, and cost price approaches to transfer pricing may be used by decentralized segments of a business.

When divisions transfer products or render services to each other, a **transfer price** is used to charge for the products or services. Since transfer prices affect the goals for both divisions, setting these prices is a sensitive matter for division managers.

Transfer prices should be set so that overall company income is increased when goods are transferred between divisions. As we will illustrate, however, transfer prices may be misused in such a way that overall company income suffers.

In the following paragraphs, we discuss various approaches to setting transfer prices. Exhibit 8 shows the range of prices that results from common approaches to setting transfer prices.[4] Transfer prices can be set as low as the variable cost per unit or as high as the market price. Often, transfer prices are negotiated at some point between variable cost per unit and market price.

---

[3]Bain & Co., "Management Tools 2003."
[4]The discussion in this chapter highlights the essential concepts of transfer pricing. In-depth discussion of transfer pricing can be found in advanced texts.

EXHIBIT 8 *Transfer Prices*

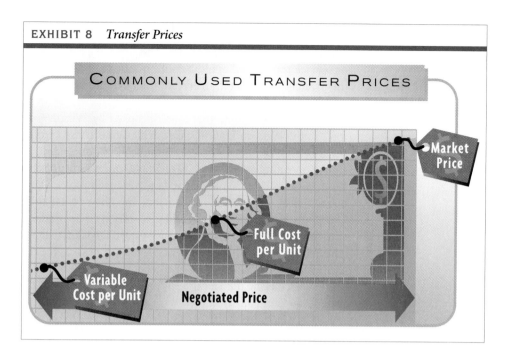

Transfer prices may be used when decentralized units are organized as cost, profit, or investment centers. To illustrate, we will use a packaged snack food company (Wilson Company) with no service departments and two operating divisions (Eastern and Western) organized as investment centers. Condensed divisional income statements for Wilson Company, assuming no transfers between divisions, are shown in Exhibit 9.

EXHIBIT 9 *Income Statement—No Transfers between Divisions*

WILSON COMPANY
Divisional Income Statements
For the Year Ended December 31, 2009

	Eastern Division	Western Division	Total
Sales:			
50,000 units × $20 per unit	$1,000,000		$1,000,000
20,000 units × $40 per unit		$800,000	800,000
			$1,800,000
Expenses:			
Variable:			
50,000 units × $10 per unit	$ 500,000		$ 500,000
20,000 units × $30* per unit		$600,000	600,000
Fixed	300,000	100,000	400,000
Total expenses	$ 800,000	$700,000	$1,500,000
Income from operations	$ 200,000	$100,000	$ 300,000

*$20 of the $30 per unit represents materials costs, and the remaining $10 per unit represents other variable conversion expenses incurred within the Western Division.

Market Price Approach

Using the **market price approach**, the transfer price is the price at which the product or service transferred could be sold to outside buyers. If an outside market exists for the product or service transferred, the current market price may be a proper transfer price.

To illustrate, assume that materials used by Wilson Company in producing snack food in the Western Division are currently purchased from an outside supplier at $20 per unit. The same materials are produced by the Eastern Division. The Eastern Division is operating at full capacity of 50,000 units and can sell all it produces to either the Western Division or to outside buyers. A transfer price of $20 per unit (the market price) has no effect on the Eastern Division's income or total company income. The Eastern Division will earn revenues of $20 per unit on all its production and sales, regardless of who buys its product. Likewise, the Western Division will pay $20 per unit for materials (the market price). Thus, the use of the market price as the transfer price has no effect on the Eastern Division's income or total company income. In this situation, the use of the market price as the transfer price is proper. The condensed divisional income statements for Wilson Company in this case are also shown in Exhibit 9.

Negotiated Price Approach

If unused or excess capacity exists in the supplying division (the Eastern Division), and the transfer price is equal to the market price, total company profit may not be maximized. This is because the manager of the Western Division will be indifferent toward purchasing materials from the Eastern Division or from outside suppliers. Thus, the Western Division may purchase the materials from outside suppliers. If, however, the Western Division purchases the materials from the Eastern Division, the difference between the market price of $20 and the variable costs of the Eastern Division can cover fixed costs and contribute to company profits. When the negotiated price approach is used in this situation, the manager of the Western Division is encouraged to purchase the materials from the Eastern Division.

The **negotiated price approach** allows the managers of decentralized units to agree (negotiate) among themselves as to the transfer price. The only constraint on the negotiations is that the transfer price be less than the market price but greater than the supplying division's variable costs per unit.

To illustrate the use of the negotiated price approach, assume that instead of a capacity of 50,000 units, the Eastern Division's capacity is 70,000 units. In addition, assume that the Eastern Division can continue to sell only 50,000 units to outside buyers. A transfer price less than $20 would encourage the manager of the Western Division to purchase from the Eastern Division. This is because the Western Division's materials cost per unit would decrease, and its income from operations would increase. At the same time, a transfer price above the Eastern Division's variable costs per unit of $10 (from Exhibit 9) would encourage the manager of the Eastern Division to use the excess capacity to supply materials to the Western Division. In doing so, the Eastern Division's income from operations would increase.

We continue the illustration with the aid of Exhibit 10, assuming that Wilson Company's division managers agree to a transfer price of $15 for the Eastern Division's product. By purchasing from the Eastern Division, the Western Division's materials cost would be $5 per unit less. At the same time, the Eastern Division would increase its sales by $300,000 (20,000 units × $15 per unit) and increase its income by $100,000 ($300,000 sales − $200,000 variable costs). The effect of reducing the Western Division's materials cost by $100,000 (20,000 units × $5 per unit) is to increase its income by $100,000. Therefore, Wilson Company's income is increased by $200,000 ($100,000 reported by the Eastern Division and $100,000 reported by the Western Division), as shown in the condensed income statements in Exhibit 10.

EXHIBIT 10   *Income Statements—Negotiated Transfer Price*

WILSON COMPANY
Divisional Income Statements
For the Year Ended December 31, 2009

	Eastern Division	Western Division	Total
Sales:			
50,000 units × $20 per unit	$1,000,000		$1,000,000
20,000 units × $15 per unit	300,000	$800,000	300,000
20,000 units × $40 per unit			800,000
	$1,300,000	$800,000	$2,100,000
Expenses:			
Variable:			
70,000 units × $10 per unit	$ 700,000		$ 700,000
20,000 units × $25* per unit		$500,000	500,000
Fixed	300,000	100,000	400,000
Total expenses	$1,000,000	$600,000	$1,600,000
Income from operations	$ 300,000	$200,000	$ 500,000

*$10 of the $25 are variable conversion expenses incurred solely within the Western Division, and $15 per unit represents the transfer price per unit from the Eastern Division.

In this illustration, any transfer price less than the market price of $20 but greater than the Eastern Division's unit variable costs of $10 would increase each division's income. In addition, overall company profit would increase by $200,000. By establishing a range of $20 to $10 for the transfer price, each division manager has an incentive to negotiate the transfer of the materials.

INTEGRITY, OBJECTIVITY, AND ETHICS IN BUSINESS

Shifting Income through Transfer Prices

Transfer prices effectively shift tax burdens of multinational corporations across different countries. For example, assume that a multinational corporation has one division in the United States and another division outside the United States. If the tax rate is lower outside the United States, the corporation has incentives to shift income to the division outside the United States. Setting the U.S. division's purchase transfer prices high and selling transfer prices low can achieve this. For example, a recent Government Accounting Office (GAO) report found that some U.S. subsidiaries bought safety pins at $29 per piece and sold pianos for $50 each and tractor tires for $7.89 each. To control this behavior, the tax codes in the United States and most other countries require transfer prices at "Basic Arm's-Length Standard" (BALS), which is often interpreted as market price. However, even within this standard, there is subjectivity. Thus, financial managers must be careful to set transfer prices to meet economic objectives within the constraints of the transfer pricing laws of the countries in which they conduct business, or they could be subject to significant fines and legal action.

HOW BUSINESSES MAKE MONEY

"Asset Light" Strategies in "Asset Heavy" Industries

The asset strategies of various companies in a given industry can be explained by examining the DuPont formula. The relationships can be graphed with the investment turnover on the vertical axis and the profit margin on the horizontal axis. Thus, each firm can be plotted on the graph according to its unique profit margin and investment turnover combination. A graph for the freight transportation industry is shown here. Each point on the graph is a firm in the freight transportation industry. For example, **FedEx Corp.** is shown in the graph as having a 5.6% profit margin and a 1.49 investment turnover. Other firms plotted on the graph are trucking companies, such as **Yellow Corp.**, railroads, such as **Union Pacific Corp.**, and logistics service providers, such as **C.H. Robinson Worldwide**.

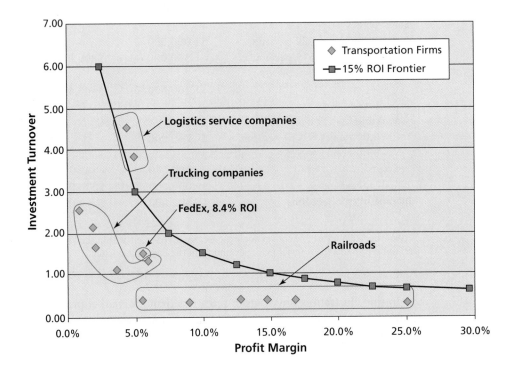

The 15% ROI frontier represents all the combinations of profit margin and return on investment that, when multiplied, equal 15%. Thus, a 15% ROI can also be achieved by many different combinations of profit margin and investment turnover. The closer a firm is to the frontier, the closer it is to a 15% ROI.

The freight transportation industry exhibits a number of different strategies. For example, the railroads are all very asset intensive; thus, their investment turnovers are the lowest of all the firms (all below 0.4). The trucking firms all have higher investment turnover than the railroads, but their profit margins are mostly lower. The trucking firms generally have ROIs of 4%–6%, which is slightly better than the railroads.

The two logistics service companies are able to exceed the 15% ROI frontier. Both companies have the highest investment turnover in the industry, while earning profit margins comparable to the truckers. These firms accomplish this by providing "door-to-door" logistics services without owning the trucks, trains, or planes that provide this service. That is, these companies arrange, manage, and purchase shipping services on behalf of their customers. This is an example of an "asset light" strategy. The logistics service companies rely on other "asset heavy" companies to supply the shipping service, while earning a margin from managing the complex logistical details.

Cost Price Approach

Under the **cost price approach**, cost is used to set transfer prices. With this approach, a variety of cost concepts may be used. For example, cost may refer to either total product cost per unit or variable product cost per unit. If total product cost per unit is used, direct materials, direct labor, and factory overhead are included in the transfer price. If variable product cost per unit is used, the fixed factory overhead component of total product cost is excluded from the transfer price.

Either actual costs or standard (budgeted) costs may be used in applying the cost price approach. If actual costs are used, inefficiencies of the producing division are transferred to the purchasing division. Thus, there is little incentive for the producing division to control costs carefully. For this reason, most companies use standard costs in the cost price approach. In this way, differences between actual and standard costs remain with the producing division for cost control purposes.

When division managers have responsibility for cost centers, the cost price approach to transfer pricing is proper and is often used. The cost price approach may not be proper, however, for decentralized operations organized as profit or investment centers. In profit and investment centers, division managers have responsibility for both revenues and expenses. The use of cost as a transfer price ignores the supplying division manager's responsibility for revenues. When a supplying division's sales are all intracompany transfers, for example, using the cost price approach prevents the supplying division from reporting any income from operations. A cost-based transfer price may therefore not motivate the division manager to make intracompany transfers, even though they are in the best interests of the company.

Key Points

1. **List and explain the advantages and disadvantages of decentralized operations.**

   The advantages of decentralization may include better decisions by the managers closest to the operations, more time for top management to focus on strategic planning, training for managers, improved ability to serve customers and respond to their needs, and improved manager morale. The disadvantages of decentralization may include failure of the company to maximize profits because decisions made by one manager may affect other managers in such a way that the profitability of the entire company may suffer.

2. **Prepare a responsibility accounting report for a cost center.**

   Since managers of cost centers have responsibility and authority to make decisions regarding costs, responsibility accounting for cost centers focuses on costs. The primary accounting tools for planning and controlling costs for a cost center are budgets and budget performance reports. An example of a budget performance report is shown in Exhibit 1.

3. **Prepare responsibility accounting reports for a profit center.**

   In preparing a profitability report for a profit center, operating expenses are subtracted from revenues in order to determine the income from operations before service department charges. Service department charges are then subtracted in order to determine the income from operations of the profit center. An example of a divisional income statement is shown in Exhibit 5.

4. **Compute and interpret the rate of return on investment, the residual income, and the balanced scorecard for an investment center.**

   The rate of return on investment for an investment center is the income from operations divided by invested assets. The rate of return on investment may also be computed as the product of (1) the profit margin and (2) the investment turnover. Residual income for an investment center is the excess of income from operations over a minimum amount of desired income from operations. The balanced scorecard combines nonfinancial measures in order to help managers consider the underlying causes of financial performance and trade-offs between short-term and long-term performance.

5. Explain how the market price, negotiated price, and cost price approaches to transfer pricing may be used by decentralized segments of a business.

Under the market price approach, the transfer price is the price at which the product or service transferred could be sold to outside buyers. Market price should be used when the supplier division is able to sell to outsiders and is operating at capacity.

Under the negotiated price approach, the managers of decentralized units agree (negotiate) among themselves as to the transfer price. Negotiated prices should be used when the supplier division is operating below capacity.

Under the cost price approach, cost is used as the basis for setting transfer prices. A variety of cost concepts may be used, such as total product cost per unit or variable product cost per unit. In addition, actual costs or standard (budgeted) costs may be used. The cost price approach should be used for supplier divisions that are organized as cost centers.

Key Terms

Balanced scorecard	Income from operations	Rate of return on investment (ROI)
Controllable expenses	Investment center	Residual income
Cost center	Investment turnover	Responsibility accounting
Cost price approach	Market price approach	Service department charges
Decentralization	Negotiated price approach	Transfer price
Divisions	Profit center	
DuPont formula	Profit margin	

Illustrative Problem

Quinn Company has two divisions, Domestic and International. Invested assets and condensed income statement data for each division for the past year ended December 31 are as follows:

	Domestic Division	International Division
Revenues	$675,000	$480,000
Operating expenses	450,000	372,400
Service department charges	90,000	50,000
Invested assets	600,000	384,000

Instructions

1. Prepare condensed income statements for the past year for each division.
2. Using the DuPont formula, determine the profit margin, investment turnover, and rate of return on investment for each division.
3. If management's minimum acceptable rate of return is 10%, determine the residual income for each division.

Solution

1.

QUINN COMPANY
Divisional Income Statements
For the Year Ended December 31, 2009

	Domestic Division	International Division
Revenues	$675,000	$480,000
Operating expenses	450,000	372,400
Income from operations before service department charges	$225,000	$107,600
Service department charges	90,000	50,000
Income from operations	$135,000	$ 57,600

2. **Rate of return on investment (ROI) = Profit margin × Investment turnover**

$$\text{Rate of return on investment: (ROI)} = \frac{\text{Income from operations}}{\text{Sales}} \times \frac{\text{Sales}}{\text{Invested assets}}$$

$$\text{Domestic Division: ROI} = \frac{\$135,000}{\$675,000} \times \frac{\$675,000}{\$600,000}$$

$$\text{ROI} = 20\% \times 1.125$$

$$\text{ROI} = 22.5\%$$

$$\text{International Division: ROI} = \frac{\$57,600}{\$480,000} \times \frac{\$480,000}{\$384,000}$$

$$\text{ROI} = 12\% \times 1.25$$

$$\text{ROI} = 15\%$$

3. Domestic Division: $75,000 [$135,000 − (10% × $600,000)]
    International Division: $19,200 [$57,600 − (10% × $384,000)]

Self-Examination Questions   *(Answers appear at end of chapter.)*

1. When the manager has the responsibility and authority to make decisions that affect costs and revenues but no responsibility for or authority over assets invested in the department, the department is called:
    A. a cost center   C. an investment center
    B. a profit center   D. a service department

2. The Accounts Payable Department has expenses of $600,000 and makes 150,000 payments to the various vendors who provide products and services to the divisions. Division A has income from operations of $900,000, before service department charges, and requires 60,000 payments to vendors. If the Accounts Payable Department is treated as a service department, what is Division A's income from operations?
    A. $300,000   C. $660,000
    B. $900,000   D. $540,000

3. Division A of Kern Co. has sales of $350,000, cost of goods sold of $200,000, operating expenses of $30,000,

and invested assets of $600,000. What is the rate of return on investment for Division A?
    A. 20%   C. 33%
    B. 25%   D. 40%

4. Division L of Liddy Co. has a rate of return on investment of 24% and an investment turnover of 1.6. What is the profit margin?
    A. 6%   C. 24%
    B. 15%   D. 38%

5. Which approach to transfer pricing uses the price at which the product or service transferred could be sold to outside buyers?
    A. Cost price approach
    B. Negotiated price approach
    C. Market price approach
    D. Standard cost approach

Class Discussion Questions

1. Differentiate between a cost center and a profit center.

2. Differentiate between a profit center and an investment center.

3. In what major respect would budget performance reports prepared for the use of plant managers of a manufacturing business with cost centers differ from those prepared for the use of the various department supervisors who report to the plant managers?

4. For what decisions is the manager of a cost center *not* responsible?

5. **Weyerhaeuser Company** developed a system that assigns service department expenses to user divisions on the basis of actual services consumed by the division. Here are a number of Weyerhaeuser's activities in its central financial services department:

   - Payroll
   - Accounts payable
   - Accounts receivable
   - Database administration—report preparation

   For each activity, identify an output measure that could be used to charge user divisions for service.

6. What is the major shortcoming of using income from operations as a performance measure for investment centers?

7. Why should the factors under the control of the investment center manager (revenues, expenses, and invested assets) be considered in computing the rate of return on investment?

8. In a decentralized company in which the divisions are organized as investment centers, how could a division be considered the least profitable even though it earned the largest amount of income from operations?

9. How does using the rate of return on investment facilitate comparability between divisions of decentralized companies?

10. The rates of return on investment for Kardin Co.'s three divisions, East, Central, and South, are 22%, 18%, and 16%, respectively. In expanding operations, which of Kardin Co.'s divisions should be given priority? Explain.

11. Why would a firm use a balanced scorecard in evaluating divisional performance?

12. What is the objective of transfer pricing?

13. When is the negotiated price approach preferred over the market price approach in setting transfer prices?

14. Why would standard cost be a more appropriate transfer cost between cost centers than actual cost?

15. When using the negotiated price approach to transfer pricing, within what range should the transfer price be established?

Exercises

E14-1

Budget performance reports for cost centers

Obj 2

✓ a. (c) $2,310

Partially completed budget performance reports for Qual-Tech Company, a manufacturer of air conditioners, are provided below.

QUAL-TECH COMPANY
Budget Performance Report—Vice President, Production
For the Month Ended April 30, 2008

Plant	Budget	Actual	Over Budget	Under Budget
North Region	$362,460	$360,920		$1,540
Central Region	259,980	258,580		1,400
South Region	(g)	(h)	$ (i)	
	$ (j)	$ (k)	$ (l)	$2,940

QUAL-TECH COMPANY
Budget Performance Report—Manager, South Region Plant
For the Month Ended April 30, 2008

Department	Budget	Actual	Over Budget	Under Budget
Chip Fabrication	$ (a)	$ (b)	$ (c)	
Electronic Assembly	74,480	75,460	980	
Final Assembly	119,980	119,560		$420
	$ (d)	$ (e)	$ (f)	$420

QUAL-TECH COMPANY
Budget Performance Report—Supervisor, Chip Fabrication
For the Month Ended April 30, 2008

Costs	Budget	Actual	Over Budget	Under Budget
Factory wages	$ 21,560	$23,100	$1,540	
Materials	60,900	60,480		$420
Power and light	3,360	3,990	630	
Maintenance	5,880	6,440	560	
	$ 91,700	$94,010	$2,730	$420

a. Complete the budget performance reports by determining the correct amounts for the lettered spaces.
b. Compose a memo to Dana Johnson, vice president of production for Qual-Tech Company, explaining the performance of the production division for April.

E14-2

Divisional income statements

Obj 3

✓ Residential Division income from operations, $80,640

The following data were summarized from the accounting records for Huggins Construction Company for the year ended June 30, 2008:

Cost of goods sold:		Service department charges:	
Residential Division	$300,800	Residential Division	$ 54,240
Industrial Division	167,840	Industrial Division	24,960
Administrative expenses:		Net sales:	
Residential Division	$80,320	Residential Division	$516,000
Industrial Division	66,560	Industrial Division	321,920

Prepare divisional income statements for Huggins Construction Company.

E14-3

Service department charges and activity bases

Obj 3

For each of the following service departments, identify an activity base that could be used for charging the expense to the profit center.

a. Accounts receivable
b. Electronic data processing
c. Central purchasing
d. Legal
e. Telecommunications
f. Duplication services

E14-4

Activity bases for service department charges

Obj 3

For each of the following service departments, select the activity base listed that is most appropriate for charging service expenses to responsible units.

Service Department	Activity Base
a. Training	1. Number of conference attendees
b. Employee Travel	2. Number of computers
c. Payroll Accounting	3. Number of employees trained
d. Accounts Receivable	4. Number of telephone lines
e. Conferences	5. Number of purchase requisitions
f. Telecommunications	6. Number of sales invoices
g. Computer Support	7. Number of payroll checks
h. Central Purchasing	8. Number of travel claims

E14-5

Service department charges

Obj 3

✓ b. Commercial payroll, $9,960

In divisional income statements prepared for Franklin Electrical Company, the Payroll Department costs are charged back to user divisions on the basis of the number of payroll checks, and the Purchasing Department costs are charged back on the basis of the number of purchase requisitions. The Payroll Department had expenses of $44,010, and the Purchasing Department had expenses of $18,720 for the year. The following annual data for Residential, Commercial, and Government Contract Divisions were obtained from corporate records:

	Residential	Commercial	Government Contract
Sales	$420,000	$500,000	$1,800,000
Number of employees:			
Weekly payroll (52 weeks per year)	144	72	108
Monthly payroll	25	20	18
Number of purchase requisitions per year	1,800	1,530	1,350

a. Determine the total amount of payroll checks and purchase requisitions processed per year by each division.

b. Using the activity base information in (a), determine the annual amount of payroll and purchasing costs charged back to the Residential, Commercial, and Government Contract Divisions from payroll and purchasing services.

c. Why does the Residential Division have a larger service department charge than the other two divisions, even though its sales are lower?

E14-6

Service department charges and activity bases

Obj 3

✓ b. Help Desk, $28,800

Harris Corporation, a manufacturer of electronics and communications systems, uses a service department charge system to charge profit centers with Computing and Communications Services (CCS) service department costs. The following table identifies an abbreviated list of service categories and activity bases used by the CCS department. The table also includes some assumed cost and activity base quantity information for each service for October.

CCS Service Category	Activity Base	Assumed Cost	Assumed Activity Base Quantity
Help desk	Number of calls	$ 73,600	2,300
Network center	Number of devices monitored	614,250	9,450
Electronic mail	Number of user accounts	53,550	6,300
Local voice support	Number of phone extensions	127,238	8,775

One of the profit centers for Harris Corporation is the Communication Systems (COMM) sector. Assume the following information for the COMM sector:

- The sector has 4,000 employees, of whom 50% are office employees.
- All the office employees have a phone, and 90% of them have a computer on the network.
- Ninety percent of the employees with a computer also have an e-mail account.
- The average number of help desk calls for October was 0.50 call per individual with a computer.
- There are 300 additional printers, servers, and peripherals on the network beyond the personal computers.

a. Determine the service charge rate for the four CCS service categories for October.
b. Determine the charges to the COMM sector for the four CCS service categories for October.

E14-7

Divisional income statements with service department charges

Obj 3

SPREADSHEET

✓ Consumer income from operations, $1,154,650

Waverunner Watersports Company has two divisions, Commercial and Consumer, and two corporate service departments, Tech Support and Accounts Payable. The corporate expenses for the year ended December 31, 2008, are as follows:

Tech Support Department	$ 588,000
Accounts Payable Department	231,000
Other corporate administrative expenses	343,000
Total corporate expense	$1,162,000

The other corporate administrative expenses include officers' salaries and other expenses required by the corporation. The Tech Support Department charges the divisions for services rendered, based on the number of computers in the department, and the Accounts Payable Department charges divisions for services, based on the number of checks issued. The usage of service by the two divisions is as follows:

	Tech Support	Accounts Payable
Commercial Division	252 computers	5,880 checks
Consumer Division	168	10,920
Total	420 computers	16,800 checks

The service department charges of the Tech Support Department and the Accounts Payable Department are considered controllable by the divisions. Corporate administrative expenses are not considered controllable by the divisions. The revenues, cost of goods sold, and operating expenses for the two divisions are as follows:

	Commercial	Consumer
Revenues	$5,600,000	$4,760,000
Cost of goods sold	2,940,000	2,240,000
Operating expenses	1,050,000	980,000

Prepare the divisional income statements for the two divisions.

E14-8

Corrections to service department charges

Obj 3

SPREADSHEET

✓ b. Income from operations, Cargo Division, $255,000

Worldwide Air, Inc., has two divisions organized as profit centers, the Passenger Division and the Cargo Division. The following divisional income statements were prepared:

WORLDWIDE AIR, INC.
Divisional Income Statements
For the Year Ended July 31, 2008

	Passenger Division		Cargo Division	
Revenues		$600,000		$600,000
Operating expenses		300,000		250,000
Income from operations before				
service department charges		$300,000		$350,000
Less service department charges:				
Training	$50,000		$50,000	
Trip scheduling	60,000		60,000	
Reservations	80,000	190,000	80,000	190,000
Income from operations		$110,000		$160,000

The service department charge rate for the service department costs was based on revenues. Since the revenues of the two divisions were the same, the service department charges to each division were also the same.

The following additional information is available:

	Passenger Division	Cargo Division	Total
Number of personnel trained	40	10	50
Number of trips	30	50	80
Number of reservations requested	4,000	—	4,000

a. Does the income from operations for the two divisions accurately measure performance?
b. Correct the divisional income statements, using the activity bases provided above in revising the service department charges.

E14-9

Profit center responsibility reporting

Objs 3, 5

SPREADSHEET

✓ Income from operations, Winter Sports Division, $11,700

Outdoor Athletic Equipment Co. operates two divisions—the Winter Sports Division and the Summer Sports Division. The following income and expense accounts were provided from the trial balance as of June 30, 2008, the end of the current fiscal year, after all adjustments, including those for inventories, were recorded and posted:

Sales—Winter Sports (WS) Division	$ 950,000
Sales—Summer Sports (SS) Division	1,437,500
Cost of Goods Sold—Winter Sports (WS) Division	512,500
Cost of Goods Sold—Summer Sports (SS) Division	687,500
Sales Expense—Winter Sports (WS) Division	150,000
Sales Expense—Summer Sports (SS) Division	205,000
Administrative Expense—Winter Sports (WS) Division	97,000
Administrative Expense—Summer Sports (SS) Division	128,000
Advertising Expense	64,500
Transportation Expense	100,700
Accounts Receivable Collection Expense	58,100
Warehouse Expense	120,000

The bases to be used in allocating expenses, together with other essential information, are as follows:

a. Advertising expense—incurred at headquarters, charged back to divisions on the basis of usage: Winter Sports Division, $28,000; Summer Sports Division, $36,500.

b. Transportation expense—charged back to divisions at a transfer price of $7.60 per bill of lading: Winter Sports Division, 6,000 bills of lading; Summer Sports Division, 7,250 bills of lading.

c. Accounts receivable collection expense—incurred at headquarters, charged back to divisions at a transfer price of $5.60 per invoice: Winter Sports Division, 4,500 sales invoices; Summer Sports Division, 5,875 sales invoices.

d. Warehouse expense—charged back to divisions on the basis of floor space used in storing division products: Winter Sports Division, 25,000 square feet; Summer Sports Division, 12,500 square feet.

Prepare a divisional income statement with two column headings: Winter Sports Division and Summer Sports Division. Provide supporting schedules for determining service department charges.

E14-10

Rate of return on investment

Obj 4

✓ a. Textbook Division, 26%

The income from operations and the amount of invested assets in each division of Deacon Publishing Company are as follows:

	Income from Operations	Invested Assets
Magazine Division	$ 96,000	$ 800,000
Textbook Division	166,400	640,000
Business Publishing Division	260,400	1,240,000

a. Compute the rate of return on investment for each division.
b. Which division is the most profitable per dollar invested?

E14-11

Residual income

Obj 4

✓ a. Magazine Division, $0

Based on the data in Exercise 14-10, assume that management has established a 12% minimum acceptable rate of return for invested assets.

a. Determine the residual income for each division.
b. Which division has the most residual income?

E14-12

Determining missing items in rate of return computation

Obj 4

✓ d. 2.0

One item is omitted from each of the following computations of the rate of return on investment:

Rate of Return on Investment	=	Profit Margin	×	Investment Turnover
24%	=	15%	×	(a)
(b)	=	8%	×	2.50
12%	=	(c)	×	0.80
24%	=	12%	×	(d)
(e)	=	10%	×	1.60

Determine the missing items, identifying each by the appropriate letter.

E14-13

Profit margin, investment turnover, and rate of return on investment

Obj 4

✓ a. ROI, 11%

The condensed income statement for the European Division of Cougar Motors Inc. is as follows (assuming no service department charges):

Sales	$875,000
Cost of goods sold	400,000
Gross profit	$475,000
Administrative expenses	282,500
Income from operations	$192,500

(continued)

The manager of the European Division is considering ways to increase the rate of return on investment.

a. Using the DuPont formula for rate of return on investment, determine the profit margin, investment turnover, and rate of return on investment of the European Division, assuming that $1,750,000 of assets have been invested in the European Division.

b. If expenses could be reduced by $52,500 without decreasing sales, what would be the impact on the profit margin, investment turnover, and rate of return on investment for the European Division?

E14-14

Rate of return on investment

Obj 4

✓ a. Media Networks ROI, 10.1%

The Walt Disney Company has four major sectors, described as follows:

- **Media Networks:** The ABC television and radio network, Disney channel, ESPN, A&E, E!, and Disney.com.
- **Parks and Resorts:** Walt Disney World Resort, Disneyland, Disney Cruise Line, and other resort properties.
- **Studio Entertainment:** Walt Disney Pictures, Touchstone Pictures, Hollywood Pictures, Miramax Films, and Buena Vista Theatrical Productions.
- **Consumer Products:** Character merchandising, Disney stores, books, and magazines.

Disney recently reported sector income from operations, revenue, and invested assets (in millions) as follows:

	Income from Operations	Revenue	Invested Assets
Media Networks	$2,749	$13,027	$26,926
Parks and Resorts	1,178	9,023	15,807
Studio Entertainment	207	7,587	5,965
Consumer Products	520	2,157	877

a. Use the DuPont formula to determine the rate of return on investment for the four Disney sectors. Round whole percents to one decimal place and investment turnover to one decimal place.

b. How do the four sectors differ in their profit margin, investment turnover, and return on investment?

E14-15

Determining missing items in rate of return and residual income computations

Obj 4

✓ c. $38,625

Data for Grobe Products Company is presented in the following table of rates of return on investment and residual incomes:

Invested Assets	Income from Operations	Rate of Return on Investment	Minimum Rate of Return	Minimum Acceptable Income from Operations	Residual Income
$643,750	$115,875	(a)	12%	(b)	(c)
$418,750	(d)	(e)	(f)	$62,813	$16,750
$275,000	(g)	12%	(h)	$44,000	(i)
$600,000	$84,000	(j)	10%	(k)	(l)

Determine the missing items, identifying each item by the appropriate letter.

E14-16

Determining missing items from computations

Obj 4

✓ a. (e) $500,000

Data for the North, East, South, and West Divisions of Tor Max Semiconductor Communication Company are as follows:

	Sales	Income from Operations	Invested Assets	Rate of Return on Investment	Profit Margin	Investment Turnover
North	$425,000	(a)	(b)	20%	10%	(c)
East	(d)	$50,000	(e)	(f)	8%	1.25
South	$400,000	(g)	$125,000	12%	(h)	(i)
West	$750,000	$180,000	$1,250,000	(j)	(k)	(l)

a. Determine the missing items, identifying each by the letters (a) through (l).
b. Determine the residual income for each division, assuming that the minimum acceptable rate of return established by management is 9%.
c. Which division is the most profitable in terms of (1) return on investment and (2) residual income?

E14-17

Rate of return on investment, residual income

Obj 4

Hilton Hotels Corporation provides lodging services around the world. The company is separated into three major divisions:

- **Hotel Ownership:** Hotels owned and operated by Hilton.
- **Managing and Franchising:** Hotels franchised to others or managed for others.
- **Timeshare:** Resort properties managed for timeshare vacation owners.

Financial information for each division, from a recent annual report, is as follows (in millions):

	Hotel Ownership	Managing and Franchising	Timeshare
Revenues	$2,215	$1,510	$421
Income from operations	394	343	99
Total assets	4,825	2,112	507

a. Use the DuPont formula to determine the return on investment for each of the Hilton business divisions. Round whole percents to one decimal place and investment turnover to one decimal place.
b. Determine the residual income for each division, assuming a minimum acceptable income of 14% of total assets. Round minimal acceptable return to the nearest million dollars.
c. Interpret your results.

E14-18

Balanced scorecard

Obj 4

American Express Company is a major financial services company, noted for its American Express® card. Below are some of the performance measures used by the company in its balanced scorecard.

Average cardmember spending
Cards in force
Earnings growth
Hours of credit consultant training
Investment in information technology
Number of Internet features
Number of merchant signings
Number of card choices
Number of new card launches
Return on equity
Revenue growth

For each measure, identify whether the measure best fits the innovation, customer, internal process, or financial dimension of the balanced scorecard.

E14-19

Balanced scorecard

Obj 4

Several years ago, **United Parcel Service (UPS)** believed that the Internet was going to change the parcel delivery market and would require UPS to become a more nimble and customer-focused organization. As a result, UPS replaced its old measurement system, which was 90% oriented toward financial performance, with a balanced scorecard. The scorecard emphasized four "point of arrival" measures, which were:

1. Customer satisfaction index—a measure of customer satisfaction.
2. Employee relations index—a measure of employee sentiment and morale.
3. Competitive position—delivery performance relative to competition.
4. Time in transit—the time from order entry to delivery.

a. Why did UPS introduce a balanced scorecard and nonfinancial measures in its new performance measurement system?
b. Why do you think UPS included a factor measuring employee sentiment?

E14-20

Decision on transfer pricing

Obj 5

✓ a. $1,000,000

Materials used by the Industrial Division of Crow Manufacturing are currently purchased from outside suppliers at a cost of $120 per unit. However, the same materials are available from the Materials Division. The Materials Division has unused capacity and can produce the materials needed by the Industrial Division at a variable cost of $95 per unit.

a. If a transfer price of $105 per unit is established and 40,000 units of materials are transferred, with no reduction in the Materials Division's current sales, how much would Crow Manufacturing's total income from operations increase?
b. How much would the Industrial Division's income from operations increase?
c. How much would the Materials Division's income from operations increase?

E14-21

Decision on transfer pricing

Obj 5

✓ b. $400,000

Based on Crow Manufacturing's data in Exercise 14–20, assume that a transfer price of $110 has been established and that 40,000 units of materials are transferred, with no reduction in the Materials Division's current sales.

a. How much would Crow Manufacturing's total income from operations increase?
b. How much would the Industrial Division's income from operations increase?
c. How much would the Materials Division's income from operations increase?
d. If the negotiated price approach is used, what would be the range of acceptable transfer prices and why?

Problems

P14-1

Budget performance report for a cost center

Obj 2

SPREADSHEET

The Southwest District of Pop Soft Drinks, Inc., is organized as a cost center. The budget for the Southwest District of Pop Soft Drinks, Inc., for the month ended May 31, 2008, is as follows:

Sales salaries	$406,725
System support salaries	222,300
Customer relations salaries	75,975
Accounting salaries	48,975
Repair and service	134,625
Depreciation of plant and equipment	45,750
Insurance and property taxes	20,475
Total	$954,825

During May, the costs incurred in the Southwest District were as follows:

Sales salaries	$406,200
System support salaries	222,075
Customer relations salaries	89,025
Accounting salaries	48,675
Repair and service	135,375
Depreciation of plant and equipment	45,750
Insurance and property taxes	20,550
Total	$967,650

Instructions

1. Prepare a budget performance report for the manager of the Southwest District of Pop Soft Drinks for the month of May.
2. For which costs might the supervisor be expected to request supplemental reports?

P14-2

Profit center responsibility reporting

Obj 3

SPREADSHEET

✓ 1. Income from operations, South Region, $280,800

Cross-Country Transport Company organizes its three divisions, the Southeast, East, and South Regions, as profit centers. The chief executive officer (CEO) evaluates divisional performance, using income from operations as a percent of revenues. The following quarterly income and expense accounts were provided from the trial balance as of December 31, 2008:

Revenues—SE Region	$1,740,000
Revenues—E Region	2,820,000
Revenues—S Region	2,340,000
Operating Expenses—SE Region	1,134,400
Operating Expenses—E Region	2,097,300
Operating Expenses—S Region	1,721,700
Corporate Expenses—Dispatching	500,000
Corporate Expenses—Equipment	525,000
Corporate Expenses—Treasurer's	375,000
General Corporate Officers' Salaries	710,000

The company operates three service departments: the Dispatching Department, the Equipment Management Department, and the Treasurer's Department. The Dispatching Department manages the scheduling and releasing of completed trains. The Equipment Management Department manages the railroad cars inventories. It makes sure the right freight cars are at the right place at the right time. The Treasurer's Department conducts a variety of services for the company as a whole. The following additional information has been gathered:

	Southeast	East	South
Number of scheduled trains	400	680	520
Number of railroad cars in inventory	4,800	6,400	5,600

Instructions

1. Prepare quarterly income statements showing income from operations for the three regions. Use three column headings: Southeast, East, and South.
2. Identify the most successful region according to the profit margin.
3. Provide a recommendation to the CEO for a better method for evaluating the performance of the regions. In your recommendation, identify the major weakness of the present method.

P14-3

*Divisional income
statements and rate of
return on investment
analysis*

Obj 4

SPREADSHEET

✓ 2, Retail Division,
  ROI, 16%

Hi-Growth Investments Inc. is a diversified investment company with three operating divisions organized as investment centers. Condensed data taken from the records of the three divisions for the year ended June 30, 2008, are as follows:

	Retail Division	*Electronic Brokerage Division*	*Investment Banking Division*
Fee revenue	$1,250,000	$750,000	$1,500,000
Operating expenses	750,000	682,500	1,170,000
Invested assets	3,125,000	250,000	2,000,000

The management of Hi-Growth Investments Inc. is evaluating each division as a basis for planning a future expansion of operations.

Instructions

1. Prepare condensed divisional income statements for the three divisions, assuming that there were no service department charges.
2. Using the DuPont formula for rate of return on investment, compute the profit margin, investment turnover, and rate of return on investment for each division.
3. If available funds permit the expansion of operations of only one division, which of the divisions would you recommend for expansion, based on parts (1) and (2)? Explain. *ignore explain*

P14-4

*Effect of proposals on
divisional performance*

Obj 4

SPREADSHEET

✓ 3. Proposal 3 ROI,
  13.6%

A condensed income statement for the Paintball Division of Outdoor Games Inc. for the year ended January 31, 2008, is as follows:

Sales	$900,000
Cost of goods sold	500,000
Gross profit	$400,000
Operating expenses	274,000
Income from operations	$126,000

Assume that the Paintball Division received no charges from service departments.

The president of Outdoor Games Inc. has indicated that the division's rate of return on a $720,000 investment must be increased to at least 20% by the end of the next year if operations are to continue. The division manager is considering the following three proposals:

Proposal 1: Transfer equipment with a book value of $120,000 to other divisions at no gain or loss and lease similar equipment. The annual lease payments would be less than the amount of depreciation expense on the old equipment by $18,000. This decrease in expense would be included as part of the cost of goods sold. Sales would remain unchanged.

Proposal 2: Reduce invested assets by discontinuing a product line. This action would eliminate sales of $75,000, cost of goods sold of $35,000, and operating expenses of $37,750. Assets of $32,500 would be transferred to other divisions at no gain or loss.

Proposal 3: Purchase new and more efficient machinery and thereby reduce the cost of goods sold by $27,000. Sales would remain unchanged, and the old machinery, which has no remaining book value, would be scrapped at no gain or loss. The new machinery would increase invested assets by $405,000 for the year.

Instructions

1. Using the DuPont formula for rate of return on investment, determine the profit margin, investment turnover, and rate of return on investment for the Paintball Division for the past year.
2. Prepare condensed estimated income statements and compute the invested assets for each proposal.
3. Using the DuPont formula for rate of return on investment, determine the profit margin, investment turnover, and rate of return on investment for each proposal.

4. Which of the three proposals would meet the required 20% rate of return on investment?
5. If the Paintball Division were in an industry where the profit margin could not be increased, how much would the investment turnover have to increase to meet the president's required 20% rate of return on investment? Round to two decimal places.

P14-5

Divisional performance analysis and evaluation

Obj 4

SPREADSHEET

✓ 2. Personal Computing Division ROI, 32%

The vice president of operations of 14 Computers Inc. is evaluating the performance of two divisions organized as investment centers. Invested assets and condensed income statement data for the past year for each division are as follows:

	Personal Computing Division	*Business Computing Division*
Sales	$800,000	$1,200,000
Cost of goods sold	460,000	780,000
Operating expenses	180,000	156,000
Invested assets	500,000	2,000,000

Instructions

1. Prepare condensed divisional income statements for the year ended December 31, 2008, assuming that there were no service department charges.
2. Using the DuPont formula for rate of return on investment, determine the profit margin, investment turnover, and rate of return on investment for each division.
3. If management's minimum acceptable rate of return is 15%, determine the residual income for each division.
4. Discuss the evaluation of the two divisions, using the performance measures determined in parts (1), (2), and (3).

P14-6

Transfer pricing

Obj 5

SPREADSHEET

✓ 3. Income from operations for Navigational Systems Division, $195,200

Goho Manufacturing Company is a diversified aerospace company, including two operating divisions, Specialized Semiconductors and Navigational Systems Divisions. Condensed divisional income statements, which involve no intracompany transfers and which include a breakdown of expenses into variable and fixed components, are as follows:

GOHO MANUFACTURING COMPANY
Divisional Income Statements
For the Year Ended December 31, 2008

	Specialized Semi-conductors Division	*Navigational Systems Division*	*Total*
Sales:			
640 units × $1,320 per unit	$844,800		$ 844,800
1,000 units × $1,984 per unit		$1,984,000	1,984,000
			$2,828,800
Expenses:			
Variable:			
640 units × $776 per unit	$496,640		$ 496,640
1,000 units × $1,560* per unit		$1,560,000	1,560,000
Fixed	195,200	254,400	449,600
Total expenses	$691,840	$1,814,400	$2,506,240
Income from operations	$152,960	$ 169,600	$ 322,560

*$1,320 of the $1,560 per unit represents materials costs, and the remaining $240 per unit represents other variable conversion expenses incurred within the Navigational Systems Division.

The Specialized Semiconductors Division is presently producing 640 units out of a total capacity of 800 units. Materials used in producing the Navigational Systems Division's product are currently purchased from outside suppliers at a price of $1,320 per unit. The Specialized Semiconductors Division is able to produce the components used by the Navigational

(continued)

Systems Division. Except for the possible transfer of materials between divisions, no changes are expected in sales and expenses.

Instructions

1. Would the market price of $1,320 per unit be an appropriate transfer price for Goho Manufacturing Company? Explain.
2. If the Navigational Systems Division purchases 160 units from the Specialized Semiconductors Division, rather than externally, at a negotiated transfer price of $1,160 per unit, how much would the income from operations of each division and total company income from operations increase?
3. Prepare condensed divisional income statements for Goho Manufacturing Company, based on the data in part (2).
4. If a transfer price of $880 per unit is negotiated, how much would the income from operations of each division and total company income from operations increase?
5. a. What is the range of possible negotiated transfer prices that would be acceptable for Goho Manufacturing Company?
   b. Assuming that the managers of the two divisions cannot agree on a transfer price, what price would you suggest as the transfer price?

Activities

A14-1

Ethics and professional conduct in business

ETHICS

Micro Tech Company has two divisions, the Semiconductor Division and the PC Division. The PC Division may purchase semiconductors from the Semiconductor Division or from outside suppliers. The Semiconductor Division sells semiconductor products both internally and externally. The market price for semiconductors is $250 per 100 semiconductors. Michael Blount is the controller of the PC Division, and Lynn Williams is the controller of the Semiconductor Division. The following conversation took place between Michael and Lynn:

Michael: I hear you are having problems selling semiconductors out of your division. Maybe I can help.

Lynn: You've got that right. We're producing and selling at about 80% of our capacity to outsiders. Last year we were selling 100% of capacity. Would it be possible for your division to pick up some of our excess capacity? After all, we are part of the same company.

Michael: What kind of price could you give me?

Lynn: Well, you know as well as I that we are under strict profit responsibility in our divisions, so I would expect to get market price, $250 for 100 semiconductors.

Michael: I'm not so sure we can swing that. I was expecting a price break from a "sister" division.

Lynn: Hey, I can only take this "sister" stuff so far. If I give you a price break, our profits will fall from last year's levels. I don't think I could explain that. I'm sorry, but I must remain firm—market price. After all, it's only fair—that's what you would have to pay from an external supplier.

Michael: Fair or not, I think we'll pass. Sorry we couldn't have helped.

Was Michael behaving ethically by trying to force the Semiconductor Division into a price break? Comment on Lynn's reactions.

A14-2

Service department charges

The Customer Service Department of Grand Lakes Technologies asked the Publications Department to prepare a brochure for its training program. The Publications Department delivered the brochures and charged the Customer Service Department a rate that was 25% higher than could be obtained from an outside printing company. The policy of the company required the Customer Service Department to use the internal publications group for brochures. The Publications Department claimed that it had a drop in demand for its services during the fiscal year, so it had to charge higher prices in order to recover its payroll and fixed costs.

Should the cost of the brochure be transferred to the Customer Service Department in order to hold the department head accountable for the cost of the brochure? What changes in policy would you recommend?

A14-3
Evaluating divisional performance

The three divisions of Monster Foods are Snack Goods, Cereal, and Frozen Foods. The divisions are structured as investment centers. The following responsibility reports were prepared for the three divisions for the prior year:

	Snack Goods	Cereal	Frozen Foods
Revenues	$1,050,000	$2,450,000	$ 875,000
Operating expenses	420,000	1,400,000	175,000
Income from operations before service department charges	$ 630,000	$1,050,000	$ 700,000
Service department charges:			
Promotion	$ 175,000	$ 350,000	$ 308,000
Legal	87,500	70,000	140,000
	$ 262,500	$ 420,000	$ 448,000
Income from operations	$ 367,500	$ 630,000	$ 252,000
Invested assets	$2,100,000	$4,200,000	$1,260,000

1. Which division is making the best use of invested assets and thus should be given priority for future capital investments?
2. Assuming that the minimum acceptable rate of return on new projects is 12%, would all investments that produce a return in excess of 12% be accepted by the divisions?
3. Can you identify opportunities for improving the company's financial performance?

A14-4
Evaluating division performance over time

The Truck Division of Yang Motors Inc. has been experiencing revenue and profit growth during the years 2006–2008. The divisional income statements are provided below.

YANG MOTORS INC.
Divisional Income Statements, Truck Division
For the Years Ended December 31, 2006–2008

	2006	2007	2008
Sales	$756,000	$972,000	$1,170,000
Cost of goods sold	475,200	558,000	616,500
Gross profit	$280,800	$414,000	$ 553,500
Operating expenses	167,400	209,880	261,000
Income from operations	$113,400	$204,120	$ 292,500

Assume that there are no charges from service departments. The vice president of the division, Terry Clark, is proud of his division's performance over the last three years. The president of Yang Motors Inc., Billy Clark, is discussing the division's performance with Terry, as follows:

Terry: As you can see, we've had a successful three years in the Truck Division.
Billy: I'm not too sure.
Terry: What do you mean? Look at our results. Our income from operations has nearly tripled, while our profit margins are improving.
Billy: I am looking at your results. However, your income statements fail to include one very important piece of information; namely, the invested assets. You have been investing a great deal of assets into the division. You had $315,000 in invested assets in 2006, $810,000 in 2007, and $1,950,000 in 2008.

(continued)

Terry: You are right. I've needed the assets in order to upgrade our technologies and expand our operations. The additional assets are one reason we have been able to grow and improve our profit margins. I don't see that this is a problem.

Billy: The problem is that we must maintain a 20% rate of return on invested assets.

1. Determine the profit margins for the Truck Division for 2006–2008.
2. Compute the investment turnover for the Truck Division for 2006–2008.
3. Compute the rate of return on investment for the Truck Division for 2006–2008.
4. Evaluate the division's performance over the 2006–2008 time period. Why was Billy concerned about the performance?

A14-5
Evaluating division performance

Casual Living Furniture Inc. is a privately held diversified company with five separate divisions organized as investment centers. A condensed income statement for the Outdoor Division for the past year, assuming no service department charges, is as follows:

CASUAL LIVING FURNITURE INC.—OUTDOOR DIVISION
Income Statement
For the Year Ended December 31, 2007

Sales	$12,800,000
Cost of goods sold	8,080,000
Gross profit	$ 4,720,000
Operating expenses	1,520,000
Income from operations	$ 3,200,000

The manager of the Outdoor Division was recently presented with the opportunity to add an additional product line, which would require invested assets of $11,000,000. A projected income statement for the new product line is as follows:

NEW PRODUCT LINE
Projected Income Statement
For the Year Ended December 31, 2008

Sales	$6,000,000
Cost of goods sold	3,360,000
Gross profit	$2,640,000
Operating expenses	1,680,000
Income from operations	$ 960,000

The Outdoor Division currently has $20,000,000 in invested assets, and Casual Living Furniture Inc.'s overall rate of return on investment, including all divisions, is 8%. Each division manager is evaluated on the basis of divisional rate of return on investment, and a bonus equal to $12,000 for each percentage point by which the division's rate of return on investment exceeds the company average is awarded each year.

The president is concerned that the manager of the Outdoor Division rejected the addition of the new product line, when all estimates indicated that the product line would be profitable and would increase overall company income. You have been asked to analyze the possible reasons why the Outdoor Division manager rejected the new product line.

1. Determine the rate of return on investment for the Outdoor Division for the past year.
2. Determine the Outdoor Division manager's bonus for the past year.
3. Determine the estimated rate of return on investment for the new product line. Round whole percents to one decimal place.
4. Why might the manager of the Outdoor Division decide to reject the new product line? Support your answer by determining the projected rate of return on investment for 2008, assuming that the new product line was launched in the Outdoor Division, and 2008 actual operating results were similar to those of 2007.

5. Can you suggest an alternative performance measure for motivating division managers to accept new investment opportunities that would increase the overall company income and rate of return on investment?

A14-6
The balanced scorecard and EVA

GROUP

Divide responsibilities between two groups, with one group going to the home page of *The Palladium Group* at **http://www.thepalladiumgroup.com**, and the second group going to the home page of *Stern Stewart & Co.* at **http://www.eva.com**. The Palladium Group is a consulting firm that helped develop the balanced scorecard concept. Stern Stewart & Co. is a consulting firm that developed the concept of economic value added (EVA), another method of measuring corporate and divisional performance, similar to residual income.

Read about the balanced scorecard at The Palladium Group Web site by clicking on "Strategy" and then clicking on "Balanced Scorecards." Prepare a brief report describing the balanced scorecard and its claimed advantages. In the Stern group, use links in the home page of Stern Stewart & Co. to learn about EVA. After reading about EVA, prepare a brief report describing EVA and its claimed advantages. After preparing these reports, both groups should discuss their research and prepare a brief analysis comparing and contrasting these two approaches to corporate and divisional performance measurement.

Answers to Self-Examination Questions

1. **B** The manager of a profit center (answer B) has responsibility for and authority over costs and revenues. If the manager has responsibility for only costs, the department is called a cost center (answer A). If the responsibility and authority extend to the investment in assets as well as costs and revenues, it is called an investment center (answer C). A service department (answer D) provides services to other departments. A service department could be a cost center, profit center, or investment center.

2. **C** $600,000/150,000 = $4 per payment. Division A anticipates 60,000 payments or $240,000 (60,000 × $4) in service department charges from the Accounts Payable Department. Income from operations is thus $900,000 − $240,000, or $660,000. Answer A assumes that all of the service department overhead is assigned to Division A, which would be incorrect, since Division A does not use all of the accounts payable service. Answer B incorrectly assumes that there are no service department charges from Accounts Payable. Answer D incorrectly determines the accounts payable transfer rate from Division A's income from operations.

3. **A** The rate of return on investment for Division A is 20% (answer A), computed as follows:

$$\text{Rate of return on investment (ROI)} = \frac{\text{Income from operations}}{\text{Invested assets}}$$

$$\text{ROI} = \frac{\$350,000 - \$200,000 - \$30,000}{\$600,000} = 20\%$$

4. **B** The profit margin for Division L of Liddy Co. is 15% (answer B), computed as follows:

$$\text{Rate of return on investment (ROI)} = \frac{\text{Profit margin}}{\times \text{ Investment turnover}}$$

$$24\% = \text{Profit margin} \times 1.6$$

$$15\% = \text{Profit margin}$$

5. **C** The market price approach (answer C) to transfer pricing uses the price at which the product or service transferred could be sold to outside buyers. The cost price approach (answer A) uses cost as the basis for setting transfer prices. The negotiated price approach (answer B) allows managers of decentralized units to agree (negotiate) among themselves as to the proper transfer price. The standard cost approach (answer D) is a version of the cost price approach that uses standard costs in setting transfer prices.

CHAPTER 15

Capital Investment Analysis

Learning Objectives

After studying this chapter, you should be able to:

Obj 1

Explain the nature and importance of capital investment analysis.

Obj 2

Evaluate capital investment proposals, using the following methods: average rate of return, cash payback, net present value, and internal rate of return.

Obj 3

List and describe factors that complicate capital investment analysis.

Obj 4

Diagram the capital rationing process.

Why are you paying tuition, studying this text, and spending time and money on a higher education? Most people believe that the money and time spent now will return them more income in the future. In other words, a higher education is an investment in future earning ability. How would you know if this investment is worth it? One method would be to compare the cost of a higher education against the estimated future increased earning power. The more your future increased earnings exceed the investment, the more attractive the investment. As you will see in this chapter, the same is true for business investments in fixed assets. Business organizations analyze potential capital investments by using various methods that compare investment costs to future earnings and cash flows.

In this chapter, we will describe analyses useful for making investment decisions, which may involve thousands, millions, or even billions of dollars. We will emphasize the similarities and differences among the most commonly used methods of evaluating investment proposals, as well as the uses of each method. We will also discuss qualitative considerations affecting investment analyses. Finally, we will discuss considerations complicating investment analyses and the process of allocating available investment funds among competing proposals.

Obj 1

Explain the nature and importance of capital investment analysis.

Nature of Capital Investment Analysis

How do companies decide to make significant investments such as the following?

- *Yum Brands Inc.* adds 375 new international Taco Bell, Pizza Hut, and KFC units.
- *The Walt Disney Company* commits to investing $315 million to build a new theme park in Hong Kong.
- *Carnival Corporation* commits $6 billion to build 13 luxury cruise ships.

Companies use capital investment analysis to help evaluate long-term investments. **Capital investment analysis** (or *capital budgeting*) is the process by which management plans, evaluates, and controls investments in fixed assets. Capital investments involve the long-term commitment of funds and affect operations for many years. Thus, these investments must earn a reasonable rate of return, so that the business can meet its obligations to creditors and provide dividends to stockholders. Because capital investment decisions are some of the most important decisions that management makes, capital investment analysis must be carefully developed and implemented.

A capital investment program should encourage employees to submit proposals for capital investments. It should communicate to employees the long-range goals of the business, so that useful proposals are submitted. All reasonable proposals should be considered and evaluated with respect to economic costs and benefits. The program may reward employees whose proposals are accepted.

Obj 2

Evaluate capital investment proposals, using the following methods: average rate of return, cash payback, net present value, and internal rate of return.

Methods of Evaluating Capital Investment Proposals

Capital investment evaluation methods can be grouped into the following two categories:

1. Methods that do not use present values
2. Methods that use present values

Two methods that do not use present values are (1) the average rate of return method and (2) the cash payback method. Two methods that use present values are (1) the net present value method and (2) the internal rate of return method. These methods consider the time value of money. The **time value of money concept** recognizes that an amount of cash invested today will earn income and therefore has value over time.

Management often uses a combination of methods in evaluating capital investment proposals. Each method has advantages and disadvantages. In addition, some of the computations are complex. Computers, however, can perform the computations quickly and easily. Computers can also be used to analyze the impact of changes in key estimates in evaluating capital investment proposals.

Methods That Ignore Present Value

The average rate of return and the cash payback methods are easy to use. These methods are often initially used to screen proposals. Management normally sets minimum standards for accepting proposals, and those not meeting these standards are dropped from further consideration. If a proposal meets the minimum standards, it is often subject to further analysis.

The methods that ignore present value are often useful in evaluating capital investment proposals that have relatively short useful lives. In such cases, the timing of the cash flows is less important.

Average Rate of Return Method   The **average rate of return**, sometimes called the *accounting rate of return*, is a measure of the average income as a percent of the average investment in fixed assets. The average rate of return is determined by using the following equation:

$$\text{Average rate of return} = \frac{\textbf{Estimated average annual income}}{\textbf{Average investment}}$$

The numerator is the average of the annual income expected to be earned from the investment over the investment life, after deducting depreciation. The denominator is the average book value over the investment life. Thus, if straight-line depreciation and no residual value are assumed, the average investment over the useful life is equal to one-half of the original cost.[1]

To illustrate, assume that management is considering the purchase of a machine at a cost of $500,000. The machine is expected to have a useful life of 4 years, with no residual value, and to yield total income of $200,000. The estimated average annual income is therefore $50,000 ($200,000 ÷ 4), and the average investment is $250,000 [($500,000 + $0 residual value) ÷ 2]. Thus, the average rate of return on the average investment is 20%, computed as follows:

$$\text{Average rate of return} = \frac{\text{Estimated average annual income}}{\text{Average investment}}$$

$$\text{Average rate of return} = \frac{\$200,000 \div 4}{(\$500,000 + \$0) \div 2} = 20\%$$

The average rate of return of 20% should be compared with the minimum rate for such investments. If the average rate of return equals or exceeds the minimum rate, the machine should be purchased.

When several capital investment proposals are considered, the proposals can be ranked by their average rates of return. The higher the average rate of return, the more desirable the proposal. For example, assume that management is considering two capital investment proposals and has computed the following average rates of return:

	Proposal A	*Proposal B*
Estimated average annual income	$ 30,000	$ 36,000
Average investment	$120,000	$180,000
Average rate of return:		
$30,000 ÷ $120,000	25%	
$36,000 ÷ $180,000		20%

If only the average rate of return is considered, Proposal A, with an average rate of return of 25%, would be preferred over Proposal B.

In addition to being easy to compute, the average rate of return method has several advantages. One advantage is that it includes the amount of income earned over the entire life of the proposal. In addition, it emphasizes accounting income, which is often used by investors and creditors in evaluating management performance. Its main disadvantage is that it does not directly consider the expected cash flows from the proposal and the timing of these cash flows.

---

[1] The average investment is the midpoint of the depreciable cost of the asset. Since a fixed asset is never depreciated below its residual value, this midpoint is determined by adding the original cost of the asset to the estimated residual value and dividing by 2.

Cash Payback Method   Cash flows are important because cash can be reinvested. Very simply, the capital investment uses cash and must therefore return cash in the future in order to be successful.

The expected period of time that will pass between the date of an investment and the complete recovery in cash (or equivalent) of the amount invested is the **cash payback period**. To simplify the analysis, the revenues and expenses other than depreciation related to operating fixed assets are assumed to be all in the form of cash. The excess of the cash flowing in from revenue over the cash flowing out for expenses is termed *net cash flow*. The time required for the net cash flow to equal the initial outlay for the fixed asset is the payback period.

To illustrate, assume that the proposed investment in a fixed asset with an 8-year life is $200,000. The annual cash revenues from the investment are $50,000, and the annual cash expenses are $10,000. Thus, the annual net cash flow is expected to be $40,000 ($50,000 − $10,000). The estimated cash payback period for the investment is 5 years, computed as follows:

$$\frac{\$200{,}000}{\$40{,}000} = \text{5-year cash payback period}$$

In this illustration, the annual net cash flows are equal ($40,000 per year). If these annual net cash flows are *not* equal, the cash payback period is determined by adding the annual net cash flows until the cumulative sum equals the amount of the proposed investment. To illustrate, assume that for a proposed investment of $400,000, the annual net cash flows and the cumulative net cash flows over the proposal's 6-year life are as follows:

Year	Net Cash Flow	Cumulative Net Cash Flow
1	$ 60,000	$ 60,000
2	80,000	140,000
3	105,000	245,000
4	155,000	400,000
5	100,000	500,000
6	90,000	590,000

The cumulative net cash flow at the end of the fourth year equals the amount of the investment, $400,000. Thus, the payback period is 4 years. If the amount of the proposed investment had been $450,000, the cash payback period would occur during the fifth year. If the net cash flows are uniform during the period, the cash payback period would be 4½ years.

The cash payback method is widely used in evaluating proposals for investments in new projects. A short payback period is desirable, because the sooner the cash is recovered, the sooner it becomes available for reinvestment in other projects. In addition, there is less possibility of losses from economic conditions, out-of-date assets, and other unavoidable risks when the payback period is short. The cash payback period is also important to bankers and other creditors who may be depending on net cash flow for repaying debt related to the capital investment. The sooner the cash is recovered, the sooner the debt or other liabilities can be paid. Thus, the cash payback method is especially useful to managers whose primary concern is liquidity.

One of the disadvantages of the cash payback method is that it ignores cash flows occurring after the payback period. In addition, the cash payback method does not use present value concepts in valuing cash flows occurring in different periods. In the next section, we will review present value concepts and introduce capital investment methods that use present value.

Present Value Methods

An investment in fixed assets may be viewed as acquiring a series of net cash flows over a period of time. The period of time over which these net cash flows will be received may be an important factor in determining the value of an investment. Present value methods use both the amount and the timing of net cash flows in evaluating an investment. Before illustrating how these methods are used in capital investment analysis, we will review basic present value concepts.

Present Value Concepts   **Present value concepts** can be divided into the *present value of an amount* and the *present value of an annuity*. We describe and illustrate these two concepts next.

Present Value of an Amount. If you were given the choice, would you prefer to receive $1 now or $1 three years from now? You should prefer to receive $1 now, because you could invest the $1 and earn interest for three years. As a result, the amount you would have after three years would be greater than $1.

To illustrate, assume that on January 1, 2008, you invest $1 in an account that earns 12% interest compounded annually. After 1 year, the $1 will grow to $1.12 ($1 × 1.12), because interest of 12¢ is added to the investment. The $1.12 earns 12% interest for the second year. Interest earning interest is called *compounding*. By the end of the second year, the investment has grown to $1.254 ($1.12 × 1.12). By the end of the third year, the investment has grown to $1.404 ($1.254 × 1.12). Thus, if money is worth 12%, you would be equally satisfied with $1 on January 1, 2008, or $1.404 three years later. This is also illustrated below.

On January 1, 2008, what is the present value of $1.404 to be received on January 1, 2011? This is a present value question. The answer can be determined with the aid of a present value of $1 table. For example, the partial table in Exhibit 1 indicates that the present value of $1 to be received three years hence, with earnings compounded at the

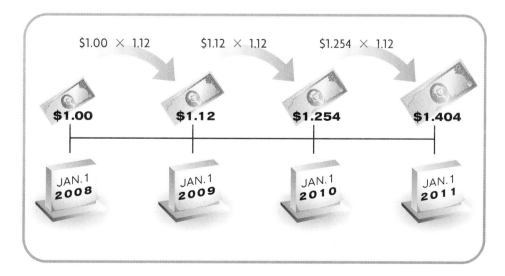

EXHIBIT 1   *Partial Present Value of $1 Table*

	Present Value of $1 at Compound Interest				
Year	6%	10%	12%	15%	20%
1	0.943	0.909	0.893	0.870	0.833
2	0.890	0.826	0.797	0.756	0.694
3	0.840	0.751	0.712	0.658	0.579
4	0.792	0.683	0.636	0.572	0.482
5	0.747	0.621	0.567	0.497	0.402
6	0.705	0.564	0.507	0.432	0.335
7	0.665	0.513	0.452	0.376	0.279
8	0.627	0.467	0.404	0.327	0.233
9	0.592	0.424	0.361	0.284	0.194
10	0.558	0.386	0.322	0.247	0.162

rate of 12% a year, is 0.712. Multiplying 0.712 by $1.404 yields $1, which is the present value that started the compounding process.[2]

Present Value of an Annuity.   An **annuity** is a series of equal net cash flows at fixed time intervals. Annuities are very common in business. Monthly rental, salary, and bond interest cash flows are all examples of annuities. The **present value of an annuity** is the sum of the present values of each cash flow. In other words, the present value of an annuity is the amount of cash that is needed today to yield a series of equal net cash flows at fixed time intervals in the future.

To illustrate, the present value of a $100 annuity for five periods at 12% could be determined by using the present value factors in Exhibit 1. Each $100 net cash flow could be multiplied by the present value of $1 at 12% factor for the appropriate period and summed to determine a present value of $360.50, as shown in the timeline at the top of next page.

Using a present value of an annuity table is a simpler approach. Exhibit 2 is a partial table of present value of annuity factors. These factors are merely the sum of the present value of $1 factors in Exhibit 1 for the number of annuity periods. Thus, 3.605 in the annuity table (Exhibit 2) is the sum of the five individual present value of $1 factors at 12%. Multiplying $100 by 3.605 yields the same amount ($360.50) that was determined in the preceding illustration by five successive multiplications.

Net Present Value Method   The **net present value method** analyzes capital investment proposals by comparing the initial cash investment with the present value of the net cash flows. It is sometimes called the *discounted cash flow method.* The interest rate (return) used in net present value analysis is set by management. This rate, sometimes termed the *hurdle rate,* is often based on such factors as the nature of the business, the purpose of the investment, the cost of securing funds for the investment, and the minimum desired rate of return. If the net present value of the cash flows expected from a proposed investment equals or exceeds the amount of the initial investment, the proposal is desirable.

To illustrate, assume a proposal to acquire $200,000 of equipment with an expected useful life of 5 years (no residual value) and a minimum desired rate of return of 10%. The present value of the net cash flow for each year is computed by multiplying the net cash flow for the year by the present value factor of $1 for that year. For example, the

[2]The present value factors in the table are rounded to three decimal places.

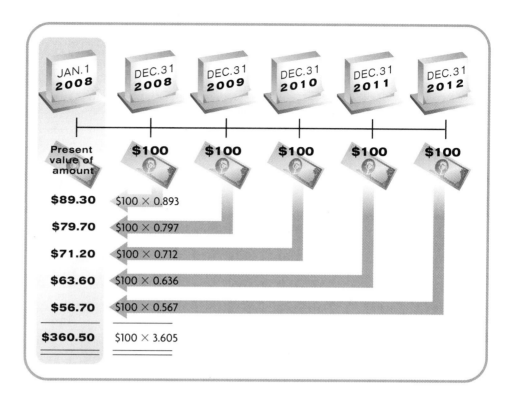

$70,000 net cash flow to be received on December 31, 2008, is multiplied by the present value of $1 for 1 year at 10% (0.909). Thus, the present value of the $70,000 is $63,630. Likewise, the $60,000 net cash flow on December 31, 2009, is multiplied by the present value of $1 for 2 years at 10% (0.826) to yield $49,560, and so on. The amount to be invested, $200,000, is then subtracted from the total present value of the net cash flows, $202,900, to determine the net present value, $2,900, as shown on the top of next page. The net present value indicates that the proposal is expected to recover the investment and provide more than the minimum rate of return of 10%.

When capital investment funds are limited and the alternative proposals involve different amounts of investment, it is useful to prepare a ranking of the proposals by using

EXHIBIT 2 *Partial Present Value of an Annuity Table*

	Present Value of an Annuity of $1 at Compound Interest				
Year	*6%*	*10%*	*12%*	*15%*	*20%*
1	0.943	0.909	0.893	0.870	0.833
2	1.833	1.736	1.690	1.626	1.528
3	2.673	2.487	2.402	2.283	2.106
4	3.465	3.170	3.037	2.855	2.589
5	4.212	3.791	3.605	3.353	2.991
6	4.917	4.355	4.111	3.785	3.326
7	5.582	4.868	4.564	4.160	3.605
8	6.210	5.335	4.968	4.487	3.837
9	6.802	5.759	5.328	4.772	4.031
10	7.360	6.145	5.650	5.019	4.192

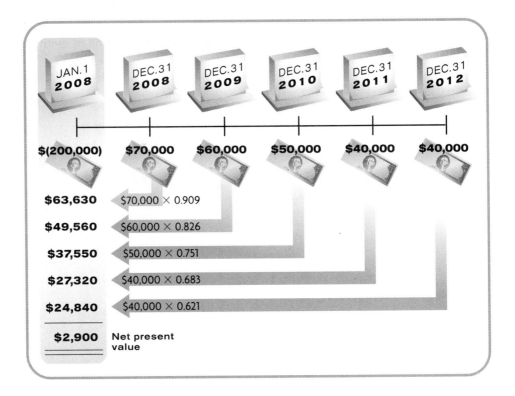

a present value index. The **present value index** is calculated by dividing the total present value of the net cash flow by the amount to be invested. The present value index for the investment in the previous illustration is calculated as follows:

$$\text{Present value index} = \frac{\textbf{Total present value of net cash flow}}{\textbf{Amount to be invested}}$$

$$= \frac{\$202{,}900}{\$200{,}000} = 1.0145$$

If a business is considering three alternative proposals and has determined their net present values, the present value index for each proposal is as follows:

	Proposal A	*Proposal B*	*Proposal C*
Total present value of net cash flow	$107,000	$86,400	$93,600
Amount to be invested	100,000	80,000	90,000
Net present value	$ 7,000	$ 6,400	$ 3,600
Present value index	1.07 ($107,000 ÷ $100,000)	1.08 ($86,400 ÷ $80,000)	1.04 ($93,600 ÷ $90,000)

Although Proposal A has the largest net present value, the present value indexes indicate that it is not as desirable as Proposal B. That is, Proposal B returns $1.08 present value per dollar invested, whereas Proposal A returns only $1.07. Proposal B requires an investment of $80,000, compared to an investment of $100,000 for Proposal A. Management should consider the possible use of the $20,000 difference between Proposal A and Proposal B investments before making a final decision.

An advantage of the net present value method is that it considers the time value of money. A disadvantage is that the computations are more complex than those for the methods that ignore present value. In addition, the net present value method assumes that the cash received from the proposal during its useful life can be reinvested at the rate of return used in computing the present value of the proposal. Because of changing economic conditions, this assumption may not always be reasonable.

Internal Rate of Return Method The **internal rate of return method** uses present value concepts to compute the rate of return from the net cash flows expected from capital investment proposals. This method is sometimes called the *time-adjusted rate of return method*. It is similar to the net present value method, in that it focuses on the present value of the net cash flows. However, the internal rate of return method starts with the net cash flows and, in a sense, works backward to determine the rate of return expected from the proposal.

To illustrate, assume that management is evaluating a proposal to acquire equipment costing $33,530. The equipment is expected to provide annual net cash flows of $10,000 per year for 5 years. If we assume a rate of return of 12%, we can calculate the present value of the net cash flows, using the present value of an annuity table in Exhibit 2. These calculations are shown in Exhibit 3.

EXHIBIT 3   *Net Present Value Analysis at 12%*

Annual net cash flow (at the end of each of 5 years)	$10,000
Present value of an annuity of $1 at 12% for 5 years (Exhibit 2)	× 3.605
Present value of annual net cash flows	$36,050
Less amount to be invested	33,530
Net present value	$ 2,520

In Exhibit 3, the $36,050 present value of the cash inflows, based on a 12% rate of return, is greater than the $33,530 to be invested. Therefore, the internal rate of return must be greater than 12%. Through trial-and-error procedures, the rate of return that equates the $33,530 cost of the investment with the present value of the net cash flows is determined to be 15%, as shown below.

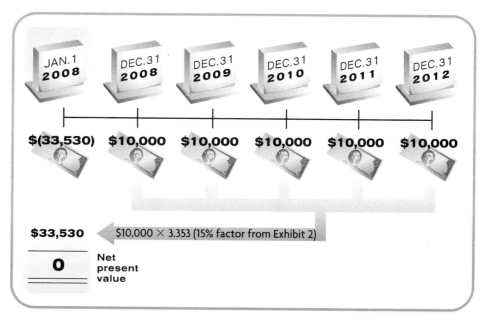

Such trial-and-error procedures are time-consuming. However, when equal annual net cash flows are expected from a proposal, as in the illustration, the calculations are simplified by using the following procedures:[3]

1. Determine a present value factor for an annuity of $1 by dividing the amount to be invested by the equal annual net cash flows, as follows:

$$\textbf{Present value factor for an annuity of \$1} = \frac{\textbf{Amount to be invested}}{\textbf{Equal annual net cash flows}}$$

2. In the present value of an annuity of $1 table, locate the present value factor determined in (1). First locate the number of years of expected useful life of the investment in the Year column, and then proceed horizontally across the table until you find the present value factor computed in (1).
3. Identify the internal rate of return by the heading of the column in which the present value factor in (2) is located.

To illustrate, assume that management is considering a proposal to acquire equipment costing $97,360. The equipment is expected to provide equal annual net cash flows of $20,000 for 7 years. The present value factor for an annuity of $1 is 4.868, calculated as follows:

$$\textbf{Present value factor for an annuity of \$1} = \frac{\textbf{Amount to be invested}}{\textbf{Equal annual net cash flows}}$$

$$= \frac{\$97,360}{\$20,000} = 4.868$$

For a period of 7 years, the partial present value of an annuity of $1 table indicates that the factor 4.868 is related to a percentage of 10%, as shown below. Thus, 10% is the internal rate of return for this proposal.

Present Value of an Annuity of $1 at Compound Interest			
Year	*6%*	*10%*	*12%*
1	0.943	0.909	0.893
2	1.833	1.736	1.690
3	2.673	2.487	2.402
4	3.465	3.170	3.037
5	4.212	3.791	3.605
6	4.917	4.355	4.111
7	5.582	4.868	4.564
8	6.210	5.335	4.968
9	6.802	5.759	5.328
10	7.360	6.145	5.650

If the minimum acceptable rate of return for similar proposals is 10% or less, then the proposed investment should be considered acceptable. When several proposals are considered, management often ranks the proposals by their internal rates of return. The proposal with the highest rate is considered the most desirable.

[3]Equal annual net cash flows are assumed in order to simplify the illustration. If the annual net cash flows are not equal, the calculations are more complex, but the basic concepts are the same.

Panera Bread Company The *Panera Bread Company* owns, operates, and franchises bakery-cafes throughout the United States. A recent annual report to the Securities and Exchange Commission (SEC Form 10-K) disclosed the following information about an average company-owned store:

Operating profit	$280,000
Depreciation	60,000
Investment	760,000

Assume that the operating profit and depreciation will remain unchanged for the next 10 years. In addition, assume that the investment salvage value will equal the original investment due to rising real estate values. The average rate of return and internal rate of return can then be estimated. The average rate of return on a company-owned store is:

$$\frac{\$280,000}{\$760,000} = 36.8\%$$

The internal rate of return is calculated by first determining the present value of an annuity of $1:

$$\text{Present value of an annuity of } \$1: \frac{\$760,000}{(\$280,000 + \$60,000)} = 2.24$$

For a period of 3 years, this factor implies an internal rate of return of nearly 15% (from Exhibit 2). However, if we more realistically assumed these cash flows for 10 years, Panera's company-owned stores generate an estimated internal rate of return of approximately 44% (from a spreadsheet calculation). Clearly, both investment evaluation methods indicate a highly successful business.

The primary advantage of the internal rate of return method is that the present values of the net cash flows over the entire useful life of the proposal are considered. In addition, by determining a rate of return for each proposal, all proposals are compared on a common basis. The primary disadvantage of the internal rate of return method is that the computations are more complex than for some of the other methods. However, spreadsheet software programs have internal rate of return functions that simplify the calculation. Also, like the net present value method, this method assumes that the cash received from a proposal during its useful life will be reinvested at the internal rate of return. Because of changing economic conditions, this assumption may not always be reasonable.

Factors That Complicate Capital Investment Analysis

Obj 3

List and describe factors that complicate capital investment analysis.

In the preceding discussion, we described four widely used methods of evaluating capital investment proposals. In practice, additional factors may have an impact on the outcome of a capital investment decision. In the following paragraphs, we discuss some of the most important of these factors: the federal income tax, unequal lives of alternative proposals, leasing, uncertainty, changes in price levels, and qualitative factors.

Income Tax

In many cases, the impact of the federal income tax on capital investment decisions can be material. For example, in determining depreciation for federal income tax purposes, useful lives that are much shorter than the actual useful lives are often used. Also, depreciation can be calculated by methods that approximate the 200-percent declining-balance method. Thus, depreciation for tax purposes often exceeds the depreciation for financial statement purposes in the early years of an asset's use. The tax reduction in these early years is offset by higher taxes in the later years, so that accelerated depreciation does not result in a long-run saving in taxes. However, the timing of the cash outflows for income taxes can have a significant impact on capital investment analysis.[4]

[4]The impact of income taxes on capital investment analysis is described and illustrated in advanced textbooks.

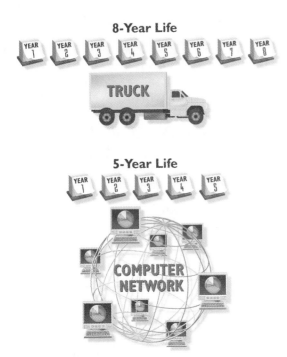

8-Year Life

TRUCK

5-Year Life

COMPUTER NETWORK

Unequal Proposal Lives

In the preceding discussion, the illustrations of the methods of analyzing capital investment proposals were based on the assumption that alternative proposals had the same useful lives. In practice, however, alternative proposals may have unequal lives. To illustrate, assume that alternative investments, a truck and computers, are being compared. The truck has a useful life of 8 years, and the computer network has a useful life of 5 years. Each proposal requires an initial investment of $100,000, and the company desires a rate of return of 10%. The expected cash flows and net present value of each alternative are shown in Exhibit 4. Because of the unequal useful lives of the two proposals, however, the net present values in Exhibit 4 are not comparable.

To make the proposals comparable for the analysis, they can be adjusted to end at the same time. This can be done by assuming that the truck is to be sold at the end of 5 years. The residual value of the truck must be estimated at the end of 5 years, and this value must then be included as a cash flow at that date. Both proposals will then cover 5 years, and net present value analysis can be used to compare the two proposals over the same 5-year period. If the truck's estimated residual value is $40,000 at the end of year 5, the net present value for the truck exceeds the net present value for the computers by $1,835 ($18,640 − $16,805), as shown in Exhibit 5. Therefore, the truck may be viewed as the more attractive of the two proposals.

Lease versus Capital Investment

Leasing fixed assets has become common in many industries. For example, hospitals often lease diagnostic and other medical equipment. Leasing allows a business to use fixed assets without spending large amounts of cash to purchase them. In addition, management may believe that a fixed asset has a high risk of becoming obsolete. This risk may be reduced by leasing rather than purchasing the asset. Also, the *Internal Revenue Code* allows the lessor (the owner of the asset) to pass tax deductions on to the lessee (the party leasing the asset). These provisions of the tax law have made leasing assets more attractive. For example, a company that pays $50,000 per year for leasing a $200,000 fixed asset with a life of 8 years is permitted to deduct from taxable income the annual lease payments.

In many cases, before a final decision is made, management should consider leasing assets instead of purchasing them. Normally, leasing assets is more costly than purchasing because the lessor must include in the rental price not only the costs associated with owning the assets but also a profit. Nevertheless, using the methods of evaluating capital investment proposals, management should consider whether it is more profitable to lease rather than purchase an asset.

Uncertainty

All capital investment analyses rely on factors that are uncertain. For example, the estimates related to revenues, expenses, and cash flows are uncertain. The long-term nature of capital investments suggests that some estimates are likely to involve uncertainty. Errors in one or more of the estimates could lead to incorrect decisions.

EXHIBIT 4 *Net Present Value Analysis—Unequal Lives of Proposals*

	Truck				Computers		
Year	Present Value of $1 at 10%	Net Cash Flow	Present Value of Net Cash Flow	Year	Present Value of $1 at 10%	Net Cash Flow	Present Value of Net Cash Flow
1	0.909	$ 30,000	$ 27,270	1	0.909	$ 30,000	$ 27,270
2	0.826	30,000	24,780	2	0.826	30,000	24,780
3	0.751	25,000	18,775	3	0.751	30,000	22,530
4	0.683	20,000	13,660	4	0.683	30,000	20,490
5	0.621	15,000	9,315	5	0.621	35,000	21,735
6	0.564	15,000	8,460	Total		$155,000	$116,805
7	0.513	10,000	5,130	Amount to be invested			100,000
8	0.467	10,000	4,670	Net present value			$ 16,805
Total		$155,000	$112,060				
Amount to be invested			100,000				
Net present value			$ 12,060				

EXHIBIT 5 *Net Present Value Analysis—Equalized Lives of Proposals*

Truck—Revised to 5-Year Life			
Year	Present Value of $1 at 10%	Net Cash Flow	Present Value of Net Cash Flow
1	0.909	$ 30,000	$ 27,270
2	0.826	30,000	24,780
3	0.751	25,000	18,775
4	0.683	20,000	13,660
5	0.621	15,000	9,315
5 (Residual value)	0.621	40,000	24,840
Total		$160,000	$118,640
Amount to be invested			100,000
Net present value			$ 18,640

Truck NPV > Computers NPV

Changes in Price Levels

In performing investment analysis, management must be concerned about changes in price levels. Price levels may change due to **inflation**, which occurs when general price levels are rising. Thus, while general prices are rising, the returns on an investment must exceed the rising price level, or else the cash returned on the investment becomes less valuable over time.

Price levels may also change for foreign investments as the result of currency exchange rates. **Currency exchange rates** are the rates at which currency in another country can be exchanged for U.S. dollars. If the amount of local dollars that can be exchanged for one U.S. dollar increases, then the local currency is said to be weakening to the dollar. Thus, if a company made an investment in another country where the local currency

INTEGRITY, OBJECTIVITY, AND ETHICS IN BUSINESS

Assumption Fudging

The results of any capital budgeting analysis depend on many subjective estimates, such as the cash flows, discount rate, time period, and total investment amount. The results of the analysis should be used to either support or reject a project. Capital budgeting should not be used in reverse. That is, the analyst should not work backward, filling in assumed numbers that will produce the desired net present value. Such a reverse approach reduces the credibility of the entire process.

was weakening, it would adversely impact the return on that investment as expressed in U.S. dollars. This is because the expected amount of local currency returned on the investment would purchase fewer U.S. dollars.

Management should attempt to anticipate future price levels and consider their effects on the estimates used in capital investment analyses. Changes in anticipated price levels could significantly affect the analyses.

Qualitative Considerations

Some benefits of capital investments are qualitative in nature and cannot be easily estimated in dollar terms. If management does not consider these qualitative considerations, the quantitative analyses may suggest rejecting a worthy investment.

Qualitative considerations in capital investment analysis are most appropriate for strategic investments. Strategic investments are those that are designed to affect a company's long-term ability to generate profits. Strategic investments often have many uncertainties and intangible benefits. Unlike capital investments that are designed to cut costs, strategic investments have very few "hard" savings. Instead, they may affect future revenues, which are difficult to estimate. An example of a strategic investment is *Nucor's* decision to be the first to invest in a new continuous casting technology that had the potential to make thin gauge sheet steel and thus open new product markets. Nucor's new investment was justified more on the strategic importance of the investment than on the economic analysis. As it turned out, the investment was very successful.

Qualitative considerations that may influence capital investment analysis include product quality, manufacturing flexibility, employee morale, manufacturing productivity, and market opportunity. Many of these qualitative factors may be as important, if not more important, than the results of quantitative analysis.

Obj 4

Diagram the capital rationing process.

Capital Rationing

Funding for capital projects may be obtained from issuing bonds or stock or from operating cash. **Capital rationing** is the process by which management allocates these funds among competing capital investment proposals. In this process, management often uses a combination of the methods described in this chapter. Exhibit 6 portrays the capital rationing decision process.

In capital rationing, alternative proposals are initially screened by establishing minimum standards for the cash payback and the average rate of return. The proposals that survive this screening are further analyzed, using the net present value and internal rate of return methods. Throughout the capital rationing process, qualitative factors related to each proposal should also be considered. For example, the acquisition of new, more

EXHIBIT 6 *Capital Rationing Decision Process*

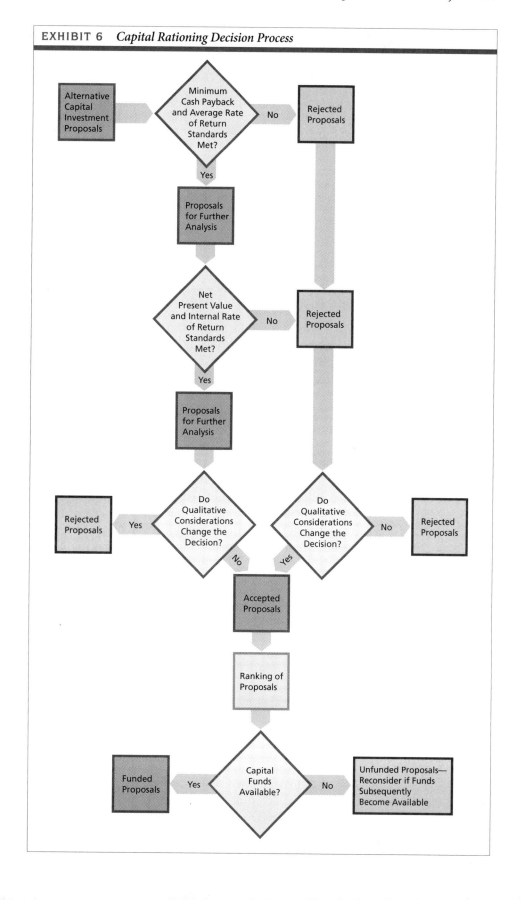

HOW BUSINESSES MAKE MONEY

Intel's "Capacity Is Strategy"

Andy Grove, Chairman of **Intel Corporation**, has stated, "You know that saying, 'The Internet changes everything'? People now are backing away from it; but I say, just wait five years. Hundreds of billions of dollars we now spend on voice telecommunications will become a freebie—just like [Cisco CEO] John Chambers has said. . . . The entire entertainment industry will be digitally distributed over broadband networks. [Media companies are] going to tip over, because one of them, with its back to the wall, will make the transition, and the others will have to follow. . . . Houses will be wireless, broadband will be delivered wirelessly, and home and portable computers and consumer electronics are going to be built to facilitate all of the above. Okay, it hasn't happened in the first five years; it's going to take ten. And there will be a lot of pain for some. But it will happen, and we'll all benefit."

Intel Corporation is betting $10 billion on four state-of-the-art computer chip factories (fabs) that Andy Grove's vision of the future is true. Intel's management believes that "capacity is strategy." As Grove says, "Henry Ford used it to revolutionize the automobile industry; the Japanese did it to push us out of the memory-chip business 25 years ago; we used it a decade ago to ignite the PC industry. Now we're using it again so we can broaden our business beyond the PC." By having the most capacity of the latest technology, Intel believes that it will be able to have the lowest cost and highest quality chip products. These new plants will produce chips that embed wireless technology, dubbed the "Radio Free Intel" strategy. Electronic devices having these new chips will be able to search and connect to wireless networks effortlessly and continuously, thus providing consumers ready access to broadband services. Intel is making a bold move. But this is not new. Over the years, Intel has made huge investments in its chip factories. As Grove has said, "Our fabs are fields of dreams. We build them and hope people will come." So far, Intel has been right.

Source: "Intel's $10 Billion Gamble," *Fortune*, November 11, 2002.

---

efficient equipment that eliminates several jobs could lower employee morale to a level that could decrease overall plant productivity. Alternatively, new equipment might improve the quality of the product and thus increase consumer satisfaction and sales.

The final steps in the capital rationing process are ranking the proposals according to management's criteria, comparing the proposals with the funds available, and selecting the proposals to be funded. Funded proposals are included in the *capital expenditures budget* to aid the planning and financing of operations. Unfunded proposals may be reconsidered if funds later become available.

Key Points

1. **Explain the nature and importance of capital investment analysis.**

   Capital investment analysis is the process by which management plans, evaluates, and controls investments involving fixed assets. Capital investment analysis is important to a business because such investments affect profitability for a long period of time.

2. **Evaluate capital investment proposals, using the following methods: average rate of return,** cash payback, net present value, and internal rate of return.

   The average rate of return method measures the expected profitability of an investment in fixed assets. It is calculated using the following formula:

   $$\text{Average rate of return} = \frac{\text{Estimated average annual income}}{\text{Average investment}}$$

   The expected period of time that will pass between the date of an investment and the complete recovery in cash (or equivalent) of the amount invested is the cash payback period. Investment proposals with the shortest cash payback are considered the most desirable.

The net present value method uses present values to compute the net present value of the cash flows expected from a proposal. The net present value of the cash flows are then compared across proposals. The present value of a cash flow is computed by looking up the present value of $1 from a table of present values and multiplying it by the amount of the future cash flow, as shown in the text.

The internal rate of return method uses present values to compute the rate of return from the net cash flows expected from capital investment proposals. When equal annual net cash flows are expected from a proposal, the computations are simplified by using a table of the present value of an annuity, as shown in the text.

3. **List and describe factors that complicate capital investment analysis.**

Factors that may complicate capital investment analysis include the impact of the federal income tax, unequal lives of alternative proposals, leasing, uncertainty, changes in price levels, and qualitative considerations. A brief description of the effect of each of these factors appears in the text.

4. **Diagram the capital rationing process.**

Capital rationing refers to the process by which management allocates available investment funds among competing capital investment proposals. A diagram of the capital rationing process appears in Exhibit 6.

Key Terms

Annuity	Currency exchange rate	Present value concept
Average rate of return	Inflation	Present value index
Capital investment analysis	Internal rate of return method	Present value of an annuity
Capital rationing	Net present value method	Time value of money concept
Cash payback period		

Illustrative Problem

The capital investment committee of Hopewell Company is currently considering two projects. The estimated income from operations and net cash flows expected from each project are as follows:

	Project A		Project B	
Year	Income from Operations	Net Cash Flow	Income from Operations	Net Cash Flow
1	$ 6,000	$ 22,000	$13,000	$ 29,000
2	9,000	25,000	10,000	26,000
3	10,000	26,000	8,000	24,000
4	8,000	24,000	8,000	24,000
5	11,000	27,000	3,000	19,000
	$44,000	$124,000	$42,000	$122,000

Each project requires an investment of $80,000. Straight-line depreciation will be used, and no residual value is expected. The committee has selected a rate of 15% for purposes of the net present value analysis.

(continued)

Instructions

1. Compute the following:
   a. The average rate of return for each project.
   b. The net present value for each project. Use the present value of $1 table appearing in this chapter.
2. Why is the net present value of Project B greater than Project A, even though its average rate of return is less?
3. Prepare a summary for the capital investment committee, advising it on the relative merits of the two projects.

Solution

1. a. Average rate of return for Project A:

$$\frac{\$44,000 \div 5}{(\$80,000 + \$0) \div 2} = 22\%$$

   Average rate of return for Project B:

$$\frac{\$42,000 \div 5}{(\$80,000 + \$0) \div 2} = 21\%$$

   b. Net present value analysis:

Year	Present Value of $1 at 15%	Net Cash Flow Project A	Net Cash Flow Project B	Present Value of Net Cash Flow Project A	Present Value of Net Cash Flow Project B
1	0.870	$ 22,000	$ 29,000	$19,140	$25,230
2	0.756	25,000	26,000	18,900	19,656
3	0.658	26,000	24,000	17,108	15,792
4	0.572	24,000	24,000	13,728	13,728
5	0.497	27,000	19,000	13,419	9,443
Total		$124,000	$122,000	$82,295	$83,849
Amount to be invested				80,000	80,000
Net present value				$ 2,295	$ 3,849

2. Project B has a lower average rate of return than Project A because Project B's total income from operations for the 5 years is $42,000, which is $2,000 less than Project A's. Even so, the net present value of Project B is greater than that of Project A, because Project B has higher cash flows in the early years.
3. Both projects exceed the selected rate established for the net present value analysis. Project A has a higher average rate of return, but Project B offers a larger net present value. Thus, if only one of the two projects can be accepted, Project B would be the more attractive.

Self-Examination Questions   *(Answers appear at end of chapter.)*

1. Methods of evaluating capital investment proposals that ignore present value include:
   A. average rate of return
   B. cash payback
   C. both A and B
   D. neither A nor B

2. Management is considering a $100,000 investment in a project with a 5-year life and no residual value. If the total income from the project is expected to be $60,000 and recognition is given to the effect of straight-line depreciation on the investment, the average rate of return is:
   A. 12%
   B. 24%
   C. 60%
   D. 75%

3. The expected period of time that will elapse between the date of a capital investment and the complete recovery of the amount of cash invested is called:
   A. the average rate of return period
   B. the cash payback period
   C. the net present value period
   D. the internal rate of return period

4. A project that will cost $120,000 is estimated to generate cash flows of $25,000 per year for 8 years. What is the net present value of the project, assuming a 10% required rate of return? (Use the present value tables in this chapter.)
   A. $11,675   C. $75,000
   B. $13,375   D. $95,000

5. A project is estimated to generate cash flows of $40,000 per year for 10 years. The cost of the project is $226,000. What is the internal rate of return for this project?
   A. 8%   C. 12%
   B. 10%   D. 15%

Class Discussion Questions

1. What are the principal objections to the use of the average rate of return method in evaluating capital investment proposals?

2. Discuss the principal limitations of the cash payback method for evaluating capital investment proposals.

3. Why would the average rate of return differ from the internal rate of return on the same project?

4. What information does the cash payback period ignore that is included by the net present value method?

5. Your boss has suggested that a one-year payback period is the same as a 100% average rate of return. Do you agree?

6. Why would the cash payback method understate the attractiveness of a project with a large salvage value?

7. Why would the use of the cash payback period for analyzing the financial performance of theatrical releases from a motion picture production studio be supported over the net present value method?

8. A net present value analysis used to evaluate a proposed equipment acquisition indicated a $7,900 net present value. What is the meaning of the $7,900 as it relates to the desirability of the proposal?

9. Two projects have an identical net present value of $9,000. Are both projects equal in desirability?

10. What are the major disadvantages of the use of the net present value method of analyzing capital investment proposals?

11. What are the major disadvantages of the use of the internal rate of return method of analyzing capital investment proposals?

12. What provision of the Internal Revenue Code is especially important to consider in analyzing capital investment proposals?

13. What method can be used to place two capital investment proposals with unequal useful lives on a comparable basis?

14. What are the major advantages of leasing a fixed asset rather than purchasing it?

15. Give an example of a qualitative factor that should be considered in a capital investment analysis related to acquiring automated factory equipment.

16. **Monsanto**, a large chemical and fibers company, invested $37 million in state-of-the-art systems to improve process control, laboratory automation, and local area network (LAN) communications. The investment was justified not merely on cost savings but also on the basis of qualitative considerations. Monsanto management viewed the investment as a critical element in achieving its vision of the future. What qualitative and quantitative considerations do you believe Monsanto would have used in its strategic evaluation of these investments?

Exercises

E15-1

Average rate of return

Obj 2

✓ Testing equipment, 10%

The following data are accumulated by Green Mountain Testing Services Inc. in evaluating two competing capital investment proposals:

	Testing Equipment	*Centrifuge*
Amount of investment	$34,000	$40,000
Useful life	6 years	8 years
Estimated residual value	0	0
Estimated total income over the useful life	$10,200	$14,000

Determine the expected average rate of return for each proposal.

E15-2

Average rate of return—cost savings

Obj 2

International Fabricators Inc. is considering an investment in equipment that will replace direct labor. The equipment has a cost of $85,000, with a $5,000 residual value and a 10-year life. The equipment will replace one employee who has an average wage of $23,000 per year. In addition, the equipment will have operating and energy costs of $6,000 per year.

Determine the average rate of return on the equipment, giving effect to straight-line depreciation on the investment.

E15-3

Average rate of return—new product

Obj 2

✓ Average annual income, $216,000

Airwave Communications Inc. is considering an investment in new equipment that will be used to manufacture a PDA (personal data assistant). The PDA is expected to generate additional annual sales of 4,800 units at $350 per unit. The equipment has a cost of $910,000, residual value of $50,000, and a 10-year life. The equipment can only be used to manufacture the PDA. The cost to manufacture the PDA is shown below.

Cost per unit:	
Direct labor	$ 52.00
Direct materials	195.00
Factory overhead (including depreciation)	58.00
Total cost per unit	$305.00

Determine the average rate of return on the equipment.

E15-4

Calculate cash flows

Obj 2

✓ Year 1: ($62,725)

Gardeneer Inc. is planning to invest $184,000 in a new garden tool that is expected to generate additional sales of 7,500 units at $38 each. The $184,000 investment includes $54,000 for initial launch-related expenses and $130,000 for equipment that has a 10-year life and a $17,500 residual value. Selling expenses related to the new product are expected to be 6% of sales revenue. The cost to manufacture the product includes the following per-unit costs:

Direct labor	$ 6.00
Direct materials	11.75
Fixed factory overhead—depreciation	1.50
Variable factory overhead	1.80
Total	$21.05

Determine the net cash flows for the first year of the project, for years 2–9, and for the last year of the project.

E15-5

Cash payback period

Obj 2

✓ Proposal 1: 5 years

First Union Bank Corporation is evaluating two capital investment proposals for a drive-up ATM kiosk, each requiring an investment of $300,000 and each with an eight-year life and expected total net cash flows of $480,000. Location 1 is expected to provide equal annual net cash flows of $60,000, and Location 2 is expected to have the following unequal annual net cash flows:

Year 1	$90,000	Year 5	$45,000
Year 2	80,000	Year 6	45,000
Year 3	65,000	Year 7	45,000
Year 4	65,000	Year 8	45,000

Determine the cash payback period for both proposals.

E15-6

Cash payback method

Obj 2

SPREADSHEET

✓ a. Cosmetics: 4 years

Family Care Products Company is considering an investment in one of two new product lines. The investment required for either product line is $600,000. The net cash flows associated with each product are as follows:

Year	Liquid Soap	Cosmetics
1	$120,000	$165,000
2	120,000	155,000
3	120,000	140,000
4	120,000	140,000
5	120,000	110,000
6	120,000	90,000
7	120,000	80,000
8	120,000	80,000
Total	$960,000	$960,000

a. Recommend a product offering to Family Care Products Company, based on the cash payback period for each product line.

b. Why is one product line preferred over the other, even though they both have the same total net cash flows through eight periods?

E15-7

Net present value method

Obj 2

✓ a. NPV ($7,700)

The following data are accumulated by Zadoc Company in evaluating the purchase of $370,000 of equipment, having a four-year useful life:

	Net Income	Net Cash Flow
Year 1	$ 67,500	$160,000
Year 2	47,500	140,000
Year 3	(12,500)	80,000
Year 4	(12,500)	80,000

a. Assuming that the desired rate of return is 12%, determine the net present value for the proposal. Use the table of the present value of $1 appearing in Exhibit 1 of this chapter.

b. Would management be likely to look with favor on the proposal? Explain.

E15-8

Net present value method

Obj 2

SPREADSHEET

✓ a. $21 million

Metro-Goldwyn-Mayer Studios Inc. (MGM), is a major producer and distributor of theatrical and television filmed entertainment. Regarding theatrical films, MGM states, "Our feature films are exploited through a series of sequential domestic and international distribution channels, typically beginning with theatrical exhibition. Thereafter, feature films are first made available for home video generally six months after theatrical release; for pay television, one year after theatrical release; and for syndication, approximately three to five years after theatrical release."

(continued)

Assume that MGM releases a film during early 2009 at a cost of $115 million, and releases it halfway through the year. During the last half of 2009, the film earns revenues of $140 million at the box office. The film requires $45 million of advertising during the release. One year later, by the end of 2010, the film is expected to earn MGM net cash flows from home video sales of $36 million. By the end of 2011, the film is expected to earn MGM $19 million from pay TV; and by the end of 2012, the film is expected to earn $4 million from syndication.

a. Determine the net present value of the film as of the beginning of 2009 if the desired rate of return is 20%. To simplify present value calculations, assume all annual net cash flows occur at the end of each year. Use the table of the present value of $1 appearing in Exhibit 1 of this chapter. Round to the nearest whole million dollars.

b. Under the assumptions provided here, is the film expected to be financially successful?

E15-9

Net present value method—annuity

Obj 2

✓ a. $50,000

Maddox Excavation Company is planning an investment of $205,000 for a bulldozer. The bulldozer is expected to operate for 1,600 hours per year for five years. Customers will be charged $95 per hour for bulldozer work. The bulldozer operator is paid an hourly wage of $25 per hour. The bulldozer is expected to require annual maintenance costing $14,000. The bulldozer uses fuel that is expected to cost $30 per hour of bulldozer operation.

a. Determine the equal annual net cash flows from operating the bulldozer.

b. Determine the net present value of the investment, assuming that the desired rate of return is 10%. Use the table of present values of an annuity of $1 in the chapter. Round to the nearest dollar.

c. Should Maddox invest in the bulldozer, based on this analysis?

E15-10

Net present value— unequal lives

Objs 2, 3

SPREADSHEET

✓ Net present value, Apartment Complex, $117,500

Blue Ridge Development Company has two competing projects: an apartment complex and an office building. Both projects have an initial investment of $720,000. The net cash flows estimated for the two projects are as follows:

	Net Cash Flow	
Year	Apartment Complex	Office Building
1	$240,000	$280,000
2	210,000	280,000
3	210,000	265,000
4	160,000	265,000
5	150,000	
6	120,000	
7	90,000	
8	60,000	

The estimated residual value of the apartment complex at the end of year 4 is $420,000.

Determine which project should be favored, comparing the net present values of the two projects and assuming a minimum rate of return of 15%. Use the table of present values in the chapter.

E15-11

Net present value method

Obj 2

✓ a. Net investment, $1,693,000

IHOP Corp. franchises breakfast-oriented restaurants throughout North America. The average development costs for a new restaurant were reported by IHOP as follows:

Land	$ 667,000
Building	800,000
Equipment	341,000
Site improvements	185,000
Total	$1,993,000

IHOP develops and owns the restaurant properties. IHOP indicates that the franchisee pays an initial franchise fee of $300,000 for a newly developed restaurant. IHOP also receives revenues from the franchisee as follows: (1) a royalty equal to 4.5% of the restaurant's sales; (2) income from the leasing of the restaurant and related equipment; and (3) revenue from the sale of certain proprietary products, primarily pancake mixes.

IHOP reported that franchise operators earned annual revenues averaging $1,500,000 per restaurant. Assume that the net cash flows received by IHOP for lease payments and sale of proprietary products (items 2 and 3 above) average $200,000 per year per restaurant, for 10 years. Assume further that the franchise operator can purchase the property for $700,000 at the end of the lease term.

Determine IHOP's:

a. Net investment (development cost less initial franchise fee) to develop a restaurant.
b. Net present value for a new restaurant, assuming a 10-year life, no change in annual revenues, and a 12% desired rate of return. Use the present value tables appearing in Exhibits 1 and 2 in this chapter.

E15-12

Net present value method

Obj 2

✓ a. $95,950,000

Carnival Corporation has recently placed into service some of the largest cruise ships in the world. One of these ships, the *Carnival Glory*, can hold up to 3,000 passengers and cost $530 million to build. Assume the following additional information:

- The average occupancy rate for the new ship is estimated to be 85% of capacity.
- There will be 300 cruise days per year.
- The variable expenses per passenger are estimated to be $80 per cruise day.
- The revenue per passenger is expected to be $310 per cruise day.
- The fixed expenses for running the ship, other than depreciation, are estimated to be $80,000,000 per year.
- The ship has a service life of 10 years, with a salvage value of $90,000,000 at the end of 10 years.

a. Determine the annual net cash flow from operating the cruise ship.
b. Determine the net present value of this investment, assuming a 12% minimum rate of return. Use the present value tables provided in the chapter in determining your answer.
c. Assume that Carnival Corp. decided to increase its price so that the revenue increased to $320 per passenger per cruise day. Would this allow Carnival Corp. to earn a 15% rate of return on the cruise ship investment, assuming no change in any of the other assumptions? Use the present value tables provided in the chapter in determining your answer.

E15-13

Present value index

Obj 2

✓ Location A, 0.95

Drive By Doughnuts has computed the net present value for capital expenditure locations A and B, using the net present value method. Relevant data related to the computation are as follows:

	Location A	Location B
Total present value of net cash flow	$306,280	$177,660
Amount to be invested	322,400	164,500
Net present value	$ (16,120)	$ 13,160

Determine the present value index for each proposal.

E15-14

Net present value method and present value index

Obj 2

✓ b. Packing Machine, 1.09

MVP Sporting Goods Company is considering an investment in one of two machines. The sewing machine will increase productivity from sewing 120 baseballs per hour to sewing 180 per hour. The contribution margin is $0.80 per baseball. Assume that any increased production of baseballs can be sold. The second machine is an automatic packing machine for the golf ball line. The packing machine will reduce packing labor cost. The labor cost saved is equivalent to $24 per hour. The sewing machine will cost $354,300, have an eight-year life, and will operate for

(continued)

1,750 hours per year. The packing machine will cost $148,300, have an eight-year life, and will operate for 1,500 hours per year. MVP seeks a minimum rate of return of 15% on its investments.

a. Determine the net present value for the two machines. Use the table of present values of an annuity of $1 in the chapter. Round to the nearest dollar.
b. Determine the present value index for the two machines. Round to two decimal places.
c. If MVP has sufficient funds for only one of the machines and qualitative factors are equal between the two machines, in which machine should it invest?

E15-15

Average rate of return, cash payback period, net present value method

Obj 2

✓ b. 5 years

Southern Rail Inc. is considering acquiring equipment at a cost of $442,500. The equipment has an estimated life of 10 years and no residual value. It is expected to provide yearly net cash flows of $88,500. The company's minimum desired rate of return for net present value analysis is 12%.
　Compute the following:

a. The average rate of return, giving effect to straight-line depreciation on the investment.
b. The cash payback period.
c. The net present value. Use the table of the present value of an annuity of $1 appearing in this chapter. Round to the nearest dollar.

E15-16

Payback period, net present value analysis and qualitative considerations

Objs 2, 3

The plant manager of O'Brien Equipment Company is considering the purchase of a new robotic assembly plant. The new robotic line will cost $1,250,000. The manager believes that the new investment will result in direct labor savings of $250,000 per year for 10 years.

a. What is the payback period on this project?
b. What is the net present value, assuming a 10% rate of return?
c. What else should the manager consider in the analysis?

E15-17

Internal rate of return method

Obj 2

✓ a. 4.487

The internal rate of return method is used by Timberframe Renovations Inc. in analyzing a capital expenditure proposal that involves an investment of $62,818 and annual net cash flows of $14,000 for each of the eight years of its useful life.

a. Determine a present value factor for an annuity of $1 which can be used in determining the internal rate of return.
b. Using the factor determined in part (a) and the present value of an annuity of $1 table appearing in this chapter, determine the internal rate of return for the proposal.

E15-18

Internal rate of return method

Obj 2

IBM recently saved $250 million over three years by implementing supply chain software that reduced the cost of components used in its manufacture of computers. If we assume that the savings occurred equally over the three years and the cost of implementing the new software was $175,500,000, what would be the internal rate of return for this investment? Use the present value of an annuity of $1 table found in Exhibit 2 in determining your answer.

E15-19

Internal rate of return method—two projects

Obj 2

✓ a. Delivery truck, 10%

Southwest Chip Company is considering two possible investments: a delivery truck or a bagging machine. The delivery truck would cost $39,918 and could be used to deliver an additional 36,250 bags of taquitos chips per year. Each bag of chips can be sold for a contribution margin of $0.40. The delivery truck operating expenses, excluding depreciation, are $0.35 per mile for 18,000 miles per year. The bagging machine would replace an old bagging machine, and its net investment cost would be $49,920. The new machine would require three fewer hours of direct labor per day. Direct labor is $16 per hour. There are 250 operating days in the year. Both the truck and the bagging machine are estimated to have seven-year lives. The minimum rate of return is 11%. However, Southwest has funds to invest in only one of the projects.

a. Compute the internal rate of return for each investment. Use the table of present values of an annuity of $1 in the chapter.

b. Provide a memo to management with a recommendation.

E15-20

Net present value method and internal rate of return method

Obj 2

✓ a. ($6,606)

Buckeye Healthcare Corp. is proposing to spend $96,030 on an eight-year project that has estimated net cash flows of $18,000 per each of the eight years.

a. Compute the net present value, using a rate of return of 12%. Use the table of present values of an annuity of $1 in the chapter.

b. Based on the analysis prepared in part (a), is the rate of return (1) more than 12%, (2) 12%, or (3) less than 12%? Explain.

c. Determine the internal rate of return by computing a present value factor for an annuity of $1 and using the table of the present value of an annuity of $1 presented in the text.

E15-21

Identify error in capital investment analysis calculations

Obj 2

Integrated Technologies Inc. is considering the purchase of automated machinery that is expected to have a useful life of four years and no residual value. The average rate of return on the average investment has been computed to be 25%, and the cash payback period was computed to be 4.5 years.

Do you see any reason to question the validity of the data presented? Explain.

E15-22

Changing prices

Obj 3

Goodwell Foods Inc. invested $10,000,000 to build a plant in a foreign country. The labor and materials used in production are purchased locally. The plant expansion was estimated to produce an internal rate of return of 20% in U.S. dollar terms. Due to a currency crisis, the currency exchange rate between the local currency and the U.S. dollar doubled from 4 local units per U.S. dollar to 8 local units per U.S. dollar.

a. Assume that the plant produced and sold product in the local economy. Explain what impact this change in the currency exchange rate would have on the project's internal rate of return.

b. Assume that the plant produced product in the local economy but exported the product back to the United States for sale. Explain what impact the change in the currency exchange rate would have on the project's internal rate of return under this assumption.

Problems

P15-1

Average rate of return method, net present value method, and analysis

Obj 2

SPREADSHEET

✓ 1. a. 45.7%

The capital investment committee of Estate Landscaping Company is considering two capital investments. The estimated income from operations and net cash flows from each investment are as follows:

	Greenhouse		Skid Loader	
Year	Income from Operations	Net Cash Flow	Income from Operations	Net Cash Flow
1	$16,000	$ 30,000	$26,000	$ 40,000
2	16,000	30,000	21,000	35,000
3	16,000	30,000	16,000	30,000
4	16,000	30,000	11,000	25,000
5	16,000	30,000	6,000	20,000
	$80,000	$150,000	$ 80,000	$150,000

(continued)

Each project requires an investment of $70,000. Straight-line depreciation will be used, and no residual value is expected. The committee has selected a rate of 12% for purposes of the net present value analysis.

Instructions

1. Compute the following:
   a. The average rate of return for each investment. Round to one decimal place.
   b. The net present value for each investment. Use the present value of $1 table appearing in this chapter.
2. Prepare a brief report for the capital investment committee, advising it on the relative merits of the two investments.

P15-2

Cash payback period, net present value method, and analysis

Obj 2

SPREADSHEET

✓ 1. b. Plant Expansion, $104,410

Unique Boutique Inc. is considering two investment projects. The estimated net cash flows from each project are as follows:

Year	Plant Expansion	Retail Store Expansion
1	$ 280,000	$ 260,000
2	260,000	260,000
3	230,000	250,000
4	260,000	250,000
5	270,000	280,000
Total	$1,300,000	$1,300,000

Each product requires an investment of $770,000. A rate of 15% has been selected for the net present value analysis.

Instructions

1. Compute the following for each project:
   a. Cash payback period.
   b. The net present value. Use the present value of $1 table appearing in this chapter.
2. Prepare a brief report advising management on the relative merits of each project.

   Not require

P15-3

Net present value method, present value index, and analysis

Obj 2

SPREADSHEET

✓ 2. Railcars, 0.97

Continental Railroad Company wishes to evaluate three capital investment proposals by using the net present value method. Relevant data related to the proposals are summarized as follows:

	Route Expansion	Acquire Railcars	New Maintenance Yard
Amount to be invested	$830,000	$480,000	$410,000
Annual net cash flows:			
Year 1	450,000	245,000	215,000
Year 2	400,000	220,000	205,000
Year 3	370,000	190,000	200,000

Instructions

1. Assuming that the desired rate of return is 20%, prepare a net present value analysis for each proposal. Use the present value of $1 table appearing in this chapter.
2. Determine a present value index for each proposal. Round to two decimal places.
3. Which proposal offers the largest amount of present value per dollar of investment? Explain.

P15-4

Net present value method, internal rate of return method, and analysis

Obj 2

✓ 1. a. Generating unit, $191,750

The management of Genco Utilities Inc. is considering two capital investment projects. The estimated net cash flows from each project are as follows:

Year	Generating Unit	Distribution Network Expansion
1	$650,000	$180,000
2	650,000	180,000
3	650,000	180,000
4	650,000	180,000

The generating unit requires an investment of $2,060,500, while the distribution network expansion requires an investment of $546,660. No residual value is expected from either project.

Instructions

1. Compute the following for each project:
   a. The net present value. Use a rate of 6% and the present value of an annuity of $1 table appearing in this chapter.
   b. A present value index. Round to two decimal places.
2. Determine the internal rate of return for each project by (a) computing a present value factor for an annuity of $1 and (b) using the present value of an annuity of $1 table appearing in this chapter.
3. What advantage does the internal rate of return method have over the net present value method in comparing projects?

P15-5

Evaluate alternative capital investment decisions

Objs 2, 3

SPREADSHEET

✓ 1. Project II, $72,626

The investment committee of Safe Hands Insurance Co. is evaluating two projects. The projects have different useful lives, but each requires an investment of $225,000. The estimated net cash flows from each project are as follows:

	Net Cash Flows	
Year	Project I	Project II
1	$70,000	$98,000
2	70,000	98,000
3	70,000	98,000
4	70,000	98,000
5	70,000	
6	70,000	

The committee has selected a rate of 12% for purposes of net present value analysis. It also estimates that the residual value at the end of each project's useful life is $0, but at the end of the fourth year, Project I's residual value would be $150,000.

Instructions

1. For each project, compute the net present value. Use the present value of an annuity of $1 table appearing in this chapter. (Ignore the unequal lives of the projects.)
2. For each project, compute the net present value, assuming that Project I is adjusted to a four-year life for purposes of analysis. Use the present value of $1 table appearing in this chapter.
3. Prepare a report to the investment committee, providing your advice on the relative merits of the two projects.

P15-6

Capital rationing decision involving four proposals

Objs 2, 4

SPREADSHEET

✓ 5. Proposal B, 1.18

Madison Capital Group is considering allocating a limited amount of capital investment funds among four proposals. The amount of proposed investment, estimated income from operations, and net cash flow for each proposal are as follows:

	Investment	Year	Income from Operations	Net Cash Flow
Proposal A:	$540,000	1	$ 42,000	$150,000
		2	42,000	150,000
		3	42,000	150,000
		4	(18,000)	90,000
		5	(18,000)	90,000
			$ 90,000	$630,000
Proposal B:	$250,000	1	$ 50,000	$100,000
		2	40,000	90,000
		3	30,000	80,000
		4	15,000	65,000
		5	15,000	65,000
			$150,000	$400,000
Proposal C:	$640,000	1	$ 92,000	$220,000
		2	82,000	210,000
		3	82,000	210,000
		4	62,000	190,000
		5	32,000	160,000
			$350,000	$990,000
Proposal D:	$310,000	1	$ 68,000	$130,000
		2	38,000	100,000
		3	(2,000)	60,000
		4	(2,000)	60,000
		5	(2,000)	60,000
			$100,000	$410,000

The company's capital rationing policy requires a maximum cash payback period of three years. In addition, a minimum average rate of return of 12% is required on all projects. If the preceding standards are met, the net present value method and present value indexes are used to rank the remaining proposals.

Instructions

1. Compute the cash payback period for each of the four proposals.
2. Giving effect to straight-line depreciation on the investments and assuming no estimated residual value, compute the average rate of return for each of the four proposals. Round to one decimal place.
3. Using the following format, summarize the results of your computations in parts (1) and (2). By placing a check mark in the appropriate column at the right, indicate which proposals should be accepted for further analysis and which should be rejected.

Proposal	Cash Payback Period	Average Rate of Return	Accept for Further Analysis	Reject
A				
B				
C				
D				

4. For the proposals accepted for further analysis in part (3), compute the net present value. Use a rate of 12% and the present value of $1 table appearing in this chapter. Round to the nearest dollar.

5. Compute the present value index for each of the proposals in part (4). Round to two decimal places.

6. Rank the proposals from most attractive to least attractive, based on the present values of net cash flows computed in part (4).

7. Rank the proposals from most attractive to least attractive, based on the present value indexes computed in part (5).

8. Based upon the analyses, comment on the relative attractiveness of the proposals ranked in parts (6) and (7).

Activities

A15-1

Ethics and professional conduct in business

ETHICS

Elisa McRae was recently hired as a cost analyst by Medlab Medical Supplies Inc. One of Elisa's first assignments was to perform a net present value analysis for a new warehouse. Elisa performed the analysis and calculated a present value index of 0.75. The plant manager, I. M. Madd, is very intent on purchasing the warehouse because he believes that more storage space is needed. I. M. Madd asks Elisa into his office and the following conversation takes place:

I. M.: Elisa, you're new here, aren't you?

Elisa: Yes, sir.

I. M.: Well, Elisa, let me tell you something. I'm not at all pleased with the capital investment analysis that you performed on this new warehouse. I need that warehouse for my production. If I don't get it, where am I going to place our output?

Elisa: Hopefully with the customer, sir.

I. M.: Now don't get smart with me.

Elisa: No, really, I was being serious. My analysis does not support constructing a new warehouse. The numbers don't lie, the warehouse does not meet our investment return targets. In fact, it seems to me that purchasing a warehouse does not add much value to the business. We need to be producing product to satisfy customer orders, not to fill a warehouse.

I. M.: Listen, you need to understand something. The headquarters people will not allow me to build the warehouse if the numbers don't add up. You know as well as I that many assumptions go into your net present value analysis. Why don't you relax some of your assumptions so that the financial savings will offset the cost?

Elisa: I'm willing to discuss my assumptions with you. Maybe I overlooked something.

I. M.: Good. Here's what I want you to do. I see in your analysis that you don't project greater sales as a result of the warehouse. It seems to me, if we can store more goods, then we will have more to sell. Thus, logically, a larger warehouse translates into more sales. If you incorporate this into your analysis, I think you'll see that the numbers will work out. Why don't you work it through and come back with a new analysis? I'm really counting on you on this one. Let's get off to a good start together and see if we can get this project accepted.

What is your advice to Elisa?

A15-2

Personal investment analysis

A Masters of Accountancy degree at Mid-State University would cost $15,000 for an additional fifth year of education beyond the bachelor's degree. Assume that all tuition is paid at the beginning of the year. A student considering this investment must evaluate the present value of cash flows from possessing a graduate degree versus holding only the undergraduate degree. Assume that the average student with an undergraduate degree is expected to earn an annual salary of $45,000 per year (assumed to be paid at the end of the year) for 10 years. Assume that the average student with a graduate Masters of Accountancy degree is expected to earn an annual salary

(continued)

of $57,000 per year (assumed to be paid at the end of the year) for nine years after graduation. Assume a minimum rate of return of 10%.

1. Determine the net present value of cash flows from an undergraduate degree. Use the present value tables provided in this chapter.
2. Determine the net present value of cash flows from a Masters of Accountancy degree, assuming no salary is earned during the graduate year of schooling.
3. What is the net advantage or disadvantage of pursuing a graduate degree under these assumptions?

A15-3

Investment analysis and qualitative considerations

The plant manager of Misson Creek Equipment Company is considering the purchase of a new robotic assembly plant. The new robotic line will cost $2,500,000. The manager believes that the new investment will result in direct labor savings of $625,000 per year for 10 years.

1. What is the payback period on this project?
2. What is the net present value, assuming a 15% rate of return?
3. What else should the manager consider in the analysis?

A15-4

Qualitative issues in investment analysis

The following are some selected quotes from senior executives:

> CEO, **Worthington Industries** (a high technology steel company): "We try to find the best technology, stay ahead of the competition, and serve the customer. . . . We'll make any investment that will pay back quickly . . . but if it is something that we really see as a must down the road, payback is not going to be that important."
>
> Chairman of **Amgen Inc.** (a biotech company): "You cannot really run the numbers, do net present value calculations, because the uncertainties are really gigantic. . . . You decide on a project you want to run, and then you run the numbers [as a reality check on your assumptions]. Success in a business like this is much more dependent on tracking rather than on predicting, much more dependent on seeing results over time, tracking and adjusting and readjusting, much more dynamic, much more flexible."
>
> Chief Financial Officer of **Merck & Co., Inc.** (a pharmaceutical company): ". . . at the individual product level—the development of a successful new product requires on the order of $230 million in R&D, spread over more than a decade—discounted cash flow style analysis does not become a factor until development is near the point of manufacturing scale-up effort. Prior to that point, given the uncertainties associated with new product development, it would be lunacy in our business to decide that we know exactly what's going to happen to a product once it gets out."

Explain the role of capital investment analysis for these companies.

A15-5

Analyze cash flows

You are considering an investment of $300,000 in either Project A or Project B for West Coast Studios Inc. In discussing the two projects with an advisor, you decided that, for the risk involved, an average rate of return of 12% on the cash investment would be required. For this purpose, you estimated the following economic factors for the projects:

	Project A	Project B
Useful life	4 years	4 years
Residual value	0	0
Net income:		
Year 1	$ 80,000	$ 40,000
2	65,000	55,000
3	55,000	73,000
4	40,000	79,200
	$240,000	$247,200

	Project A	*Project B*
Net cash flows:		
Year 1	$155,000	$115,000
2	140,000	130,000
3	130,000	148,000
4	115,000	154,200
	$540,000	$547,200

Although the average rate of return exceeded 12% on both projects, you have tentatively decided to invest in Project B because the rate was higher for Project B. You noted that the total cash flow from Project B is $547,200, which exceeds that of Project A by $7,200.

1. Determine the average rate of return for both projects.
2. Why is the timing of cash flows important in evaluating capital investments? Calculate the net present value of the two projects at a minimum rate of return of 12% to demonstrate the importance of net cash flows and their timing to these two projects. Round to the nearest dollar.

A15-6
Capital investment analysis

GROUP

In one group, find a local business, such as a copy shop, that rents time on desktop computers for an hourly rate. Determine the hourly rate. In the other group, determine the price of a mid-range desktop computer at **http://www.dell.com**. Combine this information from the two groups and perform a capital budgeting analysis. Assume that one student will use the computer for 35 hours per semester for the next three years. Also, assume that the minimum rate of return is 10%. In performing your analysis, use the present value factor of an annuity of $1 for 5% compounded for six semiannual periods of 5.07569.

Does your analysis support the student purchasing the computer?

Answers to Self-Examination Questions

1. **C** Methods of evaluating capital investment proposals that ignore the time value of money are categorized as methods that ignore present value. This category includes the average rate of return method (answer A) and the cash payback method (answer B).

2. **B** The average rate of return is 24% (answer B), determined by dividing the expected average annual earnings by the average investment, as follows:

$$\frac{\$60,000 \div 5}{(\$100,000 + \$0) \div 2} = 24\%$$

3. **B** Of the four methods of analyzing proposals for capital investments, the cash payback period (answer B) refers to the expected period of time required to recover the amount of cash to be invested. The average rate of return (answer A) is a measure of the anticipated profitability of a proposal. The net present value method (answer C) reduces the expected future net cash flows originating from a proposal to their present

values. The internal rate of return method (answer D) uses present value concepts to compute the rate of return from the net cash flows expected from the investment.

4. **B** The net present value is determined as follows:

Present value of $25,000 for 8 years at 10%	
($25,000 × 5.335)	$133,375
Less: Project cost	120,000
Net present value	$ 13,375

5. **C** The internal rate of return for this project is determined by solving for the present value of an annuity factor that when multiplied by $40,000 will equal $226,000. By division, the factor is:

$$\frac{\$226,000}{\$40,000} = 5.65$$

In Exhibit 2, scan along the n = 10 years row until finding the 5.65 factor. The column for this factor is 12%.

Double-Entry Accounting Systems

Throughout this text, we recorded and summarized transactions by using the accounting equation. Each financial statement item was represented in the equation. Transactions were recorded as pluses or minuses for each item affected by the transaction. Monitoring the equality of the accounting equation facilitated the detection and prevention of errors in processing transactions. That is, total assets must equal total liabilities plus stockholders' equity.

Double-entry accounting systems use these same concepts. Double-entry accounting systems use debit and credit rules as an additional control on the accuracy of recording transactions. In this appendix, we describe the basic elements of double-entry accounting systems.

In a double-entry accounting system, transactions are recorded in accounts. An **account**, in its simplest form, has three parts. First, each account has a title, which is the name of the item recorded in the account. Second, each account has a space for recording increases in the amount of the item. Third, each account has a space for recording decreases in the amount of the item. The account form presented here is called a **T account** because it resembles the letter *T*. The left side of the account is called the *debit side,* and the right side is called the *credit side.*[1]

Title	
Left side	Right side
debit	*credit*

Amounts entered on the left side of an account, regardless of the account title, are called **debits** to the account. When debits are entered in an account, the account is said to be *debited* (or charged). Amounts entered on the right side of an account are called **credits**, and the account is said to be *credited*. Debits and credits are sometimes abbreviated as *Dr.* and *Cr.*

In the T account for the cash account that follows, transactions involving cash receipts are listed on the debit side of the account. The transactions involving cash payments are listed on the credit side. If at any time the amount of the total cash receipts ($10,950) is needed, the entries on the debit side of the account are added. The

---

[1]The terms *debit* and *credit* are derived from the Latin *debere* and *credere*.

total of the cash payments on the credit side, $6,850 in the example, is determined in a similar manner. Subtracting the payments from the receipts, $10,950 – $6,850, determines the amount of cash on hand, $4,100. This amount is called the **balance of the account**. This balance should be identified as a debit balance in some way, such as showing the balance on the debit side of the account or simply listing it as a debit balance.

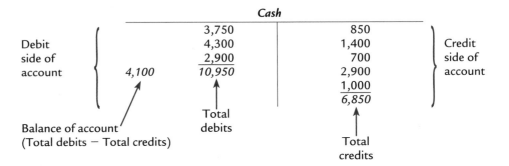

Rules of Debit and Credit

Why did we record increases in the cash account as debits and decreases as credits? The simple answer is to follow convention. That is, a standardized method of recording increases and decreases in accounts is essential so that businesses record transactions in a similar manner. If each business recorded transactions differently, the result would be chaotic and comparability between and among companies would be lost.

The standardized **rules of debit and credit** are shown in Exhibit 1. These rules are used by all businesses—from the corner gas station to the largest public corporation.

Exhibit 1 shows several important characteristics of the rules of debit and credit. First, the normal balance of an account is the side of the account used to record increases. Thus, the normal balance of an asset account is a debit balance, and the normal balance of a liability account is a credit balance. This characteristic is often useful in detecting errors in the recording process. That is, when an account normally having a debit balance actually has a credit balance, or vice versa, an error could have occurred or an unusual situation could exist.

EXHIBIT 1 *Rules of Debit and Credit*

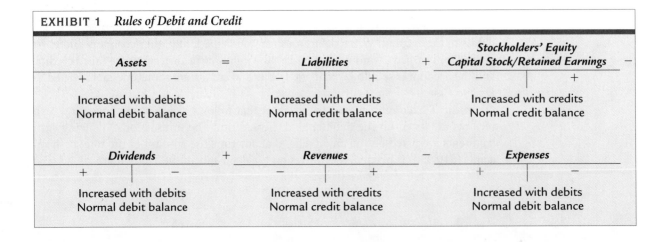

To illustrate, assume that at the end of the period, the cash account has a credit balance. In this case, either an error has occurred or the company has overdrawn its bank account. Likewise, if accounts payable has a debit balance, an error has occurred or the company has overpaid its accounts payable. On the other hand, a credit balance in the office equipment or land account can result only from an error in the recording process. That is, a company cannot have negative office equipment or land. Thus, the normal balances of accounts provide a degree of control in the recording process.

The second characteristic shown in Exhibit 1 is that accounts on the left side of the accounting equation (the assets side) are increased by debits and have normal debit balances while accounts on the right side of the accounting equation (liability and stockholders' equity side) are increased by credits and have normal credit balances. On the asset (left-hand) side of the equation, the only exception to the preceding relationship is that some asset accounts, called *contra asset accounts*, are normally increased by credits and have normal credit balances. As the words *contra asset* imply, these accounts offset the normal debit balances of asset accounts. For example, accumulated depreciation, an offset to plant assets, is increased by credits and has a normal credit balance. Thus, accumulated depreciation is a contra asset account.

On the liability and stockholders' equity (right-hand) side of the equation, the only exceptions to the preceding relationship are the dividend and expense accounts. The payment of dividends decreases stockholders' equity (retained earnings); thus, the dividends account is increased by debits and has a normal debit balance. In this sense, the dividends account can be thought of as a type of contra account to retained earnings. However, unlike contra asset accounts, the dividends account is closed to Retained Earnings at the end of the period. In this way, dividends for each period are recorded and accounted for separately.

Revenue increases stockholders' equity (retained earnings); thus, revenue accounts are increased by credits and have normal credit balances. In contrast, expenses decrease stockholders' equity (retained earnings). Thus, expense accounts are increased by debits and have a normal debit balance. Like dividends, expense accounts can be thought of as a type of contra account. In this case, expenses can be thought of as contra accounts to revenues. Like dividends, expense accounts are closed at the end of the period.

The third characteristic of the rules of debit and credit is that for each transaction, the total debits equal the total credits. That is, each transaction must be recorded so that the total debits for the transaction equal the total credits. For example, assume that a company pays cash of $500 for supplies. The asset account Supplies is debited (increased) by $500 and Cash is credited (decreased) by $500. Likewise, if the company provides services and receives $2,000 from customers, Cash is debited (increased) and Fees Earned is credited (increased) by $2,000. Debits equaling the credits for each transaction provides a degree of control in the recording process.

To summarize, each transaction is recorded under the rules shown in Exhibit 1. Under these rules, the total debits equal the total credits for each transaction. In addition, the equality of the debits and credits is built into the accounting equation: Assets = Liabilities + Stockholders' Equity.

The Journal

Each transaction is initially entered in chronological order in a record called a **journal**. In this way, the journal documents the history of the company. The process of recording transactions in the journal is called **journalizing**. The specific transaction record entered in the journal is called a **journal entry**.

In practice, a business can use a variety of formats for recording journal entries. It can use one all-purpose journal, sometimes called a **general journal**, or several journals. In the latter case, a **special journal** is designed to record a single type of transaction that occurs frequently. To simplify, we will use a basic, two-column general journal in the remainder of this appendix to illustrate the journalizing of transactions.

Assume that on November 1, 2009, Lee Dunbar organizes a corporation that will be known as Web Solutions. The first phase of Lee's business plan is to operate Web Solutions as a service business that provides assistance to individuals and small businesses in developing Web pages and in configuring and installing application software. Lee expects this initial phase of the business to last 1 to 2 years. During this period, Web Solutions will gather information on the software and hardware needs of customers. During the second phase of the business plan, Web Solutions will expand into an Internet-based retailer of software and hardware to individuals and small businesses.

To start the business, Lee deposits $25,000 in a bank account in the name of Web Solutions in return for shares of stock in the corporation. This first transaction increases Cash and Capital Stock by $25,000. The transaction is entered in the general journal by first listing the date, the title of the account to be debited, and then the amount of the debit. Next, the title of the account to be credited is listed below and to the right of the debit, followed by the amount to be credited. The resulting journal entry follows.

2009 Nov.	1	Cash	25 000 00	
		Capital Stock		25 000 00

The increase in the asset is debited to the cash account. The increase in stockholders' equity (capital stock) is credited to the capital stock account. As other assets are acquired, the increases are also recorded as debits to asset accounts. Likewise, other increases in stockholders' equity will be recorded as credits to stockholders' equity accounts.

Web Solutions entered into the following additional transactions during the remainder of November:

Nov. 5 Purchased land for $20,000, paying cash. The land is located in a new business park with convenient access to transportation facilities. Web Solutions plans to rent office space and equipment during the first phase of its business plan. During the second phase, the company plans to build an office and warehouse on the land.

10 Purchased supplies on account for $1,350.

18 Received $7,500 for services provided to customers for cash.

30 Paid expenses as follows: wages, $2,125; rent, $800; utilities, $450; and miscellaneous, $275.

30 Paid creditors on account, $950.

30 Paid stockholder (Lee Dunbar) dividends of $2,000.

The journal entries to record these transactions follow.

Nov.	5	Land	20 00 00	
		Cash		20 00 00
	10	Supplies	1 35 0 00	
		Accounts Payable		1 35 0 00
	18	Cash	7 50 0 00	
		Fees Earned		7 50 0 00
	30	Wages Expense	2 12 5 00	
		Rent Expense	8 00 00	
		Utilities Expense	4 50 00	
		Miscellaneous Expense	2 75 00	
		Cash		3 65 0 00
	30	Accounts Payable	9 50 00	
		Cash		9 50 00
	30	Dividends	2 00 0 00	
		Cash		2 00 0 00

Posting to the Ledger

As we discussed in the preceding section, a transaction is first recorded in the journal. The journal thus provides a chronological history of transactions. Periodically, the journal entries must be transferred to the accounts. The group of accounts for a business is called its **general ledger**. The list of accounts in the general ledger is called the **chart of accounts**. The accounts are normally listed in the order in which they appear in the financial statements, beginning with the balance sheet and concluding with the income statement. The chart of accounts for Web Solutions is shown in Exhibit 2.

EXHIBIT 2 *Chart of Accounts for Web Solutions*

Balance Sheet Accounts	*Income Statement Accounts*
Assets	**Revenue**
Cash	Fees Earned
Accounts Receivable	Rent Revenue
Supplies	**Expenses**
Prepaid Insurance	Wages Expense
Office Equipment	Rent Expense
Accumulated Depreciation	Depreciation Expense
Land	Utilities Expense
Liabilities	Supplies Expense
Accounts Payable	Insurance Expense
Wages Payable	Miscellaneous Expense
Unearned Rent	
Stockholders' Equity	
Capital Stock	
Retained Earnings	
Dividends	

The process of transferring the debits and credits from the journal entries to the accounts in the ledger is called **posting**. To illustrate the posting process, Web Solutions' November 1 transaction, along with its posting to the cash and capital stock accounts, is shown in Exhibit 3.

EXHIBIT 3 *Posting a Journal Entry*

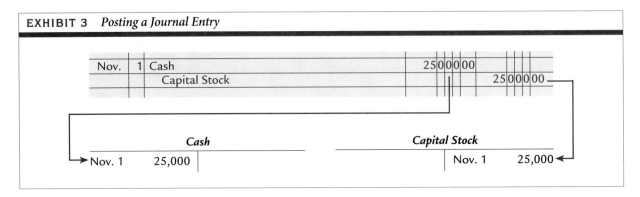

The debits and credits for each journal entry are posted to the accounts in the order in which they occur in the journal. In posting to the accounts, the date is entered followed by the amount of the entry. After the journal entries have been posted, the ledger becomes a chronological history of transactions by account. The posting of Web Solutions' remaining journal entries is shown later in Exhibit 7.

Trial Balance and Financial Statements

How can you be sure that you have not made an error in posting the debits and credits to the ledger? One way is to determine the equality of the debit and credit balances of accounts in the ledger. This equality should be proved at the end of each accounting period, if not more often. Such a proof, called a **trial balance**, can be in the form of a computer printout or as shown in Exhibit 4.

EXHIBIT 4 *Trial Balance*

WEB SOLUTIONS
Trial Balance
November 30, 2009

	Debit Balances	Credit Balances
Cash	5,900	
Supplies	1,350	
Land	20,000	
Accounts Payable		400
Capital Stock		25,000
Dividends	2,000	
Fees Earned		7,500
Wages Expense	2,125	
Rent Expense	800	
Utilities Expense	450	
Miscellaneous Expense	275	
	32,900	32,900

The trial balance does not provide complete proof of accuracy of the ledger. It indicates only that the debits and the credits are equal. This proof is of value, however, because errors often affect the equality of debits and credits. If the two totals of a trial balance are not equal, an error has occurred. In such a case, the error must be located and corrected before financial statements are prepared. This ability to detect errors in recording when the trial balance totals are not equal is the primary control feature and advantage of the double-entry accounting system.

The trial balance can be used as the source of data for preparing financial statements. The financial statements prepared in a double-entry accounting system are similar to those we described and illustrated in the text. For this reason, the financial statements are not illustrated in this appendix.

Review of Double-Entry Accounting

As a review of the double-entry accounting financial reporting system, we continue our illustration of Web Solutions. During December, assume that Web Solutions entered into the following transactions:

Dec. 1 Paid a premium of $2,400 for a comprehensive insurance policy covering liability, theft, and fire. The policy covers a 2-year period.

  1 Paid rent for December, $800. The company from which Web Solutions is renting its store space now requires the payment of rent on the first day of each month rather than at the end of the month.

  1 Received an offer from a local retailer to rent the land purchased on November 5. The retailer plans to use the land as a parking lot for its employees and customers. Web Solutions agreed to rent the land to the retailer for three months with the rent payable in advance. Web Solutions received $360 for three months' rent beginning December 1.

  4 Purchased office equipment on account from Executive Supply Co. for $1,800.

  6 Paid $180 for a newspaper advertisement.

  11 Paid creditors $400.

  13 Paid a receptionist and a part-time assistant $950 for two weeks' wages.

  16 Received $3,100 from fees earned for the first half of December.

  16 Earned fees on account totaling $1,750 for the first half of December.

  20 Paid $1,800 to Executive Supply Co. on the debt owed from the December 4 transaction.

  21 Received $650 from customers in payment of their accounts.

  23 Purchased $1,450 of supplies by paying $550 cash and charging the remainder on account.

  27 Paid the receptionist and the part-time assistant $1,200 for two weeks' wages.

  31 Paid $310 telephone bill for the month.

  31 Paid $225 electric bill for the month.

  31 Received $2,870 from fees earned for the second half of December.

  31 Earned fees on account totaling $1,120 for the second half of December.

  31 Paid dividends of $2,000 to stockholders.

The journal entries for the December transactions are shown in Exhibit 5. The posting of the journal entries to the ledger accounts is shown later in Exhibit 7.

EXHIBIT 5 *Journal Entries: December Transactions for Web Solutions*

Date		Account	Debit	Credit
Dec.	1	Prepaid Insurance	2 400 00	
		Cash		2 400 00
	1	Rent Expense	800 00	
		Cash		800 00
	1	Cash	360 00	
		Unearned Rent		360 00
	4	Office Equipment	1 800 00	
		Accounts Payable		1 800 00
	6	Miscellaneous Expense	180 00	
		Cash		180 00
	11	Accounts Payable	400 00	
		Cash		400 00
	13	Wages Expense	950 00	
		Cash		950 00
	16	Cash	3 100 00	
		Fees Earned		3 100 00
	16	Accounts Receivable	1 750 00	
		Fees Earned		1 750 00
	20	Accounts Payable	1 800 00	
		Cash		1 800 00
	21	Cash	650 00	
		Accounts Receivable		650 00
	23	Supplies	1 450 00	
		Cash		550 00
		Accounts Payable		900 00
	27	Wages Expense	1 200 00	
		Cash		1 200 00
	31	Utilities Expense	310 00	
		Cash		310 00
	31	Utilities Expense	225 00	
		Cash		225 00
	31	Cash	2 870 00	
		Fees Earned		2 870 00
	31	Accounts Receivable	1 120 00	
		Fees Earned		1 120 00
	31	Dividends	2 000 00	
		Cash		2 000 00

The trial balance shown in Exhibit 6 indicates that after posting December transactions to the general ledger, the total of the debit balances of accounts equals the total of the credit balances. Exhibit 7 shows the journal entries posted to the ledger accounts of Web Solutions.

EXHIBIT 6 *Trial Balance for Web Solutions*

WEB SOLUTIONS
Trial Balance
December 31, 2009

	Debit Balances	Credit Balances
Cash	2,065	
Accounts Receivable	2,220	
Supplies	2,800	
Prepaid Insurance	2,400	
Office Equipment	1,800	
Land	20,000	
Accounts Payable		900
Unearned Rent		360
Capital Stock		25,000
Dividends	4,000	
Fees Earned		16,340
Wages Expense	4,275	
Rent Expense	1,600	
Utilities Expense	985	
Miscellaneous Expense	455	
	42,600	42,600

EXHIBIT 7 *Ledger for Web Solutions*

Cash

Nov.	1	25,000	Nov.	5	20,000
	18	7,500		30	3,650
				30	950
				30	2,000
		32,500			26,600
Nov. 30	Bal.	5,900	Dec.	1	2,400
Dec.	1	360		1	800
	16	3,100		6	180
	21	650		11	400
	31	2,870		13	950
				20	1,800
				23	550
				27	1,200
				31	310
				31	225
				31	2,000
		12,880			10,815
Dec. 31	Bal.	2,065			

Supplies

Nov.	10	1,350	
Dec.	23	1,450	
Dec. 31	Bal.	2,800	

Prepaid Insurance

Dec.	1	2,400	

Land

Nov.	5	20,000	

Office Equipment

Dec.	4	1,800	

(continued)

EXHIBIT 7   *Ledger for Web Solutions (continued)*

Accounts Receivable				
Dec. 16	1,750	Dec. 21		650
31	1,120			—
Dec. 31 Bal.	2,220			

Accounts Payable				
Nov. 30		950	Nov. 10	1,350
			Nov. 30 Bal.	400
Dec. 11		400	Dec. 4	1,800
20		1,800	23	900
		2,200		3,100
			Dec. 31 Bal.	900

Unearned Rent		
	Dec. 1	360

Capital Stock		
	Nov. 1	25,000

Wages Expense	
Nov. 30	2,125
Dec. 13	950
27	1,200
Dec. 31 Bal.	4,275

Dividends		
Nov. 30	2,000	
Dec. 31	2,000	
Dec. 31 Bal.	4,000	

Rent Expense	
Nov. 30	800
Dec. 1	800
Dec. 31 Bal.	1,600

Fees Earned		
	Nov. 18	7,500
	Dec. 16	3,100
	16	1,750
	31	2,870
	31	1,120
	Dec. 31 Bal.	16,340

Utilities Expense	
Nov. 30	450
Dec. 31	310
31	225
Dec. 31 Bal.	985

Miscellaneous Expense	
Nov. 30	275
Dec. 6	180
Dec. 31 Bal.	455

Exercises

E1

Rules of debit and credit

The following table summarizes the rules of debit and credit. For each of the items (a) through (1), indicate whether the proper answer is a debit or a credit.

	Increase	Decrease	Normal Balance
Balance sheet accounts:			
Asset	(a)	Credit	(b)
Liability	(c)	(d)	Credit
Stockholders' Equity:			
Capital Stock	Credit	(e)	Credit
Retained Earnings	Credit	Debit	(f)
Dividends	(g)	(h)	Debit
Income statement accounts:			
Revenue	(i)	(j)	(k)
Expense	Debit	(l)	Debit

E2

Identifying transactions

Eos Co. is a travel agency. The nine transactions recorded by Eos during March 2008, its first month of operations, are indicated in the following T accounts:

Cash			
(1)	30,000	(2)	1,800
(7)	10,000	(3)	9,000
		(4)	3,050
		(6)	7,500
		(8)	2,500

Equipment	
(3)	24,000

Dividends	
(8)	2,500

Accounts Receivable			
(5)	15,000	(7)	10,000

Accounts Payable			
(6)	7,500	(3)	15,000

Service Revenue			
		(5)	15,000

Supplies			
(2)	1,800	(9)	1,050

Capital Stock			
		(1)	30,000

Operating Expenses		
(4)	3,050	
(9)	1,050	

Indicate for each debit and each credit: (a) whether an asset, liability, capital stock, dividends, revenue, or expense account was affected and (b) whether the account was increased (+) or decreased (−). Present your answers in the following form, with transaction (1) given as an example:

	Account Debited		Account Credited	
Transaction	Type	Effect	Type	Effect
(1)	asset	+	capital stock	+

E3

Journal entries

Based upon the T accounts in Exercise 2, prepare the nine journal entries from which the postings were made. Journal entry explanations may be omitted.

E4

Trial balance

SPREADSHEET

✓ Total Debit column: $52,500

Based upon the data presented in Exercise 2, prepare a trial balance, listing the accounts in their proper order.

E5

Normal entries for accounts

During the month, Witherspoon Labs Co. has a substantial number of transactions affecting each of the following accounts. State for each account whether it is likely to have (a) debit entries only, (b) credit entries only, or (c) both debit and credit entries.

1. Accounts Payable
2. Accounts Receivable
3. Cash
4. Fees Earned
5. Insurance Expense
6. Dividends
7. Supplies Expense

E6

Normal balances of accounts

Identify each of the following accounts of Sydney Services Co. as asset, liability, stockholders' equity, revenue, or expense, and state in each case whether the normal balance is a debit or a credit.

a.	Accounts Payable	f.	Fees Earned
b.	Accounts Receivable	g.	Office Equipment
c.	Capital Stock	h.	Rent Expense
d.	Dividends	i.	Supplies
e.	Cash	j.	Wages Expense

E7

Cash account balance

During the month, Harpoon Co. received $479,250 in cash and paid out $312,380 in cash.

a. Do the data indicate that Harpoon Co. earned $166,870 during the month? Explain.
b. If the balance of the cash account is $241,925 at the end of the month, what was the Cash balance at the beginning of the month?

E8

Account balances

✓ c. $5,100

a. On June 1, the cash account balance was $11,150. During June, cash receipts totaled $72,300 and the June 30 balance was $15,750. Determine the cash payments made during June.
b. On July 1, the accounts receivable account balance was $25,500. During July, $115,000 was collected from customers on account. Assuming the July 31 balance was $27,500, determine the fees billed to customers on account during July.
c. During December, $60,500 was paid to creditors on account, and purchases on account were $77,700. Assuming the December 31 balance of Accounts Payable was $22,300, determine the account balance on December 1.

E9

Transactions

The Boa Co. has the following accounts in its ledger: Cash; Accounts Receivable; Supplies; Office Equipment; Accounts Payable; Capital Stock; Retained Earnings; Dividends; Fees Earned; Rent Expense; Advertising Expense; Utilities Expense; Miscellaneous Expense.

Journalize the following selected transactions for October 2008 in a two-column journal. Journal entry explanations may be omitted.

Oct. 1. Paid rent for the month, $2,500.
 3. Paid advertising expense, $1,100.
 4. Paid cash for supplies, $725.
 6. Purchased office equipment on account, $7,500.
 10. Received cash from customers on account, $3,600.
 12. Paid creditor on account, $600.
 20. Paid dividends, $1,000.
 27. Paid cash for repairs to office equipment, $500.
 30. Paid telephone bill for the month, $195.
 31. Fees earned and billed to customers for the month, $20,150.
 31. Paid electricity bill for the month, $315.

E10

Journalizing and posting

On July 27, 2008, Colorcast Co. purchased $1,875 of supplies on account.

a. Journalize the July 27, 2008, transaction.
b. Prepare a T account for Supplies. Enter a debit balance of $735 as of July 1, 2008.
c. Prepare a T account for Accounts Payable. Enter a credit balance of $11,380 as of July 1, 2008.
d. Post the July 27, 2008, transaction to the accounts.

E11

Transactions and T accounts

SPREADSHEET

The following selected transactions were completed during August of the current year:

1. Billed customers for fees earned, $13,750.
2. Purchased supplies on account, $1,325.
3. Received cash from customers on account, $8,150.
4. Paid creditors on account, $800.

a. Journalize the above transactions in a two-column journal, using the appropriate number to identify the transactions. Journal entry explanations may be omitted.

b. Post the entries prepared in (a) to the following T accounts: Cash, Supplies, Accounts Receivable, Accounts Payable, Fees Earned. To the left of each amount posted in the accounts, place the appropriate number to identify the transactions.

E12

Trial balance

SPREADSHEET

✓ Total Credit column: $1,393,050

The accounts in the ledger of Matice Co. as of July 31, 2008, are listed in alphabetical order as follows. All accounts have normal balances. The balance of the cash account has been intentionally omitted.

Accounts Payable	$ 56,130	Notes Payable	$120,000
Accounts Receivable	112,500	Prepaid Insurance	9,000
Capital Stock	25,000	Rent Expense	180,000
Cash	?	Retained Earnings	234,920
Dividends	60,000	Supplies	6,300
Fees Earned	930,000	Supplies Expense	23,700
Insurance Expense	18,000	Unearned Rent	27,000
Land	255,000	Utilities Expense	124,500
Miscellaneous Expense	26,700	Wages Expense	525,000

Prepare a trial balance, listing the accounts in their proper order and inserting the missing figure for cash.

Problems

P1

Journal entries and trial balance

SPREADSHEET

On March 1, 2008, Kara Frantz established Mudcat Realty, which completed the following transactions during the month:

a. Kara Frantz transferred cash from a personal bank account to an account to be used for the business in exchange for capital stock, $15,000.
b. Paid rent on office and equipment for the month, $2,500.
c. Purchased supplies on account, $850.
d. Paid creditor on account, $400.
e. Earned sales commissions, receiving cash, $15,750.
f. Paid automobile expenses (including rental charge) for month, $2,400, and miscellaneous expenses, $600.
g. Paid office salaries, $3,250.
h. Determined that the cost of supplies used was $575.
i. Paid dividends of $1,000.

Instructions

1. Journalize entries for transactions (a) through (i), using the following account titles: Cash; Supplies; Accounts Payable; Capital Stock; Dividends; Sales Commissions; Office Salaries Expense; Rent Expense; Automobile Expense; Supplies Expense; Miscellaneous Expense. Explanations may be omitted.
2. Prepare T accounts, using the account titles in (1). Post the journal entries to these accounts, placing the appropriate letter to the left of each amount to identify the transactions. Determine the account balances, after all posting is complete. Accounts containing only a single entry do not need a balance.
3. Prepare a trial balance as of March 31, 2008.

P2

Journal entries and trial balance

SPREADSHEET

✓ 4. Total of Debit column: $430,650

Passport Realty acts as an agent in buying, selling, renting, and managing real estate. The trial balance on October 31, 2008, is shown on the following page.

(continued)

The following business transactions were completed by Passport Realty during November 2008:

Nov. 1. Paid rent on office for month, $5,000.
   2. Purchased office supplies on account, $1,750.
   5. Paid annual insurance premiums, $4,800.
   10. Received cash from clients on account, $52,000.
   15. Purchased land for a future building site for $90,000, paying $10,000 in cash and giving a note payable for the remainder.
   17. Paid creditors on account, $7,750.

Passport Realty
Trial Balance
October 31, 2008

	Debit Balances	Credit Balances
Cash	26,300	
Accounts Receivable	67,500	
Prepaid Insurance	3,000	
Office Supplies	1,800	
Land	—	
Accounts Payable		13,020
Unearned Rent		—
Notes Payable		—
Capital Stock		5,000
Retained Earnings		27,980
Dividends	2,000	
Fees Earned		260,000
Salary and Commission Expense	148,200	
Rent Expense	30,000	
Advertising Expense	17,800	
Automobile Expense	5,500	
Miscellaneous Expense	3,900	
	306,000	306,000

Nov. 20. Returned a portion of the office supplies purchased on November 2, receiving full credit for their cost, $250.
   23. Paid advertising expense, $2,100.
   27. Discovered an error in computing a commission; received cash from the salesperson for the overpayment, $700.
   28. Paid automobile expense (including rental charges for an automobile), $1,500.
   29. Paid miscellaneous expenses, $450.
   30. Recorded revenue earned and billed to clients during the month, $48,400.
   30. Paid salaries and commissions for the month, $25,000.
   30. Paid dividends of $8,000.
   30. Rented land purchased on November 15 to local merchants association for use as a parking lot in December and January, during a street rebuilding program; received advance payment of $2,500.

Instructions

1. Record the November 1, 2008, balance of each account in the appropriate balance column of a T account, and write *Balance* to identify the opening amounts.
2. Journalize the transactions for November in a two-column journal.
3. Post the journal entries to the T accounts, placing the date to the left of each amount to identify the transaction. Determine the balances for all accounts with more than one posting.
4. Prepare a trial balance of the ledger as of November 30, 2008.

Process Cost Systems

As we discussed in Chapter 10, the job order cost system is best suited to industries that make special orders for customers or manufacture different products in groups. Industries that use job order cost systems include special-order printing, custom-made tailoring, furniture manufacturing, shipbuilding, aircraft building, and construction. Process manufacturing is different from job order manufacturing. Process manufacturers typically use large machines to process a flow of raw materials into a finished state. For example, a petrochemical business processes crude oil through numerous refining steps to produce higher grades of oil until gasoline is produced. The cost accounting system used by process manufacturers is called the **process cost system**.

In some ways, the process cost and job order cost systems are similar. Both systems accumulate product costs—for direct materials, direct labor, and factory overhead—and allocate these costs to the units produced. Both systems maintain perpetual inventory accounts with subsidiary ledgers for materials, work in process, and finished goods. Both systems also provide product cost data to management for planning, directing, improving, controlling, and decision making. The main difference in the two systems is the form in which the product costs are accumulated and reported.

Exhibit 1 illustrates the main differences between the job order and process cost systems. In a job order cost system, product costs are accumulated by job and are summarized on job cost sheets. The job cost sheets provide unit cost information and can be used by management for product pricing, cost control, and inventory valuation. The process manufacturer does not manufacture according to "jobs." Thus, costs are accumulated by department. Each unit of product that passes through the department is similar. Thus, the production costs reported by each department provide unit cost information that can be used by management for cost control. In a job order cost system, the work in process inventory at the end of the accounting period is the sum of the job cost sheets for partially completed jobs. In a process cost system, the amount of work in process inventory is determined by allocating costs between completed and partially completed units within a department.

EXHIBIT 1   *Job Order and Process Cost Systems Compared*

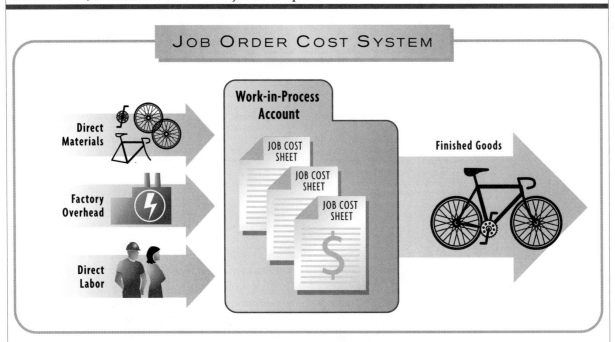

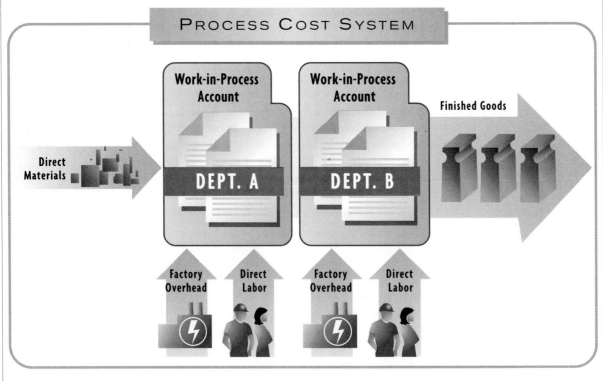

Physical Flows and Cost Flows for a Process Manufacturer

Exhibit 2 illustrates the physical flow of materials for a steel processor. Direct materials in the form of scrap metal are placed into a furnace in the Melting Department. The Melting Department uses conversion costs (direct labor and factory overhead) during the melting process. The molten metal is then transferred to the Casting Department, where it is poured into an ingot casting. The Casting Department also uses conversion costs during the casting process. The ingot castings are transferred to the finished goods inventory for shipment to customers.

EXHIBIT 2 *Physical Flows for a Process Manufacturer*

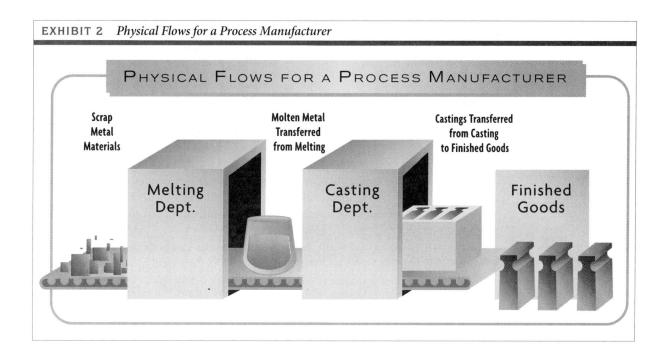

The cost flows in a process cost system reflect the physical materials flows and are illustrated in Exhibit 3. Purchased materials increase Materials (a) and Accounts Payable (not shown). Direct materials (scrap metal) used by the Melting Department increase Work in Process—Melting and decrease Materials (b). In addition, indirect materials and other overhead incurred increase department factory overhead accounts and decrease Materials (d) and other accounts. Direct labor in the Melting Department increases the department's work in process account (c) and Wages Payable (not shown). Applied factory overhead increases Work in Process—Melting using a predetermined overhead rate (e). The cost of completed production from the Melting Department is transferred to the Casting Department by increasing Work in Process—Casting and decreasing Work in Process—Melting (f). The transferred costs include the direct materials and conversion costs for completed production of the Melting Department. The direct labor and applied factory overhead costs in the Casting Department increase Work in Process—Casting (g and h). The cost of the finished ingots is transferred out of the Casting Department by increasing Finished Goods and decreasing Work in Process—Casting (i). The cost of

---

EXHIBIT 3   *Cost Flows for a Process Manufacturer*

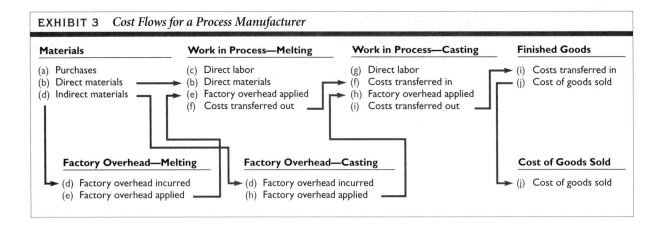

---

ingots sold to customers is transferred out of finished goods with an increase to Cost of Goods Sold and a decrease to Finished Goods (j).

The Average Cost Method

In a process cost system, the costs transferred in and out of each department must be determined. The costs transferred in minus the cost transferred out determine the ending work in process for each department. Like a merchandising business, a manufacturer uses a cost flow assumption in determining the costs flowing into, flowing out of, and remaining in each manufacturing department. The manufacturer can use a **first-in, first-out; last-in, first-out;** or **average cost flow assumption**. To simplify, we use the average cost flow assumption.[1]

Most process manufacturers have more than one department. In the illustrations that follow, McDermott Steel Inc. has two departments, Melting and Casting. McDermott melts scrap metal and then pours the molten metal into an ingot casting.

To illustrate the average cost method, we simplify by using only the Melting Department of McDermott Steel Inc. The following data for the Melting Department are for July of the current year:

Work in process inventory, July 1, 500 tons (70% completed)	$28,050
Direct materials cost incurred in July, 1,000 tons @ $50	50,000
Direct labor cost incurred in July	4,000
Factory overhead applied in July	4,350
Total production costs to account for	$86,400
Cost of goods transferred to Casting in July (includes units in process on July 1), 1,100 tons	?
Cost of work in process inventory, July 31, 400 tons, 25% completed as to conversion costs	?

Using the average cost system, our objective is to allocate the total costs of production of $86,400 to the 1,100 tons completed and transferred to the Casting Department and the costs of the remaining 400 tons in the ending work in process inventory. These

---

[1]The first-in, first-out and last-in, first-out cost flow assuptions are described and illustrated in advanced cost accounting textbooks and courses.

costs are represented in the preceding table by two question marks. We determine these amounts by using the following four steps:

1. Determine the units to be assigned costs.
2. Calculate equivalent units of production.
3. Determine the cost per equivalent unit.
4. Allocate costs to transferred and partially completed units.

Step 1: Determine the Units to Be Assigned Costs

The first step in our illustration is to determine the units to be assigned costs. A unit can be any measure of completed production, such as tons, gallons, pounds, barrels, or cases. We use tons as the definition for units in McDermott Steel.

McDermott Steel's Melting Department had 1,500 tons of direct materials to account for during July, as shown here:

Total tons to account for:	
Work in process, July 1	500 tons
Received from materials storeroom	1,000
Total units to account for by the Melting Department	1,500 tons

As we noted earlier, there are two categories of units to be assigned costs for the period: (1) units completed and transferred out and (2) units in the ending work in process inventory. During July, the Melting Department completed and transferred 1,100 tons to the Casting Department. Of the 1,000 tons started in July, 600 tons were completed and transferred to the Casting Department. Thus, the ending work in process inventory consists of 400 tons.

The total units (tons) to be assigned costs for McDermott Steel can be summarized as follows:

(1) Transferred out to the Casting Department in July	1,100 tons
(2) Work in process inventory, July 31	400
Total tons to be assigned costs	1,500 tons

Note that the total units (tons) to be assigned costs (1,500 tons) equals the total units to account for (1,500 tons).

Step 2: Calculate Equivalent Units of Production

Process manufacturers often have some partially processed units remaining in production at the end of a period. When this happens, the costs of production must be allocated between the units that have been completed and transferred to the next process (or finished goods) and those that are only partially completed and remain within the department. This allocation is determined by using equivalent units of production.

Equivalent units of production are the number of units that *could* have been completed within a given period. In contrast, **whole units** represent the number of units in production during a period whether completed or not. For example, 400 tons of whole units are in the work in process inventory for the Melting Department on July 31. Since these units are 25% complete, the number of equivalent units in process in the Melting Department on July 31 is 100 tons (400 tons $\times$ 0.25).

Since the units transferred to the Casting Department have been completed, the whole units (1,100 tons) transferred are the same as the equivalent units transferred.

The total equivalent units of production for the Melting Department is determined by adding the equivalent units in the ending work in process inventory to the units transferred and completed during the period as shown here:

Equivalent units completed and transferred to the Casting Department during July	1,100 tons
Equivalent units in ending work in process, July 31	100
Total equivalent units	1,200 tons

Step 3: Determine the Cost per Equivalent Unit

In step 3, we calculate the cost per equivalent unit. The **cost per equivalent unit** is determined by dividing the total production costs by the total equivalent units of production as follows:

$$\text{Cost per equivalent unit} = \frac{\text{Total production costs}}{\text{Total equivalent units}} = \frac{\$86,400}{1,200 \text{ tons}} = \$72$$

We use the cost per equivalent unit in step 4 to allocate the production costs to the completed and partially completed units.

Step 4: Allocate Costs to Transferred and Partially Completed Units

In step 4, we multiply the cost per equivalent unit by the equivalent units of production to determine the cost of transferred and partially completed units. For the Melting Department, these costs are determined as shown:

(1) Transferred out to the Casting Department:	
1,100 tons × $72	$79,200
(2) Work in Process Inventory, July 31:	
400 tons × 0.25 complete × $72	7,200
Total production costs assigned	$86,400

The Cost of Production Report

A **cost of production report** is normally prepared for each processing department at periodic intervals. The July cost of production report for McDermott Steel's Melting Department is shown in Exhibit 4. The cost of production report in Exhibit 4 summarizes the following:

1.   The units for which the department is accountable and the disposition of those units.
2.   The production costs incurred by the department and the allocation of those costs between completed and partially completed units.

The cost of production report is also used to control costs. Each department manager is responsible for the units entering production and the costs incurred in the department. Any failure to account for all costs and any significant differences in unit product costs from one month to another should be investigated.

EXHIBIT 4 *Cost of Production Report for McDermott Steel's Melting Department*

McDERMOTT STEEL INC.
Cost of Production Report—Melting Department
For the Month Ended July 31, 2009

Units	Whole Units (step 1)	Equivalent Units of Production (step 2)
Units to account for during production:		
Work in process inventory, July 1	500	
Received from materials storeroom	1,000	
Total units accounted for by the Melting Dept.	1,500	
Units to be assigned cost:		
Transferred to Casting Department in July	1,100	1,100
Inventory in process, July 31 (25% complete)	400	100
Total units to be assigned cost	1,500	1,200
Costs		
Cost per Equivalent Unit (**step 3**):		
Total production costs for July in Melting Dept.		$86,400
Total equivalent units (from step 2 above)		÷ 1,200
Cost per equivalent unit		$ 72
Costs assigned to production:		
Inventory in process, July 1		$28,050
Direct materials costs incurred in July		50,000
Direct labor cost incurred in July		4,000
Factory overhead applied in July		4,350
Total production costs accounted for by the Melting Dept.		$86,400
Costs allocated to transferred and partially completed units (**step 4**):		
Transferred to Casting Dept. in July (1,100 units × $72)		$79,200
Inventory in process, July 31 (400 units × 0.25 × $72)		7,200
Total costs assigned by the Melting Dept.		$86,400

Cost Flows for a Process Cost System

Exhibit 5 shows the flow of costs for each transaction. Note that the highlighted amounts in Exhibit 5 were determined from assigning the costs charged to production in the Melting Department. These amounts were computed and are shown at the bottom of the cost of production report for the Melting Department in Exhibit 4. Likewise, the amount transferred out of the Casting Department to Finished Goods would have also been determined from a cost of production report for the Casting Department.

Using the Cost of Production Report for Decision Making

The cost of production report is one source of information that can be used by managers to control and improve operations. A cost of production report normally lists costs in more detail than the one in Exhibit 4. This increased detail helps management isolate

EXHIBIT 5   *McDermott Steel's Cost Flows*

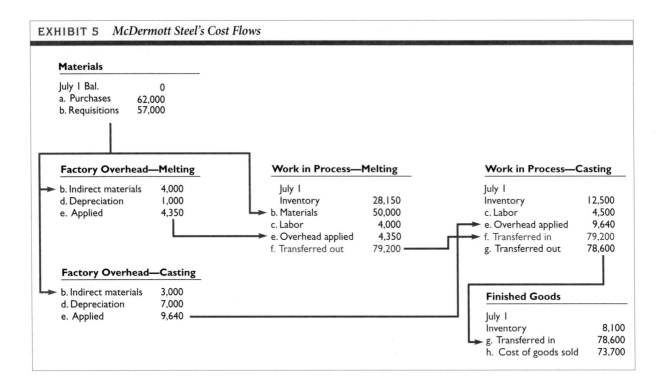

problems and opportunities. To illustrate, assume that the Blending Department of Holland Beverage Company prepared cost of production reports for April and May. In addition, assume that the Blending Department had no beginning or ending work in process inventory either month. Thus, in this simple case, there is no need to determine equivalent units of production for allocating costs between completed and partially completed units. The cost of production reports for April and May in the Blending Department are as follows:

Cost of Production Reports Holland Beverage Company—Blending Department For the Months Ended April 30 and May 31, 2009		
	April	May
Direct materials	$ 20,000	$ 40,600
Direct labor	15,000	29,400
Energy	8,000	20,000
Repairs	4,000	8,000
Tank cleaning	3,000	8,000
Total	$ 50,000	$ 106,000
Units completed	÷ 100,000	÷ 200,000
Cost per unit	$ 0.50	$ 0.53

Note that the preceding reports provide more cost detail than simply reporting direct materials and conversion costs. The May results indicate that total unit costs have increased from $0.50 to $0.53, or 6% from the previous month. What caused this increase? To determine its possible causes, the cost of production report can be restated in per-unit terms, as shown here.

Blending Department
Per-Unit Expense Comparisons

	April	May	% Change
Direct materials	$0.200	$0.203	1.50%
Direct labor	0.150	0.147	(2.00)
Energy	0.080	0.100	25.00
Repairs	0.040	0.040	0.00
Tank cleaning	0.030	0.040	33.33
Total	$0.500	$0.530	6.00%

Both energy and tank cleaning per-unit costs increased dramatically in May. Further investigation should focus on these costs. For example, a trend indicating increased energy costs could indicate that the machines are losing fuel efficiency, thereby requiring the company to purchase an increasing amount of fuel. This unfavorable trend could motivate management to repair the machines. The tank-cleaning costs could be investigated in a similar fashion.

In addition to unit production cost trends, managers of process manufacturers are concerned about yield trends. **Yield** is the ratio of the materials output quantity to the input quantity. A yield of less than 1.0 occurs when the output quantity is less than the input quantity due to materials losses during the process. For example, if 1,000 pounds of sugar entered the packing operation but only 980 pounds of sugar were packed, the yield is 98%. During the packing process, 2% or 20 pounds of sugar were lost or spilled.

Exercises

E1

Entries for materials cost flows in a process cost system

The Hershey Company manufactures chocolate confectionery products. The three largest raw materials are cocoa beans, sugar, and dehydrated milk. These raw materials first go into the Blending Department. The blended product is then sent to the Molding Department, where the bars of candy are formed. The candy is then sent to the Packing Department, where the bars are wrapped and boxed. The boxed candy is then sent to the distribution center, where it is eventually sold to food brokers and retailers.

Indicate the accounts increased and decreased for each of the following business events:

a. Materials used by the Blending Department.
b. Transfer of blended product to the Molding Department.
c. Transfer of candy to the Packing Department.
d. Transfer of boxed candy to the distribution center.
e. Sale of boxed candy.

E2

Flowchart of accounts related to service and processing departments

Alcoa Inc. is the world's largest producer of aluminum products. One product that Alcoa manufactures is aluminum sheet products for the aerospace industry. The entire output of the Smelting Department is transferred to the Rolling Department. Part of the fully processed goods from the Rolling Department are sold as rolled sheet, and the remainder of the goods are transferred to the Converting Department for further processing into sheared sheet.

(continued)

Prepare a chart of the flow of costs from the processing department accounts into the finished goods accounts and then into the cost of goods sold account. The relevant accounts are as follows:

Cost of Goods Sold	Finished Goods—Rolled Sheet
Materials	Finished Goods—Sheared Sheet
Factory Overhead—Smelting Department	Work in Process—Smelting Department
Factory Overhead—Rolling Department	Work in Process—Rolling Department
Factory Overhead—Converting Department	Work in Process—Converting Department

E3

Equivalent units of production

The Converting Department of Stay-Soft Napkin Company had 760 units in work in process at the beginning of the period, which were 75% complete. During the period, 15,400 units were completed and transferred to the Packing Department. There were 1,000 units in process at the end of the period, which were 30% complete.

a. Determine the number of whole units to be accounted for and to be assigned costs for the period.
b. Determine the number of equivalent units of production for the period.

E4

Equivalent units of production

✓ a. 25,400

The Converting Department of Kwan Napkin Company uses the average cost method and had 1,500 units in work in process that were 60% complete at the beginning of the period. During the period, 24,500 units were completed and transferred to the Packing Department. There were 900 units in process that were 40% complete at the end of the period.

a. Determine the number of whole units to be accounted for and to be assigned costs for the period.
b. Determine the number of equivalent units of production for the period.

E5

Equivalent units of production: average cost method

✓ a. 94,500 units to be accounted for

Units of production data for the two departments of Frontier Cable and Wire Company for March of the current fiscal year are as follows:

	Drawing Department	Winding Department
Work in process, March 1	1,700 units, 50% completed	1,000 units, 30% completed
Completed and transferred to next processing department during March	92,000 units	90,400 units
Work in process, March 31	2,500 units, 65% completed	2,600 units, 25% completed

Each department uses the average cost method.

a. Determine the number of whole units to be accounted for and to be assigned costs and the equivalent units of production for the Drawing Department.
b. Determine the number of whole units to be accounted for and to be assigned costs and the equivalent units of production for the Winding Department.

E6

Equivalent units of production: average cost method

✓ a. 9,000

The following information concerns production in the Finishing Department for March. The Finishing Department uses the average cost method.

ACCOUNT Work in Process—Finishing Department

Date	Item	
Mar. 1	Bal., 12,000 units, 40% completed	22,820
31	Direct materials, 125,000 units	325,000
31	Direct labor	174,500
31	Factory overhead	93,200
31	Goods transferred, 128,000 units	(586,240)
31	Bal., ? units, 70% completed	28,780

a. Determine the number of units in work in process inventory at the end of the month.
b. Determine the number of whole units to be accounted for and to be assigned costs and the equivalent units of production for March.

E7

Equivalent units of production and related costs

SPREADSHEET

✓ b. 82,720 units

The charges to Work in Process—Baking Department for a period as well as information concerning production are as follows. The Baking Department uses the average cost method, and all direct materials are placed in process during production.

Work in Process—Baking Department

Bal., 5,000 units, 70% completed	10,000
Direct materials, 81,500 units	195,700
Direct labor	123,036
Factory overhead	89,000
To Finished Goods, 11,100 units	?
Bal., 5,400 units, 30% completed	?

Determine the following:

a. The number of whole units to be accounted for and to be assigned costs.
b. The number of equivalent units of production.
c. The cost per equivalent unit.
d. The cost of the units transferred to Finished Goods.
e. The cost of ending Work in Process.

E8

Cost per equivalent unit: average cost method

✓ a. $20.00

The following information concerns production in the Forging Department for April. The Forging Department uses the average cost method.

ACCOUNT Work in Process—Forging Department

Date	Item	
Apr. 1	Bal., 3,000 units, 40% completed	24,000
30	Direct materials, 28,500 units	355,800
30	Direct labor	128,200
30	Factory overhead	100,500
30	Goods transferred, 27,200 units	?
30	Bal., 4300 units, 75% completed	?

(continued)

a. Determine the cost per equivalent unit.
b. Determine the cost of the units transferred to Finished Goods.
c. Determine the cost of ending Work in Process.

E9

Cost of production report: average cost method

SPREADSHEET

✓ Cost per equivalent unit, $2.15

The increases to Work in Process—Cooking Department for Boston Beans Company for January 2008 as well as information concerning production are as follows:

Work in process, January 1, 1,000 pounds, 40% completed	$ 900
Beans added during January, 58,200 pounds	92,400
Conversion costs during January	33,593
Work in process, January 31, 600 pounds, 70% completed	—
Goods finished during January, 58,600 pounds	—

Prepare a cost of production report, using the average cost method.

E10

Cost of production report: average cost method

SPREADSHEET

✓ Cost per equivalent unit, $5.98

Prepare a cost of production report for the Cutting Department of North Georgia Carpet Company for May 2008. Use the average cost method with the following data:

Work in process, May 1, 13,000 units, 75% completed	$ 58,000
Materials added during May from Weaving Department, 205,000 units	914,780
Direct labor for May	158,600
Factory overhead for May	100,500
Goods finished during May (includes goods in process, May 1), 202,000 units	—
Work in process, May 31, 16,000 units, 25% completed	—

E11

Decision making

SPREADSHEET

Oasis Bottling Company bottles popular beverages in the Bottling Department. The beverages are produced by blending concentrate with water and sugar. The concentrate is purchased from a concentrate producer. The concentrate producer sets higher prices for the more popular concentrate flavors. Below is a simplified Bottling Department cost of production report separating the cost of bottling the four flavors.

	Orange	Cola	Lemon-Lime	Root Beer
Concentrate	$ 5,400	$110,000	$ 63,000	$1,800
Water	1,800	30,000	18,000	600
Sugar	3,000	50,000	30,000	1,000
Bottles	6,600	110,000	66,000	2,200
Flavor changeover	3,000	6,000	3,600	3,000
Conversion cost	2,400	25,000	15,000	800
Total cost transferred to finished goods	$22,200	$331,000	$195,600	$9,400
Number of cases	3,000	50,000	30,000	1,000

Beginning and ending work in process inventories are negligible, so are omitted from the cost of production report. The flavor changeover cost represents the cost of cleaning the bottling machines between production runs of different flavors.

Prepare a memo to the production manager analyzing this comparative cost information. In your memo, provide recommendations for further action, along with supporting schedules showing the total cost per case and cost per case by cost element.

Problems

P1

Cost of production report

✓ Cost per equivalent
   unit, $4.00

Robusta Coffee Company roasts and packs coffee beans. The process begins in the Roasting Department. From the Roasting Department, the coffee beans are transferred to the Packing Department. The following is a partial work in process account of the Roasting Department at July 31, 2008:

ACCOUNT Work in Process—Roasting Department

Date	Item	
July 1	Bal., 18,000 units, 25% completed	18,450
31	Direct materials, 345,000 units	968,750
31	Direct labor	229,000
31	Factory overhead	203,600
31	Goods finished, 340,000 units	?
31	Bal., ? units, 65% completed	?

Instructions

Prepare a cost of production report, using the average cost method, and identify the missing amounts for Work in Process—Roasting Department.

P2

Equivalent units and related costs; cost of production report

✓ Transferred to Packag-
   ing Dept., $865,060

Blue Ribbon Flour Company manufactures flour by a series of three processes, beginning in the Milling Department. From the Milling Department, the materials pass through the Sifting and Packaging Departments, emerging as packaged refined flour.

The balance in the account Work in Process—Sifting Department was as follows on October 1, 2008:

Work in Process—Sifting Department (15,000 units, 75% completed) $42,000

The following costs were charged to Work in Process—Sifting Department during October:

Direct materials transferred from Milling Department: 235,800 units	$632,600
Direct labor	160,735
Factory overhead	76,900

During October, 233,800 units of flour were completed. Work in Process—Sifting Department on October 31 was 17,000 units, 75% completed.

Instructions

Prepare a cost of production report for the Sifting Department for October, using the average cost method.

Glossary

A

Accelerated depreciation method: A depreciation method that provides for a higher depreciation amount in the first year of the asset's use, followed by a gradually declining amount of depreciation.

Account: A record in which increases and decreases in a financial statement element are recorded.

Accounting: An information system that provides reports to stakeholders about the economic activities and condition of a business.

Accounting cycle: The process that begins with the analysis of transactions and ends with the preparation of the accounting records for the next accounting period.

Accounting equation: Assets = Liabilities + Stockholders' Equity.

Accounting period concept: An accounting concept in which accounting data are recorded and summarized in a period process.

Accounts payable: Liabilities for amounts incurred from purchases of products or services in the normal operations of a business.

Accounts receivable: Receivables created by selling merchandise or services on credit.

Accounts receivable turnover: Measures how frequently during the year the accounts receivable are being converted to cash by dividing net sales by the average net accounts receivable.

Accrual basis of accounting: A system of accounting in which revenue is recorded as it is earned and expenses are recorded when they generate revenue.

Accruals: Revenues or expenses that have not been recorded.

Accrued expenses: Expenses that have been incurred at the end of an accounting period but have not been recorded in the accounts; sometimes called *accrued liabilities.*

Accrued revenues: Revenues that have been earned at the end of an accounting period but have not been recorded in the accounts; sometimes called *accrued assets.*

Accumulated depreciation: An offsetting or contra asset account used to record depreciation on a fixed asset.

Activity base (driver): A measure of activity that is related to changes in cost and is used in the denominator in calculating the predetermined factory overhead rate to assign factory overhead costs to cost objects.

Activity cost pools: Cost accumulations that are associated with a given activity, such as machine usage, inspections, moving, and production setups.

Activity-based costing (ABC): An accounting framework based on determining the cost of activities and allocating these costs to products using activity rates.

Adequate disclosure concept: An accounting concept that requires financial statements to include all relevant data a reader needs to understand the financial condition and performance of a business.

Adjustment process: A process required by the accrual basis of accounting in which the accounts are updated prior to preparing financial statements.

Administrative expenses: Expenses incurred in the administration or general operations of the business.

Aging the receivables: The process of analyzing the accounts receivable and classifying them according to various age groupings, with the due date being the base point for determining age.

Allowance for Doubtful Accounts: The contra asset account for accounts receivable.

Allowance method: The method of accounting for uncollectible accounts that provides an expense for uncollectible receivables in advance of their write-off.

Amortization: The periodic transfer of the cost of an intangible asset to expense.

Annuity: A series of equal cash flows at fixed intervals.

Assets: The resources owned by a business.

Average cost method: The method of inventory costing that is based upon the assumption that costs should be charged against revenue by using the weighted average unit cost of the items sold.

Average rate of return: A method of evaluating capital investment proposals that focuses on the expected profitability of the investment.

B

Bad debt expense: The operating expense incurred because of the failure to collect receivables.

Balance sheet: A list of the assets, liabilities, and owner's equity as of a specific date, usually at the close of the last day of a month or a year.

Balanced scorecard: A performance evaluation approach that incorporates multiple performance dimensions by combining financial and nonfinancial measures.

Bank reconciliation: The analysis that details the items responsible for the difference between the cash balance reported in the bank statement and the balance of the cash account in the ledger.

Bank statement: A summary of all transactions mailed to the depositor by the bank each month.

Bond: A form of interest-bearing note used by corporations to borrow on a long-term basis.

Bond indenture: The contract between a corporation issuing bonds and the bondholders.

Bonds payable: A type of long-term debt financing with a face amount that is in the future with interest that is normally paid semiannually.

Book inventory: The amount of inventory recorded in the accounting records.

Book value: The cost of a fixed asset minus accumulated depreciation on the asset.

Bottleneck: A condition that occurs when product demand exceeds production capacity.

Break-even point: The level of business operations at which revenues and expired costs are equal.

Budget: An accounting device used to plan and control resources of operational departments and divisions.

Budget performance report: A report comparing actual results with budget figures.

Budgetary slack: Excess resources set within a budget to provide for uncertain events.

Business: An organization in which basic resources (inputs), such as materials and labor, are assembled and processed to provide goods or services (outputs) to customers.

Business entity concept: An accounting concept that limits the economic data in the accounting system of a specific business or entity to data related directly to the activities of that business or entity.

Business stakeholder: A person or entity who has an interest in the economic performance of a business.

C

Capital expenditures: The costs of acquiring fixed assets, adding a component, or replacing a component of fixed assets.

Capital expenditures budget: The budget summarizing future plans for acquiring plant facilities and equipment.

Capital investment analysis: The process by which management plans, evaluates, and controls long-term capital investments involving fixed assets.

Capital rationing: The process by which management allocates available investment funds among competing capital investment proposals.

Capital stock: Types of stock a corporation may issue.

Cash: Coins, currency (paper money), checks, money orders, and money on deposit available for unrestricted withdrawal from banks and other financial institutions.

Cash basis of accounting: A system of accounting in which only transactions involving increases or decreases of the entity's cash are recorded.

Cash budget: A budget of estimated cash receipts and payments.

Cash dividend: A cash distribution of earnings by a corporation to its shareholders.

Cash equivalents: Highly liquid investments that are usually reported with cash on the balance sheet.

Cash payback period: The expected period of time that will elapse between the date of a capital expenditure and the complete recovery in cash (or equivalent) of the amount invested.

Cash short and over account: The account used to record the difference between the amount of cash in a cash register and the amount of cash that should be on hand according to the records.

Classified balance sheet: A balance sheet prepared with various sections, subsections, and captions that aid in its interpretation and analysis.

Common stock: The basic type of stock issued to stockholders of a corporation when a corporation has issued only one class of stock.

Common-size statement: A financial statement in which all items are expressed in percentages.

Contingent liabilities: Potential liabilities if certain events occur in the future.

Continuous budgeting: A method of budgeting that provides for maintaining a 12-month projection into the future.

Contract rate: The periodic interest to be paid on the bonds that is identified in the bond indenture; expressed as a percentage of the face amount of the bond.

Contribution margin: Sales less variable cost of goods sold and variable selling and administrative expenses.

Contribution margin ratio: The percentage of each sales dollar that is available to cover the fixed costs and provide income from operations.

Controllable expenses: Costs that can be influenced by the decisions of a manager.

Controllable variance: The difference between the actual amount of variable factory overhead cost incurred and the amount of variable factory overhead budgeted for the standard product.

Conversion costs: The combination of direct labor and factory overhead costs.

Copyright: An exclusive right to publish and sell a literary, artistic, or musical composition.

Corporation: A business organized under state or federal statutes as a separate legal entity.

Cost: A payment of cash (or a commitment to pay cash in the future) for the purpose of generating revenues.

Cost accounting system: A system used to accumulate manufacturing costs for decision-making and financial reporting purposes.

Cost allocation: The process of assigning indirect costs to a cost object, such as a job.

Cost behavior: The manner in which a cost changes in relation to its activity base (driver).

Cost center: A decentralized unit in which the department or division manager has responsibility for the control of costs incurred and the authority to make decisions that affect these costs.

Cost concept: An accounting concept that determines the amount initially entered into the accounting records for purchases.

Cost of goods sold: The cost of the manufactured product sold.

Cost of goods sold budget: A budget of the estimated direct materials, direct labor, and factory overhead consumed by sold products.

Cost of merchandise sold: The cost that is reported as an expense when merchandise or a manufactured product is sold; also called *cost of goods sold.*

Cost price approach: An approach to transfer pricing that uses cost as the basis for setting the transfer price.

Cost variance: The difference between the actual cost and the standard cost at actual volumes.

Cost-volume-profit analysis: The systematic examination of the relationships among costs, expenses, sales, and operating profit or loss.

Cost-volume-profit chart: A chart used to assist management in understanding the relationships among costs, expenses, sales, and operating profit or loss.

Credit memorandum: A form used by a seller to inform the buyer of the amount the seller proposes to decrease the account receivable due from the buyer.

Credit period: The amount of time the buyer is allowed in which to pay the seller.

Credit terms: Terms for payment on account by the buyer to the seller.

Currency exchange rate: The rate at which currency in another country can be exchanged for local currency.

Current assets: Cash and other assets that are expected to be converted to cash or sold or used up through the normal operations of the business within 1 year or less.

Current liabilities: Liabilities that will be due within a short time (usually 1 year or less) and that are to be paid out of current assets.

Current ratio: The ratio of current assets to current liabilities.

Currently attainable standards: Standards that represent levels of operation that can be obtained with reasonable effort.

D

Debit memorandum: A form used by a buyer to inform the seller of the amount the buyer proposes to decrease the account payable due the seller.

Decentralization: The separation of a business into more manageable operating units.

Deferrals: Delayed recordings of expenses or revenues.

Deferred expenses: Items that are initially recorded as assets but are expected to become expenses over time or through the normal operations of the business; sometimes called *prepaid expenses*.

Deferred revenues: Items that are initially recorded as liabilities but are expected to become revenues over time or through the normal operations of the business; sometimes called unearned revenues.

Depletion: The process of transferring the cost of natural resources to an expense account.

Depreciation: The systematic periodic transfer of the cost of a fixed asset to an expense account during its expected useful life.

Differential analysis: The area of accounting concerned with the effect of alternative courses of action on revenues and costs.

Differential cost: The amount of increase or decrease in cost expected from a particular course of action compared with an alternative.

Differential revenue: The amount of increase or decrease in revenue expected from a particular course of action as compared with an alternative.

Direct labor cost: Wages of factory workers who are directly involved in converting materials into a finished product.

Direct labor rate variance: The cost associated with the difference between the standard rate and the actual rate paid for direct labor used in producing a commodity.

Direct labor time variance: The cost associated with the difference between the standard hours and the actual hours of direct labor spent producing a commodity.

Direct materials cost: The cost of materials that are an integral part of the finished product.

Direct materials price variance: The cost associated with the difference between the standard price and the actual price of direct materials used in producing a commodity.

Direct materials purchases budget: A budget that uses the production budget as a starting point.

Direct materials quantity variance: The cost associated with the difference between the standard quantity and the actual quantity of direct materials used in producing a commodity.

Direct write-off method: The method of accounting for uncollectible accounts that recognizes the expense only when accounts are judged to be worthless.

Discount on bonds payable: The excess of the face amount of bonds over their issue price.

Dividend yield: A profitability measure that is computed by dividing the annual dividends paid per share of common stock by the market price per share on a specific date.

Dividends: Distributions of the earnings of a corporation to stockholders.

Divisions: Decentralized units that are structured around a common function, product, customer, or geographical territory.

Double-declining-balance method: A method of depreciation that provides periodic depreciation expense based on the declining book value of a fixed asset over its estimated life.

DuPont formula: An expanded expression of return on investment determined by multiplying the profit margin by the investment turnover.

E

Earnings per share (EPS) on common stock: A measure of profitability computed by dividing net income, reduced by preferred dividends, by the number of common shares outstanding.

Electronic data interchange (EDI): An information technology that allows different business organizations to use computers to communicate orders, relay information, and make or receive payments.

Electronic funds transfer (EFT): A system in which computers rather than paper (money, checks, etc.) are used to effect cash transactions.

Elements of internal control: The control environment, risk assessment, control activities, information and communication, and monitoring.

Employee fraud: The intentional act of deceiving an employer for personal gain.

Employee involvement: A philosophy that grants employees the responsibility and authority to make their own decisions about their operations.

Expenses: Costs used to earn revenues.

F

Factory overhead cost: All of the costs of operating the factory except for direct materials and direct labor.

Financial Accounting Standards Board (FASB): The authoritative body that has the primary responsibility for developing accounting principles.

Financial accounting system: A system that includes (1) a set of rules for determining what, when, and the amount that should be recorded for economic events, (2) a framework for facilitating preparing financial statements, and (3) one or more controls to determine whether errors could have arisen in the recording process.

Financial statements: Financial reports that summarize the effects of events on a business.

Financing activities: Business activities that involve obtaining funds to begin and operate a business.

Finished goods inventory: The cost of finished products on hand that have not been sold.

Finished goods ledger: The subsidiary ledger that contains the individual accounts for each kind of commodity or product produced.

First-in, first-out (fifo) method: A method of inventory costing based on the assumption that the costs of merchandise sold should be charged against revenue in the order in which the costs were incurred.

Fixed assets: Long-lived or relatively permanent tangible assets that are used in the normal business operations; sometimes called *plant assets.*

Fixed costs: Costs that tend to remain the same in amount, regardless of variations in the level of activity.

Flexible budget: A budget that adjusts for varying rates of activity.

Fringe benefits: Benefits provided to employees in addition to wages and salaries.

FOB (free on board) destination: Freight terms in which the seller pays the transportation costs from the shipping point to the final destination.

FOB (free on board) shipping point: Freight terms in which the buyer pays the transportation costs from the shipping point to the final destination.

G

Generally accepted accounting principles (GAAP): Rules for the way financial statements should be prepared.

Goal conflict: Situation when individual self-interest differs from business objectives.

Going concern concept: An accounting concept that assumes a business will continue operating for an indefinite period of time.

Goodwill: An intangible asset of a business that is created from favorable factors such as location, product quality, reputation, and managerial skill, as verified from a merger transaction.

Gross pay: The total earnings of an employee for a payroll period.

Gross profit: Sales minus the cost of merchandise sold.

H

High-low method: A technique that uses the highest and lowest total cost as a basis for estimating the variable cost per unit and the fixed cost component of a mixed cost.

Horizontal analysis: A method of analyzing financial performance that computes the percentage of increases and decreases in related items in comparative financial statements.

I

Ideal standards: Standards that can be achieved only under perfect operating conditions, such as no idle time, no machine breakdowns, and no materials spoilage; also called theoretical standards.

Income from operations (operating income): The excess of gross profit over total operating expenses.

Income statement: A summary of the revenue and expenses for a specific period of time, such as a month or a year.

Indirect method: A method of preparing the statement of cash flows that reconciles net income with net cash flows from operating activities.

Inflation: A period when prices in general are rising and the purchasing power of money is declining.

Intangible assets: Long-lived assets that are useful in the operations of a business, are not held for sale, and are without physical qualities.

Interest payable: A liability to pay interest on a due date.

Internal control: The policies and procedures used to safeguard assets, ensure accurate business information, and ensure compliance with laws and regulations.

Internal rate of return method: A method of analyzing proposed capital investments that focuses on using present value concepts to compute the rate of return from the net cash flows expected from the investment.

Inventory shrinkage: The amount by which the merchandise for sale, as indicated by the balance of the merchandise inventory account, is larger than the total amount of merchandise counted during the physical inventory.

Inventory turnover: Measures the relationship between the volume of goods (merchandise) sold and the amount of inventory carried during the period.

Investing activities: Business activities that involve obtaining the necessary resources to start and operate the business.

Investment center: A decentralized unit in which the manager has the responsibility and authority to make decisions that affect not only costs and revenues but also the fixed assets available to the center.

Investment turnover: A component of the rate of return on investment computed as the ratio of sales to invested assets.

Invoice: The bill that the seller sends to the buyer.

J

Job cost sheet: An account in the work in process subsidiary ledger in which the costs charged to a particular job order are recorded.

Job order cost system: A type of cost accounting system that provides for a separate record of the cost of each particular quantity of product that passes through the factory.

Just-in-time (JIT) manufacturing: A business philosophy that focuses on eliminating time, cost, and poor quality within manufacturing processes.

L

Last-in, first-out (lifo) method: A method of inventory costing based on the assumption that the most recent merchandise inventory costs should be charged against revenue.

Lead time: The elapsed time between starting a unit of product into the beginning of a process and its completion.

Leverage: The tendency of the rate earned on stockholders' equity to vary from the rate earned on total assets because the amount earned on assets acquired through the use of funds provided by creditors varies from the interest paid to these creditors.

Liabilities: The rights of creditors that represent a legal obligation to repay an amount borrowed according to terms of the borrowing agreement.

Lifo conformity rule: A financial reporting rule requiring a firm that elects to use lifo inventory valuation for tax purposes to also use lifo for external financial reporting.

Lifo reserve: A required disclosure for lifo firms, showing the difference between inventory valued under fifo and inventory valued under lifo.

Limited liability company (LLC): A form of corporation that combines attributes of a partnership and a corporation in that it is organized as a corporation, but it can elect to be taxed as a partnership.

Long-term liabilities: Liabilities that will not be due for a long time (usually more than 1 year).

Lower-of-cost-or-market (LCM) method: A method of valuing inventory that reports the inventory at the lower of its cost or current market value (replacement cost).

M

Management Discussion and Analysis (MDA): An annual report disclosure that provides management's analysis of the results of operations and financial condition.

Managerial accounting: The branch of accounting that uses both historical and estimated data in providing information that management uses in conducting daily operations, in planning future operations, and in developing overall business strategies.

Manufacturing: A type of business that changes basic inputs into products that are sold to individual customers.

Margin of safety: The difference between current sales revenue and the sales at the break-even point.

Market price approach: An approach to transfer pricing that uses the price at which the product or service transferred could be sold to outside buyers as the transfer price.

Market rate of interest: The effective rate of interest at the time bonds are issued.

Markup: An amount that is added to a "cost" amount to determine product price.

Master budget: The comprehensive budget plan linking the individual budgets related to sales, cost of goods sold, operating expenses, projects, capital expenditures, and cash.

Matching concept: An accounting concept that requires expenses of a period to be matched with the revenue generated during that period.

Materials inventory: The cost of materials that have not yet entered into the manufacturing process.

Materials ledger: The subsidiary ledger containing the individual accounts for each type of material.

Materials requisitions: The form or electronic transmission used by a manufacturing department to authorize the issuance of materials from the storeroom.

Maturity value: The amount that is due at the maturity or due date of a note.

Merchandise available for sale: The cost of merchandise available for sale to customers.

Merchandise inventory: Merchandise on hand (not sold) at the end of an accounting period.

Merchandising: A type of business that purchases products from other businesses and sells them to customers.

Mixed cost: A cost with both variable and fixed characteristics.

Multiple-step income statement: A form of income statement that contains several sections, subsections, and subtotals.

N

Negotiated price approach: An approach to transfer pricing that allows managers of decentralized units to agree (negotiate) among themselves as to the transfer price.

Net income: The excess of revenues over expenses.

Net loss: The excess of expenses over revenues.

Net pay: Gross pay less payroll deductions; the amount the employer is obligated to pay the employee.

Net present value method: A method of analyzing proposed capital investments that focuses on the present value of the cash flows expected from the investments.

Net realizable value: For a receivable, the amount of cash expected to be realized in the future. For inventory, the estimated selling price of an item of inventory less any direct costs of disposal, such as sales commissions.

Net sales: Gross sales less sales returns and allowances and sales discounts.

Nonvalue-added lead time: The time that units wait in inventories, move unnecessarily, and wait during machine breakdowns.

Note payable: A type of short- or long-term financing that requires payment of the amount borrowed plus interest.

Note receivable: Written claim against debtors who promise to pay the amount of the note plus interest at an agreed-upon rate.

Number of days' sales in inventory: The relationship between the volume of sales and inventory, computed by dividing the inventory at the end of the year by the average daily cost of goods sold.

Number of days' sales in receivables: The relationship between sales and accounts receivable, computed by dividing the net accounts receivable at the end of the year by the average daily sales.

Number of times interest charges are earned: A ratio that measures the risk that interest payments to debt holders will continue to be made if earnings decrease.

O

Objectivity concept: An accounting concept that requires accounting records and data reported in financial statements be based on objective evidence.

Operating activities: Business activities that involve using the business's resources to implement its business strategy.

Operating leverage: A measure of the relative mix of a business's variable costs and fixed costs, computed as contribution margin divided by income from operations.

Opportunity cost: The amount of income forgone from an alternative to a proposed use of cash or its equivalent.

Other expense: Expenses that cannot be traced directly to operations.

Other income: Revenue from sources other than the primary operating activity of a business.

Outstanding stock: The stock in the hands of stockholders.

Overapplied factory overhead: The amount of factory overhead applied in excess of the actual factory overhead costs incurred for production during a period.

Owners' equity: The financial rights of the owner.

P

Par: The monetary amount printed on a stock certificate.

Partnership: A business owned by two or more individuals.

Patents: Exclusive rights to produce and sell goods with one or more unique features.

Payroll: The total amount paid to employees for a certain period.

Period costs: Those costs that are used up in generating revenue during the current period and that are not involved in the manufacturing process.

Periodic inventory method: The inventory method in which the inventory records do not show the amount available for sale or sold during the period.

Perpetual inventory method: The inventory system in which each purchase and sale of merchandise is recorded in an inventory account.

Petty cash fund: A special-purpose cash fund to pay relatively small amounts.

Physical inventory: A detailed listing of the merchandise for sale at the end of an accounting period.

Predetermined factory overhead rate: The rate used to apply factory overhead costs to the goods manufactured. The rate is determined from budgeted overhead cost and estimated activity usage data at the beginning of the fiscal period.

Preferred stock: A class of stock with preferential rights over common stock.

Premium on bonds payable: The excess of the issue price of bonds over their face amount.

Premium on stock: The excess of the issue price of a stock over its par value.

Prepaid expenses: Assets resulting from the prepayment of future expenses such as insurance or rent that are expected to become expenses over time or through the normal operations of the business; often called *deferred expenses.*

Present value concept: Cash today is not the equivalent of the same amount of money to be received in the future.

Present value index: An index computed by dividing the total present value of the net cash flow to be received from a proposed capital investment by the amount to be invested.

Present value of an annuity: The sum of the present values of a series of equal cash flows to be received at fixed intervals.

Price-earnings (P/E) ratio: The ratio of the market price per share of common stock at a specific date to the annual earnings per share.

Process: A sequence of activities linked together for performing a particular task.

Process cost system: A type of cost accounting system in which costs are accumulated by department or process within a factory.

Process-oriented layout: Organizing work in a plant or administrative function around processes (tasks).

Product cost concept: A concept used in applying the cost-plus approach to product pricing in which only the costs of manufacturing the product, termed the *product costs,* are included in the cost amount to which the markup is added.

Product costs: The three components of manufacturing cost: direct materials, direct labor, and factory overhead costs.

Production budget: A budget of estimated unit production.

Product-oriented layout: Organizing work in a plant or administrative function around products; sometimes referred to as *product cells.*

Profit center: A decentralized unit in which the manager has the responsibility and the authority to make decisions that affect both costs and revenues (and thus profits).

Profit margin: A component of the rate of return on investment computed as the ratio of income from operations to sales.

Profitability: The ability of a firm to earn income.

Profit-volume chart: A chart used to assist management in understanding the relationship between profit and volume.

Proprietorship: A business owned by one individual.

Pull manufacturing: A just-in-time method wherein customer orders trigger the release of finished goods, which trigger production, which triggers release of materials from suppliers.

Purchase discounts: Discounts taken by the buyer for early payment of an invoice.

Purchase return or allowance: From the buyer's perspective, returned merchandise or an adjustment for defective merchandise.

Push manufacturing: Materials are released into production and work in process is released into finished goods in anticipation of future sales.

Q

Quick assets: The sum of cash, receivables, and marketable securities.

Quick ratio: A financial ratio that measures the ability to pay current liabilities with quick assets (cash, marketable securities, accounts receivable).

R

Rate earned on stockholders' equity: A measure of profitability computed by dividing net income by total stockholders' equity.

Rate earned on total assets: A measure of the profitability of assets without regard to the equity of creditors and stockholders in the assets.

Rate of return on investment (ROI): A measure of managerial efficiency in the use of investments in assets computed as income from operations divided by invested assets.

Ratio of fixed assets to long-term liabilities: A solvency measure that indicates the margin of safety of the noteholders or bondholders.

Ratio of liabilities to stockholders' equity: A solvency measure that indicates the margin of safety for creditors.

Receivables: All money claims against other entities, including people, business firms, and other organizations.

Receiving report: The form or electronic transmission used by the receiving personnel to indicate that materials have been received and inspected.

Relevant range: The range of activity over which changes in cost are of interest to management.

Report form: The form of balance sheet in which assets, liabilities, and stockholders' equity are reported in a downward sequence.

Residual income: The excess of divisional income from operations over a "minimum" acceptable income from operations.

Residual value: The estimated value of a fixed asset at the end of its useful life.

Responsibility accounting: The process of measuring and reporting operating data by areas of responsibility.

Retained earnings: Net income retained in a corporation.

Retained earnings statement: A summary of the changes in the retained earnings in a corporation for a specific period of time, such as a month or a year.

Revenue: The increase in assets from selling products or services to customers.

Revenue expenditures: Costs that benefit only the current period or costs incurred for normal maintenance and repairs of fixed assets.

S

Sales: The total amount charged to customers for merchandise sold, including cash sales and sales on account.

Sales budget: A budget that indicates for each product (1) the quantity of estimated sales and (2) the expected unit selling price.

Sales discounts: From the seller's perspective, discounts that a seller can offer the buyer for early payment.

Sales mix: The relative distribution of sales among the various products available for sale.

Sales returns and allowances: From the seller's perspective, returned merchandise or an adjustment for damaged or defective merchandise.

Sarbanes-Oxley Act of 2002: An act passed by Congress to restore public confidence and trust in the financial statements of companies.

Selling expenses: Expenses that are incurred directly in the selling of merchandise.

Service: A type of business that provides services rather than products to customers.

Service department charges: The costs of services provided by an internal service department and transferred to a responsibility center.

Setup: The effort required to prepare an operation for a new production run.

Single-step income statement: A form of income statement in which the total of all expenses is deducted from the total of all revenues.

Solvency: The ability of a firm to pay its debts as they come due.

Special-purpose fund: A cash fund used for a special business need.

Standard cost: A detailed estimate of what a product should cost.

Standard cost systems: Accounting systems that use standards for each manufacturing cost entering into the finished product.

Stated value: A value, similar to par value, approved by the board of directors of a corporation for no-par stock.

Statement of cash flows: A summary of the cash receipts and cash payments for a specific period of time, such as a month or a year.

Static budget: A budget that does not adjust to changes in activity levels.

Stock dividend: A distribution of shares of stock to its stockholders.

Stock split: The reduction in the par or stated value of common stock and issuance of a proportionate number of additional shares.

Stockholders: Investors who purchase stock in a corporation.

Stockholders' equity: The stockholders' rights to the assets of a business.

Straight-line method: A method of depreciation that provides for equal periodic depreciation expense over the estimated life of a fixed asset.

Sunk cost: A cost that is not affected by subsequent decisions.

Supply chain management: The coordination and control of materials, services, information, and finances as they move in a process from the supplier, through the manufacturer, wholesaler, and retailer to the consumer.

T

Target costing: A concept used to design and manufacture a product at a cost that will deliver a target profit for a given market-determined price.

Taxable income: The income of a corporation that is subject to taxes as determined according to the tax laws.

Temporary differences: Differences between taxable income and income before income taxes that are created because items are recognized in one period for tax purposes and in another period for income statement purposes.

Theory of constraints (TOC): A manufacturing strategy that attempts to remove the influence of bottlenecks (constraints) on a process.

Time tickets: The form on which the amount of time spent by each employee and the labor cost incurred for each individual job, or for factory overhead, are recorded.

Time value of money concept: The concept that an amount of money invested today will earn interest.

Total cost concept: A concept used in applying the cost-plus approach to product pricing in which all the costs of manufacturing the product plus the selling and administrative expenses are included in the cost amount to which the markup is added.

Trademark: A name, term, or symbol used to identify a business and its products.

Transaction: An economic event that under generally accepted accounting principles affects an element of the accounting equation and, therefore, must be recorded.

Transfer price: The price charged one decentralized unit by another for the goods or services provided.

Treasury stock: Stock that a corporation has once issued and then reacquires.

U

Underapplied factory overhead: The actual factory overhead costs incurred in excess of the amount of factory overhead applied for production during a period.

Unearned revenues: Items that are initially recorded as liabilities but are expected to become revenues over time or through the normal operation of the business; often called deferred revenues.

Unit contribution margin: The dollars available from each unit of sales to cover fixed costs and provide income from operations.

Unit of measure concept: An accounting concept requiring that economic data be recorded in dollars.

V

Value-added lead time: The time required to manufacture a unit of product or other output.

Variable cost conept (variable costing): A method of reporting variable and fixed costs that includes only the variable manufacturing costs in the cost of the product.

Variable costs: Costs that vary in total dollar amount as the level of activity changes.

Vertical analysis: A method of analyzing comparative financial statements in which percentages are computed for each item within a statement to a total within the statement.

Voucher: Any document that serves as proof of authority to pay cash.

Voucher system: A set of procedures for authorizing and recording liabilities and cash payments.

W

Work in process inventory: The direct materials costs, the direct labor costs, and the factory overhead costs that have entered into the manufacturing process but are associated with products that have not been finished.

Z

Zero-based budgeting: A concept of budgeting that requires all levels of management to start from zero and estimate budget data as if there had been no previous activities in their units.

Index